THE FRANK LLOYD WRIGHT COMPANION

THE FRANK LLOYD WRIGHT COMPANION

William Allin Storrer

THE UNIVERSITY OF CHICAGO PRESS CHICAGO AND LONDON

WILLIAM ALLIN STORRER is the author of
*The Architecture of Frank Lloyd Wright:
A Complete Catalog.*

This work is supported in part by a grant
from the Graham Foundation for Advanced Studies
in the Fine Arts

The University of Chicago Press, Chicago 60637
The University of Chicago Press, Ltd., London

02 01 00 99 98 97 96 95 94 93   5 4 3 2 1
ISBN: 0-226-77624-7 (cloth)

Library of Congress Cataloging in Publication Data

Storrer, William Allin.
     The Frank Lloyd Wright companion / William Allin Storrer.
          p.   cm.
     Includes index.
     1. Wright, Frank Lloyd, 1867–1959—Catalogs.   2. Wright, Frank
     Lloyd, 1867–1959—Criticism and interpretation.   I. Wright, Frank
     Lloyd, 1867–1959.   II. Title. 3. Architecture, Modern
     NA737.W7A4   1993   ÷y 20th century.
     720'.92—dc20   93-30127
     W931St   CIP

This book is printed on acid-free paper.

Contents

Acknowledgments

This publication could not have been done without the guidance of Lloyd Wright and documentation provided by John H. Howe.

Production of the graphics in this publication was aided by a grant from the Graham Foundation for Advanced Studies in the Fine Arts.

John G. Thorpe, AIA, and John A. Eifler, AIA, not only provided documentation but also guidance on matters architectural.

My wife Pat read the text more times than anyone but myself.

Bruce Brooks Pfeiffer not only opened the archives of the Frank Lloyd Wright Foundation to me but, long before general access was possible, also brought to my attention projects not published until many years later, which aided me in my continued investigations of Wright's design philosophy and methods. Richard Carney, Tom Casey, John and Kay Rattenbury, Greg Williams, Indira Berndtson, Kenn and Sue Lockhart, Charles and Minerva Montooth, Anneliese and David Dodge and everyone else at Taliesin West were not only generous with their time but helpful in many ways that demonstrated their love and understanding of Mr. Wright's life philosophy. Wes Peters's encouragement and advice were invaluable.

Paul E. Sprague, Jonathan Lipman, AIA, Don Aitken, and Jeanne Rubin provided insights not elsewhere discoverable.

John Tilton, AIA, Mary Jane Hamilton, John O. Holzhueter, W. R. Hasbrouck, AIA, Eric Wright, AIA, Curtis Besinger, Tom Rickard, George Stefan, and the Michigan Society of Architects each helped with information on several projects.

William Marlin, Scott Elliott, Richard Twiss, John Geiger, Robert A. Bell, Bradley Ray Storrer, AIA, Denis C. Schmiedeke, AIA, Ben Raeburn,

Henry-Russell Hitchcock, Steve Danforth, and Cheryl Barenfeld each provided information in several areas of my research.

Meg Klinkow and Elaine Harrington of the Frank Lloyd Wright Home and Studio Foundation Research Center provided information from that invaluable collection.

The following persons provided information about and/or access to Wright structures:

Sandra Wilcoxon, Rev. Msgr. Gregory R. Kennedy, Paul Minor, Edsel Ruddiman, Sonia Cooke, Ruth Michaels, Janet and Anthony Walters, Alice Shaddle, Emmond and Catherine Thompson, Kathryn and Charles Gale, Tom Longhi, Paul Sorensen, Vicki and Kenneth Prouty, Joan Walker, Jeanette and Jerry Goldstone, Dick and Joanne Lazarski, Mr. and Mrs. Lou Mercuri, Mr. and Mrs. Watson, Mary Lofgren, Richard W. Vernon, Patty and William Saltenberger, James and Audrey Kouvel, William Ryan, Dorothy and Robert Tharp, Irene and Tom DeCaro, Ron Moline, Milt and Sylvie Robinson, David and Joyce McArdle, William and Jan Dring, W. Gordon Yadon, Jeanette S. and Ellis K. Fields, Mr. and Mrs. Walter Swardenski, Mark Heyman, W. R. Hasbrouck, AIA, Jack Pfeiffer, Jack Prost, Yates Smith, Gilbert H. and Charles Marquardt, Todd Lunsford, Jr., Clive and Laurel Cooper, Mike Panyard, Kay and John Heep, Brian Spencer, AIA, Mary Ann and William Mueller, Donald and Jean Clark, Burr Robbins, Terry Robbins, Mr. and Mrs. Robert Wright, James and Holly Campbell, John Faulds, Ann Peterson, Art J. Potter, Rudy Cooper, Wilfred Myrmel, Marshall Salzman, Joe d'Angelo Blatz, Dale Smirl, Donna Bretzer, Nancy Elwood Schmidt, Mr. and Mrs. Donald J. Poore, Staci and Jim Cannon, Jack and Nancy Sutherland, Lois Fineberg, Paul and Suzanne Peck-Collier, James Yoghourtjian, Uwe and Gabriella Freese, Kathy and Keith Hult, Patricia P. and James MacLachlan, Mark and Terry Allen, Robert J. Blackburn, Maya Moran, Darlene Larson, Donna Hawkins, Alden Odt, Tom Knoebel, Mr. and Mrs. Niketas Sahlas, Christine Holt Craig, Carolyn and Jim Howlett, Edward Marcisz, Mr. and Mrs. Frank Lucente, Jr., Delton D. Ludwig, L. Milnarik, Nelle Weiss, Karen Brown, Louise Newcomb, Joan Lupton, the children of Meyer May, Walter Sobol, Les Nelson, Paul and Clare Obis, Jr., Robert Ooley, Jim and Jane Blockman, Alice Sloan, Mr. and Mrs. Ben Bouck, Patrick J. Meehan, AIA, Mrs. Stephenson, Ted Smith and Susan Shipper-Smith, Frank Paluch, Harold and Doris Blumenthal, Ross Edman, Susan Solway, Harvey Siegel, Ted and Sonia Block, Tony and Vonnie Macaitis, Carole Nolen, Jane Marie Smith, Eleanor Pateira, Drs. Fedor F. and Sirirat R. Banuchi, Sian Evans, Masami Tanigawa, Masaru Sekino, Barbara and Robert Elsner, Mr. and Mrs. William Kagianas, Louis and Consetta Briatta, Jill and David Arena, J. Scott McDonald, Terry Koch, David Craig, Tim Samuelson, Barbara Buchbinder-Green, Gwen Sommers Yant, Rebecca and Peter Olafsen, William Kincaid, Mr. Shichiro Hayashi, Virginia Kazor, Roderick Grant, Eleanor Pettersen, Raku Endo.

Nicole Daniels, Joel Silver, Samuel and Mabel Freeman, Augustus Brown, Patrick J. Mahoney, R. Murray McCune, Dr. and Mrs. Dwight Holden, Lynda Waggoner, Edgar Kaufmann, Jr., Christopher Wilk, James Dennis, Paul and Jeanne Hanna, Abby Beecher Roberts, John Lautner, Mary Roberts, Karol Peterson, Richard Kinch, E. J. Rebhuhn, Ed and Mary Anzalone, Robert de Silets, Donald M. Aucutt, Grace Block, Ray

Fischer, Betty and Louis Frank, John and Patricia Peterson, Jessica Stevens and Stan Loring, Bruce and Linda Haines, Mildred Rosenbaum, Alvin Rosenbaum, Mary Leighey, Anne Garrison, Elizabeth Halsted, Edith Anderson, Jack Larson, Jeff Bridges, Mr. and Mrs. John C. Pew, Dr. John S. and Cynthia Edwards, Gregor and Elizabeth Affleck, Mary Ann Lutomski, Mary and Anthony Gholz, Theodore Baird, Sultan Amerie, Richard Stern, Cynthia Weaver, Carl and Margaret Wall, Frank DeRoski, Angela Oliveri, Richard and Catherine Macintosh, Herbert and Katherine Jacobs, Lowell and Agnes Walter, Joanne Arms, Mrs. Arnold Friedman, Mel and Sara Smith, Douglas, Jackie, and David Grant, Chauncey and Johanna Griggs, Charlotte Helstad, A. H. Bulbulian, Mr. and Mrs. Nels Jorgenson, Dr. David and Christine Weisblatt, Eric and Pat Pratt, Mr. and Mrs. James Hemenway, Curtis and Lillian Meyer, Heather McCartney, Mr. and Mrs. Tom Parachini, Richard R. Williams, Ward and Helen McCartney, Eric V. and Anne Brown, Dr. and Mrs. Larry Ruppert, Mr. and Mrs. Hermann T. Mossberg, J. Willis Hughes, Robert Parker Adams, Robert McCormick, Mrs. Della Walker, Ollie and Edie Adelmann, Mr. and Mrs. Maynard Buehler, Karen Anderson, Ellen Johnson, Mr. and Mrs. Erling Brauner, Mr. and Mrs. William T. Martin III, Mr. and Mrs. Henry J. Neils, Paul and Mary McGee, Richard Lindenfeld, Scott Elliott, David Henken, Michael Osheowitz, Doris Abramson, Roland and Ronny Reisley, Kenneth and Phyllis Laurent, Wilbur Pearce, Llewellyn Pearce, David and Gladys Wright, John H. Shoaff, AIA, Dr. and Mrs. Richard Davis, Dr. and Mrs. G. Michael Ball, Muriel Sweeton, Christian Peterson, J. O. Carr, Don and Mary Lou Schaberg, Thelma Cappell, Gloria Berger, Mr. Sox, William and Mary Palmer, Lucille Zimmerman, Robert

Muirhead, Karl Staley, Dr. Susan and Jack Turben, Mr. and Mrs. Warren Plunkett, Richard Smith, John Gillen, Seamour and Gerte Shavin, Mr. and Mrs. Russell W. M. Kraus, Larry Smith and Victoria Mondae, Mr. and Mrs. Patrick Kinney, Nathan Rubin, Mrs. Gardina K. McCarthy, Bertram V. Karpf, Roy Palmer, Harris Klein, Carlos Meija, Welbie L. and Ardah Fuller, Leonard R. Spangenberg, Jr., AIA, Ray Brandes, Quin and Ruth Blair, Patricia and Archie Boyd Teater, Henry Whiting, Mr. and Mrs. R. W. Lindholm, David Lee, R. G. Robinson, Luis Marden, Robert and Elizabeth Wright, George and Clifton Lewis, Andrew and Maude Cooke, Lucille Kinter, John J. and Syd Dobkins, Caroline Price Barton, Jack Cook and Karen Wood, Louis, Paul, and Debra Penfield, Lawrence and Sharon Tarantino, Karen Johnson and William Boyd, Morton Delson, John Geiger, Ellis Feiman, James and Bonnie Gwin, Dr. Maurice Greenberg, Bob Weil, Mr. and Mrs. E. Clarke Arnold, John E. Christian, Mr. and Mrs. Louis B. Fredrick, Mr. and Mrs. I. N. Hagan, Harold Price, Sr., Patricia Neils Boulter, David Gosling, H. R. and Carol Ruth Shepherd, Ranko and Susan Santric, Mr. and Mrs. Randall Fawcett, Gerald and Beverly Tonkens, Dr. Toufic H. and Mildred Kalil, Dorothy Turkel, Tom Monaghan, William and Elizabeth Tracy, Mrs. Emily Fisher Landau, Donald and Virginia Lovness, Ted and Bette Pappas, Mr. and Mrs. Robert Sunday, Dr. Robert and Hollis Cassidy, Anthony Scott, Dr. Karl Kundert, Dr. James Apesos, Ida Trier, Mary Karageannes, Mr. and Mrs. Allen J. Friedman, Dr. and Mrs. Samuel H. Fraerman, Frank and Eloise Bott, Irene and Ralph Hatfield, Michael and Rebecca Wissell, Jane Sindt, Mr. and Mrs. Don Duncan, Marcia Martin, Mr. and Mrs. Frank Iber, Ric Wytmar, Catherine Cass, Morton Delson, Socrates and Celeste

Zaferiou, Paul and Eugenia Gengler, Dr. Edward and Lora Jane LaFond, Mr. and Mrs. Walter Rudin, Mr. and Mrs. James McBean, Aaron Green, FAIA, Dr. George Platt, Conrad Edward and Evelyn Gordon, Julia and Duey Wright, Dr. Robert G. and Mary Walton, Dorothy and Sterling Kinney, Drs. Joseph Kugler and John W. Thibodo, Richard G. Brown, Mr. and Mrs. Dwain Rauhoff, Jack and Fredda Sparks, Helen and Paul Olfelt, Dr. George and Millie Ablin, Mr. and Mrs. Don Stromquist, Audrey Laatsch, Aime Lykes.

Preface

The true archive of Wright's genius as an architect exists not in a storage vault, but in cities and towns throughout this country and a few others in the form of buildings designed between 1886 and 1959. This book documents in plans, photographs, drawings, and commentary Wright's nearly five hundred known works built from over twenty thousand drawings, including about one hundred structures that have been destroyed.

As a companion—not an encyclopedia—a main purpose of this book is to identify uniquely each and every built structure designed by Frank Lloyd Wright or under his direction. If I stopped here, this book would be no more than a catalog. Through textual comment, photographs, and plans presented together, this book offers new vistas for comprehending Wright's work. The text places the structure in a context, by client, by the time and/or place of the design's conception or construction, or a combination of these. If any of the work can be called minor, the information supplied for some will be encyclopedic. For the best known, it might seem no more than basic, but avenues for further study or discovery may be identified. I have avoided conjecture as much as possible, although for some plans where evidence is minimal, I have completed a reasonable presentation of Wright's space.

Each work is presented on its own terms; no formula is followed, except in the presentation of basic facts in the heading; Storrer catalog number (**S.**, unique to each building), a project number (**T.**, Taliesin number, the first two digits of which identify the year the first plan was drawn for the project—which may contain many schemes and thus does not uniquely define a project—and the last two digits of which identify that year's clients in alphabetical order), an identifying name (with the parts necessary for unique identification in boldface type), the date the project first took a form fully identifiable in the final built work, the location of the project by municipality and state, and notes on the current status of the original work. Because plans are a key to understanding the work, they are not only shown but described in the text for those who have difficulty "reading" a plan.

A room to Frank Lloyd Wright was space, not the walls surrounding the space, but "the space within to be lived in," as Wright quoted Lao Tse. He was unique in his ability to see a whole house, its spaces, in his mind's eye before he put pencil to paper. Few architects can do this easily; many who profess architecture cannot do it at all. Yet it is the "why" of why Wright was a genius and why he put that genius to the test of architecture. By combining photos, text, and plans of buildings in a single book, I attempt to provide the experience of Wright and Wrightian space, as far as can be achieved on the printed page, for the architect's entire career. For this reason, I avoid the word "room" as much as is practical on the plans, even as Wright changed "kitchen" to "workspace" in his Usonian homes. We are dealing with space, not rooms, with an artist, not a designer, with an architect, not a builder.

No one has yet explained "how" Wright designed a building. Wright never did. Instead, he sent his apprentices out into the desert to see how Nature designed. Science cannot provide the answer, for science is the process of reducing to a single phenomenon all the diverse expressions in Nature thereof. Conversely, art seeks to express all the possibilities inherent in a single idea. The artist sees in an idea a possibility that only he or she can express, and in such expression is found the unique signature of that artist. Nature has expressed all possible structure; each architect must decipher the organic code for him or herself.

People have been trying to define Prairie architecture, and Usonian architecture, and Organic architecture for decades. Usonian grew out of Prairie when Wright attempted to turn an architecture suited to a Victorian American upper-middle class and the rich into a Democratic American architecture; both are Organic. Many of Wright's "students," whether office staff in Oak Park or apprentices at Taliesin, became excellent architects in the organic manner: Walter Burley Griffin, Barry Byrne, Marion Mahony, William Drummond, John H. Howe, Karl Kamrath, Aaron Green, William Wesley Peters, Nils Schweizer, James Fox, and Morton Delson (to name but a few, and with apologies to the many now carrying on the tradition who are not named here). It is not Wright's fault that many have failed in the effort, nor the fault of those who have attempted to define Wright's methods.

Perhaps the most successful at following in Wright's footsteps is John H. Howe. His houses are Baroque to Wright's Renaissance, and thus easily distinguished from his master's designs by the discerning eye. Yet they are not an era apart, as such a description implies, but of the same ethos. Even the best Howe should not be mistaken for Wright, and yet it need be no less organic.

It is one thing to study Wright in theory, another in practice. Among the major contributions of this book are schematic drawings of Wright's built work, the practice of architecture. Previous books have dealt largely with theory (even when they spoke of practice) because published plans did not correctly represent the built work. Wright was a dreamer, but also a pragmatist at architecture.

Those who have wanted to study Wright's architecture—his organization of spaces—by "reading" schematic/diagrammatic plans of the built work have been frustrated over the years by a lack of resource materials. The most comprehensive presentation has been that of my mentor, Henry-Russell Hitchcock. His *In the Nature of Materials* contains only 18 percent of the built work, and no other book, until now, has challenged this offering. With the publication of the *Monographs* by Taliesin archivist Bruce Brooks Pfeiffer, the floodgates opened. To study the plans, however, required purchase of eight beautifully produced but expensive volumes.

Further complicating such study was the fact that the *Monograph* volumes presented photographic halftones of original drawings at one-eighth their original size or smaller. Such reduction diminishes line weights, often to virtual nothingness. Even plans redrawn for reproduction by Wright or his studio staff sometimes lost so much, especially the grids of Usonian plans, that the lines would disappear, partially or completely. A good schematic, drawn for reproduction at a given size, can overcome such problems, and this is a major reason for the project that led to inclusion of plans in this book.

Furthermore, neither Hitchcock nor Pfeiffer presented us "as-built" plans, the works as Wright-the-artist allowed them to be built as practical architecture. Many of the *Monograph* plans were the preliminary drawings for the project, Wright's original concept, one or more generations removed from the working drawings from which the works, with on-site revisions, were built. Some of Wright's most famous drawings, those in the *Wasmuth Portfolio,* show the structures as Wright idealized them. Here the works are presented, as much as possible, in their ultimate built form. But, as Taliesin archivist Bruce Brooks Pfeiffer notes, "Frank Lloyd Wright frequently said that a good plan is also a good abstraction, something beautiful in itself, with grace and rhythm" (Pfeiffer, *Monograph,* vol. 8). In my "redrawings," I have sought to preserve—where it does not deny the reality of the building—this beautiful, graceful, rhythmic abstraction.

The question remains, what plan to use or what enhancements to make. Wright's published plans gave precedence to beauty over accuracy. "Truth is beauty, beauty truth, that is all ye know, and that is all ye need to know." Never mind that this is not a literal quote. It is the truth. Wright, as an artist even more than an architect, instinctively chose to present the "truth" of his design in a beautiful drawing, however it came out when built. Changes were almost always made during construction to realize the practical structure in as much of its beauty as was affordable by the client, but they are not reflected in these published "official" drawings. So we must admit that a collection of Wright's original published drawings does not fully add to our knowledge of Wright's architectural oeuvre. Wherever possible in this publication, I show the works as built. Even some of the most important of Wright's works, the first Prairie house (Willits, S.054) and the first so-called Usonian era house (Jacobs first, S.234) are obvious examples, for neither of them has been published previously in an accurate as-built form. An accurate plan of the Willits reveals the grid to which it conforms. In the Jacobs, in order to relocate utilities from the original single-level design to a below-grade arrangement, Wright added 2 feet to a 2-by-4-foot grid in order to sandwich in the required stairway; published plans do not show the "corrected" grid.

Where there is a "standard" published drawing, I have tried to use it with as little alteration as possible. Yet even here, changes are required to make the plan "read well" in book size. Thus, labels are most often subject to change.

At times my source is not a published drawing (however much I may need to revise it to reflect as-built conditions), but a composite of the original architectural drawings and on-site measurements. These must be redrawn for reproduction in a space rarely larger than 5 inches square. Sometimes I have been able to maintain the distinct imprint of Wright's studio; at other times the item required total computer redrawing. Those who find Wright's own hand sacrosanct (even when it was William Drummond's, Marion Mahony's, John H. Howe's, Davey Davison's or someone else's) will have to turn to the aforementioned *Monograph* series. Here I have sought maximum clarity, while keeping as much as I could of the beauty of Wright's original drawings.

There is no single design standard for these drawings, for Wright had many fine draftspersons in his Oak Park studio and the studios at Taliesin and Taliesin West. Each had his or her own style. I have tried to follow this or Wright's "style" as much as possible. What, "Wright's style"? Of course, there is no such thing. There is only a grammar of organic architecture and Wright's apprentices, in trying to use this grammar, have created a significant number of works that even at a casual glance look "Wrightian." But that is not style, nor "a style." It is a grammar of design. Everyone who speaks English (or even "American") speaks with a shared grammar, but this is not an American or English "style."

Over the years Wright changed his ideas about what a drawing should look like, just as he changed his own homes—Oak Park, Spring Green, Scottsdale—yearly, if not sometimes daily. Generally, I have tried to follow Wright's own practices for each specific drawing, but there are many occasions when this proved impractical. Often the preserved plan in Taliesin's archives has warped or otherwise been damaged over the years and cannot be accurately "read" into a computer program. Sometimes the original is a drawing other than the standard ground plan, such as the electrical systems drawing, because it provides some needed details. When on-site changes are entered, a new graphic standard may impose its own regulations. Given the variety of problems, some drawings are totally redrawn. For redrawings of Usonian era houses, a common computer graphic standard has usually been applied.

The typeface for plans of the pre-Prairie era is Times, Prairie is Lubalin Graph, and late work (1923 on) is Avant Garde (the sans serif version of Lubalin Graph). All arrows are in the "down" direction, so that they do not need labeling. If the head is "on" stairs, the tail indicates the floor from which one is starting down. If the head is on a floor, that is the level to which the stairs lead down. In many instances, bathtubs are not given specific orientation. While it will not always be obvious what a particular object in a floor plan may be, I have avoided extra labeling to keep the plans graphically clean. It is usually more important to know that some object is occupying a space than to know the specific nature of that object. Key objects, such as chairs and beds, toilets, baths and sinks, should be self-explanatory from their shapes.

These drawings are for study of Wright's spaces; they are not construction drawings. Even a 300 dpi scanner and computer resolution capability mean that for the largest number of drawings, I cannot resolve closer than three-fourths of an inch. A one-sixteenth-inch error in the 2-foot blocks of the Tonkens house (S.386), when multiplied by the 50-block length of the structure, would have produced a 3-inch error. Computer technology employed in production of the drawings for this book, state of the art at the start of the project, allowed a cumulative error a dozen times this great, or 3 feet. Since that Tonkens drawing is done on a grid, no 3-foot error occurs, yet at any point an inch or two error is possible.

By following the principles and practices outlined above, I have been able to achieve approximately a 93 percent coverage of the built work. The remaining 7 percent consists of items for which plans do not add significantly to what a photograph can tell us (such as sculptural works) or for which no plans survive in the Taliesin archives and the building was demolished before measured drawings could be made.

Photographs of Wright's work present problems not usually faced in the work of most other architects, and Wright had his own ideas of what constituted good architectural photography. Wright's prescription demanded a natural context. Exterior photos would include foliage, particularly if he or one of his associates did the landscaping. Interior photographs were to be shot with "natural light," "from a seated position." These two conditions remove many famous photographs from serious consideration. Work by such photographic legends as Ezra Stoller almost always employed significant amounts of artificial lighting. More recent color photographs seem to be shot by photographers who have never heard Wright's first condition and are even occasionally shot looking downward, a viewpoint incongruous for Wright, at 5 feet, 8 inches.

Which is not to say that photographs of Wright's works should not be beautiful or "colorful." The beauty should derive from the subject architecture, not from photographic wizardry. Color, however, is not a "natural" medium for architecture because the eye sees two ways, simultaneously, in black and white as well as in color. Architecture is space. The eye sees in depth with its black and white receptors, the 75 to 150 million rods. It sees color with the 7 million cones that detect blue-violet, green, and yellow-red spectra. In twilight or darkness, we lose color capability. The cones also detect fine lines and points of an image. We see shape (the two-dimensional aspect of an object), form (the three-dimensional aspect, the space), texture (surface variation), and color. Color can overpower the others and has a strong appeal, but it very easily leads us away from the subject and so must be used with extreme caution in architectural representation.

Wright's first condition conflicts with our desire to "see the building." It has meant that I have returned to each of the extant works, once, twice, sometimes five or six times, in search of a season, a particular position of the sun, the year after the bushes have been trimmed and new growth naturalizes the setting—whenever it has been possible to reveal Wright's architecture fully without removing it altogether from its natural setting. Wright's second condition has been met in my interior photographs as much as possible. Occasionally the camera position may be a bit higher where no one would or could sit down, such as on a stairway, or when looking over a dining table, where the table will dominate if the camera is too low. There are also circumstances where a shot may be from an especially low angle. In all instances, I have tried to observe the principle of Wright's injunctions.

In some instances I have been unable to make quality photographs. Where the building still stands, I often obtained a photograph from a local photographer or some Wrightian who has made a suitable photograph. At other times, particularly for buildings that have been demolished or altered beyond recognition as Wright's work, I have chosen what to me is the most representative historical photograph from a wide range of archives.

Of course, this book is incomplete, at times inconsistent, and occasionally (unintentionally) inaccurate, as the time to study it will reveal. I should like to think it is, however, a coherent whole, as much as any one person can make it. This has been a quarter-century long project, some would say over four decades. In the spring of 1950 I met Mr. Wright at Taliesin. Fourteen years later I visited Taliesin West for the first time. Not until the spring of 1968, while teaching an undergraduate course in architectural history at Ohio University, did I first study Wright's work seriously. That autumn, while photographing my brother Bradley's buildings in Michigan, I parked in front of the Dorothy Turkel house (S.388), a side visit to my brother's teacher's work. Someone walked up to me, pointed to a list of Wright's built work in a book he held, and asked me if I knew where a particular house on the list was. I answered, "it was not built." He thanked me and drove off. To this day I'm not certain why or how I knew that house was not built, but that moment was the beginning of what became in 1974 *The Architecture of Frank Lloyd Wright: A Complete Catalog,* and also what is now *The Frank Lloyd Wright Companion.*

While readers of this volume have their own special areas of interest regarding Wright and his work, I hope they will find something here to send them off to further discoveries. There never will be a "complete" book on the man or his work. Each generation, with new tools for discovery and research, will provide new insights to the depths of Wright's genius, even though such insights are flawed by their distance from the original subject of the study. It takes time to understand the work of a genius. I have been granted more time than most to understand the nature of organic architecture as Mr. Wright created it. This is my testimony to that American Democratic architectural heritage.

FRANK LLOYD WRIGHT BUILDINGS

S.000
Unity Chapel (1886)
Spring Green, Wisconsin

While working in the office of J. Lyman Silsbee, a successful Chicago architect, Wright practiced his drafting skills. The Japanese prints that decorated the office walls were provided by Silsbee's cousin, the noted orientalist Ernest Francisco Fenollosa, who was in the United States from 1890 to 1897 between stints in Japan. Thus it was that Wright became acquainted with Japanese art in his formative years.

Wright's first design (unbuilt, published in 1887), for a Unitarian chapel in Sioux City, is similar to the Unity Chapel long thought to have been designed by Silsbee and drawn by Wright for the Jones family in Helena Valley within view of today's Taliesin. The perspective drawing of the chapel, by Wright, is an example of uncommonly good draftsmanship for one so young.

Yet, did Wright perhaps design the entire building? Recent discoveries of correspondence indicate that, indeed, Wright may have done not only the perspective sketch, but the building it describes, under Silsbee's tutelage. *Unity* magazine of August 1886 states that "a boy architect belonging to the family looked after the interior." So this is the minimum that must be attributed to Wright.

While we may never know with certainty the true story of this project, unless drawings in Wright's own hand and with his signature appear in some long-lost file or in someone's attic, it commands inclusion because it is at least an "interior" design and fits with Wright's own dictum, from Lao Tse, that it is the space within to be lived in that is architecture, not the exterior clothing.

UNITY CHAPEL, HELENA, WIS.

Unity Chapel, as drawn by Master Wright

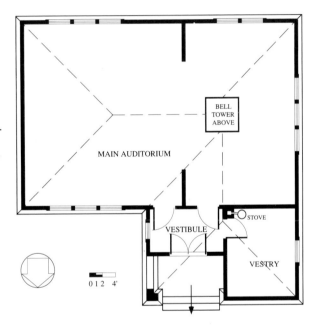

MAIN AUDITORIUM

BELL TOWER ABOVE

VESTIBULE

STOVE

VESTRY

0 1 2   4'

Unity Chapel, as built

Unity Chapel

S.001   T.8703
Hillside Home School I (1887) for Nell and Jane Lloyd Jones
Spring Green, Wisconsin
Demolished 1950

The first Hillside Home School follows the style Wright had absorbed from his first architectural mentor, J. Lyman Silsbee, who popularized the Shingle style in Chicago and gave Wright his first experience in an architectural office late in the 1880s. Silsbee's Queen Anne designs were very fashionable.

Wright's aunts, Nell and Jane Lloyd Jones, taught in this private school for many years. Hillside, noted for its progressive approach to education, was the first coeducational boarding school in the nation, taking children from five to eighteen years of age and teaching boys and girls together.

A larger, more complex structure was erected in 1903 (S.069) to serve the needs of the school, though this building, Wright's first, was not torn down until the early 1950s. It has been suggested that Wright had it torn down because he thought it did not represent his architectural principles. Little documentation survives to reveal what, if any, elements of Wright's design genius were present in this structure.

Hillside Home School I

S.002   T.8901
Frank Lloyd Wright Residence
(1889),
S.003   T.9307
Playroom Addition with new
Dining Room and Kitchen (1895),
and
S.004   T.9506
Studio (1897), "Frank Lloyd Wright
Home and Studio"
S.002–S.004A   T.1125
**Home and Studio Apartment
Conversion** with Garage and
Caretaker's Quarters (1911)
Oak Park, Illinois
Apartment Conversion altered in 1956
by Wright. Residence, Playroom, and
Studio restored to about 1909 during
the 1970s and 1980s. Garage
converted into the Ginkgo Tree
Bookshop.

Frank Lloyd Wright Home, west facade, with later library to the left

Wright chose to live in Oak Park in
1887, or rather, he joined his mother
and two sisters who were living in the
home of an Oak Park friend, Augusta
Chapin, an ordained minister. Miss
Chapin introduced the Wrights to the
congregation of Unity Temple (see
S.096), from which many of the
architect's clients would come. Two
years later, he built a home for his wife
Catherine and himself. This, the oldest
extant house by Wright, is surfaced
with wood shingles.

In the interior space the architect
defines door tops with stringcourses
rather than the more common architraves. Because Wright was his own
client, his expression was not reserved; ornament became one with
architecture, structure and design one
with each other, and the whole and its
parts could not be separated.

The original 1889 house layout was
typical of early Wright design. The
entry is spacious and well appointed in
oak. Here, a visitor is forced to turn left
into the living room; straight ahead
was the kitchen and to the right are
stairs to the second floor, well-lit by a
window at the first landing. In the corner farthest from this foyer was the formal dining room. Above were the one
bedroom, bath, and nursery, and a studio for the architect. While in its own
way highly original, neither it nor any
other of his pre-Prairie homes chal-
lenges the dominant Victorian standards of domestic living of the time.

In 1895, Wright began an association with the Luxfer Prism Company

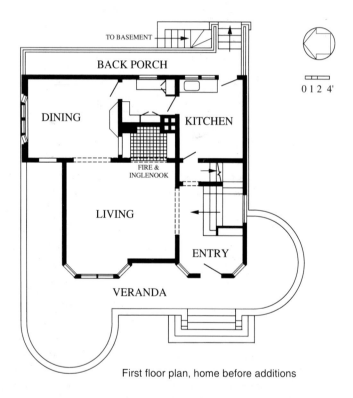

First floor plan, home before additions

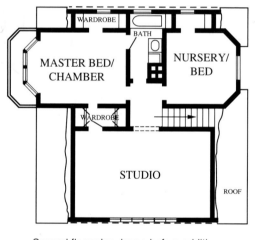

Second floor plan, home before additions

and, perhaps foreseeing financial security, began plans for expanding his
home to accommodate a growing
family and architectural practice. He
extended the house east from the original kitchen to gain a servant's room
and new kitchen, with a barrel-vaulted
children's playroom above. By adding
a bay to the original kitchen, he created a new dining room on the sunlit
side of the house; the original dining
room became a study. Another bay

was added to the north wall of the
living room, creating an octagonal corner, a geometry favored early by
Wright as a means of breaking down
the square.

Upstairs, the original studio was
divided by a low wall so that the
girls and boys would have separate
sleeping and dressing spaces. Such
a wall, or screen (common in Japan),
rather than a floor-to-ceiling partition,
appears often in Wright's domestic

design and becomes a feature of many
Usonian bedroom wings.

In 1898, Wright opened new offices
in Chicago and Oak Park. His Rookery
Building office was next to that of the
Luxfer Prism Company. In Oak Park,
he created a showpiece for his radical
architectural style, his own studio and
offices. Octagonal geometry appears
throughout in the plan of the library as
well as in several interlockings of
square and octagon in the drafting

studio. The studio was connected to the home by a passageway leading to the study. The Magnesite (oxichloric cement, sawdust, and pigment) flooring throughout the studio looks like aged leather and is very durable. A complex public entry (added in about 1906) is created by a low wall that admits the prospective client to one or the other end of a low terrace, where he is forced to turn and enter a very narrow covered portico before arriving at the reception room proper. This is the continual compression of space, from below, then above, and finally at the sides, before expansion at the main activity space, that typifies much of Wright's mature design of entries.

The reception hall is now lit by three art glass skylights composed of green, gold, and clear rectangular glass (installed about 1906). The two figures flanking the porch, called *The Boulders* and "typifying the struggle of the oppressed and shackled soul to break its bonds and find self expression" (the words of Robert C. Spencer, Jr.) are by Richard Bock, whose association with Wright was both long and fruitful.

Wright left Oak Park in 1909 to prepare the *Wasmuth Portfolio* in Europe. When he returned to the United States, he moved to Spring Green, Wisconsin. In 1911 he remodeled the Oak Park structures into two apartments to provide income for his wife, Catherine, who moved with four of their children from the home to the altered studio. A firewall separated the studio from the house. The original studio office became a dining room, while the two-story-high studio was split into two floors, the lower a living room, the upper four bedrooms. The original house provided rental income to support Catherine and the family. A three-car garage was constructed, with an additional apartment above, as part of this studio conversion. Further remodeling, specifically in the studio, was undertaken by Clyde Nooker (S.405) in 1956.

Dating of the three structures has been established by the Frank Lloyd Wright Home and Studio Foundation. Design of the studio began in 1897 (the date assigned here), and it was constructed during the winter and spring of 1898 (the date assigned by the foundation). The official dates established by Taliesin for the play-

Frank Lloyd Wright Residence living room, fireplace inglenook

Playroom Addition to
Frank Lloyd Wright Residence

(Continues)

room and the studio are 1893 and 1895, both a bit too early since Wright did not expand the house until his association with the Luxfer Prism Company provided the funds he needed.

The Frank Lloyd Wright Home and Studio Foundation, formed in 1974, is in charge of preservation of these buildings and conducts tours of the premises, which are owned by the National Trust for Historic Preservation. Under the foundation's direction, the two buildings and the playroom addition have been restored, for the most part, to their 1909 appearance, the last year Wright was in regular residence (some elements of the original house entry were initially chosen over a pure 1909 re-creation). There is a workable argument that different parts of the house should have been restored to different dates, to represent Wright's continual reworking of the structure. The studio existed in its 1911 condition, and this original Wright work had to be destroyed to re-create a sense of the 1909 studio. Research and construction to achieve a multistage restoration revealing Wright's developing design principles would have been monumental. As is, the restoration progressed largely in an ad hoc fashion, rather than by any unified plan for renovation. The 13-year, $2.25-million restoration won a National Honor Award from the American Institute of Architects in 1987. The structure has been designated by the American Institute of Architects as one of seventeen buildings to be retained as an example of Wright's architectural contribution to American culture.

Those wishing to visit the Home and Studio or tour the architecture in the Frank Lloyd Wright–Prairie School of Architecture National Historic District should contact the Oak Park Visitors Center.

The Oak Park Studio

Frank Lloyd Wright Studio lobby with art-glass ceiling light

The Oak Park Studio drafting room restored to 1909, view from balcony

Studio library

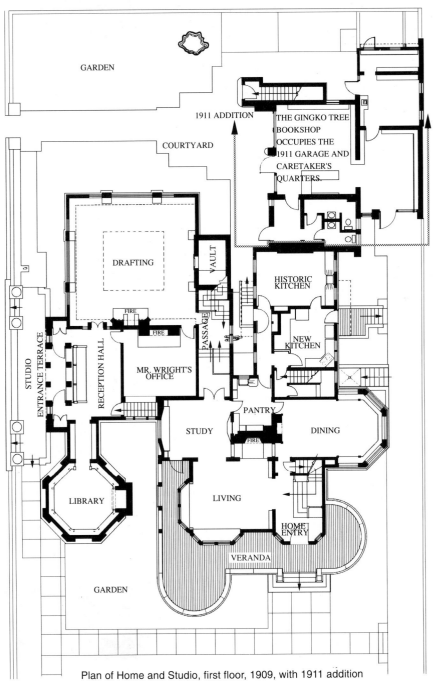

GARDEN

1911 ADDITION

COURTYARD

THE GINGKO TREE BOOKSHOP OCCUPIES THE 1911 GARAGE AND CARETAKER'S QUARTERS.

DRAFTING

VAULT

HISTORIC KITCHEN

FIRE

FIRE

PASSAGE

NEW KITCHEN

STUDIO

ENTRANCE TERRACE

RECEPTION HALL

MR. WRIGHT'S OFFICE

STUDY

PANTRY

FIRE

DINING

LIBRARY

LIVING

HOME ENTRY

VERANDA

GARDEN

Plan of Home and Studio, first floor, 1909, with 1911 addition

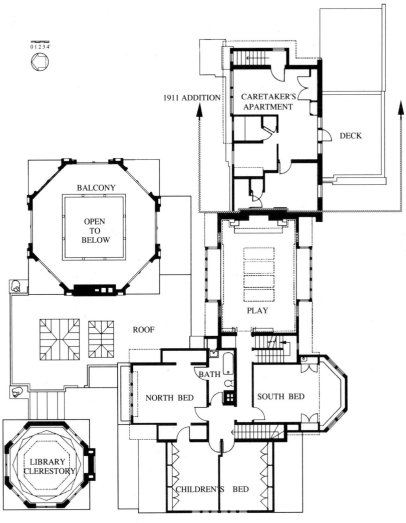

0 1 2 3 4'

1911 ADDITION

CARETAKER'S APARTMENT

DECK

BALCONY

OPEN TO BELOW

PLAY

ROOF

BATH

NORTH BED

SOUTH BED

LIBRARY CLERESTORY

CHILDREN'S BED

Plan of Home and Studio, second floor, 1909, with 1911 addition

S.005 T.9003
Louis Sullivan Bungalow (1890),
S.006A T.9003
Stables (1890), and
S.006B T.9003
Servant's Quarters (1890)
Ocean Springs, Mississippi
Stables demolished, 1942. Bungalow
restored, with addition to rear and east
side in imitation of original building,
1990.

Louis Sullivan, exhausted from designing the Auditorium Building, took his
first vacation in fifteen years. First he
went to California, then New Orleans
where, encountering Chicagoans
Helen and James Charnley, he was led
to the Gulf Coast town of Ocean
Springs. He was entranced with local
horticulture. On March 10, for one
dollar, the Charnleys transferred five of
their 21 acres to Sullivan on the condition he plan a house for them. "He
planned for two shacks or bungalows,
300 feet apart, with stables far back.
. . . The building was let to a local carpenter." Thus goes Sullivan's account,
in *Autobiography of an Idea.*

Wright, in *An Autobiography,*
states, "Adler and Sullivan refused to
build residences. The few imperative,
owing to social obligations to important
clients, fell to my lot out of office hours.
. . . Sullivan's brother's own home on
Lake [Park] Avenue was one of these,
as were the southern house at Ocean
Springs and the house next door there
for the Charnleys." Perhaps this was
mere boasting by Wright about "the
country house I had designed for him"
(Genius and the Mobocracy), but
Sullivan designed half a dozen other
houses during this period that Wright
did *not* claim. What is likely, and consistent with all known facts, is that they
were designed in Chicago by Wright
and the plans sent to the carpenter,
who had possibly quoted Sullivan a
price based upon square footage and
number of rooms, for construction of
the exterior before the late autumn
rains arrived and completion by
Sullivan's return to Chicago in the
winter of 1890/91.

The basic plan is the "dog trot
house," a common layout for cottages
on the Mississippi Gulf coast, as well

Louis Sullivan Bungalow in 1970, from the west. The opening for the original chimney can
barely be seen under the eaves of the bedroom (right center).

Plan of Louis Sullivan Bungalow

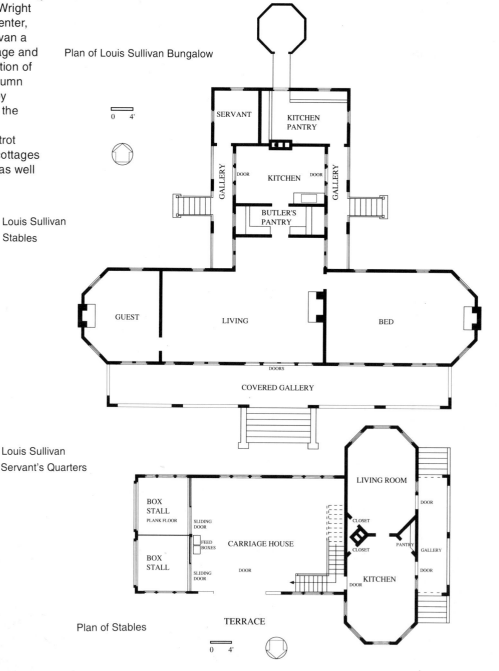

Louis Sullivan
Stables

Louis Sullivan
Servant's Quarters

Plan of Stables

as bungalows found well inland, where a central breezeway separates rooms to the sides. For nearly two decades, until he became financially incapable of supporting his southern "paradise, the poem of spring, Louis's other self," Sullivan vacationed there.

The Sullivan bungalow plan has a full-width veranda facing south to Davis Bayou on the Gulf of Mexico. The main entry opens to a living room, on either side of which are the guest and master bedrooms, each with its own fireplace. Due to the need of a kitchen, this plan is extended into a **T,** behind the living room. Down the stem of the **T** is a butler's pantry, with verandas on either side, servant's quarters, and kitchen pantry. Finally, to the rear, is an octagonal water tower, later converted to a library (there was an artesian well on the property, from which Sullivan drew water for his extensive gardens and for both his and the Charnleys' bungalow). The verandas, with their extensive eaves' overhang, provide shade on the south, east, and west. Paneling is tongue-and-groove in local pine.

The Sullivan stable, or "carriage house," preserved the **T** plan on a small scale, with kitchen and living room in the head of the **T,** carriage space and two box stalls in the stem. The servant's quarters have undergone many changes; originally the east end (shown in the photograph) was open and used as a carriage stall, with a sleeping room in the far end.

Photographs from the early 1970s show the building exterior much as it was in a 1900 photograph published in *Architectural Record*. A "renovation" done in the 1930s and a new dining room added in 1970 to the east half of the **T** plan once disfigured the main structure. In the late 1980s, full restoration including the water tower (as a wine cellar) "in the style of early Wright" was begun by Samuel Wilson of Kock & Wilson in New Orleans. This, together with an addition at its northeast corner in the style of the main building, has made the structure usable for year-round living.

Charnley Guesthouse (left) and Bungalow (right)

S.007 T.9001
James **Charnley Bungalow** (1890),
S.008A T.9001
Guesthouse (1890), and
S.008B T.9001
Stable Cottage (1890)
Ocean Springs, Mississippi
Stable Cottage demolished. Guesthouse altered on side and added to at the rear.

The Charnley bungalow is similar in its **T** plan to the neighboring Sullivan bungalow (S.005). Both have the living room's long axis pointing toward the gulf, acting as a breezeway to catch the on-shore/off-shore cycle of light winds. Wright preferred the Charnley residence over his Lieber Meister's cottage; the detailing is finer and better reveals his contribution to the design. Octagonal bays at the corners of the Charnley bedrooms make it an enlarged version of the Sullivan bungalow. Fireplaces in these bedrooms provide relief from the chill of damp winter evenings. A 1930s restoration was followed by enlargement of the northeast veranda; then both side and front verandas were enclosed, and the wood steps were replaced with brick.

The guesthouse was originally an octagon divided by a single wall into two rooms.

A photograph reproduced as the Sullivan home in Hitchcock's *In the Nature of Materials*, as Charnley's cottage in Manson's *Frank Lloyd Wright to 1910*, and as Sullivan's stables in Twombly's *Louis Sullivan, His Life and Work* was actually the "stable cottage" (now demolished), toward the rear of the Charnley acreage.

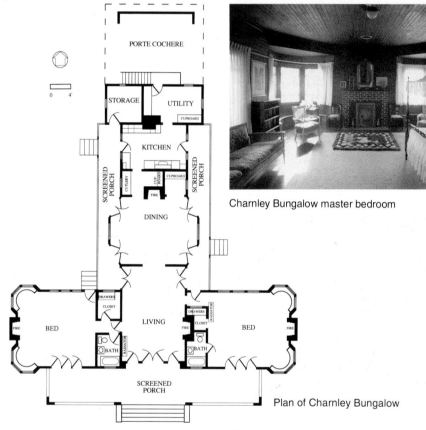

Charnley Bungalow master bedroom

Plan of Charnley Bungalow

Charnley Stable Cottage

The Charnley Residence, as restored

S.009   T.9101
James **Charnley Residence** (1891)
Chicago, Illinois
Restored in 1988 for the SOM
Foundation

The architectural firm of Adler &
Sullivan was essentially devoted to
large commercial work and avoided
domestic commissions. The general
assertion has been that Sullivan let
Wright work on such domestic commissions as the Charnley townhouse
outside office hours, allowing the
young designer to earn overtime pay.
Even so, some residential designs that
came from their offices have to be attributed to Louis Sullivan or Dankmar
Adler, not to Wright.

James Charnley was head of a
lumber company. The plan of his
house is a rectangle broken by a
dining room bay on the south. Instead
of windows in its three sides, the center of the bay is a fireplace, blocking
the view of a building too close by in
crowded Chicago. The central stairwell, with finely carved woodwork, is
also a skylit atrium. The structure is
advanced beyond its time in terms of
simplicity of ornamentation and in the
way the exterior reflects interior space.
Comparison of the second-floor log-
gias of the Charnley with Sullivan's

Babson residence (1907; demolished)
in Riverside reveals the elder architect
still using arches which his junior had
abandoned in favor of rectilinear forms
here in the Charnley house seventeen
years earlier.

In 1986, the Chicago architectural
firm of Skidmore, Owings & Merrill purchased the house, which had been
designated a Chicago Landmark in
1972, to be headquarters for the SOM
Foundation. Restoration, completed in
1988 by John A. Eifler, reveals a dining
room with Sullivan's choice of Mexican
(Tabasco) mahogany and a living room
with Wright's American white oak. The
original brick has darkened from a
lighter orange, having been sprayed
with linseed oil, a common masonry
sealant of the 1890s. New brick on the
south facade has been similarly sealed.

Wrightian Charnley living room mantelpiece

Sullivanian Charnley dining room mantelpiece

Stairwell, from second floor

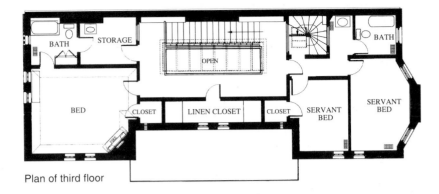

Plan of third floor

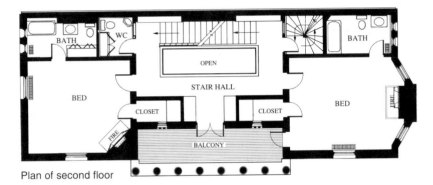

Plan of second floor

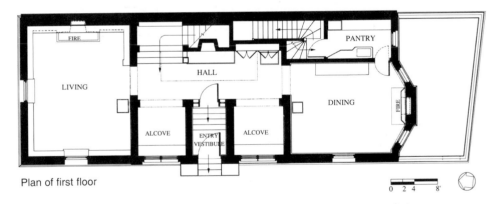

Plan of first floor

0 2 4 8'

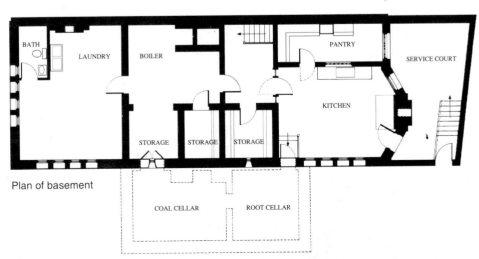

Plan of basement

MacHarg Residence

S.010   T.9002
William Storrs MacHarg Residence
(1891)
Chicago, Illinois
Demolished

Out of his salary, Wright was paying back to Sullivan the loan that had allowed the aspiring architect to buy land and build his home in Oak Park. To support his growing family and obtain the luxuries he felt proper to his life-style, Wright turned to working at night on commissions of his own. Such moonlighting violated the express provisions of Wright's five-year contract with Adler & Sullivan.

It has long been suggested that the MacHarg house was the first of what Grant Manson termed the bootlegged houses. Since W. S. MacHarg was a plumbing contractor and specifically a consultant to Adler & Sullivan, it is unlikely that this house would not have been known to the firm. Since Sullivan focused his efforts on commercial architecture, he may have given the commission to Wright as "overtime" work to help him pay off his indebtedness. Whatever the situation, little is known of the work, for no plans and only one photo have survived.

McArthur Residence

McArthur dining
room sideboard

McArthur Garage

S.011   T.9205
Warren **McArthur Residence**
(1892),
S.011A   T.0014
Residence Remodeling (1900) and
S.011B   T.0014
Garage (1900)
Chicago, Illinois

Warren McArthur was a partner with E. E. Boynton (S.147) in the Ham Lantern Company. The McArthur family was an important Wright client. In 1927, Wright's collaboration with McArthur's son Albert on the Arizona Biltmore Hotel (S.221–S.222) introduced the Wisconsin architect to warm Arizona winters. Then, in the winter of 1928, he built a desert camp (S.224) at Chandler, just south of Phoenix.

Eventually the appeal of Arizona's winter climate led Wright to establish Taliesin West as the winter home for his fellowship.

Wright disguised his bootlegged work by publishing it under the name of Cecil S. Corwin, with whom he had worked in Silsbee's office. In the McArthur residence Roman brick is used up to the windowsill, with plaster above. The entry is to the side at ground level rather than facing the street. Once inside, one must turn right and move up several steps to the first-floor level. The entry is spacious, separating the reception and living rooms (right) from activities of secondary importance. The fireplace is in the living room on the outside wall and is faced with 1 1/2-by-3-inch tile.

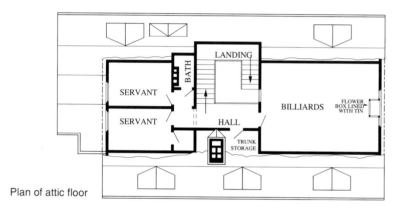

Plan of attic floor

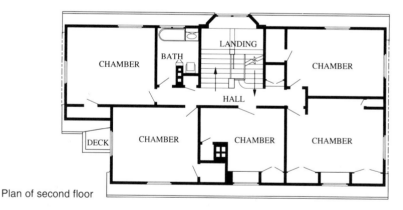

Plan of second floor

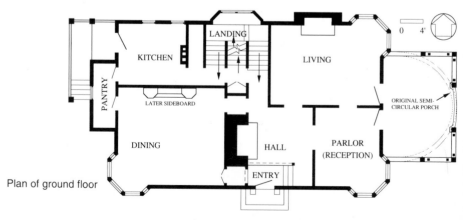

Plan of ground floor

Corner octagonal bays required cantilevering, though hardly of a daring sort. The stairwell, opposite the entry, is particularly large and well-lit by tall windows (known as lites) as it winds to a third floor that is dominated by a barrel-vaulted front room, designed a year or more before Wright used this feature in his children's playroom (see S.003). There are five bedrooms on the second floor. The finished attic and basement utilities (laundry, heater, and coal rooms) make this a four-story structure. In the houses he designed over the next decade, Wright eventually raised the main floor well above ground level (see S.047), then eliminated the basement as such, and finally, after the Robie house (S.127), dispensed with the attic (but for one last demand in the Bogk house, S.196).

Surviving plans show an additional bathroom as part of a 1900 remodeling, with some changes in the pantry and at the rear entry; the work may not have been carried out until 1902. In that year, as best we can discern (since these plans do not survive), there was also a particularly interesting remodeling of the dining room. Here a California oak sideboard and a pair of French doors are linked by stringcourses. One set of French doors leads only to a useless balcony directly above the entry well. Curved art glass is feathered with small pieces of glass. Stemlike forms in wood columns and the design of leaded glass are similar to those of the Thomas house (S.063), supporting the 1902 date. The dining room remodeling was featured in *House Beautiful* (March 1904) as "A Yellow Dining Room."

The covered porch was originally an open terrace. Drawings show it as semicircular, with the rectilinear porch sketched over it, and this is how it was built: the half-circle of porch remains today, inside the false square facade.

The garage has quarters upstairs for chauffeur and servants and a turntable inside the single garage door to turn vehicles around since at that time automobiles had no reverse gear.

David and Ruth Michael became the third owners of this property and are responsible for its remarkably good condition.

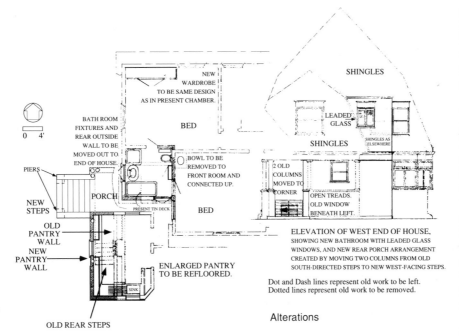

ELEVATION OF WEST END OF HOUSE, SHOWING NEW BATHROOM WITH LEADED GLASS WINDOWS, AND NEW REAR PORCH ARRANGEMENT CREATED BY MOVING TWO COLUMNS FROM OLD SOUTH-DIRECTED STEPS TO NEW WEST-FACING STEPS.

Dot and Dash lines represent old work to be left.
Dotted lines represent old work to be removed.

Alterations

Plan of upper level of garage

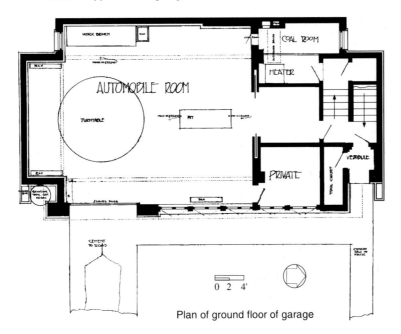

Plan of ground floor of garage

S.012
Kenwood Dining Room Remodeling (1903)
Chicago, Illinois
Dining table and chairs removed; sideboard and trim remain

Two houses to the north of the McArthur residence (S.011) in the Kenwood district is another dining room remodeling of the same year as its neighbor (though some evidence suggests it could have been as late as 1907). It included a sideboard and a dining table and chairs, probably built by John Ayers, Wright's furniture craftsman before the architect's long association with George Niedecken, which began in 1903. The client is not yet known, and no drawings have been found in the Taliesin archive.

Sideboard in the remodeled dining room

W. Irving **Clark** Residence (1893)
LaGrange, Illinois
Restored late 1980s

Plans found at Taliesin in 1966 provide evidence of Wright's authorship of a building previously attributed, even by Wright, to E. Hill Turnock. *Inland Architect* (August 1894) carried a photo of the house with a caption identifying Wright as its architect.

The Clark residence looks back to Wright's three-year earlier Oak Park home (S.002) in its crossed roof forms, high front gable, Palladian window over twin bays and open front porch. The plan, at least on the ground floor, is more complex but otherwise somewhat similar to that of the nearby Emmond house (S.015), particularly in its porches. Thus a design evolution may be seen from MacArthur (S.011) through Clark to Blossom (S.014), Emmond, and Harlan (S.018). The main entry, board-and-batten-paneled, leads to a hall, reception room to the right, drawing room to the left, then an inglenook with a fireplace faced in 1 1/2-by-5 1/4-inch tile, typical of Wright's design for this period. Here one must choose to turn left to stairs, jog left to the dining room, or turn right into the sitting room (stairs from this room to the nursery above, shown on plans, were not built). Behind the dining room is the kitchen. There are entries centered in each facade, the front one obviously for guests, a side entry for the family to reach the carriage, a back entry for servants, and a south side exit from the sitting room opening, as in the Emmond house, to the yard. The second floor seems more Victorian than Wrightian. The third-floor front is a ballroom. The flooring in the half octagonal south porch is pie-segmented, a detail identical to one in the Young house (S.036) alterations of 1895.

In 1892–93 Wright was busy with three bootlegged designs in LaGrange. The Clark house may be the earliest of these, for its plan shows an organization that was simplified and clarified in the Emmond house. Almost five decades later Henry-Russell Hitchcock, querying Wright on his LaGrange projects, was told that the Clark house was Turnock's. Turnock, Wright's senior by a decade, was respected in his profession, but his designs are jumbled collections from architectural textbooks. Perhaps his most coherent design is immediately behind the Clark home, on Sixth Street. It shows none of the organizational brilliance demonstrated by Wright at this time and reveals Turnock as incapable of having designed the Clark structure. Was Wright, who often remembered dates incorrectly for Hitchcock, rejecting Clark because he was remembering the Orrin Goan fiasco (see Peter Goan, S.029, for a discussion of this) and confusing Goan's architect John Tilton with Turnock? Evidence in hand points to this as one possible solution that brings together all relevant pieces of the puzzle.

John Thorpe was the restoration architect for work done in 1988 to return the building to its 1893 appearance. As restoration progressed, the true Wrightian character of the house, previously clad in aluminum, was revealed.

Clark Residence, restored

Plan of first floor

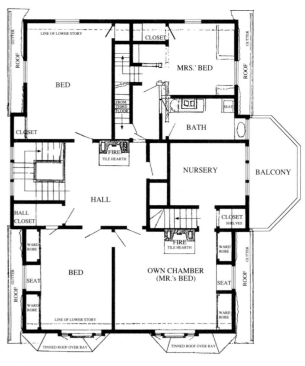

Plan of second floor

S.014 T.9201
George **Blossom Residence** (1892)
Chicago, Illinois

With the Blossom house, Wright demonstrated that, had he chosen to, he could have been a great academic architect. The work is a fine example of academic Colonial Revival. With the exception of the conservatory at the rear, the plan is essentially symmetrical. The semicircular conservatory is balanced by the rear porch entry, sketched as a semicircle on the original plan. The balcony above the conservatory is now enclosed, as shown in the sketch on Wright's plan. The house has clapboard siding, and the south dormer is a later addition.

Many characteristics of early Wrightian design are here apparent. Entry is gained by stairs to a covered porch, then passing into a narrow ante room. To the right is a dead-end reception room, to the left a parlor, and straight ahead a double-banded archway framing the fireplace inglenook beyond. The fireplace is faced with a 1-by-4-inch olive tile. Beyond the living room on the south is the formal dining room. The north side of the living room is the stairwell, protected by a balustrade of rectilinear balusters that looks back to the Charnley stairwell (see S.009). There is a separate servant's stair to the half-level landing, allowing the servant to go upstairs unseen, a feature common in the period which Wright used throughout his pre-Prairie homes. The third level is a full-length studio in balloon construction.

Many features, such as archways, reveal Sullivan's influence on Wright. Perhaps more interesting, however, are elements possibly derived from the thirteen Froebel Gifts, those educational puzzles and toys that were a major influence during his childhood. Board siding is beaded, suggesting the peas of the ultimate Gift, and the windows have leaded glass in a pattern created by a compass, which strongly resembles what would easily be created from the eleventh Froebel Gift.

The Blossom house is another of the bootlegged houses. Alice Shaddle is but the third owner of this property, having purchased it from a Blossom relative in 1957. Built-in seating has been removed from the conservatory, but the home is otherwise in excellent condition.

Queen Anne style Blossom Residence, front

Blossom living room fireplace, through anteroom arch

Blossom Residence, rear, with Prairie-style garage (S.133) at left

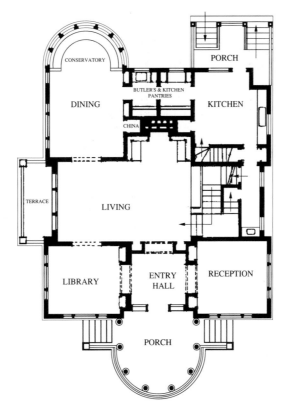

Plan of first floor

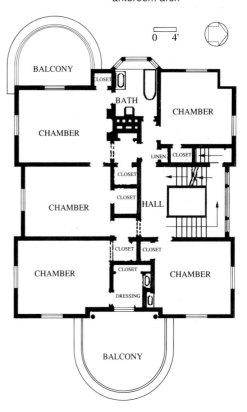

Plan of second floor

S.015 T.9202
Robert G. **Emmond** Residence
(1892)
LaGrange, Illinois
Brick resurfacing at lower story.
Terraces enlarged and enclosed

Another bootlegged venture, the Emmond house is the most elaborate of three houses (the others, Thomas Gale, S.016, and Robert Parker, S.017) using the same square plan, made a bit more elegant by octagonal bays at two corners, which define the reception and dining rooms, with a library (which he called the living room) between them. Typically, the main entry leads three ways, to stairs to the second floor, on one side, a door hiding the side entry and kitchen, and a large opening to the reception room, beyond which, in the farthest corner, is the formal dining room. All three houses have their public entries looking toward the street, yet each faces sideways on its lot. The Emmond house has a complete lot to itself at the side while the Thomas H. Gale and Robert Parker homes are crowded in their Oak Park settings.

All three were originally clapboard structures, but the Emmond has been resurfaced with brick on its lower story; the terraces have also been enlarged and enclosed (about 1935), and the house otherwise altered. Oak is used on the main floor, pine above.

Family history suggests that Emmond had a room on Washington Boulevard, Chicago, which he shared with Orrin Goan (see S.029), who, at one point, owned the entire LaGrange city block. The owners in the 1980s, Emmond and Catherine Thompson, are responsible for exterior renovation that suggests some of the original elegance of Wright's design. Emmond Thompson's maternal grandfather was Robert Emmond, the original client.

Across the street is the Peter Goan (S.029) residence and to the immediate south the house by John Tilton for Orrin Goan.

Emmond Residence

View through dining room window to yard

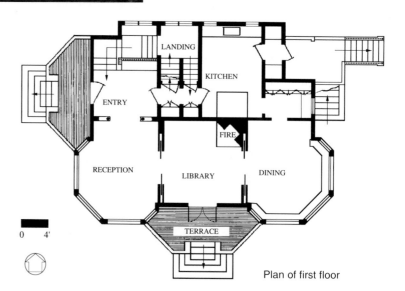

Plan of first floor

S.016 T.0905
Thomas H. Gale Residence (1892)
Oak Park, Illinois

The Gales were a very prominent Oak Park family. Edwin Oscar Gale was born in 1835 and came from Europe to Chicago in 1837 on a steamship named the *Illinois;* eventually the Gales settled on Lake Street at Kenilworth. Two of Oscar's sons, Walter and Tom, moved into Wright-designed homes on Chicago Avenue (see also S.020) to raise their families; Walter remained childless, but Tom and his wife Laura, who met at the University of Michigan, raised two children.

This house in a rectilinearized Queen Anne style built for realtor, speculator, developer, and attorney Thomas H. Gale and the Emmond (S.015) and Parker (S.017) residences have plans that are very similar, the Emmond being a mirror of the others. They differ more in details, such as arched entries and windows (on Wright's plan, pencilled over the origi-nal rectilinear treatment) in the Emmond versus lintels in Gale and Parker, than in spatial arrangements. Comparison of the octagonal bays reveals varied treatment of the second-story fenestration. Mr. Gale built two houses on Chicago Avenue, sold one to attorney Robert Parker and, for reasons long buried in history, their ownership, according to historian Frances H. Steiner, has been reversed in most publications; Tom and Walter Gale were, accordingly, neighbors (the photograph shows the Walter Gale house in the background). Charles Gale, their nephew, argues for the tradi-tional assignment of ownership on the authority of his first cousin, Sally Gale, yet the plan marked with Parker's name and county records substantiate Steiner's findings. The Gales later built three designs by Wright, two cottages (S.088 and S.088.1–3) and a home (S.098).

Zona Gale, an author from Portage, Wisconsin, who is mentioned in Wright's *Autobiography,* is not one of the Oak Park Gales.

Robert P. Parker Residence

S.017 T.9206
Robert P. **Parker** Residence (1892)
Oak Park, Illinois

The Parker house is similar in plan to the Emmond (S.015, a mirrored plan) and Thomas H. Gale (S.016) resi-dences. A porch intended for the side was never built, and the front porch reveals more affinity with the Woolley residence (S.023) than the postless half-octagon planned by Wright. Com-pare the corner turrets of this and the Thomas Gale house, and the more interesting treatment of the second-story windows in the latter is apparent; both, however, represent Queen Anne style tending toward the rectilinearity that characterized Wright's work a decade later. Ownership of these two houses was long reversed in listings, but the plan in the Taliesin archives clearly identifies this unit as the one designed for Robert Parker. This, however, must be countered by the argument that the house was built by Walter and Thomas H. Gale as an investment. It was then purchased by Parker. Sally Gale remembered this as the home in which she was born and raised, according to Gale family historians, Kathryn Gale and nephew Charles Gale, first cousin of Sally Gale.

Thomas H. Gale Residence

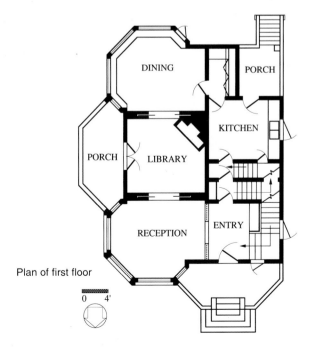

Plan of first floor

0   4'

An Historical Overview of Frank Lloyd Wright's Career

In his first architectural period (1887–1900), Wright groped for an artistic ethos. Only with the "discovery" of the grid and the use of a unit system in the design of his first Prairie houses did his architecture take on an immediately recognizable quality which, when other architects picked up its grammar, gained the title Prairie school architecture.

A period of exploration, the nineteen-teens, led Wright to expand his unit system. From the simple square units of his first Prairie home (see the Ward Willits Residence, S.054), he developed rectangles, triangles, and other geometric possibilities. In the twenties, he invented a construction system of concrete blocks fully suited to his newly developed Usonian architecture. This time the Great Depression interrupted his line of artistic development, and Wright retreated to his Wisconsin home, Taliesin (Welsh for "shining brow"; the house was set into the brow of the hill), and started a school of architecture. In 1935, the first homes he specifically called Usonian appeared, though the Usonian principle was completely developed as early as 1921, and Wright stated in 1952 that La Miniatura (S.214; 1923) was the first Usonian home.

Wright's earliest work (1887–1900) was both eclectic and experimental, yet geometric forms occur in his earliest structures. Octagonal bays appear in the plans for his earliest designs, such as the first Hillside Home School (S.001; 1887), as well as his own Oak Park residence (S.002; 1889), one of whose gables is an equilateral triangle. Semicircles and hexagonal elements abound in his moonlighted designs of 1892.

The Prairie era emerged from various experiments in the nineties in which Wright developed his own style, often hesitatingly or through his own "perfecting" of other popular styles. Wright's Prairie school years (1901–9) are characterized by consistent use of a grid comprised of squares, most often centered on door and window mullions. Within this grid, a unit system provided Wright a method with which to express both a coherent vision of an American architecture as well as his transcendentalism (essentially Swedenborgian, though Wright never acknowledged European influences and would relate publicly only to American transcendentalists; he seems to have read Coleridge extensively and incorporated many of his ideas into *An Autobiography*). This first golden era came to an abrupt end publicly in 1909, when it became clear to Wright that his ideas were not to be accepted by such establishment leaders as Harold McCormick, for whom Wright had produced a magnificent design, possibly the most important of his life to that point. At this juncture, capitalism and democracy had failed to unite in Wright to produce an American democratic architecture.

The years 1913–19 saw Wright actively develop his architectural art for the average (democratic) American

more than for establishment leaders. The American Ready-Cut System of prefabricated houses and apartments (S.201–S.204) and the Ravine Bluffs Development (S.185–S.192) reveal this tendency. What was missing was a system of construction that would meet the new democratic ideal.

He found his solution early in the twenties. With his eldest son Lloyd, he developed a concrete block system of construction. His first design for this method was the Doheny Ranch (1921, not constructed), but it was first fully employed in a house designed for Mrs. George Madison Millard (S.214; 1923) in Pasadena.

By the end of the twenties, Wright had explored the concrete block system with significant results. This was called a textile block method of construction, for 3 1/2-inch-thick concrete blocks were woven together by reinforcing rods in edge reveals. Wright began to develop wholly new grids: rectangles (double squares), equilateral triangles, equilateral parallelograms, eventually hexagons, and circular segments that spelled the final destruction of the right angle in his house design.

In the postwar years, Wright reintroduced textile block to his domestic work (now with the vertical dimension completely free of the plan grid) in a

group of do-it-yourself houses in Michigan (S.294–S.301) and in a form with full block roofing, the Usonian Automatic (see Pieper, S.349, Tonkens, S.386, Kalil, S.387). Variants on this led to prefabricated versions in the late fifties in both block (for Walter Bimson in Arizona, never built) and board and batten (for Marshall Erdman, S.406–S.412, of Madison, Wisconsin).

Interchanging his materials freely on a great variety of modules, Wright created most of his finest work in these later Usonian years. Yet it is an architecture—diverse and democratic, thus truly American—that is much too little known, for architectural historians have concentrated their efforts on the more easily understood Prairie houses from Wright's simplest architectural grammar.

S.018   T.9204
Dr. Allison W. Harlan Residence
(1892)
Chicago, Illinois
Demolished, 1963

Of the many houses Wright moonlighted while still with the firm of Adler & Sullivan, the Harlan residence stands out both in design and as the one that could have caused Wright's separation from the firm. The facade was not broken by an entryway; rather, that element was placed on the side facing south (left in the photograph), as in the McArthur (S.011) and later Heller (S.038) residences, and was reached by a walled walkway. While the McArthur and Heller houses were crowded by neighbors to the south, the arrangement here gained maximum exposure to southern sunlight. Wright would make this a feature of his later designs by setting the house close to or on the north lot line, shifting the main entry to that side as well, gaining maximum exposure to the south (Moore, S.034, Fricke, S.059, Beachy, S.117, May, S.148, and Bach S.193 are some examples).

The living room was later altered at the insistence of Dr. Harlan, a professor of dental surgery; originally it spanned the full width of the facade, an arrangement that became standard in most of Wright's square-plan houses. This space was isolated from the remainder of the first floor by the large entry hall, which had a double fireplace, the rear one facing a library. Then further to the rear separate dining and breakfast rooms, all finally terminated in a pantry and kitchen. The full-width terrace and second-story balcony emphasized the horizontality of the structure.

The house was built on a section owned by Elbert Hubbard, of the Roycroft community and later the Larkin enterprise (see S.093).

Late in 1988, Tom Longhi and Paul Sorensen of Schema Design Group discovered art glass in a home a few lots north of the Harlan site. Though the glass evidenced several design patterns and not one coherent scheme, art evaluator Ross Edman determined that they were by Wright. Although the house shows bits and snatches of Wright, no one element may be said to be his and his only at this time. This house was designed by Webster Tomlinson in 1900, half a year before Tomlinson and Wright initiated their short partnership. The client was Jay Morton, president of Diamond Steam Lines, who was living a few blocks away when the Harlan residence was erected. Sharing in the commission of a $15,000 house early in 1900 would have been tempting to Wright, who had seen only four of his designs of the previous three years built. Commissions had been plentiful in the early 1890s (there were 13,100 new housing starts in Chicago in 1892) but were scarce at the turn of the century (3,500 starts in 1900). The plan is Victorian, revealing none of the principles with which Wright was experimenting on his way to the Prairie house, which would emerge within the year. At most, then, one may see Wright as having provided art-glass designs, perhaps to help Tomlinson complete a project that, given his other work, was probably stretching his creative resources.

Harlan Residence

© Rossita Byrne Sweeney, used with permission

Living room

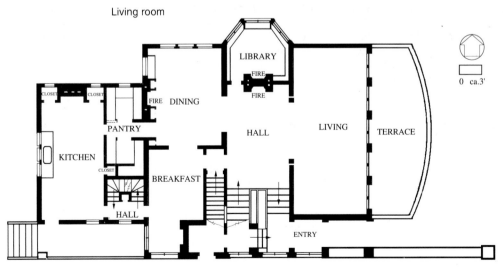

Plan of first floor

S.019   T.9207
Albert Sullivan Residence (1892)
Chicago, Illinois
Demolished, 1970

The Albert Sullivan house was apparently designed for Louis's mother, Adrienne, but she died before construction was completed. Sullivan himself lived in the house some four years before his brother Albert, after whom Wrightians name the building, occupied the quarters with his family.

The facade of this rowhouse revealed Sullivanian tracery in its detail but the work was one of those that Louis Sullivan passed on to his draftsman Wright while he, the master architect, dealt with large commercial projects. Note particularly that the main floor was well above street level, and the entry created a strong effect of compressed space, both elements characteristic of Wrightian design. Louis's career declined after the firm of Adler & Sullivan dissolved in 1895, while Albert's, with the Illinois Central Railroad, soared; the brothers were estranged for the remainder of their lives.

This building and others (S.005, S.006A, S.006B, S.007, S.008A, S.008B, S.009) could all be attributed to Sullivan on the principle that they originated in his office. That would, however, misrepresent Wright's contribution, though Wright would claim to have been only the pen in the master's hand.

Albert Sullivan Residence

S.020   T.9302
Walter M. Gale Residence (1893)
Oak Park, Illinois
Porch restored in 1977. Additional restoration begun late 1980s

Walter Gale, a University of Illinois pharmacy graduate and elder brother of Thomas H. Gale, had the most interesting and gracious of three early homes that Wright designed for one block on Chicago Avenue. This house is located immediately west of his brother's residence (S.016). The rounded forms are more typical of Queen Anne style than the neighboring structures.

One of the first houses Wright designed after he opened his own office, this, like his moonlighted designs, shows few of the characteristics that revealed a truly individual style later in the same year. The entry hall, which faces to the side and not the street, is quite grand and has beaded-edge wood paneling (see also S.014). From here one can turn left into the dead-end reception room, move forward to the library (which today would be a living room), turn right to a door leading to the kitchen, or turn around to the stairs. An octagonal bay with a seat at the landing level in the stairwell admits light to this otherwise dark room. There are two fireplaces on the main level. The one in the living room is on the outside wall, that in the dining room on the inside wall; each is faced with 1 1/2-by-6-inch tile. The dormer rises from the second floor, where it is framed by closets, to the third story. The three-story turret is reminiscent of Silsbee. Windows upstairs are curved and diamond-paned, which obscures the view and thus eliminates the need for curtains; the window at each end opens as a casement. Although stringcourses are used downstairs, they are absent upstairs and on the third floor; the servant's quarters were probably generous, for there was a bathroom at this level. The original front terrace, long since destroyed, was restored in 1977. New owners Vicki and Kenneth Prouty continued restoration into the late 1980s.

Walter Gale Residence

Walter Gale entry hallway

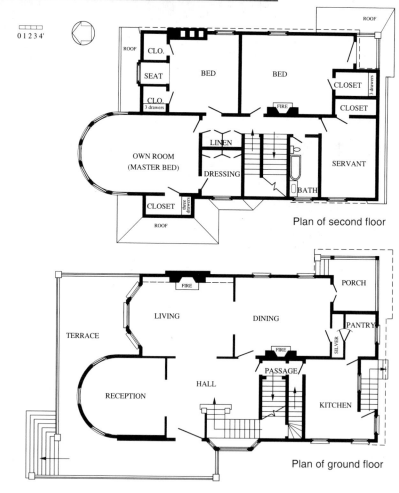

Plan of second floor

Plan of ground floor

S.021   T.9301
Robert M. Lamp Cottage, Rocky Roost (1893),
S.021A
Additions and Alterations (1901)
Rocky Roost, northwest of Governor's Island, Lake Mendota, Wisconsin
Destroyed by fire in 1934 or 1935. Normal lake water level now covers Rocky Roost

Though living in Oak Park in 1893, Wright maintained contact with his native area around Madison, Wisconsin. Two works came from this association, both on the shores of the lake that often inspired him to his best achievements. One of these was for Robert Lamp, a boyhood friend whom

Wright always called Robie; he was to have another Wright-designed home eleven years later (S.097).

It cannot be determined with any assurance how closely Rocky Roost adhered to any design of Wright's, because we know of it only from a limited number of photographs. Apparently a number of buildings were erected on this rocky outcrop hardly above water in the early 1890s. Then, in the early part of the first decade of the 1900s, Wright regrouped these buildings and added a second story to all, with a surrounding porch. The photograph here reproduced was made at about the time the Lamp residence was in construction, namely, the early 1900s.

S.022   T.9308
Municipal Boathouse (Lake Mendota Boathouse) for the Madison Improvement Association (1893)
Madison, Wisconsin
Dismantled 1926

In May 1893, Wright won a competition for design of the Municipal Boathouse. Its large arch, facing the lake, may also be seen as a design feature of later lakeside structures, such as the Jones house (S.083) and the George Gerts Double House (S.077).

The only general source of information on this structure is the June 1900 issue of *Architectural Review,* which contained an article on Wright by Robert C. Spencer, Jr., critic and Prairie school architect. A plan (too small to be of much use) and two photos of this structure were printed. What does not show in the photograph here is the pair of piers reaching into the lake, providing shelter and docking space for boats. Inside, the semicircular two-story section had berthing places for boats and a crane on a circular tram above. At the second level was a pergola leading visitors from the street side to the two observation towers.

Madison Municipal Boathouse

Lamp Cottage called Rocky Roost (1909)

Courtesy of the State Historical Society of Wisconsin

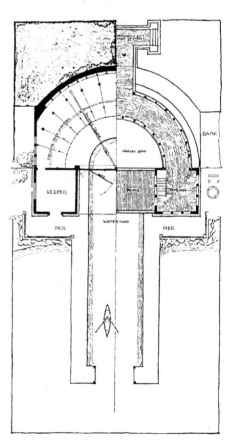

Plan, lower and upper levels

S.023 T.9405
Francis **Woolley** Residence (1893)
Oak Park, Illinois
Original clapboard siding now covered
with vinyl clapboard

Back-to-back with the Robert Parker
house (S.017), of which it seems to be
a further, less-inspired, variant is the
"Wooley" (as Wright spelled it) residence, for Francis and Cora L.
Woolley. Originally it featured clapboard to the second-floor sill line and
shingles to the soffit. This carrying of
the lower floor exterior to the sill line
of the second floor was a design feature
of Wright's at this time and may be
seen in such diverse structures as the
Winslow (S.024), Goan (S.029),
Goodrich (S.042), Rollin Furbeck
(S.044), and Davenport (S.068) residences. The structure was covered in
1987 with vinyl clapboard siding.

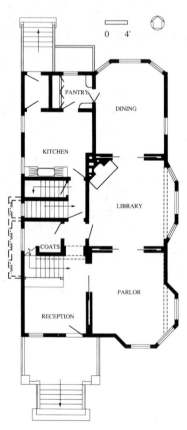

Plan of first floor

Woolley Residence, 1988

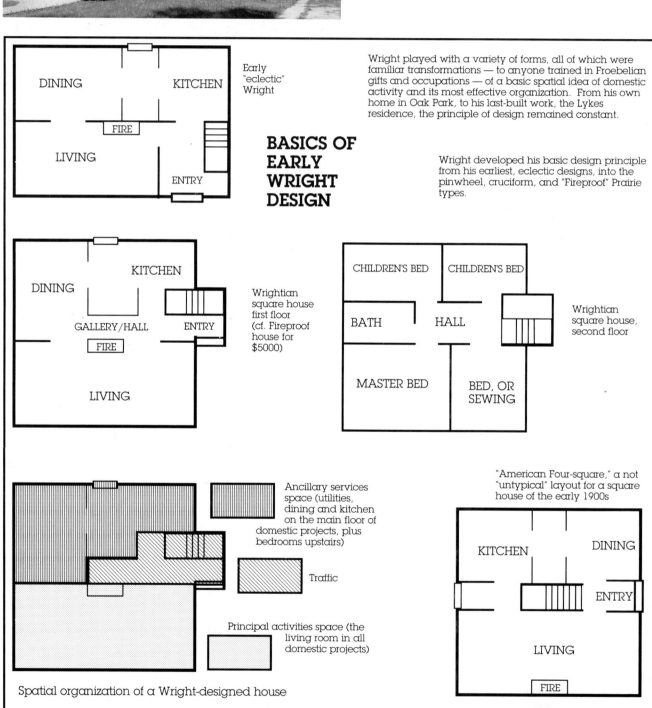

Early
"eclectic"
Wright

Wright played with a variety of forms, all of which were
familiar transformations — to anyone trained in Froebelian
gifts and occupations — of a basic spatial idea of domestic
activity and its most effective organization. From his own
home in Oak Park, to his last-built work, the Lykes
residence, the principle of design remained constant.

**BASICS OF
EARLY
WRIGHT
DESIGN**

Wright developed his basic design principle
from his earliest, eclectic designs, into the
pinwheel, cruciform, and "Fireproof" Prairie
types.

Wrightian
square house
first floor
(cf. Fireproof
house for
$5000)

Wrightian
square house,
second floor

Ancillary services
space (utilities,
dining and kitchen
on the main floor of
domestic projects, plus
bedrooms upstairs)

Traffic

Principal activities space (the
living room in all
domestic projects)

"American Four-square," a not
"untypical" layout for a square
house of the early 1900s

Spatial organization of a Wright-designed house

S.024 T.9305
William Herman **Winslow Residence** and
S.025 T.9305A
Stable (1894)
River Forest, Illinois

Winslow Residence

William Winslow, president of Winslow Bros. Ornamental Ironworks, a national supplier of quality ironwork, acquired the property in Auvergne Place early in 1894 from Edward C. Waller, whose own dwelling was across the street. This fact requires refiguring the date of the house design from the commonly accepted 1893. Wright certainly knew Winslow, however, from meetings in the Adler & Sullivan offices well before the design was commissioned. With Wright, Winslow published a special edition of *The House Beautiful* by Unitarian minister William C. Gannett in the winter of 1896/97 at Winslow's Auvergne Press, in a room at the side of the stable. The stable, picturesque in its own right, was later equipped with a turntable for an automobile.

This, then, was Wright's first major commission ($20,000) after he left Sullivan's office. He claimed it as his first independent commission. It suggests an influence from the 1893 World Columbian Exposition Turkish exhibition building. More important, perhaps, it is a descendant, or reworking to perfect the design, of the lost Orrin Goan commission (see the discussion of the Peter Goan residence, S.029). Certain stylistic characteristics were to stay with Wright throughout his life: a stylobate-like foundation that firmly sets the house on the earth; first-floor living quarters that dominate the structure; low, hipped-roof above broad overhanging eaves; and, in two-story structures, a second story that is like a gallery, never dominating the first floor. The house has a full basement and a finished attic floor for servants.

In the Winslow house, the masonry elements are treated to a foliage ornament in the manner of Louis Sullivan. Tapestry brick of Roman dimensions is the basic material, while stone and plaster (in the frieze, which is not terra-cotta) are also employed. Here, double hung windows are used, a rarity among the architect's Prairie and later designs; casement windows were the norm.

Wright here establishes the hearth as the focus of the domestic scene;

Reception hall

View through dining room window to the Stable

Plan of Winslow Residence, second floor

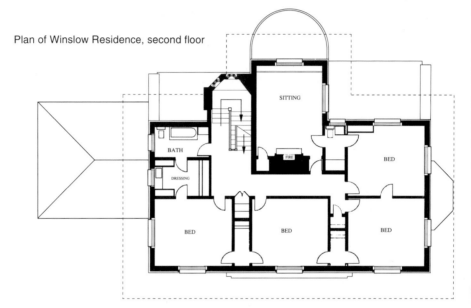

Plan of Winslow Residence, first floor

(Continues)

(**S.024** *continued*)

the front door opens directly to a hall
with a fireplace set behind ornate columns. It is back-to-back with another
fireplace, in the dining room; the two
are at the geometric center of the building's basic rectangular plan.

The porte-cochere on the north
side was balanced on the south in
Wright's plan by a pavilion, intended,
but never built, in the architect's octagonal geometry, which was ubiquitous
in the early years. The arch of the
porte-cochere led directly to the similarly arched central doorway of the
stable before its conversion to a
garage. The southeast corner porch
(not visible in the exterior photograph)
was enlarged by architect Norman
Steenhof in 1962.

This structure has been designated
by the American Institute of Architects
as one of seventeen American buildings designed by Wright to be retained
as an example of his architectural contribution to American culture.

Winslow Stable, as built

Winslow Stable in more recent times

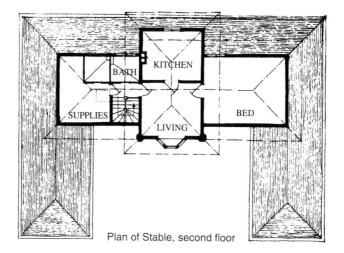
Plan of Stable, second floor

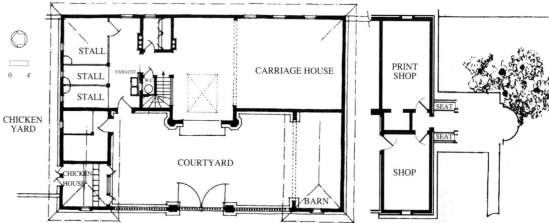
Plan of Stable, first floor, as done for the Auvergne Press (detail) and as later redone

S.026   T.9404
Robert W. **Roloson Rowhouses**
Remodeling (1894)
Chicago, Illinois
The four Roloson rowhouses are
numbered from north to south S.026.1
through S.026.4. Interior gutted in
1981; only the exterior reflects original
Wright

Robert Roloson purchased four
rowhouses set on three 25-foot-wide
city lots and commissioned Wright to
remodel them. Individual units were,
however, rather large, some 3000
square feet, as each "house" was on
seven "half" levels (including basement). Entry at ground level led to a
reception room to the side, then a
full-width skylighted stairwell that rose
the full four-floor front height of the
house. Behind this, rooms drop off at
half level.

Having been designated a Chicago
Landmark did not prevent the 1981 gut-
ting of the interiors after deterioration
and fire. Wright's work is now evident
only in the exterior, whose stonework
is abstract, like Sullivan's early period,
not Gothic. Wright intended to have the
gables removed, but this was never
done.

Robert Marshall Roloson, son of
Robert W., was married to the daugh-
ter of E. C. Waller (see S.030, S.031,
S.047, S.065, S.066).

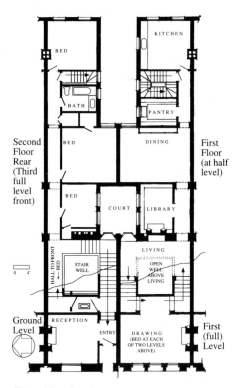

Plan of four levels

Roloson Rowhouses, 1988

Bassett Remodeling

S.027   T.9402
H. W. **Bassett** Residence
Remodeling (1894)
Oak Park, Illinois
Demolished

Wright's remodeling for Dr. H. W.
Bassett turned a residence into a
combination office on the ground floor
and residence above. The first floor
was given a shingle-and-batten siding
up to the second-floor sill level, a
surfacing that led eventually to a
favored Wright exterior, board and
batten. (For the first known use of this
shingle-and-batten surfacing, see the
Peter Goan house, S.029, 1893.)
Above this wood, light-colored plaster
was used, which in the soffit brought
light into the upper level; Wright used
this treatment often in Prairie designs
to counteract the darkening effect of
wide overhangs.

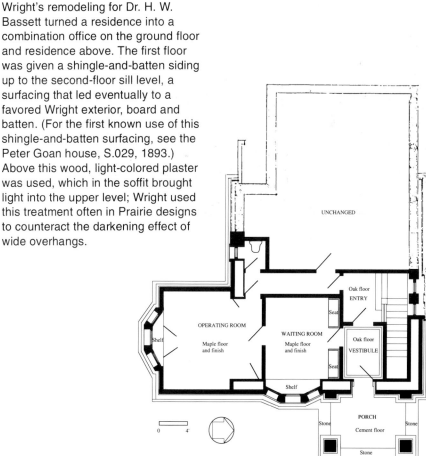

Frederick Bagley Residence

S.028   T.9401
Frederick Bagley Residence (1894)
Hinsdale, Illinois
Extended to the rear with enclosed
porch and detached pergola

Frederick Bagley was a marble
importer. He had Wright design a
communion rail and altar sculpture for
his Chicago company in 1894, which, if
built, have never been located, though
there is photographic evidence that a
baptismal font by Wright was built.

In the same year, Bagley built this
house, where he resided for fifteen
years. Many of Wright's early houses
reflect the eclectic tastes of the clients.
While the Bagley house reveals influences from Silsbee and Richardson,
Wright makes a strong statement of his
own. The general layout of the first-
floor rooms, with the exception of
the front porch, is a mirror image of
Wright's own home (S.002). The entry,
to one side of the full-length veranda,
leads to the stairs to the second floor,
the hall to the kitchen, or the living
room. The dining room is in the most
remote corner from the entry. The
marble-faced living room fireplace is
on an inside wall, with an inglenook
framed by two Ionic columns. Both

living room entries feature full pocket
doors. The octagonal library (17 feet, 4
inches in diameter) was an after-
thought and follows the geometry
Wright was to employ in his own library
(S.004). Here, however, it is raised far
above ground level, for its archway
opens from the first landing of the
stairs. The home has five bedrooms
and a bathroom. There is also a full
attic, perhaps originally with servants'
quarters.

Hinsdale was both farming country
and a summer home to Burlington Rail
Road executives. Each building,
therefore, had a telegraph but no
phone. The Bagley home, however,
was a year-round residence, for it was
heated. Originally the shingle exterior
was stained but is now covered with
white siding. The veranda is stone,
and the carriage step and basement
window wells are done in marble. The
basement has a laundry room. The
expansion of the single south living
room window to a picture window
framed with side panels is an addition
by the second owners, the Lamb family.

In 1976, Jerry and Jeannette
Goldstone acquired the property. They
found that much of the trim in the
dining room ceiling as well as stringcourses had been removed, and a
room had been added over the original
kitchen. They have preserved the
streetside view but have extended the
rear with an enclosed porch and
detached pergola and have fully
modernized the kitchen.

Plan of first floor

Peter **Goan** Residence (1893)

LaGrange, Illinois

Wright never expressed any love of clapboard, which he used by choice only as an economic alternative. Board and batten, laid horizontally, became his clear preference in wood siding after 1898. Here we see shingles, laid to give a board effect between horizontal battens, rising to the second-story sills. Stucco trimmed the area above and the soffits. Over the years the Goan house has lost a full-width front porch, which enhanced the horizontal character of the structure. Both siding and stucco have been altered. The Goan may be the last of the designs Wright moonlighted while with the firm of Adler & Sullivan. The 1894 date previously assigned the design is too late; instead, that date represents completion of construction.

Orrin S. Goan, a National Biscuit Company executive, was the son of Peter Goan. He wanted a Wright-designed house on a lot south of the Emmond house (S.015), which was just across the street from his father's house. Wright provided a design, and construction was set for (and may have begun on) this structure. Although the dating of the plan is uncertain, the design may have been in progress while Wright was still employed by Adler & Sullivan and thus forbidden to do any work on his own. Therefore, the design, however much it met Goan's specifications, would have been less dramatic than Wright might otherwise have produced, so as to avoid calling attention to his involvement therein. This house, then, may be seen as an early version of the Winslow residence (S.025), less daring and not so ornamental. Evidence of this is found in *The Architectural Review* (June 1900) in an article by Robert C. Spencer, Jr., where it is identified as the "Goare" house, probably only a poor transcription of Spencer's handwritten manuscript. Wright and Mrs. Goan had a falling out, and Wright abandoned the project. Work on the Emmond, Peter Goan (S.029), and Clark (S.013) houses continued. Orrin went to Wright and obtained the plans for his house, such as they were. A plan based on Wright's ideas was completed by architect John Tilton in about 1895, and this is the house that sits on the site today.

Goan Residence

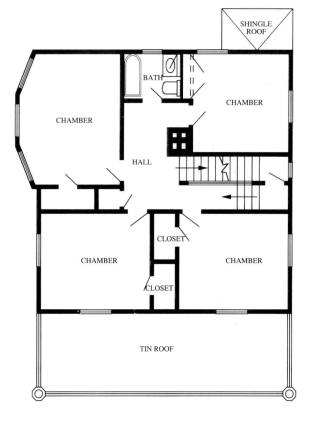

Goan Residence in more recent times, with porch removed

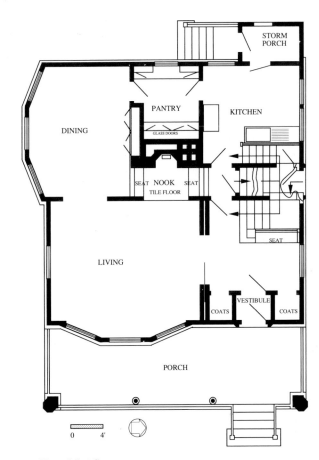

Plan of first floor

Plan of second floor

Francisco Terrace Apartments for
Edward Carson Waller (1895)
Chicago, Illinois
Demolished, March 1974 (entry
archway reconstructed at Euclid Place,
Oak Park, August 1977)

Edward C. Waller, neighbor of William
H. Winslow (S.024–S.025) in Auvergne
Place, was one of Wright's most important early clients, and Waller's son
Edward, Jr., commissioned Midway
Gardens (S.180). In 1895 Waller built
two sets of apartments at the corner of
Francisco and West Walnut streets.
Francisco Terrace was the more original of the two, reaching deep into its
lot, with a half-circle terra-cotta archway framing the entrance to an interior
court, rather like a mid-twentieth-
century motel. The second-story balcony ringing the court was wood.
Towers at the four inside corners held
stairwells. Most of the apartments had
a sitting room, kitchen, bathroom, and
two bedrooms. A center pair of apartments above the archway at the front
had a third bedroom. Two one-bedroom units were sandwiched between
three two-bedroom units at the rear.

All apartments opened onto the
garden courtyard, though front apartments also had direct access to the
street. Wright's usual three-entry
system for single-family domestic
dwellings is here reduced, for apartments, to two. By ingenious planning,
all had separate entries into the sitting
room and the kitchen.

General neglect led to vandalism,
then demolition. The archway has
been preserved on Lake Street at
Euclid Place in Oak Park in an
apartment building which, though
smaller, imitates much of Wright's
original idea.

Francisco Terrace Apartments

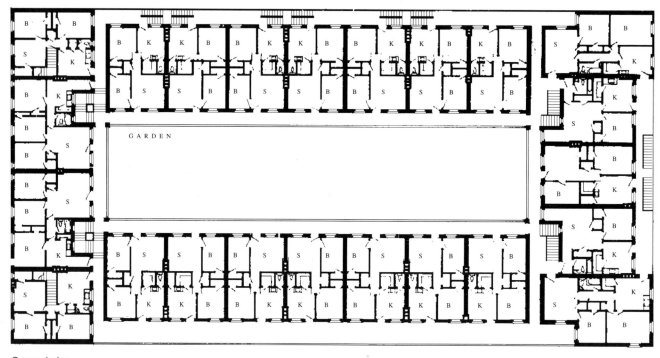

General plan

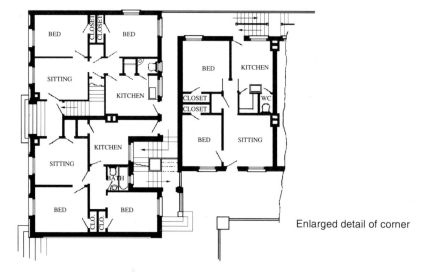

Enlarged detail of corner

S.031　T.9504

Edward C. **Waller Apartments**
(1895)

Chicago, Illinois

The five units are numbered from east to west S.031.1 to S.031.5. The individual apartments, a pair on each of two floors per unit, are numbered (east to west) S.031.11 and S.031.12 for downstairs apartments through S.031.53 and S.031.54 for upstairs apartments.

One of the five units, S.031.4, demolished by fire, 1968. Others in various states of alteration or disrepair, 1992. Restoration, including rebuilding of demolished unit, in development stages in late 1992

The Waller Apartments, although designed later, were constructed before Francisco Terrace, which was immediately behind these five units at Jackson Boulevard and Kedzie Avenue. Entry details vary, such as arches versus lintels. The plans vary from first to second floor to accommodate entry and stairs, the upper apartments being smaller. Plans are otherwise the same for all apartments except the end ones (S.031.11, S.031.13, S.031.52, and S.031.54), which have side windows and are mirror images of each other.

Each apartment had a parlor, chamber (bedroom), dining room, kitchen, bathroom, and closets. The arrangement accordingly was planned to be quite different from the Francisco Terrace units, but shortly after construction began, the plan was revised so that each apartment was arranged much like the Francisco Terrace units.

None were supervised by Wright during construction. Later usage suggests that some units were combined vertically so that the "chamber" became a sitting or reception room and the upstairs sleeping quarters.

The fifth unit (S.031.5) from the east is shown in the photograph. The fourth (S.031.4) was demolished by fire and the remains torn down in 1968. The others have long been threatened with demolition because of urban blight. As the nearby neighborhoods have revived from the blight, efforts to save the Waller units led to hiring in 1992 of John Eifler to submit plans for complete restoration and rebuilding of the demolished unit.

Waller Apartments, westernmost unit

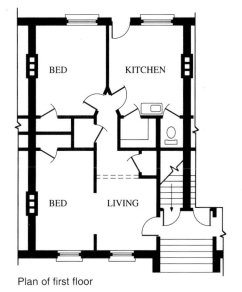

Plan of first floor

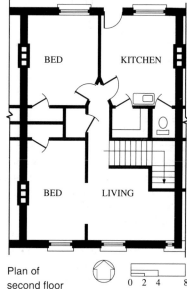

Plan of second floor

Francis
Apartments

S.032 T.9501
Francis Apartments for the Terre Haute Trust Company (1895)
Chicago, Illinois
Demolished, 1971

Above a prominent stylobate-like "base and water table of buff bedford," as Wright described the limestone, the ground floor of this four-story structure was faced in cream white vitreous terra-cotta with a circular geometric pattern in the manner of Sullivan. The pattern was carried into ironwork gates. Above, Wright used a yellow fire-clay Roman brick surface. Upper floors had eight apartments of three (rear),

four (front outside corners) or five (front courtyard) rooms. The top floor was similarly laid out but lacked bay windows. On the ground floor the north wing (right in the photo) contained four shops; thus, the south wing gained a five-room apartment where two three-room apartments were centered above. Entries to the two wings were at the far rear corners of the courtyard, leading directly to stairwells and short hallways that were typical of Wright. Trim was the wood Wright preferred for over two decades, quarter-sawn American white oak. The photograph shows the Francis Apartments shortly before demolition.

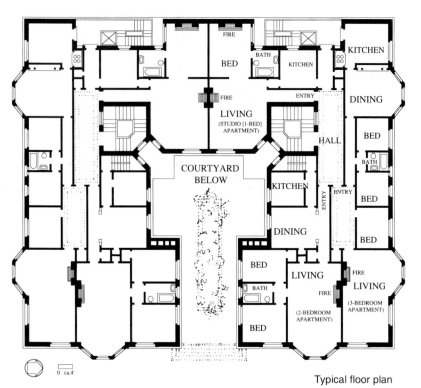

Typical floor plan

S.033 T.9505
Chauncey L. **Williams Residence** (1895) and
S.033A T.9505
Dormer Alterations (after 1900)
River Forest, Illinois
Enclosed porch added west of living room

Chauncey Williams, a publisher, came to River Forest from Madison, where he had known Wright. The design Wright provided for him was one of the first to reveal oriental influence. Stone boulders, in the manner of a Japanese garden, set off the foundation and entry. With its steeply pitched roof, articulation of plaster between eaves and sill line, and Roman brick below, this dwelling creates a colorful impression.

In his dormer remodeling, Wright called for ventilation openings every three courses of shingles, which would have emphasized the horizontal element more than the current even layering of cedar shakes that now approximates the original shingle roof design.

Wright made several designs for the dormers, at least two of which have been used in other structures (S.042, S.051). The earlier version framed the dormer window in a half circle, echoing the entry. One of these original designs remains, toward the rear on the north. The living room is at the rear rather than the front or the side where it usually was in Prairie designs. Both the dining room and library are octagons, a form Wright favored in the early nineties. No floor plans survive in the archives of the Frank Lloyd Wright Foundation at Taliesin West, though sketches of the dormer alterations reveal something of the architect's design methods.

The Dormer Alterations, in the archives under an 1895 date, raise a question of when the home and the alterations were originally done; how soon after the house was constructed would changes have been considered necessary? Since the photo with Robert C. Spencer's article in *The Architectural Review* (June 1900) shows the original dormers, the alterations were probably made after the turn of the century.

Williams Residence as first constructed

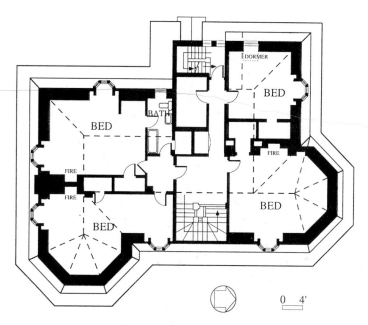

Conjectural plan of second floor as originally built

Williams Residence, showing original dormer on north side

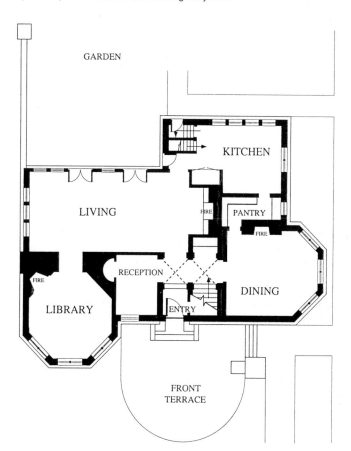

GARDEN

KITCHEN

LIVING

PANTRY

FIRE

FIRE

RECEPTION

DINING

LIBRARY

FIRE

ENTRY

FRONT
TERRACE

Conjectural plan of ground floor as originally built

Williams Residence after Dormer Remodeling

S.034 T.9503
Nathan G. Moore Residence
(1895)
S.034A T.2303
Residence Remodeling (1923)
and
S.035
Stable (1895 or later)
Oak Park, Illinois
Two-car garage added between
garden house and main structure.
Interior altered

This cross-gabled Roman brick house
for attorney Nathan Moore is studious-
ly Tudor in character. As built in 1895,
it was set on the northernmost limit of
the lot to gain maximum southern exposure for its porch. This porch is inconsistent with the Elizabethan character
elsewhere so aptly expressed. After a
fire in 1922, it was rebuilt, from the
foundations in some places, above the
first floor everywhere. At that time, the
steeply pitched roof was made even
more dramatic by extending the roof
downward, from just above the second-
floor window lintels to the first-floor
lintel line. Chimneys were enlarged, the
tile roof, which had impeded fire-
fighting efforts, was replaced by slate,
and the horizontal trim was removed
so that the vertical nature of the structure was emphasized. The small wing
to the west, according to the original
plans, was an unfinished garden
house. Between this garden house
and the main house is now a two-car
garage. There have been some interior
alterations. Directly south is the Hills
residence (S.051), which Moore had
Wright remodel for his daughter.

There is little reason to believe that
Moore would have built a house of
such size and cost without a stable.
The stable is nearly behind the Hills
residence but, according to historical
photographs, was probably entered by
a drive just north of the Hills house.
Upper filigree detail, rakes on the
eaves, as well as over-all proportions
are like those of the 1895 house.
Board-and-batten siding replaces the
brick of the main house. The board is
rough-sawn and cut at an angle to drip
properly in rain. Therefore, though
some stylistic evidence suggests a
date as late as 1900, it is dated 1895
and would represent Wright's first use
of board and batten.

Moore Residence, rear (southern exposure,
1923 remodeling)

Moore Residence, rear (southern exposure,
1895 design)

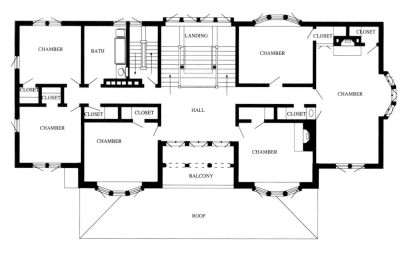

Plan, Original (1895) Moore Residence, second floor

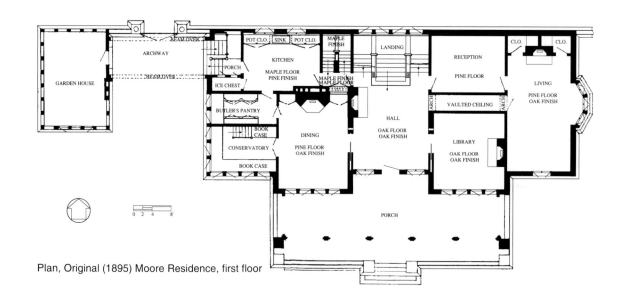

Plan, Original (1895) Moore Residence, first floor

Moore Residence, entry side (northern exposure, 1895 design)

Moore Residence, entry side (northern exposure, 1923 remodeling)

Moore Stable

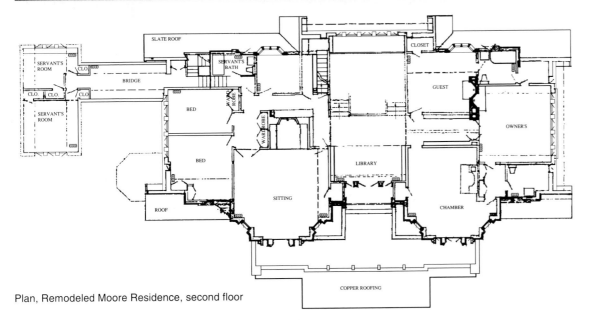

Plan, Remodeled Moore Residence, second floor

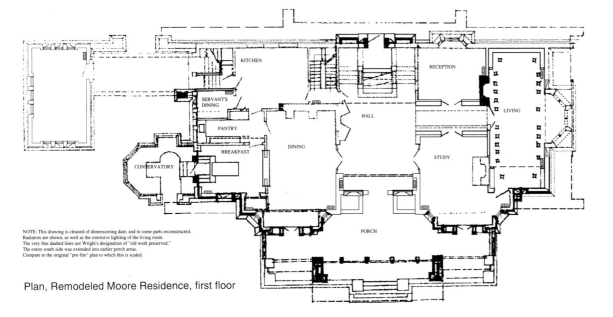

NOTE; This drawing is cleaned of dimensioning date, and in some parts reconstructed.
Radiators are shown, as well as the extensive lighting of the living room.
The very fine dashed lines are Wright's designation of "old work preserved."
The entire south side was extended into earlier porch areas.
Compare to the original "pre-fire" plan to which this is scaled.

Plan, Remodeled Moore Residence, first floor

S.036 T.9507

Harrison P. Young Residence
Additions and Remodeling (1895)
Oak Park, Illinois
Partially restored late 1980s and early 1990s

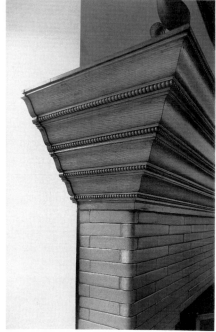

Fireplace mantel

As part of Wright's design, an existing wide-clapboard house was moved back 16 1/2 feet, and a narrow clapboard addition, consisting of new living room, broad porch, and two second-floor bedrooms, was built in front on the original foundations. These new and existing areas are keyed in three colors on the original drawing. Basic building forms that may hark back to Wright's experience with Froebel Gifts appear in the massings and include the cube, crossed triangular prisms, half cones, and cylinders, as well as an octagonal bay window. Some of the interior changes have classic details, such as Tuscan columns and spindles that screen the reception room from the entrance hallway. In the den, egg and dart detailing is used. Hardware is red brass.

The added living room spreads across the full front of the house, as those in most of Wright's square-plan houses do. Here, however, a row of windows opens the porch wall, extending the interior space to the outdoors in a way that would carry his signature throughout many later designs, but is only hinted at in the planimetrically similar Frederick Bagley home (S.028). Fireplaces in living room and master bedroom are by Wright, with intricate beaded work in the mantel, faced with an orangish tan Roman brick with a glazed surface, curved at the corners. The north end of the porch cantilevers over the driveway and a specially built carriage step. The entry veranda steps, recently restored, parallel the porch and lead the visitor up toward the porch cantilever, Wright's means here of compressing the architectural space as one approaches the entry. The south end of the porch is now enclosed. The stucco in the gable has been imitation half-timbered and was not part of Wright's design.

Screen between hallway and reception room

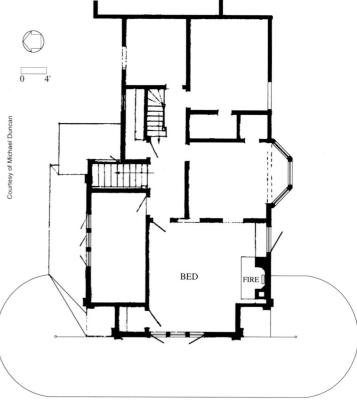

BED   FIRE

Plan of second floor

S.037   T.9607
Romeo and Juliet Windmill for
Nell and Jane Lloyd Jones (1896)
S.037A
Romeo and Juliet (II) (1938)
Spring Green, Wisconsin
Original windmill covered with
shingles, resurfaced in 1938 with
board and batten. Torn down in 1990.
New structure erected on original
stone base and capped with roof
saved from original structure

The plan of Romeo and Juliet reveals
a diamond penetrating an octagon.
This represents Romeo and Juliet,
Shakespeare's lovers, embracing (and
structurally supporting) each other,
though it is also a simple arrangement
of Froebel forms. The windmill was
constructed in the fall of 1897, about a
year after the idea was probably first
conceived. The *Weekly Home News* of
Spring Green suggests 1897 as both
the conception and construction date.
The 60-foot tower supplied water to
the coeducational Hillside Home
School (S.001). Wright later attached a
loudspeaker to the top of the tower
and wired it to a record player at the
"new" Hillside, the Taliesin Fellowship
complex (S.228), enabling him to play
Beethoven to cows as well as the
apprentices.
   In 1938 the original wood shingles
were replaced with horizontal cypress
board-and-batten siding. Wright tried,
at one point, to save the windmill by
pouring concrete into the structure
halfway to its top. Several later
attempts at restoration failed until, in
1990, serious efforts led to scaffolding
and fund-raising efforts; $150,000 was
the estimated cost of restoration. In
1992, two days before the celebration
at Taliesin of the 125th anniversary of
Wright's birth, a new Romeo and Juliet
was dedicated.

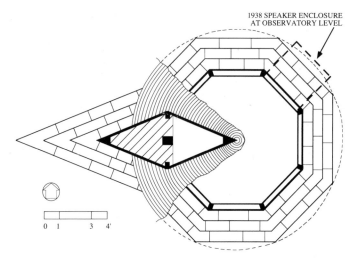

Romeo and Juliet Windmill

1938 SPEAKER ENCLOSURE
AT OBSERVATORY LEVEL

0   1   3   4'

Romeo and Juliet (II), detail of observatory level
with speaker enclosure (1992)

S.038   T.9606
Isidore **Heller Residence** (1896)
and
S.038A   T.9606
Alterations (1896?)
Chicago, Illinois

The primary axis of the Heller house is east-west, with its entry on the south side rather than on the street facade. This arrangement was often used by Wright to gain southern exposure, but this is not the case here because of the narrowness of the lot. The living room occupies the front quarter of the house. The main hallway runs from the center of the living room past the entry and reception room, with stairs on the opposite side, to the fireplace end of the dining room. To the rear are a kitchen and a servants' dining room. Yellow roman brick is complemented by white stone outside, waxed white oak inside, with plaster "saturated with pure color" in a rough sand finish.

This is among the earliest of Wright's explorations of three-story residence designs. Though there are occasional "finished attics" in some earlier houses (the Clark house, S.013, has a ballroom in the third-floor front), here Wright begins an exploration of third-floor possibilities that he will end with the Tomek (S.128) and Robie (S.127) houses. The third story is decorated in sculpted figures (not nude, as some texts suggest, but draped) by Richard Bock.

Wright also designed alterations at the second level which would have provided a new bedroom for Mrs. Heller with more windows on both the south and north, over the kitchen and servant's dining area. An elevator, rising from ground to attic floor, was installed. No coherent plans bearing a single date seem to exist, and the available attic plan does not show the house as it was constructed.

The stable, shown on most published plans, and previously listed as item S.039, was apparently never built. S.039 is thus an unassigned number.

Heller Residence

Heller Residence, rear

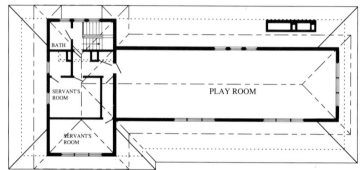

Plan of attic level

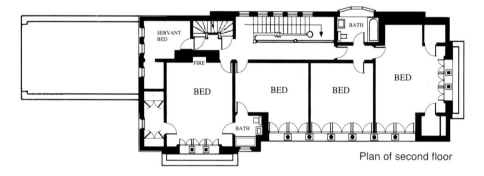

Plan of second floor

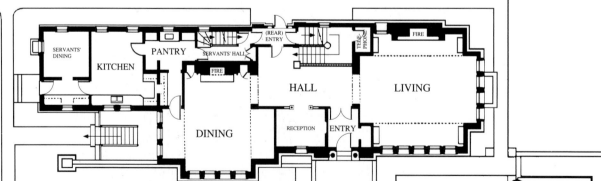

Plan of first floor

S.040   T.9603

Charles E. Roberts Residence Remodeling (1896)
Oak Park, Illinois
Wright's full-width veranda completed 1990

Charles E. Roberts, president of the Chicago Screw Company, was a member of the Board of Trustees at Unity Temple and chairman of its building committee. Not only did he influence his relatives in Kankakee to build Wright designs (S.052–S.053, S.056), but he also commissioned a number of projects himself. Strangely, the only works that came directly to fruition from this client were this residence remodeling and a stable (S.041).

The original Roberts structures were designed in 1879 by Daniel H. Burnham of Burnham and Root; the house was built in 1883. Changes to the house—"additions" Wright called them—were marked in color on the plan; these simplified Burnham's arrangement, both exterior (roof details and veranda) and interior. Extensive revision of the woodwork was Wright's major contribution, including changing architraves into stringcourses to humanize the scale. The southwest corner was redesigned as a downstairs bedroom. The central stairwell was redesigned at both levels. Wright also designed a perforated screen cabinet in his favorite wood of this period, American oak, for the living room fireplace mantel. Like one of his early signature squares, this screen features circles within the square, and a pattern between circle and square.

Implementation of a large full-front veranda was achieved in 1990.

Exterior with full-width veranda

Plan of Charles E. Roberts
Residence Remodeling ground floor

CLOSET

PORCH

REF

FIRE

NEW WORK IN THIS REAR QUADRANT PROVIDED A BEDROOM WITH CLOSETS AND PRIVATE BATHROOM: NOT ALL OF WRIGHT'S ALTERATIONS WERE COMPLETED.

KITCHEN

STAIRWELL REDESIGNED AT BOTH LEVELS

FIRE

FIRE

CABINET ABOVE FIREPLACE

0 1 2 3 4'

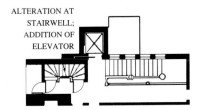

ALTERATION AT STAIRWELL; ADDITION OF ELEVATOR

Plan of second floor Alterations

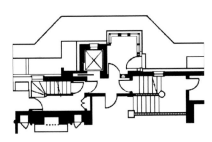

Plan of first floor Alterations

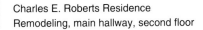

Charles E. Roberts Residence
Remodeling, main hallway, second floor

S.041 T.9602
Charles E. Roberts Stable (ca. 1900)
Oak Park, Illinois

Drawings have not survived to prove or disprove Wright's efforts regarding the stable, but local documents indicate that a barn may have been replaced about 1900 by a Wright-designed stable. The stable later became a garage for Roberts's electric automobile. Remodeling of the stable in 1929 by Charles E. White, Jr., merely adds confusion to the question of Wright's contribution. White married Alice Roberts in 1901 and worked in Wright's Oak Park office from 1903 to 1905, and supposedly lived in the stable after he remodeled it. White had his own residence and office in 1905 at 321 N. Euclid, the address of the Roberts Residence (S.040). This address would also have applied to the stable/garage at the rear but, if Wright were involved in the barn's replacement, a "317 N. Euclid" address should have applied.

In 1917, White had an office at 717 Columbia, but by 1926 (the next recorded date) he was back at 321, where he stayed until the property was sold sometime after 1936. Further research is needed to clarify all of White's residency and Wright's involvement in the design of the structures at 317 and 321 N. Euclid.

Charles E. Roberts Stable

S.042 T.9601
Harry C. Goodrich Residence (1896)
Oak Park, Illinois
Kitchen remodeled, dormer added in slate roof

Harry C. Goodrich, a successful inventor, made his fortune on an attachment for sewing machines. With this house for the inventor, Wright reached a baker's dozen of built projects in Oak Park and River Forest and had yet to begin the Prairie era. Here the architect took a step further away from historicism and toward geometry as the dominating factor in design. Here may be found another of Wright's circles within squares arrangements, a window pattern, in the small room next to the vestibule; this window alone is lead-camed.

The plan is a reworking—"improvement" by Wright's standards—of one of five low-cost designs originally offered to Charles Roberts (S.040–S.041) and may date from 1895; the house was built in the summer of 1896. The plan is not atypical of this era in the architect's developing sense of spatial organization, a public entry at the front, plus side and rear entries, with separate sitting room and library, and a centralized hearth.

Goodrich Residence

Many elements point to later Wright compositions. The second-story windows are located directly below the eaves and are linked by the light color of the clapboards, probably the last time Wright would choose this kind of siding which he used only for economic, not design, reasons. The lower boards conceal a basement that is partly above ground. The second level has maple floors and a foot-tub off the southwest bedroom. The attic is not finished, and the dormer in the slate roof is a later addition. The once open porch has been enclosed and parts of the interior altered.

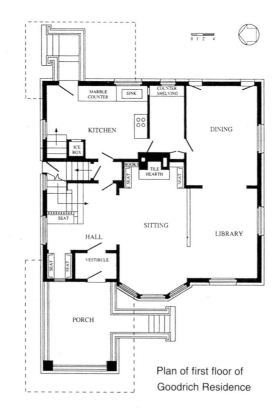

Plan of first floor of Goodrich Residence

Plan of second floor

S.043 T.9701

George Furbeck Residence (1897)
Oak Park, Illinois
Original porch enlarged and enclosed.
Third-floor dormer added to south

There are two Furbeck homes, wedding gifts from Warren Furbeck to George, his first son, and Rollin (S.044), third of his five sons. In September 1899, George moved to another house.

If one ignores the expanded porch and concentrates on the lower, brick-faced facade, one will recognize some of Wright's earliest purely rectilinear design. The octagon, which Wright used extensively in his own Studio (S.004), designed at about the same time as this home, permeates the plan. On either side of the entry are two towers, octagons inscribed within circles, 10 feet, 10 inches in diameter. Beyond them is the main space, an octagonal living room whose radius equals the tower diameter, with a fireplace to the right and a seat to the left. Continuing west, the next opening leads to a 17-foot-deep dining room, terminated by a fireplace, with an alcove to the left; the ends of this alcove repeat the octagonal geometry with a dimension half that of the towers. Behind this second fireplace are the kitchen, laundry, and rear porch. A single-story passageway along the north wall allows servants to reach the front door from the kitchen without having to pass through either dining or living room. Windows in the outside (north) wall are repeated in the north living room wall so that light can penetrate to the innermost reaches of the living room space.

The main stairwell is in the north tower, and the master bedroom at the second floor with library below in the south tower. Two bathrooms, four additional bedrooms, and a second set of stairs complete the composition at this level.

The brickwork for the front and towers and for the lower story (between stone courses) is specified in the earliest drawings as Flemish bond, in which header and stretcher alternate in each course. The shingles above were replaced with brick when detailing around the bay (far left in the photograph) and elsewhere was simplified. One must note the "buttressing" and prowlike forms in the

exterior, which also appear in Rollin's house and the Mary M. W. Adams house (S.108). Inside one finds the usual oak and Roman brick in both fireplaces.

Portions of the George Furbeck house no longer appear as originally constructed. The pinkish brick and wood trim remain, but a vastly enlarged third-floor dormer intrudes upon Wright's complex yet cohesive composition. The open-roofed porch was enclosed in 1922 by extending the original roof with splayed eaves to reach beyond the low, original un-

covered wall. Corner piers of new brick were erected, then glazing enclosed the new space, altering Wright's balance of proportions between the single-story porch and two-story main structure.

James and Audrey Kouvel acquired the house in 1969. Restoration of their home has been difficult; cleaning of the brick required use of hydrofluoric acid (normally used for etching glass) because the brick was too soft for abrasives. After cleaning, the brick was coated with silicone to prevent further deterioration.

George Furbeck Residence

George Furbeck Residence as altered

Living room, 1980s

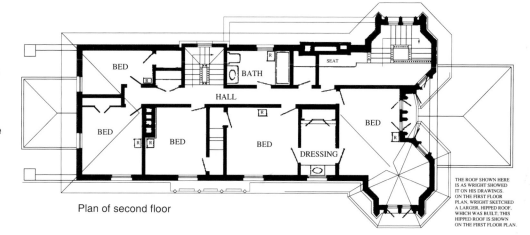

Plan of second floor

THE ROOF SHOWN HERE IS AS WRIGHT SHOWED IT ON HIS DRAWINGS. ON THE FIRST FLOOR PLAN, WRIGHT SKETCHED A LARGER, HIPPED ROOF, WHICH WAS BUILT; THIS HIPPED ROOF IS SHOWN ON THE FIRST FLOOR PLAN.

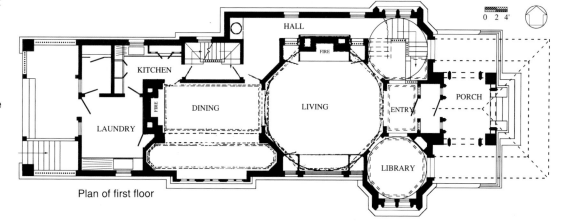

Plan of first floor

Dining room with concealed radiator

S.044　T.9801
Rollin Furbeck Residence (1897)
and
S.044A
Residence Remodeling (1907)
Oak Park, Illinois
Restored in the 1980s

This and the house for Rollin's brother George (S.043) were wedding gifts from their father, Warren Furbeck, a stockbroker, but it was probably Sophia Wapples Furbeck who chose Wright as the architect. Judson L. Wapples sold the property to his son-in-law in 1896 and construction was under way the following spring according to the *Oak Park Vindicator*, May 7, 1897. The house was built at a cost of $6000 plus $2250 for the property. Rollin Judson Furbeck, third of five sons, kept the house for only a year before moving to a $12,000 home, again financed by his father, from plans drawn by George W. Maher. Then, in November 1899 Rollin moved to New York City to head, as a member of the New York Stock Exchange, the east coast offices of the newly formed W. F. Furbeck Company.

The house is essentially square in plan with first-floor extensions. These are open porches at the north half of the front and rear facades and a porte-cochere on the south at the rear. Thus the house is a major transitional work from early square and rectangular plans, such as the 1896 Heller house (S.038), to the Prairie cruciform and pinwheel designs of the architect's first mature design period. Two design trends are evident; first, the brick base rising to the second-floor sill, Bedford limestone trim, window symmetry, broad hip roofs, central chimney, and porte-cochere like the Winslow house (1893, S.024), and, second, a central three-story mass with decorative columns like the Heller house (1896, S.038). The living and dining rooms feature picture windows, the first residential use of this architectural element. Wright employed another of his favorite devices, that of running the surface of a lower floor to the sill of the next higher floor, at both second and third levels. This building also features one of the last of Wright's square, semidetached entry porches (see also S.016, S.023, S.042, S.045, and S.051), most of which had flared eaves. The sculptural staircase to the

Rollin Furbeck Residence

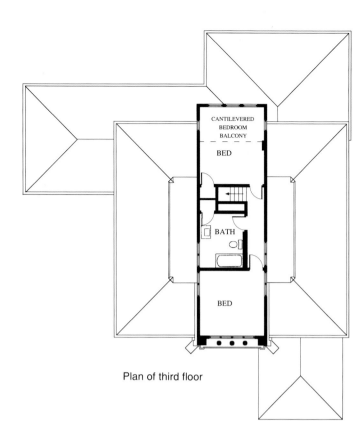

Plan of third floor

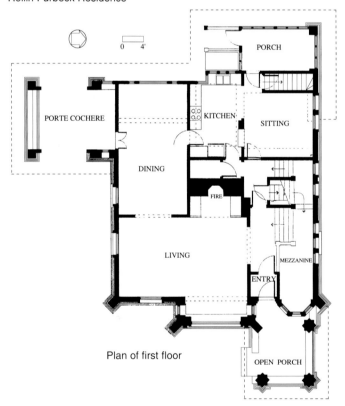

Plan of first floor

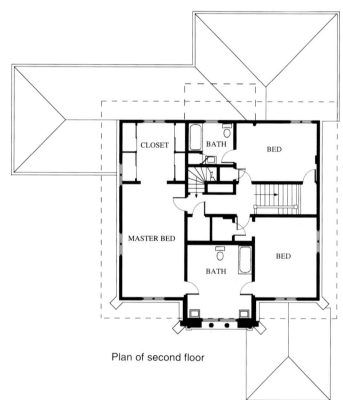

Plan of second floor

north of the gallery connects entry, living room, and kitchen, turns toward the center of the north wall to reach the second floor; in the opposite direction is an alcove that overlooks the entry porch. Under the stairwell is a half-level bathroom in what would otherwise have been stairs to the basement. The true basement staircase is at the rear of the kitchen, the original northwest corner of the main floor, and represents a step back from Wright's usual compact arrangement of stairwells at the main entry.

The third floor "attic" probably provided servants' quarters, for there is a bathroom at this level. The provision of unusually spacious arrangements for servants carries into other houses of the period for Walter Gale (S.020) and Harry Goodrich (S.042), though not into early three-story Prairie structures such as the Fricke (S.058) and William E. Martin (S.061) houses, which feature billiards and play rooms. Here, however, we have an unusual experiment by Wright, a rear room part of which is cantilevered well beyond the second-floor exterior wall structural support. This appears to be Wright's first use of such cantilevering in domestic design, a feature which would become common in later Prairie structures.

Extension of first floor rooms to fill in a long rear porch, dated 1907 and costing $2000, along with enclosure of the porte-cochere, may have been by Wright.

Restoration was begun in the mid-1980s by Linda and William F. Ryan, with John G. Thorpe as architect. During restoration, much was learned of the original nature of this structure. There were the usual three entries; front for guests, side for carriage, and rear, which the servants could reach from the carriage entry under the porte-cochere. At the second level rear was an open porch, possibly originally cantilevered by Wright; this has been enclosed and supported from below to provide needed space. Exterior restoration has included a new wood-shingled roof, single-beaded copper gutters and downspouts, and chemical stripping of paint from exterior masonry and the plaster columns (a lingering influence of Sullivan) as well as full tuckpointing.

S.045   T.9803
George W. Smith Residence (1896)
Oak Park, Illinois
Altered

The George W. Smith house, built in 1898, may come from a plan first submitted in 1896 to Charles Roberts (S.040) as part of a group of four low-cost homes for the community of Ridgeland, Illinois, now the east half of Oak Park. Its use of shingle siding looks back to earlier years; Wright had already begun to employ horizontal board-and-batten siding, a hallmark of many Prairie and Usonian structures. The original roofing was red-stained shingles, which, with its flaring eaves and steep pitch, gave an oriental flavor to the composition. Note the size of the lower-level living room windows, large even for double-hung sash. This amount of glazing on the west wall is necessary because there are no windows on the north wall of the living room, which is but a few feet away from the house to the north.

The roofing material has been changed, and the entry porch enclosed; other interior alterations are not documented.

George W. Smith Residence

Dining room

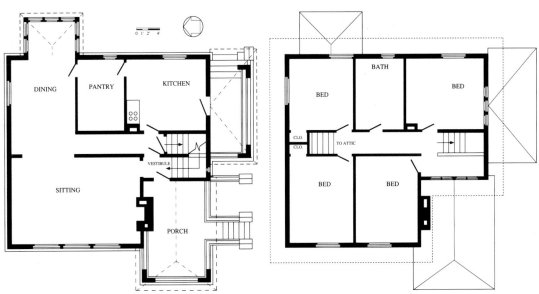

Conjectural plan of first floor   Conjectural plan of second floor

Joseph and Helen **Husser**
Residence (1899)
Chicago, Illinois
Demolished in 1923 or 1924

Joseph Husser was an executive for John M. Williams, real estate broker on Dearborn, living in Chicago as early as 1895. His Wright-designed dwelling was built in the Buena Park addition of James B. Waller, one of Edward C. Waller's three brothers, at 178–80 (now 730 West) Buena Avenue. Several blocks east of Graceland Cemetery, it was shorefront property long before landfill allowed what is now Lake Shore Drive to be built. Husser lived in the house until 1923.

This design takes several strides toward the soon-to-emerge Prairie style house. Prior to the Husser house, Wright's work had gradually moved away from the Queen Anne and Shingle style, making use of square or rectilinear plans, often with a projecting or engaged porch, terrace, porte-cochere, tower, library, and so forth. In the Husser house, for the first time, the appendages become natural extensions or wings, and the cross-axial plan, hinted at in the plans and roof shapes of buildings as early as his own home (S.002), finally make a strong, dynamic architectural statement. The concept of linear elements moving out in several directions from a central chimney core, affording maximum light, view, isolation or separation of internal functions, would become a standard in both cruciform and pinwheel Prairie, then **L** and in-line Usonian, plans.

Wright apparently never liked attics any better than he liked "cellars." Many of his early (to 1909) basements were used for laundries, servants' quarters, and such, beyond the rudiments of coal storage and heating unit. He eliminated both basement and attic altogether in his Usonian houses. In Prairie houses, he raised living quarters above ground level. In the Husser residence, the basement was at ground level, and the house rose yet two floors higher, thereby affording a magnificent view of nearby Lake Michigan. This design innovation may also be seen as a means of avoiding flooding of living quarters.

Octagonal forms soften the terminus of all the wings except the servants' wing. The west-east extensions—entry stairwell and dining room overlooking Lake Michigan—of this basically north-south structure are too shallow to suggest that the plan is tending to Wright's favorite Prairie forms, the cruciform and pinwheel. The surface ornament at the upper story and the window arches represent perhaps the last time such obvious influence of Sullivan will appear in Wright's design.

Husser Residence

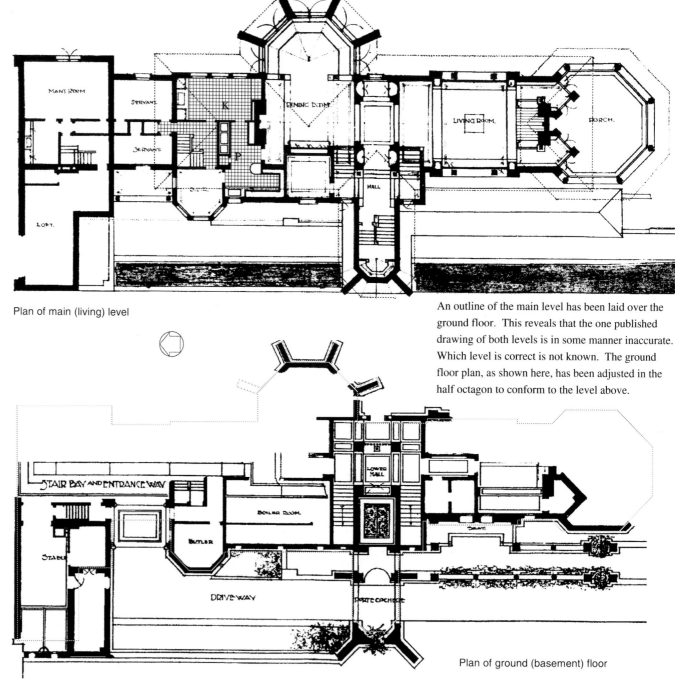

Plan of main (living) level

An outline of the main level has been laid over the ground floor. This reveals that the one published drawing of both levels is in some manner inaccurate. Which level is correct is not known. The ground floor plan, as shown here, has been adjusted in the half octagon to conform to the level above.

Plan of ground (basement) floor

S.047 T.9902
Edward C. **Waller Residence Remodeling** (1899)
River Forest, Illinois
Demolished 1939

Though Wright produced many designs for Edward C. Waller, few came to fruition, principally, only two apartment projects (S.030, S.031). In the late 1890s Wright kept a Chicago office in the Rookery Building (S.113), which was managed by Waller. William H. Winslow was also a tenant of the Rookery Building at that time.

This remodeling of a large house in Auvergne Place across the street from the Winslow house and stable (S.024–S.025) included the dining room and other interior work. Apparently this involved extensions for a kitchen and pantry suitable to serve the new dining room and for bedrooms above, but little documentation of this work survived the building's demolition. The ground floor plan shown here is a conflation of two drawings by Wright, a master plan altered by another drawing marked as a replacement for work in the upper right quarter of the master.

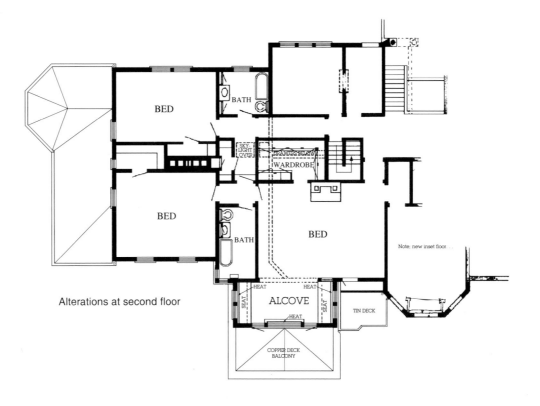

Alterations at second floor

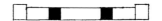

PORTE COCHERE

Waller dining room

On the original drawing, old walls were shown in red. Dotted lines indicate old work to be removed. New work was shown in solid purple.

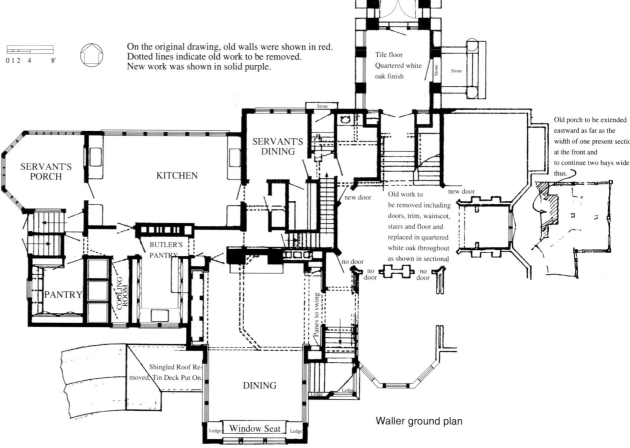

Waller ground plan

Jessie M. Adams Residence

S.048   T.0001
William and Jessie M. Adams
Residence (1900)
Chicago, Illinois

William Adams, contractor for the
Husser (S.046) and Heller (S.038) residences, registered this house in the
name of his wife, Jessie. Locally, and
to historical agencies, it is known as
the William Adams house. The exterior
of the home is hardly Wrightian,
double-hung windows being particularly uncharacteristic by 1900. Some
historians have suggested a fore-
shadowing of the "Fireproof House for
$5,000" (see S.138), but that would be
true at best for the second story,
where, four bedrooms are set at the
four corners, with bathroom between
two of these on one side. Stairs are
at the rear and jut out only slightly beyond the basic square rather than sufficiently to define the main entry, as
developed later for the Fireproof
House plan. Downstairs a reception
room still takes away space that will be
given to a full-width living room in
Wright's later square-plan houses.
Moreover, there is a full, finished three-
room attic with a fireplace in the largest room.

Plan of main floor

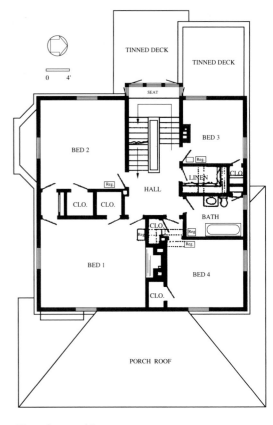

Plan of second floor

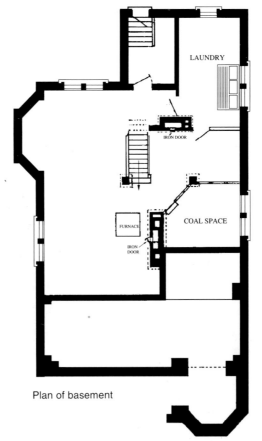

Plan of basement

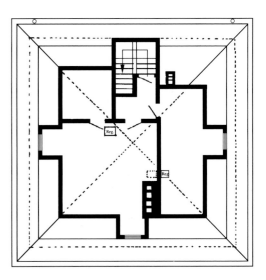

Plan of attic floor

S.049   T.0003
S. A. **Foster Residence** and
S.050   T.0003
Stable (1900)
Chicago, Illinois
Altered and enlarged to the rear. Trellis
between residence and stable removed

While the plans describe this as a
story and a half, they show it to be a
two-story-plus-attic summer cottage
for attorney (later judge) Stephen A.
Foster. Yet those who have lived in
the house have always known it as
a year-round dwelling in this West
Pullman, or Roseland, district of
Chicago on marshland once dominated by an Indian cemetery. Ykema
Roberts, who came to the United
States in 1890 from Holland, bought
the house from Judge Foster in 1914.
Roberts's daughter Dorothy was born
here in 1917 and has lived in the
house since, now with her husband
Robert Tharp. Mrs. Tharp once met the
judge's daughter, thus learning of
changes in the house and of how similar their experiences of growing up in
the house were.

The design is typical of Wright in
his pre-Prairie years, both in its
essentially standardized plan and in
those special touches that reveal the
impress of the architect's genius. The
roof lines of this dwelling, with flared
ridgepole (angular rake in the eaves),
suggest the possible influence of
Japanese prints. This same design
feature appears in the Bradley (S.052)
and Hickox (S.056) residences of the
same year, though in neither is it as
pronounced as it is here. The public
entry is concealed by a screen on the
side of a small porch that faces the
drive rather than the street. It leads to
a northwest corner reception area.
Stairs fill the center of the north side
together with passage to the kitchen
at the northeast corner. Though the
wood has been painted, some of the
kitchen cabinets are those built in
1900. Stairs to the basement also led
to a ground-level carriage entry, still
common to Wright's designs up to the
Prairie era. From the reception room,
one enters a combined living-dining
room. This is a very early example of
Wright's later practice of making dining
activities share the living space.
Central to the common room is a
keystone arched fireplace of tan brick
on the inside wall. South of this

common room is the full-width porch
facing a large yard on this northeast
corner lot. Upstairs are five bedrooms
(the stairs and hall pass between pairs
of chimney flues) and bathroom, and
the attic was laid out for a maid's room.

Changes to the building may, in
many instances, be due to a 1929 fire.
The kitchen has gone through
extensive alterations, being enlarged
to include the full northeast, or first,
quadrant of the house. The pantry,
once a quarter of that corner, was
moved south into space taken from a
dining room now separated from the
living room by a wall that crowds the
fireplace. The main floor rear has
been extended east. The porch was
lengthened with stairs to the yard, and
a room was added to the rear of the
kitchen. The rear entry was moved
beyond the basic square of the plan
and oriented to the north, rather than
toward the stable to the east. This
stable includes gardener's quarters
and was once linked to the house by
extensive trellising.

Foster Residence

Fireplace in Foster Residence

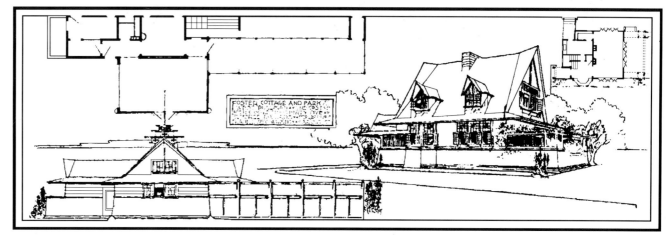

Plan of main floor and stable with perspective of Residence and Stable

Foster Stable

The Victorian Frank S. Gray house

The Hills Residence, remodeled from the Gray house

S.051 T.0102
Edward R. **Hills** Residence **Remodeling** (1900, 1906)

Oak Park, Illinois
Known locally as the Hills-DeCaro residence after rebuilding following a fire in 1976

The original structure for Frank S. Gray, a Victorian dwelling one lot north of its present location—the back yard of Nathan Moore (S.034–S.035)—was built in 1883. Gray agreed to sell to Moore in 1900, at which time Wright designed a remodeling. Actual work, including the relocation and reorientation of the structure, was delayed by legal problems and did not begin until the spring of 1906 and cost between $4000 and $5000. Moore presented the house as a wedding gift to his daughter Mary and her husband Edward R. Hills, an attorney, who were married on New Year's day, 1908. The Hills family lived here for forty-five years; the home then passed through two owners and fell into disrepair.

Tom and Irene DeCaro purchased the building in 1975 and immediately began restoration. On the night of January 3, 1976, Mrs. DeCaro was removing old paint from the last of 136 windows when fumes caught fire. The

structure burned down to the tops of the first-floor windows, but some first-floor built-ins and art glass survived. Restoration architect John D. Tilton returned to the original plans to rebuild the house as designed, with details not included in the original construction. This involved milling of wood to 1906 sizes, among other difficulties. Some mortar had crumbled, but the Roman brick fireplaces, notably the one in the second-floor north bedroom, were still in place.

The 1900 plan is an advance on earlier work. The house is entered at its northeast corner by way of a left-handed pinwheeled entry porch (see also S.016, S.042, S.044 and S.045). The library and living room occupy the front of the main floor. A spacious hallway connects entry, living room, dining room, and main stairwell. At the rear are the kitchen, the dining room, and a family room with stairs to a modernized basement. The formal dining room features a Wright-designed sideboard and stringcourses that give human scale to the space. The stairwell is grand, with an octagonal bay breaking the plane of the north wall, giving Mary a view of her father's house.

In 1977, the restoration won the Orchid Award from a local AIA chapter, and the Oak Park Landmark Commission renamed the restored building the Hills-DeCaro House.

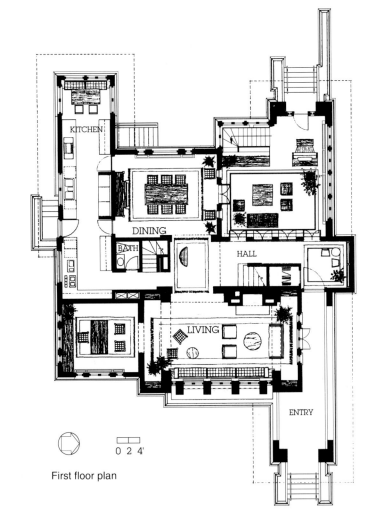

First floor plan

The Hills-DeCaro Residence

Dining room sideboard

Upstairs hallway

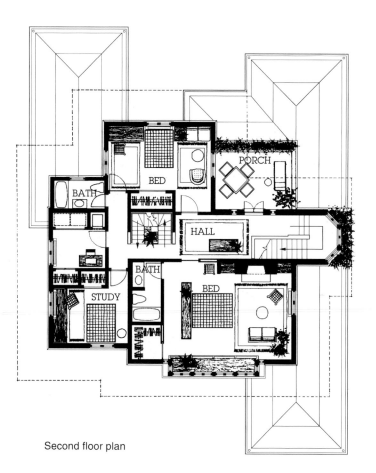

Second floor plan

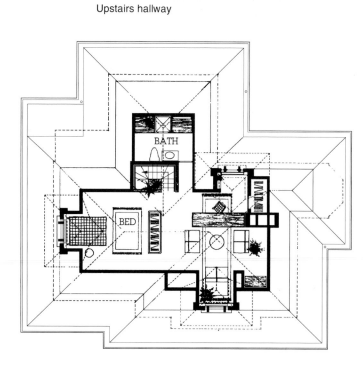

Third floor plan

Glenlloyd

S.052 T.0002
B. Harley **Bradley Residence,**
Glenlloyd, and
S.053 T.0002
Stable (1900)
Kankakee, Illinois
Renovated for use as professional
offices, 1990

Glenlloyd was built for the B. Harley
Bradleys; she was the sister of Mrs.
Charles Roberts (S.040–S.041) and
Warren Hickox (S.056). This, like the
Husser house of the previous year
(S.046), is a major transitional work
between eclectic experiments and
mature Prairie structures. Here the
influence of Japanese prints on Wright
becomes apparent in such elements
as flaring of the gable ridges and raked
eaves.

The basic plan is cruciform, the
main axis the living room and kitchen.
The cross axis is the dining room and
reception room, each extended, the
former by a screened porch, the latter
by a porte-cochere. The plan could be
the basis for the Willits house (S.054),
but here there is a back corner with
sitting, dressing, and bath rooms,
denying a pure cross-axial plan. Structural elements, however, differentiate
Glenlloyd even more clearly from its
Prairie cousin in Highland Park. A large
girder in the first-floor ceiling, hung
from the roof, makes possible the large

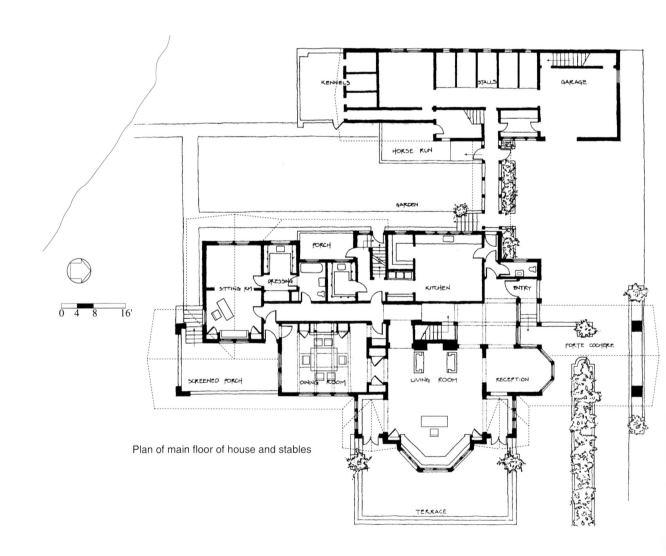

Plan of main floor of house and stables

Living room

Living room

Dining room

later in the Willits and successive Prairie structures. Plaster with wood trim and leaded art glass windows articulate the surface. Furniture was designed by John W. Ayers. Typical of Wright, "public" areas were treated to the highest quality materials, "private" areas were given utility wares. Thus, the outside of downstairs servants' rooms is oak, but the inside, seen only by servants, is pine. The stable is actually a combination of kennels, five stalls, and garage, with servant's quarters above.

Located on the right (north) bank of the Kankakee River, which flows into the Illinois from headwaters near South Bend, Indiana, this large residential structure has seen many lives, including that of the restaurant Yesteryear. Under project architect John A. Eifler, restoration work on the main floor was begun and various additions removed in the mid-eighties. After five years of vacancy as a result of the death of its owner Stephen B. Small, work was begun again to complete renovation and initiate reconstruction to convert the building to use as law and architectural offices. Original colors have been restored and where original art glass was unavailable, re-creations were installed. Once-open porches have been glass-enclosed. Ronald L. Moline, L. Lee Thacker, Michael L. Dietchweiler, and Robert B. Labeau were the sponsors of the ultimate renovation.

To the immediate north is the Hickox house (S.056), which may have been used as the builder's office/house while Glenlloyd was being constructed.

living room span. The hangers are located on either side of the entry to the front bedroom. In the Willits house, the architect created a wider space for the bedroom by suspending double girders from the roof with the hangers at the inside corners of the second-floor double balconies. Thus, even structurally, and thereby spatially, the Prairie Willits improves on proto-Prairie Bradley.

The series of compressive, then expansive spaces that lead one from the porte-cochere to the living room is not as strongly defined here as it is

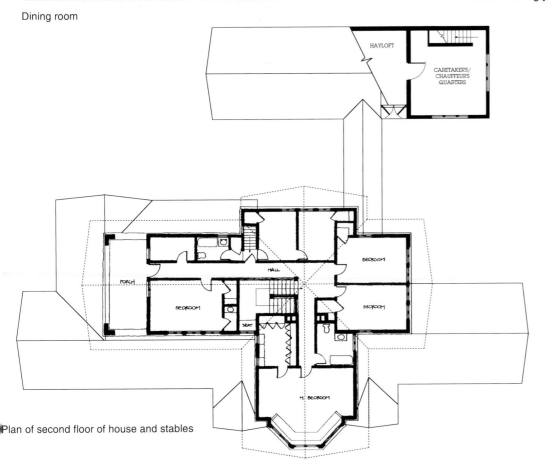

Plan of second floor of house and stables

Bradley Stable

Ward Winfield **Willits Residence**
(1901)
Highland Park, Illinois
Renovated 1980s

Ward Willits was born in New Boston, Illinois, on the Mississippi River, in 1859. His parents moved to Chicago so that Ward could obtain a proper education. By the time he was twenty, he was employed by Adams and Westlake Company, a brass foundry; by 1891 he was the vice-president, and in 1904 was made its president. Orlando Giannini went to work with the firm in 1887 and later did glass for Wright. It was probably Giannini who provided the connection between client and architect. In 1905, Willits and his wife Cecelia Mary Berry accompanied the Wrights on a trip to Japan. Thereafter, there seems to have been little interest on the part of the Willits in continuing the relationship. Ward Willits still lived in the house when he died at the age of ninety-two.

The home Willits built in 1902–3 represents a radical step forward in Wright's emerging design maturity. Gone are any suggestions of Tudor half-timber trim, such as are hinted at in Glenlloyd (S.052) and remain in Hickox (S.056). Here is the first house in true Prairie style, with first-floor living quarters raised slightly above ground level on a stylobate-like base. Construction, constantly delayed by slow delivery of plans and updates by Wright, was supervised by Walter Burley Griffin.

The living room of the Willits house relates the indweller to the site in a manner new to Wright's work although closely approximated in the Husser house (S.046). Its end wall is floor-to-ceiling glass, open to the yard, to nature, across a large terrace. On the sides, high windows lead the eye neither to the neighbor's home nor to the ground but to the sky. From this concept, the Prairie ideal would develop to more open, yet interlocked, spaces. Structural steel is concealed within the walls; wood and plaster hint at later steel and concrete designs. Oak is used on the main floor, pine above, and stringcourses are used on both floors.

Each wing extends from a massive central Roman brick fireplace. While the rooflines present a reasonably

Ward W. Willits Residence, front and entry

Ward W. Willits Residence, entry and rear

Entry hallway; view from balcony above

View from living room to dining room

balanced cruciform, the dining room is offset. This adjustment to an otherwise regular plan, together with use of screening, simultaneously isolates and interlocks each wing from and with the others, giving a human scale to buildings that might otherwise be overbearing in their monumentality. The cruciform plan provided more space than could be achieved in a square or rectangular layout, without overwhelming the occupant. Some of Wright's large pre-Prairie designs employ the more irregular pinwheel to

achieve this. Later Wright would reverse the principle. In the **L**-plan Usonian houses he would locate the dining space just off the living room or in one corner so as to share its space and thus seem larger.

In the Willits house, a 39-inch unit dominates, although one set of drawings indicates an enlarging of the dining room by the simple expedient of changing the unit to 41 inches. Wright did lengthen the porch by "breaking" the plan and revising the dimension. Also, the living room was enlarged

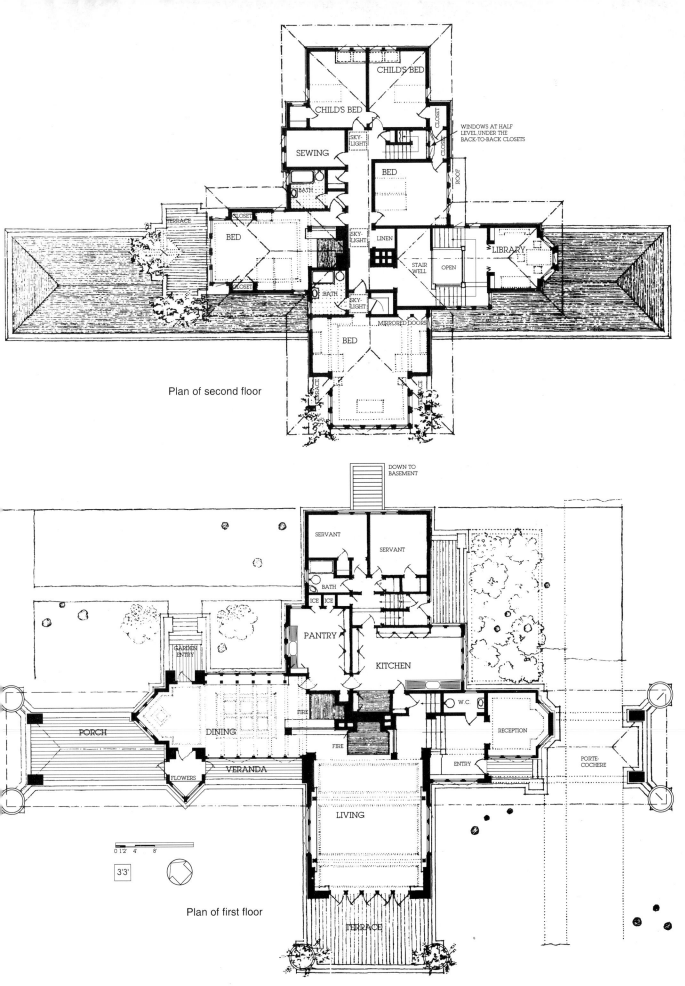

CHILD'S BED

CHILD'S BED

SEWING

SKY-LIGHT

BED

CLOSET

CLOSET

ROOF

WINDOWS AT HALF LEVEL UNDER THE BACK-TO-BACK CLOSETS

BATH

CLOSET

TERRACE

BED

SKY-LIGHT

LINEN

STAIR WELL

OPEN

LIBRARY

CLOSET

BATH

SKY-LIGHT

MIRRORED DOORS

BED

Plan of second floor

DOWN TO BASEMENT

SERVANT

SERVANT

BATH

ICE ICE

PANTRY

KITCHEN

GARDEN ENTRY

W.C.

PORCH

DINING

FIRE

FIRE

RECEPTION

FLOWERS

VERANDA

ENTRY

PORTE-COCHERE

LIVING

0 1 2' 4'   8'

3'3'

Plan of first floor

TERRACE

from original plans, and the stairwell altered, despite Willits's always pleading with Wright not so much to reduce costs, but to be efficient.

The spatial organization of the Willits house is typical of Prairie designs; one must pass through a series of alternating expansive (relaxation)—porte-cochere, stairwell—and compressive (tension)—entry, short stairway, and left turn—spaces to reach the main living (relaxing) area which, at the end of these spatial manipulations, seems larger than it is. This series of transitions is the architectural equivalent of a series of musical suspensions, where two notes are placed so close to each other (a musical second) that they create tension, which is then resolved (relaxed) by one note moving away to create harmony (a third).

Before Milton Robinson purchased the property, a deck had extended the dining area and a garage had been added at the rear. Upstairs the bedroom over the original kitchen had been extended outward one unit. In the late eighties, Robinson commissioned architect John A. Eifler to provide full renovation of this residence, designated by the AIA as one of seventeen American buildings designed by Frank Lloyd Wright to be retained as an example of his architectural contribution to American culture. Robinson and his artist wife Sylvie did much of the work themselves. Changes represent an attempt to maintain the spirit of Wright without forfeiting modern conveniences. Wright originally called for a base of green in living and dining rooms; later he called for the living room to be done in a thin green glaze with bronze powder, achieving a gold effect. The dining room was done, then, with gold flecks. The dining room has been redone in dark ("forest") green, and the living room in gold lamé to achieve something of the original effect.

Former servants' quarters have been converted to a master bedroom. The kitchen, moved to the original butler's pantry, has been fully modernized, as have bathroom facilities. The entrance to the front bedroom has been moved. Forced air climate control has replaced radiators; the original living room featured recirculating air ducts.

S.055 T.0208
Ward W. **Willits Gardener's
Cottage with Stables** (1901)
Highland Park, Illinois
Remodeled into house

Behind the Willits residence stands a
gardener's cottage with stables. This
wood-and-stucco structure is in the
same new Prairie idiom as the main
house, with broad overhanging eaves
and hipped roof. The original plan was
a pinwheel at the ground floor, with a
carriage room extending from under
the second floor into its own wing (left
in the photo), stalls, and a single-story
cow stable (right in the photo), now
enlarged. Over the stalls was a hay
loft, and over the carriage room
quarters for the gardener, essentially a
square, half of which was the living
room, the remainder divided equally
between a bedroom and a kitchen. The
cottage has since been remodeled into
a separate house.

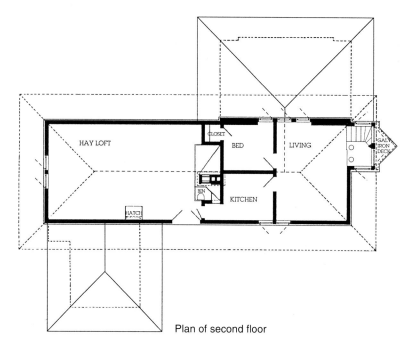

Plan of second floor

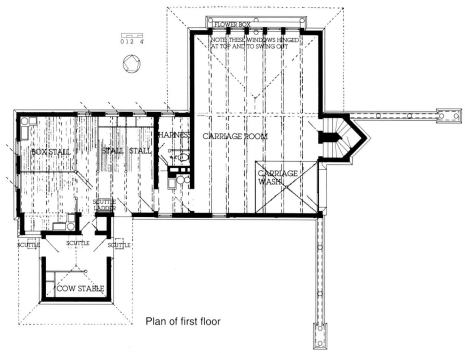

Plan of first floor

Hickox Residence

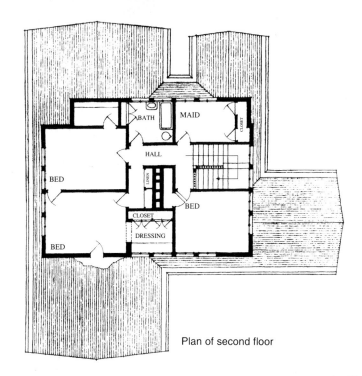

Plan of second floor

S.056   T.0004
Warren **Hickox** Residence (1900)
Kankakee, Illinois
Enclosed bay entry added at living
room, where original terrace was
located

The Hickox house still retains in its
trim suggestions of Tudor half-timber
framing, which is structural in British
building. The plan, however, has a
Prairie organization of spaces, like its
mirror-imaged twin, the Henderson
residence (S.057). The basic plan may
be seen as a pinwheel altered only by
continuing the dining room in line with
the library and living room, to allow a
full terrace outside the living room.
This flowing together of three spaces
is typical of Prairie school principles.
As in all but a few early designs,
Wright's chimney is in the center of the
house. Furthermore, there are still
three entries, the covered guest entry
leading to the reception room, an
adjacent ground-level entry, and a rear
servants' entry. If the octagonal bays of
the music room—library and dining
room were removed and the terrace
covered, this would be a mirror image
of the pre-Prairie Foster house
(S.049), though the use of stucco and
timber now shows this to be a major
step in Wright's rethinking of all
elements of domestic design that will
lead in less than a year to the
Henderson Prairie house. All wood trim
is pine, only the floors being oak. Four
bedrooms are served by a single bathroom upstairs, and closets conceal the
masonry of the chimney. The Hickox
dwelling is located just north of the
Bradley house (S.052).

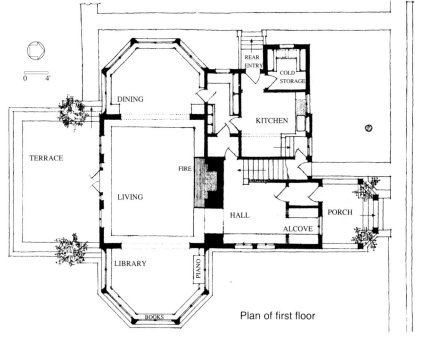

Plan of first floor

Henderson Residence

S.057   T.0104
F. B. **Henderson** Residence (1901)
Elmhurst, Illinois
Restored 1980s and early 1990s

In terms of plan, the Henderson is a
virtual mirror of the Hickox structure
(S.056), both plans set sideways to the
main road. The open porch and entry
are extended, but absence of a
separate servant's entry at the rear
suggests a tendency toward cruciform
design (this would be more obvious if
the terrace were enclosed) as well as
the beginnings of Wright's changed
attitude toward the social structure and
hierarchy of democratic living. Here
the alcove rooms of the Hickox are
identified as dining room and library.
Upstairs, the chimney flue has been
split to serve fireplaces in each of the
bedrooms above the living room.
Wright used the split flue again in 1909
in cottages for Mrs. Gale (S.088.1–3)
and the Stewart house (S.160), among
other buildings.

Regularity of fenestration (mullions
on 41-inch centers), suggests this as
the basis for a unit system in the
design. Differences between earlier
proto-Prairie Hickox and Prairie
Henderson include gabled versus
hipped roof, though Wright would
continue to use gables in Prairie
designs through 1906. The house was
done in collaboration with Webster
Tomlinson, the only "partner" whom
Wright ever admitted having. In later
years, a covered second-story porch
was added, over the original terrace.
Joan and Roger A. Schmiege began
restoration of the house to its original
design in 1975. Further restoration
was done in the late 1980s (exterior)
and early 1990s (interior).

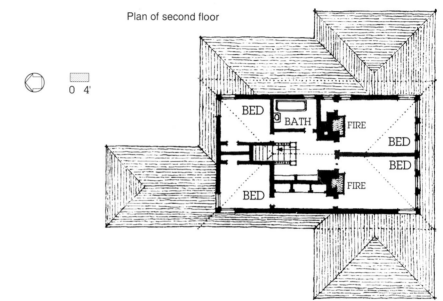

Plan of second floor

0   4'

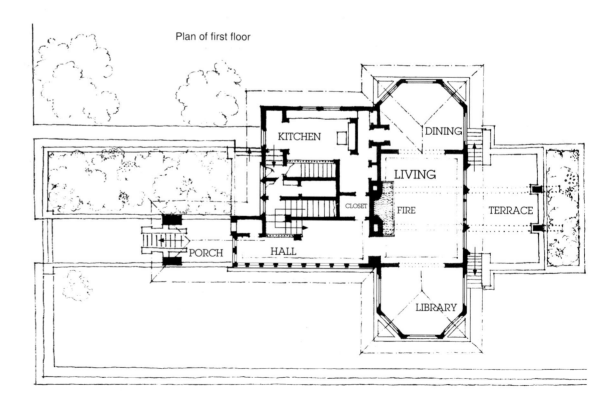

Plan of first floor

Prairie Architecture: The Unit System, the Grid

In 1925 Frank Lloyd Wright proclaimed, "All the buildings I have built—large and small—are fabricated upon a unit system." Typically, Wright the iconoclast was overstating the case. Charles E. White, Jr., who worked in Wright's office from 1903 to 1906, the early years of the Prairie era, wrote:

"All his plans are composed of units grouped in a symmetrical and systematic way . . . [Wright's] process in getting up a new design is the reverse of that usually employed. Most men outline the strictly utilitarian requirements . . . whereas Wright develops his unit first, then fits the design to the requirements as much as possible . . . and never allows any of the petty wants of his client to interfere with the architectural expression of his design."

The unit system was based on a square module with a length, a "unit," equal to some specific architectural element, most often, as in the Willits house, the distance between center lines of mullions. It represented the final elimination of historical references in Wright's design and the new dominance of rectilinear geometry, evolved out of earlier Queen Anne efforts. Before the 1920s, the grid appears only rarely on Wright's plans and seems not to carry with it the ethical and symbolic values it would obtain in the architect's Usonian designs.

The unit system and the grid it generated, together with the cantilever (the third dimension to the grid plan's two), constitute the grammar of organic architecture. The Prairie school architecture Wright developed from these elements, albeit sporadically, created a wholly unified architecture of the Prairie. Two basic designs come from this in domestic architecture, the "four-square" plan and the pinwheel/cruciform plans. Simultaneously Wright developed a basic tripartite organization for all his urban public buildings.

Although Wright may have experimented occasionally with the idea of a unit system in his earliest, eclectic work, the first Prairie house where it informs the entire design is the Ward Willits (S.054). Throughout the Prairie period, Wright employed the unit system inconsistently, particularly in its relationship to the vertical element of space. Only when he encountered the concrete block in California in the 1920s did Wright find a material totally suited to interrelating the necessities of design with the requirements of aesthetically beautiful space. Faced with the requirement of lowering the cost of building, Wright promulgated his Usonian system of design in the 1930s. With the basement eliminated and a slab floor providing radiant heating his standard, the unit system came into its own, even showing in lines scored on the concrete mat, to which the walls were aligned. Here, the vertical unit system finally became totally detached from the horizontal dimensioning.

The unit system, determining a grid, and the cantilever, the element that freed the third dimension, are the basic elements in the grammar of organic architecture. They seem more related to human scale than any abstract idea, such as the Froebel blocks of which scholars have made such a point. The Japanese lay out space in numbers of tatami mats, their basic "human scale" unit (3 feet by 6 feet). Wright had encountered this at the World's Columbian Exposition in Chicago in 1893, though he would not see its full expression until he visited Japan in 1905.

Wright's two major periods of design are traditionally identified as the Prairie era, 1901–10, and the Usonian era, 1935–55. Before the Prairie ideal was developed, Wright was quite eclectic, though he infused his designs with more abstract shapes than other architects of the time. He could do as good a shingle style or Queen Anne as any of his contemporaries.

Realizing the futility of his pursuit of establishment clients and conventional living, Wright left for Europe in 1909 with Mamah Borthwick Cheney, wife of one of his clients. Upon his return to America, he explored inexpensive approaches to design and building, particularly in his most extensive project, the American System-Built (Ready-cut) homes, prefabricated designs for the Arthur L. Richards Company of Milwaukee, Wisconsin. The failure of this venture and the size and success of the Imperial Hotel and Barnsdall Park projects led him to the West Coast, where he moved in on his son Lloyd and, with four California clients, developed the textile block method of construction in which, for the first time, a unit system was consistent in both the horizontal plane and the vertical.

None of this provided any security for Wright. With the onset of the Great Depression, Wright retreated to the family homestead in central Wisconsin. There he invited young students to come study with him, in a Taliesin Fellowship. He rethought his design procedures, and "invented" the Usonian home, a refinement of ideas already in place in the California block houses. Now, with a thin sandwich-wall construction and masonry limited primarily to what was needed to support his cantilevers, Wright set his vertical unit system to the nature of the materials (essentially the true dimensions of a finished 1 inch by 12 inch board with batten, which was also commensurate with brick and mortar or concrete block courses).

William G. **Fricke** (Fricke-Martin) **Residence (**1901)

Oak Park, Illinois
Original semidetached pavilion
demolished

William Fricke died half a decade after
he moved into the house, which was
then sold to Emma Martin (S.060).
While alterations to the house were
once attributed to Mrs. Martin, no
evidence of these has been discovered by current owners, who have
preserved the house while modernizing only as necessary.

Several elements such as
masonry-like treatment of stucco walls
and lack of clarity in plan have suggested to some a date earlier than the
"Dec. 9, 1901" neatly inscribed by
Wright on the plan. But this house, an
experiment in monolithic stucco and
therefore a precursor of Unity Temple
(S.096), is essentially vertical, even as
Wright was moving toward a principle
of horizontal dominance in his designs.
The broad overhanging eaves, thin-
edged in profile, and dark horizontal
banding of windows are in precarious
balance with the verticals of the mullions, projecting reception room and
living room bays, and a three-story
central tower. This last architectural
element may also be found in various
forms in the Heller (S.038) and Rollin
Furbeck (S.044) houses and others
where it leads to little more than a
finished attic. The floor of a rear
second-level porch is concealed by
balusters, thus hiding the true height of
interior rooms and giving added
emphasis to the vertical element.
There is a main entry leading to a
central hall from which spin, clockwise,
an alcove reception room, side entry,
stairs, hall to kitchen, dining room and
living room. The living room, bedroom
above, and third-story billiards room
have fireplaces. There is much built-in
furniture, and Wright's hand is apparent in detailing on all levels. This
dwelling was a collaboration with
Webster Tomlinson.

The alterations previously listed as
S.059 appear to be the garage addition to the property (S.060).

Fricke Residence,
north side, showing
Emma Martin
Garage under
construction

Fricke
Residence from
the southeast,
showing pavilion
(to left) and
southeast corner
of the house

Fricke Residence, from the west, showing pavilion

Billiards room

Dining area, view toward living room

Entry hallway; side entry, stairs, hall to kitchen

Plan of third floor, Fricke Residence

Plan of second floor, Fricke Residence

Plan of ground floor of Fricke Residence with pavilion,
and of Emma Martin Garage, both floors

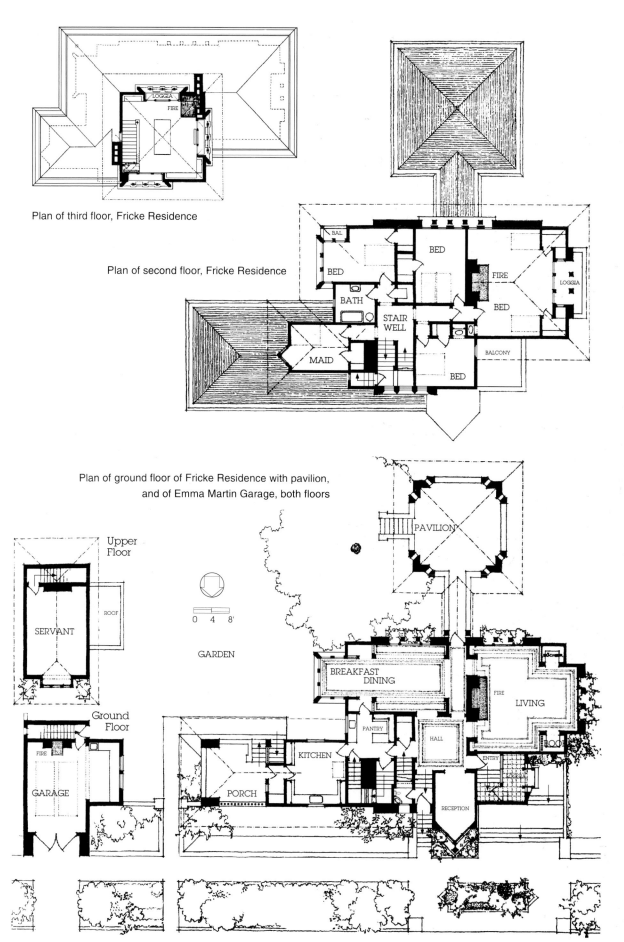

LOGGIA
FIRE

BAL
BED
BED
BED
FIRE
LOGGIA
BATH
STAIR
WELL
BED
MAID
BALCONY
BED

Upper
Floor
SERVANT
ROOF

Ground
Floor
FIRE
GARAGE

GARDEN

0 4 8'

PAVILION

BREAKFAST
DINING
FIRE
LIVING
PANTRY
HALL
KITCHEN
ENTRY
PORCH
RECEPTION

S.060   T.0707

Emma Martin Garage (1907)
Oak Park, Illinois

Emma Martin added a garage in the Prairie idiom of the house to this property when she acquired it from the estate of William Fricke in 1907. The plaster-surfaced structure had a pit for servicing a car from below. To the side, Wright designed a workshop with lavatory, but this was not built. Upstairs he designed a single room with fireplace at one end. For many years the Fricke house was known as the Emma Martin house, since her tenure was longer than his.

Emma Martin Garage

S.061 T.0304
William E. Martin Residence
(1902) and
S.061A T.0921
Pergola (1909)
Oak Park, Illinois
Pergola demolished

The stucco and wood trim of this three-story dwelling for W. E. Martin, brother of Darwin D. Martin (see E-Z Polish Factory, S.114, and other Martin-related listings, S.090, S.093, S.100–S.102, S.225, S.226) are like those of the Fricke residence (S.058), but the extension of fenestration and trim to and around corners gives much more horizontality to the Martin composition. The plan is also clearer. The front entry gives one the choice of turning left to the hall or right to the veranda, which, as in the Willits residence (S.054), is on the side as an extension of the dining room. The fireplace is on one short wall of the living room. Fireplaces also appear in the bedroom above and the third-floor playroom. This is the last of Wright's visually obvious trilevel Prairie homes (see also S.067, S.127, and S.128 for three-story homes without "true" basements). At one point the building was subdivided into three apartments, but in 1945 it was restored to single-family use.

The pergola was a centerpiece in a design with extensive plantings, including trellises and pools. Walter Burley Griffin, who designed the gardens, also supervised construction of the entire project.

It was a visit to his brother William and a tour of Oak Park that led Darwin D. Martin to visit Wright's studio (though Wright was not there at the time) and eventually to commission his own home in Buffalo. Thus, the Larkin Company's other officers also came to know of Wright.

William E. Martin Residence

Hall with skylight

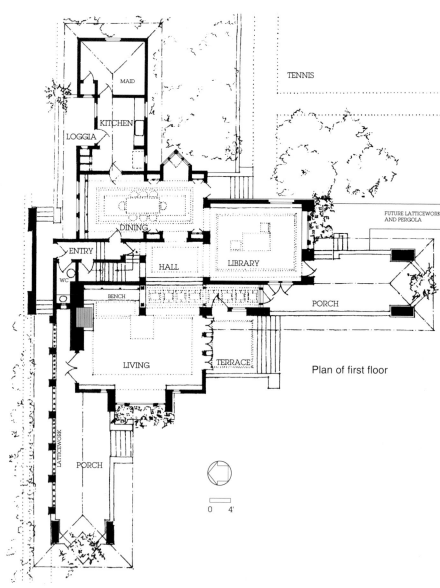

Plan of first floor

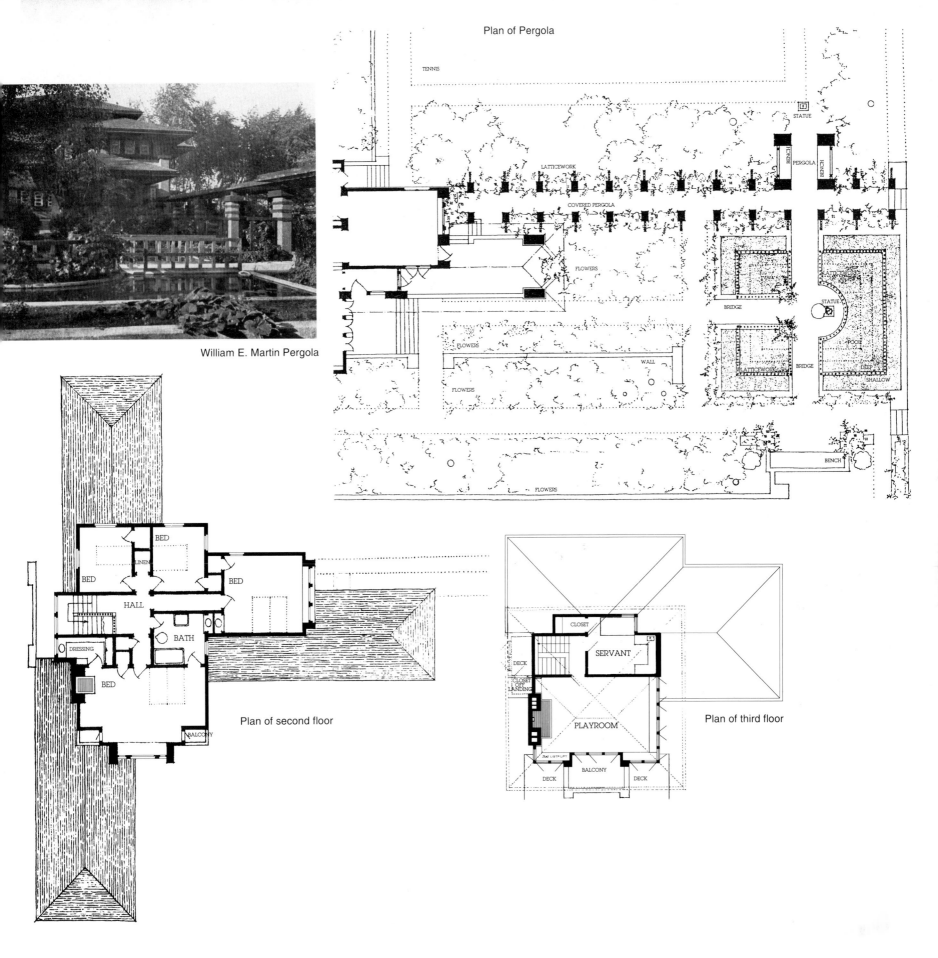

Plan of Pergola

TENNIS

STATUE

LATTICEWORK

PERGOLA

BENCH

BENCH

COVERED PERGOLA

FLOWERS

LATTICEWORK

STATUE

BRIDGE

POOL

FLOWERS

WALL

LATTICEWORK

BRIDGE

DEEP

FLOWERS

SHALLOW

BENCH

FLOWERS

William E. Martin Pergola

BED

LINEN

BED

BED

HALL

BED

DRESSING

BATH

BED

BALCONY

Plan of second floor

CLOSET

DECK

SERVANT

CLOSET
OF
LANDING

PLAYROOM

DECK

BALCONY

DECK

Plan of third floor

S.062 T.9802, T.0217
River Forest Golf Club (1898) and
S.062A T.0105
Additions and Alterations (1901)
River Forest, Illinois
Demolished

The River Forest Golf Club was a single-story structure of horizontal board-and-batten siding, making it possibly the earliest known major work of Wright's to employ this surfacing (see Moore Stable, S.035). Originally it was a small structure with nothing more than a porch, an assembly room, and men's and women's lounges set behind a fireplace.

In 1901 the building was considerably enlarged with the addition of a full octagonal lounge (clubroom) with a fireplace on either side, behind the original fireplace. Side wings provided expanded men's locker rooms on one side and a dining room on the other with open terraces at both ends. A kitchen was attached to the dining room, caretaker's quarters to the lockers.

The second Taliesin number, T.0217, is that assigned the drawing that fits the 1898 River Forest Golf Club as built. The T.9802 number fits a plan that seems to be a first scheme for the 1901 additions and alterations.

River Forest Golf Club, terrace entry, before alterations

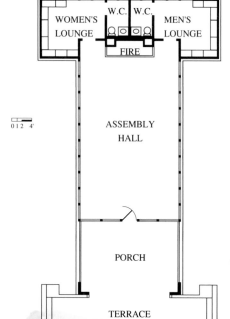

Original plan

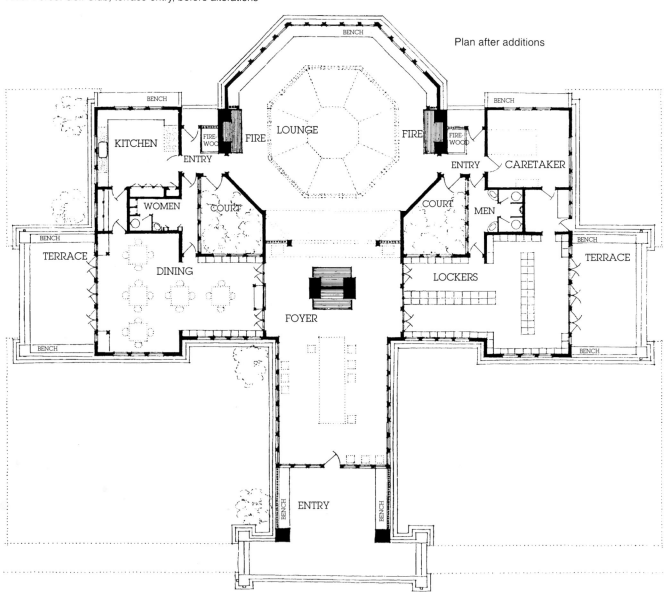

Plan after additions

Buffalo Exposition Pavilion for
the Universal Portland Cement
Company (1901)
Buffalo, New York
Demolished

Although the Universal Portland
Cement Company (Cement Department of Illinois Steel) never commissioned a permanent building from
Wright, it did construct a pavilion for
the 1901 Pan-American Exposition in
Buffalo (see also S.163). Neither
photographs nor plans seem to have
survived.

In the Nature of Materials: Cement and Concrete

Cement has been with us for a long
time. The Greeks had it, the Romans
used it widely, and even the Mayans
employed it before Columbus arrived
on this continent.

It has to be mixed with sand and
gravel (in proportions of 1:2:4 normally) and water to become concrete,
which is fireproof and therefore the
basis of the true Fireproof House (see
S.138), had anyone built it with this
material (see also S.184). It is plastic
and can be shaped while it is curing as
no other material available to Wright
could. It can be precast, as it was in
the California block houses (S.214–
S.217) and Usonian Automatic designs
(S.386–S.389, S.392), reinforced with
steel, or prestressed (reinforced under
compression, which strengthens the
concrete). From the first time he used
it in a major building, Unity Temple
(S.096), Wright was enamored with its
possibilities, which he explored end-
lessly for the remainder of his architectural practice.

"Portland cement" is not the name
of a company, but of a type of cement.
It is made from natural cement specially processed. It was patented in 1824
by a British bricklayer, Joseph Aspdin
(possibly just after a similar patent

lapsed). The name derived from the
Isle of Portland, where the stone was
quarried, though Aspdin, who worked
in Leeds, where Portland stone was
not available, described his invention
by its coloration.

Cement is a mixture of three major
ingredients and a few minor ones. In
1901 there were nearly a hundred different formulas but in 1917, percen-
tages were set by the U.S. Bureau of
Standards and Testing at 60 lime (cal-
cium oxide), 25 silica (silicon dioxide,
or sand), 10 alumina (aluminum dioxide), plus other minor elements.
Cement is a bonding agent for other
masonry, but it is in concrete—particularly if it is reinforced with iron or steel
mesh, rods, or beams inside—that it
has gained its greatest architectural
significance. Cement, mixed with sand
and gravel, is concrete. It was this
form that held a fascination for Wright,
who explored it in poured forms, with
reinforcing steel, in his own textile
block method of construction (see
S.214–S.217, S.221–S.222, S.227,
S.294–S.296, S.298–S.301, S.386–
S.389, and S.392), as well as the
common concrete block.

Concrete by itself can work only
in compression, but reinforced it can
handle tensile and shearing stresses.
William E. Ward, of Port Chester, New
York, built his own home between
1871 and 1876 entirely of reinforced
concrete. The 13,000 square feet of
flooring was so over-reinforced that the
parlor floor could hold a 26-ton load in
the center of its 1,888-foot span. The

ceilings are coffered; Wright also employed this design feature as a means
of reducing the weight of the structure,
particularly in his Usonian Automatic
houses.

It was Ernest L. Ransome, however, who led the way to standardiza-
tion of building practice with reinforced
concrete. From a modest reinforced
concrete sidewalk in Stockton, California, in 1883, Ransome built an
empire. In 1889 he achieved a complete reinforced concrete building; roof
tiles, domed skylight, slabs, and
columns arose as the museum at
Stanford University.

Concrete, so important to Wright, is
primarily a first-world construction
material; worldwide, adobe is the most
commonly used masonry material, and
bamboo the most widely used wood.

S.064   T.0217

Lake Delavan Yacht Club (1902)
Delavan Lake, Delavan, Wisconsin
Demolished

Lake Delavan Yacht Club

Limited photographic evidence of the Lake Delavan Yacht Club survives to show that a structure approximating Wright's plan was built. While not large, it had a ladies' parlor, dancing floor, a dining room, and a kitchen. It was situated on the shore of the lake where Wright designed several summer homes (Johnson, S.087; Jones, S.083–S.086; Ross, S.082; Spencer, S.081; and Wallis, S.079–S.080).

Wright sketched a variety of options and trial possibilities over his basic plan.   One such is shown to the side of the ladies' parlor.

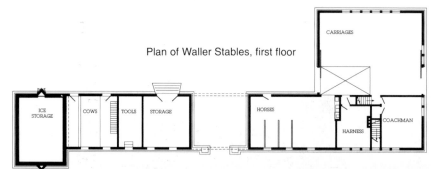

NO SCALE IS GIVEN ON MR. WRIGHT'S DRAWING

THE STRUCTURE, AS BUILT, HAD STEPS AS SHOWN HERE THAT LEAD FROM TERRACE DOWN TO PIER AND ANOTHER SET OUTSIDE THOSE SHOWN ON THE PLAN. LEADING FROM PIER TO WALKS AT EACH SIDE OF THE BOATHOUSE PAVILION

S.065   T.0108
Edward C. **Waller Gates** and
S.066   T.0108
Stables (1901)
River Forest, Illinois
Stables demolished. Gates refurbished

Wright's work for Edward Waller (S.030, S.031, S.047, S.065–S.066, S.166), of Auvergne Place, is mostly gone. The gates to Waller's estate on Auvergne Place, however, retain six original stone pylons and some iron-work. Lanterns and swinging iron gates for both drives and walks are lost. A committee of preservationists in River Forest and Oak Park, including the Frank Lloyd Wright Home and Studio Foundation, was organized to restore these works. By the late 1980s, over $5000 had been raised and was used to restore stonework and put in electrical connections for the lanterns. Future plans call for full restoration of the ironwork and lanterns. Curiously, the Historic District in River Forest stops one block east, excluding the Waller Gates and the most famous home in the town, that for William Winslow.

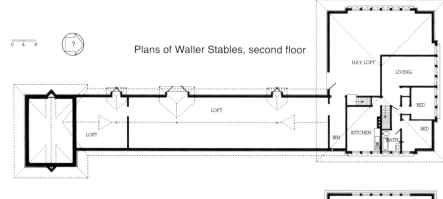

Waller Gates

Alan Thatcher

Waller Stables, elevation

NORTH ELEVATION

Plans of Waller Stables, second floor

Plan of Waller Stables, first floor

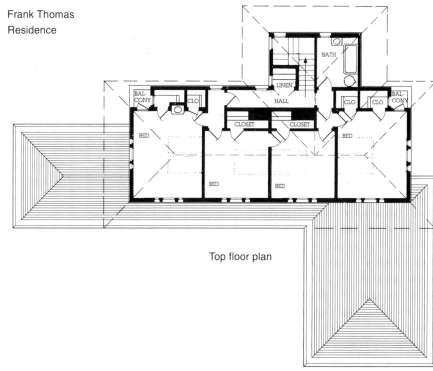

Top floor plan

S.067   T.0106
Frank Wright **Thomas** Residence,
The Harem (1901) for James C.
Rogers
Oak Park, Illinois
Two-story addition by Tallmadge and
Watson, 1922. Exterior restored 1975.
Additional restoration 1980s

The Frank W. Thomas house is
the first Prairie-style house in Oak
Park. It was commissioned by James
C. Rogers and given to his daughter
and son-in-law, Mr. and Mrs. Frank
Thomas, upon completion. They
moved out after only a brief residence.

Here is an early example of
Wright's placing the "basement" fully
above ground, enclosing three stories
in a building no taller than its traditional two-story-plus-attic neighbors
(see also S.127 and S.128). The main
entry at the second level is reached
through a labyrinth starting at the front
walk with high walls leading to an archway, then stairs to the left, a landing to
reverse direction, more stairs, and a
glazed breezeway.

Various historians give credit for
the **L** plan (as opposed to a traditional
Prairie cruciform, **T** plan or pinwheel)
to Walter Burley Griffin, who came to
Wright's office after serving as drafts-

man to Webster Tomlinson, but Marion
Mahony, later Griffin's wife (her name
seems to have been pronounced
MAH-huh-nee), claimed the design
as her own. The house plan features
a ground floor with spacious quarters
for servants (Wright's contribution to
democratic architecture at this point in
his career, also incorporated into the
Heurtley house [S.074]). The living
room is to the left of the entry, the dining room around to the right, in the
single-story wing. Here we find another
situation in which Wright brings together several flues in one visible
chimney, creating interior passageways at three levels between fireplace
and heater flues on one side, laundry
and kitchen stove flues and kitchen
vent on the other (see also S.088.1–3).
On the top floor are four bedrooms in
line, a feature Wright would transfer to
his Usonian homes, with stairs and
bathroom to the rear.

A large, two-story addition, not
visible from the street, was added in
1922 by local Prairie school architects
Thomas E. Tallmadge and Vernon S.
Watson. For many years the Thomas
residence was surfaced with shingles,
but in 1975 it was returned to its
original plaster. Additional restoration
was carried out in the 1980s.

Plan of main floor

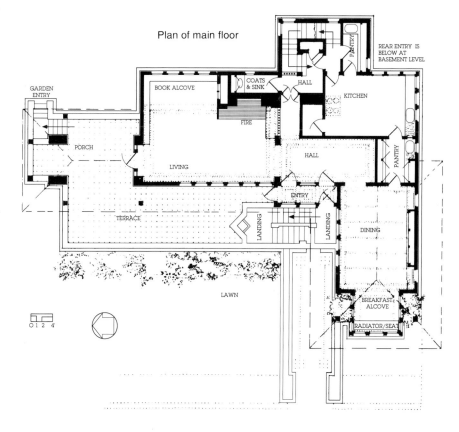

Detail at entry porch

Davenport Residence, ca. 1901

Davenport Residence

Living room

S.068   T.0101
E. Arthur **Davenport** Residence (1901)
River Forest, Illinois
Veranda removed. Restoration ongoing

E. Arthur Davenport was with the Pullman Company for 52 years. He was active in civic affairs and served as River Forest's first township supervisor and in a number of other posts. Mrs. Susan Davenport was president of the River Forest Women's Club.

The *Ladies Home Journal* published Wright's "Small House with 'Lots of Room in It'" in July 1901. The Davenport house as originally built, with front veranda and a different window treatment in the living room but without porte-cochere, is essentially a mirror image of that prescription. Features of the period include raked eaves, leaded ribbon windows, with stained board-and-batten siding. The "Small House" was a cruciform plan with offset side wings, but a slight shift in the Davenport house makes it a regular cruciform. At the second level a study overlooks the stairwell.

The front elevation was changed, and the veranda removed, probably in the early 1900s, possibly by Wright or William Drummond, his draftsman of seven years. The house is being restored under direction of the fourth owners, Jeanette S. Fields (editor of *A Guidebook to the Architecture of River Forest*) and Ellis Fields.

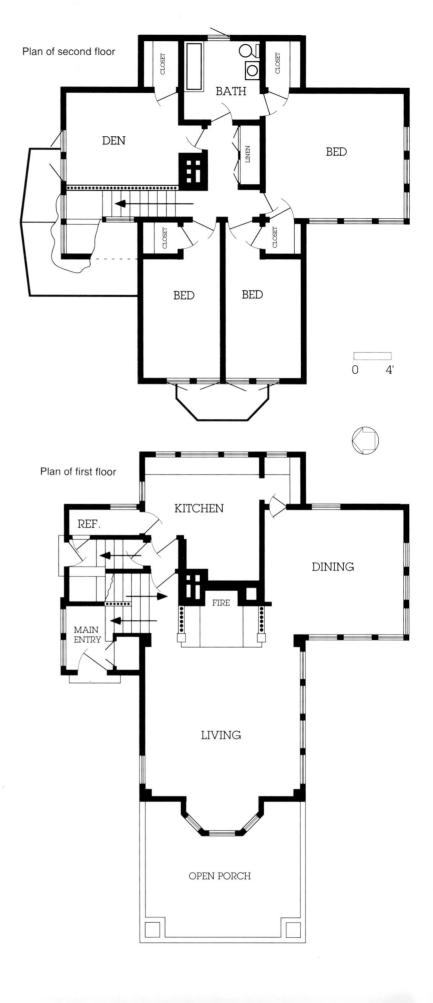

Plan of second floor

CLOSET
BATH
CLOSET
DEN
BED
LINEN
CLOSET
CLOSET
BED
BED

0   4'

Plan of first floor

KITCHEN
REF.
DINING
FIRE
MAIN ENTRY
LIVING
OPEN PORCH

The Lesson of Louis Sullivan

Frank Lloyd Wright called Louis Sullivan his "Lieber Meister." Why, we might ask, did the greatest master elevate his teacher to an even higher position than his own?

Sullivan said that "form follows function." He made his buildings beautiful, modern by their time's Victorian standards, with extensive natural decorative patterns. Wright saw in his beloved master's design a higher principle, one that would help an artist consistently achieve the beauty he desired. Wright learned from Sullivan that, in fact, "form and function are one." Wright only achieved this unity through great struggle. The prin- ciple he found in Sullivan he eventually articulated as a grammar of organic architecture. He may have been led to his understanding of Sullivan's design by his own study of the Japanese print: "Go deep enough into your experience to find that beauty is in itself the finest of morality— ethical, purely—the essential fact, I mean, of all morals and manners" (Frank Lloyd Wright, *The Japanese Print: An Interpretation* [New York: Horizon Press, 1967]; quotes not otherwise specifically identified are from this text). In this study, Wright demonstrates his real attachment to "things Oriental," so often misinterpreted in terms of the specific architectural features that Wright supposedly "brought back" from Japan.

Wright first visited the Orient in 1905, though in 1893 he certainly saw the Japanese pavilion, Ho-o-den, at the World's Columbian Exposition. In the late 1880s, Wright was surrounded by Japanese prints in Silsbee's office. Eventually, Japanese design philosophy captivated him. Wright, in his *Autobiography,* freely admitted, "If Japanese prints were deducted from my education, I don't know what direction the whole might have taken." They were not, of course, and the direction is evidenced in all his mature design.

"A flower is beautiful, we say—but why? Because in its geometry and in its sensuous qualities it is an embodiment and significant expression of that precious something in ourselves which we instinctively know to be Life, 'An eye looking out upon us from the great inner sea of beauty,' a proof of the eternal harmony in the nature of a universe too vast and intimate and real for mere intellect to seize."

Beauty Is the First Principle of All Art . . .

Beauty, to Wright, was the heart of all art, and it was not "in the eye of the beholder," but a matter of something in the object.

"We are familiar with the assertion that, should a man put eleven stove-pipe hats on top of the cornice of his building and find them beautiful, why then they are beautiful. Yes, perhaps to him: but the only possible conclusion is that, like the eleven hats on the cornice, he is not beautiful, because beauty to him is utter violation of all the harmonies of any sequence or consequence of his own nature.

"To find inorganic things of no truth of relation beautiful is but to demonstrate the lack of beauty in oneself and one's unfitness for any office in administering the beautiful, and to provide another example of the stultification that comes from the confusion of the curious with the beautiful. Education seems to leave modern man less able than the savage to draw the line between these qualities." (*Frank Lloyd Wright, Buildings, Plans, and Designs* [New York: Horizon Press, 1963], Introduction)

. . . Especially the Mother Art, Architecture

Wright's architectural practice, then, was directed towards educating humankind back to a sense of beauty. Architecture, as the "Mother of All Arts," was his means of revealing beauty "too vast and intimate and real for mere intellect to seize."

Because many of his admirers have seized upon the literal possibilities of design, which he called attention to by his own example (such as the "praying hands" image in the glazing of the Unitarian Church, S.291, in Madison, Wisconsin), Wright would have to call them back to the less obvious and more difficult response:

"it is this quality of absolute and essential beauty in the result of the artist's creative efforts that is the Life of the work of art, more truly than any literal import or adventitious significance it may possess."

What, then, is the link between Wright's philosophy of beauty and his architectural designs?

"Now, as it is with the flower, so is it with any work of art and to greater degree: because a work of fine art is a blossom of the human soul, and so more humanly intimate."

The flower image leads us to the principle of beauty and design and forges Wright's close connection with the Orient in his entire design thought:

"Japanese art is a thoroughly structural art; fundamentally so in any and every medium. It is always, whatever else it is or is not, structural. The realization of the primary importance of this element of "structure" is also at the very beginning of any real knowledge of design. And at the beginning of structure lies always and everywhere geometry."

It is really all so simple, yet how easily it escapes us. The nature of any organic process is revealed in its structure. Geometry is the grammar of organic architecture.

It is this root principle of geometry as architecture's grammar that unites all of Wright's mature designs, that underlies both Prairie and Usonian architecture. It is his greater use of geometric methods in his later years that makes Usonian work perhaps a more important statement of Wright's creative principles:

"So, in design, that element we call its structure is primarily the pure form, an organization in a very definite manner of parts or elements into a larger unity—a vital whole. So, in design, that element which we call its structure is primarily the pure form, as arranged or fashioned and grouped to "build" the idea; an idea which must always persuade us of its reasonableness. Geometry is the grammar, so to speak, of the form. It is its architectural principle."

What forms are particularly significant to Wright, and why? For him, a psychic correlation existed between the geometry of form and its symbolic value, which we perceive through the ideas, moods, or sentiments we ascribe to that form. The artist sees beneath the geometry, not just the structural skeleton, but also the aesthetic one, the suggestive soul of the work. Structure is not derived from the space within to be lived in. Structure is that space. Thus, to Wright:

the circle = infinity
the triangle = structural unity
the spire* = aspiration
the spiral = organic progress
the square = integrity

*Though Webster gives "spiral" as one definition of "spire," Wright used it in the alternative meaning of "a tapering roof or analogous pyramidal construction . . . loosely, a steeple."

In his later years, Wright the artist "signed" his works of architectural art with a red tile (signifying the blood of life) on which he had inscribed his initials. The tile was placed in the masonry near the main entry. The tile was square.

Assembly room

S.069 T.0216
Hillside Home School II (1902) for
Nell and Jane Lloyd Jones
Spring Green, Wisconsin
Converted in 1933 to the Taliesin
Fellowship Complex

Hillside has gone through many transformations. The first building, dating from 1887 (S.001), was demolished in 1950. The second school, designed in 1902 and built in 1903, was also for Wright's aunts, Nell (Ellen) and Jane. This building is rose-colored sandstone with oak beams, capped by a red tile roof. Two cruciform units comprise the main part of the school, a gymnasium dominating the west wing and a three-story assembly room with gallery (prelude to Unity Temple, S.096) the right, with classrooms linking the wings. Rooms to the north of the assembly room are linked by a bridge-gallery over the driveway.

The historical photograph presents a close-up view of the original assembly room. The mullions were load supporting, a means of reducing the load on the principle cantilever supports. In later Usonian design, Wright would occasionally conceal steel within mullions, though most of his Usonian cantilevers did not require such additional help.

The remodeling of the buildings since 1933 is listed as part of a separate project: Taliesin Fellowship Complex (S.228) for Frank Lloyd Wright.

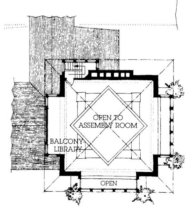

Plan, second floor of assembly room

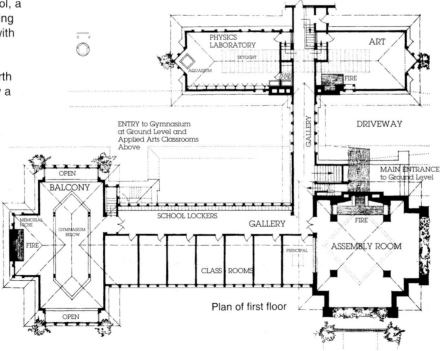

Plan of first floor

S.070 T.0009
Francis W. and Mary **Little** (Little-Clarke) **Residence I** and
S.071 T.0009
Stable (1902)
Peoria, Illinois
Veranda enclosed. Children's bedroom extended to enclose porch

The first residence by Wright for Francis W. and Mary Trimble Little was a brick home with a separate, large stable. It is notable for high-quality art glass (the maid's room and kitchen have less-interesting leaded glass, without gold tinting). The main floor plan is a truncated cruciform, nearly a **T** as emphasized by its long porch. If the kitchen and dining room of the Willits residence (S.054) were switched and the servant's quarters deleted, a clear similarity could be seen. There is a greater flow of space in the Little house, from front living room to rear dining room, with entry and stairwell between. The master bedroom is over the living room; both feature a fireplace. In May 1903, Mary Little, in whose name the property was registered, took out a mortgage for $8000.

Less than a year later, with Mr. Little in financial troubles, the home was sold to Cora G. and Robert D. Clarke (see S.152). The Clarkes spent fifteen years in the house, then sold to Frank S. Foster, who died in 1927. In 1930, Charles T. and Laura Hill Buehler purchased the property. Mrs. Buehler found the entry was leaking, so she extended the children's bedroom to cover it fully, scavenging two windows each side from the shallow bay to make two side windows on the front of the house. Ruth and Walter Swardenski, who purchased from the Buehler family in 1962, enclosed the veranda. The house is in excellent condition with little upkeep, original steel I-beams having held all cantilevers level.

The Littles built a second house (S.173), Northome, in Minnesota a decade later, when Mr. Little was again financially secure.

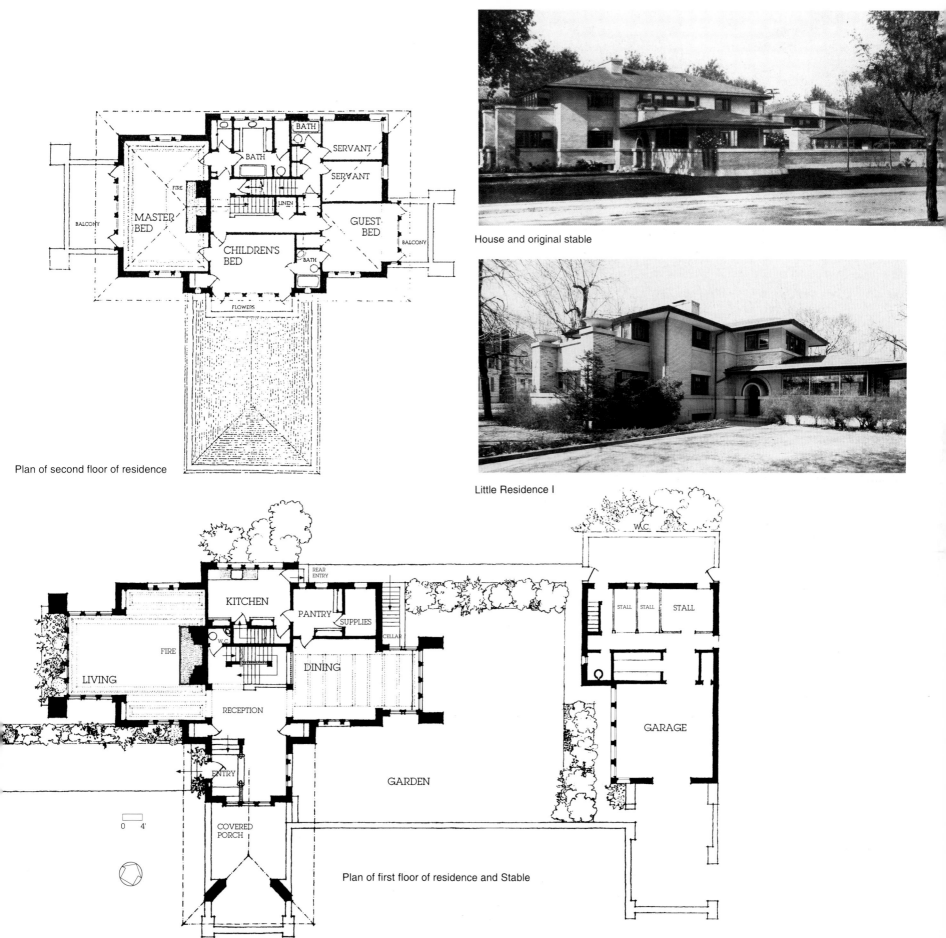

Plan of second floor of residence

House and original stable

Little Residence I

Plan of first floor of residence and Stable

MASTER BED

BATH

BATH

SERVANT

SERVANT

GUEST BED

CHILDREN'S BED

LINEN

FIRE

BALCONY

BALCONY

FLOWERS

LIVING

FIRE

KITCHEN

PANTRY

SUPPLIES

W.C.

REAR ENTRY

CELLAR

DINING

RECEPTION

ENTRY

COVERED PORCH

GARDEN

W.C.

STALL

STALL

STALL

GARAGE

0   4'

S.072　T.9905
Susan Lawrence Dana
(Dana-Thomas) **Residence** and
S.072A
Stable Remodeling (1902) and
S.072B
White Cottage basement (ca. 1902)
Springfield, Illinois
Restoration of house, and conversion
of stable to bookstore and main tour
center, completed in 1990

Susan Lawrence Dana was born five
years before Frank Lloyd Wright. In
1883 she married Edwin Dana, a
mining engineer, who was killed in a
mining accident in Oregon in 1900. A
year later, Susan's father, Rheuna
Lawrence, died. Mr. Lawrence had
made his money through investments
in a Springfield bank, stock raising,
railroading, lumbering, real estate, and
mining of gold, silver, and coal.

In 1902, Susan, at the age of forty,
decided to remodel and enlarge the
family homestead (thus, earlier 1900
attributions of the plan are incorrect;
the final design was dated 18 January
1903). Wright gave her a design "incorporating" part of the home. Photos
show the old Italianate Lawrence
home still standing, even as the
ground-floor walls of Wright's Prairie
structure began to rise around it. The
original basement was retained as well
as wall sections of the library and its
marble fireplace with butterfly motif,
which may be the source of Wright's
geometrically abstract butterfly
chandeliers in the dining room and
gallery. This gallery (at left in photo)
and the reception and dining rooms all
rise two stories. In December 1904,
the house was opened with parties
given by mother Mary and daughter
Susan. Mrs. Lawrence died in 1905,
and Susan made the house a social
center, living alone with her invalid
cousin, Flora Lawrence. Susan then
married her childhood friend Charles
Gehrmann in 1915; they were divorced
in 1930, though the marriage had gone
sour as much as a decade earlier. In
1928, when Flora died, Susan moved
to the White Cottage (see below) the
other side of the railroad tracks from
Lawrence House. Her health failed in
1942, when she was eighty; she was
placed in St. John's Hospital. In 1943
her possessions were auctioned.

Sculptor Richard Bock and the
Linden Glass Company, regular col-

Dana Residence

Fountain in entry hallway

Dana dining room

Dana Stable, remodeled as tour center

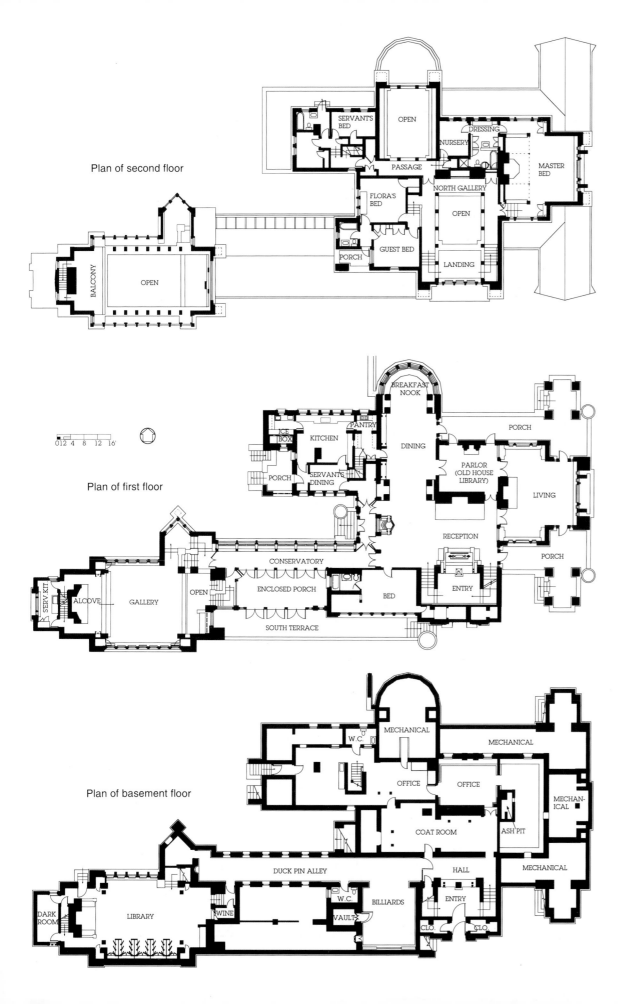

Plan of second floor

BALCONY

OPEN

SERVANT'S BED

OPEN

DRESSING

NURSERY

PASSAGE

MASTER BED

FLORA'S BED

NORTH GALLERY

OPEN

PORCH

GUEST BED

LANDING

Plan of first floor

0 1 2 4 8 12 16'

BREAKFAST NOOK

PANTRY

ICE BOX

KITCHEN

DINING

PORCH

PORCH

SERVANT'S DINING

PARLOR (OLD HOUSE LIBRARY)

LIVING

SERV. KIT.

ALCOVE

GALLERY

OPEN

CONSERVATORY

ENCLOSED PORCH

BED

RECEPTION

ENTRY

PORCH

SOUTH TERRACE

Plan of basement floor

MECHANICAL

MECHANICAL

W.C.

OFFICE

OFFICE

MECHANICAL

COAT ROOM

ASH PIT

DARK ROOM

LIBRARY

DUCK PIN ALLEY

WINE

W.C.

VAULT

BILLIARDS

ENTRY

HALL

MECHANICAL

CLO.

CLO.

laborators with Wright in this period, contributed to the project. Though the designs for details are abstract patterns, they derive largely from prairie sumac. The stained glass and much of the Wright-designed furniture remain intact. Original art glass is of particular note; it has several different abstractions of the sumac, outlined in the lead caming. This glass was manufactured primarily by the Kokomo (Indiana) Opalescent Glass Company and fabricated into windows by the Linden Glass Company of Chicago. The Stable/Carriage House was remodeled at the same time construction proceeded on the house; this included replacing the roof with one of lower pitch and altering all upper-level windows.

Immediately to the west of "Lawrence House," as Susan called it, is a house known as the White Cottage whose basement may have been used by Wright during construction, and which most certainly was remodeled by him; its fireplace is identical to one in the main house.

In 1944 the house was purchased by Mr. and Mrs. Charles C Thomas with art glass (approximately 450 pieces) and Wright-designed furniture (103 pieces) intact. The house later became the center for Mr. Thomas's publishing firm. The Dana-Lawrence residence is now called the Dana-Thomas House to recognize the preservation efforts of the Charles C Thomas Company, which occupied the building for thirty-six years, until 1981, when the State of Illinois (whose capitol building is but a few blocks away) purchased the structure, which had been designated a National Historic landmark in 1976, for a million dollars. Major restoration to its 1910 condition was carried out by Hasbrouck Peterson Associates, Wilbert Hasbrouck architect in charge, in 1986–90.

The Illinois State Historic Preservation Agency opens the house, now the Dana-Thomas House Historic Site, for free tours. The public entry and balcony over it are the only places visitors are allowed to see the building as Wright envisioned it. Sitting is not permitted, since only original furniture is used.

S.073   T.0509
Lawrence Memorial Library (1905)
Springfield, Illinois
Mostly demolished; rebuilt from
original plans, opened 1993

The Lawrence Memorial Library was
located not in the Dana house gallery,
as many have supposed, but in the
West Room of the Rheuna D. Lawrence School, named after Susan's
father, who was, at his death in 1901,
president of the School Board of
Springfield.

The Lawrence School has been
converted into an adult center. In
1993 restoration of the library was
completed.

Lawrence Memorial Library reading room in the R. D. Lawrence School

S.074   T.0204
**Arthur and Grace Heurtley
Residence** (1902)
Oak Park, Illinois

In 1902, Arthur Heurtley, an amateur
musician and president of the Apollo
Society and a banker with the Northern
Trust, commissioned two works, a
home half a block away from Wright's
studio and a cottage remodeling in
northern Michigan (S.075). In this
almost square-plan home, the tawny,
standard-sized (8 1/4 by 2 1/4 inches)
face brick is laid so that, at a distance,
it suggests a slightly battered board-
and-batten siding. This is achieved by
stacking courses as follows; a protruding course below and above a deeply
recessed course, then another set of
three courses, each stepped back
slightly. Eight such groups take brick
from stylobate base to upper-level sills.

The house, like many others on
Forest Avenue, was originally heated
by a neighborhood system of underground hot water pipes connected to a
central, public utility steam source; it
was known locally as the "Yaryan"
system after the engineer who
developed it. After the Second World
War regional utility systems were
consolidated. When, in 1955, the
Yaryan system was shut down, a
ground floor space was available for
conversion to a furnace room, since
Wright had placed the primary living
quarters on the floor above. The plan
shows the first level has servant's
quarters and laundry, plus additional
bedrooms and children's playroom.

On the second level is the dining
room with breakfast alcove on the
north, flowing uninterruptedly into the
living room in the center, and the porch
to the south, now enclosed. Three
bedrooms are to the rear, and the
kitchen is centered on the north
between a bedroom and the dining
room. Here, then, are all the spaces
Wright would combine on a single
ground level in most of his Usonian
designs, but now raised a story above

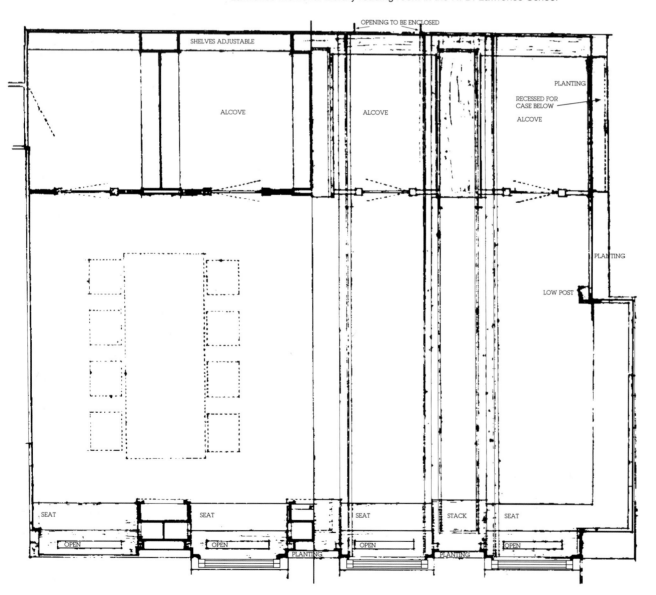

Living room

Heurtley Residence

 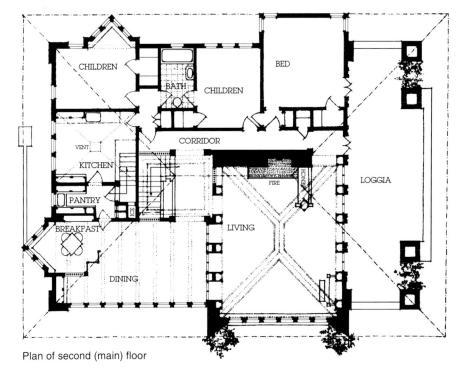

the "prairie." In the Heurtley residence, all these rooms are directly under the broad overhang of the hip roof, drawing their light from soffit-hugging art glass casement windows. This creates a cavelike sense of security. Wright embraced this cave effect in various manners throughout his Prairie years. In the Usonian era, broad overhangs would often be replaced by trellises, bringing light into the interior.

Second floor hallway, living room to left, dining room ahead

Dining room

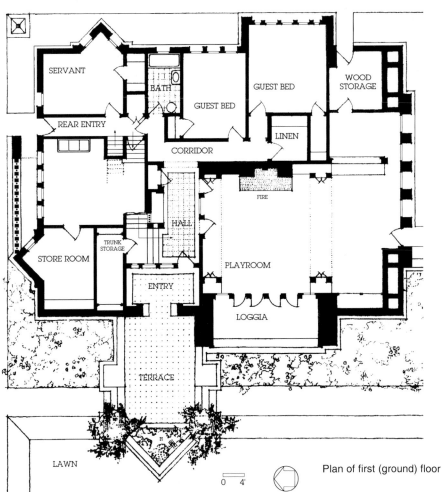

SERVANT

BATH

GUEST BED

GUEST BED

WOOD STORAGE

REAR ENTRY

CORRIDOR

LINEN

FIRE

HALL

TRUNK STORAGE

STORE ROOM

ENTRY

PLAYROOM

LOGGIA

TERRACE

LAWN

0   4'

Plan of first (ground) floor

CHILDREN

BATH

CHILDREN

BED

VENT

CORRIDOR

KITCHEN

PANTRY

FIRE

BENCH

LOGGIA

BREAKFAST

LIVING

DINING

Plan of second (main) floor

Heurtley Cottage

S.075 T.0214
Arthur **Heurtley Cottage Remodeling** (1902)
Marquette Island, Michigan
Altered, particularly at the lower level.
Bay window added to island side of cottage

The Heurtley remodeling is one of many cottages on the properties of Les Cheneaux ("The Channels") Club. Wright made alterations to a corner main-floor bedroom and converted the basement into a large dining room with kitchen, maid's room, and storage by removing partitions and supporting the original main floor with added steel beams. A fireplace of his own design, under the original fireplace in the upper floor, marked the rear of this dining space.

Original windows that opened the dining room to a lake view have been replaced by French doors, and the once-stained, battered board-and-batten siding is now painted. A balcony has been added to the southwest corner and a bay window to the second bedroom of the main level. Below the hillside lakefront retreat is a boathouse with similar exterior treatment, perhaps by Wright but not authenticated for lack of surviving drawings.

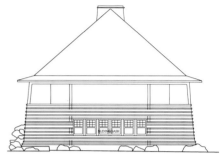

Front (lakeside) elevation

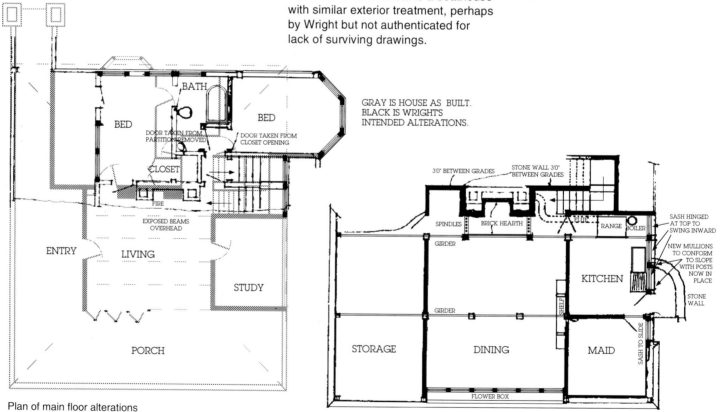

Plan of main floor alterations

GRAY IS HOUSE AS BUILT.
BLACK IS WRIGHT'S
INTENDED ALTERATIONS.

Plan of basement alterations

S.076 T.0005
E. H. **Pitkin** Residence (1900)
Sapper Island, Desbarats, Ontario,
Canada

Wright designed several cottages in
this period, all in the Great Lakes
states. The E. H. Pitkin residence, one
of the first, is near the Heurtley cottage
by boat, though some distance via
Sault Sainte Marie and ground trans-
portation. Pitkin visited the area on a
summer cruise, apparently expecting
to find a thriving colony of vacationers.
Few were there, but on a side cruise
he found this lovely location, the
westernmost promontory of Sapper
Island, with an incomparable view of
northern sunsets. Some of the Swiss
chalet character about this building
has been lost in the current structure,
which is enlarged and somewhat
altered from Wright's original plan.
That plan, excluding the veranda
around three sides, is strikingly similar
to, though not as elegant as, the later
Mrs. Gale cottages (S.088.1–3) in its
layout of living room in front of a fireplace, behind which are kitchen, stairs,
and servant's room. The plan seems to
conform to a regular 4-foot unit system
except where 6-inch corner posts
intrude. Many nearby cottages reveal
the influence of this Wright work in
their imitation of roof lines and
board-and-batten construction.

Pitkin Residence

Fireplace

Plan of ground floor

Plan of upper floor

S.077   T.0202
George Gerts Double House,
Bridge Cottage (1902)
Whitehall, Michigan
Second-story addition to rear. Porch
roof extended to cover bridge, then
enclosed

George Gerts lived next door to the
Gale family patriarch, Edwin Oscar
Gale, in Oak Park. He built his cottage
on the south shore of White Lake on
the easternmost limit of land held in
common by his son Walter (S.078) and
Edwin Gale's son Thomas (S.016,
S.088.0). Birch Brook flows under the
bridged loggia of this **T**-plan (double-**L**)
cottage and fifty yards farther empties
into White Lake. South Shore Drive
is well above the cottage, which is
entered halfway down a steep hill.
Though there is a suggestion that a
wall once divided the two **L**s, grandchildren remember drawn sheets on a
stretched clothesline as the only separation. Each **L** has its own fireplace,
sharing a common chimney. The plan
is drawn on a 3-foot square unit, interrupted only by a 2-by-3 unit where the
bridge joins the main house.

In mid-1988, Laurel and Clive
Cooper began renovation of the
structure, including proper bracing of
the bridge so that jury-rigged post-and-
beam supports could be removed.
Earlier owners extended the roof to
cover three-fourths of the bridge,
instead of the called-for half, then
enclosed the entire area as a porch,
and added a floor to the rear above the
main living space. The grandchildren,
who visited the cottage from its second
summer, remember it only with the
second-story rear addition.

Bridge Cottage

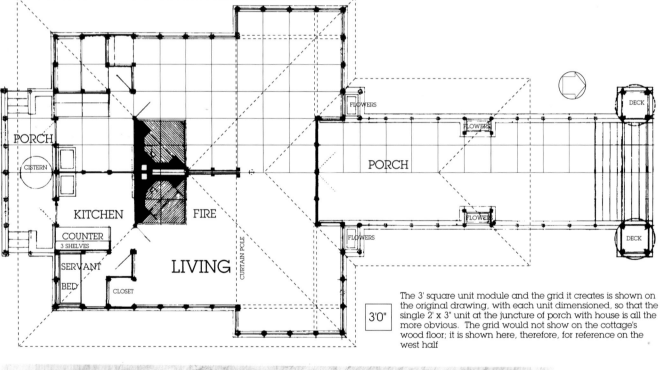

The 3' square unit module and the grid it creates is shown on
the original drawing, with each unit dimensioned, so that the
single 2' x 3' unit at the juncture of porch with house is all the
more obvious. The grid would not show on the cottage's
wood floor; it is shown here, therefore, for reference on the
west half

Drawing from Wright's Studio
of the Double Cottage

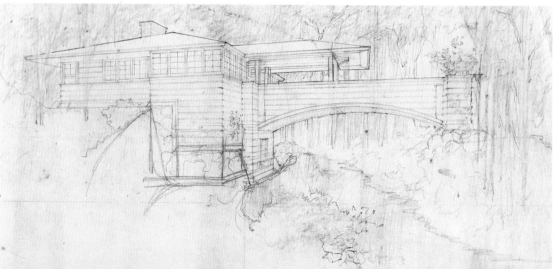

S.078   T.0203
Walter Gerts Cottage (1902)
Whitehall, Michigan
Mostly demolished

The original building for Walter S. Gerts, son of George Gerts (S.077), and his wife Ethel, concert violinist and sister of Laura Gale (S.088), was a single-story board-and-batten structure of rectangular plan, with a central fireplace. A 3-foot-square unit was employed in the design. The house is divided into thirds; the seven-by-ten-unit central section (21 by 30 feet) was balanced by a north-and-west-facing living room with fireplace in the front and two bedrooms behind. The west porch was framed by unit-wide pilasters that functioned as closets inside. The cantilever-supporting piers break the unit system slightly, being 2 feet by 3. A kitchen and dining room faced onto a shallow porch. Twenty-three windows and eight doors brought considerable light into this "tree in its birch forest setting." The living room originally was approximately parallel to the shoreline, gaining excellent views of the setting sun, but the cottage has been rotated 90 degrees clockwise on its lot, resurfaced, and gutted.

Walter Gerts Cottage

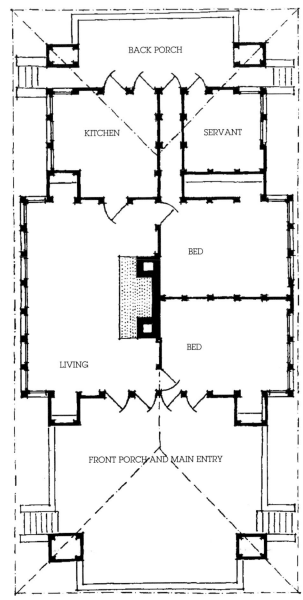

3'0"

Living room

75

S.079　T.0114
Henry Wallis (Wallis-Goodsmith)
Cottage (1900) and
S.080　T.9703
Boathouse (1897)
Delavan Lake, Delavan, Wisconsin
Boathouse demolished. Main cottage
altered immediately upon sale

Henry Wallis was an Oak Park resident
and real estate agent. He led others,
many from Oak Park, to a tract of land
that he held on the south shore of
Delavan Lake. To these business and
social contacts he sold subdivided
sections, many of which had Wright-
designed buildings placed on them
(S.079–S.087). The first of these, the
Wallis cottage, was the second
scheme done by Wright for the client.
It was unsupervised and sold upon
completion to H. Goodsmith. Wright's
design unit seems to be 39 inches and
is one of the earliest uses by Wright of
the unit system (39 inches is also used
in the Willits house) predating Prairie
era designs.

　The fireplace, central to the originally enclosed space, is actually in
a gallery that connects entry to the dining room (jutting out on the side). The
living room was bounded on the front
by a porch and on the side by a
terrace; upon sale all this was
enclosed as a living room for Mr.
Goodsmith; it has always been known
in this altered version. Behind the
fireplace are a pantry, kitchen, and
servant's bedroom.

　Extensions, particularly from the
porch back to the main entrance,
obscure the original design, which is
an early precursor of the "Fireproof
House for $5000" plan. The stairwell
tower juts well outside the basic rectangle of the main floor plan. The living
room was originally the whole front half
of the enclosed space; expanded for
Goodsmith, it fills the entire width of
the lakeside facade. The master bedroom takes advantage of the dining
room extension below, allowing five
bedrooms and bathroom to crowd the
upper floor. H. Goodsmith, from Oak
Park, was one of two brothers, both
doctors, married to twins, so the
bedrooms were enlarged and made
identical in size.

Wallis cottage, view as restored, with additions by which the cottage has always been known

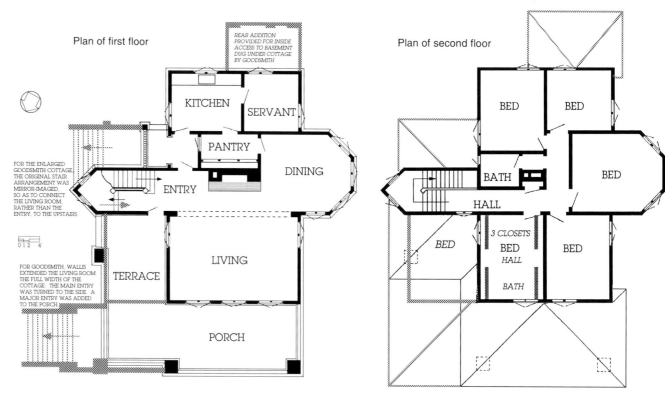

Plan of first floor

REAR ADDITION
PROVIDED FOR INSIDE
ACCESS TO BASEMENT
DUG UNDER COTTAGE
BY GOODSMITH

KITCHEN　　SERVANT

PANTRY

ENTRY　　DINING

FOR THE ENLARGED
GOODSMITH COTTAGE,
THE ORIGINAL STAIR
ARRANGEMENT WAS
MIRROR-IMAGED,
SO AS TO CONNECT
THE LIVING ROOM,
RATHER THAN THE
ENTRY, TO THE UPSTAIRS.

0 1 2　4'

FOR GOODSMITH, WALLIS
EXTENDED THE LIVING ROOM
THE FULL WIDTH OF THE
COTTAGE. THE MAIN ENTRY
WAS TURNED TO THE SIDE. A
MAJOR ENTRY WAS ADDED
TO THE PORCH.

TERRACE　　LIVING

PORCH

Plan of second floor

BED　　BED

BATH　　BED

HALL

BED

3 CLOSETS
BED
HALL

BED　　BED

BATH

　Enlargement of the Wallis design
for Goodsmith was by Wallis; if Wright
was involved, it cannot be proved with
any certainty.

　The exterior was resurfaced in
asbestos shingles by its third owner
who also installed dropped ceilings.
Renovation was begun in 1988, by
then owner John O'Shea and architect
Brian Spencer. Original rough-sawn
pine was replaced with rough-sawn
cedar stained as originally intended in
dark green.

　All the lakeside projects (S.079–
S.087) are on lands subdivided by
Wallis. When at Delavan Lake this
Chicago businessman lived in the
gatehouse to the Wallis Cottage. The
gatehouse may have been designed
by Wright, but no plans, correspondence, or other documents are known
that could verify this possibility.

S.081   T.0207
George W. Spencer Residence
(1902)
Delavan Lake, Delavan, Wisconsin
Two-story addition at rear mirrors
original, unaltered, building

One local tale has it that Wright dis-
owned the George Spencer cottage
when, during construction, the architect arrived at the site on horseback
and discovered that the second-
level boards had been laid vertically.
Wright's elevation drawings, however,
show this vertical treatment. The plan
reveals a dining alcove off the living
room, with a central fireplace, plus
kitchen and veranda on the first floor,
with three bedrooms above.

Even as a cottage, this is rather a
small building. In 1988–89 it was
enlarged by an extension to the rear
with a two-story arrangement that
mirrors the plan of the veranda at the
front. The original building remained
unaltered.

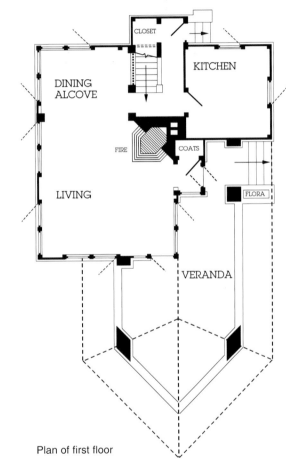

Plan of first floor

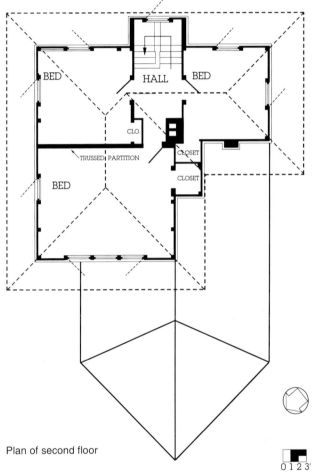

Plan of second floor

S.082 T.0206
Charles S. Ross Residence (1902)
Delavan Lake, Delavan, Wisconsin
Significantly altered

Charles S. Ross was a stock broker in
Chicago. His cottage was a cruciform-
plan, board-and-batten, Prairie style
structure. Photographs of it as originally constructed reveal an obvious
kinship to the Stewart house (S.160),
which is a mirror image of the Ross cottage, with some ideas incorporated
also from the Cheney and Isabel
Roberts houses (S.104, S.150), such
as a garage at the basement level
within the house shell, an interesting
idea that was not carried out in this or
the other houses.

This structure has been utterly
altered inside, and its original back-
woods charm is gone. Yellow paint
covers what was dark-stained, rough-
sawn boards. The open porch is
enclosed, and additions have been
placed to front and rear at the upper
level. The entire structure is winterized
for year-round use.

Of interest is the water storage and
pump house to the south. Electricity
did not come to these lake cottages
until about 1920, so catching and
storing of rain water, or hand pumping
or windmills for ground water, were
methods of obtaining fresh drinking
water.

The two-car garage is not a Wright
design.

Charles S. Ross Residence

Charles S. Ross Residence
(1970s photo)

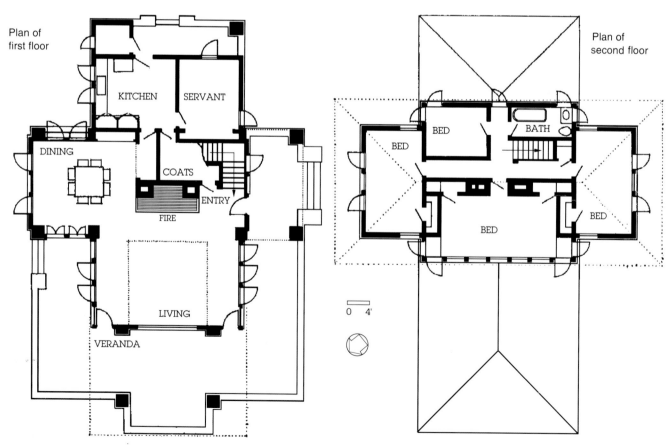

Plan of
first floor

KITCHEN   SERVANT

DINING

COATS

ENTRY

FIRE

LIVING

VERANDA

Plan of
second floor

BED   BATH

BED

BED

BED

0   4'

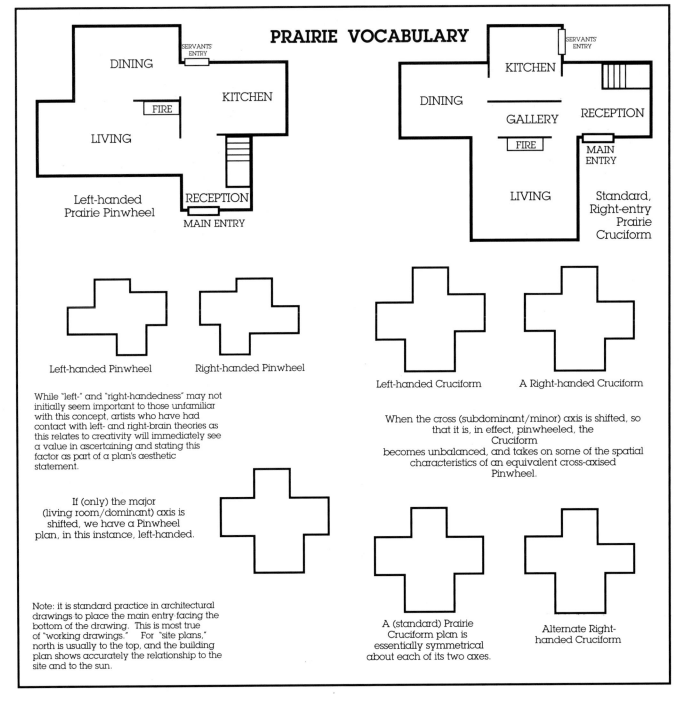

PRAIRIE VOCABULARY

DINING

SERVANTS' ENTRY

KITCHEN

FIRE

LIVING

RECEPTION

Left-handed
Prairie Pinwheel

MAIN ENTRY

KITCHEN

SERVANTS' ENTRY

DINING

GALLERY

RECEPTION

FIRE

MAIN ENTRY

LIVING

Standard,
Right-entry
Prairie
Cruciform

Left-handed Pinwheel

Right-handed Pinwheel

Left-handed Cruciform

A Right-handed Cruciform

While "left-" and "right-handedness" may not initially seem important to those unfamiliar with this concept, artists who have had contact with left- and right-brain theories as this relates to creativity will immediately see a value in ascertaining and stating this factor as part of a plan's aesthetic statement.

When the cross (subdominant/minor) axis is shifted, so that it is, in effect, pinwheeled, the Cruciform becomes unbalanced, and takes on some of the spatial characteristics of an equivalent cross-axised Pinwheel.

If (only) the major (living room/dominant) axis is shifted, we have a Pinwheel plan, in this instance, left-handed.

Note: it is standard practice in architectural drawings to place the main entry facing the bottom of the drawing. This is most true of "working drawings." For "site plans," north is usually to the top, and the building plan shows accurately the relationship to the site and to the sun.

A (standard) Prairie
Cruciform plan is
essentially symmetrical
about each of its two axes.

Alternate Right-
handed Cruciform

S.083 T.0103
Fred B. Jones Residence
Penwern (1900),
S.084 T.0103A
Gate Lodge with Water Tower and
Greenhouse (1901),
S.085 T.0103A
Barn with Stables (1901) and
S.086 T.0016
Boathouse (1900)
Delavan Lake, Delavan, Wisconsin
Major addition to the south corner of
house; rear porch altered. Greenhouse
demolished. Barn altered. Boathouse
destroyed by fire, 1975. Water tower
torn down

Based on dating of the plans in the
Taliesin archives, these would have
been among the earliest, and certainly
most extensive, of the Delavan Lake
projects. In the main building, arches
at the porte-cochere and front veranda
distinguish it from all the other lakeside
cottages. The board-and-batten siding
was originally stained but is now
painted.

Little seems to be known of Fred B.
Jones. He was a bachelor, possibly
living in Oak Park, and vice president
for the Westlake Company of Chicago,
which produced fixtures such as door
handles for the Pullman railroad cars
being assembled south of Chicago. He
ran his summer home somewhat like a
hotel for those with whom he worked.
The tower room was a place where his
summer visitors played poker. At his
death in 1934, he left over $750,000
to various charities. The will was con-
tested by five of his cousins. The bank
apparently took the entire property,
and it lay empty until purchased by
Burr Robbins in 1939. Robbins lived in
the house (by then weatherized
against Wisconsin winters) for five
decades.

The living room runs the width of
the lakefront facade, with the veranda
surrounding it on three sides. The
fourth side is a central entry, with a
stairway leading to a balcony that
opens over the living room as well as
the dining room. Back-to-back Roman
brick fireplaces serve both the living
room and dining room, but the billiards
room, behind which is the kitchen, has
a separate fireplace. Five bedrooms

Fred B. Jones Residence

are served by one bathroom. One
bedroom has its own fireplace.

There is new partitioning and
woodwork in the house, but more
important, there is a large two-story
addition on the southwest next to the
original servant's room and an altered
rear porch, which destroy the building's proportions. These alterations
were made in 1921 to house Jones's
grandmother. Elsewhere the ensemble remains largely as originally
constructed—apparently without
Wright's supervision. A water tower,
not shown on the plans and now torn
down, was by Wright.

The Jones gate lodge, directly on
South Shore Road, was originally
equipped for year-round living with a
furnace and coal bin in the basement,
and four bedrooms plus bath above
the living and dining room and the
kitchen facilities. It was connected to a
water tower via the gateway to the
property, and a greenhouse, since
demolished, extended into the property
from the tower. Storage for vegetables
is in the lodge basement. A new greenhouse, of recent vintage, is off one
corner of the lodge.

The boathouse repeated the
arches of the main building and its
board-and-batten siding. The roof to
the upper-level pavilion had a flared
ridgepole as in the Foster residence
(S.049), designed the same year.

The barn is at one side of the lot
and has been altered so that the
original design is not readily in
evidence.

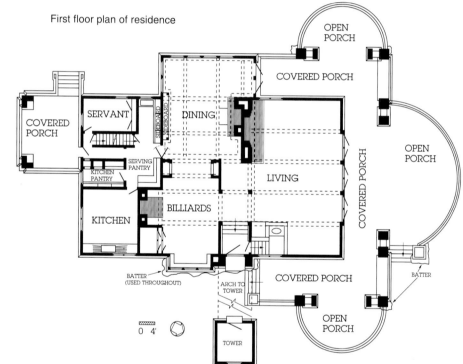

First floor plan of residence

Fred B. Jones Gate Lodge

Fred B. Jones Barn

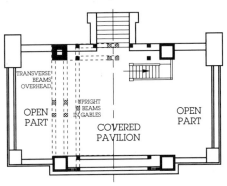

Plan of Boathouse at ground level

TRANSVERSE BEAMS OVERHEAD

OPEN PART

COVERED PAVILION

OPEN PART

UPRIGHT BEAMS IN GABLES

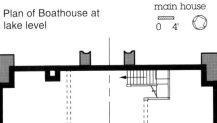

Plan of Boathouse at lake level

Same scale as main house

0   4'

BATTERED WALL

DOORS ON HANGERS

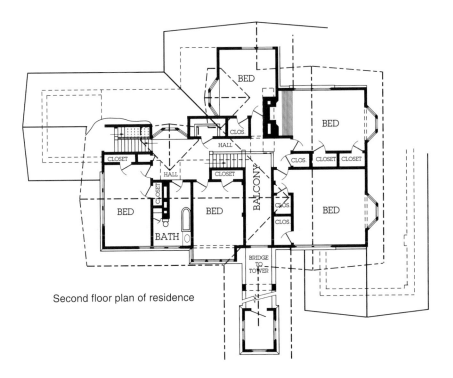

BED

BED

CLOS

HALL

CLOSET

CLOS.   CLOSET   CLOSET

HALL

CLOSET

BED

BED

BALCONY

BED

BATH

CLOS

CLOS

BRIDGE TO TOWER

Second floor plan of residence

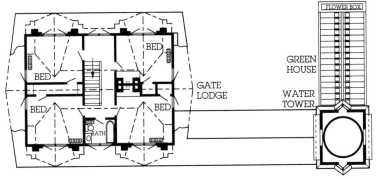

Fred B. Jones Boathouse

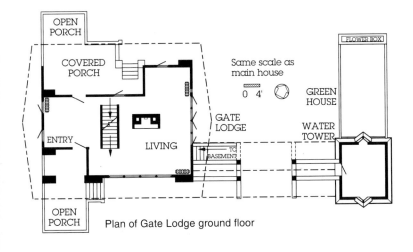

OPEN PORCH

COVERED PORCH

ENTRY

LIVING

OPEN PORCH

TO BASEMENT

Plan of Gate Lodge ground floor

Same scale as main house

0   4'

GATE LODGE

GREEN HOUSE

WATER TOWER

FLOWER BOX

BED

BED

BED

BED

BATH

Plan of Gate Lodge second floor

GATE LODGE

GREEN HOUSE

WATER TOWER

FLOWER BOX

S.087   T.0508
A. P. Johnson Residence (1905)
Delavan Lake, Delavan, Wisconsin
Interior significantly altered

It is said that when Wright, approaching on horseback via the dirt driveway to supervise final stages of work on this Prairie style house, saw it painted white, he rode away and never returned. Renovation, begun in 1970 by Robert Wright (no relation to the architect), included a new kitchen and toning of the exterior to darker colors more in keeping with the architect's known tastes. Continuation of renovation by several later owners included insertion of steel beams in cantilevered sections, addition of a full basement, and returning the exterior color to lighter, though not white, hues.

The plan is approximately cruciform with the veranda on the lake side connecting covered porches at each end. Five bedrooms, the front central one with a fireplace, and bathroom, forming a square around the stairwell, surmount the main-level cruciform above its crossing. To the rear at ground level are a kitchen, hall, and maid's room.

This is an excellent example of how the architect emphasized his roof cantilevers; he carried the buttress-like pilasters on the face of the central square part of the house only to the second-story sill line. Less imaginative architects would have taken them up to the soffit as supporting elements. The gap between pilaster cap and soffit calls attention to Wright's architectural daring (though note how even more daring is the veranda cantilever).

Tongue-and-groove horizontal boards are cut to look like board and (sunk) batten. The original leaded art-glass windows have been sandwiched between sheets of glass for protection from further weathering. Like others of the Delavan Lake cottages, electricity was originally unavailable; the building was gas-lit.

A freestanding, four-car garage with second-story apartment, built in the 1980s and imitating the main structure's design, is not by Wright. The main building was placed on the National Register of Historic Places in 1982, but the interior has undergone such changes, before that date and since, as to alter Wright's spatial concept beyond recognition.

A. P. Johnson was in the furniture business.

A. P. Johnson
Residence

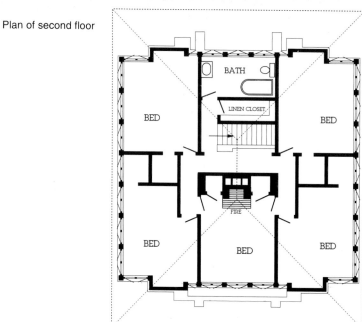

Plan of second floor

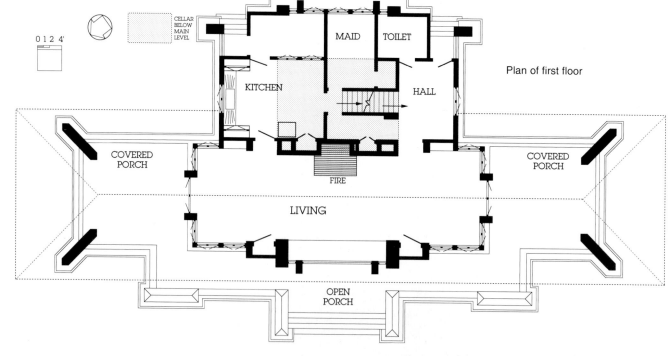

Plan of first floor

S.088.0
Mr. **Thomas H. Gale Cottage**
(1897)

Whitehall, Michigan
Relocated on site. Extended to the
rear and east side. Rear half (from
fireplace) altered

Five years after Wright designed a
home for Thomas H. and Laura
Robeson Gale (S.016) in Oak Park,
the clients returned for a summer
cottage at Whitehall, Michigan. White
Lake opens to Lake Michigan, and
Chicagoans could take a steamer to
their front door. Thomas Gale and
Walter Gerts, whose wives were
sisters from Port Huron, Michigan,
together purchased the whole of Lot 4
of Section 5 on Birch Brook.

The Thomas Gale cottage was the
first to be built. While highly altered,
what remains is sufficient to recreate
what most likely was built (no plans
survive in Taliesin archives). This may
represent Wright's first residential work
in board-and-batten siding. The boards
(7 inch) and battens (1 3/8 by 1 inch
with a 45-degree mitre on the top side)
are smaller than those used in the later
Gale and Gerts cottages (7 1/2-inch
boards, 2 1/2-by-1-inch battens). Its
18-by-24-foot living room was separated from a 10-foot-deep rear kitchen
by the fireplace column, the whole
balanced by a 10-foot-deep porch.
Ceiling beams are eight feet above
floor beams. Window panes on the
lower floor were laid on their long
ends, adding to the horizontal emphasis of the structure. Upstairs, under a
hip roof, were four bedrooms. At least
one window in each front bedroom was
a casement type, to help direct air flow.

This cottage remained Laura
Gale's summer home until her death in
1943. Her unmarried daughter Sally
used the cottage until 1961, when she
sold it to Adolph J. Struven. (Sally's
brother Edwin Oscar, who died in
1953, seems to have had little interest
in the property.) The building was
moved 9 feet west in 1966 to fit a
50-foot lot carved out of the original

Mr. Thomas H. Gale Summer Residence (1897)

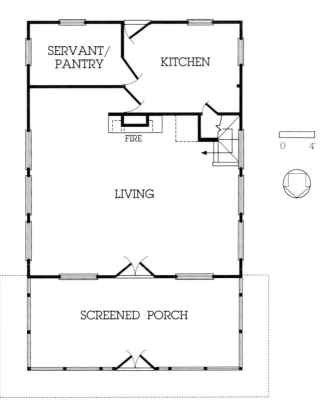

Conjectural reconstruction of Mr. Thomas Gale Cottage main floor

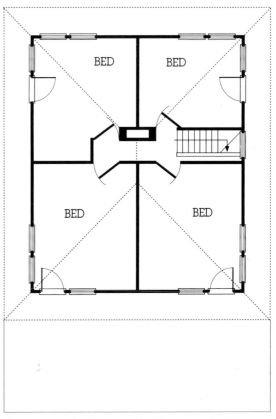

Conjectural reconstruction of Mr. Thomas Gale Cottage upper floor

plat. Much of the board-and-batten
siding was replaced with standard
lapped siding during modernizations
and alterations. A porch was added on
the east side. The kitchen was moved
into a rear addition which also allowed
for an inside bathroom. The original
rear space became a fifth bedroom,
furnace room, and dining room.

Discovery of this building resulted
from the researches of two historians,
Paul G. Sprague and Frances H.
Steiner. The latter notes in her *Frank
Lloyd Wright in Oak Park and River
Forest* (1983), the *Oak Park*

Vindicator, July 2, 1897, as calling Mr.
Gale's cottage (a decade before the
"Mrs." Gale rental cottages) "in the
happiest style." Sprague found the
building referred to, so highly altered
as to have escaped earlier
identification, adjacent to the first Mrs.
Gale rental cottage.

Mrs. Thomas H. (Laura R.) **Gale**
Rental **Cottage 1,**
Cottage 2, and
Cottage 3 (1909)
Whitehall, Michigan
Cottages 2 and 3 mostly demolished.
Cottage 1 enlarged and porch enclosed

The similarity between this structure and the earlier cottage for the Gales (S.088.0) is striking, suggesting that the earlier unit was a prototype ready for Prairie updating in these three rental units for Mrs. Gale. The compact arrangement is organized on a 3-foot unit, seven units wide and twelve deep. Three units deep are devoted each to the porch and the kitchen plus servant's room and the living room in between is allotted five units (extending to the rear of the fireplace mass), with an additional unit for the hallway. Four 3-foot windows, one on the side and three at the rear of the kitchen, had screens rather than glazing, to aid in carrying away cooking odors. Up-stairs are four bedrooms, the front pair having casement windows opening fully their entire exterior walls, both front and side. The almost flat roofline, tilted sufficiently to aid drainage of heavy Michigan snowfalls, is more distinctive than the hip roof of the first Gale cottage. The only inside plumbing was a hand pump in the kitchen.

Tom and Laura met at the University of Michigan, and friends always wondered "how that nice Tom Gale" could marry Laura, who was "a real heller." Tom died young, in his forties in 1907, of cancer. Normally 1905 has been considered the earliest possible dating for these buildings, but the property did not become Mrs. Gale's via Tom's estate until early 1909. Specific 50-foot lots were quit-claimed to Mrs. Gale from Walter and Ethel Gerts, who held the land in common with the Gales, only in the spring of 1910. It is possible, then, that the design is 1909, with unsupervised construction as late as 1910.

The first of these three has been more fully enclosed, lost its planters, and has had a room added to the west

side. It was once thought that this was the cottage in which Mrs. Gale spent her summers. Instead, it seems that she used the original 1897 cottage as her summer home until her death in 1943.

The second of the three, which like Mrs. Gale's own cottage faces north, was renovated in 1970–71 and has been further winterized and modern-ized since; structural problems caused virtual destruction of the fireplace, and vertical siding is hardly Wright's recommendation, but its dark brown stain is welcome. The third unit, on the westernmost lot of the Gerts-Gale properties has been fully upgraded to year-round living and its fireplace moved to the side wall, though the exterior retains some of the characteristic original shape.

Mrs. Gale Cottage, south side

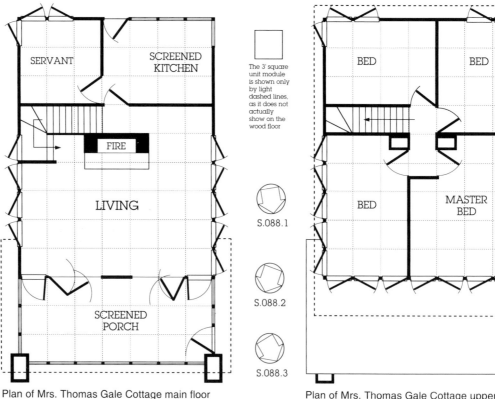

Mrs. Thomas H. (Laura Robeson) Gale Cottage, north side (1909)

The 3' square unit module is shown only by light dashed lines, as it does not actually show on the wood floor

SERVANT

SCREENED KITCHEN

FIRE

LIVING

SCREENED PORCH

S.088.1

S.088.2

S.088.3

BED

BED

BED

MASTER BED

Plan of Mrs. Thomas Gale Cottage main floor

Plan of Mrs. Thomas Gale Cottage upper floor

S.089   T.0112
A. W. **Hebert** Residence
Remodeling (1902)
Evanston, Illinois
Mostly demolished after 1959 fire

The revisions supplied by Wright to Dr. A. W. Hebert, who "prairie-fied" a number of houses in Evanston, gave the structure an enclosed entry on the north side that provided the usual compression of space before expansion into the living room. An enclosed front porch was dropped so a clerestory could enliven the living room, and a new slat floor was laid. Dropped ceiling beams gave character to the dining room and possibly elsewhere. A note on Wright's drawing, "This addition to be removed from rear of lot and attached to house," suggests that part of another structure was used in the remodeling. Evidence of Wright's work was largely destroyed in the rebuilding of the upper story after a fire in 1959.

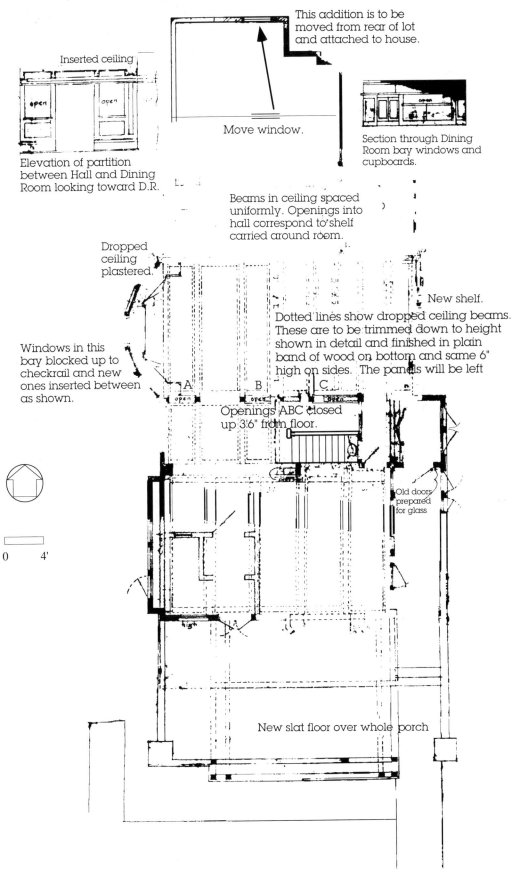

Inserted ceiling

Elevation of partition between Hall and Dining Room looking toward D.R.

This addition is to be moved from rear of lot and attached to house.

Move window.

Section through Dining Room bay windows and cupboards.

Beams in ceiling spaced uniformly. Openings into hall correspond to shelf carried around room.

Dropped ceiling plastered.

New shelf.

Dotted lines show dropped ceiling beams. These are to be trimmed down to height shown in detail and finished in plain band of wood on bottom and same 6" high on sides. The panels will be left

Windows in this bay blocked up to checkrail and new ones inserted between as shown.

Openings ABC closed up 3'6" from floor.

Old doors prepared for glass

0   4'

New slat floor over whole porch

Wright's sketches for the remodeling

S.090   T.0530
Darwin D. Martin Gardener's Cottage (1905, 1908)
Buffalo, New York
Single-story enclosed porch to rear, added in 1990

This house, unlike its illustrious neighbor, the Darwin D. Martin house, is plaster on a wood frame. When *The Architecture of Frank Lloyd Wright: A Complete Catalog* was first published in 1974, the plans were not on the list of items in the Taliesin archives. Furthermore, stylistic evidence argued against its inclusion; the fact that the overhang is not as broad as in other Wright houses of this type suggests that it may have been designed by one of the draftsmen in Wright's employ, such as William Drummond.

The plan is not as regular or compact as was usual in Wright's four-square designs. First the entry porch is recessed into the side facade and does not lead to the stairwell, which is reached only by crossing through the living room. Upstairs this creates a hallway that is wasteful of space, limiting the house to three bedrooms; the bath is in a corner rather than in the center along the longer wall as was typical of Wright's four-square designs. The plan is first dated 1905, with revision in 1908 suggesting a later construction date.

The rear of the structure, once altered by a clumsy addition, has been renovated with a newer single-story addition imitating Prairie Wright, and a terra-cotta tile roof has been installed. Leaded glass windows and doors copied from the adjacent Darwin D. Martin residence (S.100) give the structure a bit of elegance never intended by the original architect for a four-square house.

Darwin D. Martin Gardener's Cottage

O 16 32 48"

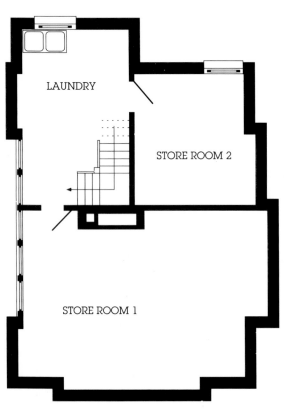

Plan of basement

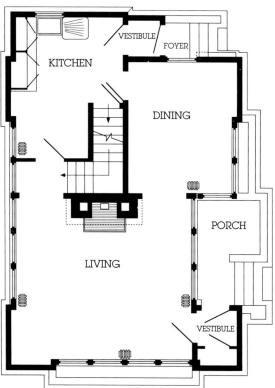

Plan of first floor

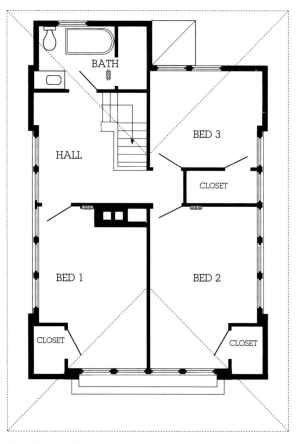

Plan of second floor

S.091　T.0306
J. J. **Walser,** Jr., Residence (1903)
Chicago, Illinois
Additions to the rear. Original art-glass windows removed

This Prairie-style house of wood and stucco now stands in rather cramped quarters between two much larger apartment buildings. In this cruciform plan the entry is at the side, opposite the kitchen, the living room is at the front, and the dining room to the rear. A full basement has space for vegetable storage as well as laundry, plus heater and coal storage. There are five bedrooms and the usual single bathroom upstairs. Alterations to the rear of the structure destroy the balance of Wright's concept. Attempts to have the house moved from its rundown urban environment have failed. To prevent their complete loss by theft, the leaded art-glass windows were removed, then sold, by Scott Elliott of Kelmscott Galleries. In the late 1980s, the structure was given minor face-lifting to help its sales appeal.

Walser Residence

Though this work has been commonly listed among Wright's completed oeuvre, no evidence, photographic or otherwise, has been found to prove that it was constructed. Contrarily, photographs do show a structure on the Freeman lot different from but contemporary with that designed for Freeman by Wright. It should also be noted that the Abbott house across the street is William Drummond's nearly exact copy of Wright's "Fireproof House for $5000" six years after its publication in the *Ladies Home Journal* (April 1907).

Plan of first floor

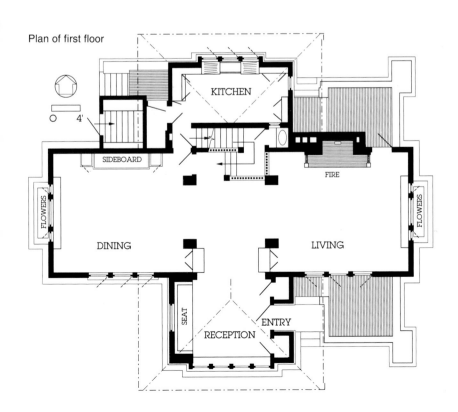

Plan of second floor

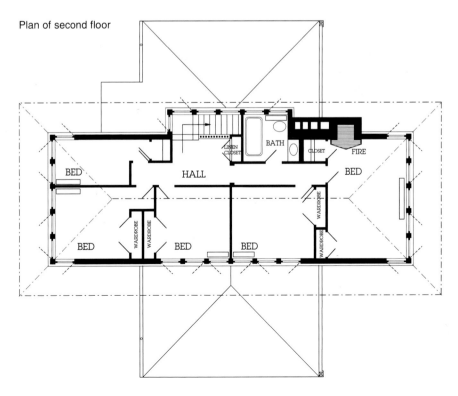

S.093 T.0403
Larkin Company Administration
Building (1903)
Buffalo, New York
Demolished, February–July 1950

The Larkin Company was a mail-order
business named after its founder John
Durant Larkin (1845–1926), who was
born in Buffalo. He became a clerk in a
soap-making firm when his sister
married its owner, Justus Weller. He
followed Weller to Chicago in 1870
but returned to Buffalo in 1875. There
he formed the company with Elbert
Hubbard, whose sister Frances
became Mrs. Larkin. Hubbard retired,
abruptly, in 1893 to establish the
Roycrofters, a community of craftsmen
in the tradition of the arts and crafts
movement, which, far more than
Gurdjieff or his writings, affected
Wright's later ideas for the Taliesin
Fellowship. All Wright's Buffalo clients
were involved with the Larkin enter-
prise in some manner. Darwin D.
Martin (see S.090, S.100–S.102,
S.114, S.225–S.226) replaced
Hubbard on the latter's retirement.
Walter V. Davidson (S.149) was a
Larkin Company manager. W. R.
Heath (S.105) was an attorney for the
Larkin enterprise. George Barton
(S.103) married Martin's sister.

The Larkin Company occupied
several buildings either side of Larkin
Street south of Seneca St. The new
administration building was to be north
of this, or just south of where Seymour
and Swan streets meet, just east of a
railroad turntable.

The new Larkin Administration
Building was one of Wright's most
important structures, though this was
long in being realized by the architectural profession. In a review of the
building in the *Architectural Record*
(April 1908), Russell Sturgis called it
"wholly repellent as a work of human
artisanship," and Wright's response
was withheld by the *Record* when their
critic died.

Wright's typical division of activities three ways is clearly observed:
ancillary services were placed in the
"annex" to one side of the public entry,
and the major activity spaces on the
other side. The main workroom was a
Roman-style atrium surrounded by
balconies which allowed light to stream
into the central building space so that
little artificial illumination was needed.

Larkin Company Administration Building, west facade facing New York Central Railroad turntable   Larkin Building, Seneca Street elevation

Larkin Building main workroom

Larkin Building, reception desk, elevator shaft behind

Larkin Building,
fifth floor,
looking across
light court

Third floor Annex plan

Multiple floor plan, three levels, with second floor Annex

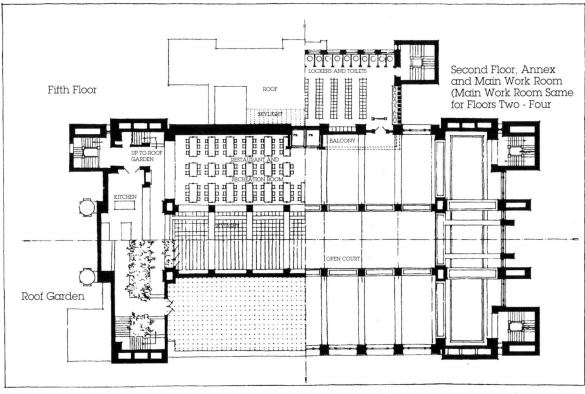

Fifth Floor

Roof Garden

Second Floor, Annex and Main Work Room (Main Work Room Same for Floors Two - Four

Ground floor plan; main workroom level

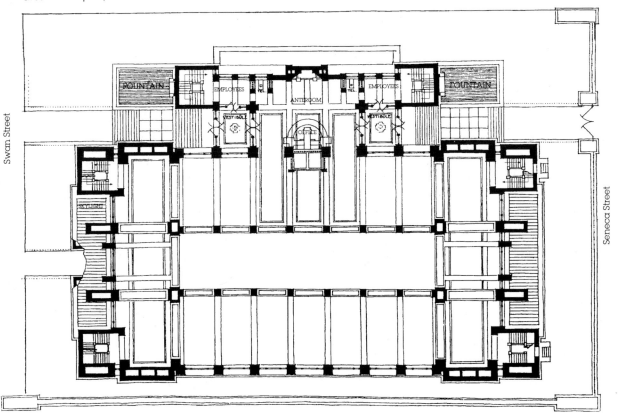

This skylighting over a central court appears as early as the Charnley stairwell (S.009) and as late as the Guggenheim Museum (S.400) and Marin Administration Building and Hall of Justice (S.416–S.417).

The annex is interesting because it rises only to the third-floor level of the main structure, yet opposite the third and second floors of that main unit the annex fits three stories, a locker below, a classroom above, and a lounge and restaurant at half-level in between, all lit by natural light provided by a special light well.

Among the firsts of the Larkin Building were use of plate glass, office furniture of metal, not wood, fireproof and noiseless magnesite flooring (which the architect had tried in his studio), all of them intended to guarantee that the building was fireproof. An "air conditioning" system was also part of the specification. This latter feature is truly notable, for Willis Carrier had invented true air conditioning just months before Wright wrote his specifications for the Larkin Building. Wright's system initially cleaned and heated the air while providing limited humidity control. William LeBaron Jenney's Chicago National Bank, which preceded Wright's Larkin Building by about two years, employed a system similar to this. Only in 1909 was cooling added to the Larkin system.

Dating of this project is problematic. Foundations were laid, some steel was in place, and construction was proceeding by October 1903, much earlier than published drawings, which are dated 1904–6. The Larkin "idea" thus predates the Yahara Boathouse project, which Wright credited as being the progenitor of all flat-topped Prairie structures and to which Henry-Russell Hitchcock, no doubt at Wright's prompting, gave a date of 1903, though recent research proves it was 1905.

Wright entrusted the working drawings to William Drummond, whose own designs were sometimes constructed near Wright's, often confusing the casual viewer (see Isabel Roberts, S.150, and Coonley residence, S.135; the Martin Gardener's Cottage, S.090, was thought to have been done by Drummond under Wright's supervision).

S.094 T.0305
Scoville Park Fountain (1903)
Oak Park, Illinois
Original demolished; replica now in
Scoville Park

In an article by Donald P. Hallmark in
the *Prairie School Review* (no. 2,
1971), this work is identified, not as
"with sculpture by Richard Bock," but
as by Bock "with the help of Wright."
As Bock's work, it is known as the
Horse Show Fountain and was dedicated on July 24, 1909. The Frank
Lloyd Wright Foundation, however,
attributes the work to Wright from a
much earlier year, 1903.

The current work, a replica of the
original fountain with new sculpture
that is an interpretation of Bock's work,
was put up in 1969 to celebrate the
hundredth anniversary of Wright's
birth. This replica may have spear-
headed the resurgence of interest in
Wright and his contemporaries in Oak
Park, leading to the designation of
much of the town as an historic district.
John Michaels designed the setting,
which is 100 feet east of its original
location (nearer the current Oak Park
Public Library); the concrete work was
by Albin Carlson.

Scoville Park Fountain replica

S.095 T.0010
Abraham Lincoln Center (1903)
for Reverend Mr. Jenkin Lloyd Jones
Chicago, Illinois
Renovated in 1978

The original project, for All Souls
Church, had more of Wright's signature on it than this construction. The
first-floor lobby reveals the imprint of
Wright, the two-story auditorium above
is his idea, and the building is designed on a 7 1/2-foot-unit system, surely a
Wright contribution.

Wright's involvement dates from
early 1894 through early 1903. He was
the designer, Dwight Heald Perkins, an
MIT graduate, the implementor. Both
were members of All Souls and had
offices in Steinway Hall, which Perkins
designed. The new building was to be
less a church than a community center, for Wright's uncle, the Rev. Jenkin
Lloyd Jones had taken All Souls out of
the Unitarian Church and made it an independent, nonsectarian organization
focused on the needs of the surrounding community. Accordingly, Jones's
center included a two-story auditorium,
an apartment for the Jones family,
rooms for meetings, reading, and
classes, as well as a library and shop.
Wright and his uncle fought each other
through three major designs. At this
point, Rev. Jones was still trying to get
Wright to further simplify the exterior,
which remained derivative of Sullivan.
Perkins tried to reconcile the differences, took over the design, and
changed the exterior to the Reverend's
satisfaction, then quit, demanding that
"Designed in accordance with specific
directions given by Jenkin Lloyd Jones
and against the protest of D. H.
Perkins" be written on the drawings.

John Lloyd Wright claimed the
original design was his father's first
architectural work and dated it 1888.
That date, however, coincides with the
original All Souls' Church designed by
Silsbee and built in Chicago. The
center was renovated in 1978 by
Andrew Heard and Associates.

Abraham Lincoln Center, auditorium as built

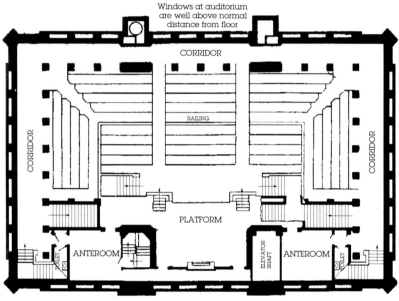

Plan of auditorium level

0 4 8 12 16'

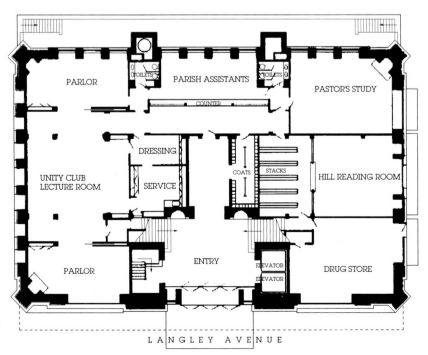

Plan of entry level

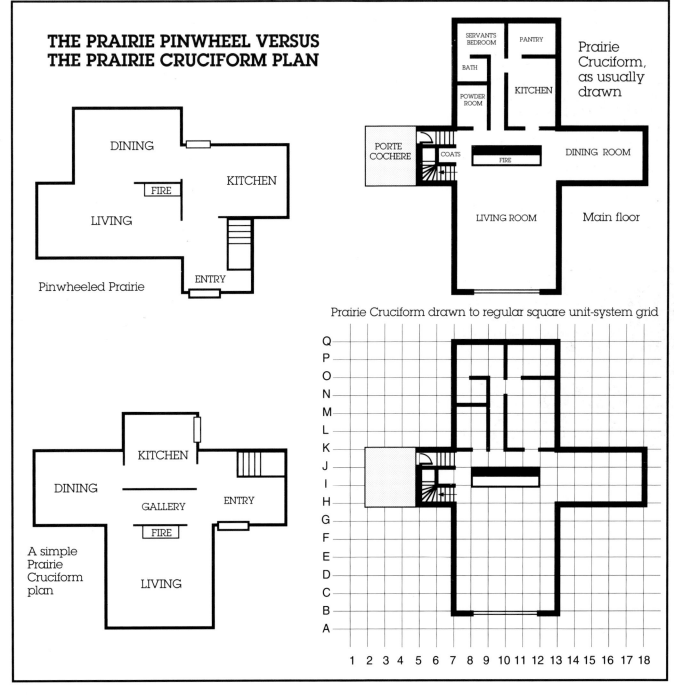

THE PRAIRIE PINWHEEL VERSUS
THE PRAIRIE CRUCIFORM PLAN

DINING

KITCHEN

FIRE

LIVING

Pinwheeled Prairie

ENTRY

SERVANT'S BEDROOM

PANTRY

BATH

KITCHEN

POWDER ROOM

PORTE COCHERE

COATS

FIRE

DINING ROOM

LIVING ROOM

Prairie Cruciform, as usually drawn

Main floor

Prairie Cruciform drawn to regular square unit-system grid

KITCHEN

DINING

GALLERY

ENTRY

FIRE

A simple Prairie Cruciform plan

LIVING

Unity Temple [Unity Church] (1904)
Oak Park, Illinois
Restored, in several stages, beginning
in 1969

Unity Temple (originally Unity Church
but now known by the name of its worship space) is composed of what
Wright called Unity Temple—the north
section, whose plan inscribes a Greek
cross in a square, used for religious
services—and Unity House, the parish
house to the south. A central entry hall
separates these two spaces, giving the
building three activities areas: worship,
traffic, and social and educational
services. This is a tripartite arrangement observed by Wright in most of his
design though it is particularly clear
here.

Wright's use of poured concrete,
while original in making no obeisance
to earlier, widely published nineteenth-
century French experiments with this
ancient building material, is but the
first expression of the architect's fascination with a material he would explore
and develop over the following fifty-five
years. The significance of his use of it,
however, is often overstated, or justi-
fied for the wrong reasons (see the
discussion of cement and concrete
after the listing for the Buffalo Exposition Pavilion, S.063, p. 61).

With its exposed pebble surface—
the coarse aggregate, which is mixed
with cement and sand to make concrete, showing through—the Unity
monolith introduced reinforced-
concrete construction to America on a
grand scale. Wright found beauty in
the concrete and made all exterior
walls and ornamentation from it.
Earlier uses of concrete, such as the
Hotel Ponce De Leon in St. Augustine,
Florida, of the late 1880s, though multistory, were usually heavily ornamented, concealing the importance of the
concrete. Wright trumpeted his choice
of the material. Its use was dictated in
part by the need to keep costs of the
new structure low; only $35,000 was
available to house the four-hundred-

Unity Temple (church), with worship
space to the left

member congregation, in which Wright
was active but never on the membership rolls. In 1952, Wright stated,
"Unity Temple is where you will find the
first real expression of the idea that the
space within the building is the reality
of that building."

The prime mover in the building
committee that chose Wright as architect was Charles Roberts (see S.040,
S.041). The working drawings were
prepared by Barry Byrne, who, after
leaving Wright's office, became one of
the more successful and imaginative of
Prairie school architects, concentrating
on other flat-roofed churches.

In the late fifties, Wright brought out
the Broadacre City model in hopes of
reusing it. It was in autumn colors; pink
and chartreuse abounded. Wright said
to John H. Howe, "let us redo it in
Spring colors!" Thus, when Unity (after
first deciding to tear down the building
and raise a conventional one) wanted
a "brighter, livelier" building, they
asked Howe and he offered pink and
chartreuse. There was no restoration
movement at that time to challenge
such a decision, but perhaps it saved
the building from demolition.

Initial restoration was actually begun in 1969. After a fire in Unity House
in 1971, restoration of the building
began in earnest. Fire damage, including that to art glass, was repaired.
The Unity Temple Restoration

Unity Temple (worship space) from north

Foundation was formed in 1973 to continue restoration and secure grants for which a religious organization would be ineligible. The rough pebble surface was repaired with a gunite coating, roofing and rewiring were redone, new painting returned the interiors to original colors, and a Historic Structures Report was completed. Visitor's donations, income from tours, and grants help with continual maintenance and ongoing restoration.

The building is owned and occupied by the congregation that commissioned it, the Unitarian Universalist Church in Oak Park. This structure has been designated by the American Institute of Architects as one of seventeen American buildings designed by Frank Lloyd Wright to be retained as an example of his architectural contribution to American culture.

The church is open daily to the public.

Unity Temple
(worship space) interior

Unity Temple (church) plan, composite of three levels

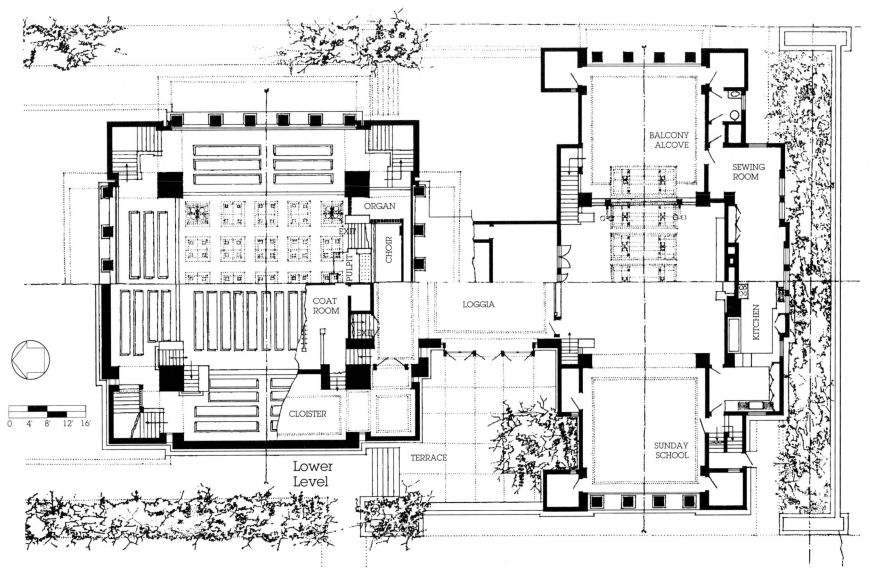

Robert M. **Lamp Residence** (1903)
Madison, Wisconsin
With rooftop trellises gone, the third
floor is now enclosed

Wright's lifelong friend Robert Lamp,
his legs crippled, loved rowing, something he could do with his strong arms.
So "Robie" as Wright called him, chose
a site that provided a view of Madison's lakes from the roof terrace, since
enclosed in a manner at odds with the
architect's conception.

The house is an early example of
Wright's Prairie four-square plan. The
living room takes up half the main
floor, and the fireplace has been
moved from its traditional American
location on the outside wall to the center. Behind this is the dining room, fully
open to the living room, and kitchen
plus stairs. An earlier sketch for Lamp
shows the stairwell protruding from the
square, much as Romeo and Juliet's
main octagon is penetrated by a
diamond member. Thus, the Lamp
residence, though not built with the
protrusion, may be the earliest design

Lamp Residence

that leads, through Wright's efforts to
perfect the plan, to the Fireproof
House (S.138).

Upstairs are four bedrooms, the
two at the front reached by a passage
between chimney flues (see Gale
cottages, S.088.1–3). The stairs continued to the rooftop terrace as the
only enclosed part of the structure at
that level, with trellises around; now
this third level is fully enclosed. The
main floor is raised well above ground
level.

There is some suggestion of the
handiwork of Walter Burley Griffin
in the external massing, particularly
the corner piers that rise only to the
second floor sill level. A 38-inch unit
seems to have infused the design,
though this is nowhere indicated on
any of Wright's drawings.

Mrs. Thomas H. (Laura R.) **Gale Residence** (1904, 1909)
Oak Park, Illinois
Restored several times, most recently
in 1984–85. Unfinished basement now
a playroom

The commonly accepted date for this
house, 1909, is that of construction.
Mrs. Thomas Gale and her children
Constance (Sally) and Edwin were at
their Michigan cottage (S.088.0),
receiving news from Oak Park friends
who reported on this "terrible thing
Wright was building" for her during her
summer's absence. The 1904 date on
Wright's presentation drawing may
have been added by the architect at a
later date, or it may represent the
delay between design and construction
that resulted from Thomas Gale's un-
expected illness and premature death
from cancer in 1907. The house remained Mrs. Gale's until her death in
1943, when it became the property of
her daughter Sally.

"Here is the progenitor of Fallingwater," said Wright in 1951. While the
use of cantilever design may anticipate
Fallingwater (S.230), the Gale house is
stylistically itself the offspring of the
Yahara Boat Club project (December
1905), which was in Wright's mind the
progenitor of most of his flat-roofed
residential-scale buildings.

Wright may have envisioned construction in concrete, which would
relate the building to both Unity Temple
and the Fireproof House for $5000
(S.138, S.139; 1907), but in the working drawings this was changed to
stucco and wood. The plan of the main
floor may be seen as an extensive
development of Mrs. Gale's Rental
Cottage (S.088.1), with the fireplace
moved to the side at the rear left
quarter of the living room. The main
passageway remains immediately
behind the fireplace, leading to stairs.
In the right rear is the dining room, fully
open to the living room but set off by
large built-in cabinets and a two-step
rise. The plan of the second floor is

Plan of first floor

Plan of second floor

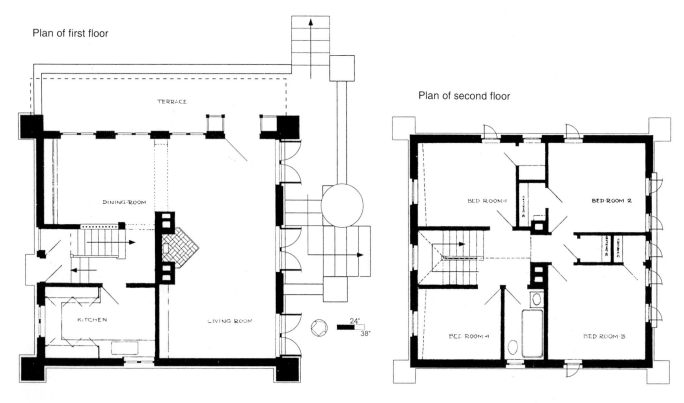

Laura (Mrs. Thomas H.) Gale Residence

Living room

Dining room light

quite different from any of Wright's contemporary work.

The Gale residence was sold by Sally Gale to the Rosenwinkels, who did considerable restoration work in the 1960s and 1970s. With John Thorpe as architect, extensive restoration was done in 1984–85, and the previously unfinished basement was turned into a playroom.

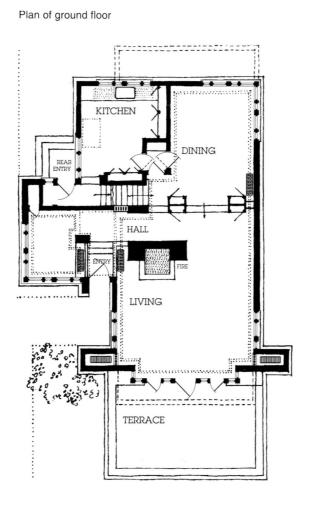

Plan of ground floor

KITCHEN

DINING

REAR ENTRY

HALL

ENTRY

FIRE

LIVING

TERRACE

0   4'

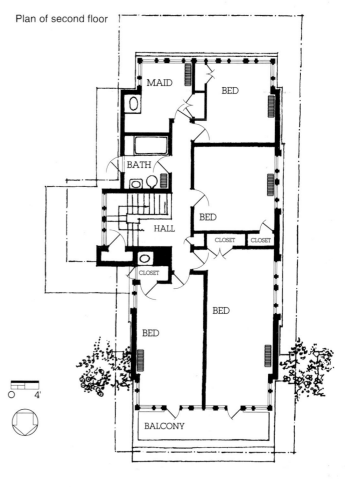

Plan of second floor

MAID

BED

BATH

BED

HALL

CLOSET   CLOSET

CLOSET

BED

BED

BALCONY

S.099   T.0712
Burton J. **Westcott Residence,**
S.099A   T.0712
Pergola and Detached **Garage**
(1904)
Springfield, Ohio
Residence converted to six-unit apartment building. Garage converted to residential use and otherwise altered

Although the Taliesin archives suggest 1907 as the date for the Burton J. Westcott residence, local sources give a 1904 date for the design and 1905 for construction. The plan features a large living room with fireplace on the back wall facing the glazing that overlooks a terrace and pool. On either side of screens that cross half the living room from the fireplace masonry are a dining room and reception room. The fireplace masonry continues to the second floor, supporting fireplaces in each of the front bedrooms; entrances are through an opening in the center of this mass (see S.088.1, S.160 among others). Each of the front bedrooms

Westcott Residence as constructed

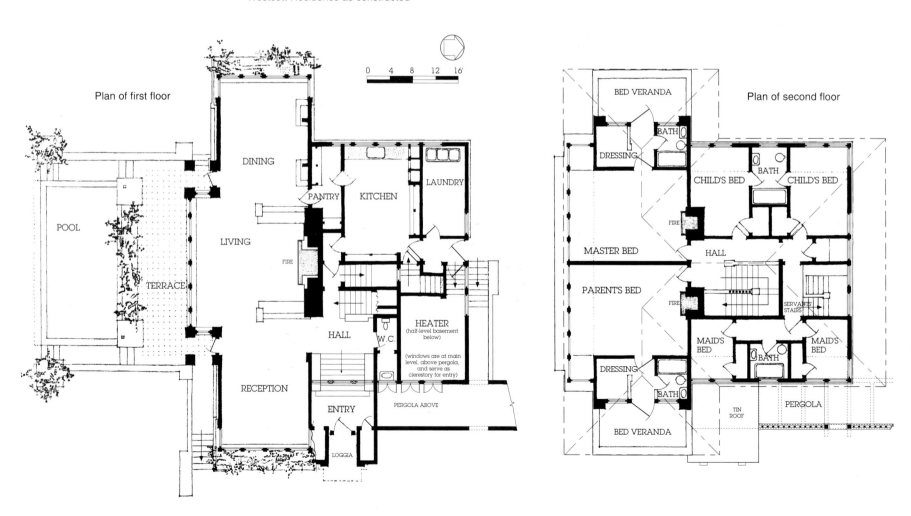

Plan of first floor

POOL

TERRACE

DINING

LIVING

FIRE

PANTRY

KITCHEN

LAUNDRY

HALL

W.C.

RECEPTION

HEATER
(half-level basement below)

(windows are at main level, above pergola, and serve as clerestory for entry)

ENTRY

PERGOLA ABOVE

LOGGIA

0 4 8 12 16'

Plan of second floor

BED VERANDA

BATH

DRESSING

BATH

CHILD'S BED

CHILD'S BED

FIRE

MASTER BED

HALL

PARENT'S BED

FIRE

SERVANTS STAIRS

MAID'S BED

MAID'S BED

DRESSING

BATH

BATH

TIN ROOF

PERGOLA

BED VERANDA

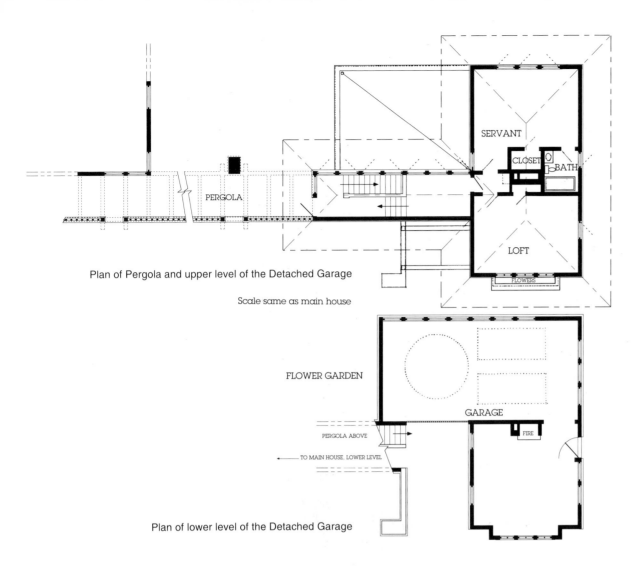

Plan of Pergola and upper level of the Detached Garage

Scale same as main house

Plan of lower level of the Detached Garage

had its own bathroom, dressing room, and porch (since enclosed), while pairs of bedrooms to the rear each share their baths.

A pergola with high wall gives privacy to the property as it leads to a garage with gardener's quarters above. In the 1980s the main house was being used as an apartment building, divided for at least six residents and superintendent. Comparison of the photo of the garage with the plan reveals alterations to the northeast corner; the east wall has been extended beyond the original flower box and the north wall squared off to the facade.

Detached Garage

The Grid and the Cantilever

There are two principles that dominate all others in Wright's method of architectural design: the unit system determining a grid, and the cantilever. The cantilever freed homes from boxiness, opened their spaces to the surrounding environment. The grid unified the artistic ideas into a flexible and diversified grammar, liberating the architect to let his fancy run free, yet assuring that no important principle of aesthetic proportion would be violated.

The importance to Wright of the grid and its related unit system cannot be overemphasized. Almost all of Wright's designs from 1901 on were created on grids, often hidden in his Prairie designs but clearly shown in most of the Usonian plans. Its absence in works prior to 1901 is apparent in their eclectic qualities. Its presence in the Prairie era is a sign of his having found his artistic grammar. Its appearance in 1935 both on the plan itself and in the concrete flooring of those first homes he called "Usonian" signifies the public arrival of a fully developed grammar of organic architecture. The Usonian idea, if not so named, was complete by 1921 in a series of houses employing concrete block as their basic material.

The grid is a simple device for organizing architectural space in the form of a plan. Rule a piece of paper with one-inch squares. Then draw the solid walls of your design *on* these lines. Since walls have thickness, you can vary your aesthetic in minute amounts simply by placing the wall so that it exactly straddles the grid line, or so that its inside or outside surface is *on* the line. That is an aesthetic choice, though it may often relate to the technology employed in construction. In the early 1900s, the grid matched the spacing of mullions. In the twenties, it matched the size of the concrete block Wright chose as his building material; three 16-inch blocks became a standard as these filled a

4-foot grid; there was no mortar between edges of Wright's "textile" blocks.

Use a grid scaled so that a door equals one square's side, a window one or two such sides. Four feet becomes the most common unit because it rationalizes the maximum number of building elements into a single module. Other units could be employed, the 48 inch being expanded to 52 or 60 inches or reduced to 42 or even 36 inches. This was a simple matter; to change the size of a house drawn to a 48-inch unit, simply re-mark the *scale* of the plan without need to

redraw it, for the integrity of the design remains locked in the grid.

"It is the space within to be lived in" (quoting from Lao Tse) was Wright's way of explaining the nature of architecture, "not the walls and roofs and floors." In each of his designs, the scale of the unit could be used to match interior spaces to their uses, giving clients the space they needed to entertain, raise children, and such. His "workspaces" were purposefully small to aid the housewife who had to prepare meals alone (servants were not common in Democratic Usonia). She could simply turn in a small circle to reach everything she needed, wasting no energy walking from one end to the other of a "graciously large" but useless kitchen.

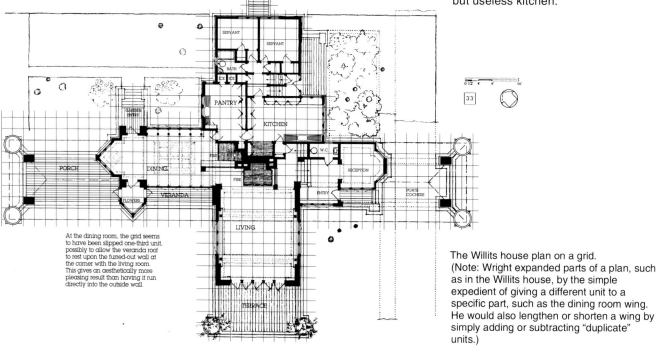

At the dining room, the grid seems to have been slipped one-third unit, possibly to allow the veranda roof to rest upon the furred-out wall at the corner with the living room. This gives an aesthetically more pleasing result than having it run directly into the outside wall.

The Willits house plan on a grid. (Note: Wright expanded parts of a plan, such as in the Willits house, by the simple expedient of giving a different unit to a specific part, such as the dining room wing. He would also lengthen or shorten a wing by simply adding or subtracting "duplicate" units.)

S.100   T.0405

Darwin D. Martin Residence,

S.101   T.0405

Conservatory with Pergola and

S.102   T.0405

Garage with Stables (1904)

Buffalo, New York
House renovated late 1960s. Garage
and Conservatory (with Pergola)
demolished in the 1950s

Darwin D. Martin and his brother W. E.
Martin (S.061) were partners in the E-Z
Polish Factory (S.114). Darwin Martin
joined the Larkin Company (S.093) in
Buffalo, New York, in 1878 as manager
of customer accounts and became its
secretary in 1893. He was a lifelong
friend of Wright's.

The Martin house, with its Conservatory and connecting gallery/pergola,
is one of the largest of the Prairie-style
houses. The plan may be seen as a
cruciform, with its main axis running
lengthwise from veranda through the
reception room fireplace; on either side
of this center line the house is essentially symmetrical. The main entry
allows one several choices. A U-turn to
the right leads to the library, while
right, around the fireplace, leads to the
living room and the veranda beyond.
Farther on is the dining room. A dogleg
to the left leads to stairs to the second
level with its eight bedrooms, four
bathrooms, and sewing room. Left
leads into the reception room with its
own fireplace, behind which is the
kitchen. Primary construction materials
are russet Roman brick and oak,
Wright's favorite wood. Its propensity
to collect dust and dirt in its open grain
causes it to darken and therefore the
original effect of Wright's color scheme
is often lost later on, and restoration is
difficult.

Orlando Giannini, who often
worked with Wright in this period,
designed the glass work. Walter Burley
Griffin designed the extensive semicircular plantings, a "flori-cycle" garden
that bloomed from early spring until
mid-autumn. After leaving Wright,
Griffin advertised himself as both
architect and landscape architect.

Apartment buildings now crowd the
lot where Garage and Conservatory
were once located. In 1967, Edgar
Tafel was retained to restore the main
building. To meet contemporary standards, a skylight was installed in the
entrance hall, fluorescent lighting was

added to supplement existing light,
and the kitchen modernized. Dutch-
metal surfaces became off-white.

The Darwin D. Martin house is a
National Historic Landmark and is
owned by SUNY Buffalo and operated
by the Darwin D. Martin House
Associates.

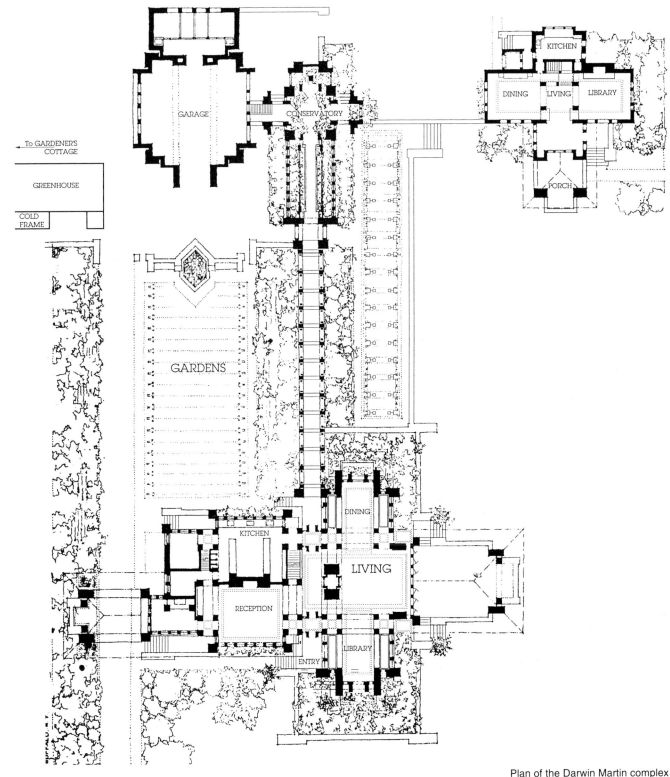

Plan of the Darwin Martin complex

(Continues)

Living room full view

Darwin D. Martin Residence

Reception room

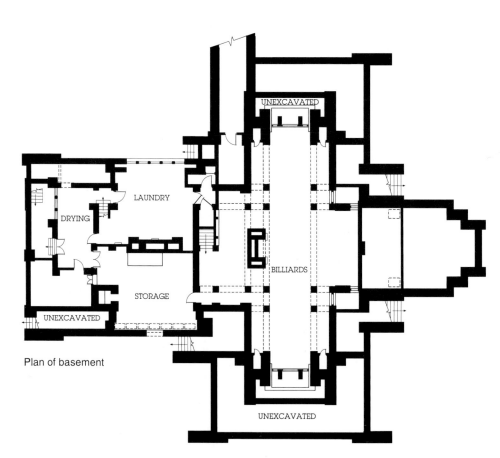

Plan of basement

Dining room

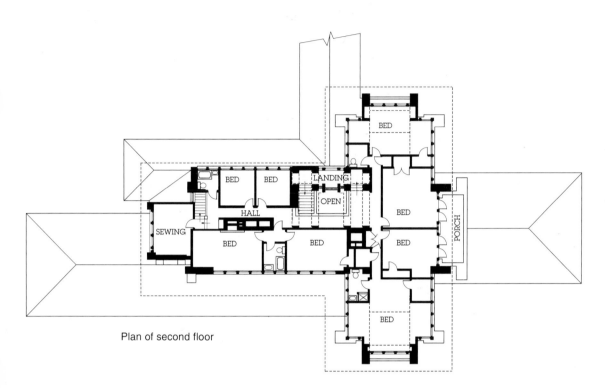

Plan of second floor

Northwest corner of living room

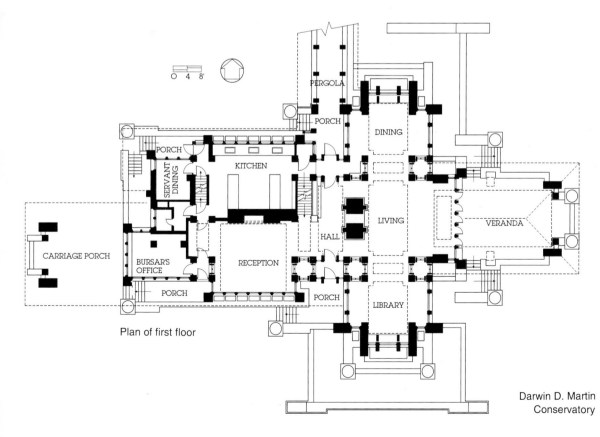

Plan of first floor

Darwin D. Martin
Conservatory

S.103 T.0301

George **Barton** Residence (1903)
Buffalo, New York

Mr. George Barton and his wife Delta Martin Barton, the sister of Darwin D. Martin, built their home on a lot immediately adjacent to the north limit of the Martin residence (S.100). The cruciform plan is articulated on the main floor by the dining room on the west, and the living room on the east, the kitchen on the north, and the veranda on the south with offset entry into the living room. The house was restored in the 1970s by Eric Larrabee and his architect wife, Eleanor.

Barton Residence

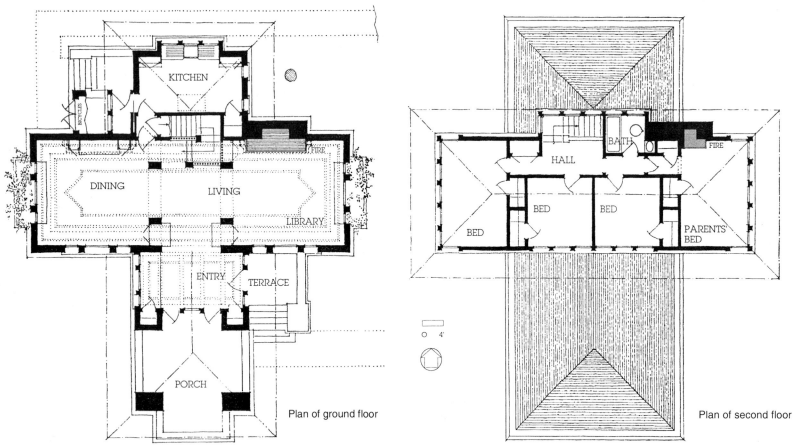

Plan of ground floor

Plan of second floor

Barton living room

The Cheney house bears a reputation more for its clients than its design, though the latter is especially interesting. What appears to be a single-story bungalow is actually a two-story house in brick with wood trim, with V-shaped gutters, particularly beautiful on this compact, low Prairie dwelling. The front of the house has a dining area on one side of the living room and a library on the other, all overlooking an extensive walled courtyard. Visitors must walk past the yard and half the house to reach the entry on the south side.

Every one of the fifty-two windows at the main level has art glass. Iridescent glass versus monocolor marks the difference between reflected and transmitted light. Lighting fixtures were designed for gas or electricity; there are eight original fixtures and five reproductions in the living room. The structural support of the living room is

Cheney Residence

a chain-link truss. Radiators are concealed, and there is an original sideboard, a favorite piece of furniture in Wright's Prairie days. Four bedrooms to the rear are mechanically vented into the attic.

The basement is at half level, concealed from the street by the retaining wall; a two-car garage, a design feature Wright would repeat in the Isabel Roberts home (S.150), was vetoed by the Oak Park city council, who feared the possibility of fire from gasoline fumes. This full basement was then turned into a separate apartment for Mrs. Cheney's

sister, a schoolteacher. The sill level of the basement windows is at ground level. The apartment living room has an iron-spot Roman brick fireplace. The flue rises through the center of the house, next to a well that brings natural light not only to the attic (which was never finished) but all the way down to the main-floor gallery. This device could brighten the innermost reaches of a building naturally.

Mamah Borthwick Cheney, wife of Edwin Cheney, went with Wright to Germany in 1909, when he was invited to prepare and publish the Wasmuth Portfolio. In 1910 (plans dated May 17) a board-and-batten garage was added at the alley and later connected to the house by a

raised breezeway. Hermann von Holst may have been the architect. The garage upper level was designed as a sleeping porch, a device Wright would use often in 1910–20 (see Sutton, S.106, and Ravine Bluffs, S.188, S.192).

In 1990 considerable exterior deterioration was corrected on eaves, the walk, perimeter walls, and the front terrace. Earlier renovation repaired damage by fires in 1965 and 1968 which required that one 10-foot wall be torn down.

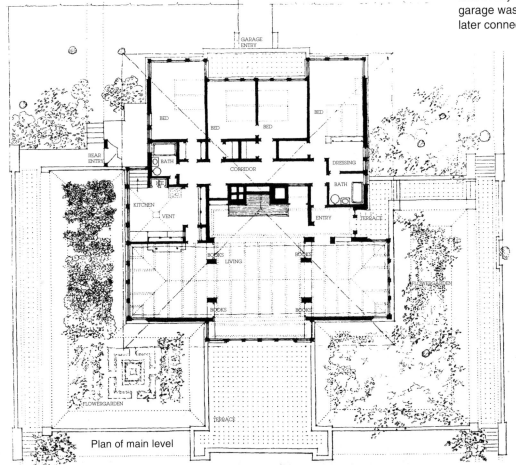

Plan of main level

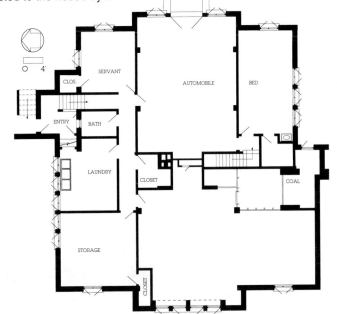

Plan of lower level

William R. **Heath** Residence (1904)
Buffalo, New York
Part of the house now given over to
alternative uses

William R. Heath, attorney for the
Larkin Company (S.093), and his wife,
a sister of Larkin's cofounder Elbert
Hubbard, built a dark red brick Prairie
style home. The main east-west axis
parallels Bird Avenue where it reaches
Soldier's Place, a vehicular traffic
circle. Originally the minor axis, entry
and dining room, were right-hand
(counter-clockwise) pinwheeled from
this. Enlargement of the reception
room and addition of a ground-level
servants' wing (two bedrooms, bath,
and dining room) west of the main
kitchen obscure this arrangement in
the final plan. There is a lavatory on
the main floor and two bathrooms
above serving seven bedrooms. The
fireplace constitutes the north wall of
the living room, with south wall
windows, and east wall doors opening
to the veranda. The mantel is Medina
sandstone, inscribed,
   The reality of the house is order
   The blessing of the house is
contentment
   The glory of the house is hospitality
   Full crown of the house is coolness
   Like the Tomek (S.128) and Robie
(S.127) houses, the Heath residence
has a basement playroom at half level,
with light admitted by a south-facing
well.The two-story garage is a 1911
addition, though Wright's published
plans show a single-story structure
attached to the main house by a
covered walkway. The original servants' quarters are now a doctor's
office.

Heath Residence, north side

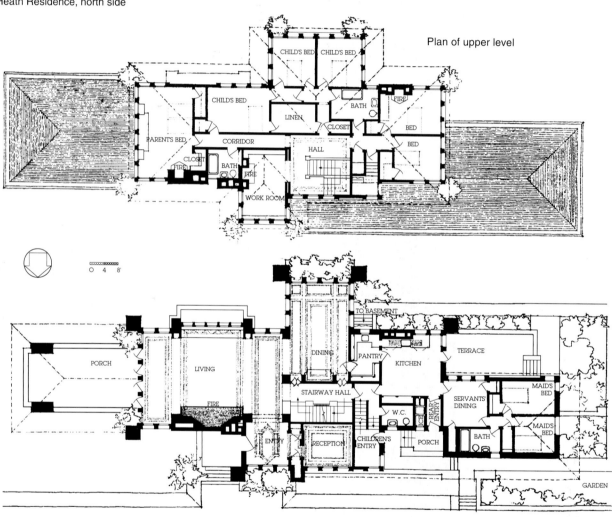

Plan of upper level

Heath Residence, south side

Two views in the living room

Sutton Residence with original entry

S.106 T.0710
Harvey P. Sutton Residence (1905)
McCook, Nebraska
Largely refurbished, but northwest
stairwell addition still in place

The Harvey P. Sutton house, the third
scheme for the client, is the only
Wright-designed work in Nebraska. A
living room opens on one side to a
dining room, the other side to a reception room, and forward to a veranda.
Behind the iron-spot tan Roman brick
fireplace is the kitchen. Breaking what
would otherwise be a standard cruciform main-floor plan is "bedroom 6" to
the right rear. Upstairs are five bedrooms, a pair over the living room, and
a sleeping porch over the main-floor
bedroom. Because the Nebraska
climate can be rather dry, a cistern
collected water which was pumped to
an attic bin.

After threats of demolition in the
late seventies, Donald J. Poore
purchased the house and began
restoration. Much damage had been
done over the years during a period
when the house was used as doctors'
offices, though all but one of the original art glass windows were intact. The
original ground-level entry into the
reception room by way of internal
stairs had been closed off, leaving only
the veranda entry for visitors. The
veranda was reduced in size and posts
put up to support the daring cantilever.

New stucco has been applied to
the exterior. Non-Wright interior
partitioning has been removed, but the
northwest corner of the cruciform has
been squared off to enclose a second
stairway to the basement and provide
for a modern laundry. The cream,
brown, and yellow color scheme was
restored, though damage to the floors
would have require complete
replacement of the wood. Oak
woodwork has been refinished. A
dining room sideboard discovered in
the basement was refinished and
returned to its proper location.

The Sutton sideboard

Sutton Residence (1990 photo)

(Continues)

Plan of second floor

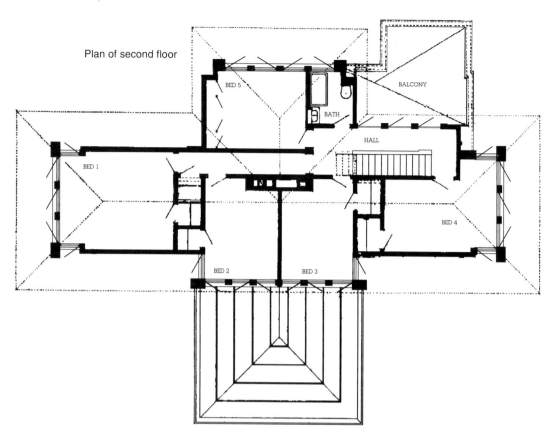

BED 5
BATH
BALCONY
BED 1
HALL
BED 4
BED 2
BED 3

Plan of first floor

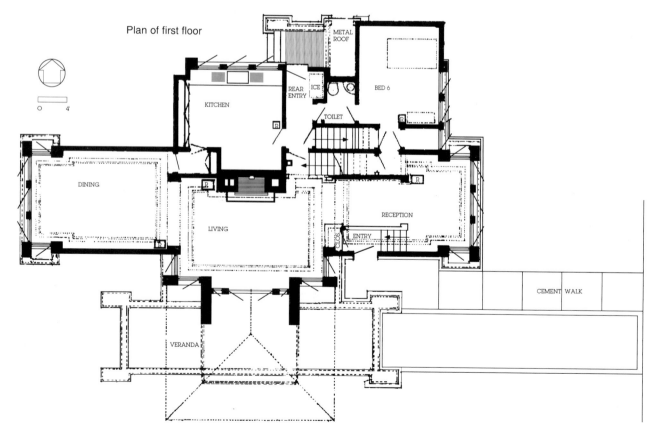

o   4'

METAL ROOF
REAR ENTRY
ICE
BED 6
KITCHEN
TOILET
DINING
RECEPTION
LIVING
CLOS
ENTRY
VERANDA
CEMENT WALK

S.107   T.0502
Hiram **Baldwin** Residence (1905)
Kenilworth, Illinois
Open porch now enclosed. Additions
to the rear

The main axis of the Baldwin house
lines up a dining room, reception room,
the fireplace massing with maid's room
offset behind, and the porch, this latter
now enclosed. The living room, a
semicircular bay, sits under a square
roof. There are two baths and four
bedrooms on the second floor. The
master bedroom, with its own fire-

place, is above the living room. A
smaller bedroom cantilevers over the
porch, though the effect is concealed
by the porch roof. In the basement are
a laundry, maid's bathroom, furnace
room, and coal storage, plus a photographic darkroom. Thus, this is
another of Wright's experiments
utilizing a three-story arrangement of
spaces, though here the basement is
not at full half-level as in the Heath
home (S.105).

Over the years there have been a
number of alterations, most notably an
addition to the rear.

Baldwin Residence

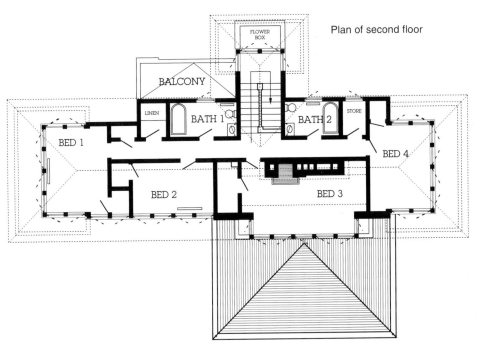

Plan of second floor

FLOWER BOX

BALCONY

LINEN · BATH 1 · BATH 2 · STORE

BED 1

BED 4

BED 2

BED 3

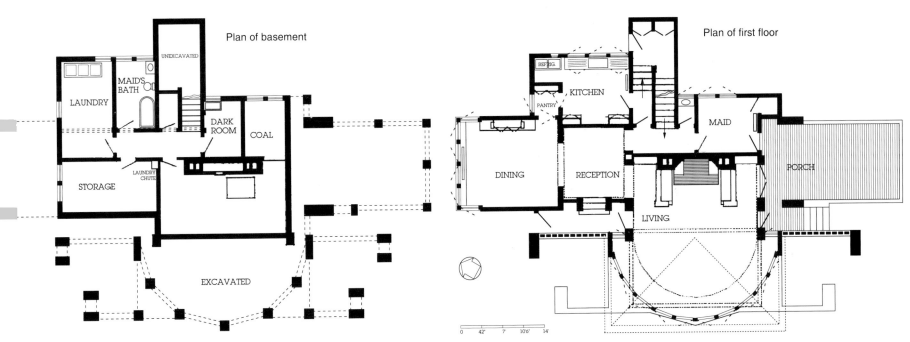

Plan of basement

UNEXCAVATED

MAID'S BATH

LAUNDRY

DARK ROOM · COAL

LAUNDRY CHUTE

STORAGE

EXCAVATED

Plan of first floor

REFRIG.

KITCHEN

PANTRY

MAID

DINING · RECEPTION

PORCH

LIVING

0   4'2"   7'   10'6"   14'

Entry

S.108   T.0501A
Mary M. W. Adams Residence
(1905)
Highland Park, Illinois
Porch enclosed

Wright supposedly intended the Mary
Adams home to be inexpensive. One
can see in it elements of the Fireproof
House (S.139; 1907) converted, in
ways recognizable to anyone familiar
with Froebelian transformations, from
square to rectangle. The first plan
shows porches at the extremities, and
an entry which is almost an annex,
as in the Larkin Building (S.093), set
to the side. From this plan, Wright
removed the south porch, inter-
changed kitchen with dining room so
that the latter obtains the open view,
and simplified the entry and stairwell.
The resultant plan could be seen as an
improvement upon the Charnley residence (S.009).

There are rooms for both a maid
and a manservant, and the house was
equipped with a call system so that
Mary Adams could beckon her help
even from the porch. Interior floors are
quarter-sawn white oak, but the porch
is pine, and fir is used upstairs. An
interesting feature of the building is its
diagonal corner "buttresses," which are
not structural but serve to emphasize
the extension of the roof. The living
room, with tan roman brick fireplace,
has been extended part way into the
porch, and the porch enclosed.

Plan of first floor

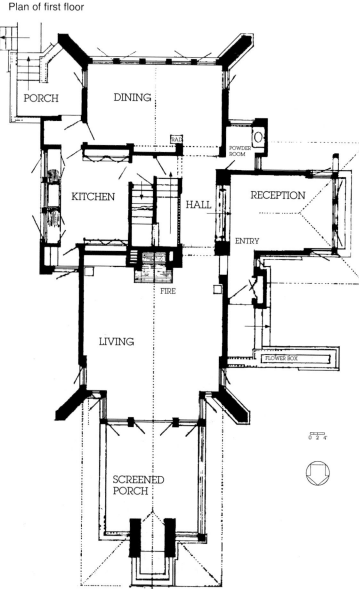

PORCH   DINING

RAD

POWDER
ROOM

KITCHEN   HALL   RECEPTION

ENTRY

FIRE

LIVING

FLOWER BOX

0 2 4'

SCREENED
PORCH

Plan of second floor

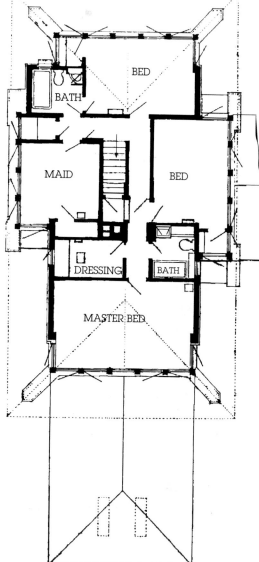

BED

BATH

MAID   BED

DRESSING   BATH

MASTER BED

William A. **Glasner** Residence (1905)

Glencoe, Illinois
East library enlarged. Basement finished. Two-car garage added. West porch enclosed. Greenhouse added

Situated on the brow of a ravine, this single-story with utilities basement house for William A. Glasner could serve as a prototype for later Usonian designs. No separate room was planned for dining. Octagonal spaces, den-library and sewing room, are attached to the living room and a corner of the bedroom. The main entry leads directly to the living room without a reception room and is diagonally opposite the kitchen. Other entries are at the rear of the house; one must enter the porch, where there are doors to the kitchen and to the corridor (the "gallery" of Usonia). There is finely detailed art glass, with multicolor inserts. Although the original plan included a bridge over one part of the ravine, that extension was never built.

Like many Prairie style houses with board-and-batten exteriors, the wood is rough sawn in finish. In many remodelings of Wright houses smooth lumber was used in the mistaken notion that this original rough wood was used for economy; in fact, it was preferred by the architect. The Glasner dwelling was renovated in 1926 and 1938, and restored in the early 1970s by Dr. and Mrs. Henry Fineberg. In an earlier renovation, the east library was enlarged, one side eliminating the octagonal plan. The originally unfinished basement containing only the laundry, coal storage, and heater has been finished, and a two-car garage added under the now-enclosed west porch. A greenhouse has been added to the south side of the porch at a lower level.

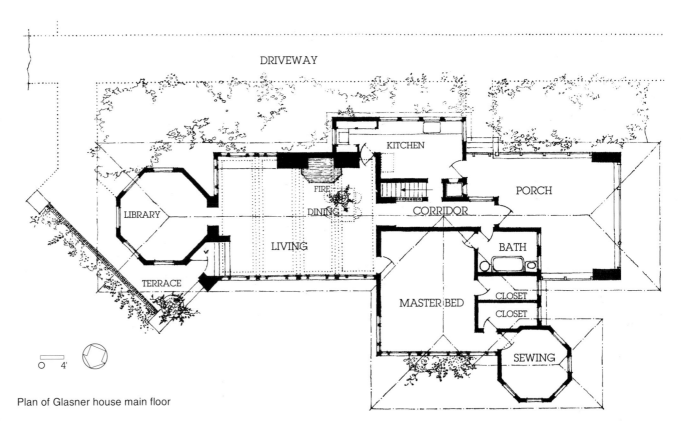

Plan of Glasner house main floor

Glasner house from across the ravine

Charles A. Brown Residence
(1905)
Evanston, Illinois
Renovated in 1980s

During the renovation of the Charles A. Brown house in the late 1980s, project architect John A. Eifler discovered evidence that this was a tract house; published drawings and the building permit identify the client. Final revisions are dated August 1905, and the building was under construction by October that year.

It has many interesting features, indicating more care in design than a tract house would suggest. The 22-foot-wide cantilever over the veranda extends more than nine feet; the piers are false, providing visual security,

Charles A. Brown
Residence

Charles A. Brown
living room

while the fulcrum is at the line of the glazing. The entry is at ground level. Inside, there are two piers, each with a coat closet. Up a few stairs and to the right is the living room, which runs the full width of the facade. Further to the right is the porch and to the left, the Roman brick fireplace—a small rectangle in a large masonry mass. To the rear and upstairs is a variation on the Wrightian four-square; the dining room and kitchen with stairs at the side lead to a second floor with four bedrooms and a bathroom.

An early mechanical air condition-

ing system is used; adjustable wood dampers in the chimney, controlled by pulleys, receive air from vents in the closets. Much leaded-glass enlivens the interior space. As needed, this has been repaired by Suzanne and Paul Peck-Collier, who discovered that sagging in one instance probably resulted from forcing a window into too small a frame. The sash is oak and pine, with double-hung windows at the front. The garage dates only to 1952; the house originally occupied its own and the corner lot.

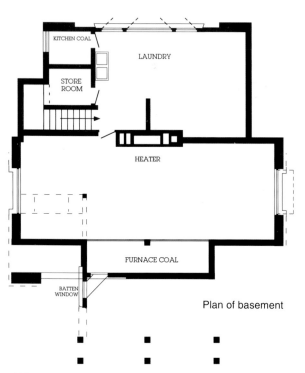

Plan of basement

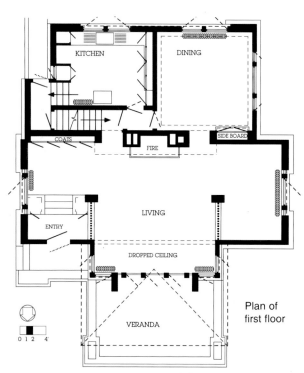

Plan of
first floor

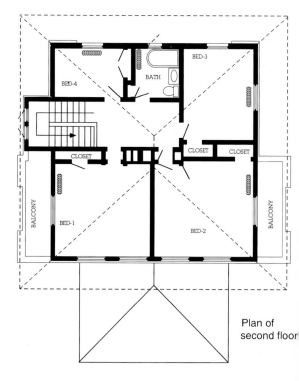

Plan of
second floor

Frank L. Smith Bank

E. W. Cummings Real Estate Office (1905)
River Forest, Illinois
Demolished

The E. W. Cummings Real Estate Office was a Prairie structure of wood and plaster with broad overhanging eaves surrounded by an imposingly high wall that also served as a sign and gates framed by urns of Wright's design. The plan is a **T**; a meeting room is in the head (viewed in the photograph), and Mr. Cummings's office in the tail, the two areas separated by a fireplace. Though the title of Cummings Real Estate Office applies, this building also served as the River Forest Land Association Building.

The front elevation of the Bitter Root Valley Irrigation Company Office (see S.145), an unbuilt project, exactly coincides with one of two photographs, as shown here, which constitutes most of the knowledge we have of this building. A plan in the Taliesin archives, T.0702, is an earlier preliminary idea for the Cummings structure; it is a variation on the Pettit Chapel (S.116).

S.111 T.0512
Frank L. Smith Bank, First National Bank of Dwight (1905)
Dwight, Illinois
Additions and renovation in 1990 reveal the original design

Correspondence between Colonel Frank L. Smith and Wright about the bank indicates that Walter Burley Griffin worked on this project, now the First National Bank of Dwight, Illinois. The rock-faced random ashlar exterior conceals the Wrightian delineation of interior spaces, which features clerestories directly under the eaves of the one and a half story interior.

The building was completely renovated in 1968 and again in 1990, at which time an addition in the style of Wright was put on and earlier non-Wright accretions were removed from the original building. Only the president's office, which divides the long, narrow plan with banking facilities at the front and offices at the back, truly suggests Wright's original intent. Its fireplace is by Wright, while the original furniture was designed by John Ayers. The building is open during regular banking hours.

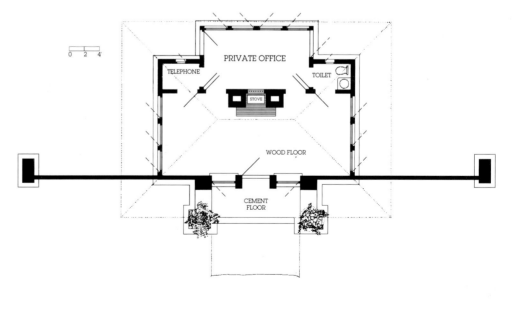

Cummings Real Estate Office

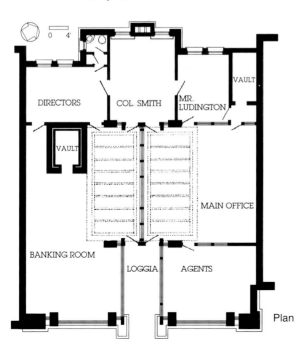

Plan

S.113 T.0511
Rookery Building Entryway and
Lobby **Remodeling** (1905)
Chicago, Illinois
Remodeled in 1931 by William
Drummond. Restored in the late 1980s

In the late 1890s, Wright, the American
Luxfer Prism Company, and William
Winslow (S.024) all had offices in the
Rookery Building, which was under the
management of another Wright client
and patron, Edward C. Waller (see
S.030, S.031, S.047, S.065, S.066,
S.166). Wright's work for the American
Luxfer Prism Company included
designs for glass prism lights, which
are pressed glass with decorative
design outside and triangular ribs
inside that are intended to help diffuse
natural light into shop interiors.

In the remodeling of the Rookery
Building, an 1886 skyscraper by
Burnham and Root, Wright contributed
entry and lobby elements; note most
specifically the white marble with decorative "Persian" motif. There has been
subsequent remodeling, including
1931 work by William Drummond. In
the late 1980s, complete restoration of
this historic building was undertaken.
The Rookery Building is open during
regular business hours.

Rookery Building Lobby view toward entry

Plan of main floor including entry and lobby

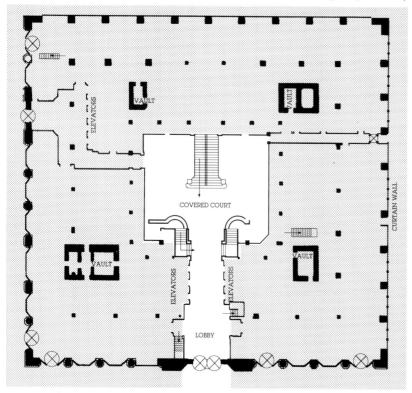

AREAS OF BUILDING NOT
ALTERED BY MR. WRIGHT

0 5 10   20'

Detail of stairway and ceiling

E-Z Polish Factory (1905) for
Darwin D. Martin and W. E. Martin
Chicago, Illinois
Expanded above second floor.
Windows bricked-in and other changes
in later years.

The brothers Martin (see S.061,
S.100–S.102) were partners in the
Martin and Martin Polish Company,
which made both shoe and stove
polishes. The building Wright designed
for their enterprise, a production and
storage facility of reinforced concrete
faced with brick, now serves other
commercial uses. The original building
was two storys high; the upper floors
were built after a fire in 1913. The
original facade was not as regularly
pierced as the now-filled sash areas
suggest. The part that may be seen
from the street was for storage.
Smaller rooms, projecting to the rear,
were for production of stove polish on
one side, shoe polish on the other. A
painted mural on the main office floor
no longer survives; it showed part of a
Prairie house, framed in geometric
patterns, but is not believed to be by
Wright.

E-Z Polish Factory (1990 photo)

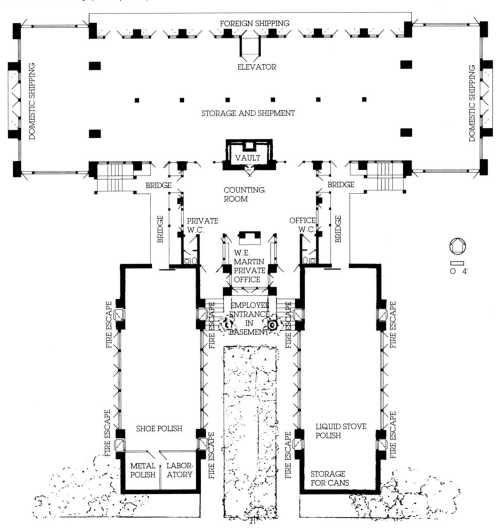

Hardy Residence, private (lakeside) facade

Living room from balcony

S.115   T.0506
Thomas P. **Hardy** Residence (1905)
Racine, Wisconsin

It seems that few people view the Hardy house as Wright envisioned it (as shown in a penned drawing in Japanese style from his own, or Marion Mahony's, hand) from the Lake Michigan shoreline. The photograph here published reveals that lakeside aspect.

Here, with a site many would have considered too difficult to build on, Wright meets the challenge of a steep embankment with a three-story arrangement. The terrace is half a story below street level, the living room half a story up with an upper-story balcony. This opens all living quarters to the Lake Michigan view. None of this is apparent from the street approach. The terrace level, or house basement, contains the dining room overlooking the terrace, the kitchen and one bedroom occupying the wings. Four additional bedrooms occupy the wings above, two on each floor. The only bathroom is on the third floor on the street side, between the flues that vent fireplaces in the living and dining rooms and provide for plumbing and house heating located in the basement.

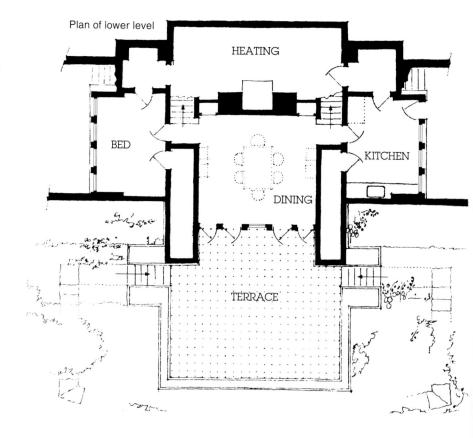

Plan of lower level

HEATING

BED

KITCHEN

DINING

TERRACE

Plan of upper level

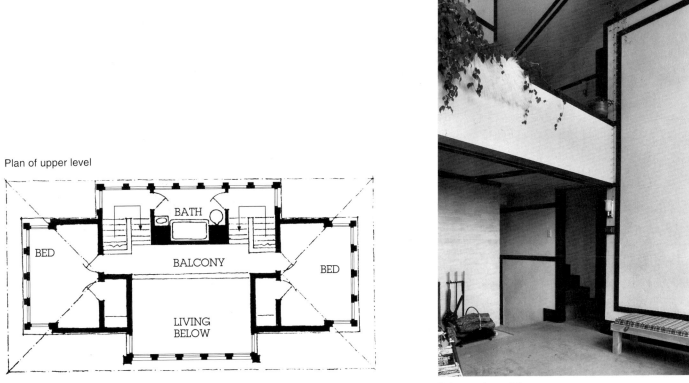

BATH

BED

BALCONY

BED

LIVING
BELOW

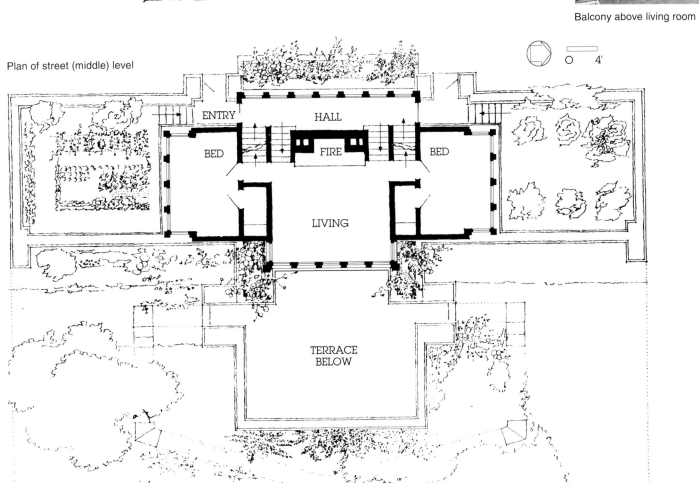

Balcony above living room

Plan of street (middle) level

ENTRY   HALL

BED   FIRE   BED

LIVING

TERRACE
BELOW

4'

Pettit Chapel from southeast

S.116   T.0619
William H. Pettit Mortuary Chapel
(1906)
Belvidere, Illinois
Restored in 1981

The chapel is a memorial by Emma Glasner Pettit to her husband, Dr. William H. Pettit, who died March 25, 1899. It is a **T**-plan configuration with its main floor raised. The surface is lime-based stucco (Portland cement-based plaster would crack in the temperature extremes of Prairie Illinois), and the wood trim is cypress outside with yellow pine in the chapel interior. The central stairs lead up to a large porch, terminated by flower boxes. The broad hip roof sheltered those who were waiting for cars, and a fireplace inside the hall provided warmth. Lavatories are at the ground level, reached by stairs in the doorways either side the central stair. The contractor was F. H. Dixon; E. B. Glass did the masonry. The building was restored in 1981 by the Belvidere Junior Women's Club and is on the National Register of Historic Places.

The gravestones of the Glasner and Pettit families are about 25 yards east of the chapel. Mrs. Pettit, sister of William A. Glasner (see S.109) died December 4, 1924. The Belvidere Cemetery is open at all times.

Plan of Chapel

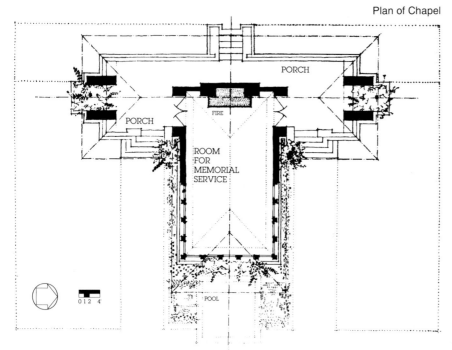

THE PRAIRIE SQUARE VERSUS THE PRAIRIE PINWHEEL

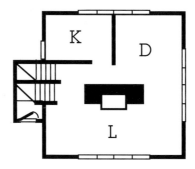

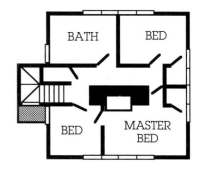

If one extends the walls of each quarter over half the quarter's width, a square becomes a pinwheel. Further adjustments make this into a *livable* pinwheel. Below is a pinwheel created from Wright's cube. Here, there is no change in the size of the original main floor rooms. Typical, however, of the pinwheel, and its planimetric sister the cruciform, are the addition of a porte-cochere and servant's quarters, with pantry and downstairs bath. Thus, a pinwheel is almost always larger and more expensive than a cube, even if only by small amounts as shown here. Lloyd Wright once said that one of the most important aspects of his father's designs was asymmetry. The pinwheel has this quality naturally, while the cruciform is naturally symmetrical. Many of Wright's buildings classified by scholars as cruciform turn out, on close inspection, to be pinwheels.

Usually, the living and dining rooms would be expanded beyond this "compact" plan, for the nature of pinwheel/cruciform is extension. Thus, this plan, so naturally suited to elaboration, is also an architecture of the wealthy, and not a democratic solution to American housing. Wright, accordingly, put Prairie architecture behind him in 1909. He experimented with prefabricated design, then tried concrete block. From these attempts at achieving a truly democratic architecture, he created the Usonian house and its concrete block development, the Usonian automatic.

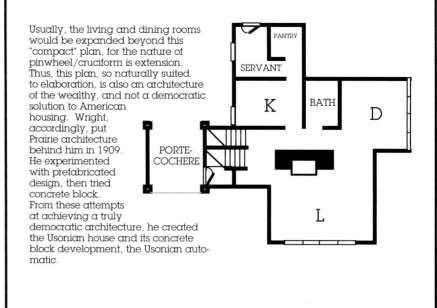

S.117　T.0601

Peter A. **Beachy** Residence (1906)
Oak Park, Illinois
House restored after 1990 fire

The Beachy residence, somewhat like the 1902 Dana house (S.072), incorporates an earlier building into its structure, the small Gothic-style Fargo family cottage. All that seems to have been retained is the foundation, perhaps under the porch. The building, placed at the north lot line like other Wright homes in Oak Park (Moore, S.034; Fricke, S.059; William E. Martin, S.061), exploits fully the 133-by-330-foot yard, gaining maximum exposure to sunlight. Note the broad bands of windows and stonework that emphasize the horizon of the prairie. The lower windows have limestone lintels, the upper ones wood. The tripartite windows on the south (left in the photo) resemble those of the Darwin D. Martin (S.100), Barton (S.103), DeRhodes (S.125), and May (S.148) houses.

The main entry is concealed on the north wall of this east-west building, much as in the May home. Dark red Roman brick is laid in the fireplaces with the mortar joints at thirds to give the surface an interesting rhythm. Cherry wood cabinets and furniture of Wright's design grace the structure. Roof framing, structural members, and partitions are redwood. Oak is used for window frames, stringcourses, and flooring. There are cedar beams supporting the porch. Many light fixtures are original; their shape is created by extending one set of parallel sides of a hexagon to a little over twice their usual length. This design is used even in the wood detailing for the ceiling. The original tile roof has been replaced, and the kitchen was remodeled in the 1950s. The brick is a hand-formed type. Wright often preferred a smooth-face or iron-spot brick.

The garage, clearly in the style of the main structure, including the flat extensions of the gable and the framing of the windows, was built in 1909, but its origin is not certain.

It has been suggested that Beachy, a banker two years younger than Wright, may have obtained his design from Walter Burley Griffin, because Wright was in Japan with the Ward Willits when the work was done, and

the design reveals a massing of masonry that is in keeping with later Griffin designs. This argument is contradicted by the fact that the Taliesin files preserve extensive drawings, indicating that it was indeed Wright's. Perhaps, however, the garage is by Griffin. Barry Byrne was involved in the preparation of working drawings and supervision of the house.

In August 1990 fire caused considerable damage to the roof at the front of the structure. Repairs based on original working drawings were completed by 1991.

Beachy Residence

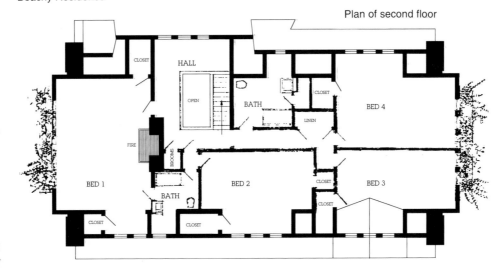

Plan of second floor

Beachy living room

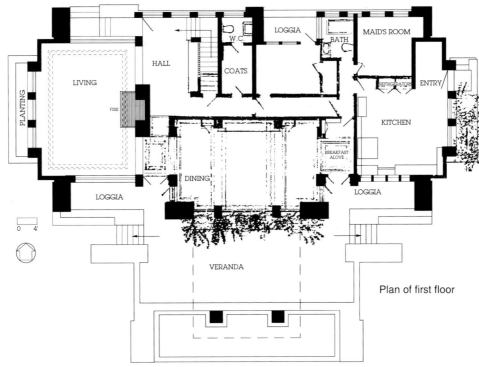

Plan of first floor

S.118 T.0607
Frederick D. **Nichols** Residence (1906)
Flossmoor, Illinois
Several alterations to the front of the structure

Wright had a penchant for misspelling clients' names, from Wooley (Woolley, S.023) to Nicholas. The person who contracted for this home was Frederick Doveton Nichols, Sr. He was one of the Chicago-area promoters of the Como Orchard (S.144) and Bitter Root (S.145) projects in Montana.

Flossmoor is on a passenger train line to Chicago, so Nichols used this as a summer house where he could escape for golf on weekends. It had no electricity and may have been heated only by its fireplace, though forced-air heating was later added by Genevieve and Melvin Evans, who lived in the house for 52 years. These tenants also added the southeast porch, using window sash from the original south and east walls but replacing 1 1/2-inch redwood or cedar siding with stained pine in 1933. The enclosed room

Nichols Residence, from southwest, the corner least changed

above this porch, extension of the entry, and room to the northeast are all additions from various years that disguise the basic layout, in mirror image, of the *Ladies Home Journal* Fireproof House (S.138). The characteristic entry-stairwell of the Fireproof House design, half within the house square and half outside, is already fully developed here; it was considered but rejected in the design for Robie Lamp (S.097).

The original mantel and fireplace have been paneled over; the flues on the second level are split to either side of the door to the master bedroom and a closet in the second bedroom.

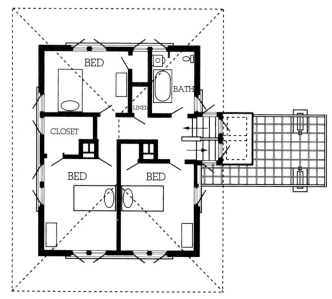

Plan of second floor

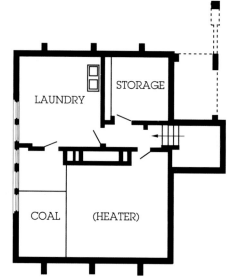

O   4'

Plan of basement

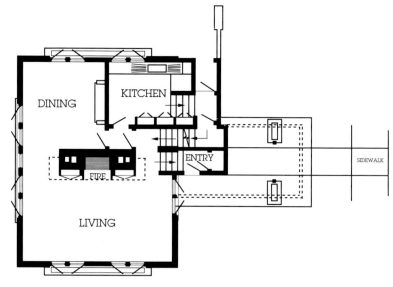

Plan of first floor

S.119 T.0510, T.0608
River Forest Tennis Club (1906)
River Forest, Illinois
1905 structure rebuilt, after fire, in
1906. Relocated in 1920

Wright was a member of the River
Forest Tennis Club, one of many
organizations that provided him social
contacts that led to commissions. On
this horizontal board-and-batten
project, Charles E. White and Vernon
S. Watson, the other architect-
members, were associated with
Wright. The building, mostly of Wright's
inspiration, was long and low, with a
central hall that was half the structure.
This hall was framed by three fireplaces—a feature of many other of
Wright's pavilion-like designs, such as
the Banff National Park Pavilion
(S.170); the fourth wall consisted of
seven pairs of glass doors facing the
tennis courts. At the ends were the
dressing rooms, men's to the north,
women's to the south, with the kitchen.
Transom-level lighting is provided by
balustraded windows, achieving
privacy while letting in natural light.

In 1920 the property, then at
Harlem and Quick, was sold to the
Cook County Forest Preserve.
Removal of the structure, in three
parts, five blocks west to the present
site, and extension to the east of the
dressing rooms, plus addition of a
stage, all of which leaves but little of
Wright's efforts, was by Watson. In
1988, new buildings to serve a
swimming pool were erected on the
east side of this site. Designed by
John D. Tilton, they look more like the
original tennis club than does Watson's
revision. The logo RFTC on the
masonry massing to the left on the
street side was also designed by
Wright.

Tennis-court side of the clubhouse

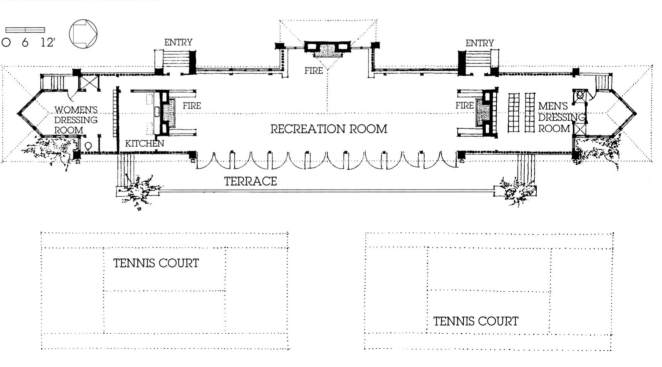

P. D. **Hoyt** Residence (1906)

Geneva, Illinois
Entry pergola at front restored in late
1980s. Addition to rear

The home for the Hoyts, he a phar-
macist, she a civic activist, was
designed to be inexpensive, with
stained fir rather than oak trim even on
the main floor. Final cost, exclusive of
property, was about $5,000.

It is thought that the commission
came to Wright from the Hoyt's son
Harrie, a student at the University of
Chicago, whose initials, H H, are
reflected in each pair of windows. The
building is a square plan, one of
Wright's many variants on the four-
square, with stucco surface. In most
designs of the period, the entry was a
separate spatial element. Here, entry
is directly to the right side of the living
room from a 17-foot pergola lined with
flower boxes and surmounted by trellis
work; the house is made square by
having an office to the right and a
pantry to the rear. Thus, the chimney,

Hoyt Residence as restored

centered in the living room, is off-
center for the plan as a whole.

This very unusual direct entry to
the living room rather than to an entry
and stairwell suggests the possibility
that the floor plan was by someone in
Wright's office. The Darwin D. Martin
Gardener's Cottage (S.090) also has
an entry direct to the living room and
separated from the stairwell and may
have been the idea of William
Drummond.

In 1980, Patricia P. and James
MacLachlan purchased the house,

added a new entry and walled the
entire yard in an attempt to recapture
something of the effect of the original
pergola, which had been removed in
1917—all on the suggestion of a
restoration architect. The effect was
not achieved, and so the original
design was rebuilt in 1989–90. The
interior, badly altered by the time the
MacLachlans gained ownership, has
been largely renovated, with the

woodwork redone in the lighter tones
restoration architects now consider the
norm for the Prairie era. A rear addition
remains in place.

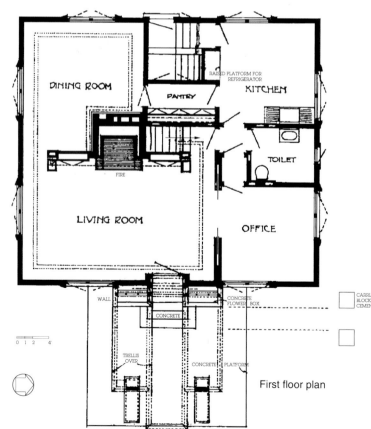

First floor plan

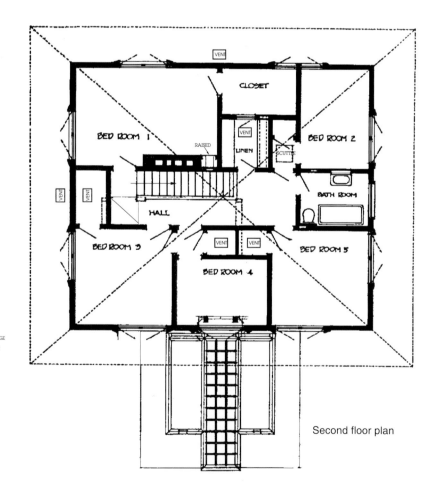

Second floor plan

Gridley Residence

S.121　T.0604
A. W. **Gridley Residence** and
S.122　T.0604
Barn (1906)
Batavia, Illinois
Barn demolished

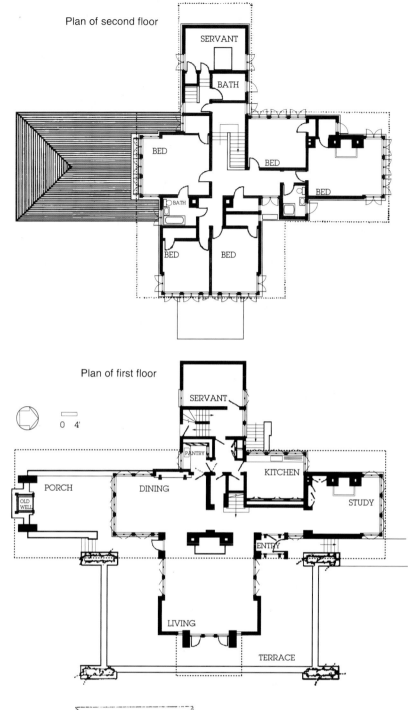

Plan of second floor

Plan of first floor

The Gridley home is set well back from the street in this rural setting, thus gaining privacy without the need for stained art-glass windows. The plaster Prairie style house with stained wood trim is a cruciform plan on the ground floor and **T** plan at the second story, which has no upper level above the long, open porch. Oak flooring and trim are used on the main level, yellow spruce above.

The ground floor resembles the Willits plan (S.054), the living room on the front, the dining room in one side wing, extended by a porch. The entry wing, with a study but no porte-cochere beyond, and the smaller rear wing make this considerably less elegant than its suburban predecessor, even as its 5000 square feet of space make it seem palatial.

There is a full basement, but the foundations, consisting of little more than rubble and cement, have settled badly and unequally. Gridley had financial problems and did not live in the house long. This may account for the lack of information about the barn and whether or not Wright's design

Sideboard

was ever built. His original design was a symmetrical arrangement with a chicken house in one wing (some documents suggest a smoke house), kennels in the other, stalls between, and a carriage room at front center. The existing barn is the 1870s Batavia fire department renovated.

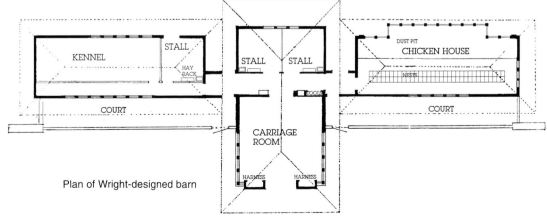

Plan of Wright-designed barn

Grace Fuller house

S.123 T.0603
Grace Fuller Residence
Glencoe, Illinois
Demolished

As Wright refined his four-square house, he experimented with a number of variants. In the Grace Fuller residence, though the living room is the full left half of the house, Wright put a short wing at the rear for a maid's room and kitchen, over the basement laundry.

This was one of the houses well-known to John H. Howe, head of Wright's drafting room during the post-Depression Usonian years, before he joined the Taliesin Fellowship.

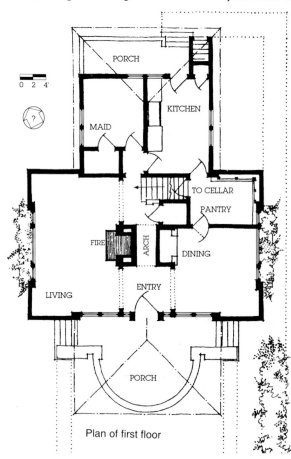

Plan of first floor

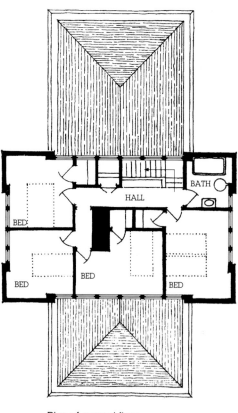

Plan of second floor

S.124 T.0610
C. Thaxter **Shaw** Residence
Remodeling (1906)
Montreal, Quebec, Canada
Demolished, ca. 1980

When C. Thaxter Shaw decided not to build Wright's magnificent stone house in the Westmount district of Montreal, he asked for a remodeling of his town house. Wright gave him a plan calling for extensive revisions, including removal of bay windows, alteration of dormers, and a new layout for fenestration based on five lites (windows) at each level.

The standard entry for row housing on this hilly site was half a level up, reached by exterior steps. Wright dropped the entry to street level, then used interior steps to lead one to the main floor, thus gaining compressed space before the expansion of the drawing room and dining room (and billiards room beyond) in his plan. Recent research indicates that most of this remodeling was probably never done. The facade and entry had no changes from their Victorian original. Access was not permitted by the last-known owners, who stated that "some of the work" had been done. A fireplace, viewed only at a distance, seemed to be faced with Roman brick. As plans and elevations were not available, it was impossible to determine if anything matched Wright's design.

A final determination of how much was built and how much was removed before Peel Plaza was erected on the site may not now be possible. There is even a possibility that none of Wright's remodeling was ever completed.

S.125   T.0602

K. C. **DeRhodes** Residence (1906)
South Bend, Indiana
Extensive restoration in 1980s

The axial symmetry of the K. C. DeRhodes house is noteworthy. Entry reception is in one short cruciform wing, the kitchen opposite, with living and dining rooms on either side of the cross space, fully open one to the other. Terraces at both ends originally completed the cruciform. Upstairs, bathrooms frame the stairwell, with bedrooms taking full advantage of long rows of soffit-hugging windows.

Comparison with the Horner (S.142) floor plans is instructive, for it is a rectilinear mirror-image of the DeRhodes idea. The home was purchased in 1978 by Suzanne and Thomas C. Miller, who immediately proceeded with restoration. The interior was reconstructed, with built-ins, art-glass windows and transoms, and the fireplace was restored to its correct location and color.

DeRhodes Residence

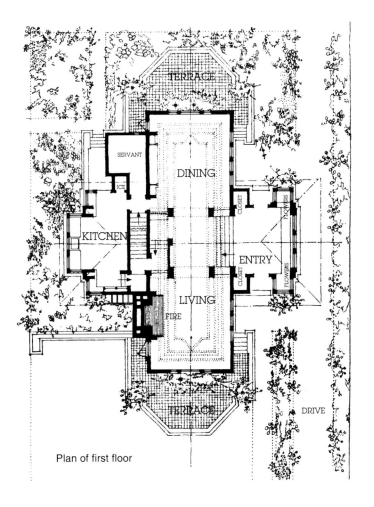

Plan of first floor

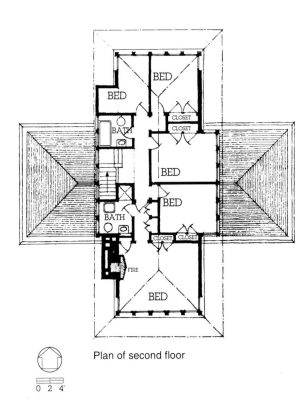

Plan of second floor

123

S.126 T.0606
George Madison **Millard** Residence (1906)
Highland Park, Illinois

Like several of Wright's Oak Park homes (S.034, S.058, S.117), the plan of the George Madison Millard house is turned sideways to the street, to give each bedroom exposure to morning sun, while placing the dining room at the westernmost reach of the **L** plan. The ground floor wing, then, is the living room, extended by a porch. Upstairs are three bedrooms, sewing room and two baths in an in-line arrangement; the master bedroom overlooks the porch roof and has its own fireplace. The house has a full basement, including quarters for a man servant, with the maid's room directly above, at the rear corner of the board-and-batten structure. Seventeen years later, Mrs. Millard built La Miniatura in Pasadena, California (S.214).

Millard Residence, west end

Millard Residence, east end

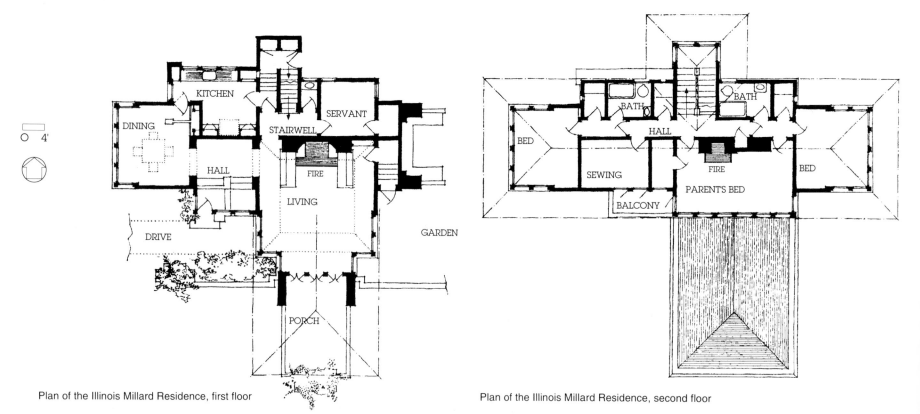

Plan of the Illinois Millard Residence, first floor

Plan of the Illinois Millard Residence, second floor

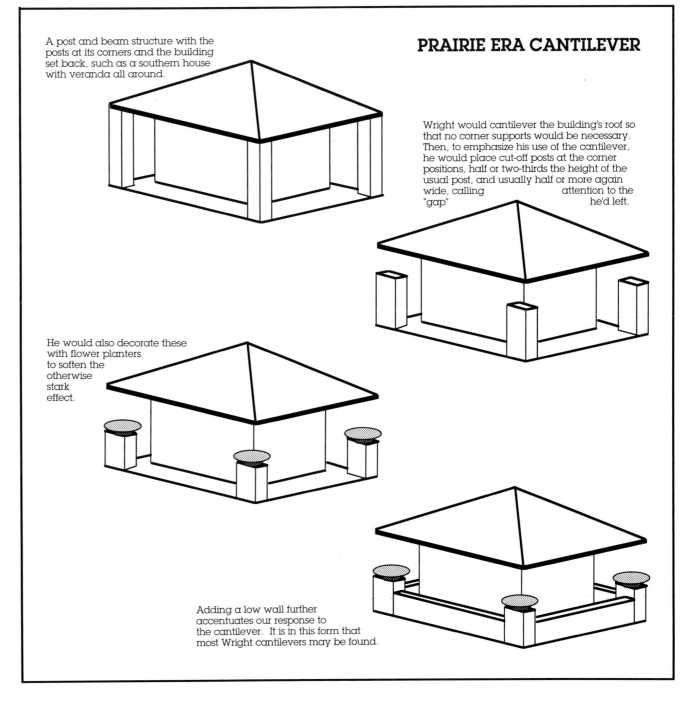

A post and beam structure with the posts at its corners and the building set back, such as a southern house with veranda all around.

PRAIRIE ERA CANTILEVER

Wright would cantilever the building's roof so that no corner supports would be necessary. Then, to emphasize his use of the cantilever, he would place cut-off posts at the corner positions, half or two-thirds the height of the usual post, and usually half or more again wide, calling   attention to the "gap"   he'd left.

He would also decorate these with flower planters to soften the otherwise stark effect.

Adding a low wall further accentuates our response to the cantilever. It is in this form that most Wright cantilevers may be found.

Robie house, view from southwest

Robie house facade, midsummer, noon, showing how overhang shades the glazing

S.127 T.0908
Frederick C. **Robie** Residence
(1906)
Chicago, Illinois

The house designed for Frederick C. Robie is Wright's best expression of the Prairie masonry structure. Sheathed in Roman brick and over-hung so perfectly that a midsummer noon sun barely strikes the foot of the long, glass-walled southern exposure of the raised living quarters, it demonstrates Wright's total control and appreciation of microclimatic effects. This is coupled with a high degree of integration of the mechanical and electrical systems designed by Wright into the visual expression of the interior. Living and dining space are in line, with only the fireplace (which is open above the mantel) providing separation. Sleeping quarters are a floor above, play and billiards rooms below at ground level—a plan first tried in the Tomek house (S.128); there is no "basement."

With the Robie house, development of the Prairie cantilever reaches maturity. The cantilever was, to Wright, the second principle of organic design (the unit system, generating a regular grid, was the first). The west veranda is shaded by a cantilevered hip roof that reaches 10 feet from the nearest

Living room (1970s photograph)

Central fireplace with split flues, in living room

Dining room

Living room of the Robie House, showing overhead lighting

Robie house lamp

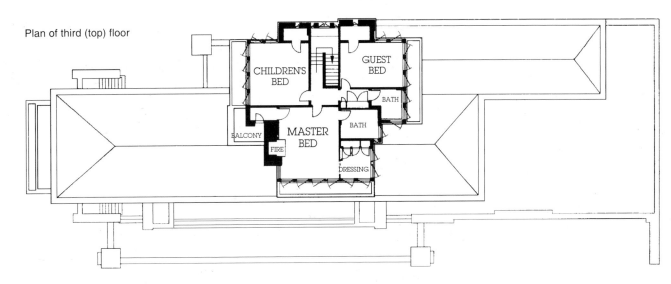

Plan of third (top) floor

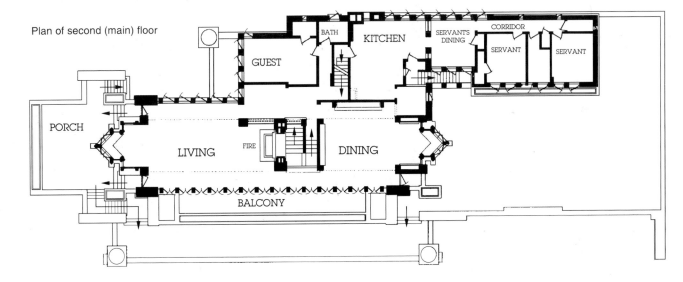

Plan of second (main) floor

possible supporting member and 21 feet from the closest masonry pier. By placing an incipient pier—a pier short of completion—beneath the cantilever, Wright emphasizes subtly, even when that pier is capped by one of the architect's planters, the daring nature of the seemingly unsupported roof. This is a device he used throughout the Prairie era.

Window mullions are consistently on 4-foot centers, suggesting this as the unit used by Wright in the design. Construction was begun in 1908 and completed the following year. The Robies lived here only two years. The garage and its surrounding wall were later altered from the original design. The building's early local nickname, "The Battleship," has never gained currency among Wright scholars. Repointing of the brickwork left the deeply raked horizontal joints flush (though more recent refurbishing has partially corrected this). The original carpet was recreated by Bentley Carpet Mills.

The Robie house is a National Historic Landmark. It has been designated by the American Institute of Architects, which awarded Frank Lloyd Wright a gold medal in 1949, as one of seventeen American buildings he designed to be retained as an example of his architectural contribution to American culture. The Robie house is owned by the University of Chicago and occupied by its Alumni Office. Guided tours are available.

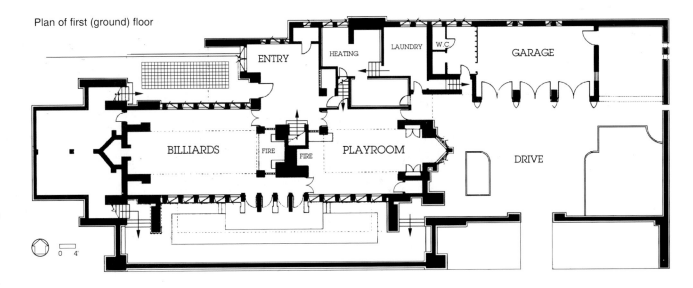

Plan of first (ground) floor

Ferdinand Frederick and Emily **Tomek** Residence (1904)

Riverside, Illinois
Unnecessary posts added to "support" terrace cantilever shortly after construction. Restoration ongoing

Wright's statement that the Tomek "plan was later elaborated into the plan of the Robie house" is an important admission. Recent findings place the design of the Tomek one to two years before that of the more famous Robie. Published plans usually show only the main and second floors of the Tomek house, the ground and main floor of the Robie; this disguises their similarity. The later-designed and built Robie is a mirror image of the Tomek in all basic elements of design. Both have ground-level playrooms and billiards rooms. Both have a central stairwell that rises through all three

Tomek house, view from west

View of full facade before false pillars were placed on the porch

Southwest wall, living room

floors. The main entry to the earlier Tomek is at the front, the later Robie at the rear. At the main level, the Tomek house has casement windows and the Robie has floor-to-soffit doors leading to a shallow balcony. Robie has servants' quarters at the main level; Tomek has a servant's room below the kitchen. The top floor of each—"in belvedere" Wright would say—has three bedrooms. The Robie has a fireplace, a later idea and improvement on Tomek where the possibility of a fireplace exists, but was denied by a closet placed at that wall.

The Tomek had a red tile roof, now asbestos, parquet floors, and Roman brick inside, with deep raking of the uncolored horizontal joints and tinted vertical mortar. The posts that rise from the terrace wall support none of the cantilever load, and were put there for psychological "family security." Each roof has a short non-functioning pier below to emphasize the daring of the cantilever. In the foreground of the exterior view from the south, these are surmounted by flower urns of Wright's design, further calling attention to the overhang. Structural steel is sufficient to support all cantilevers. After two years vacancy, the house was purchased in 1972 by Maya Moran, who has since been carefully restoring the property.

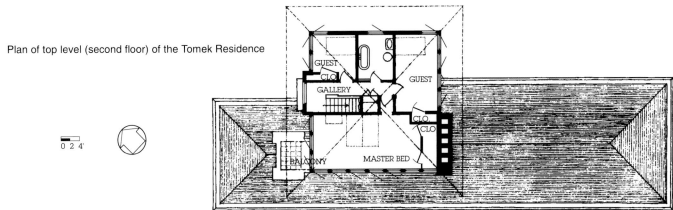

Plan of top level (second floor) of the Tomek Residence

GUEST
CLO.

GUEST

GALLERY

CLO.
CLO.

BALCONY

MASTER BED

0 2 4'

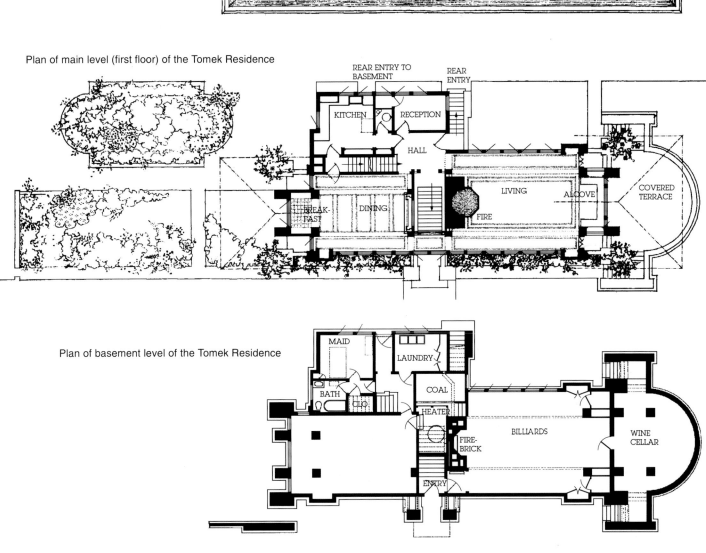

Plan of main level (first floor) of the Tomek Residence

REAR ENTRY TO
BASEMENT

REAR
ENTRY

KITCHEN

RECEPTION

HALL

LIVING

ALCOVE

COVERED
TERRACE

BREAK-
FAST

DINING

FIRE

Plan of basement level of the Tomek Residence

MAID

LAUNDRY

BATH

CLO.

COAL

HEATER

FIRE-
BRICK

BILLIARDS

WINE
CELLAR

ENTRY

Fabyan Villa, west side

S.129   T.0703
Colonel George **Fabyan**
Remodeling, Fabyan Villa (1907)
Geneva, Illinois
Restoration ongoing in early 1990s

For Wright, one client invariably led to another. Wright designed the Hoyt house (S.120) in 1906, and this led to the Gridley commission (S.121–S.122). While Wright was supervising construction of these two works, he met Colonel Fabyan, who commissioned remodeling of two structures on his estate, which he called Riverbank. One of these was the Fox River Country Club (S.130), the other his residence, the Fabyan Villa.

George Fabyan was active in the areas of cryptology, acoustics, physiology of the body, and horticulture. During World War I he trained soldiers in code on the Riverbank grounds at his own expense, in effect establishing the U.S. Signal Corps. For this, he was awarded the honorary title

of colonel by the State of Illinois. He and his wife Nelle shared a wide range of interests, including the development of improved concrete, which might have caught Wright's attention.

Like many other of Wright's "remodelings," the work left little trace of the **L**-shaped original. Obvious changes included details of the main-floor living room, the north room of the second story, and the exterior. Three verandas turned it into a cruciform plan. The largest of these extended east toward the river, but two enormous concrete piers that supported the main deck are all that remain. A spindle-wall, a fence-like structure providing some privacy for the service entry on the southwest, was removed long ago. While the property remains in the hands of the Kane County Forest Preserve District, the Friends of Fabyan are replacing missing verandas and the spindle-wall, thus restoring Colonel George and Nelle Fabyan's Villa to its remodeled horizontal nature and architectural magnificence.

Fabyan Villa, east side

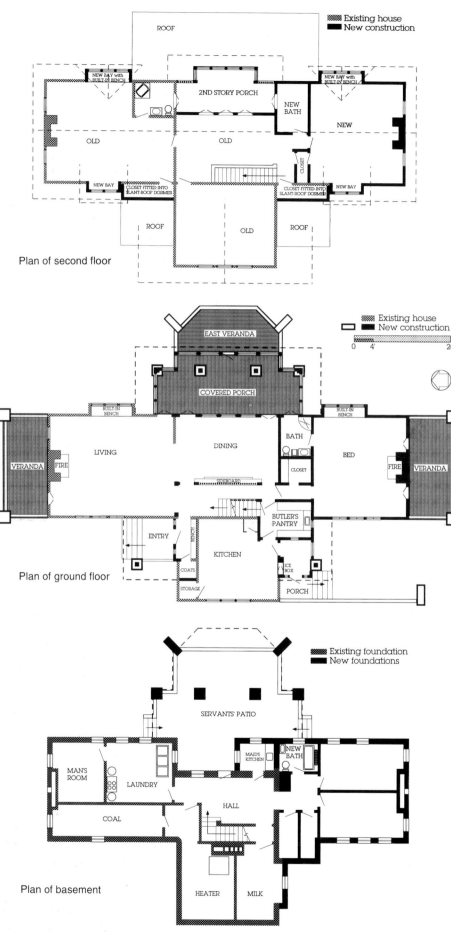

Plan of second floor

Plan of ground floor

Plan of basement

S.130   T.0704

Fox River Country Club Addition

(1907)
Geneva, Illinois
Destroyed by fire at midnight, March 21, 1910

The Fox River Country Club was located on the Fox River estate of Colonel George Fabyan, southwest of Fabyan Villa (S.129). Wright's 30-by-75-foot addition—20 by 70 feet was the architect's original suggestion—became the north wing of an existing Victorian structure on gently sloping ground so that basement windows were fully exposed to the view. The basement featured two alleys for bowling plus tables for billiards and pool. The dance hall above gained a rustic flavor from exposed timber roof beams but stringcourses with plaster articulated the space in Wrightian Prairie manner. Outside, a broad porch extended the full length of the gable-roofed structure, protected by the overhanging eaves. The Fabyan estate included property on the east side of the Fox River, an island in the river, and research facilities which still stand, west of the villa.

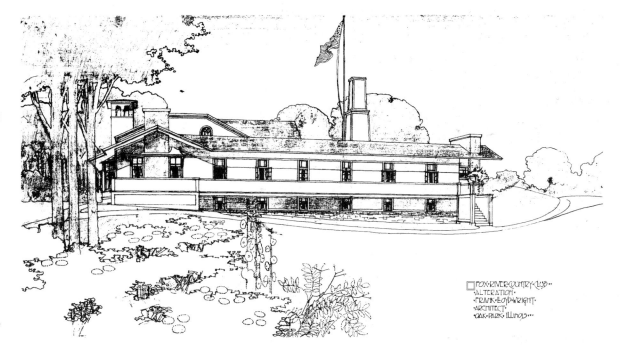

Wright's drawing of the addition as originally conceived

The dance hall

Wright's north end addition as built

The basement bowling alley

Pebbles & Balch
Shop storefront

Pebbles & Balch Shop interior

S.131 T.0708
Pebbles & Balch Shop
Remodeling (1907)
Oak Park, Illinois
Demolished

The remodeling of a building on Lake Street for interior decorators Pebbles & Balch reveals the influence on Wright of his 1905 visit to Japan, both in the interior treatment and the exterior. Inside, natural woods, oiled paper for glass, and plain surfaces were seen side by side with lighting fixtures of geometrical forms used by Wright for over a decade. Wright also transformed the exterior to maximize display space.

Wright also designed a home for shop-partner Oscar B. Balch (S.168).

Plan, with Wright's
hand-sketched changes

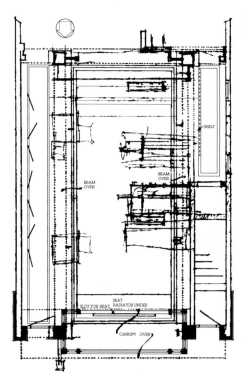

S.132 T.0706
Jamestown Exhibition Pavilion
(1907) for the Larkin Company
Sewell Point, Norfolk, Virginia
Demolished

The Official Blue Book of the Jamestown Ter-Centennial Exposition, published two years after the event, contains photographs revealing that Wright's pavilion was constructed as it was drawn for the *Ausgeführte Bauten und Entwürfe von Frank Lloyd Wright.* It was symmetrical about one axis, had about 1500 square feet, and contained exhibition space and an auditorium where a film about Niagara Falls, Buffalo, and the "newly completed" Larkin Company building (S.093) was shown.

(Note: The Martin Gardener's cottage, which held this number in the second edition of *The Architecture of Frank Lloyd Wright: A Complete Catalog,* is now listed as S.090.)

Jamestown Exhibition Pavilion

Plan

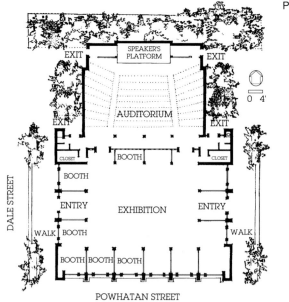

Blossom Garage

S.133　T.0701
George **Blossom Garage** (1907)
Chicago, Illinois

Fourteen years after he designed the Queen Anne house for George Blossom (S.014), Wright did a Prairie style garage in Roman brick, stucco, and wood for him. This circumstance provides dramatic testimony of his design evolution during the period 1893–1907.

This was Wright's second design for the project, though the two are quite similar. The first provided stabling for horses, while the second is specifically for the automobile, including a turntable. Upstairs were quarters for the chauffeur. A 3-foot-6-inch unit module was employed in the design. The work is contemporary with the garage for Emma Martin (S.060), in a similar Prairie idiom.

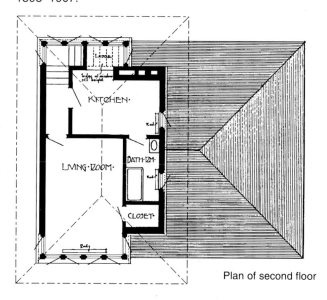

Plan of second floor

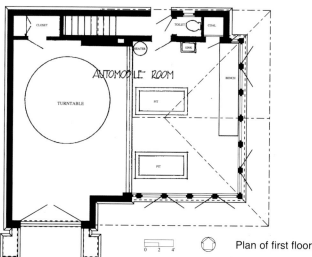

Plan of first floor

S.134　T.0709
Andrew T. **Porter** Residence, Tanyderi (1907)
Spring Green, Wisconsin
Altered in various ways over the years to suit changing activities at Taliesin

Tanyderi

Tanyderi ("under the oaks" in Welsh) is an apt name for this shingled building under the trees in Wisconsin that Wright built for his sister Jane and her husband, Andrew T. Porter, who came to Taliesin to be head of the Hillside Home School (S.069). The plan is typical of Wright's square Prairie houses; the living room takes half the main floor and continues without interruption in an **L** to the dining room. Since the main entry is half inside and half outside the main building square, this could be a shingled precursor of the Fireproof House for $5000. Interior trim transforms the casement windows into frames for the exterior view, letting nature paint the picture.

The plan that survives in the Taliesin archives is more a sketch than working drawings, yet it fully suggests the building that was built. Current porch treatment follows the lines of the sketched plan, but the finished work has an upper enclosed rectangular porch and a walled terrace below.

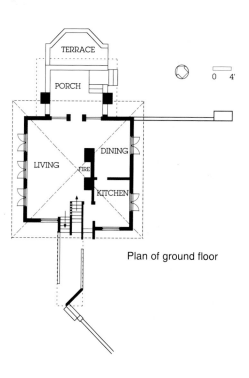

Plan of ground floor

S.135 **T.0803**
Avery **Coonley Residence** (1907),
S.136 **T.1103**
Gardener's Cottage (1911), and
S.137 **T.1103**
Original Garage with Stables (now known as the **Coach House**) (1911)
Riverside, Illinois
Estate divided among five owners in late 1950s, with house divided into two. Main quarters restored after 1978 fire. Garage and stables remodeled as Coach House

Perhaps no built project by Wright exceeds the seeming splendor of the estate he designed for Avery Coonley, a successful Chicago industrialist, and his wife, Queene Ferry, of the Detroit-based Ferry Seed Co. Both were active Christian Scientists; their commitment to the religion brought about a move to the East Coast eight years after the completion of the main residential building in 1909.

Here a low Prairie house, Wright's first "zoned plan," is twice extended from central spaces. In effect, this is two pinwheel plans linked at the tips of their cross axes. By raising living quarters a full story—the entry and a playroom are set at ground level, as in the Tomek (S.128) and Robie (S.127) houses—Wright places the main living room directly under the hip roof so that its ceiling partakes of the protective drooping overhang and attendant cavelike quality first achieved in the Heurtley house (S.074). Living and dining rooms, as well as the kitchen and servants' quarters, occupy this section. Linked at this upper level by a long corridor is the bedroom wing, with children's bedrooms, master bedroom, and guest bedrooms. The ground floors, playroom in the main wing and a basement in the bedroom wing, are not linked.

This main ensemble, then, is further integrated with a garage/stable (now Coach House), Gardener's Cottage, and raised garden around an extensive sunken garden. The property was once a single town block. Frederick Law Olmsted planned the

Coonley living room, view toward windowall

Living room

layout of Riverside in 1869, creating thereby the beautiful sites for the Coonley estate and the later Playhouse (S.174). He also planned both South Park and Jackson Park in Chicago as well as the World's Columbian Exposition of 1893.

Between 1952 and 1957 the Coonley property was divided among five owners. The secondary wing, minus its study, had five bedrooms above the ground-level basement; this became another property. The Gardener's Cottage became its own property. The stable was remodeled into living quarters for Carolyn and James W. Howlett by Arnold P. Skow; the sunken gardens are part of this property. The raised gardens were

Stairwell with skylight

134

Coonley living room, exterior

Dining room

separated, and a house built on that property. The living room was destroyed by fire, June 11, 1978, only eighteen months after Mr. and Mrs. Niketas Sahlas purchased the main residence; they spent the next eighteen months restoring the space. The Avery Coonley House has been designated a National Historic Landmark.

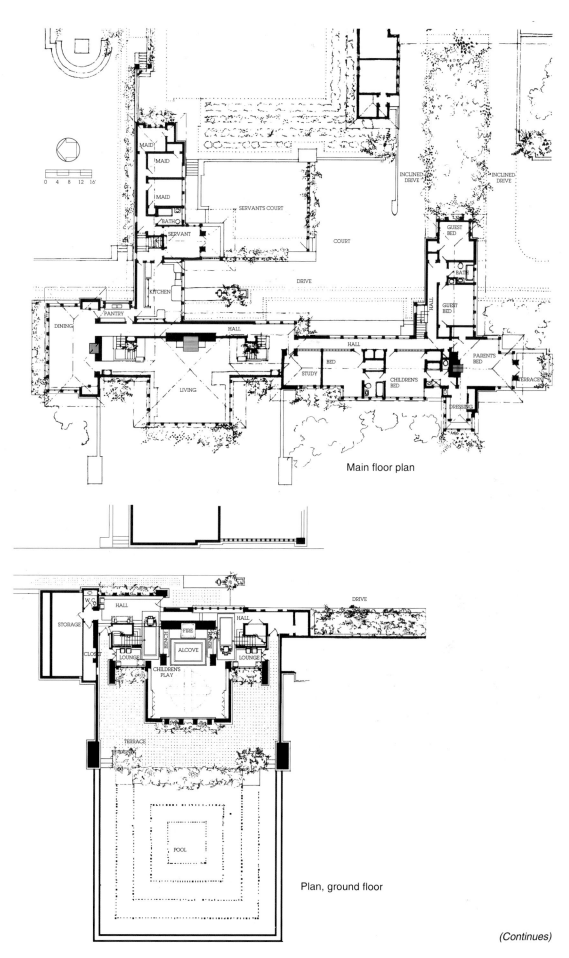

Main floor plan

Plan, ground floor

(Continues)

Gardener's Cottage

Plan of Gardener's Cottage and Coach House

Coonley Coach House

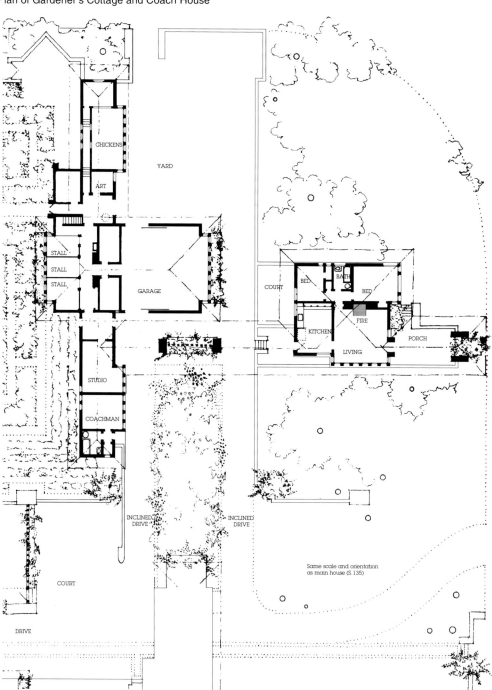

THE AMERICAN BOX VERSUS WRIGHT'S CUBE

American "4-square" (one of many possibilities)

Wrightian 4-square (based on "A Fireproof House for $5000")

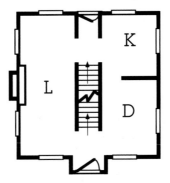

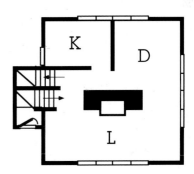

The ground floor is several steps above street level.

Wright's "cube" was never quite that. His square-plan houses were always a bit wider than they were tall. Wright would experiment with vertical unit systems, perhaps with some hope that a "perfect" system, in which elevation and plan units were identical, could be found. Only with Arizona and California block projects did he approximate this goal.

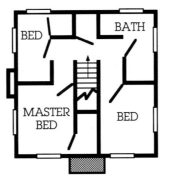

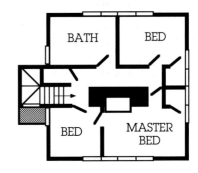

It may look like a simple adjustment, but moving the hearth from an outside wall to a central location was key to Wright's design. The line "from the center of the earth to the heavens above" passed directly up the chimney. Wright's bands of windows brought a more open quality to the interior space than did single or paired double-hung windows of standard designs.

Wright moved the entry to the house to one side, and moved half of its volume outside the square, so that it no longer split the house in two. "Traffic" could flow more freely. Dining and living rooms were "enlarged" by seeming to share each other's space.

Stephen M. B. **Hunt Residence I**
(1907)
LaGrange, Illinois

The Stephen Hunt residence is the best-constructed example of "A Fireproof House for $5000" published in the *Ladies Home Journal* (April 1907). Originally planned for construction in concrete, which would have made it truly fireproof, if too expensive for the space it would provide, it represents the maturation of Wright's thoughts on how best to arrange space in a square plan, or what might have been his American four-square house. In Hunt's version, the fireplace is moved from the outer wall to the center of the structure with the living room occupying fully half the main floor. The dining room continues from this space as an **L.** The kitchen occupies the other quarter. Wright then added a small entry space onto the

Hunt I

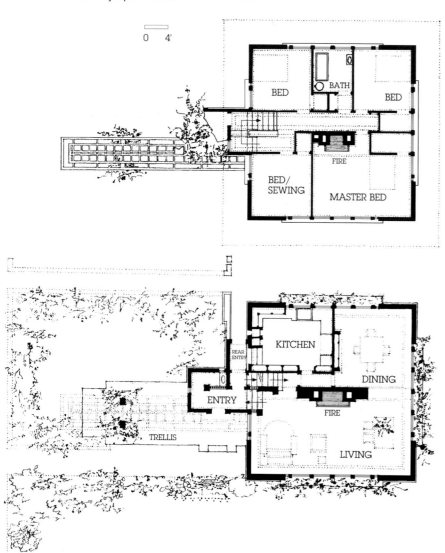

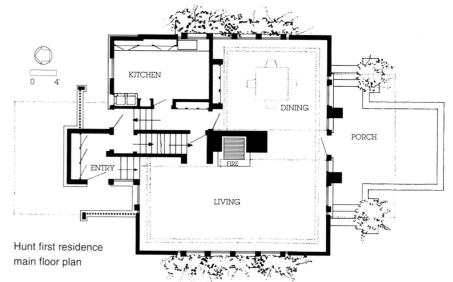

Hunt first residence
main floor plan

Ladies Home Journal "Fireproof House for $5000" plans, first and second floors side opposite the dining room, with stairs adjacent but within the house square and cross traffic flowing behind the chimney masonry. The standard square geometry in this built version of the Fireproof House is violated by the dining room, which is larger than a quarter of the square, pushing the kitchen beyond the square. Upstairs this allows for a larger second bedroom.

This arrangement shows the coherence of all of Wright's designs in a basic tripartite spatial organization. It places the main activity (in a house, the living room) in one area, separated by the traffic area (entry, hallway, stairs) from ancillary activity areas (kitchen, utilities, sleeping quarters). Wright continued to use this spatial idea in Usonian dwellings as well as nonresidential structures as a basic element of organic design.

A terrace wing, later enclosed, was added to this residence for the Hunts (see the second, S.203.4). The Tiffany brick fireplace and oak woodwork have been fully restored by Edward M. Marcisz.

Since construction plans could be purchased from the *Ladies Home Journal,* many of these houses were built with no connection to Wright. Local architects and builders would make their own alterations. For example, one in San Francisco has a Spanish flavor and internal partitions added that defeat Wright's spatial innovation.

S.139   T.0809

G. C. **Stockman** Residence (1908)
Mason City, Iowa
Moved to new site in 1989 and restored 1991–92

The G. C. Stockman house, Wright's first extant work in Iowa, is a mirror image of the first Hunt residence (S.138), therefore derivative of the "Fireproof House for $5000." A full-width veranda centered on the side extends both dining and living room space toward the outdoors. The entry is also larger than the Fireproof House standard and featured a cantilevered roof (no posts were called for by Wright).

Dark wood bands turn the corner of the house (partially concealed by vines) while they frame the plaster panels of the Hunt residence. Wright often used this device, which he called "back-band trim," in the late 1890s through the mid-1910s because it could easily be made by machine, and it bound one material to another, such as plaster to wood (see also Hills, S.051 for an early example, and Hoyt, S.120, versus Fuller, S.123).

Threatened by demolition, the house was moved in 1989 to a new site near the Rock Crest Rock Glen subdivision, where houses by other Prairie architects, notably Barry Byrne and Walter Burley Griffin, abound. Here it was oriented to the west; on its original site it faced north on an east-west street. Restoration was begun in 1991 and completed in 1992 under the direction of Jonathan Lipman, who was the first to develop a theory of tripartite spatial arrangement in Wright's non-residential designs.

Stockman Residence, as re-sited

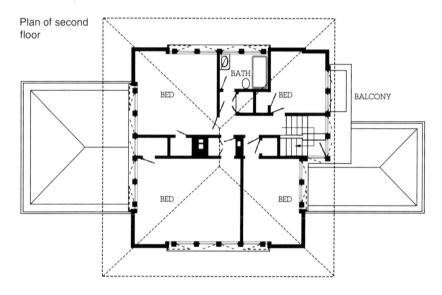

Plan of second floor

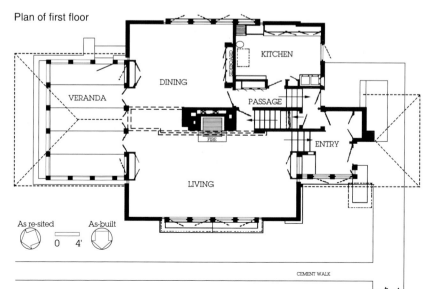

Plan of first floor

Living room, as restored

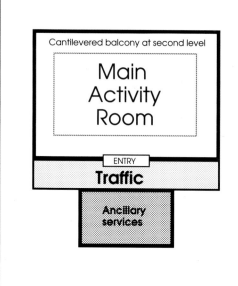

Cantilevered balcony at second level

Main Activity Room

ENTRY

Traffic

Ancillary services

In plan, Wright's urban public buildings are rather consistently organized into three clearly defined zones. The largest of these is the main activity room, the space in which the purpose of the structure is fully realized. This typically is entered on one side only, and is overlooked by a cantilevered balcony.

Second is the traffic area including the main entrance to the structure.

Third is the space that contains ancillary services, which vary according to the purpose of the main activity room.

FRANK LLOYD WRIGHT'S TRIPARTITE ARRANGEMENT OF SPACE IN HIS URBAN PUBLIC BUILDINGS

Johnson Wax
Administration **Building**

Garage

Driveway

ENTRY

Office desks

Sanctuary

Loggia

Sunday School

Unity Temple

Larkin Administration Building

Annex

ENTRY

Office desks

(The original "traffic" area was to have been a driveway, as in the Johnson Wax Administration Building.)

Guggenheim Museum

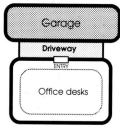
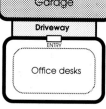

Main

ENTRY

Greek Orthodox Church

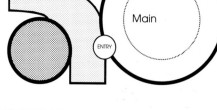
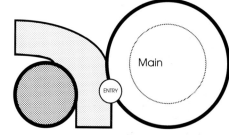

Sanctuary

Spiral stair well

ENTRY

Chapel and Hall

Here the tripartite arrangement of spaces shows clearly in the section. The ancillary elements are below ground. The main entry leads to the sanctuary only. Three spiral stairwells lead up to the balcony, cantilevered away from the altar, and down to the assembly hall and chapel below ground.

Beth Sholom Synagogue

To show the spatial principle at work in this synagogue, one must look at a section. Entry to the sanctuary is above the public entry, and one walks down into the space devoted to worship.

Sanctuary

ENTRY

Lower level chapel

S.140   T.0805
Raymond W. Evans Residence
(1908)
Chicago, Illinois
Porch later enclosed, possibly by
Wright. Plaster front facade stone-
veneered. All movable furniture
removed

The Raymond W. Evans structure
commands a hilly site on Chicago's
South Side in an area known as
Beverly. In basic plan it is a "Fireproof
House for $5000," and the expansion
of that plan makes it very similar to the
Brigham home (S.184), built seven
years later. In both a narrow passageway leads from the porte-cochere to
the reception area, separated from
the living room only by a screen. The
living room spans the full depth of the
house and is extended by a porch
(now enclosed). It differs from the
Brigham home in its northwest corner,
where there is a dining room with
magnificent art glass in the ceiling,
which can be lit three different ways.
The butler's pantry, kitchen, and
servant's quarters pinwheel out to the
rear.

   The chimney flues split at the upper
floor, and entry to a south bedroom is
between masonry masses (for the
most dramatic use of this device, see
Stewart, S.160). There are two baths
and four bedrooms above. Front-facing
stucco surfaces have been resurfaced
with concrete that is colored and
formed to look like stone. Structural
beams are failing. The house was
completely furnished by Wright, but all
furniture has gone to museums or
been removed by early owners. A later
enclosure, apparently by Wright, is
undocumented in any known archive.
Recent research identifies the client as
Raymond W. Evans, though the name
on Wright's plans is Robert W. Evans.

Evans house with original stucco

Plan of second floor

Dining room ceiling light

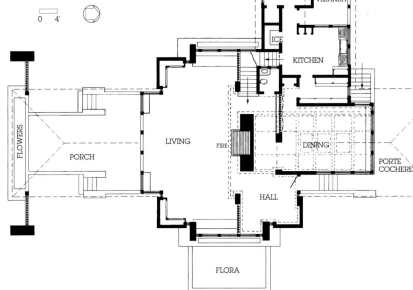
Plan of first floor

Living room

Browne's Bookstore, outside main entry

Browne's Bookstore, inside main entry

Browne's Bookstore, view along corridor
(from left to right on plan)

S.141 T.0802
Browne's Bookstore (1908)
Chicago, Illinois
Demolished

In a narrow space in the Fine Arts Building, Wright created alcoves around tables for Browne's Bookstore. With gray oak trimming it, cream-colored plaster enlivening it, and magnesite floors shaded ivory brightening it, he helped the space seem larger than it was. This was the first of three shops Wright designed for the Fine Arts Building, the others being art galleries (S.154, S.181).

Browne's Bookstore, the main reading room; note fireplace, which does not show on the plan

Browne's Bookstore, end cove

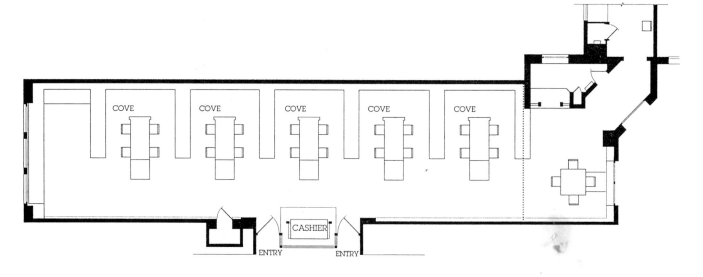

S.142 T.0807
L. K. **Horner** Residence (1908)
Chicago, Illinois
Demolished

The L. K. Horner plan is more rectilinear than the DeRhodes home
(S.125), and both predate, in terms of
construction though possibly not
design, the Mrs. Thomas Gale residence (S.098), the fullest expression
of this basic architectural idea. The
ground-floor plan is cruciform; the
entry was opposite the kitchen and the
interior opened the full length to
terraces on each end. Upstairs, the
symmetry was maintained only about
the shorter cross axis. Balconies were
added to emphasize the cruciform.

Horner Residence

View to entrance

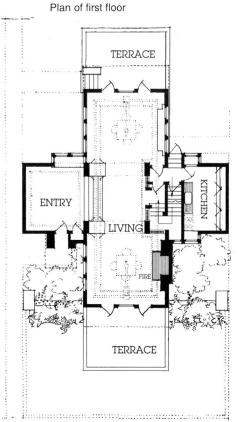

Plan of first floor

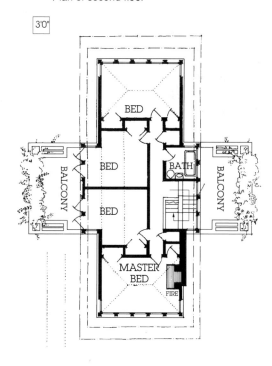

Plan of second floor

S.143   T.0814

Horseshoe Inn (1908) for Willard
Ashton
Estes Park, Colorado
Demolished

Little is known of this structure, though
it is likely that it was the same genre
as the Como Orchard Summer Colony
project (S.144). Wright's description is
of a summer hotel in pine-clad hills, in
horizontal undressed (rough-cut)
board-and-batten siding. *Dos à dos*
fireplaces face a large central entry at
the front, a dining hall to the rear.
Extending on both sides were **T**-wings
of sleeping rooms, one of which goes
over a stream (see Bridge Cottage,
S.077), with dormitory-style lavatory
facilities. The heads of the **T**s are two
stories high.

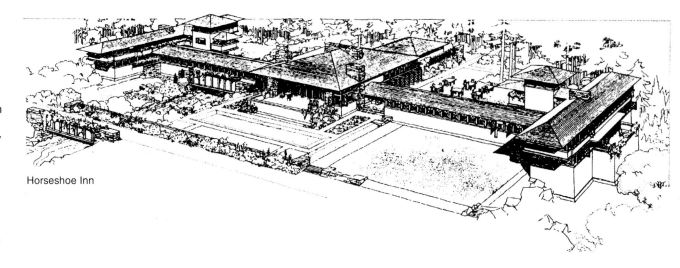

Horseshoe Inn

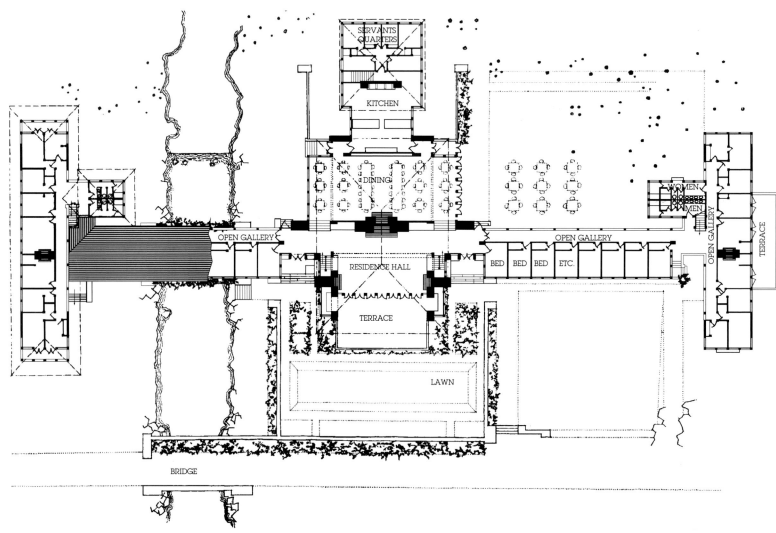

Plan, showing first and second floors

S.144 T.1002
Como Orchard Summer Colony
(1909) for the Como Orchard Land
Company, a subdivision of the Bitter
Root Valley Irrigation Company
S.144A T.1002
Como Orchard Clubhouse (Inn)
S.144B T.1002
One-room Cottage/**Manager's**
Office (Land Office Building)
S.144C T.1002
Three-bedroom Cottage
S.144D T.1002
Small **Cottage**
University Heights, Darby, Montana

The three-bedroom cottages are
identified as follows: clockwise from
northeast, S.144.1C to S.144.5C. The
small cottages are identified as
follows: from the west to east,
S.144.1D to S.144.6D. All six small
cottages (S.144D) demolished. Of the
five constructed three-bedroom
cottages, only one (S.144.3C)
remains, and it is in a form revised
from Wright's standard plan. The
One-room Cottage survives in its form
as the Manager's Office. The
Clubhouse was torn down in 1945.

Six miles north of Darby, Montana, the
broad Bitterroot Valley gives way to
canyons and arroyos. The rail line
down from Missoula through Stevensville (see S.145) ends abruptly at Old
Darby and University roads, where
steep hills block useful extension.
Bunkhouse Road is a continuation of
University Road, which leads to the
former University Heights and Wright's
summer escape for Chicago professors on property logged clear in 1907
except on the steep part of the hill.

This is Ravalli County, named after
Father Ravalli, S.J., a missionary from
northern Italy who brought with him the
name of Lake Como for the body of
water 2 miles northwest of this project,
which is also known by various
promoters as the Dinsmore Irrigation
and Development Company project
and McIntosh-Morello Orchards. The
orchards that were planted to reforest
the area take their name from the lake.

There would have been no project
had not both irrigation and railroads
come to the area. The Northern Pacific
Railroad built a spur from Missoula,
the main railroad center in western
Montana, through the Bitterroot Valley
south to Darby, and the Great Northern

(Continues)

General view of Como Orchards. The clubhouse is in the center. Four cottages
are shown, as well as a large, unidentified single-story building (probably a garage) behind the
clubhouse, and a small shed.

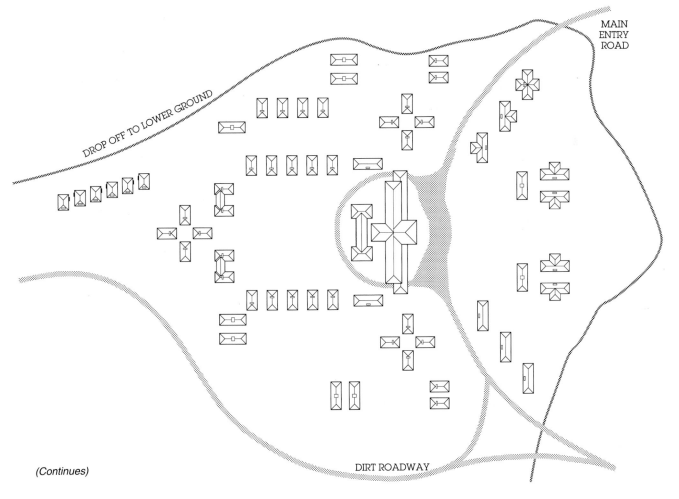

MAIN
ENTRY
ROAD

DROP OFF TO LOWER GROUND

DIRT ROADWAY

145

(**S.144** *continued*)

Railroad opened a line north of Missoula to Wenatchee, Washington (Wright designed both the site and the World War I Memorial Community Center for Columbia River in 1919). Then in 1909 the Chicago, Milwaukee and St. Paul Railroad extended its services into Missoula. The good growing season of the dry inter-mountain region required irrigation for successful agriculture, and Samuel Dinsmore contacted Chicago financier W. I. Moody for help in building what quickly became known as the Big Ditch, an irrigation scheme extending from a dam at Lake Como north to a juncture with the Bitterroot River north of Stevensville. The rest is local history.

Professors visiting Darby could stay as transients in the main Como Orchard Clubhouse, with its two-story lounge and dining rooms in both wings below guest rooms, kitchen to the rear below servants quarters. The main intent, however, in luring these academics west during summer months was to induce them to purchase ten acres of irrigated apple orchard at

Como Orchard Clubhouse

Type 3C Cottage

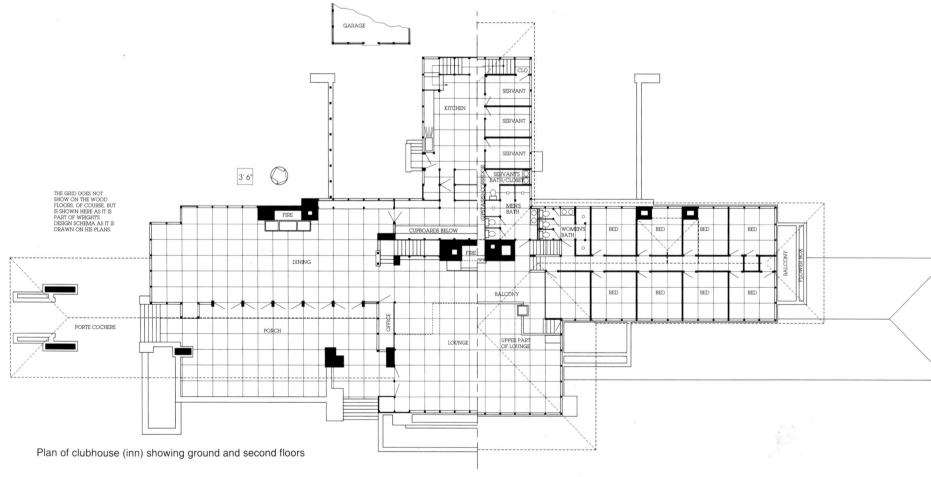

THE GRID DOES NOT SHOW ON THE WOOD FLOORS, OF COURSE, BUT IS SHOWN HERE AS IT IS PART OF WRIGHT'S DESIGN SCHEMA AS IT IS DRAWN ON HIS PLANS.

Plan of clubhouse (inn) showing ground and second floors

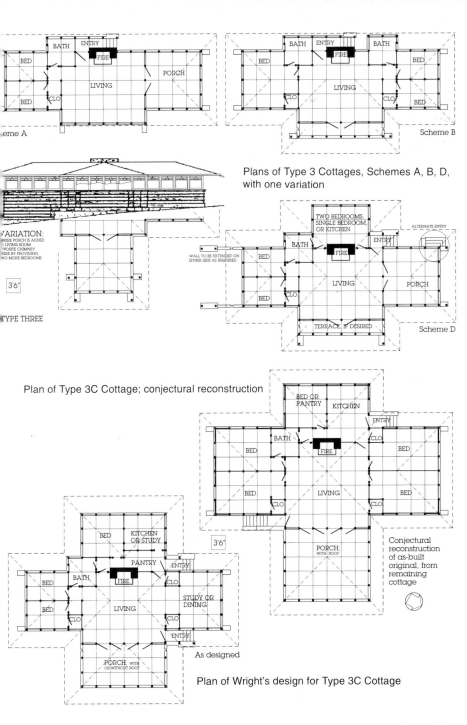

eme A

Scheme B

Plans of Type 3 Cottages, Schemes A, B, D, with one variation

VARIATION:
WHERE PORCH IS ADDED
O LIVING ROOM
OPPOSITE CHIMNEY
ERE BY PROVIDING
WO MORE BEDROOMS

3'6"

TYPE THREE

TWO BEDROOMS,
SINGLE BEDROOM,
OR KITCHEN

ALTERNATE ENTRY

WALL TO BE EXTENDED ON
EITHER SIDE AS REQUIRED

BATH

ENTRY

FIRE

BED

BED

CLO

LIVING

PORCH

TERRACE, IF DESIRED

Scheme D

Plan of Type 3C Cottage; conjectural reconstruction

BED OR
PANTRY

KITCHEN

ENTRY

BATH

CLO

FIRE

BED

BED

BED

CLO

LIVING

CLO

3'6"

PORCH,
WITH ROOF

Conjectural
reconstruction
of as-built
original, from
remaining
cottage

BED

KITCHEN
OR STUDY

PANTRY

ENTRY

BED

BATH

FIRE

CLO

BED

LIVING

STUDY OR
DINING

CLO

CLO

ENTRY

PORCH, WITH
OR WITHOUT ROOF

As designed

Plan of Wright's design for Type 3C Cottage

$400 an acre together with a cottage site at University Heights. The Chicago-based operation was promoted by Frederick D. Nichols (S.118), a friend of Chicago financier W. I. Moody. Wright visited the area in February 1909.

Fourteen buildings from Wright's plans were built, but only two remain—a three-bedroom cottage (in front of the clubhouse in the overall view) and a now-abandoned land office building. Construction began on May 1, 1909. The clubhouse was sited as Wright had instructed, but was simplified during construction. Second-level balconies, piers, and flower boxes were eliminated, but the two-story lobby was retained. To the sides, portes cocheres framed the structure over the oval dirt road that connected to Bunkhouse Road where it crests the hill after a hairpin reverse leading to the site. During the Prairie era, Wright often concealed his use of the square module in his design process, but this 4-foot unit is clearly ruled on the drawing paper.

The small cottage design, without cross-axis, was certainly intended for those who would eat in the clubhouse; it provided shelter and privacy on a more individual basis than rooms in the clubhouse did. Of these six, three were located on the north road behind the inn and two others in approximate alignment with Wright's intent, while the sixth was oddly angled. Of the five cruciform three-bedroom cottages, two were along the main entry road much as in Wright's site plan, while the other three retained alignment with Wright's site grid. The land office building is much altered; supports were added for the cantilevered roof as well as a room behind the fireplace. At one time there was a vault in a basement below the office.

The remaining cottage, a cruciform plan (type 3C), is built to a 42-inch-square unit module. It was enlarged at the time of construction with two additional units in the cross-axis to make the bedrooms more commodious and with two more to extend the living room and porch, now enclosed. The main entry has been flipped on the plan from the north to the south side, while the rear entry remains on the north. The space to the rear of the cobblestone fireplace, which Wright designed as a bedroom plus study (or kitchen with pantry for those who did not take their meals at the clubhouse), has been modernized into a kitchen, and the northwest corner fully enclosed as a winterized entry. Both the cottage and the land office building retain windows with a simple design created by the muntin frames, by Wright.

By 1913 blight and lawsuits had hit the project and the bank foreclosed in 1916. In 1923 the property was known as McIntosh-Morello Orchards. In 1937 a local rancher owned the property. In the early 1970s, Leonard Melnarik took over the property as a farm and ranch.

Manager's (Land Office) Cottage, original part

One-room Cottage fireplace, typical of Wright's design for all the cabins

S.145   T.0918A
Bitter Root Inn (1908) for the Bitter
Root Valley Irrigation Company
Bitter Root, near Stevensville, Montana
Destroyed by fire, July 28, 1924

The town of Stevensville is "where
Montana began" in 1883. The state
flower of Montana, whose "official"
centennial was 1989, is the Bitterroot,
Lewisia rediviva, named after Captain
Meriwether Lewis of the Lewis and
Clark Expedition. The Bitterroot Valley
begins about where the Bitterroot
River is formed from its west and east
forks, the latter originating at the Continental Divide, the former starting
where the Bitterroot Range meets
Idaho. Between these two, U.S. 93
rises to an altitude of 7014 feet at Lost
Trail Pass, where it then dives down
toward the Salmon River in Idaho. Just
west of here Lewis and Clark crossed
back into Montana over what has since
become the Montana-Idaho border.

Stevensville is about a mile east of
the river, and the town is laid out
another half mile east to the railroad
tracks.

Wright's project, a complex of
structures in the north end of the Bitter
Root Irrigation District and for the
company originally of that name, was
laid out some 6 miles north of
Stevensville, where the valley is wide
and flat. The plan included public
buildings either side of a long, central
east-west green. Around these were
suburbanlike square blocks divided for
construction into quadrants, a device
Wright first developed in 1900, and

published in the *Ladies Home Journal*
(February 1901).

The inn that was built was hardly
the grand scheme on a hillside
overlooking the main boulevard that
Wright illustrated in his German
portfolio, but a much scaled-down
version of the inn and clubhouse at
University Heights (S.144A). This was
located instead at the north end of
town immediately east of the planned
railroad line, and had dining and
reception rooms on either side of the
central office, behind which was the
kitchen and above which were guest
rooms. Siding was board and batten,

and the ensemble was designed to
require the least possible amount of
off-season maintenance, while providing suitable accommodations for
summer transients. Frederick D.
Nichols (S.118) was the Chicago-
based promoter of this and the
University Heights projects.

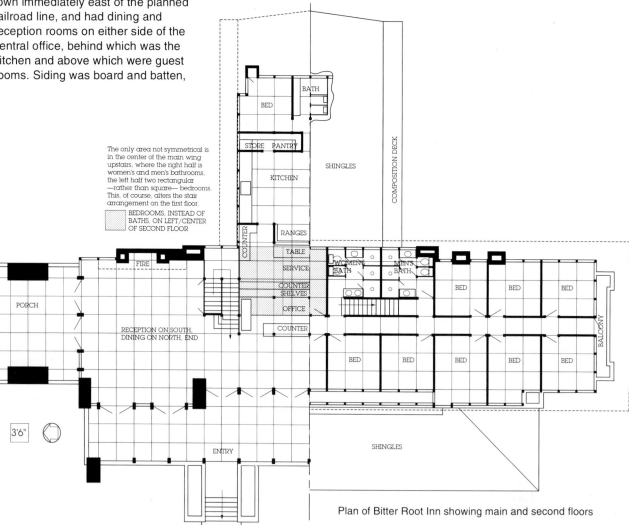

The only area not symmetrical is
in the center of the main wing
upstairs, where the right half is
women's and men's bathrooms,
the left half two rectangular
—rather than square— bedrooms.
This, of course, alters the stair
arrangement on the first floor.

▨ BEDROOMS, INSTEAD OF
BATHS, ON LEFT/CENTER
OF SECOND FLOOR

Plan of Bitter Root Inn showing main and second floors

S.146 T.0806
Eugene A. **Gilmore** Residence, Airplane House (1908)
Madison, Wisconsin
Enclosed second-level entry added.
Additions to the rear

Eugene A. Gilmore was a professor in the law school at the University of Wisconsin. His later success, leading to the deanship at Wisconsin, then similar positions at the universities of Iowa and Pittsburgh as well as the presidency at Iowa, did not affect his concern for economy at some level; he supervised construction. Even so, the house has servant's quarters at the ground level, beneath a library on the main floor and the fourth bedroom on

Gilmore's first architect did not provide a satisfactory design. A university colleague showed Gilmore "In the Cause of Architecture," recently published in *Architectural Record* (March 1908). Soon after, Wright was hired.

The small porches of the Gilmore house represent a break with Wright's rather consistent rectangular and octagonal modules. They frame the three bedrooms in the cross-axis of the house, which is turned sideways to the street to face the morning sun and provide privacy. Underneath, the living room spans two-thirds of this segment of the structure, and the dining room fills the other third.

Howard and Nelle Weiss acquired the property in 1928. During their

tenure, a second (main) floor exterior entry with stairs that face west was added; originally visitors entered the basement on the ground level and took inside stairs to the living level. Further additions were made to the rear: a new service wing where the south and west wings meet, with its own chimney; a

three-car garage at ground level surmounted by an expanded kitchen, new servant's quarters with a sitting room and a bedroom and porch, and two bathrooms on the top level.

Courtesy of the State Historical Society of Wisconsin

Gilmore house with original entry

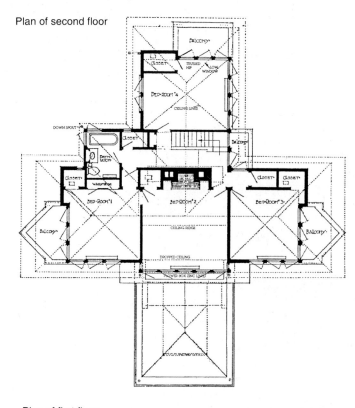

Plan of second floor

Gilmore house from northwest, with revised entry

the second level, which comprise the rear wing of the home.

Gilmore purchased his University Heights subdivision lot with another University of Wisconsin professsor, Michael V. O'Shea, in 1904. Each purchased a single lot and shared a third. Gilmore eventually bought O'Shea's half lot, gaining a property 140 feet deep with nearly 180 feet of frontage.

Plan of ground (entry) floor

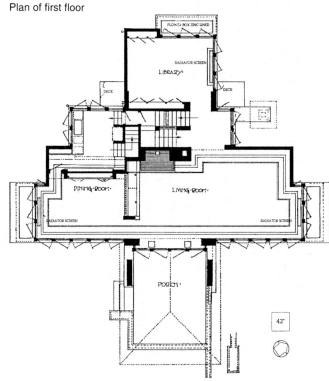

Plan of first floor

S.147 T.0801

Edward E. **Boynton** Residence (1908)
Rochester, New York
Partially restored in the 1980s

Edward Boynton lost his wife, sister of George Gerts (S.077), and his two sons early in the marriage. He and his surviving daughter Beulah decided to build in Rochester, New York. Boynton knew of Wright through Warren McArthur, his partner in the Ham Lantern Company (see S.011, S.221–S.222).

Wright's desire to be not just architect, but artistic designer of all parts of the house, met with approval from Boynton. Despite the distance from Chicago, Wright visited the site many times, often sleeping in make-shift sheds set up by the workmen. Every detail had his careful attention. All main-floor windows are leaded, with separate designs for casements and for clerestory lights. The living room is extended west by a veranda, now enclosed with the same glasswork designs as those found elsewhere (made by the original supplier), though the original plans show it as open (preliminary drawings are dated 1903). The dining room is a particularly fine space, graciously large with plentiful lighting including a large clerestory and overhead light panels. The dining table, seating eight to fourteen, is supported by four posts surmounted by lights of simple yet elegant geometry. Upstairs, a long gallery extending from the main hallway, separated father (west end) from daughter (center south). Both the kitchen and the master bath remain as they were built with original plumbing, a rarity for a building of this age. Mullions on 51-inch centers suggest that as the unit used throughout the design.

Restoration, including replacement of the badly damaged tin roof with asphalt shingle surrounded with copper gutter, and copper in flat-roof sections, and removal of paint from wood trim, has been completed by Karen and Burt Brown. The Landmark Society of Western New York owns the full complement of Wright-designed furniture and has a covenant on the deed to the house.

Boynton Residence

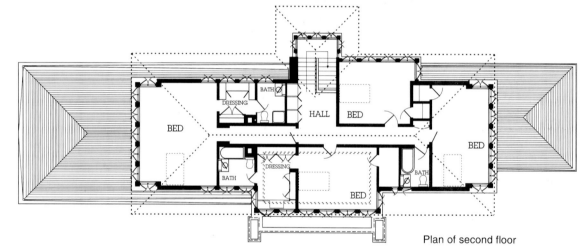

Original bathroom shower fixture

Dining room, with original sideboard and dining table, and overhead electric lights plus clerestory lighting

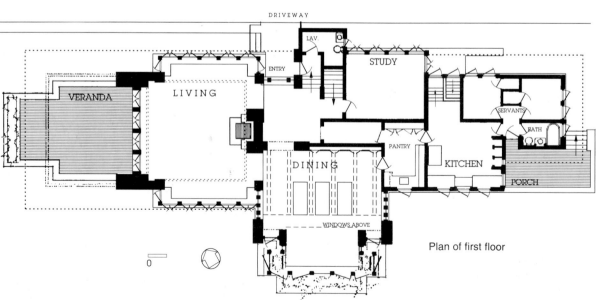

Plan of second floor

Plan of first floor

May Residence, south facade

Living room; fireplace with light in mortar

Shadows and lights; morning room

S.148   T.0817
Meyer **May** Residence (1908)
Grand Rapids, Michigan
Restored 1987–88

The Meyer May home, built for a local clothier, is Michigan's Prairie masterpiece. It is a tan brick structure with red Belgian tile roof, copper detailing, and leaded art-glass windows.

The entry is concealed to the rear (a feature first fully developed in the Beachy house, S.117), in the middle of a wall that maintains privacy by placing the main windows well above ground level, where they serve the stairwell and second-level gallery. In the living room, art glass in a south alcove softens and varies the lighting throughout the day; overhead art-glass panels, with electric lighting, continue the effect past sunset. The sills are low and the alcove not very high, reflecting Meyer May's own short stature. The lighting effects are further modified by the firelight glimmering through golden glass embedded in the horizontal mortar joints of the fireplace.

In the dining room, vertical elements dominate. The dining room table, which seats six, is supported by four near-corner piers, surmounted by lights that translate the planes of the art-glass windows into three-dimensional boxes, the angled tops of which are further translated into the design of the carpet, unifying all these Wright-designed features. The Niedecken mural is noteworthy.

The house was fully restored in 1987–88 by Steelcase Inc., the builders of the Johnson Wax furniture (S.237–S.238), with Carla Lind as project director and Tilton+Lewis Associates as restoration architects.

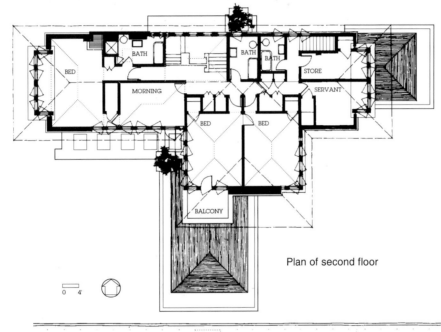

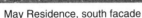

Plan of second floor

Dining room with light piers in table

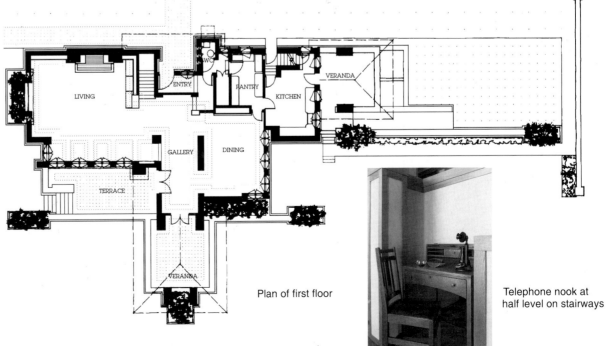

Plan of first floor

Telephone nook at half level on stairways

151

S.149 T.0804
Walter V. **Davidson** Residence
(1908)
Buffalo, New York

The house for a manager appointed by
Darwin Martin at the Larkin Company
(S.093) is an unbalanced cruciform in
plan, heavier to the rear than the front.
This rear section is split level and
contains utilities, kitchen, laundry, and
maid's room at main level (there is no
true basement), three bedrooms and
bathroom above. The living room is
two stories high. The single-story arms
of the cruciform contain the dining
room and porch.

Like most of Wright's plaster-
exterior buildings, the original color
was not white. A pastel blue underlies
many successive coats of paint.

Note: This residence has been
erroneously listed as the Alexander
Davidson residence (see Manson,
Frank Lloyd Wright to 1910, pp. 138,
147, and *The Architecture of Frank
Lloyd Wright: A Complete Catalog,* 2d
ed.).

Davidson Residence from the street

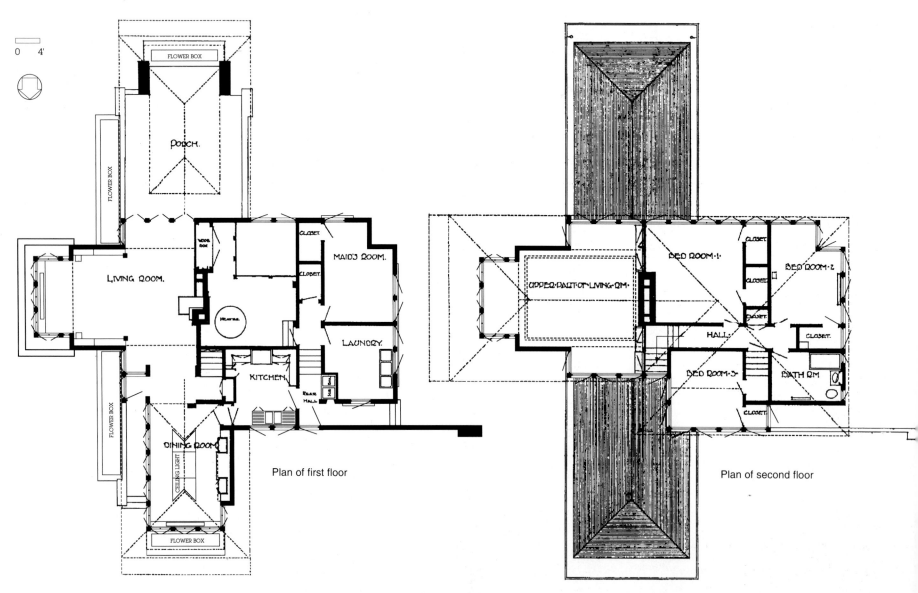

Plan of first floor

Plan of second floor

S.150   T.0808
Isabel Roberts (Roberts-Scott)
Residence (1908)
River Forest, Illinois
Altered by Wright in 1955 for Warren
Scott (S.394)

The Isabel Roberts house represents
Wright's most mature development of
the Prairie cruciform plan, first promulgated in the Willits house (S.054). The
cross is seen in the main floor front
narrow living room, which rises one
and a half floors with a balcony above
the fireplace to the rear. The kitchen
and various ancillary functions (which
originally included an "in-house"
garage, as in the Cheney house,
S.104, and similarly vetoed by local
authorities) are in a wider rear wing.
Bedrooms and servant's quarters are
to the rear at the upper level. The
dining room and porch are in subsidiary single-story cross-axis wings. The
entry, at the corner where the dining
room and living room meet, is as
suppressed as it ever would be in
the Prairie house, where it often com-
manded its own wing.

The actual plans and permit were
in the name of Mary Roberts, but it
was designed for her daughter, Isabel,
a bookkeeper of five years' standing in
Wright's Oak Park studio, possibly as
early as 1905. Wright thought of it as a
working out for a narrow lot of the
William Norman Guthrie project for
Sewanee, Tennessee, later built for
Frank J. Baker (S.151). The original
structure was wood with a stucco surface. The living room clerestory starts
only after an interrupting section of
wall next to the floor-to-ceiling front
windows, as in the Davidson house
(S.149) but not the Baker. The south
porch, originally open, is built around a
British elm tree that rises through the
roof. The flooring and roof framing
around this have twice been redone to
allow the tree to live on, once in the
1955 remodeling for Warren Scott and
again late in the 1980s.

The cruciform plan makes the
actual square footage seem smaller
than it would be in a rectangular layout. Though Wright usually made
spaces flow one into the another,
extending the eye's view, the historical
photograph of the living room hearth
with the dining room beyond suggests
instead relative isolation. In Wright's
square houses, the dining room is

Isabel Roberts
Residence, as
originally built

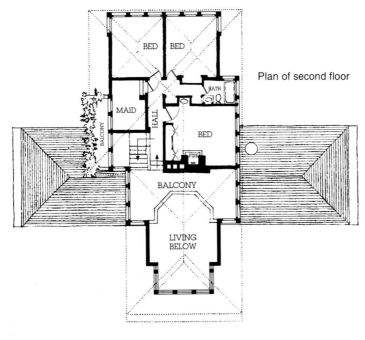

Plan of second floor

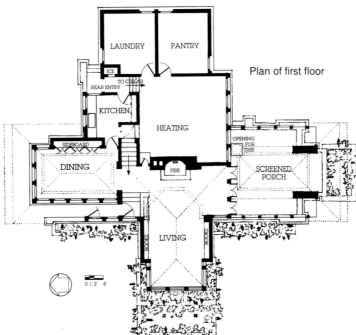

Plan of first floor

Living room under balcony, view to dining room

directly linked to the living room with
no wall or screen shielding the view, as
here or as in the Willits, the prototype
of all cross plans.

Immediately to the south and
across the street are houses by Prairie
school disciple, William Drummond,
who prepared the working drawings for
the Isabel Roberts house. Harry
Robinson, who in 1926 was designing
an addition to the Greene house
(S.176), was also responsible for the
resurfacing of the house with a brick
veneer. Wright, admitting that the original had been done cheaply, remodeled
the house for Warren Scott in 1955,
employing blonde Philippine mahogany throughout the interior and
replacing the roof with a copper cover.
Additional work to accommodate
growth of the tree in the porch was
done in 1988 for son Anthony W. Scott.
The photograph shows the house as
originally constructed. For a photograph of the building as remodeled,
see the Scott Remodeling (S.394).

S.151   T.0901
Frank J. **Baker Residence** (1909)
and
S.151A   T.0901
Carriage House (1909) and
S.151B
Residence **Additions** (early 1920s)
Wilmette, Illinois
1920s additions attributed to Wright's
office

Twenty-two-foot porches terminate the
wings of this nonsymmetrical cruciform
plan. The longer wing aligns a reception room and a dining room, extended
by a porch, with kitchen adjacent. One
must walk the full length of this wing to
reach the entry; such a long approach
was seldom used by Wright, but always dramatically (see a similar use in
a late Usonian design, S.421). The
rear, bedroom half of the plan is at half
level, running nearly the full length of
the house exclusive of the porches.
This split-level arrangement is quite different from that of the Roberts (S.150)
house, but it serves to keep the whole
close to the ground. The living room is
a story and a half in height, with clerestory windows on both sides; the only
support for the living room roof cantilever is in the corner mullions. Mullion
centers of 4 feet, 6 inches define the
unit to which the design is related.

An early 1920s addition to the rear
is attributed to Wright because of total
coherence of style and structure, but
no documentation of this is available
from any reliable source. The Bakers
lived in the house until the late
twenties, and no reason is known as to
why they would have sought out a
different architect for the addition. It is
also possible that Harry Robinson,
who was doing additions and alterations to other Wright buildings at this
time, produced this addition.

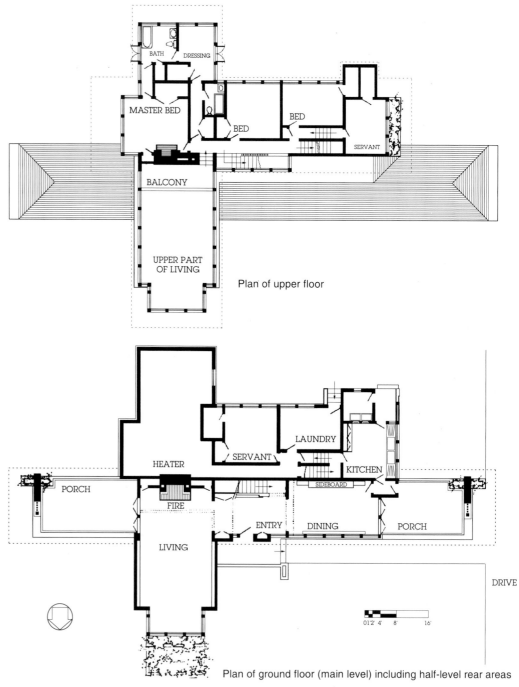

Plan of upper floor

Plan of ground floor (main level) including half-level rear areas

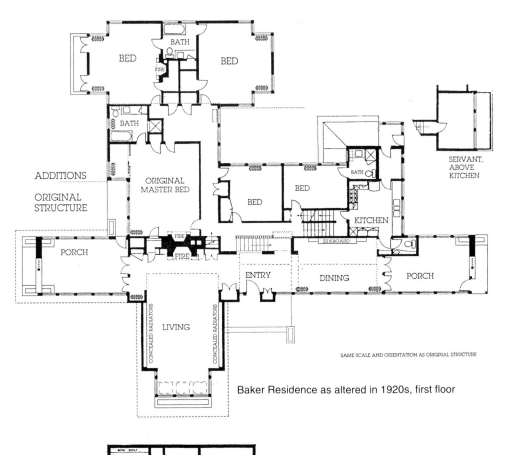

ADDITIONS

ORIGINAL
STRUCTURE

BED

BATH

BED

BATH

ORIGINAL
MASTER BED

BED

BED

BATH

SERVANT,
ABOVE
KITCHEN

KITCHEN

SIDEBOARD

PORCH

FIRE

FIRE

CONCEALED RADIATORS

CONCEALED RADIATORS

ENTRY

DINING

PORCH

LIVING

SAME SCALE AND ORIENTATION AS ORIGINAL STRUCTURE

Baker Residence as altered in 1920s, first floor

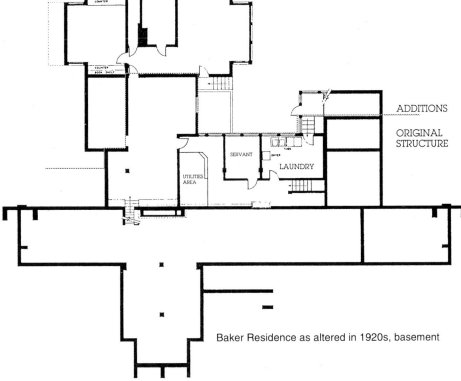

WORK SHELF

COUNTER

COUNTER
BOOK SHELF

ADDITIONS

ORIGINAL
STRUCTURE

SERVANT

DRYER

UTILITIES
AREA

LAUNDRY

Baker Residence as altered in 1920s, basement

Clarke Stable

S.152   T.0903
Robert D. **Clarke Additions** to the
Little Stable (1909)
Peoria, Illinois

Despite his obtaining plans for a
Wright-designed home in 1905, Robert
Clarke did not build. In March 1904 the
Little residence (S.070) was sold to
Cora G. Clarke, who assumed the
Little's $8000 mortgage. She and her
husband made Wright-designed revisions to the original stable (S.071),
turning an upstairs hay loft into living
space. New stable stalls were added
on the west end, which have been
converted to additional garage space,
by cutting through the original brick
wall (far left garage door). The larger
area to the east includes a pit for
changing oil and doing other
maintenance.

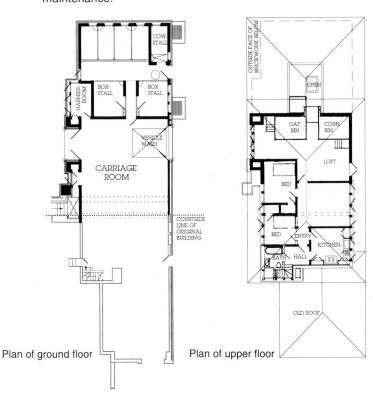

COW
STALL

HARNESS
ROOM

BOX
STALL

BOX
STALL

VEHICLE
WASH

CARRIAGE
ROOM

COURTSIDE
LINE OF
ORIGINAL
BUILDING

OUTSIDE FACE OF
BRICKWORK BELOW

OPEN

OAT
BIN

CORN
BIN

LOFT

BED

BED

ENTRY

KITCHEN

BATH

HALL

OLD ROOF

Plan of ground floor   Plan of upper floor

S.153   T.0909

Oscar **Steffens** Residence (1909)
Chicago, Illinois
Demolished

The Steffens house sat on a hilltop near Lake Michigan before it was taken down in the 1950s, after years of neglect. The plan was a variation on the Davidson dwelling (S.149). There was no basement; utilities were directly behind the fireplace with the kitchen to the side, an arrangement Wright explored further in Usonian house plans. As in the Isabel Roberts house, over the living room is a balcony which leads nowhere. Alterations of the fenestration at the front and rear were made during construction.

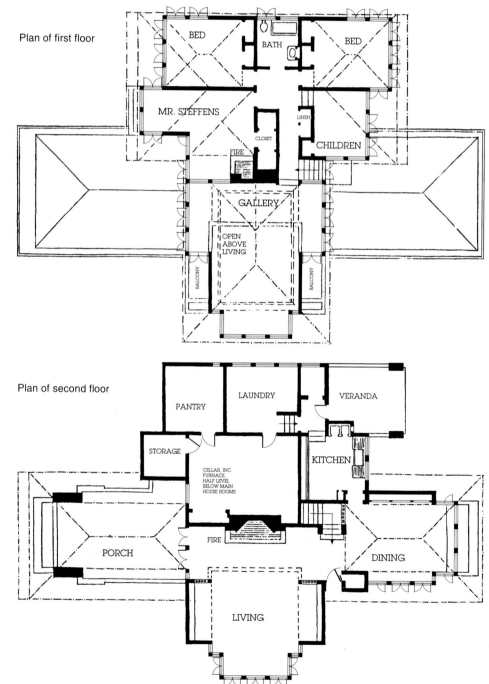

Plan of first floor

Plan of second floor

S.154 T.0911
W. Scott **Thurber Art Gallery** (1909)
Chicago, Illinois
Demolished

Two long panels of leaded art glass
provided lighting for the gallery, by sun
or by concealed electric bulbs at night.
Articulation of space into stalls divided
by display cases makes the compact
sales area seem large. The gallery,
like Browne's Bookstore (S.141) and
the much later Mori Oriental Art Studio
(S.181), was in the Fine Arts Building.

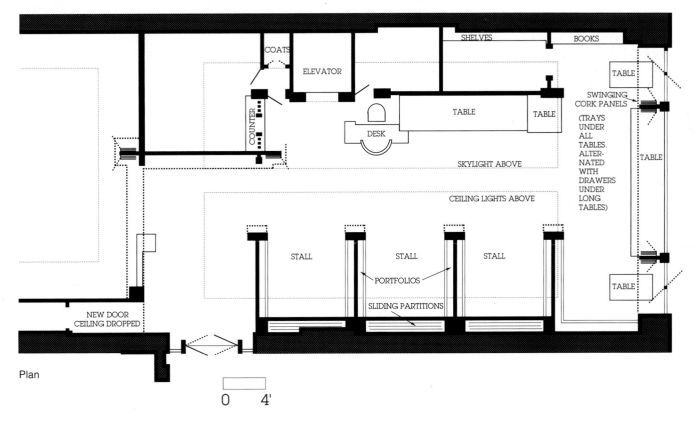

Plan

0   4'

S.155　T.0902
City National Bank Building and
S.156　T.0902
Park Inn **Hotel** (1909) and
S.157　T.1006
Law Offices Remodeling (1910)
for James E. Blythe and J. E. E.
Markley
Mason City, Iowa
Hotel remodeled many times over the
years. Bank remodeled at ground level
into commercial store

J. E. E. Markley's eldest daughter had
been a student at Wright's aunts'
Hillside Home School in Spring Green,
Wisconsin; the two men thus met in
the normal course of events, leading to
the client-architect relationship. Wright
provided an ingenious solution to the
needs of his Mason City clients. The
bank and hotel are essentially separate buildings. The main banking room
is symmetrical under a two-story vault.
To the left side is a single-story area
with president's office, cashier's room,
and directors' room. Above the vault, a
third story provides a baker's dozen
offices. A side entry gives direct
access to basement shops. The original fenestration provided full lites for
the offices, and a clerestory for the
main banking area.

The small hotel had rooms for
hardly four dozen guests. The main
floor held a central lobby with lunch
room to the left, bakery to the left rear
corner, and cafe and kitchen to the
rear. To the open street side to the
right of the lobby were shops. Basement cisterns were fed from several
rooftop catch basins.

There were twenty-six rooms on
the third floor. Some second-floor

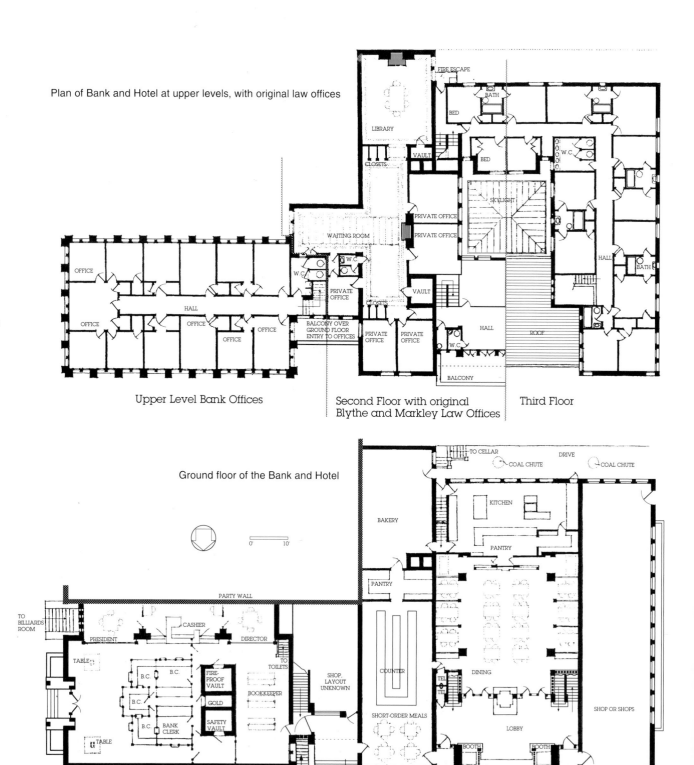

Plan of Bank and Hotel at upper levels, with original law offices

Upper Level Bank Offices

Second Floor with original
Blythe and Markley Law Offices

Third Floor

Ground floor of the Bank and Hotel

City National Bank as originally built

Plan showing alterations for law offices

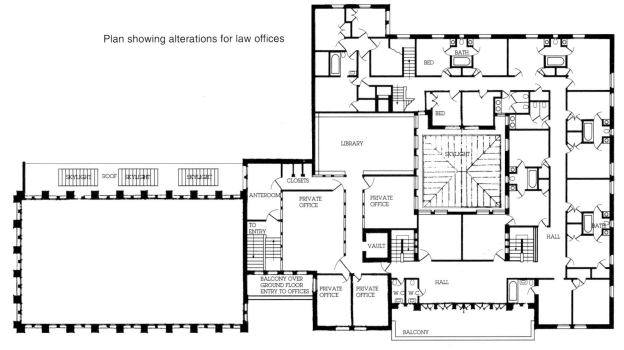

The Hotel

Bank at Clerestory Level

Second Floor of Hotel with Remodeled
Blythe and Markley Law Offices

rooms were converted into offices for the firm of Blythe, Markley, Rule & Smith. These were situated in the east (left) wing of the building and could be reached directly from the central entry between the bank and the hotel, which also gave access to the rear of the bank, a ground-level shop, and the lunch room. The remodeling provided the law partners with a smaller reception room to gain a library. Mahogany board-and-batten trim is used throughout. Interior clerestory windows allow natural light into a hallway at the safe.

The project was nearly two years in construction and was completed by William Drummond during Wright's 1910 travels in Europe. Had Wright been present, Markley's business partner, James E. Blythe, might have become the kind of client that so often failed to materialize for the architect, one with many commissions at his command. The law firm of Blythe, Markley was involved in the 1912 Rock Crest–Rock Glen project, designed by Walter Burley Griffin. Blythe built a Griffin-designed house and commissioned several others, including one for Arthur Rule, partner in the firm. Wright had also designed at this time a house similar to that for Isabel Roberts for J. C. Melson; Melson built a Griffin design. William Drummond and Barry Byrne each designed houses that were built in or near the Rock Glen area. But as these former Wright apprentices were becoming independent of their master, the master himself was breaking free of his own past and looking westward in the second decade of the century for his future in architecture.

This bank and the hotel beside it have been so thoroughly altered by store window fronts cut into the lower wall and other "modernizing" alterations as to disguise their once-elegant appearance. In the 1980s a pedestrian mall was created in front of the bank, and much of the clutter removed. In the late 1980s, Les Nelson Investments purchased the hotel in order to renovate it fully and turn guest rooms into professional offices.

S.158　T.0904
William H. **Copeland Residence Alterations** (1909) and
S.159　T.0922
Garage Alterations (1908)
Oak Park, Illinois
Kitchen remodeled and rear terrace added. Some renovation of the garage done about 1973

Dr. Copeland built his house on one acre of wooded property in 1875. He came to Wright for garage alterations in 1908, then for house alterations a year later. After plans to remodel the house into a three-story Prairie structure with hip roof were rejected, Wright presented Dr. Copeland with a more modest scheme. Of the many alterations intended to give more light to the interior and lower the profile of the structure, few were carried out. The roof pitch was lowered, but the dormer, which was to have run the width of the floor it serves, was left unchanged. A second-story band of windows was not built. After removal of the side porch, the full-length front porch roof was to have been supported only by two substantial symmetrically placed piers, thus replacing post and beam with cantilever. The bays at two levels on the front left were to have been removed. A large bay at the end of the dining room was to have been replaced by a shallow, rectilinear design.

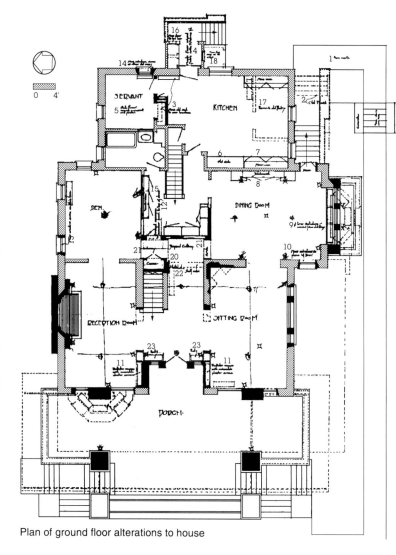

Plan of ground floor alterations to house

THE BLACKENED WALL AREAS AND NUMBERS INDICATE ALTERATIONS. CONSIDERABLE ATTENTION WAS PAID TO NEW ELECTRICAL CONNECTIONS, THE THREE SYMBOLS BELOW INDICATING NEW "BRACKET LIGHTS," OUTLETS IN BASE(BOARDS), AND FLOOR OUTLETS.

ORIGINAL WALLS RETAINED

WALL AND WINDOW AREAS ALTERED BY WRIGHT

WRIGHT'S LABELS AND INSTRUCTIONS INCLUDE:

1. NEW WALK
2. OLD PORCH
3. MOVE OLD RADIATOR TO NEW LOCATION
4. MAPLE FLOOR RAISED FLUSH WITH KITCHEN
5. OAK FLOOR, REMOVE WAINSCOT AND PLASTER
6. OLD SINK
7. NEW CASE
8. SIDEBOARD
9. LOW RADIATORS MOVED FROM OLD BAY
10. NEW WINDOW IN PLACE OF DOOR
11. RADIATOR RECESS WITH REMOVABLE PLASTER SCREEN
12. ARCHED OPENING; CIRCULAR PANEL IN TOP OF DOOR
13. NEW WINDOW SAME AS THIS ONE
14. NEW WINDOWS SAME AS OTHER OLD ONES
15. WARDROBE
16. NEW DOOR TO TOP BOX
17. REMOVE OLD PANTRY
18. NEW FLAT ROOF ON OLD SHED
19. SLOPE OF TERRACE
20. DROPPED CEILING
21. ARCHWAY
22. SHELF OVER
23. RADIATOR

Copeland Residence, entry hall, view to living room

Sideboard by Wright

160

Some detailing, such as the vertical members of the railings, may be by Wright, but his important contributions are to the interior.

Inside, the main floor received a major transformation, from a house of cubicles to one with spaces flowing each to the next, under original 11-foot ceilings. Stringcourses replaced architraves. For the dining room, Wright designed a sideboard, table and chairs, and outward-swinging beveled-glass porch doors. The living room fireplace was remodeled, though not exactly as intended if the plan is an accurate guide. The stairwell was remodeled fully to the second floor in such a manner as to conceal the lack of any Prairie updating to the upper level. The kitchen has been remodeled, and a terrace added at the back.

The 20-by-40-foot garage, to the rear of the lot, had its original steep-pitched roof dropped to a Prairie hip angle. The upper floor was dropped to accommodate living quarters. The side shop, now a separate garage entry, was also added.

Of particular interest is Wright's use of narrow slit windows at the sides of the main garage door framing columns (with wider ones at the second level). This may be his first use of slit windows, and one must wonder why he tried it in a garage. The Brigham residence (S.184) makes a design feature of this device, and the similarity of the stucco and wood trimmed Copeland garage facade with the Brigham concrete and wood trim front facade is striking, lending credence to the latter work's being redated to 1908.

Copeland Garage, front (west) elevation

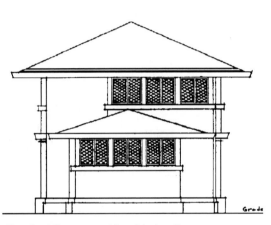

Copeland Garage, end (south) elevation

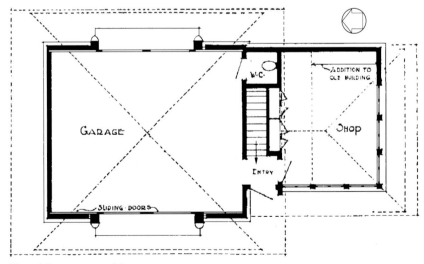

Plan of Garage ground floor

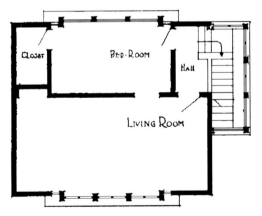

Plan of Garage second floor

S.160   T.0907
Emily and George C. Stewart
Summer Residence, Butterfly
Woods (1909)
Montecito, California
Rear extended at both levels. Front of
house renovated in 1980s

The Stewart family hailed from the
vicinity of Edinburgh, Scotland. The
elder Stewart bought land for Sunny-
side Vineyard in Fresno in the mid-
1800s. A booklet on the seventy-fifth
anniversary of the vineyards mentions
an R. W. Millard as a director, but
whether or not he was related to the
Millard family who built two Wright
designs (S.126, S.214) has not been
ascertained.

In 1906 George C. Stewart
acquired land in Montecito. His wife,
Emily, was interested in design and
was probably responsible for choosing
Wright as their architect. Wright drew
plans for "a board house for Mr.
Stewart at Fresno, California,"
although the house is not in the hot
central valley of California, where the
family was living, but within a mile of
the Pacific Ocean at the Santa
Barbara Channel. Wright sent but six
blueprints, not a full set. This alone
cannot account for significant changes
between design and construction,
which was essentially complete by the
end of 1911. Since Wright was in
Europe from late 1909 to early 1911,
changes had to be effected without the
architect's help.

The first of Wright's California
houses and his only Prairie design in
that state, the Stewart dwelling reveals
Wright's use of Midwestern Prairie
concepts on the Pacific Coast—
two-story-high living room, broad
overhanging roof, and raised living
quarters. The tall, oak-floored living
room is the main feature of the structure. This living room and the house
plan suggest a board-and-batten
reworking of the Isabel Roberts house
(S.150), itself a development and
improvement on the Charles S. Ross
cottage (S.082). The flues of the iron-
spot, standard-sized brick fireplace
split at the second level, providing

Stewart Residence

Living room

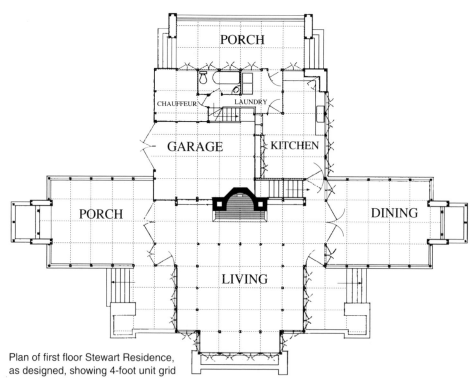

Plan of first floor Stewart Residence,
as designed, showing 4-foot unit grid

access to the balcony overlooking the living room and from there to two bedrooms. The split flue is also employed in the summer cottages for Mrs. Gale (S.088.1–S.088.3) and several other works, including the Ross cottage. At the attic level, a thousand gallon water storage tank is supported by this masonry mass.

The original design called for a garage built into the main floor of the house next to the chauffeur's quarters, an interesting variant on basement garage ideas for Edwin Cheney (S.104, 1903) and Isabel Roberts (S.150, 1908). Instead, the plan was a mirror image, with the servant's quarters and laundry enlarged. Multiple levels abound, some rooms a few steps up, others down, originally so designed with the interior garage arrangement in mind, but retained when that garage was removed.

A separate stable and work shed, now remodeled as a private residence, imitated the all-redwood board-and-batten construction of the main house, but attribution to Wright is doubtful given his other travels.

The windows feature a pattern in clear glass. Wood muntins, rather than zinc cames, create a stylized tree—whether eucalyptus or local pine is not known.

A 4-foot unit is used rigorously throughout but Wright, as if not trusting the contractor, has marked 4′0″ between each grid line. The cruciform plan, symmetrical about the prime axis, is 18 units wide, 15 deep, with the living room a 6-by-6-unit square. This unit is not employed in the vertical dimension.

Almost immediately after construction the rear porch was enclosed, and in the 1930s sleeping porches were added above. Renovations without the help of a preservation-trained architect (the rear additions were left in place) were completed in the 1980s by Gerald Peterson, only the fourth owner of the house.

Reconstruction of plan of second floor Stewart Residence as built

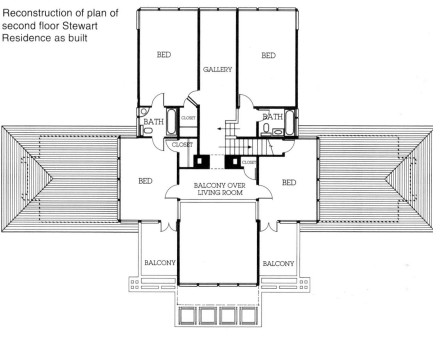

Exterior of living room at entry

Reconstruction of plan of first floor Stewart Residence as built

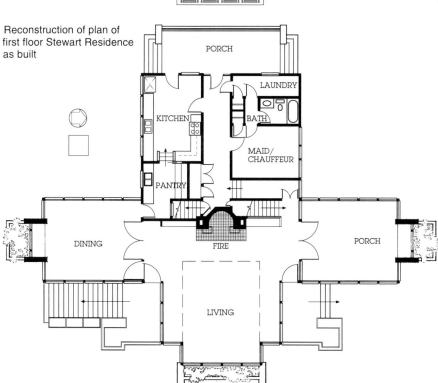

This was joined at the stairwell, with additional storage space that partially supported an added study and lavatory at the second level. In 1981, John D. Tilton removed the porch, modernized the kitchen and added a cruciform family room and open terrace beyond. The original house remains essentially as Wright designed it, unchanged from the rear of the fireplace forward, yet much-needed space was gained by the owner-architect.

Ingalls Residence

S.161   T.0906

J. Kibben **Ingalls** Residence (1909)
River Forest, Illinois
Several additions by William Drummond. House restored in 1981, with single-story family room and terrace added to rear

The Kibben Ingalls structure is an elegantly compact Greek cross in stucco and oak. Entry and dining room provide nearly symmetrical wings south and north of the fireplace mass, with kitchen and pantry to the rear, living room to the front. Above half of the living room is the master bedroom; thus, it lies under the cross roofing, and overlooks the living room roof. Above each wing is a bedroom with cantilevered sleeping balcony. The plan, particularly at the upper story, is very open, for the Ingalls wanted sunlight and fresh air to help cure their children of tuberculosis. The entry has a **U**-shaped wall designed to frame an upright piano and provide a rail for the stairs. The dining room has a unique Wright-designed sideboard that frames a window open to the rear of the 330-foot-deep lot. The porch features an 11-foot cantilever. Art-glass windows are camed with copper, and there are copper sconces to match.

In 1917, William Drummond added a detached garage and in 1926 a porch extending halfway around the kitchen, to the rear of the entry wing.

Sideboard

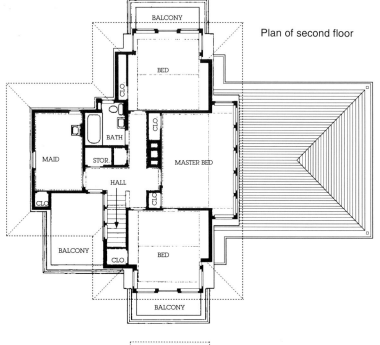

Plan of second floor

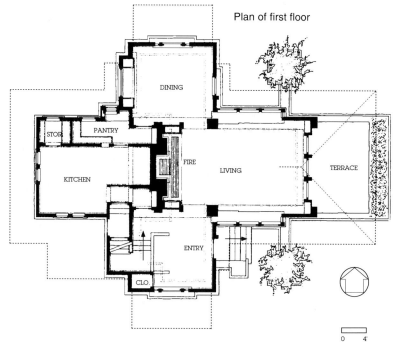

Plan of first floor

0   4'

S.162 T.0910
Peter C. **Stohr Arcade Building**
(1909)
Chicago, Illinois
Demolished, December 1922

The Stohr Arcade was located at the
Wilson Avenue Station of the Chicago
elevated transit system. Most of it was
under the "el" tracks—the structure
incorporated stairs to the ticket booths
and railway—but where the arcade
ducked out from under the tracks, it
rose to three stories. The main-level
row of shops extended the predomi-
nantly horizontal motif from the three-
tiered section. The second-level
windows reveal the influence of one of
the Froebel Gifts, that of rings and
circular segments, three years before
the famous Coonley Playhouse
(S.174) windows.

Stohr Arcade Building

S.163 T.1004
New York City Exhibition (1910)
for the Universal Portland Cement
Company
New York, New York
Demolished

The Universal Portland Cement
Company never had Wright design
them a permanent structure. Wright
did, however, design two works, both
for public fairs. The first was for the
Pan-American Exposition in Buffalo in
1901 (S.063), and the second was this
sculpture for the New York City Exhibition held in the old Madison Square
Garden.

"Portland Cement" in the company
name is not a trademark, but a type of
cement, and can thus be used by any
manufacturer employing the correct
mix and manufacturing process (see
the discussion on p. 61).

New York Exhibition Sculpture

Ziegler Residence

S.164   T.1007
Reverend Jessie R. **Ziegler** Residence (1910)
Frankfort, Kentucky
Rear porch enclosed and room added above it

Presbyterian minister Jessie Ziegler met Wright in Europe, either in or on the way to Italy; local lore claims it was the summer of 1910, but the plans for the Ziegler house are dated February and March 1910. Wright could easily have described what he wanted for this commission (his only built work in Kentucky) in terms of his "Fireproof House for $5000" by telling his Chicago office (Mahony and von Holst) to add a front porch to the living room, change the windows to French doors, and add a half porch to the rear, at the dining room.

As construction was to be unsupervised, the plans are more detailed than usual. Among the more interesting items are the copper-camed sideboard, zinc-camed clear-glass window designs, and oak-framed glass-windowed bookcases dropped from the ceiling over the fireplace mantel, wrapping into the dining room. Outside, the main entry is screened from the neighboring house that hugs the lot line.

Ziegler relinquished ownership after five years to Mr. and Mrs. James Owen Roberts. A succession of owners followed until 1948, when Mrs.

W. C. Weitzel took possession for two dozen years. During her tenure, Wright visited, and later wrote concerning "liberties" taken with the design. The rear porch has been enclosed, and a new room built over the porch.

Dining room sideboard and bookcases dropped from the ceiling

S.165   T.1003
Edward P. and Florence Bernice **Irving Residence** with
S.165A   T.1003
Detached Garage (1909)
Decatur, Illinois
There are interior alterations to modernize the kitchen

This commission came to Wright from Edward P. Irving, an energetic executive president and treasurer of the Faries Manufacturing Company, president and treasurer of Walrus Manufacturing Company, vice-president of Home Ice Cream Company and the Polar Company. Edward died in 1923, but his wife, Florence, remained in the house until 1950. Three owners followed, and the house was vacant in 1972 when purchased by Alice L. Sloan.

This was the last commission that Wright worked on before heading to Europe, with Mamah Borthwick Cheney (S.104), to produce the Wasmuth Portfolio. Drawings on thin onionskin paper, signed by Wright, bear the date October 22, 1909. These plans reveal the architect working as the total artist he wanted to be, designing not only the house but all its furnishings, down to "the maid's uniforms, silverware, china, and fabric, which was loomed in Belgium, and rugs made in Austria," according to a grandson of the original owners. Built-ins are everywhere, and there are grills with zinc-camed art glass in both the upstairs ceiling and stairwell, each lit by skylights in the attic with supplemental electric lighting for night time use. Standard lighting included provision for gas or electricity. Banding of interior plaster deserves special note. Whether or not the furniture delivered to Irving while Wright was in Europe (and sold at auction in 1986) was that designed by Wright or a different design by George M. Niedecken is not certain; it is possible that Niedecken built some of Wright's designs and some of his own and delivered a mixed set.

The plan shows a library and dining room flanking a living room, each over 20 feet long. The extension is nearly doubled by porches to east and west, while interior volume is further doubled by a reception hall, kitchen, and servants' dining room. Four bedrooms for the family, one for the maid, and two sleeping porches (to counter the humid

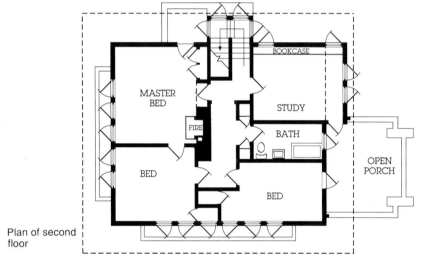

Plan of second floor

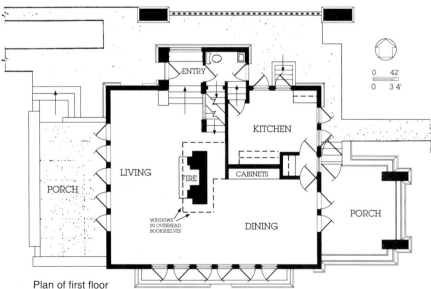

Plan of first floor

Irving Residence

View through art-glass windows to Irving homestead

summers on the prairie), complete the expansive design. Red tile caps the main structure. The garage design is separate, but of the same vernacular, in tan brick.

The property was deeded to Irving in 1909, and construction ran from 1910 to 1913. Between October 1909 and February 1910, Marion Mahony and Hermann V. von Holst, operating out of Wright's Chicago office at 907 Steinway Hall, changed the plaster to brick and moved the foundation 30 feet west so as not to intrude upon the Mueller property (and house by Mahony and von Holst). Mahony enclosed the second-level porch with glass and squared off the entry.

An extensive landscape plan was prepared by Walter Burley Griffin for both the Wright-designed Irving house and the Mahony-designed Mueller house, which was long attributed to Wright.

The kitchen and pantry have been modernized into a single room, and the original coat room combined into the powder room. A mural by George Niedecken has long since been covered. Garage doors were restored from photographs.

Hot water heat was specified, with the heating plant in the basement of the detached garage to the rear. A separate transformer-power building is west of the garage.

Plan of ground floor

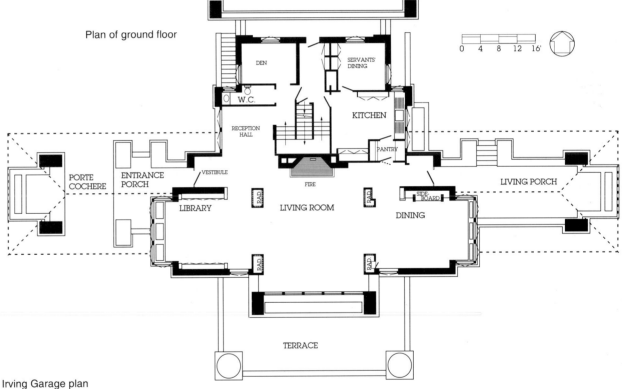

0 4 8 12 16'

Irving Garage plan

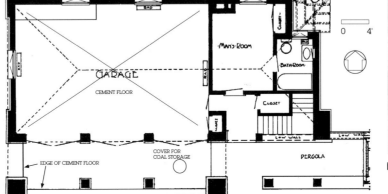

0 4'

Irving Detached Garage

Waller Bathing Pavilion

S.166 T.0916
Edward C. **Waller Bathing Pavilion** (1909)
Charlevoix, Michigan
Demolished by fire 1922 or 1923

One end of Waller Road on the north side of Charlevoix is the main U.S. highway in this part of the woods. The other comes to a **T** intersection just a stone's throw from an enormous sand hill, the other side of which drops to a rocky beach at the edge of Lake Michigan. Rocks are mixed with sand, not a typical or traditional bathing beach, but normal here in Charlevoix. Roughly north and east of this Waller Road dividing line, Edward C. Waller (S.030, S.031, S.047, S.065, S.066) purchased 2,000 acres of clearcut timber land "halfway to Petosky," as the editor of the Charlevoix *Courier* put it. He replanted it with pine trees and built his bathing pavilion on a dune rise overlooking Lake Michigan and Beaver Head Lighthouse seven leagues away on Beaver Island.

Chicagoans often vacationed in Michigan or nearby Canada—Grand Beach (S.197–S.199), the Gales and Gerts at Whitehall (S.077–S.078, S.088.0–S.088.4), Les Cheneaux Club on Marquette Island (S.075), and Sapper Island (S.076) involved Wright clients. For places close to Chicago, they arrived by train; further up the Lake Michigan coast, they arrived by steamer. Charlevoix was a steamer stop. Lake Charlevoix opens to Lake Michigan via a channel, much like White Lake opens Whitehall and its Wright clients to water-borne traffic. On high sand bluffs on the north and east side of Lake Charlevoix lies the Chicago Club for vacationers from nearly 300 miles south; on the opposite shore the Belvidere Club was for summering St. Louisians.

Based on Wright's drawings for Waller (who first bought an 1882 house, then commissioned Wright for a suitable design), a 12-bedroom summer house was to be built on the Chicago Club bluffs. Neither the first nor a second, more detailed, scheme was built. After a six-year hiatus, attempts to build in Charlevoix apparently produced only the bathing pavilion. The relatively large structure, 64 feet along the beach frontage with an 18-foot-deep living room dominated by a fireplace, was board-and-batten construction, single story with shingled, hipped roof. There were nicely detailed windows and a large front terrace.

(Note: the work originally listed as S.166, the J. Hattie Amberg residence, was designed by Marion Mahony while she and Herman V. von Holst were maintaining the Steinway Hall office in Chicago during Wright's sojourn in Europe.)

S.167
Women's Building (1914)
Inter-County Fairgrounds, Spring Green, Wisconsin
Demolished

The Spring Green *Home News* of Thursday, July 16, 1914, provides the following notice: "It is proposed that a Neighborhood club be formed. This club will include both men and women of Spring Green and the surrounding country, who are interested in the improvement of Spring Green and neighborhood, in sanitation, education, beauty, and other conditions which shall conduce to the health, morality, happiness and general good citizenship of its people. Any person may become a member of this club by signing the constitution and paying fifty cents annually to the treasurer."

The illustration in the newspaper hardly resembles what was finally built, though both the open children's play yard and covered exhibition space are present in the low, gabled wood structure that was erected. Inside were burlap-covered partitions, and the exterior walls could apparently be entirely removed when weather permitted.

The building was to be formally dedicated on September 2. On Thursday, August 13, Wright went to Chicago to work on Midway Gardens; that Saturday, Julian Carlton set fire to Taliesin, killing Mamah Bouton Borthwick Cheney and her two children, John and Martha. The manuscript copy of her Goethe biography was also destroyed in the fire—what irony in light of the fact that Margaret Fuller, Transcendentalist compatriot of Ralph Waldo Emerson, had died at sea returning from Europe to Boston with her completed Goethe biography.

Despite the tragedy, Wright provided a full exhibition of his oriental pottery, brocades, and such for the (September Inter-County) fair, and shortly thereafter took rural mailmen attending a picnic at the fairgrounds on an auto tour of Taliesin, already being rebuilt.

(Note: The Robert Mueller Residence, immediately east of the Irving residence, S.165, once assigned this number, is most certainly not by Wright. The majority of the design may be by Marion Mahony, and the hand of Walter Burley Griffin, later to be her husband, seems evident. The design in the stucco between the four pilasters is stylistically similar to Mahony's house for David or J. Hattie Amberg in Grand Rapids, formerly listed as S.166, giving additional credence to her participation in the authorship of this building.)

Women's Building

Balch Residence

S.168   T.1102
O. B. **Balch** Residence (1911)
Oak Park, Illinois
Balconies enclosed. Renovated in 1991

Oscar B. Balch was an interior decorator for whom Wright had remodeled a shop in 1907 (S.131). The Balch residence, one of Wright's earliest designs after his return from Europe, is very formal, axially symmetrical (library and dining room framing the living room with central, tan Roman brick fireplace). Further, privacy, which seems to become an obsession with the architect, is provided by the concealing of the entry, the high-walled terrace, the security wall to the south, and other elements of design.

Fifty windows, most of the casement type, open the structure to natural air conditioning. Renovation and upgrading of the kitchen and some exterior design elements were completed in 1991. Once open balconies have long since been enclosed.

Wright's hand-drawn perspective sketch reveals an affinity between this built work and the Yahara Boat Club project designed six years earlier for Madison, Wisconsin, claimed by the architect as the spiritual progenitor of all his flat-roofed designs.

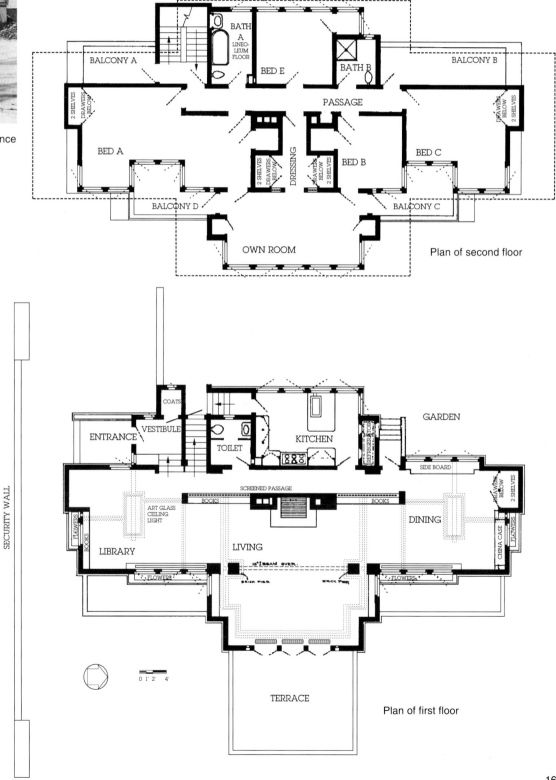

Plan of second floor

Plan of first floor

Herbert Angster Residence (1911)
Lake Bluff, Illinois
Demolished

In 1909, the major project on Wright's drafting table was a "summer" residence for Harold McCormick in Lake Forest, a magnificent multi-pavilioned design for a site overlooking Lake Michigan. Construction of it would have meant acceptance of Wright by the country's conservative industrial magnates. The project seems to have been scuttled largely by Edith Rockefeller McCormick because her advocacy of Jung did not meet with Wright's approval. Some evidence suggests that Mrs. Angster, a sister of Sherman Booth, Jr., may have been a secretary to Harold McCormick, perhaps the first connection for the Angsters with the architect, which became a long-term and strong relationship.

Angster Residence

The Angster dwelling is essentially a single-story building of cement plaster and cypress trim with the master bedroom on the ground floor. The entry well gives one many choices: kitchen on the left, the stairs ahead, the living room on the right, and the master bedroom. A dropped ceiling articulates an area in front of the fireplace. The master bedroom and its porch extension form a **T** plan. The upstairs is quite shallow, with only a small guest bedroom, with a closet between the fireplace flues, and a servant's room.

Landscaping of the grounds was extensive. Even after a contemporary house was placed over the footprint of the Wright design in the 1960s, evidence of the layout, including a multicar garage (Angster was an automobile enthusiast) remained.

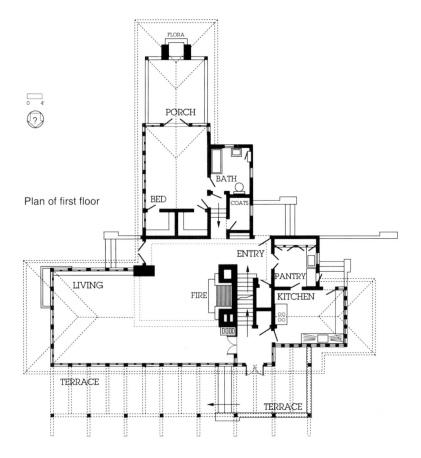

Plan of first floor

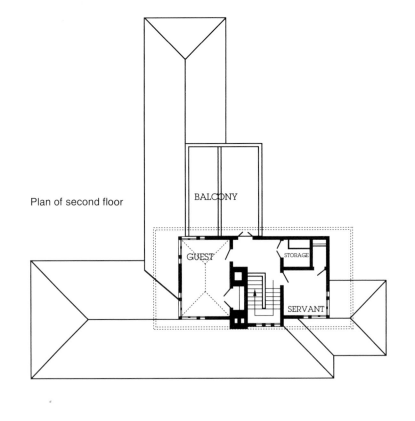

Plan of second floor

View looking east to Mount Rundle

S.170   T.1302
Banff National Park Pavilion
(1911)
Alberta, Canada
Demolished, 1939

A very long, board-and-batten structure supported by stone massings with steel beams holding the cantilevered roofing, this pavilion was somewhat similar to the River Forest Tennis Club (S.119), particularly in the framing of the interior space on three sides by fireplaces. A ladies' powder room was in one terminus, men's retiring room in the other, of this narrow building. A clerestory lighted the interior pavilion.

Wright worked as designer in association with Francis C. Sullivan, a Canadian architect, on this and perhaps three other projects. Sullivan had worked in Wright's Oak Park studio and set up his own practice in Ottawa in 1911. Over the next five or

six years, Sullivan would see some twenty of his designs built, but his overbearing demands on contractors and his public arguments with "eclectic" architects would cost him his practice. While the pavilion is clearly Wright's design, the other three projects, a library, a post office, and a house, are less so. Though the public library in Pembroke, Ontario, is composed of Prairie elements, it looks more like other buildings done by Sullivan outside his association with Wright than anything to which Wright might have contributed. An Ottawa post office building is presumed demolished and not otherwise known, and documents on a Double House (compare S.077) in Ottawa are lacking.

Interior

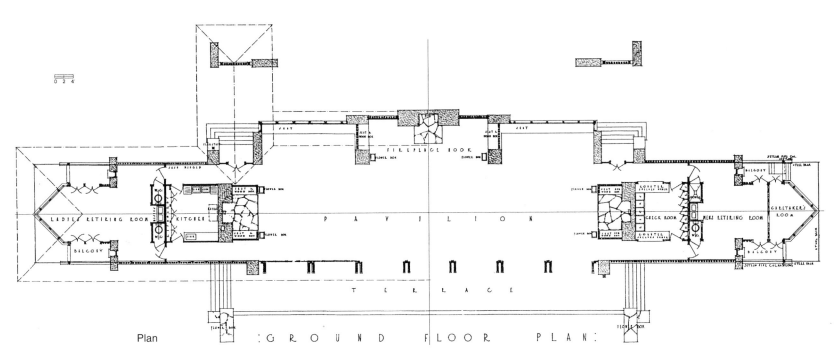

Plan

Lake Geneva Hotel

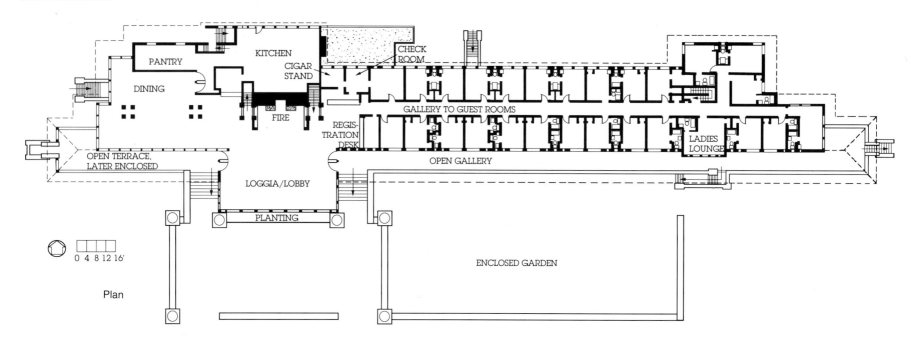

Plan

S.171   T.1202
Lake Geneva Hotel (1911) for
Arthur L. Richards and John J.
Williams
Lake Geneva, Wisconsin
Demolished, 1970

This was the first design from Wright
built by Arthur L. Richards, a real
estate developer from Milwaukee
(S.201–S.204). It was developed as a
project by the Artistic Building Company, formed by John J. Williams and
Richards. While in its last years, the

hotel was known as the Geneva Inn, it
was christened the Lake Geneva
Hotel. It was a Prairie-style structure of
wood frame, with the main lobby
featuring a large Roman brick fireplace. Dining and entertainment
facilities were west of the entry, guest
rooms in the east wing. Plain and identical, these rooms could have allowed
for indefinite extension of this wing to
accommodate any number of guests.

The original plan shows that
detached guest cottages were considered, but they were erased and the
current plan drawn over that design.
Further, a major three-story cross-axis

section, shown in a watercolor perspective, was never built.

The hotel had a major effect upon
the town, which it once dominated; a
local water supply had to be established, and the coal-burning ships on
the lake were required to use a coal
which would give off limited ash and
smoke.

S.172   T.1104
Taliesin I (1911) for Frank Lloyd
Wright
Spring Green, Wisconsin
Fire destroyed living quarters, August
15, 1914

The first Taliesin was built in the Valley
of the Lloyd Joneses within view of
Unity Chapel (S.000). Taliesin provided
a home for Wright's mother, Anna
Lloyd Jones Wright, and a meeting
place for Wright's local Welsh breth-
ren. It also provided a haven for Wright
and Mamah Borthwick Cheney, wife of
a former client (S.104), with whom the
architect had gone to Europe in 1909.
It was around the hill from the second
Hillside Home School (S.069). Taliesin
grew from a home into a farm and
architectural studio over the years and
was rebuilt twice because of fire
damage (see S.182 and S.218). The
grounds also included additional
buildings, some by Wright and some
not, such as a dam and power house.
Living quarters of the main house were
destroyed by fire; other quarters survive in today's Taliesin III (S.218). The
disaster was caused by Julian Carlton,
a black from Chicago, whose father

may have been a slave, from Cuba or
Barbados. Carlton locked all the doors
but one, where he stood, with hatchet
in hand. Jailed in Dodgeville, Carlton
died while on a hunger strike. Mamah
Borthwick and her two children Martha
and John, with four others, died in the
fire.

Taliesin I with main driveway, garden, and loggia

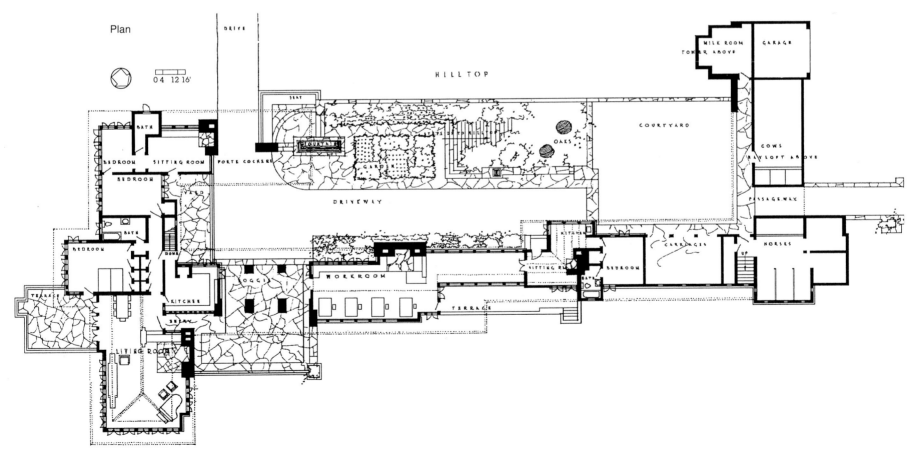

Plan

S.173   T.1304
Francis W. **Little Residence II,**
Northome (1912)
Deephaven, Minnesota
Demolished, 1972
Living room reconstructed in the
Metropolitan Museum of Art, New York
City. Library reconstructed in the
Allentown Art Museum, Pennsylvania.
Bedroom wing stored at Domino's
Farms, Ann Arbor, Michigan

Wright's first building in Minnesota
used its site most effectively. Overlooking Robinson Bay of Lake Minnetonka,
the 55-foot living room, perhaps
Wright's most spacious domestic interior from this Prairie period, opened its
secondary view inland. Sleeping quarters were also on the main and upper
floors, opposite the living room and
over the dining space, which nestled in
a hilly depression. Two adjacent buildings, though of Prairie board-and-

Little Residence II living room (photograph made while the building was on its original site, from west end)

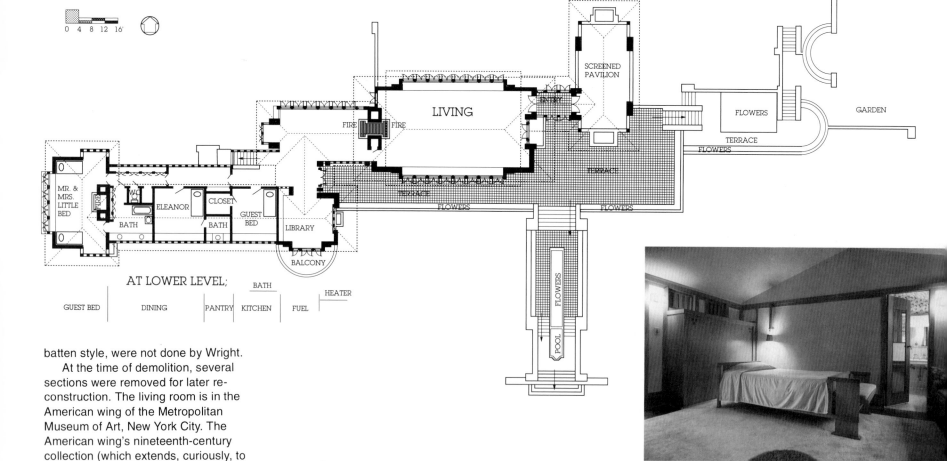

batten style, were not done by Wright.
   At the time of demolition, several
sections were removed for later reconstruction. The living room is in the
American wing of the Metropolitan
Museum of Art, New York City. The
American wing's nineteenth-century
collection (which extends, curiously, to
World War I) is housed on the ground
floor. This means that the reconstructed living room has been set in a
depression like the original dining

Bedroom in Little Residence II (photograph from the
house on its original site)

Bathroom in Little Residence II (photogra[ph]
from the house on its original si[te]

174

Little Residence II Library as rebuilt
in Allentown

room, where its only exterior view is of
rising grass to the south; perched on a
knoll at its original site, the room had
as primary view the blue of northern
sky and lake. Fortunately, even in this
indoor setting, natural light prevails, in
decided and welcome contrast to most
historic room re-creations. The original
northern exposure is necessarily
blocked, in this museum setting, by
masonry. Passing through the room
is not permitted, nor is one allowed to
sit and view the space as Wright
intended. Craig Miller was project
director for the rebuilding.

The library now opens on an
enclosed courtyard at the Allentown
Art Museum in eastern Pennsylvania.
Reconstruction was by architect and
former Taliesin apprentice Edgar Tafel.

Windows from the Second Little
Residence are in the collections of
museums in Dallas, Minneapolis, and
Karlsruhe.

S.174   T.1201
Avery **Coonley Playhouse** (1912)
Riverside, Illinois
Converted to domestic use. Original
windows replicated

Scaled-down from original plans,
this is still an imposing design. At Mrs.
Coonley's famous original "cottage
school," theatrical activity was expected from the students. This new
building, then, featured a stage at the
back of the cruciform crossing, the
usual centrally located fireplace being
a permanent backdrop thereto. The
kitchen (countertops were specially
built to child's height) and shop
straddled the crossing, which was part
of the assembly room. This design
feature reappears in nicely modified
form in the Wyoming Valley Grammar
School (S.401) forty-four years later.
The beautiful "balloons and confetti"
triptych windows have been removed
to the Metropolitan Museum of Art in
New York, and the clerestory windows
have been placed into separate private
ownership. Development of the fanciful
designs in glass may have been
triggered by a visit in 1910 to Paris,
where Wright would have seen a
similar design on the floor of the Petit
Palais.

Following a long-term program
prepared by John Vinci, recent owners
have renovated the structure by
removing various accretions of the
years. There are 22 clerestory
windows. Replicas were installed in
1988–89. The flash opal-colored
glass was redeveloped and hand-
blown in Germany for assembly at
the Oakbrook-Esser Studios in
Oconomowoc, Wisconsin. This art
glass is 3/16 inch thick and white; a
separate micro-thin layer of color is
flashed onto the surface. This allows
the glass to appear plain outside
during the day, yet the design inside is
brightly colored; stained glass would
be visible outside and would not be as
bright inside. At night, the pattern is
visible outside, but appears as pastel
color; with stained glass, the color
would be bright outside at night. A
garage to the rear was designed by
William Drummond about 1919.

Coonley Playhouse

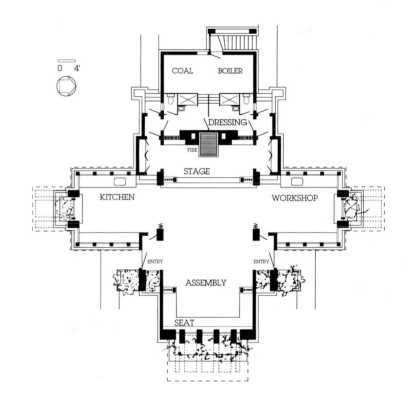

175

Park Ridge Country Club
Remodeling (1912)
Park Ridge, Illinois
Demolished

Two existing buildings (the larger outside the photograph to the right, the
smaller left center) were linked in
Wright's alterations by a covered
walkway. Additional spaces, a "19th
hole" terrace and dancing court, were
defined by the new layout, and the
whole was given a horizontal character
by the board-and-batten siding,
liberally applied. Rows of screens
open the interior to summer breezes.

William B. **Greene** Residence
(1912)
Aurora, Illinois
Significantly enlarged by Harry
Robinson. Screened veranda replaced
by enclosed, heated porch

Familiar elements are present here:
plaster surface, wood trim, hipped roof.
Upstairs is a minor variation of the
Fireproof House in its Stockman
version. The main floor has the living
room running along two-thirds of the
east wall between veranda and fireplace. Connected to it on the southwest corner is the dining room. Harry
Robinson, Wright's draftsman, was
involved in the original drawings and
supervision of construction and was
called upon in 1926 to add a new,
larger dining room and master bedroom wing. The old veranda, once
screened, was removed, and an
enclosed, heated porch added in 1961
by Robert Mall, for William A. Greene,
son of the original client. There is also
a full basement.

Park Ridge Country Club Remodeling

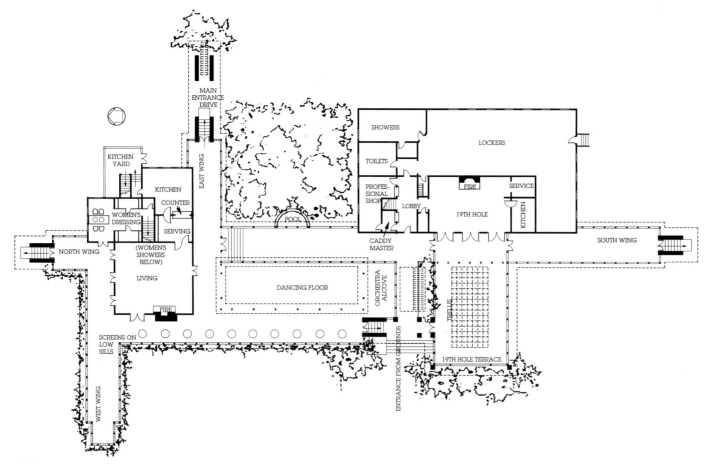

Greene house
from southwest,
before addition

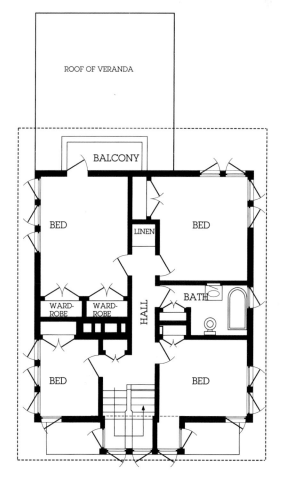

The Greene house from the north, showing Harry Robinson's additions on the right

Living room, veranda through doors on left, dining room to right

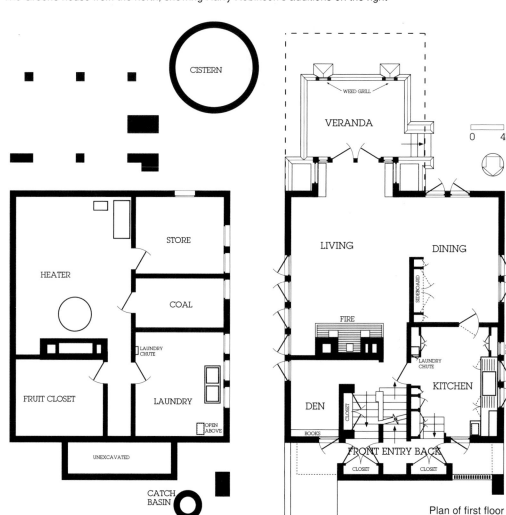

CISTERN

STORE

HEATER

COAL

LAUNDRY
CHUTE

FRUIT CLOSET

LAUNDRY

UNEXCAVATED

CATCH
BASIN

Plan of basement

VERANDA

WEED GRILL

0   4'

LIVING

DINING

SIDEBOARD

FIRE

LAUNDRY
CHUTE

ICE
DOOR

DEN

CLOSET

KITCHEN

BOOKS

OPEN
ABOVE

FRONT ENTRY BACK

CLOSET

CLOSET

Plan of first floor

ROOF OF VERANDA

BALCONY

BED

LINEN

BED

WARD-
ROBE

WARD-
ROBE

HALL

BATH

BED

BED

Plan of second floor

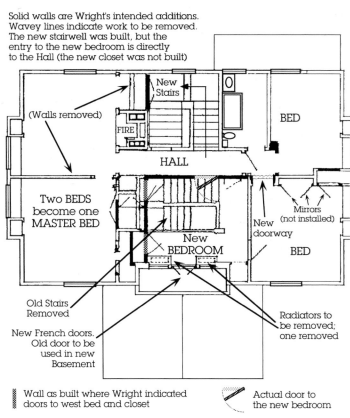

Solid walls are Wright's intended additions.
Wavey lines indicate work to be removed.
The new stairwell was built, but the
entry to the new bedroom is directly
to the Hall (the new closet was not built)

▌▌ Wall as built where Wright indicated
doors to west bed and closet

⟋ Actual door to
the new bedroom

Plan of second floor remodeling

S.177   T.1114
Walter Gerts Residence
Remodeling (1911)
River Forest, Illinois

This house was originally designed by
Charles E. White, Jr., and built in 1905.
It was published by Herman V. von
Holst in his *Modern American Homes*
(1928) as "A Frame and Stucco
Country House." After a fire, Walter
Gerts (see also S.078) asked Wright
for a remodeling.

The major part of Wright's work
involved relocation of the stairwell from
its central location to the rear of the
house, gaining thereby an open foyer
and much freer flow of traffic. This
remains, though the intended offset
entry to the newly created front bedroom has been moved to a place
directly opposite the stairs. Leaded
glass designs remain unexecuted, and
glass doors were never installed as
Wright had desired.

(Note: The Florida Cottage in Palm
Beach, Florida, once listed under this
number, was a design by Walter Burley
Griffin. It was demolished in the mid-
1970s.)

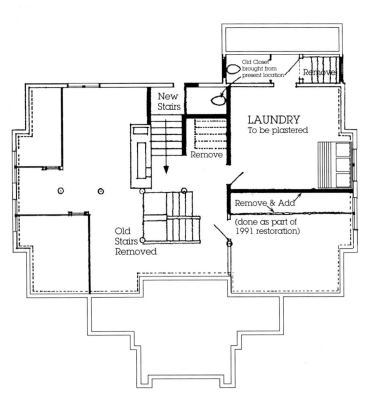

Plan of basement remodeling

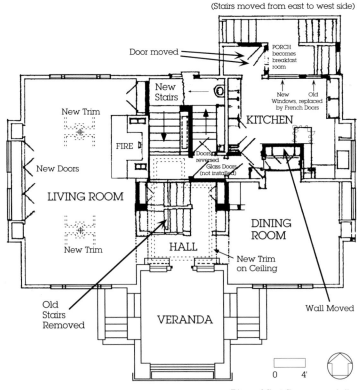

Plan of first floor remodeling

178

Detail of leaded glass window in Booth Cottage

S.178   T.1119
Sherman M. **Booth Cottage** (1911)
Glencoe, Illinois

Local lore has it that this was a honeymoon cottage for "Sylvan" Booth (Sylvan Road is the northeast entry to the subdivision) and that the original plan was hand-sketched by Wright on a brown paper bag. The original plan has since been found, proving the structure to be by Wright though it was hardly built to his standards. This was

the first house in the area that became the Ravine Bluffs Development (S.185–S.192), and apparently was moved from its original site to its present location in 1916.

(No evidence of construction of the M. B. Hilly residence, previously listed as S.178, has been found.)

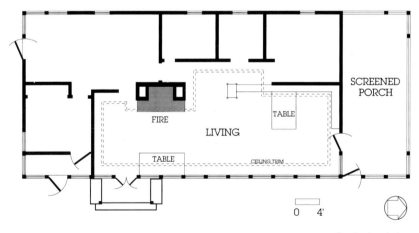

Conjectural plan

S.179   T. 1301
Harry S. Adams Residence with
S.179A
Detached **Garage** (1913)
Oak Park, Illinois

This large brick structure, 70 feet end to end, with its horizontality emphasized by limestone bands at the sill level of both stories, is Wright's valedictory statement to Oak Park. It represents a summation of his Prairie

Harry S. Adams Residence

Door panel with glass insets

ideals just as he was turning the page in his career to Midway Gardens and new ideas. It is the second scheme for the client after many revisions to the first proved futile. From the porte-cochere, one steps up to a soffit-shielded walkway that passes an office and the living room on the way to the entry. Adams, who lived only three years in the house (apparently his wife did not enjoy it) was a physician; the office here, however, was for meeting tradesmen who came to present their bills. It has been converted to a sun room with bar.

The front door deserves special mention for its art glass, the colored glass transmitting inside a range of colors from gold to green, outside reflecting a different set of colors. The entry hallway separates the living room from the dining room, kitchen, and breakfast porch (since enclosed). Above were four bedrooms, three baths (two small ones now converted to one commodious unit) and a sewing

(Continues)

room, now part of the master bedroom. White oak is used for trim, with stringcourses unifying elements, and vertical bands, especially articulating corners, framing the light buff plaster. The building is notable for Wright's design of perforated copper lighting fixtures both overhead and attached to moldings. Thin leaded windows and furniture, especially a dining room buffet, by Wright reveal the architect's complete mastery of a style he was at the time seeking to abandon or utterly transform.

Detached Garage

Living room

Dining room sideboard

Ceiling light in the dining room

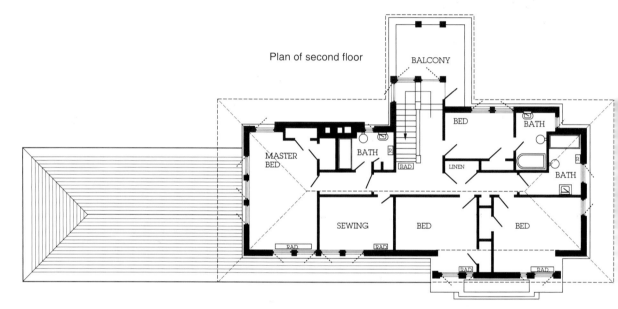

Plan of second floor

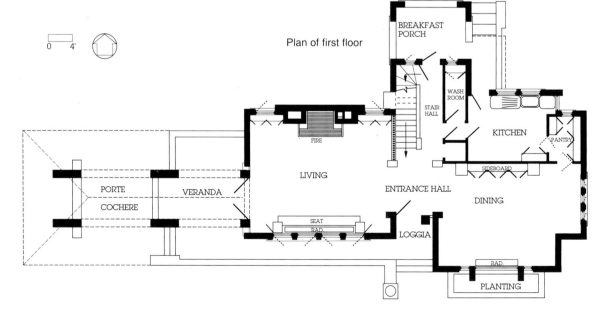

Plan of first floor

S.180 T.1401
Midway Gardens (1913) for
Edward C. Waller, Jr.
Chicago, Illinois
Demolished 1929

The Wallers were good clients for Wright. Edward, Sr., commissioned many designs and built several (S.030, S.031, S.047, S.065, S.066, S.166). Edward, Jr., built Midway Gardens. The richness of architectural expression, in patterned concrete block and brick, was exceptional. A double (thus square) city block, the southwest corner of Cottage Grove Avenue and 60th Street, where Midway Plaisance meets Washington Park, was enclosed by the structure, while the interior court was open to the elements yet separated from the harshness of urban life. This courtyard was the Summer Garden, a dancing and eating area. To the sides were low arcades, also for eating and dancing, with a band shell at one end. The Winter Garden opposite, enclosed for year-round activity, was four floors high with a covered area roughly equal to the Summer Garden. The first floor was embraced by a series of three terraces around the main floor area. This was capped by a roof garden.

John Vogelsang joined Waller in this project, guiding Wright on matters of quality food preparation; the kitchen was in the basement, thus nearer the areas served. Sculptures by Alfonso Ianelli adorned the work, and John Lloyd Wright, a son of the architect, assisted in construction supervision. Paul Mueller was in charge of construction; he seemed to find building Wright's complex structures a particular joy, working on such others as Unity Temple (S.096) and the Imperial Hotel (S.194).

Prohibition was but one of the many factors that destroyed the Midway Gardens pleasure palace. The First World War forced revenues below the break-even point. Then, two years after being opened, it was purchased by the Edelweiss Brewing Company and converted to serve the needs of a clientele hardly accustomed to its refined surroundings.

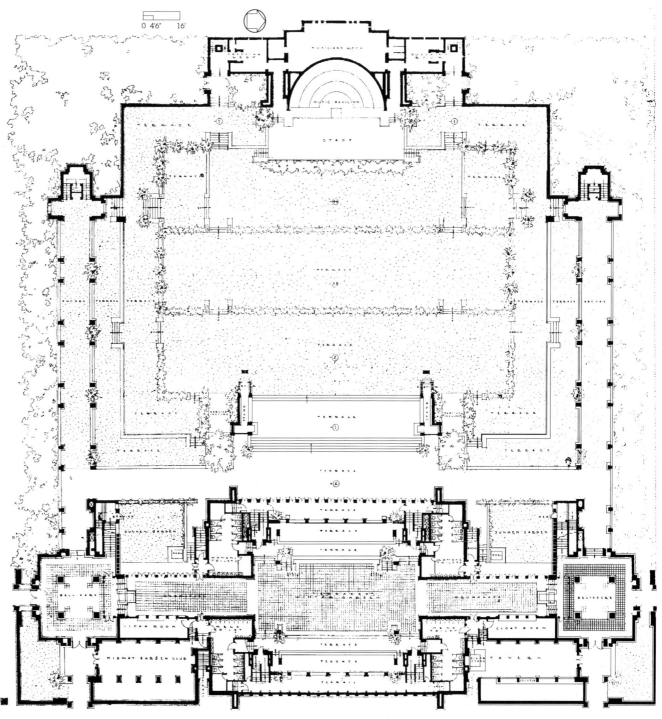

Midway Gardens overall plan

Cottage Grove Avenue

(Continues)

(**S.180** *continued*)

Midway Gardens, on Cottage Grove Avenue

Midway Gardens main floor of Winter Garden with terraces
and balcony above

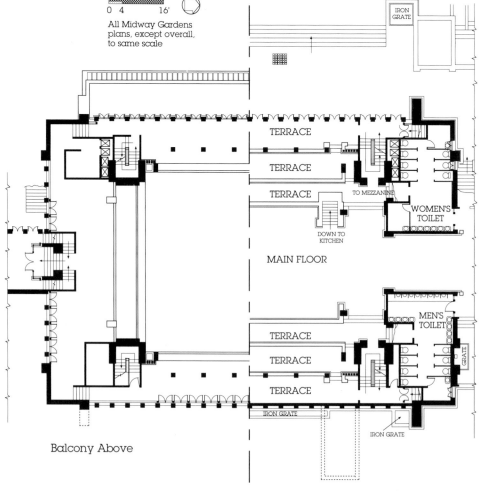

All Midway Gardens
plans, except overall,
to same scale

0 4   16'

IRON GRATE

TERRACE

TERRACE

TERRACE

TO MEZZANINE

DOWN TO KITCHEN

WOMEN'S TOILET

MAIN FLOOR

MEN'S TOILET

TERRACE

TERRACE

TERRACE

GRATE

IRON GRATE

IRON GRATE

Balcony Above

Plan of Winter Garden first floor (with terraces) to right, balcony above (mirror-imaged) to left

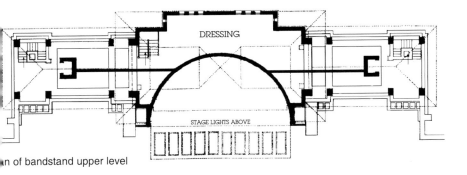

n of bandstand upper level

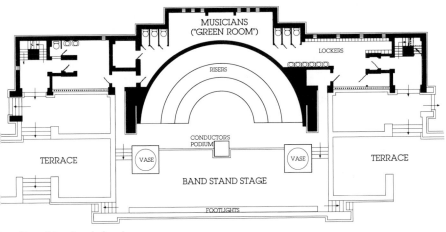

an of bandstand main level

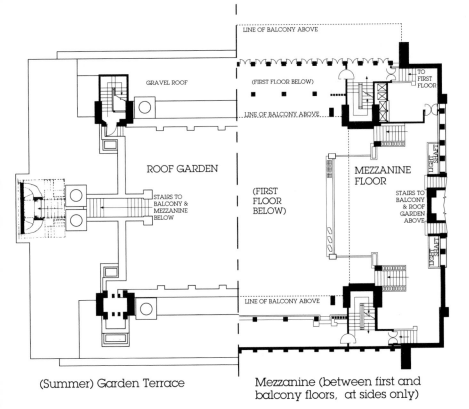

(Summer) Garden Terrace   Mezzanine (between first and balcony floors, at sides only)

Plan of Winter Garden rooftop Garden Terrace to left, mezzanine level to right

Mori Oriental Art Studio (1914)
Chicago, Illinois
Demolished

The southeast, high-ceilinged corner room on the eighth floor of the Fine Arts Building on Michigan Avenue is quite large, larger than the rooms used for two other Wright-designed shops in the same building, Browne's Bookstore (S.141) and the Thurber Art Gallery (S.154). Here, however, in keeping with the nature of the product being offered for sale—Japanese prints—spaces were divided neither by traditional stalls nor by walls. The stalls and display screens that Wright designed were made of fabric on frames. The one known photo of the studio has been lost, but the display cases and furniture survive, since they were removed from the Fine Arts Building and used at other locations. One characteristic feature of Wright's work was the geometrical design of the lighting fixtures; similar types can be seen in the interiors previously mentioned as well as the Rookery Building Remodeling (S.113).

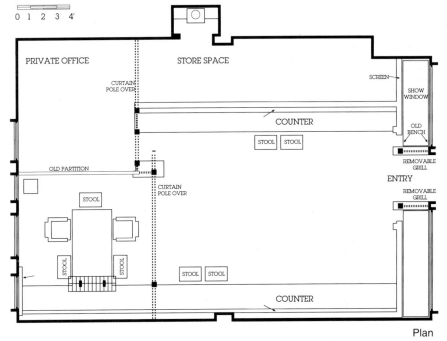

Plan

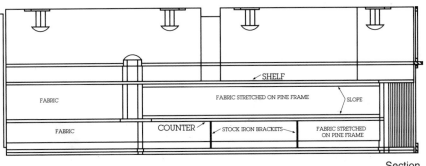

Section

Taliesin II, dining area in living room

S.182   T.1403
Taliesin II (1914) for Frank Lloyd
Wright
Spring Green, Wisconsin
Destroyed by fire, 1925

Wright's sprawling home in the Lloyd
Jones Valley had its living quarters
destroyed by fire twice. This listing
represents Taliesin as rebuilt when
living quarters of Taliesin I (S.172)
were destroyed in 1914. The building,
as it survives today, is Taliesin III
(S.218). The basic shape of Taliesin is
determined by its masonry, and this
has been changed little by fire. Each
rebuilding brought about enlargement
and changes in detail.

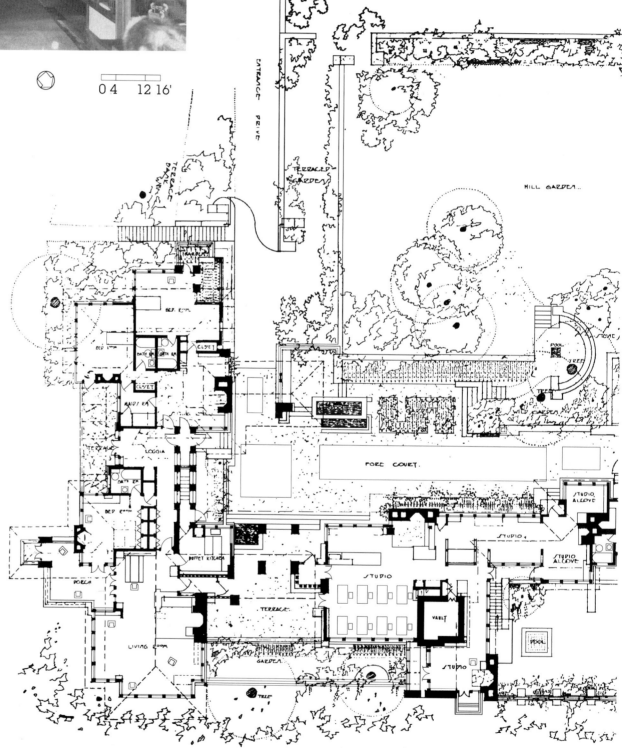

Detail plan of living quarters

0 4   12 16'

S.183 T.1504
A. D. German Warehouse (1915)
Richland Center, Wisconsin
Converted to a variety of alternative uses

Frank Lloyd Wright was born in or near Richland Center on June 8, 1867, Albert Dell German on December 18, 1875; both claimed Welsh descent. After Wright moved from Chicago to Spring Green, he did much of his shopping at A. D. German, dealer in coal, hay, grain, and cement. In 1912 German built a two-story (plus basement) warehouse next to the Badger Hotel, which he had purchased in 1907, when it was called the Mitchell and was owned by his father-in-law, Dr. George Mitchell. When Wright could not pay his bills, German took payment in the form of a design for a new warehouse to meet the demands of a rapidly growing business. Demolition of the hotel began in December 1916.

The new building was to be a place for storing and selling wholesale goods as well as providing space for a teahouse restaurant, retail shops, and art gallery. It was to be built of reinforced concrete, with a brick face, capped by a patterned block encircling the fourth floor. The job of mixing the concrete, for which the U.S. Bureau of Standards and Testing had just set standards when construction began (though few seemed to notice or follow them) in 1917 fell to the son of John Daughhetee Dillard; the cement was Chicago AA. River sand helped this become concrete; its tan color and cleanliness was prized.

Construction proceeded slowly. The original $30,000 projected cost was soon passed, $125,000 approached. Construction stopped in 1921, the building unfinished. Finances had not been good for German during the war, and things did not significantly improve thereafter. Unpaid taxes cost him the building in

1932; he bought it back in 1935 but lost it finally in 1937.

After a succession of owners, in 1980 the structure came under the ownership of Harvey Glanzer, who had bought the Willey house (S.229) in 1975, and Beth Caulkins, who operates the gift shop. John H. Howe, who had worked on drawings for the Willey house, was hired as renovation architect. The building is on the National Register of Historic Places.

German Warehouse

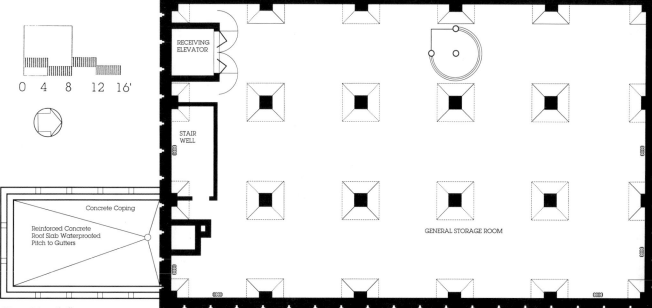

Plan of fourth floor

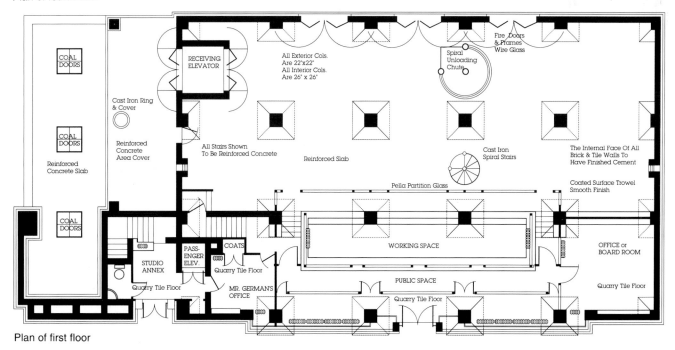

Plan of first floor

185

Edmund F. **Brigham Residence** and
S.184A
Detached **Garage** (1908/15)
Glencoe, Illinois
Porch enclosed. Kitchen area altered.
Restoration of house begun in late
1980s. Garage demolished 1968

Though apparently built the same year
as the projects for Sherman Booth
(S.178, S.185–S.192), the design concept dates to 1908. Brigham was a Chicago and Northwestern Rail Road executive from 1914 to the end of the
decade and construction of his 1908
design (and preparation of working
drawings) may have been put off until
his circumstances improved. Preliminary plans were done in Wright's Oak
Park office, which the architect did not
use after 1909. Wright did not supervise construction of this house, but it
was built much as he specified; most
of the changes were made at the rear
area in the kitchen, which was widened one unit (mullion centers of 45
inches suggest the unit used; the
poured-in-forms concrete walls are half
this thick).

The plan, like that of the Evans
house (S.140), begins as a version of
the "Fireproof House for $5000"—this
being the only known version actually
done in concrete—and is then expanded by wings to two sides. Particularly
important in this version is the veranda, which significantly extends the
main floor to the south. There is no
separate dining room; space on one
side of the living room serves this
purpose. The area behind the fireplace
leads to stairs and a maid's room. The
entry was concealed on the north side,
with steps leading up from the porte-
cochere (as in the Evans house). A
later change created an opening to the
street front. The reception area flows
into the living room. An inglenook was
intended for the fireplace; a pair of
benches was to have extended from
the fireplace masonry to two brick
piers. There is also a full basement,
with laundry, root cellar, furnace room
and coal storage, and servant's bathroom. The bedroom story was flipped
front to rear. Instead of corner flower
boxes, the upstairs corner "piers" are
closets and baths.

Of particular note is Wright's use of
narrow (3 inches wide) slit windows.
They serve as "frames" for the corner

Brigham Residence

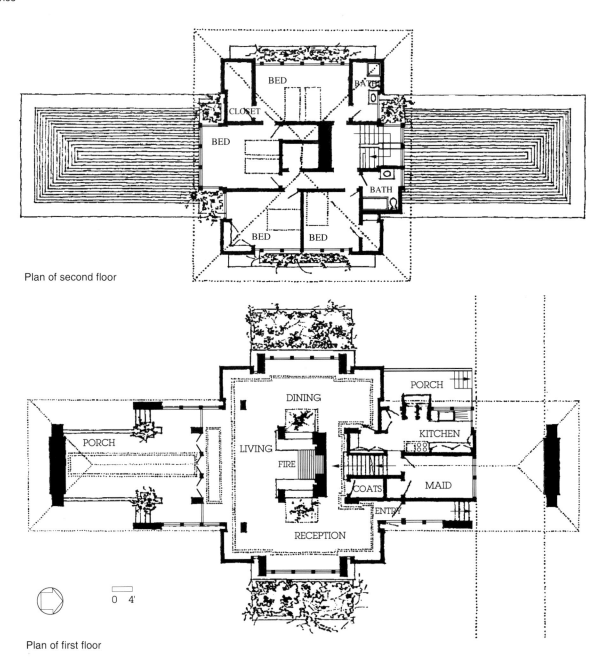

Plan of second floor

Plan of first floor

Living room, French doors to veranda

Fireplace in living room

piers, making the corners seem to float free from the main mass of the living room (for further discussion, see the Copeland garage, S.159). Note, too, that the front tripartite window columns, set just inside these slit windows, rise only to the second-level sill line, where the horizontal porch wall trim, backed by the darkness of glazing against the light painted concrete, strongly emphasizes the cantilever of the roof. (For a variant, without slit windows, see the Root house, S.189.) To the less-public rear of the building, the columns extend to the roof.

A. G. Mills enclosed the porch during his tenure in the twenties through forties. Richard Freeman installed a bathroom off the kitchen during his ownership, 1964–79. Susan Solway and Howard Siegel (former owners of the Kissam house, S.192), working with restoration architect John Thorpe, intend to return the entry to its original design and to remove many other accretions not of Wright's design. This includes removal of terra-cotta roof tiles, repair and strengthening of the roof with steel, and replacement of tiles.

A combined stable and "automobile room," with "man's room," was built; the foundations stand but the original structure has been torn down.

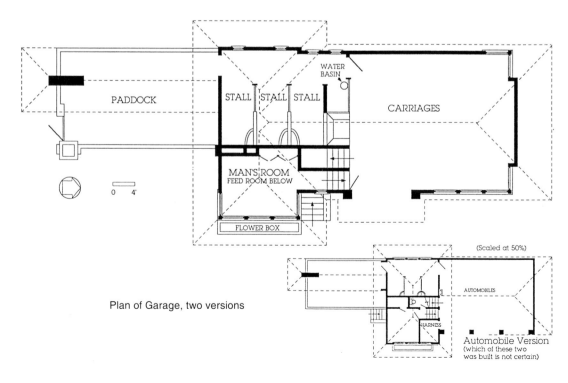

Plan of Garage, two versions

PADDOCK

STALL STALL STALL

WATER BASIN

CARRIAGES

MAN'S ROOM
FEED ROOM BELOW

FLOWER BOX

0   4'

(Scaled at 50%)

AUTOMOBILES

HARNESS

Automobile Version
(which of these two
was built is not certain)

Ravine Bluffs Development

S.185–S.192
(1915) for Sherman M. Booth
Glencoe, Illinois

Sherman M. Booth commissioned a complete plan for a housing development just west of a ravine in Glencoe, Illinois. Six houses, including his own, were built, along with three sculptures in poured concrete.

Sherman Booth, Jr., whose father was a noted Wisconsin journalist, humanitarian, and civil-rights leader, was Wright's attorney at this time. He had grandiose ideas, and as early as 1911 Wright was drawing up designs for his building schemes. A town hall, two waiting stations on the Chicago & Milwaukee Electric railroad line, park features reminiscent of the work of Richard Bock, stables, an art gallery for the north side of Chicago, and the first, ostentatious residence design for Booth's own home at Ravine Bluffs all date from 1911. None was built.

The Ravine Bluffs Development included five houses for rent. Each is named for its first-known independent owner. All are plaster surfaced, with wood trim, and none was supervised by Wright. All may be variants of designs prepared for Edward C. Waller and his son (S.030, S.031, S.047, S.065, S.066, S.166, S.180), for the Waller Estate in River Forest.

Ravine Bluffs Development sculpture at the west end of Sylvan Road

Ravine Bluffs Development sculpture at Franklin and Meadow Roads

S.185
Ravine Bluffs Development Sculptures, and
S.186 T.1505
Bridge (1915)
Glencoe, Illinois

The three sculptures are S.185.1, at the west end of Sylvan Road; S.185.2, at Franklin Road at Meadow; and S.185.3, at the east end of Sylvan Road.
Bridge rebuilt in the 1980s, and two sculptures redone

Although it has been suggested that the Ravine Bluffs sculptures were executed by Alfonso Ianelli, who collaborated with Wright in the early part of this decade on several projects including the Midway Gardens (S.180), recent evidence does not support the claim. One might also see in these sculptures some influence of Richard Bock on Wright. The northeastern entrance to the development is by way of a bridge over the ravine from which the project takes its name. The bridge, in a state of near collapse, was rebuilt in the 1980s, and the two sculptures at the entrances to the project were rebuilt.

Ravine Bluffs Development bridge

Ravine Bluffs Development

S.187 T.1502
Sherman M. Booth **Residence**
Remodeling (1915)
Glencoe, Illinois

The home constructed for Sherman Booth is the second scheme, actually an extensive remodeling of, and addition to, an existing structure. Wright called for three bedrooms on the ground floor in the wing that guides the visitor to the front door; these have been remodeled. Originally the hallway had a tile floor, but it has been replaced by wood laid to a pattern from the Frank Lloyd Wright Home and Studio (S.003–S.005). The dining room is the only one with detailed windows, wood frames with colored-glass inserts. Living spaces are large, the living room being 36 feet long, the living porch that extends it 23 feet, now enlarged to 28 feet and fully enclosed. Three more bedrooms are on the floor above, the master bedroom featuring canopied beds by Wright, and all having built-in closets with drawers. A belvedere-style roof garden, with fireplace and screened sleeping porch, caps all. There is a basement under the main, three-story section only. Some of the timber used includes Western tamarack (larch) and Montana cypress, which is not water resistant. A landscaping plan, dated 1912, is by Jens Jensen.

Booth Residence

View to northeast corner

Living room

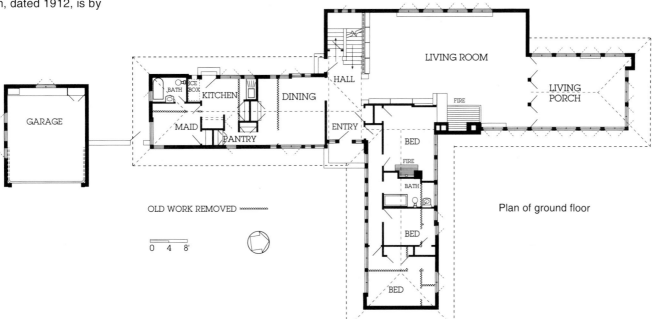

OLD WORK REMOVED ✕✕✕✕✕✕

0 4 8'

Plan of ground floor

189

Ravine Bluffs Development

S.188   T.1516
Charles R. **Perry** Residence (1915)
Glencoe, Illinois

Four Ravine Bluffs rental houses share a basic square plan, a refinement of the Fireproof House. By looking at the elevations, one can see whether the plan of a given floor is standard or mirrored front to back or side to side, and whether the porch is to the side of the living room or juts from the front (long wall). The chimney will reveal the basic orientation of the house, toward the street (Perry, Root, Kissam) or to the side (Kier).

The Perry residence is from this family of square-plan houses to which Wright often returned. The living room occupies half the main floor in front of the central fireplace. The plan is extended by a porch to one side, a smaller covered entry opposite (one of the Waller designs initiated this plan). Upstairs there are three bedrooms and a bath, plus a sleeping porch, which in each of the Ravine Bluffs houses has been enclosed.

Whereas the Waller units had double-hung windows, the Ravine Bluff windows are casements with two to four panels in the grouping. The roofline adds visual interest where the flat cornice is broken by gabling; the axis of the main-level porch entry extension is at 90-degrees to that of the second-story roof. In essence, for these rental houses Wright took a basic floor plan, sometimes mirror-imaging one floor, capped them with flat, gabled, or hipped roofs, and thereby created a variety of buildings without having to provide a different design for each house. He oriented them variously on their sites, some to the street, others to the side. The William F. Ross house (S.191) is the unique plan in the grouping.

Perry Residence

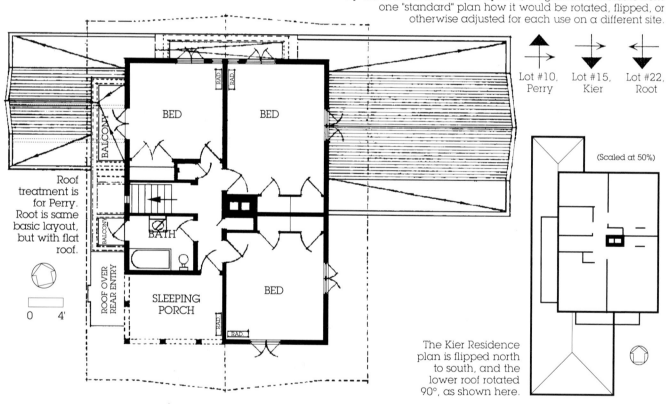

By use of a full co-ordinate system, Wright could indicate from one "standard" plan how it would be rotated, flipped, or otherwise adjusted for each use on a different site.

Lot #10, Perry   Lot #15, Kier   Lot #22, Root

Roof treatment is for Perry. Root is same basic layout, but with flat roof.

(Scaled at 50%)

The Kier Residence plan is flipped north to south, and the lower roof rotated 90°, as shown here.

Plan of second floor; type for Perry (and Root), with Kier variant

Ravine Bluffs Development

S.189   T.1516
Hollis R. **Root** Residence (1915)
Glencoe, Illinois
Renovated in the late 1980s

The Root house (on lot 22) is virtually identical in plan to the Perry residence (on lot 10) but is capped with flat roofs. Fourth owners Tony and LaVonne Macaitis, with help from restoration architect John G. Thorpe, have returned the structure to its original form and color. In the basic plan the living room is in front of the fireplace, kitchen and dining room behind. First floor trim is sweet gum. Wood joists in multiples of two to four are used as structural beams. Framing at the roof perimeter is with 2-by-12-inch and 2-by-10-inch joists, in pairs or triplets. Early failure of the cantilevers, particularly in the porch, is thus not so much due to the quality of the materials as to how and where they were joined during construction. Steel flitch beams (steel sandwiched between wood members) have corrected this. Similarity in details of the built Ravine Bluffs units suggests that construction was to Wright's specifications.

Three bedrooms on the second floor have recently been made into one large rear bedroom and a library. Unvarnished oak and painted yellow pine have been replaced with cherry, stained to match the original scheme. Steam radiators have been replaced with a combination system with forced air heating and cooling. Roof pitches were restored to their original central drain (inside the chimney mass).

Root Residence

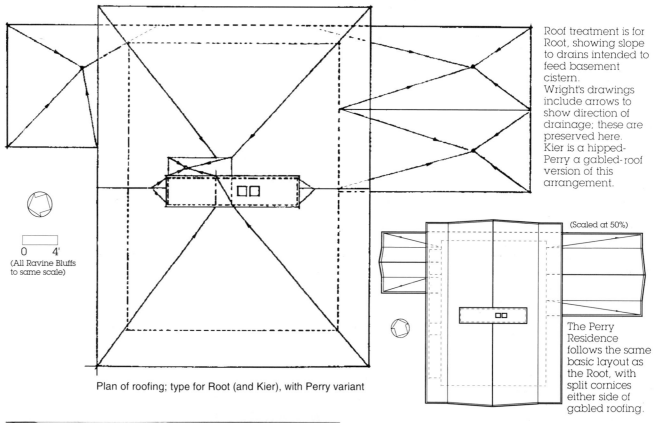

0   4'
(All Ravine Bluffs to same scale)

Plan of roofing; type for Root (and Kier), with Perry variant

Roof treatment is for Root, showing slope to drains intended to feed basement cistern.
Wright's drawings include arrows to show direction of drainage; these are preserved here.
Kier is a hipped-Perry a gabled-roof version of this arrangement.

(Scaled at 50%)

The Perry Residence follows the same basic layout as the Root, with split cornices either side of gabled roofing.

Living room

Ravine Bluffs Development

S.190   T.1516
William F. **Kier** Residence (1915)
Glencoe, Illinois
Original open porch altered to allow
access to a later, detached garage.
New, enclosed porch to rear

Four Ravine Bluffs rental houses share
a basic square plan, a refinement of
the "Fireproof House for $5000." The
hip-roofed Kier house utilizes a mirror-
image of the Perry house (S.188)
(flipped north to south on the primary
axis) with the entire plan turned 90
degrees from the street. This places
the kitchen at the northwest, dining
room to the northeast, thus giving the
living room the southern exposure.

As a variant on the Fireproof
design, the porch projects from the
long side of the living room at the
entry, rather than from the short side
near the dining room. This has been
cut through to allow access to an
attached garage, not designed by
Wright. The doorway in the center of
the street facade was then cut through
to replace the porch entry. Note the
lattice framing treatment of some
upper-level windows; each house in
the Ravine Bluffs Development had a
different treatment of this element.

A new, enclosed porch has been
added to the rear.

Kier Residence

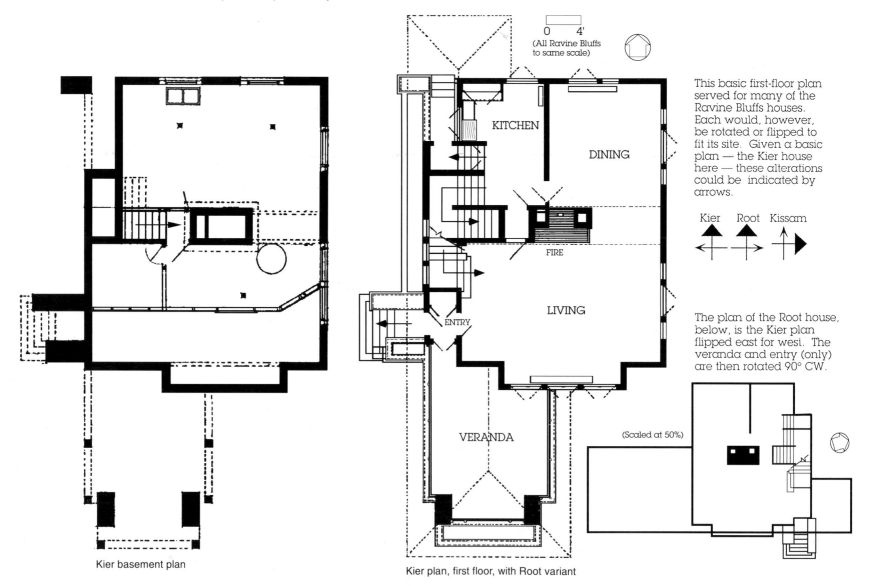

0   4'
(All Ravine Bluffs
to same scale)

KITCHEN

DINING

FIRE

LIVING

ENTRY

VERANDA

This basic first-floor plan
served for many of the
Ravine Bluffs houses.
Each would, however,
be rotated or flipped to
fit its site. Given a basic
plan — the Kier house
here — these alterations
could be indicated by
arrows.

Kier   Root   Kissam

The plan of the Root house,
below, is the Kier plan
flipped east for west. The
veranda and entry (only)
are then rotated 90° CW.

(Scaled at 50%)

Kier basement plan

Kier plan, first floor, with Root variant

William F. Ross Residence (right),
with Kier Residence (left)

S.191   T.1516
William F. Ross Residence (1915)
Glencoe, Illinois
Enclosed entry added

Of the rental homes built for Sherman
Booth and his Ravine Bluffs Development project, this is the only one not
sharing the basic square plan. The
chimney, rather than being the centerpiece of the design, is set well to one
side, acting as a screen for the entry
(now enlarged and enclosed) immediately behind. The living room
occupies two-thirds of the street
facade, sharing a door to the veranda,
now enclosed, with the dining room to
the rear. The kitchen occupies the

remaining main-floor quarter. Upstairs,
there are four bedrooms (one replacing the sleeping porch of the other
designs) and a bath. The master bedroom has a balcony, like the four other
houses in this project. Details reveal
the influence of the Sherman Booth
design (S.187) on all the Ravine Bluffs
houses.

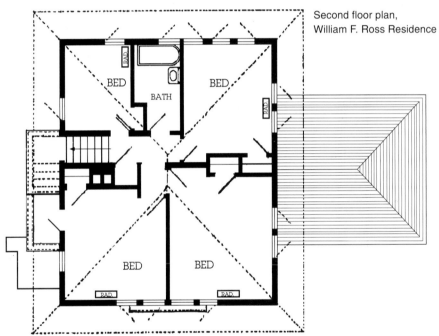

Second floor plan,
William F. Ross Residence

BED

BED

BATH

BED

BED

RAD.

RAD.

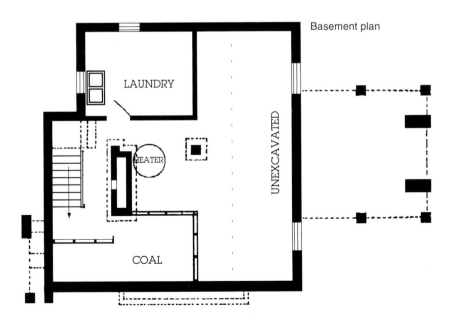

Basement plan

LAUNDRY

UNEXCAVATED

HEATER

COAL

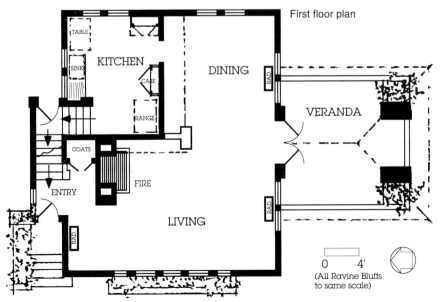

First floor plan

TABLE

KITCHEN

DINING

SINK

CASE

RANGE

VERANDA

COATS

ENTRY

FIRE

RAD.

LIVING

RAD.

0   4'
(All Ravine Bluffs
to same scale)

Ravine Bluffs Development

Ravine Bluffs Development
S.192 T.1516
Lute F. and Daniel **Kissam**
Residence (1915)
Glencoe, Illinois
Failure of roof cantilever corrected in 1980s

Again, the basic Ravine Bluffs square plan dominates. The entry to the Kissam residence is through the main porch, which is rotated 90 degrees around the plan. In the Perry, Root, and Kier houses, the second floor is split down the middle; after mirror-imaging, that central wall is shifted one unit to the side to enlarge the two main bedrooms. The sun room, or enclosed sleeping porch, is to the northeast.

    Eventual sagging of the cantilevered porch roof was due less to materials than to the fact that, instead of single, long wood members, the supporting beams were assembled from shorter pieces; it was the joints that failed. The original flat roof has now been given a slight pitch to improve drainage and has been resurfaced. As in the other houses, every inch of available space has been put to some good use.

Kissam Residence

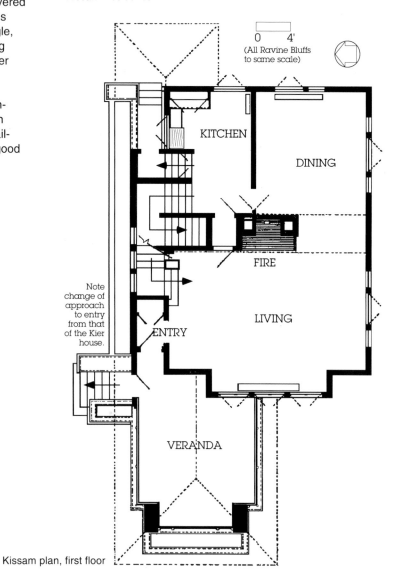

Note change of approach to entry from that of the Kier house.

0 4'
(All Ravine Bluffs to same scale)

KITCHEN

DINING

FIRE

ENTRY

LIVING

VERANDA

Kissam plan, first floor

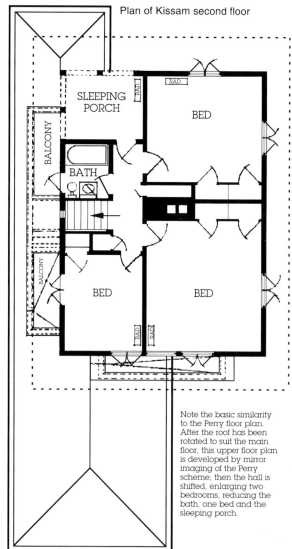

Plan of Kissam second floor

SLEEPING PORCH

BALCONY

BATH

RAD

RAD

BED

BED

BED

BALCONY

RAD RAD

Note the basic similarity to the Perry floor plan. After the roof has been rotated to suit the main floor, this upper floor plan is developed by mirror imaging of the Perry scheme; then the hall is shifted, enlarging two bedrooms, reducing the bath, one bed and the sleeping porch.

Bach Residence

Living room

S.193 T.1501
Emil **Bach** Residence (1915)
Chicago, Illinois
Various alterations, including
modification of basement room into a
wine cellar

During the First World War, Emil Bach
was a government information officer,
with access to a supply of walnut, then
controlled by the army. A single tree
was used throughout for the trim.
Wright employed a cantilever design to
allow the second story to overhang the
first. The brick is unchanged, but some
wood and plaster have been painted.
The basic square plan becomes a
clear cruciform at the upper level,
where each of three bedrooms has its
own bay, four windows forward with
one on each side. The maid's room,
bath, and stairwell are to the rear. The
original rear porch has been enclosed,
after shoring up the foundations, and a
separate room created above by Drs.
Fedor and Sirirat Banuchi.

The living room occupies the south
side of the house, sharing space on
the west with a dining table integrated
around the fireplace masonry. The
house is set almost flush with the north
lot line. This is typical of most Wright
designs where a side lot, as here,
allowed extensive southern exposure.
The main entry is concealed, to the
rear of the south wall, and on the north
there is a servant's entry. The garage,
at the back of the lot, is not by Wright.

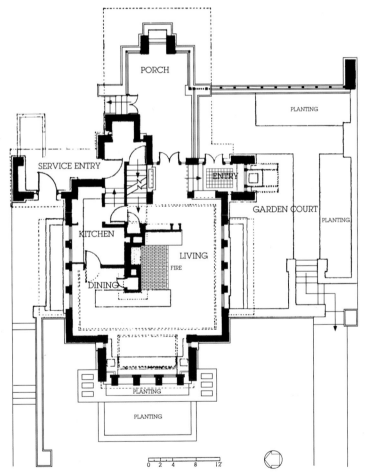
Plan of first floor

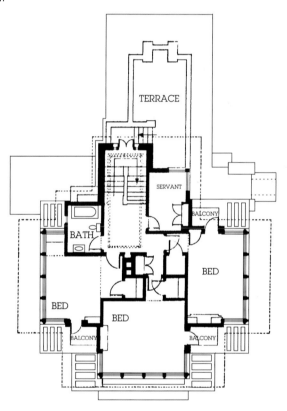
Plan of second floor

S.194 T.1509
Imperial Hotel (1915) and
S.195 T.1604
Annex (1919)
Tokyo, Japan
Hotel demolished, 1968 (entrance, lobby, and pool reconstructed at Meiji Village near Nagoya, Japan, 1976)
Annex demolished, 1923

Wright's major work in Japan, the Imperial Hotel, made liberal use of soft lava block, or Oya stone. The softness of Oya permitted carvings of great subtlety, revealed in such items as brackets topping piers in the dining room. The guest rooms, slightly over one hundred on each of the three floors of the two side wings, were unremarkable; the hotel's interest spatially was in its three-story grand lobby, two-story dining room, and ballroom. There was also a two-story auditorium above a rear lobby, with a banquet hall above it, all designed to a 4-foot unit. Paul Mueller was the builder.

The hotel's floating foundation and steel-reinforced construction permitted it to survive, with little damage, the great Kanto earthquake of September 1, 1923, the day of the hotel's completion ceremony. This floating foundation has long been considered a triumph of Wright's engineering, but the idea was likely picked up and transformed, as genius is wont to do, from an 1870 building by Josiah Conder in Hokaido which, though not articulated, was set on piers. Conder was professor of engineering at the Imperial University, a meeting place for the few English-speaking people in this part of the Orient. Wright had read Conder's *Floral Art of Japan* in its 1899 second edition and would certainly have met him on his visits and stays in Tokyo. (The Wright connection with Conder was made by Sian Evans with Elaine Harrington and me at the research center of the Frank Lloyd Wright Home and Studio in August 1988.)

The old Imperial Hotel was built between May 1888 and November 1890 and had but seventy guest rooms and ten suites. The original annex was built in 1906 with more accommodations than the main building. This old annex burned down in December 1919, and Wright provided a new design in ten days. The new structure included among other things Wright's

Imperial Hotel lobby reconstruction, exterior across the reflecting pool

The lobby well (entrance) from the lobby, with tea balcony above

Guestroom

The promenade

own living quarters and architectural offices, as well as guest rooms brought into line with the design he had established for the new Imperial Hotel.

Wright actually spent much time at the site between 1916 and 1919. He did not travel well, but the steamship crossing of the Pacific took less than three weeks; when he was ill in Japan his mother, Anna, visited him. He returned to America often, crossing the country by car to supervise what little work he had and to seek new commissions.

The hotel was altered during the occupation by the American army

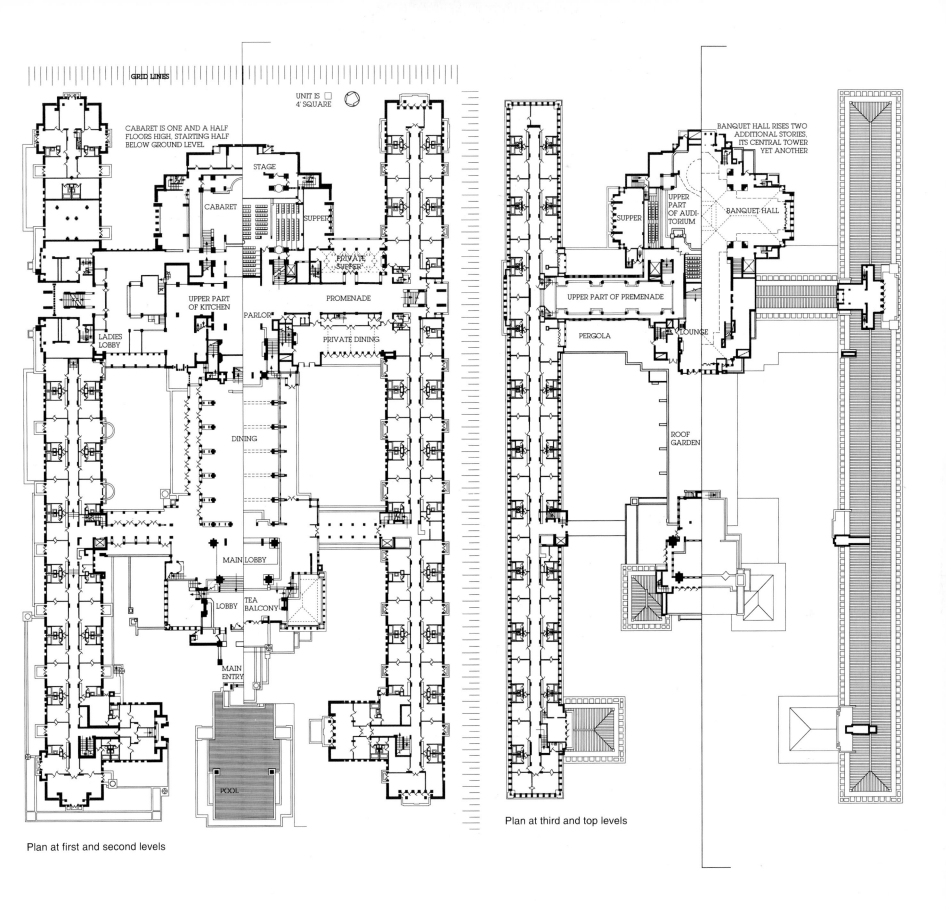

GRID LINES

CABARET IS ONE AND A HALF
FLOORS HIGH, STARTING HALF
BELOW GROUND LEVEL

UNIT IS ☐ ⬡
4' SQUARE

STAGE

CABARET

SUPPER

PRIVATE
SUPPER

UPPER PART
OF KITCHEN

PROMENADE

PARLOR

LADIES
LOBBY

PRIVATE DINING

DINING

MAIN LOBBY

LOBBY

TEA
BALCONY

MAIN
ENTRY

POOL

Plan at first and second levels

BANQUET HALL RISES TWO
ADDITIONAL STORIES,
ITS CENTRAL TOWER
YET ANOTHER

SUPPER

UPPER
PART
OF AUDI-
TORIUM

BANQUET HALL

UPPER PART OF PREMENADE

PERGOLA

LOUNGE

ROOF
GARDEN

Plan at third and top levels

(Continues)

(**S.194** *continued*)

following World War II. Apparently Wright was offered the opportunity to remodel the structure at this time but refused. As downtown-Tokyo land values rose, it became more feasible to tear down the building than to renovate it.

Japan's tradition of beauty, however, would not allow the building to vanish completely; the entrance and lobby were dismantled and taken to Nagoya. It was reconstructed on the western reaches of the Meiji-Mura open-air architectural museum and opened to the public in March 1976. New artificial Oya of precast concrete and tile are used in the right side (stereo photographs of the original guided robot stone-cutting machines). Those original stones that were usable are on the left side of the structure. There is a long-range possibility that additional spaces may be rebuilt.

Ballroom

Main dining room

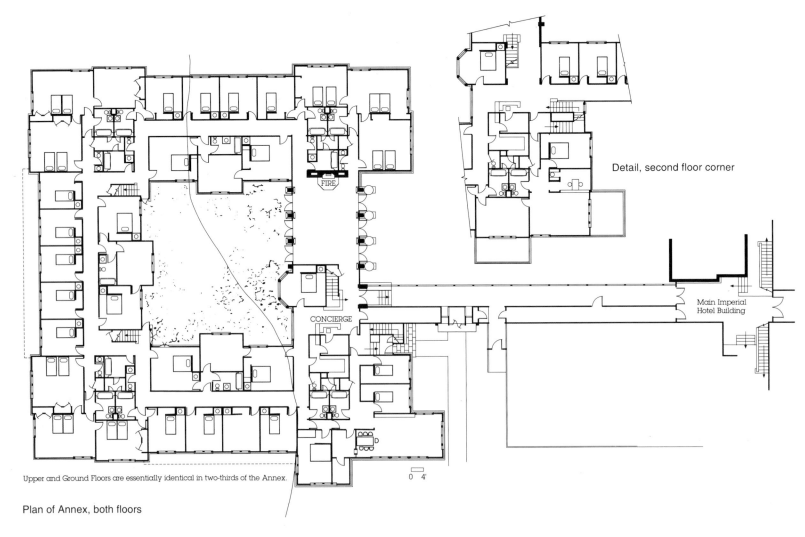

Detail, second floor corner

Main Imperial Hotel Building

CONCIERGE

FIRE

Upper and Ground Floors are essentially identical in two-thirds of the Annex.

0   4'

Plan of Annex, both floors

S.196   T.1602
Frederick C. **Bogk** Residence (1916)
Milwaukee, Wisconsin

Because of Arthur L. Richards (S.171, S.201–S.204), Milwaukee became a center of activity for Wright. Among those who came to Wright through Richards were Arthur Munkwitz (S.201) and Frederick C. Bogk. Bogk's father was a butcher, but Frederick went early into land sales and later insurance. He entered politics successfully in 1902. Though Bogk's connections with Richards could have brought client and architect together, it is also possible that Mrs. Bogk chose the architect after a visit to the Coonleys in their Riverside home (S.135).

The design for Bogk's house may date as early as 1911, when Wright also drew up designs for A. H. Esbenshade and Edward Schroeder; all three were living within two blocks of each other, and Munkwitz was only a few more blocks away. For many years Schroeder's business offices were in the same building as those of Richards.

The house is constructed of ferro-concrete, to support the thirty-five thousand pounds of roof tile. The facade of Bogk's home, brick framing windows capped by a cast concrete ornament under broad (5 1/2-foot) eaves and hipped roof, reveals the aesthetic of the Imperial Hotel (S.194), under construction at this time. Wide and deep brick mullions increase the privacy on this narrow city lot. Privacy is further protected by amber glass in narrow window frames.

Entry is at the side of the living room, on the edge of the division cre-

Bogk Residence

ated by the back-to-back fireplaces. Had the entry been set behind the fireplace masonry, the planimetric similarity to the Gale house (S.098) could not be ignored. The rear fireplace is raised to face the dining room. To the rear on the second floor are a bath and maid's room and above the basic square are four bedrooms, one with its own bath. The intricate patterning of the street facade conceals the fact that this house has an attic, which Mrs. Bogk demanded so she could dry her laundry indoors. Walnut, which had become a favorite wood with Wright, is used downstairs, gum upstairs. Furniture was designed by Wright, not his local associate, George Niedecken. Credit for the high quality of this structure must go to Russell Barr Williamson, who supervised construction while Wright was in Japan and on the West Coast, relaying what instructions he could by cable.

Living room, view toward dining room

Dining room with sideboard

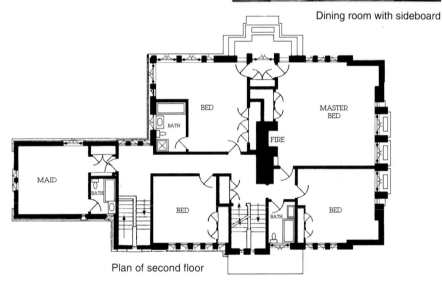

Plan of second floor

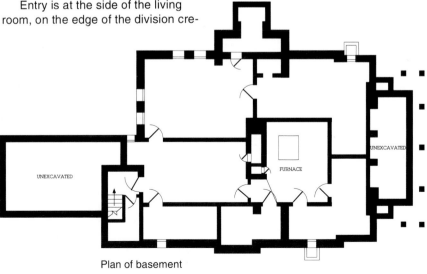

Plan of basement

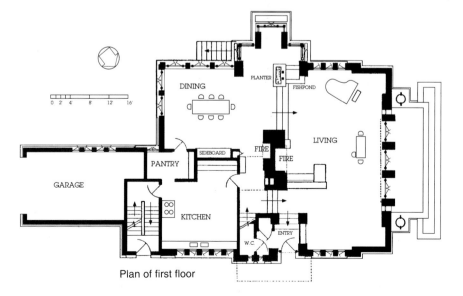

Plan of first floor

Vosburgh Residence

S.197   T.1607
Ernest Vosburgh Summer
Residence (1916)
Grand Beach, Michigan
Rear porch and terrace enclosed,
interior paneled

Wright designed three houses in
Grand Beach, and only the Vosburgh
remains essentially as built. It is a
Prairie gem with a pinwheel plan and a
two-story-high living room set near a
creek that flows through the woods to
nearby Lake Michigan. It is based on
a 4-foot unit, surfaced with stucco,
trimmed with oak and cedar, and
capped by a hipped roof. The fireplace
is red Norman brick. Cedar shakes
have been replaced with asbestos
shingles. Both the rear porch and the

terrace have been enclosed, and the
kitchen and the storage area modernized. Once-open studs, typical of
Wright cottages, are now paneled. A
stair leads to a short balcony overlooking the living room, the only space
at the two-story level.

Living room

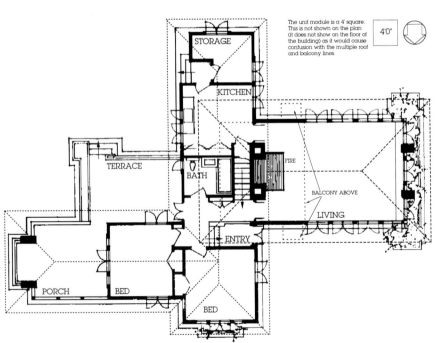

The unit module is a 4' square.
This is not shown on the plan
(it does not show on the floor of
the building) as it would cause
confusion with the multiple roof
and balcony lines.

4'0"

S.198   T.1601
Joseph J. Bagley Summer
Residence (1916)
Grand Beach, Michigan
Mostly demolished

The Bagley summer residence is a
rambling structure under hipped roofs
and is based on a 4-foot unit. The
living room is 5 by 7 units, attached to
pairs of 3-by-5-unit rooms, further
connected to 6-by-3-unit terminals.

W. S. Carr Residence, entry on south s*

S.199   T.1603
W. S. Carr Summer Residence
(1916)
Grand Beach, Michigan
Stone veneer over original plaster.
Terrace enlarged and enclosed, and
entry enlarged

This cottage sits just on the edge of a
bluff high above Lake Michigan. The
original was designed to a 4-foot unit
on a flat site. Because of the ridge
topping the bluff, Wright's single-story
bungalow was set on a basement
below the bedroom wing of the structure. The entire structure, in being
resited, was rotated 180 degrees from
Wright's intent. The main space (44
feet long) is divided by the fireplace
and living room to one side and the
kitchen, servant's room, and bath
behind. A gallery links four bedrooms,
each 10 feet wide. The rear hall was
originally screened and reached only
to the door of the back bedroom; it has

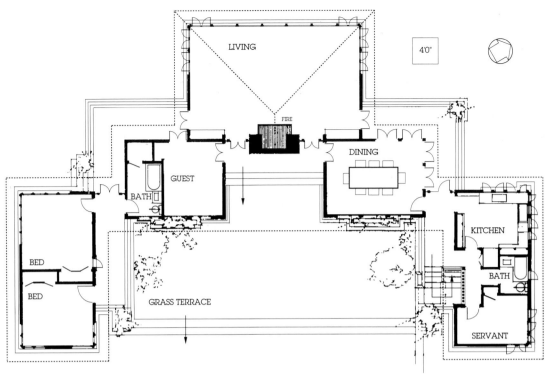

Joseph J. Bagley
Residence

LIVING

FIRE

DINING

GUEST

BATH

KITCHEN

BED

BATH

BED

GRASS TERRACE

SERVANT

4'0"

One wing contains the dining room, kitchen, and servant's quarters, the other a bathroom and bedrooms. The building has been altered and added to so that only the outer shell reveals Wright's intentions. Casement windows and screens have been eliminated or replaced with plate glass and storm windows. Interior partitioning has been altered. Exposed studs have been sided, and insulation inserted to winterize the structure, which is now heated and air conditioned. The kitchen has been modernized.

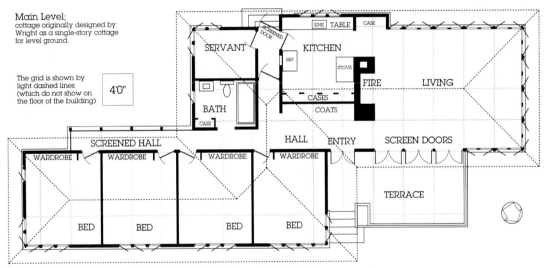

Main Level;
cottage originally designed by Wright as a single-story cottage for level ground.

The grid is shown by light dashed lines (which do not show on the floor of the building)

4'0"

SINK TABLE CASE
SCREENED DOOR
SERVANT
KITCHEN
REF
STOVE
FIRE
LIVING
CASES
BATH
COATS
CASE
SCREENED HALL
HALL ENTRY SCREEN DOORS
WARDROBE WARDROBE WARDROBE WARDROBE
TERRACE
BED BED BED BED

been extended to square off the rear and enclosed.

Stucco and wood trim have given way to stone veneer. The terrace and entry have been enlarged, the terrace enclosed, and the kitchen modernized. The fireplace was to have been slightly to one side of the living room axis, but at some point it was centered.

W. S. Carr Residence, view of northern side

Munkwitz Apartments

S.200 T.1606
Arthur R. **Munkwitz Duplex Apartments** (1916)
Milwaukee, Wisconsin
From north to south, the first duplex is numbered S.200.11 for the north unit and S.200.12 for the south, the second building is S.200.21 for the north wing and S.200.22 the south. The upper level units would number S.200.13–14 and S.200.23–24.
Demolished 1973

As early as 1911, Wright was designing his American System Ready-Cut structures with "prefabricated" construction integral to their concept. Here, however, prefabricated meant "ready-cut" parts, rather than whole wall units cut to size and shipped to the site where they would be fabricated. In 1916, the idea was again taken up, resulting in these buildings for Arthur R. Munkwitz and Arthur L. Richards, who had first come together as president and vice-president, respectively, of the American Realty Service Company. They are based on the American Model home marked A4 in Wright's drawings, but identified as Model J-521 on City of Milwaukee plans.

Each apartment features a living room the full width of the front facade. An adjoining dining space overlooks the entry, and the kitchen occupies the balance of the front. The stairwells and hall separate these front spaces from the bathroom and a pair of bedrooms at the rear of each unit. Two of the Model A4 units, one above the other, form a duplex, and two mirrored duplexes are joined at a common entryway. The main stairwells thus meet at this central entry, but side entries are also provided for each unit, allowing separation of each "quadraplex" from the other. What looks like four units in a group is really two separate buildings, each with four apartments.

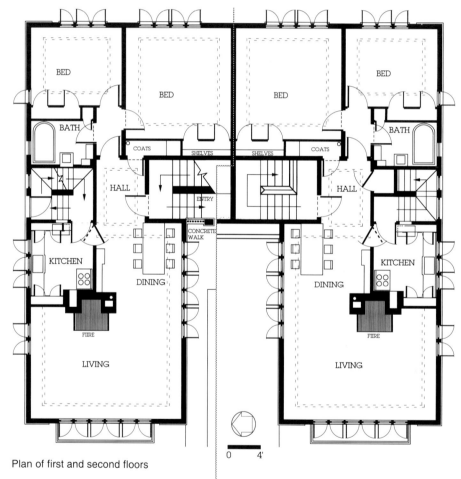

Plan of first and second floors

0   4'

S.201 T.1605
Arthur L. **Richards Duplex Apartments** (1916)
Milwaukee, Wisconsin
The four duplex structures are numbered S.201.1–S.201.4 from east to west. The individual apartments of each duplex are numbered (east to west) S.201.11 and S.201.12 through S.204.11 and S.204.12.
The units are in various states of repair, with some fully restored.

Arthur L. Richards was born in Milwaukee on August 21, 1877. By 1904 he was building houses, claiming that by building forty at one time, he could realize great savings over the individual buying a house part by part. Such an idea would sit well with Wright a bit over a decade later. Then Richards built all the structures on Burnham Street in the block west of Layton Boulevard.

The duplex apartments are four separate buildings, each with upper and lower apartments, using one plan from the American System Ready-Cut "prefabricated" plans of 1911. To identify each, they are given decimal suffixes. The first three buildings (S.201.1–3), from east to west (right to left in the photo), are identical in plan. The fourth (S.201.4), which is on a corner lot, employs a mirror-image plan to satisfy needs of security.

Supervision of construction of the Burnham Street project, the Bogk house (S.196), and the Munkwitz Duplex Apartments (S.200) was by Russell Barr Williamson, Wright's chief drafting room assistant following the fire at Taliesin. The first unit has been restored, the second given protective vinyl siding, and work on the exterior of the third was completed in 1988. Then, in 1990, the Milwaukee Common Council approved creation of an historic district for these duplexes, the small Richards house (S.202), and the Richards bungalow (S.203.1).

Richards Apartments

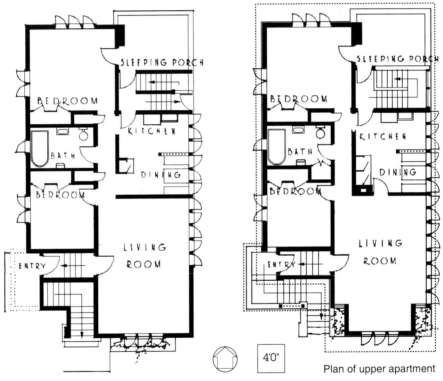

Plan of lower apartment

Plan of upper apartment

Close-up of restored, easternmost apartment

Richards Small House

S.202 T.1506A
Arthur L. **Richards Small House**
(1915)
Milwaukee, Wisconsin
Terrace enclosed

Just east of the Richards Apartments (S.201) is the small, single-story, flat-roofed American System-Built (Ready-Cut) prefab plan identified as type B-1 on drawings. There are no eaves, the water being drained by a spout at the chimney, which also has vents receiving air from soffit openings and a kitchen vent—an early mechanical form of air conditioning. The entry is concealed on the side, opening behind the fireplace that faces into the

dual-purpose living and dining room. Two bedrooms and bath are at the side, kitchen to the rear. The basement has rooms for laundry, heater, and coal supply. Its cost of $1835 may be compared with that of $15,000 for the Bogk (S.196) home.

The design may be as early as 1913. More drawings were made for this American System-Built project, or rather group of projects, than for any other Wright worked on. Only those that were built are cataloged here. They range from very small, flat-roofed houses, such as this, through larger bungalows to three-story designs with hanging garden terraces, both in single-family and multifamily units. For all of them, the parts were to be cut and shipped from Richards's Milwaukee factory to the site, where they would be assembled by local labor.

Plan of basement foundation

Plan of ground floor

S.203   T.1506A
Arthur L. **Richards** American System-Built Homes **Bungalow** (1915) (Cottage "A")
S.203.1
Richards Bungalow
Milwaukee, Wisconsin
S.203.2
Lewis E. **Burleigh** Residence,
Wilmette, Illinois
S.203.3
Richards Bungalow
Lake Bluff, Illinois
S.203.4   T.1703
Stephen M. B. **Hunt Residence II**
(1917)
Oshkosh, Wisconsin
Milwaukee bungalow has been re-sided. Burleigh has been expanded to the north and east. The Lake Bluff house is in serious disrepair

Wright designed more than three dozen different housing units, from bungalows through two-story houses to duplex apartments, for construction by various companies of Arthur L. Richards. All were American System Ready-Cut structures, designed to be cut at the factory and shipped to the site ready for construction. The project was announced in the *Chicago Sunday Tribune,* March 4, 1917, offering small homes from $2,750 to $3,500 and larger ones from $5,000 to $100,000 (advertising copy and brochures were written by novelist Sherwood Anderson). More than a dozen suburban dealers were licensed to sell American System-Built Homes. The United States entered World War I a month after the announcement in the newspaper, perhaps scuttling this early example of Wright's desire to provide inexpensive, beautiful housing to Americans of any income.

Original drawings show a side porch entry, which is enclosed in all built units. The fireplace is on the side of the dual-purpose living-dining room. The two bedrooms are separated by a bathroom. The kitchen is at the rear, where stairs lead to a full basement with laundry, heating system, and coal storage. Construction of the Milwaukee demonstration house was begun

October 26, 1915, and finished July 5 the following year.

Several of these homes have come to light since publication of *The Architecture of Frank Lloyd Wright: A Complete Catalog* (2d ed.), requiring changes in listings S.203 and S.204 to accommodate the various types now known to have been built. Type 203 are all bungalows, centered about a massive fireplace at the entry. One, next to the Richards small house (S.202), was resurfaced with precast coral stone veneer in 1956. The Lake Bluff unit is in severe disrepair and so deeply buried in foliage as to be beyond photographing.

Another was erected in Wilmette by Thomas E. Sullivan & Co. and sold to Lewis E. Burleigh in 1919. (There is an unresolved discrepancy here: the Recorder of Deeds files indicate that Sullivan sold the property to J. J. O'Connor in 1916.) A formal dining room was added at the rear (opening into the foyer and the kitchen), with an another bedroom added to the right side of the house (entered from the front bedroom), probably in the 1950s. Further, a partition was added to create a hall to the new bedroom and provide privacy for the front bedroom. Next to this is a building resembling the two-story American System Built House (see S.204) designed by John S. Van Bergen, where Thomas E. Sullivan lived.

The Stephen Hunt (S.203.4, formerly S.204) residence shares the basic bungalow floor plan but was altered for the individual, reflecting the better financial circumstances of this client. The kitchen is 2 feet, 2 inches deeper, but also equally narrower. The porch has a second exit, to the rear, and is lengthened one unit, the back entry is directly to the rear rather than the side. The bedrooms each have two casement windows (and one corner window) to the side, instead of the standard, and cheaper, one, though the Bungalow compensates partially with three to the front. This admits more, and more even, light to the Hunt corner rooms by giving them more northern exposure. The whole structure is enlarged by adding one unit to the Richards grid system. Wright provided drawings directly to the client, thus gaining the full architect's fee, rather than having such monies go to Richards.

Richards Bungalow, Milwaukee

Burleigh Residence

Lake Bluff Residence

Alan Thatcher

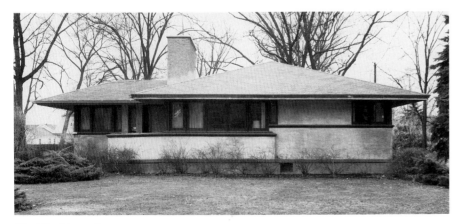

Hunt Residence II

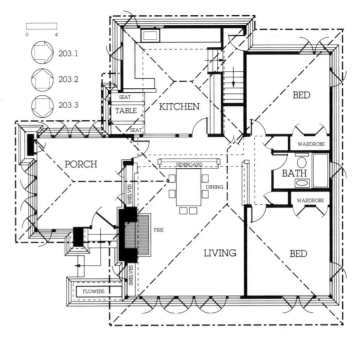

Plan of Richards Bungalow

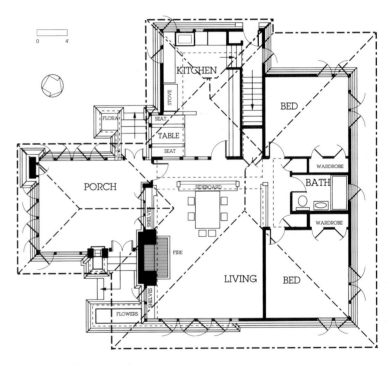

Plan of Hunt Residence II

205

Guy C. Smith Residence

S.204 T.1506A
Arthur L. Richards American System-Built Homes **Two-Story** Residence (1917)

S.204.1
Guy C. Smith Residence
Chicago, Illinois

S.204.2
H. H. **Hyde** Residence
Chicago, Illinois

S.204.3
Oscar A. Johnson Residence
Evanston, Illinois

S.204.4
Delbert W. **Meier** Residence
Monona, Iowa

Guy C. Smith residence undergoing renovation early 1990s. Hyde residence expanded to northeast and rear. Meier residence has entry expanded and garage added.

Wright produced many variations on each of his Richards themes, but with sufficient family resemblance that the two-story units are grouped together here rather than being listed individually.

The first house (S.204.1) is in Beverly, also known as the Ridge Historic District of Chicago. Its plan is a mirror image of the one widely advertised in Chicago newspapers. The wing opposite the porte-cochere has been deleted, perhaps to economize on total cost. It was constructed in stucco and painted wood trim (a standard for prefabrication) by builder P. D. Diamond & Company, whose offices were a few blocks south.

The second house is but a short distance south of the first; its plan is the same as that of the Meier house, but with additional windows (see below).

The Johnson house in Evanston was built by Hanney & Son. The building permit of March 1917, signed by Wright, indicates that it was to be a stucco house requiring 2,500 brick, 110 cubic yards of concrete, 650 square yards of plastering, all included in a total cost not to exceed $4,000. The chimney is a small square, rather

Hyde Residence, showing addition to rear beyond downspout

Plan of basement
Guy C. Smith Residence

DRYING
LAUNDRY
VEGETABLES
HALL
FUEL
HEATER

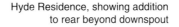

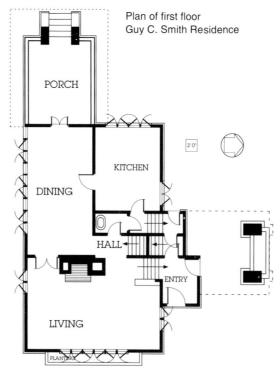

Plan of first floor
Guy C. Smith Residence

PORCH
KITCHEN
DINING
HALL
ENTRY
LIVING
PLANTING

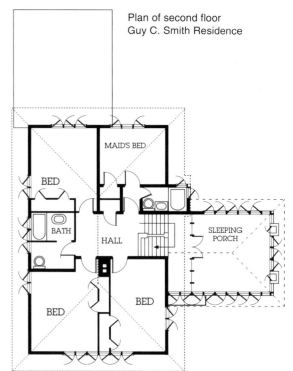

Plan of second floor
Guy C. Smith Residence

MAID'S BED
BED
BATH
HALL
SLEEPING PORCH
BED
BED

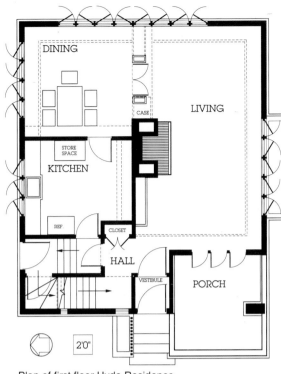

DINING

CASE

LIVING

STORE
SPACE

KITCHEN

REF.

CLOSET

HALL

VESTIBULE

PORCH

2'0"

Plan of first floor Hyde Residence

BED

BED

WARDROBE

BATH

WARDROBE

WARDROBE

HALL

CLOSET

BED

Plan of second floor Hyde Residence

Oscar A. Johnson Residence

Meier Residence

Plan of first floor Meier Residence

DINING

CASE

LIVING

STORE
SPACE

KITCHEN

REF.

CLOSET

HALL

VESTIBULE

PORCH

2'0"

Plan of second floor Meier Residence

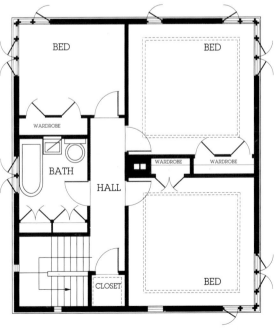

BED

BED

WARDROBE

BATH

WARDROBE

WARDROBE

HALL

CLOSET

BED

than the wide thin masonry stack that would define the orientation of the fireplace within most of his houses. Wright's chimneys were wide because they usually contained several flues, for separate furnace, water heater, one or two fireplaces, even a kitchen stove in the earliest houses. This design feature reveals at the exterior the orientation of the living room fireplace. The legendary quality of the architect's fireplaces, and their ability to draw properly, may be due, at least in part, to the fact that he often did not combine flues, but kept them independent.

The Smith and Johnson two-story houses are derived all too obviously from the "Fireproof House for $5000" concept, which served as Wright's basic plan for a square or rectangular two-story compact house after 1907.

The Iowa building for attorney Delbert W. Meier (like the Hyde structure) follows another floor plan, with its second-story windows at the corners, rather than centered in the walls. The plan shows Wright's basic square—living and dining rooms and kitchen—extended with porch and main entry, as well as stairs and secondary entry to the side. This gives a rectangular plan, allowing larger-than-usual bedrooms. The building has been altered by the addition of a side porch and garage.

S.205   T.1701
Henry J. **Allen Residence** and
S.205A   T.1701
Detached **Garden House** (1917)
Wichita, Kansas
Renovated 1971. Restoration being
carried out in 1990s

In the fiftieth year of his fruitful life,
Wright was feeling the call of the West;
he was in California and Japan more
than Wisconsin. Nevertheless, he had
time to design this marvelously refined
building for Henry Allen, editor of the
Wichita Beacon and governor of
Kansas from 1919 to 1923. Allen, who
lived in the house until 1948, wanted to
be president of the United States and
refused the vice-presidency, which
went to Calvin Coolidge.
    The total structure is roughly a
square, enclosing a large pool and
garden while shutting out traffic noise.
The house encloses two sides with its
L plan, a two-story east-west section
and a single story north-south living

Allen Residence

Dining room

Living room

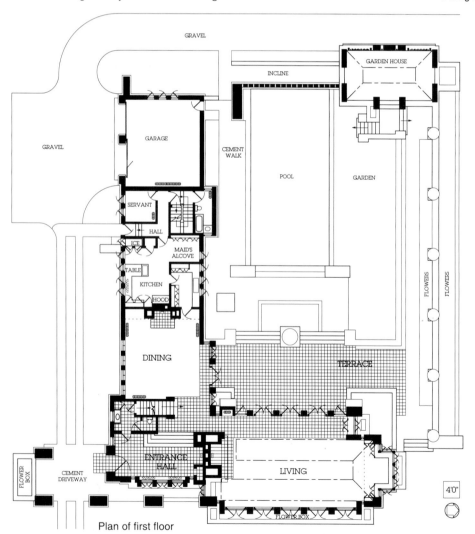

Plan of first floor

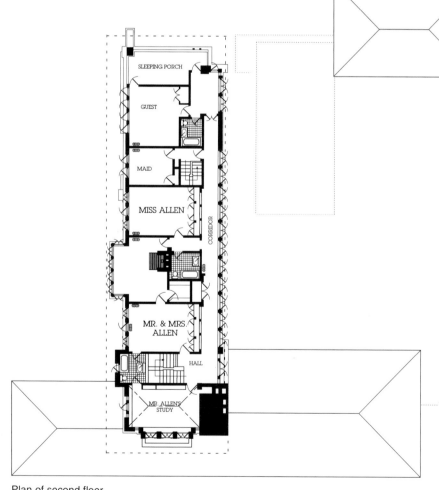

Plan of second floor

room. The culinary and servant facilities and a two-car garage are under the bedrooms and sleeping porch, which drop off a long tunnel gallery. A 3-foot unit seems to be operative. It should be noted that at 6 feet 8 inches tall, Mr. Allen could not put on a sweater in his own room.

Materials are interesting, particularly in the living room. Quarter-sawn oak provides living room flooring. A cover board is used between wall and baseboard. Gold leaf is applied to the recessed (raked) masonry joints. Rice paper in the ceiling lights has a Japanese maple-leaf stencil applied. The radiators are "under" the exterior planters along the main facade. Cypress is used upstairs, for its heavier grain pattern to enliven smaller trim.

Paul Mueller, builder of the Imperial Hotel (S.194), was the contractor. When Mrs. Allen became an invalid, an elevator replaced the rear stairs. The house and grounds were completely renovated for A. W. Kincade in 1971–72. In the late eighties, Kincade bequeathed the house to Wichita State University, which constructed the only other Wright-designed building in the state (S.418) over forty years after the Allen design. The university then sold the house to the Allen-Lambe House Foundation, named after Charles Lambe, who was involved in real estate in the College Hill area where the Allen house is located, and his artist wife Polly. The foundation has restored the house, which is now open to public view upon application.

Courtyard

S.206   T.1702
Aisaku **Hayashi** Residence (1917)
Tokyo, Japan
Remodeled

It was Aisaku Hayashi, general manager of the "old" Imperial Hotel, who brought Wright the commission for the "new" Imperial (S.194). It is not known if the entire house designed for Hayashi by Wright, and dated April 10, 1917, was constructed. Though Wright spent much time in Japan while the Imperial was under construction, he also took the short (less than three weeks each way) trips back to the United States to supervise work there, particularly the Barnsdall projects (S.208–S.211). Accordingly, this building may have received little if any supervision. The structure, such as it survives, north of Komazawa Olympic Park, is owned by Dentsu Advertising Company of Tokyo. The main entry as built suggests Wright's design but leads only to a single-story structure, not the two-story unit planned.

Taliesin archive drawings show a two-story main building, half of which was a combined 20-by-40 foot living and dining room, with an entry, stairs,

Hayashi Residence

and a small office. Four rooms, not marked as to use, were to be above, and a greenhouse was attached to one corner. To the other side a single level had brother's, sister's, and mother's rooms, segregated from the servant quarters and kitchen by a series of passageways. All this was combined in a second, single-level design, but plans do not survive. Oya stone (soft lava block) is trimmed with wood.

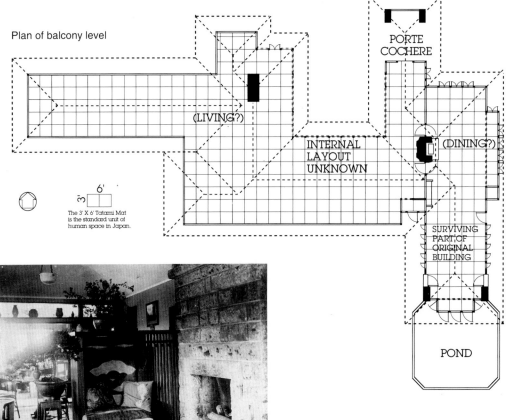

Plan of balcony level

(LIVING?)

INTERNAL
LAYOUT
UNKNOWN

PORTE
COCHERE

(DINING?)

SURVIVING
PART OF
ORIGINAL
BUILDING

POND

6'

3'

The 3' X 6' Tatami Mat
is the standard unit of
human space in Japan.

Hayashi interior

S.207 T.2801
Arinobu **Fukuhara** Residence (1918)
Gora, Hakone, Japan
Destroyed by the great Kanto earthquake, 1923

Little is known of the Fukuhara residence. The client was actually Shinzo Fukuhara, founder of the Japan Amateur Photographer's Association and son of Arinobu Fukuhara, founder of the Shiseido Company. The plans are lettered in Japanese characters, probably by Arata Endo, Wright's local representative. A large two-story living room with a balcony overlooking it dominates the structure, with a terrace at the front, a fireplace to the right side of the center line, and dining space to the left. Behind this was a courtyard, with galleries leading to three bedrooms and a veranda on the right side.

Fukuhara
Residence

At the back were bathrooms and culinary and laundry facilities. To the left, angled at 45 degrees, was a separate bedroom with a private bath and fireplace. This large house was destroyed by an earthquake.

S.208 T.1705A
Aline **Barnsdall Hollyhock House** (1917),
S.209
Spring House (1920),
S.210 T.2002
Residence A (1920), and
S.211 T.2003
Studio **Residence B** (1920)
Los Angeles, California
Hollyhock House was restored on several occasions, once by Lloyd Wright in the 1970s. Studio Residence B demolished ca. 1950

Aline Barnsdall was born in Bradford, Pennsylvania, on April Fools day, 1882. She was the granddaughter of William Barnsdall, who drilled the second oil-producing well in the United States. Miss Barnsdall met Wright in Chicago in 1914; she was codirector of the Players Producing Company. She first proposed to Wright a theatre for Chicago but then moved to the coast, and designs for her "California Romanza" were produced mostly in Japan. The 36-acre Olive Hill site was purchased by this patroness of the arts in 1919, and 11 acres of the summit, with structures, were donated to Los Angeles in 1927. Plans for a community of theatrical artists called not only for the four buildings that were built, but also for retail shops, small residences, an apartment building for

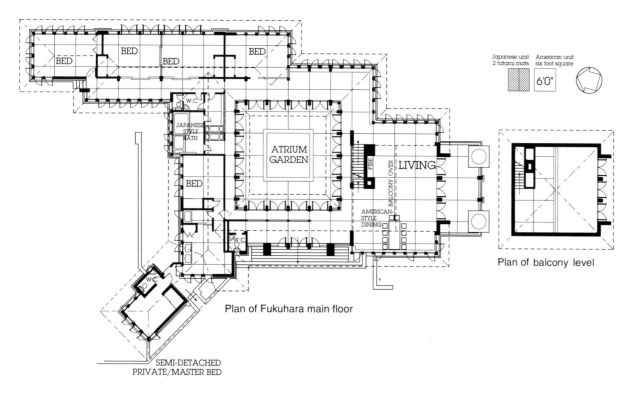

Plan of Fukuhara main floor

Plan of balcony level

SEMI-DETACHED
PRIVATE/MASTER BED

Fireplace in living room; Lloyd Wright restoration

Hollyhock House

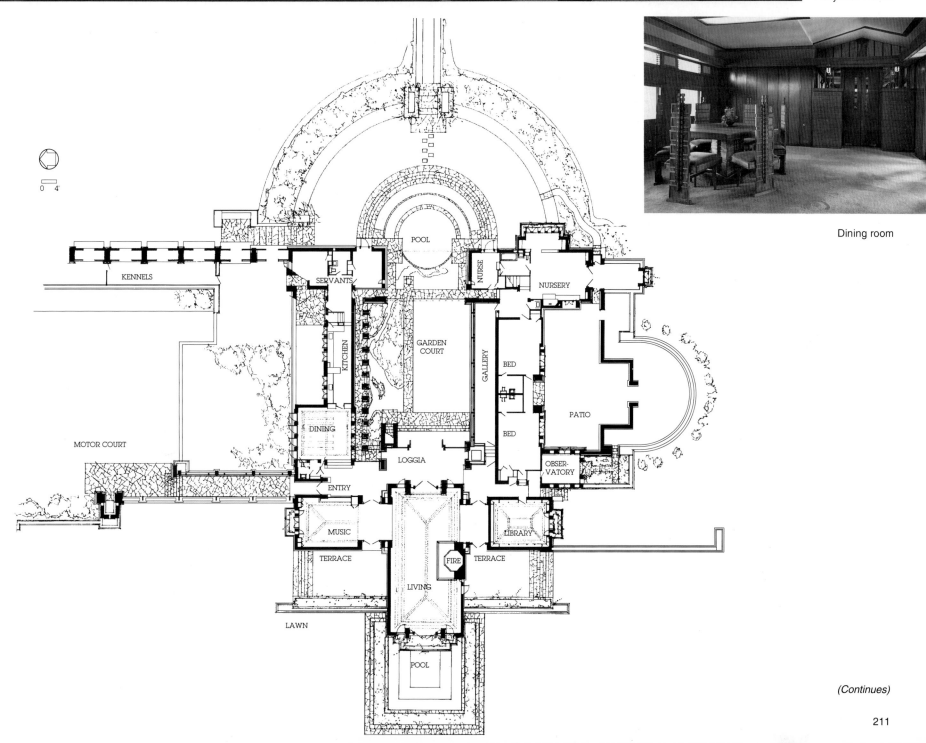

Dining room

KENNELS

SERVANTS

NURSE

NURSERY

MOTOR COURT

KITCHEN

GARDEN COURT

GALLERY

BED

PATIO

DINING

BED

OBSER-VATORY

LOGGIA

ENTRY

MUSIC

LIBRARY

TERRACE

FIRE

TERRACE

LIVING

LAWN

POOL

POOL

0   4'

(Continues)

visiting thespians, and a motion picture theatre.

Hollyhock House, named for Miss Barnsdall's favorite flower, from which Wright abstracted the ornamental forms that infuse the design, suggests to some a Mayan temple as it commands the western view from Barnsdall Park. Others have argued that the resemblance is only superficial, not a design intention of Wright. In 1915 there was a major exhibition in Los Angeles on Mayan architecture, and Wright visited it with Alfonso Ianelli and shortly thereafter received a set of photos of Mayan temples.

Wright had originally wanted a poured-concrete construction similar to Unity Temple (S.096). Instead, the basic material is structural clay tile, a fired-clay product with hollow cells commonly used in stucco construction before "cinder," then concrete, block replaced it at a lower cost.

Hollyhock House is richly ornamented with cast concrete forms, which Wright called art stone. Their tawny gold color, which came from crushed, decomposed granite at the site, provided a delightful contrast to the "silver green" of the house,

according to Pam Edwards (*Hollywood Citizen News,* September 2, 1921). There is also extensive decorative art glass in the windows and ceiling lights, trimmed with oak. The living room, facing west, is the main space of the structure; the fireplace rises from a pool on the south wall. The living room is bracketed by a music room and a library; the wings extend beyond, one for dining with the kitchen adjacent, the other for beds and the nursery, the ensemble encompassing a garden court.

The Spring House is a small structure down the hill from Hollyhock House. Like other Barnsdall Park buildings, it is structural clay tile and art stone. Whether it was fed originally by a natural spring or by pumped water is not known.

Residence A is another part of Wright's grand concept still standing; it, too, was done in clay tile. A second-story dining room, with adjacent kitchen, looks over the living room. Some possible alterations to the entry have given rise to the myth that the building was done by R. M. Schindler.

Residence B, known as the director's residence, also used clay tile and had art stone decoration; it featured a rooftop sleeping porch, suitable to the local climate. Miss Barnsdall gave Wright a budget of $30,000, not a penny more, to remodel the structure

Barnsdall Residence A, entry side

Barnsdall Residence A, north wall

Spring House

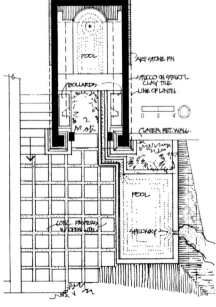

Plan of Spring House

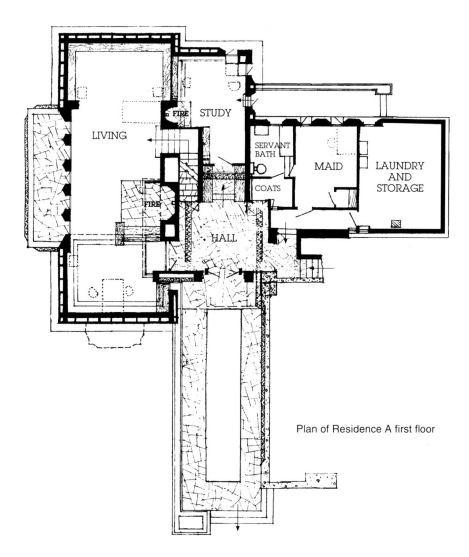

Plan of Residence A first floor

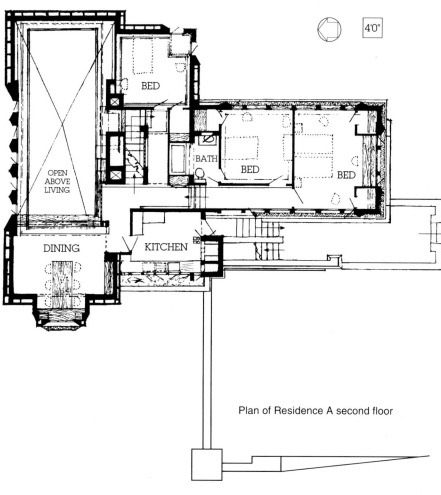

Plan of Residence A second floor

4'0"

in 1923. When this figure was reached, construction stopped, but the sleeping porch roof was not completed. So it stayed until it was condemned and later torn down. The remodeling featured Wright's first-known use of the mitred corner window. It also had finely detailed paint trim on the wood parts of the facade, which was a factor in the cost overrun.

The Little Dipper Kindergarten building (formerly S.209) was designed in textile block, suggesting a date of 1923 or later for its design. A triangular fireplace expanded into a stage, then a large two-story classroom, beyond which was a circular sand-floored terrace. Construction never got beyond the retaining walls, which remain to

this day, so it is now deleted from the listing of constructed works.

The original landscaping of Olive Hill was designed by Lloyd Wright; it has long since been altered beyond recognition. Hollyhock House, which was restored between 1974 and 1976 under the direction of Lloyd Wright, has been designated by the American Institute of Architects as one of seventeen American buildings designed by Wright to be retained as an example of his architectural contribution to American culture. The house and Residence A are open to the public

Barnsdall Residence B

(Continues)

(S.208-211 *continued*)

through the City of Los Angeles Department of Cultural Affairs.

In 1988, a propitious earthquake hit the hill, leaving some walls damaged. The county was thus encumbered with the expense of repairs. Chemical tests, not in use during Lloyd Wright's restoration, were employed to determine the architect's original colors; these were then applied during the repainting. In 1989, reproductions of furniture were installed where originals were no longer available, completing the return of Hollyhock House to its earlier splendor.

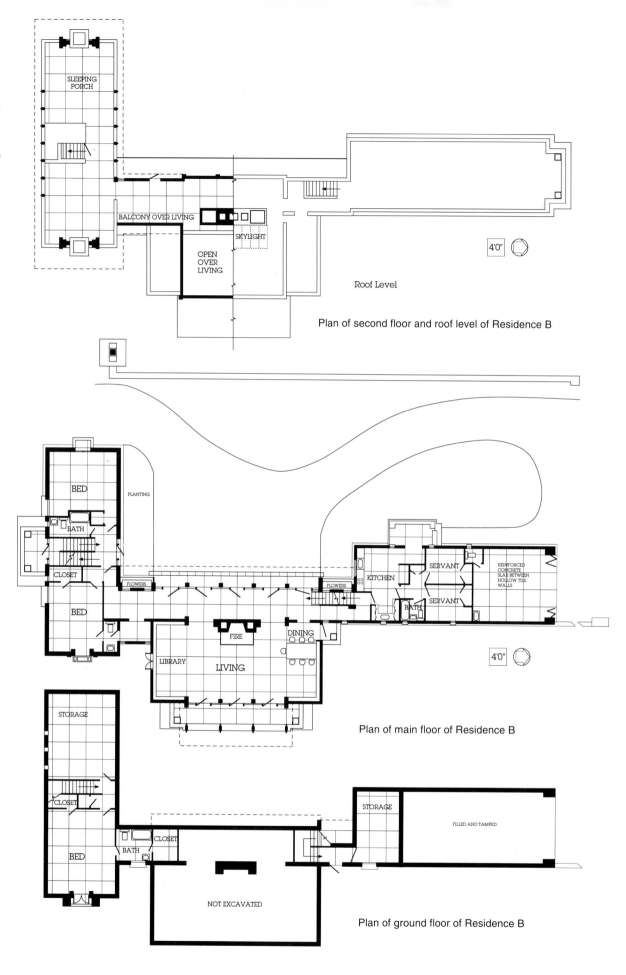

Plan of second floor and roof level of Residence B

Plan of main floor of Residence B

Plan of ground floor of Residence B

S.212   T.1803

Tazaemon **Yamamura** Residence (1918)
Ashiya, Japan
Converted to dormitory use

The house for sake brewer Tazaemon Yamamura is perched on a promontory above the left bank of the Ashiyagawa River, facing south to Osaka Bay. Four stories lift it up the hillside, and one 120-degree bend take it around its eastern slope. The lowest level is the entry with carport, while at top is a roof terrace outside a dining room with dramatic high peaked ceiling. The third floor is the largest, with two galleries spanning the length of the eastern exposure, bedrooms and other activities rooms to the west and both sides of the 120-degree juncture. Oya stone, plaster, and Lauan (Philippine mahogany) are the prime construction materials. The building has served in recent years as a company dormitory for the Yodagawa Seiko (Yodagawa Steel Company) of Osaka.

Terrace and dining room exterior

Dining room

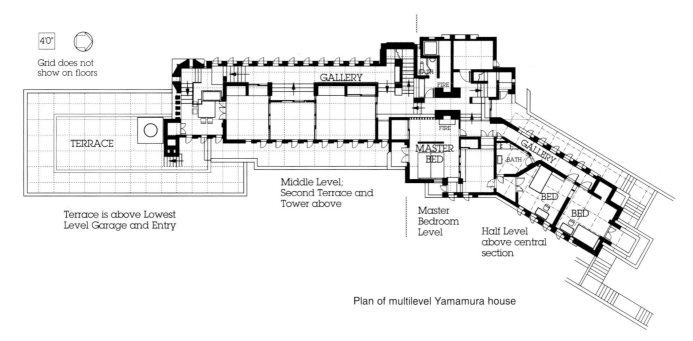

4'0"

Grid does not show on floors

TERRACE

GALLERY

Terrace is above Lowest Level Garage and Entry

Middle Level; Second Terrace and Tower above

Master Bedroom Level

MASTER BED

BATH

GALLERY

BED

BED

Half Level above central section

Plan of multilevel Yamamura house

Jiyu Gakuen Girls' School (1921)

Tokyo, Japan
Dining room expanded, and classroom wings added

Jiyu Gakuen is known to many in English as the School of the Free Spirit. The central area plan is composed of two rectangles, with a second-story 42-foot-long dining room at the rear and a two-story high, 32-foot-wide living room and classroom in the front. Pairs of 28-by-32-foot rooms on the sides are connected to the main building by the protective roof, creating breezeways that relate the structure and the students intimately to nature even in a crowded urban center. The whole is drawn to a 4-foot-square unit module.

Classrooms forming a **U**-shaped plan were added to the original structures later on, yet are perfectly integrated. The dining room has also been expanded by enclosing the 16-foot-square, flat-roofed spaces above the main-floor lavatories, and by a similar addition to the rear through former windows over flower boxes. All these additions are most likely the work of Arata Endo, who supervised Wright's work in Japan and whose son continues his father's practice of organic architecture following his Taliesin apprenticeship. This father-son team is largely responsible for the new Jiyu Gakuen School in the countryside west of Tokyo.

Main classroom, exterior, Jiyu Gakuen

Dining room

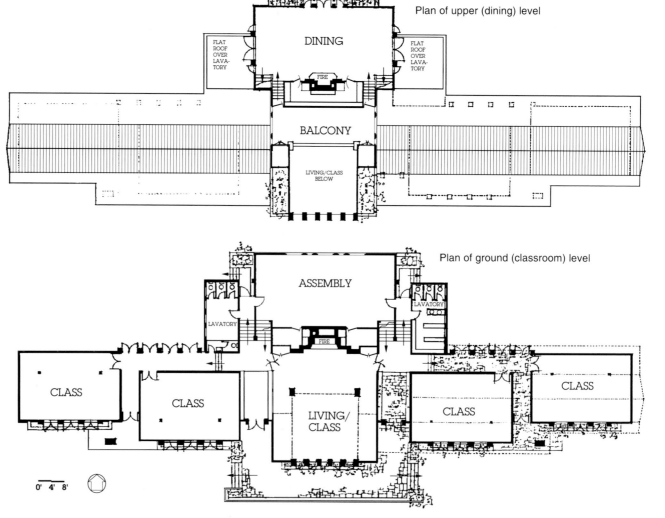

Plan of upper (dining) level

Plan of ground (classroom) level

Main classroom interior from balcony

S.214   T.2302
Mrs. Alice (George Madison)
Millard Residence, La Miniatura
(1923)
Pasadena, California

Alice Millard moved from a typical
Prairie house in Illinois (S.126) to one
in California that represented a new
direction, even for the pioneering
Wright. Built in 1923, the Millard house
was the first of four textile-block
houses constructed in the Los Angeles
area. Thirty years later Wright called
this his first Usonian house. Its two-
story-high living room is delicately lit
by pierced, patterned block and overlooks a lovely pool surrounded by lush
gardens deep in the ravine-traversed
site.

The face relief patterns vary for
each of the four textile-block projects.
The method of construction consisted
of laying concrete blocks three inches
thick, cast in molds, next to and on top
of one another without visible mortar
joints. In all but La Miniatura, steel
reinforcing rods were run horizontally
and vertically in edge reveals of the
blocks, then filled with thin concrete
(grouting), "knitting" the whole
together. A double wall was common,
held together by steel cross ties, the
air space serving as insulation. After
World War II, this knitting process,
called "knit block" (not to be confused
with W. B. Griffin's totally different
"knitlock" system), gave rise to the
Wright textile block. All four of the
California block houses (S.214–S.217)
were supervised in construction by
Lloyd Wright, eldest son of the architect. He also provided the landscaping
as well as design of the 1926 studio to
the side of the ravine below La
Miniatura.

La Miniatura

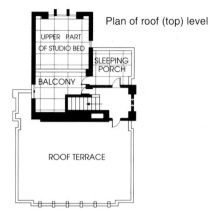

Plan of roof (top) level

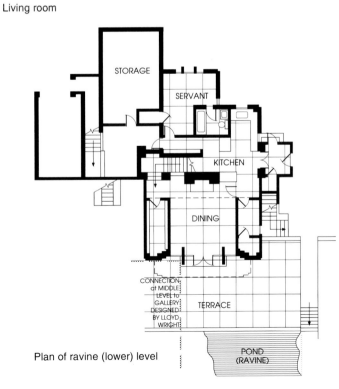

Living room

Plan of mezzanine
(upper) level

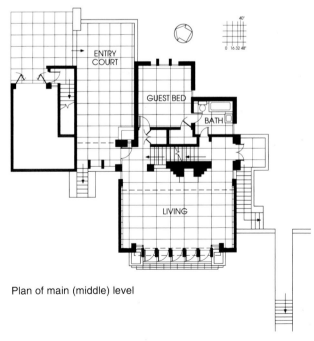

Plan of ravine (lower) level

Plan of main (middle) level

Transition from Prairie to Usonia

When Wright left Oak Park for Europe in the autumn of 1909, he knew that single-minded Prairie architecture, beautiful as it was, had not led to a democratic American architecture as he had hoped. Instead, Wright kept getting led into projects such as that for Harold McCormick, expensive schemes for the leaders of society rather than projects that would serve the American middle class.

From 1913 to 1919, Wright sought a new direction for his architecture. He tried prefabrication in the various Richards projects (S.201–S.204) and means of standardizing design by rotating and mirroring axes in the Ravine Bluffs units (S.188–S.192).

While Wright had more than a hundred projects in his Prairie decade, he had less than fifty between his sojourn in Europe and settling in California in the early twenties. Fortunately, one of these was the Imperial Hotel, whose construction occupied Wright for half the decade.

For Wright, the four California block houses (S.214–S.217) mark a new era. From this point on, the unit system, which he had experimented with throughout the Prairie era, became a standard upon which all his designs depended. The square

module, its size defined by a unit that was constant for the project, was the initial module, later supplanted by various equilateral polygons and eventually circular segments.

The California block houses, like the majority of their Prairie predecessors, were multilevel structures. The organization of activities in them was not as simplified and compact as it was in the single-story Usonians produced from 1935 on. In only two of these, the John Storer and Samuel Freeman houses, is the kitchen next to the living room, as would be standard after 1935; La Miniatura and the Mabel and Charles Ennis house feature formal dining rooms.

At the age of 86, Wright would declare that the California block houses (S.214–S.217) constituted four of the first five Usonian System houses (the other would be the Richard Lloyd Jones home, S.227). Though historians identify the beginning of the Usonian period with the first Jacobs residence (S.234), the system was in place with the development of the knit-block method of construction, which Wright developed, though did not fully employ, in the house for Alice Millard (S.214). Wright called the textile (patterned concrete) block "stone," and the regularity with which he would return to it, as the economic situation allowed or dictated, showed it to be a preferred material. It was only the Great Depression that caused Wright

to rethink his new direction and temporarily abandon block construction. Two Michigan subdivisions (S.294–S.301), the Usonian Automatic designs (S.386–S.389, S.392) including the Turkel house (S.388), which returns to California-style two-story construction, and unbuilt designs that became two types of prefabs for Marshall Erdman (S.406–S.412) are testimony to this. They are evidence that the "Usonian ideal" was fully compatible with all-masonry construction employing wood essentially as trim and was an (possibly the) operative principle in Wright's architecture from the early twenties to the architect's death.

TRANSFORMATION FROM PRAIRIE TO USONIA

START with a basic Prairie Cruciform plan suitable for a family of four, plus servant. First alter the living room, giving it a full glass "windowall" to its long side.

THEN reduce the kitchen, pantry and servant's space to a compact "Workspace" suitable for preparation of the family's meals by the modern American woman. Eliminate the formal dining room, and place dining activities in a convenient place just outside the workspace where it will share space with the living area and be seemingly enlarged thereby.

NEXT, bring all second floor activities down to ground level, placing them along a gallery running from the Workspace entry (so the housewife can watch at all times household activity while working in her space). This obviates the stairwell; the porte cochere is simplified into a carport, usually dramatically cantilevered. You achieve a Usonian house that is much more compact than was the Prairie ideal. It was also infinitely variable on a number of unit-modules to suit any site, any climate, and any size family.

START with a basic Cruciform plan. . .

ALTER the living room. . .
REDUCE the kitchen, pantry and servant's space. . .
ELIMINATE the formal dining room. . .

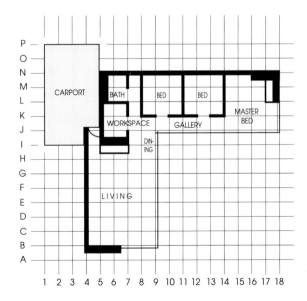

BRING all second floor activities down to ground level. . . the porte cochere is simplified into a carport. . .

Storer Residence, south terrace

Living room

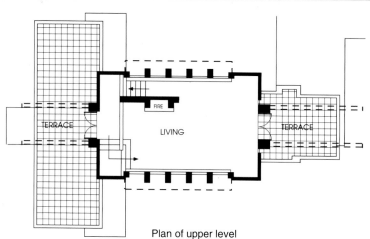

Plan of upper level

S.215   T.2304
John **Storer** Residence (1923)
Hollywood, California
Swimming pool added in sunken garden area. Structure restored in 1980s

The design of this house for John Storer, the second of the four Los Angeles area textile-block houses, is the culmination of an unbuilt G. P. Lowes idea translated to textile block from frame and cement plaster. The head of its **T**-plan is three levels, capped by an open terrace set at half level to the main-floor dining room and two-story living room above. The southern exposure has a view of Hollywood and Los Angeles. The northern view is into a courtyard, carved out of the rising hillside. The Storer house was supervised during construction by Lloyd Wright, who also designed the landscaping. Eric Wright, son of Lloyd Wright, grandson of Frank Lloyd Wright, was the architect for the restoration of the building by Joel Silver in the 1980s. A swimming pool is now fitted in where patriarch Wright had originally designed a sunken garden.

The Storer family name originated in Chûr, a town in the Swiss canton of Graubunden, over 500 years ago. A third "r" distinguishes those Storrers who migrated northeast, to what is now known as Bavaria, from the traditional Swiss family line, one of whom was John Storer.

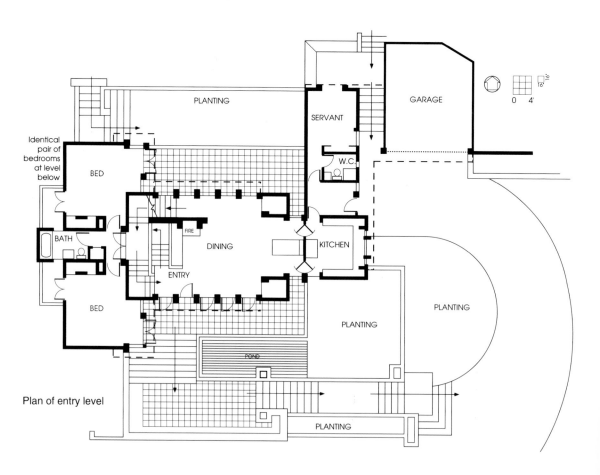

Plan of entry level

View across terrace to private facade

S.216 T.2402
Harriet and Samuel Freeman
Residence (1923)
Los Angeles, California
Undergoing restoration in 1990s

This third, or possibly last, of the California textile-block houses, clings to the Hollywood foothills of the Santa Monica Mountains. The living room, kitchen, balcony, and garage are on the entry level, and sleeping quarters and terrace are one story below. Eucalyptus (for appearance) and fir (structural) painted redwood red and both plain and patterned textile block are the materials employed in construction. The project was supervised by Lloyd Wright, who also did the working drawings and landscaping; one of the architect's students, R. M. Schindler, designed the Freeman's furniture. The house passed to the University of Southern California ownership via a living trust, upon Mrs. Harriet Freeman's death in 1986; her husband died in 1980. The university intends to restore the building and use it as quarters for visiting distinguished professors.

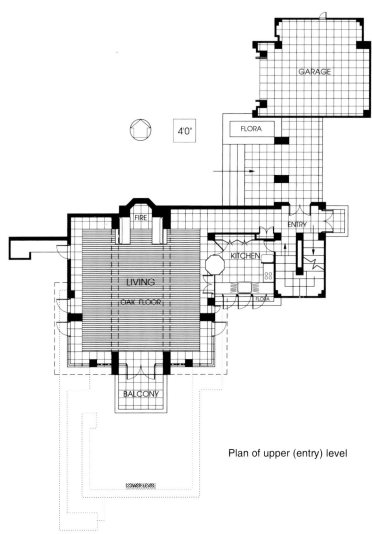

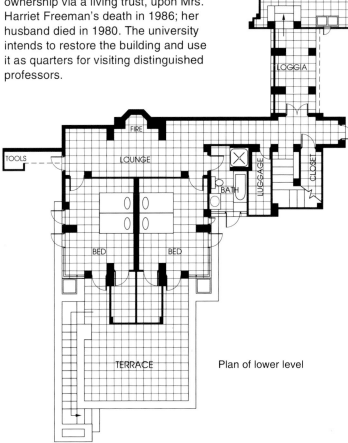
Plan of lower level

Plan of upper (entry) level

S.217   T.2401
**Mabel and Charles Ennis
Residence** (Ennis-Nesbitt) with
S.217A   T.2401
Detached **Chauffeur's Quarters**
(1923)
S.217B   T.4017
John **Nesbitt Alterations** to the
Ennis Residence (1940)
Los Angeles, California
East bedroom converted to alternate
uses. South retaining wall in serious
disrepair, sections collapsing in the
1980s. Now usually known as the
Ennis-Brown house.

North side of the
Ennis house

The last of the four Los Angeles
textile-block houses, the Ennis, is the
most monumental. Anywhere along
Vermont Avenue, looking north, one
sees it completing its ridge on the
southern reaches of the Santa Monica
Mountains, looking more like a Mayan
temple than any other Wright building
except Hollyhock House (S.208). Its
views are to Griffith Park, on the north,
and the Los Angeles metropolitan
area, on the south.

Entry is below the main level. A
long loggia on the north side at
half-level passes the living room on the
way to two bedrooms, which are
separated by a terrace. The dining
room, a half-level further up, looks
south; this level also features a guest
room, pantry, and kitchen. The "loggia," which connects all these rooms,
will become the "gallery" of Wright's
later Usonian homes. The plan is laid
out on a 4-foot unit, or three blocks (as
are all these California block houses).
The textile-block pattern is almost
symmetrical about the diagonal of its
sixteen-inch square surface. While in
the Freeman house (S.216) blocks are
paired, one mirroring the other, here
they usually are given the same
orientation, and in the Arizona Biltmore
Hotel and Cottages (S.221–S.222), the
pattern is complete only when the
blocks are paired. Teak provides
contrast to the neutral blocks. Art glass
windows—abstractions of wisteria—
are the last designed by Wright for
domestic use; hereafter he would use
cutouts in wood panels, throughout the
Usonian era. Lloyd Wright supervised
construction, prepared the working
drawings, and designed the landscaping, most of this after his father
had returned to Wisconsin.

Charles Ennis died at the age of
seventy in 1926; his wife Mabel occupied the house until 1936. Tenancy
passed through several owners over
the next 32 years. When his Wright-
designed 5000-square-foot, three-
tiered Carmel house project was
halted by World War II, radio personality John Nesbitt purchased the
Ennis house. He had it altered by
Wright with a north-terrace swimming
pool and ground-floor billiards room as
well as the first heating system for the
structure, a forced air system. In 1968,
Mr. and Mrs. August Brown became its
eighth owners, for $119,000, $31,000

less than the cost of original construction. They replaced a bath, bedroom,
and stucco wall with a Japanese
garden, opposite the swimming pool.
With structural deficiencies too expensive to correct fully, the building was in
serious disrepair by the 1980s, the
south retaining wall having partially
collapsed. Much of this results from
Wright's use of decomposed granite
from the construction site to color the
block. While intended to blend the
block with its site, it introduced natural
impurities to the concrete mix, which,
when combined with the Los Angeles
basin's high levels of air pollution,
caused early decay. The Browns have,
however, corrected leaking roofs and
many other inherited problems.

Mr. Brown established the Trust for
Preservation of Cultural Heritage to
insure maintenance of the house in
perpetuity, and donated the house to
this nonprofit corporation. The house's
name was then changed to Ennis-
Brown in recognition of the contributions to its restoration by its longest-
term tenant. While Brown remains in
residence as its curator, the building is
open for tours on the second Saturday
of each odd month by reservation only.
To obtain funds for restoration, the
structure has been used as a film site
for such items as *Black Rain* and
various television commercials.

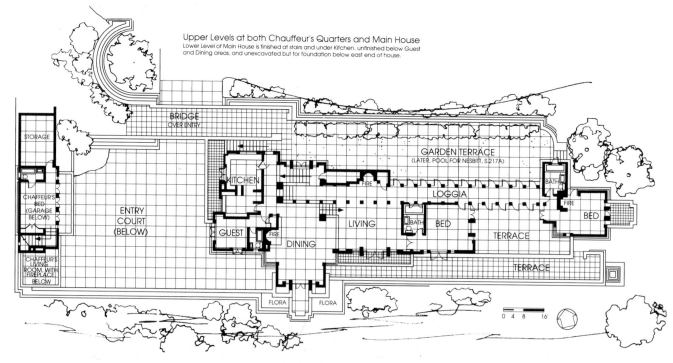

Upper Levels at both Chauffeur's Quarters and Main House
Lower Level of Main House is finished at stairs and under Kitchen, unfinished below Guest
and Dining areas, and unexcavated but for foundation below east end of house.

S.218   T.2501
Frank Lloyd Wright, Taliesin III,
Taliesin (1925–) and
S.219   T.4509
Dams (1945)
S.220   T.5910
Mrs. Frank Lloyd Wright, **Enclosed Garden at Taliesin** (1959)
Spring Green, Wisconsin
Enclosed Garden converted to other uses

Taliesin is the name of Wright's home in Wisconsin. It is from the Welsh, meaning "shining brow"; Taliesin does not sit atop the hill but rather clings to the brow above the left bank of the Wisconsin River, looking north and east. There have been two major rebuildings at Taliesin (S.172) since it was first built in 1911 (S.182 and this). Taliesin West (S.241) was built in Arizona in 1937, and there is perhaps even a "Taliesin the Third" or "Taliesin East," the Hotel Plaza Apartment Remodeling (S.381). Taliesin in Wisconsin is sometimes called "Taliesin North." The current Taliesin was rebuilt in 1925 after destruction by fire. As in 1914, only living quarters were destroyed, and much of Taliesins I and II remains in Taliesin III.

Constructed mostly of native limestone, wood, and plaster surfacing, it has been continually altered over the years in keeping with the needs of the Wrights and the Taliesin Fellowship. After the second, 1925, fire, Wright planned and executed extensive westward additions. The hill garden was partially terraced. A formal terrace was completed south of Mr. Wright's bedroom. The dams in the valley have created a small lake that is used for recreation as well as to control water flow through the farm land. The garden was built for Mrs. Wright by the Fellowship in the summer of 1960. Taliesin is one of seventeen buildings designated by the AIA to be retained as an example of Wright's architectural contribution to American culture.

Taliesin III from across the lake

Taliesin III from northwest: (l. to r.); Mrs. Wright's bedroom, loggia, bird walk, living room

Taliesin III living room

(Continues)

Taliesin III guest bedroom

Taliesin III: (l. to r.); loggia, Mr. Wright's bedroom, terrace

Taliesin III tower with dining room and kitchen

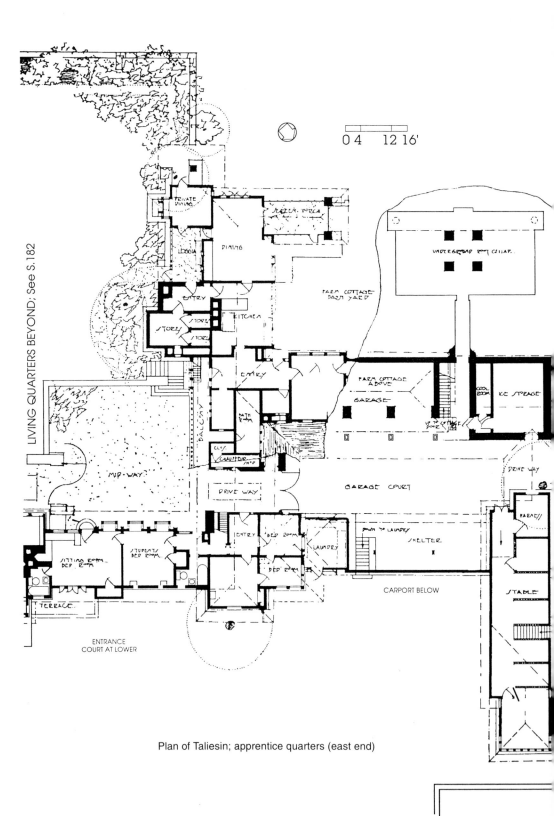

Plan of Taliesin; apprentice quarters (east end)

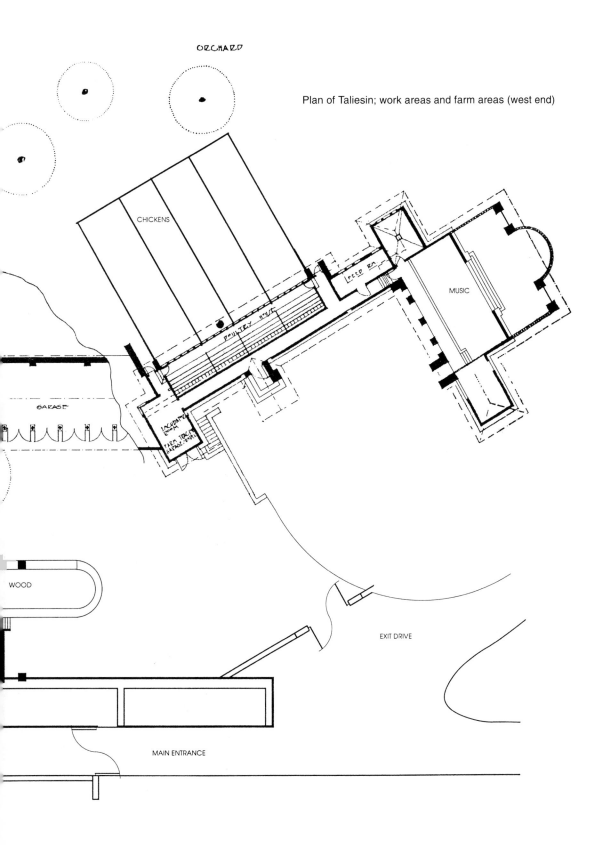

ORCHARD

Plan of Taliesin; work areas and farm areas (west end)

CHICKENS

MUSIC

GARAGE

WOOD

EXIT DRIVE

MAIN ENTRANCE

(Continues)

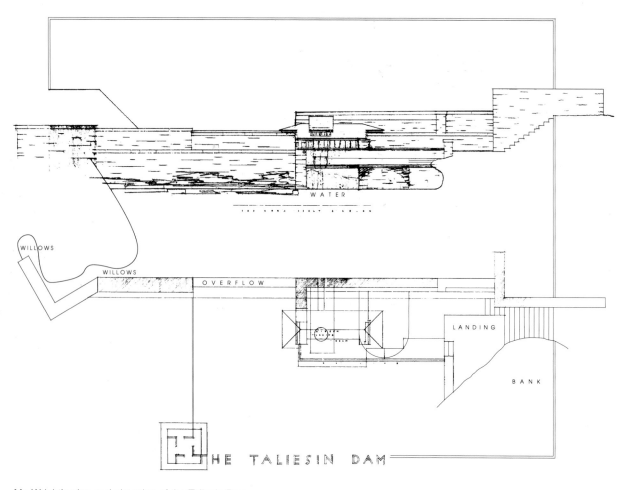

WATER

WILLOWS

WILLOWS

OVERFLOW

LANDING

BANK

THE TALIESIN DAM

Mr. Wright's plan and elevation of the Taliesin Dam

S.221   T.2710
Arizona Biltmore Hotel and
S.222   T.2710
Fifteen **Cottages** (as listed below)
S.222A   T.2710
Six **Single-story Type 1** (four
apartment) **Cottages**
S.222B   T.2710
Five **Single-story Type 2** (five
apartment) **Cottages**
S.222C   T.2710
Four **Two-story Cottages** (1927)
for Warren, Charles, and Albert
McArthur
Phoenix, Arizona
The six single-story four-apartment
cottages are numbered as follows: the
southern group, clockwise from the
southwest unit S.222.1A to S.222.3A,
the northern group, west to east,
S.222.4A and S.222.5A. A demolished
unit is S.222.6A.
The five single-story five-apartment
units are numbered as follows:
clockwise from the southeast S.222.1B
to S.222.4B for the four extant units,
S.222.5B for the demolished unit.
The four two-story units are numbered
as follows; clockwise from the
southeast S.222.1C to S.222.4C.
Two single-story cottages demolished,
as noted above. Cottage units S.222A
gained terraces and enlarged bathrooms in 1982.
The hotel was renovated after a fire in
June 1973. There have been additions
by Taliesin Associated Architects using
textile block to blend old with new.

Much confusion remains concerning
attribution of these designs. Three
sons of Warren McArthur (S.011),
Warren, Jr., Charles, and Albert
Chase, were building a resort hotel in
Phoenix. Albert's two brothers asked
Wright to come to Arizona to help
Albert with the design. Wright, often
short of cash, was happy to do so and
was paid $10,000 for the "patent" that
Albert thought existed on the textile
block system. The basic layout may be
credited to McArthur, but certain parts
of the design reveal Wright's hand with
few or no adjustments by Albert
McArthur: the Aztec theatre, the
Arizona room, and the cottages, in
particular. Drawings for the detailing
and the textile block method of
construction took Wright five months
(January–May 1928) in the desert heat
to complete and confirm that, without
his effort, the Arizona Biltmore as we

Biltmore main entry

Biltmore lobby

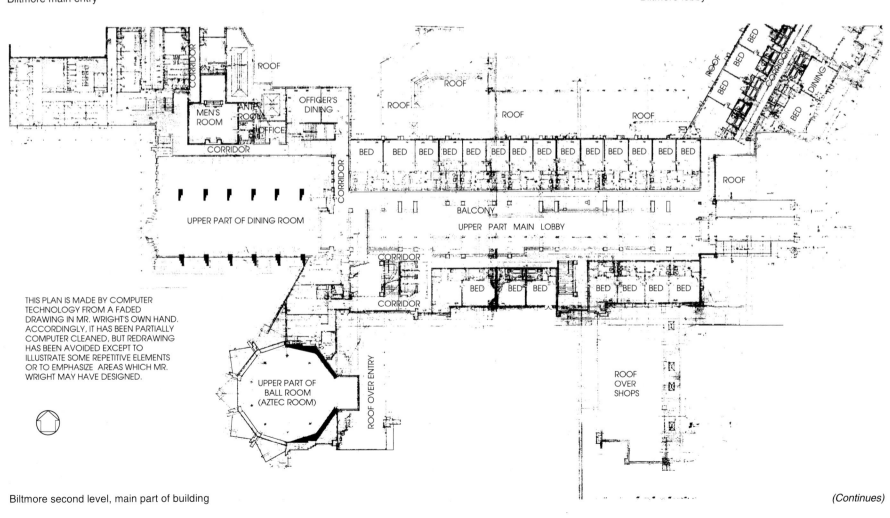

THIS PLAN IS MADE BY COMPUTER
TECHNOLOGY FROM A FADED
DRAWING IN MR. WRIGHT'S OWN HAND.
ACCORDINGLY, IT HAS BEEN PARTIALLY
COMPUTER CLEANED, BUT REDRAWING
HAS BEEN AVOIDED EXCEPT TO
ILLUSTRATE SOME REPETITIVE ELEMENTS
OR TO EMPHASIZE AREAS WHICH MR.
WRIGHT MAY HAVE DESIGNED.

Biltmore second level, main part of building

(Continues)

Biltmore Gold Room, with Frank Lloyd Wright Building Conservancy conference diners at far end, March 1990

Biltmore Aztec Room

know it today would have been an impossibility.

When Wright left Phoenix, McArthur made changes in Wright's beautiful proportions. Albert had studied at the Armour Institute of Technology in Chicago and at Harvard and in 1908 he worked as a draftsman for Wright. He seemed to think four floors better than three, or three than two, wherever possible. McArthur, author of a few undistinguished residences and office buildings, is architect of record. Wright, who considered the building "even worse" than he thought it would be, wrote, on June 2, 1930, "Albert McArthur is the architect of that building—all attempts to take credit for that performance are gratuitous and beside the mark."

McArthur produced "his" designs for John McEntee Bowman, president of Bowman Biltmore Hotels. The Arizona Biltmore was but one of fourteen Bowman Biltmore establishments, commissioned when Phoenix was a town of only 70,000. The Arizona Biltmore Company board of directors consisted of John H. Gage, chairman, James Woods, first vice-president, Charles Baad, vice-president, F. A. Reid (president, Salt River Valley Water Users Association), Frank J. Mangham, Charles H. McArthur, secretary and treasurer, and Warren McArthur, selling agent. When supplemental funding was required, additional stockholders were brought in; James A. Talbot (president, Richfield Oil), Herbert Fleishhacker of San Francisco, C. W. Clark (United Verde Copper Co.), James F. Gorman (president of the Chicago, Rock Island and Pacific Railroad) and William Wrigley, Jr. (of the chewing gum empire, and owner of the Chicago Cubs baseball team).

The original Biltmore was situated on 200 acres in the foothills of Squaw Peak, with 400 acres reserved for a residential park. The complex had its own water system and underground electrical facilities, the first such in Arizona. It also has a nursery growing fresh vegetables and fruits for the hotel restaurants.

Wright had wanted 12-inch-square, 3-inch-thick blocks (coffered to reduce weight); McArthur used 18-by-13 1/2-inch-high blocks, saving almost 50 percent on the production of blocks. The face design is an abstraction of the "criss-crossed pattern of freshly trimmed trunks of palm trees" according to Anna, the wife of Emry Kopta, the "Rodin of the southwest," fifth sculptor to work from Wright's drawings. Kopta's efforts led to the design of aluminum forms that, with adjustments, served to produce, on-site, the multitude of inside and outside corner and half-block variations necessary for construction of the main hotel building and the cottages.

The copper roof consists of 32,500 pounds of Sun Belt copper; the lobby ceiling is the largest gold-leafed ceiling in the world, actually a design economy, since it never requires maintenance.

The opening, scheduled for December 1928, was delayed until February 23, 1929, eight months before the stock market crashed. At the reopening, for the second season, on November 10, Wrigley was the effective owner. His home, La Colina Solana, an Earl Heitschmidt design, is the most recognizable landmark, perched on its hill, as one approaches the Biltmore; here Wrigley died in 1932, but the Biltmore and surrounding estates remained in the Wrigley family, guided by the only son Philip, until 1973. Air-conditioning was "ordered" by Philip in 1963, and the cottages were air-conditioned a year later and the Breakfast Room converted to a Ballroom.

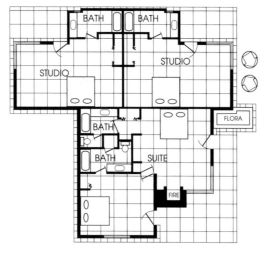

Single-story Type 1 Cottage

Single-story Type 2 Cottage

Arizona Biltmore Cottage, Single-story, four unit

Arizona Biltmore Cottage, two-story

Talley Industries acquired the Biltmore properties, now grown to 1100 acres (which does not include the Fashion Park mall) in 1973 for $21,500,000; on June 20, Phoenix's first six-alarm fire destroyed the fourth floor and damaged lower floors and the roof. Only 82 days were available to correct $6,000,000 damage and reopen on time, September 29. This was accomplished by the Taliesin Associated Architects and the J. R. Porter Construction Company of Phoenix. "Saguaro Forms and Cactus Flowers," a back-lit mural of stained glass in the foyer, is a 1929 Wright design added during reconstruction. The lobby carpet is also a Wright design, from that originally used in the Imperial Hotel.

Since this 1973 renovation, the Taliesin Associated Architects, with John Rattenbury as project architect, have been restoring the Biltmore complex as well as adding to it a Conference Center and other rooms.

S.223   T.2711
Beach Cottages, Dumyât, Egypt
(1927)
Six built, all demolished

The beach cottages at Dumyât (or Damietta), six to be set in a circle angled as 60-degree spokes of a pinwheel, were prefabricated structures designed to be disassembled each year and stored during the spring flood season. Looking like origami butterflies, these canvas-roofed box-board tents were designed to be bolted to concrete mats.

Dumyât is the last town in the delta of the east branch of the Nile River, 30 miles west of Port Said and the Suez Canal. The cottages were a few miles beyond the town, at Râs el Barr. Lake Manzala is on one side of this cape and the Mediterranean on the other; the cottages may have been located on the lake rather than on the seaside.

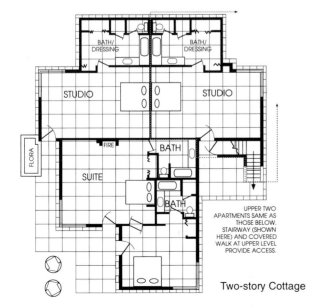

Two-story Cottage

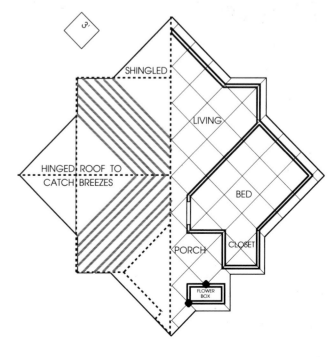

Ocatillo Desert Camp

S.224 T.2702
Frank Lloyd Wright, **Ocatillo Desert Camp** (1928)
Chandler, Arizona
Demolished. The site remains, with some evidence of Wright's occupancy, but suburbs are rapidly approaching.

Ocatillo (Wright spelled it "Ocatilla"), "candle flame," the name given the red triangular forms created by the one-two (30–60-degree) triangle, and painted in the gables, was a group of buildings around a hill, with a board-and-batten wall to link them and enclose the area against various dangers. Indoor areas were covered by white canvas, diffusing the brilliant desert sun; Wright did not forget this magic when he built Taliesin West. The Ocatillo Desert Camp, constructed of wood and canvas much like the Egyptian Beach Cottages (S.223), was a temporary residence for Wright in 1929, when the architect's designs for the Chandler, Arizona, area were in progress. Wright's association with client Dr. Alexander Chandler was, for the most part, unfruitful. Projects never realized from this year and for this client alone included San Marcos-in-the-Desert (a resort hotel), San Marcos Hotel alterations, San Marcos Water Gardens, a simple block house, and a residence for Owen D. Young. All these projects died in the stock market crash.

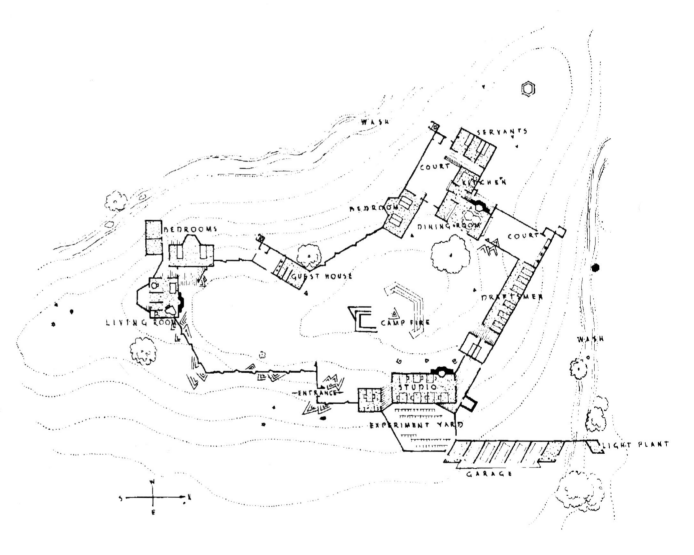

S.225   T.2701
Isabel Martin Residence, Graycliff
and
S.226   T.2701
Garage (1927)
Derby, New York
Garage converted to school building

Mrs. Darwin D. ("Bel") Martin built *her* summer home in Derby and furnished it with comfortable wicker furniture. It was here that the gray-haired Christian Scientist Martins, he with a large white moustache, would spend long periods in summer with their children and grandchildren.

Graycliff was a scant 25 yards from the bluff whose precipice drops directly to Lake Erie. The residence, probably originally of plaster surface with wood trim, has been resurfaced. A grand living room with an enormous stone fireplace is the central feature of the building. The kitchen is at one end of the plan, below the servants' quarters. The master bedroom has its own fireplace, but shares its bath with another bedroom. Two other bedrooms have their own bathrooms. A screened sleeping porch provided relief from summer heat.

The town of Derby is fictive, existing as a post office, established first in the railroad station on the tracks of the Lake Shore and Michigan Southern Rail Road in 1873, but no defined town center. It is named after Henry G. Derby, an official of the New York Central Rail Road, who was responsible for construction of stations on rail lines that were often shared by several companies.

In recent years the property has served as a residence for the Piarist Fathers, who are dedicated to educating the young. The garage may have been started in 1926 and is now used as a school building. Wright did not supervise the construction of either building.

Graycliff entry

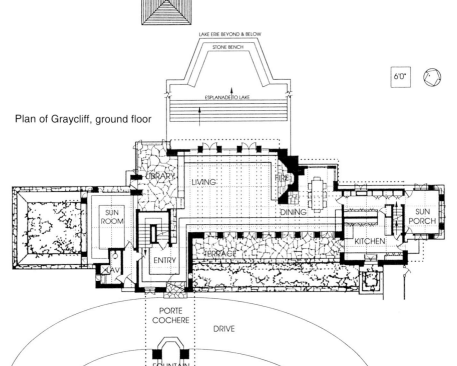

Plan of Graycliff, upper floor

Plan of Graycliff, ground floor

Isabel Martin's living room as she furnished it

Graycliff Garage

Richard Lloyd Jones Residence, entry, with "conservatory" (right)

S.227 T.2902
Richard Lloyd Jones Residence,
Westhope, with
S.227A T.2902
Detached **Garage** and Servants'
Quarters (1929)
Tulsa, Oklahoma
Various alterations, including addition
of concealed air conditioning system,
and several resizings of the kitchen

Wright's first project in Oklahoma was
for his first cousin, Richard Lloyd
Jones, founder of *The Tulsa Tribune.*
Though Frank and Richard fought as
children, the newspaper editor
supported Wright when no commissions were coming in, hired him as his
architect, and lived in the Wright-
designed house until his death at age
ninety.

No one view reveals the true
dimension of this accomplishment in
glass and textile block. The dwelling,
two stories high for only one-third of
the plan, encloses a raised inner
courtyard with a swimming pool. Built
on a 5-foot-square unit module, it
employs dry-tamped concrete blocks

inside and out, colored a dull orange-
brown to blend with the local sandstone. The blocks are one-third by
one-fourth of the module in surface
dimension; previous domestic textile
block construction (S.214–S.217)
utilized square-faced block (while the
Arizona Biltmore, S.221–S.222,
employed rectangular blocks), freeing
the vertical unit system from the
dominant horizontal one. Typically
inside, four plain blocks are stacked
before the designed block is laid. The
lights in the grills are dipped in orange
shellac to provide a candlelike glow.

The house, on 4 acres, is large by
any standard, especially Wright's, at
10,000 square feet. The living room is
flanked by a study and three bedrooms; a second floor imitates this with
children's bedrooms opening to a roof
garden. A half-level below were
kitchen, pantry, and billiards room. A
five-car garage with servants' rooms,
considerably altered, are in a detached
structure.

The building has gone through various modifications and renovations,
primarily by architect Murray McCune
in 1965, then the Nelson family, and
more recently by Sandra Holden and
Dr. Dwight Holden. The structure has
been modified for modern conveniences such as air conditioning (with

Richard Lloyd Jones living room

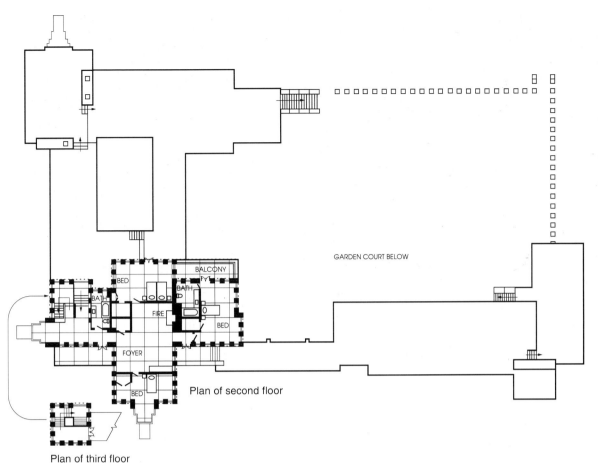

BALCONY

BED

BATH BATH

FIRE

BED

FOYER

BED

Plan of second floor

GARDEN COURT BELOW

Plan of third floor

vents concealed behind the grillwork of the cut-out Mayan-design blocks), the kitchen enlarged by combining with the pantry, then renovated again in favor of its original arrangement. The open terrace has been made into an enclosed patio. The stairwell to the top floor was added during construction and is not on Wright's original plans. Three decorative extensions or conservatories off the interior space may have served as aviaries but were also supplied with water to serve as winter greenhouses.

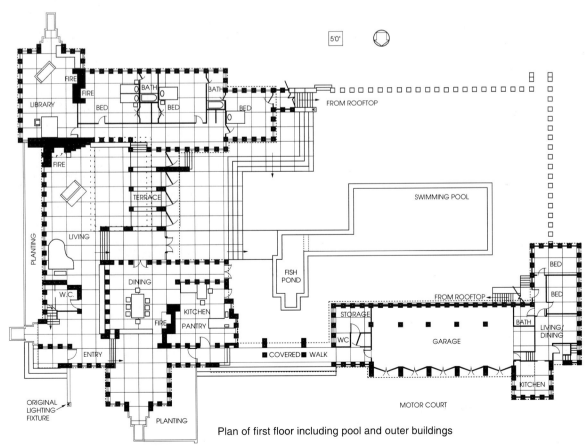

5'0"

FIRE
FIRE

LIBRARY

BATH
BED
BED
BATH
BED

FROM ROOFTOP

FIRE

TERRACE

LIVING

PLANTING

DINING

W.C.

KITCHEN

FIRE

PANTRY

ENTRY

ORIGINAL LIGHTING FIXTURE

PLANTING

SWIMMING POOL

FISH POND

FROM ROOFTOP

BED
BED

STORAGE

BATH

LIVING/ DINING

WC

GARAGE

COVERED WALK

KITCHEN

MOTOR COURT

Plan of first floor including pool and outer buildings

Taliesin Fellowship Complex, new Theatre with foyer to the left, living room to the right

S.228   T.3301
Frank Lloyd Wright, **Taliesin Fellowship Complex,** Hillside (1932–), including
S.228A
Hillside Drafting Studio (1932),
S.228B   T.3302
Hillside Playhouse (1933) and
S.228C   T.5213
Hillside Theatre (1952)
Spring Green, Wisconsin
Playhouse destroyed by fire, 1952, rebuilt as Hillside Theatre. Fellowship Complex remodeled many times over the years, including the Playhouse foyer (1944) and the kitchen (1952)

The Great Depression left Wright with few commissions. Instead of retiring in 1932 at the age of sixty-five, he entered a whole new era of creativity. He founded the Taliesin Fellowship (three of the first apprentices were William Wesley Peters, John H. Howe, and Edgar Tafel). He remodeled the Hillside Home School II (S.069),

converting the gymnasium into the Hillside Playhouse, for use by the fellowship. The playhouse was destroyed by fire in 1952. Wright built a new theater, giving it its own foyer, and re-did adjacent classrooms as a new dining room at a balcony level to the stage and overlooking it from behind.

Across the bridge to the north of the main entry is the great hall of the drafting studio, a major expansion in 1932 of the original laboratory classrooms of Hillside School, the Dana Gallery, and Roberts Room. This was refurbished in 1978–80 and is the center of activity for the Taliesin Associated Architects (Taliesin Architects as of 1990). Tours of the Fellowship Complex are offered daily during the warmer months of the year; the fellowship still spends its winters in Arizona.

With the fellowship, Wright began work on his concept of Broadacre City and the Usonian home. In the drafting room of the complex, each apprentice would draw his idea of a good American home; Wright would rework the student sketch, breathe life into it, and

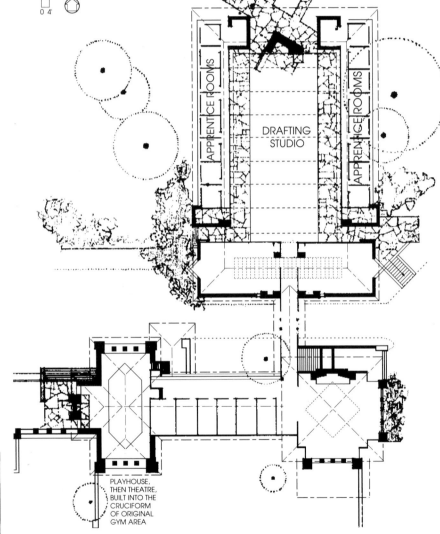

Plan of Hillside

Dining room in Hillside

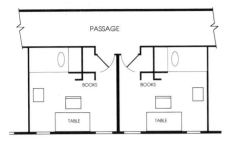

Apprentice rooms to the side of
the Drafting Studio

Hillside: living room to the left, Drafting Studio to the right

Hillside Drafting Studio

The Theatre in the Fellowship Complex

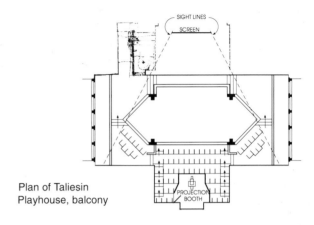

Plan of Taliesin
Playhouse, balcony

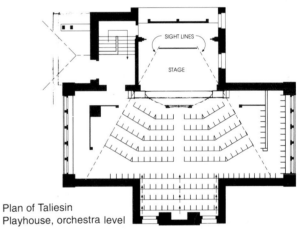

Plan of Taliesin
Playhouse, orchestra level

thus help the student develop his skills. But Wright's scheme for a truly American city was realized on a grand scale only in models and in a few scattered works—for example, the Affleck and Abby Beecher Roberts houses (S.274, S.236), Suntop Homes (S.248), and the Lindholm Service Station (S.414)—but never in the way Wright wanted, in a complete city or in a new concept of American city planning universally applied.

As Taliesin entered its fourth decade since Wright's death, former Taliesin Fellows carried on the practice of organic architecture. Tom Casey, Charles and Minerva Montooth, John Rattenbury, Cornelia Brierly, John Hill, Ling Po, Dick Carney, Bruce Brooks Pfeiffer, Kenn and Sue Lockhart, David and Anneliese Dodge are but a few of those who were with Mr. Wright in the 1950s. William Wesley Peters was the dean among these; this author and Taliesin archivist Greg Williams had lunch and a long sharing of ideas thereafter at Taliesin less than an hour before Peters had his fatal heart attack. Mr. Wright, Olgivanna, Wes—one by one the giants of Taliesin history have left us all rich memories.

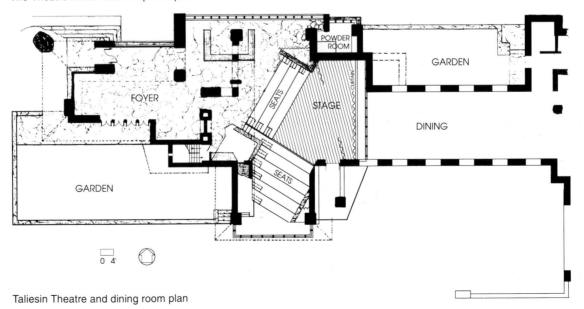

Taliesin Theatre and dining room plan

Willey Residence

S.229   T.3401
Malcolm E. **Willey** Residence (1933)
Minneapolis, Minnesota

The house Wright built for Malcolm Willey, a college administrator, was the second of two designs. It is a single-story structure of dark red sand and paving bricks with cypress trim located above the Mississippi River on a bluff that was disfigured in the 1960s by the intrusion of Interstate Highway 94. With its central workspace—Wright's term for a kitchen and utilities core—directly adjoining the living-dining room, it represents the major bridge between the Prairie style and the soon-to-appear standard **L**-plan Usonian house.

Actually all the features of a Usonian in-line plan are here but are not in the usual order. The workspace is on one side of the living room and the gallery linking the quiet spaces on the other, an arrangement Wright used in his first true in-line Usonian, for Lloyd Lewis (S.265), but soon abandoned for a workspace at the juncture of the living room and gallery, as in **L**-plan houses. The Willey-Lewis layout was used again in the Erdman Prefab #1 (S.406–S.411) units. The use of cypress is important. Wright had always preferred American woods, particularly oak, whose major fault was that its open grain held dirt and dust, quickly darkening. Cypress, particularly east coast red Tidewater cypress, became a favorite wood for all Usonian construction. It was a beautiful wood with fine grain and warm coloration and was highly resistant to rot. Wright specified it regularly, agreeing to substitutions when it was unavailable or too costly for the client.

S.230   T.3602
Liliane S. and Edgar J. **Kaufmann,** Sr., **Residence Fallingwater** (1935)
Mill Run, Pennsylvania
Restoration is ongoing

Aside from his own Taliesin Fellowship Complex, Wright had seen only two of his projects constructed over a period of almost eight years, from 1928 to 1935. Then, when the architect was sixty-nine, came Fallingwater, the Johnson Administration Building (S.237), and the structure commonly known as the first-built Usonian home (S.234), all in one year, and Wingspread (S.239) in the following year.

Fallingwater is perhaps the best-known private home for someone not of royal blood in the history of the world. Perched over a waterfall deep in the Pennsylvania highlands, it seems part of the rock formations to which it clings. Reinforced-concrete cantilever slabs project from the rock band to carry the house over the stream. From the square living room, one can step directly down a suspended stairway to the stream. Immediately above, on the third level, terraces open from sleeping quarters, emphasizing the horizontal nature of the structural forms; "the apotheosis of the horizontal" it has been called. Robert Mosher did the early supervision of Fallingwater. Edgar Tafel, who had arrived at Taliesin but four years earlier, completed the work from the second level and above.

Fallingwater's features are too many to describe in a few paragraphs, but a few must be listed. The stone is known as Pottsville sandstone; the

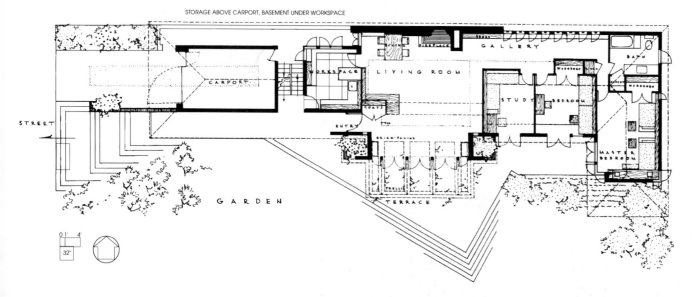

STORAGE ABOVE CARPORT, BASEMENT UNDER WORKSPACE

ridge from which the stone is quarried starts in Pottsville (between and slightly north of Harrisburg and Allentown). Nonstructural wood is North Carolina black walnut. The several centuries old chairs at the dining table were found by Mrs. Kaufmann in Italy and have only three legs, which makes them stable on the rough stone floor. The kettle at the fireplace, which allows mulling of wine, holds 18 gallons. The kitchen has its original St. Charles cabinets.

At one point, whether in jest or not is uncertain, Wright suggested to Kaufmann that Fallingwater ought to be gold-leafed inside and out. Kaufmann loved the idea, hired a leafer who spent one day working, at the end of which he said the idea was absurd, and left. Thus, the "dead rhododendron" color was adopted for masonry surfaces.

No matter how high the quality of design or how much care goes into its construction, a building requires upkeep. Long-term maintenance of Fallingwater is entrusted to WASA

Fallingwater, the Kaufmann Residence

Dining area with three-legged chairs from Italy, Liliane S. Kaufmann's solution to chairs on the rough stone floor

Fireplace in the living room

Living room

(Continues)

237

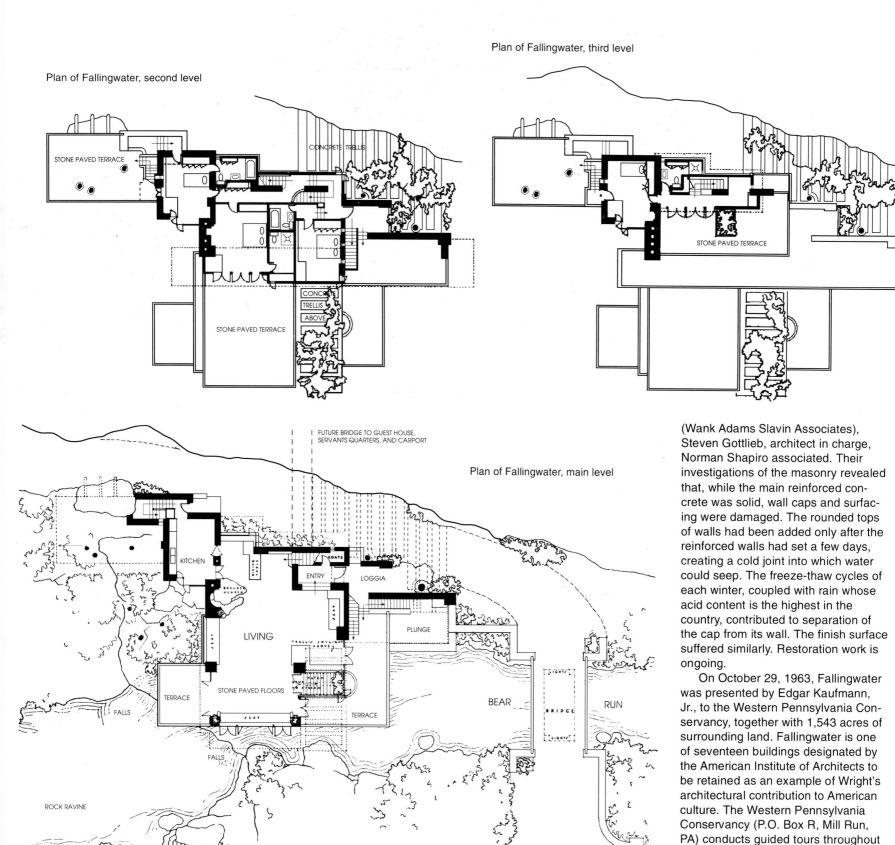

Plan of Fallingwater, second level

Plan of Fallingwater, third level

STONE PAVED TERRACE

CONCRETE TRELLIS

STONE PAVED TERRACE

CONCRETE TRELLIS ABOVE

STONE PAVED TERRACE

FUTURE BRIDGE TO GUEST HOUSE, SERVANTS QUARTERS, AND CARPORT

Plan of Fallingwater, main level

KITCHEN

COATS

ENTRY

LOGGIA

BOULDER HEARTH

SEAT

LIVING

PLUNGE

SEAT

STONE PAVED FLOORS

TRELLIS SKYLIGHT ABOVE

TERRACE

FALLS

TERRACE

SEAT

BEAR

RUN

BRIDGE

LIGHTS

LIGHTS

FALLS

ROCK RAVINE

0 2 4   10   15'

ENTRANCE DRIVEWAY

(Wank Adams Slavin Associates), Steven Gottlieb, architect in charge, Norman Shapiro associated. Their investigations of the masonry revealed that, while the main reinforced concrete was solid, wall caps and surfacing were damaged. The rounded tops of walls had been added only after the reinforced walls had set a few days, creating a cold joint into which water could seep. The freeze-thaw cycles of each winter, coupled with rain whose acid content is the highest in the country, contributed to separation of the cap from its wall. The finish surface suffered similarly. Restoration work is ongoing.

On October 29, 1963, Fallingwater was presented by Edgar Kaufmann, Jr., to the Western Pennsylvania Conservancy, together with 1,543 acres of surrounding land. Fallingwater is one of seventeen buildings designated by the American Institute of Architects to be retained as an example of Wright's architectural contribution to American culture. The Western Pennsylvania Conservancy (P.O. Box R, Mill Run, PA) conducts guided tours throughout the year; these are limited to weekends during the cold winter months. Reservations are advised.

Edgar J. **Kaufmann,** Sr., **Guesthouse** (1938)
Mill Run, Pennsylvania

Three years after Fallingwater was designed, Mr. Kaufmann was seeking a place to put an overflow of guests. Fallingwater had room for one guest couple on the second floor where the separate bedrooms for Mr. and Mrs. Kaufmann were located. Another bedroom on the third floor could be pressed into service when Edgar, Jr., was not in residence, but this was not sufficient, so a guesthouse was built above and behind the main building, reached by a serpentine covered walkway. This guesthouse has its own lounge with fireplace, bath, and bedroom with terrace and pool (this latter item sketched in 1938 and added later). These are east of the stair; to the west are a laundry room and four-car garage at the same level, and two single bedrooms, one double bedroom, and bath at an upper level. This upper-level section has been converted to offices for Fallingwater's staff.

In 1947, Wright designed an addition, a garage at the upper level, but this was never built.

Kaufmann Guesthouse

Fireplace in Guesthouse

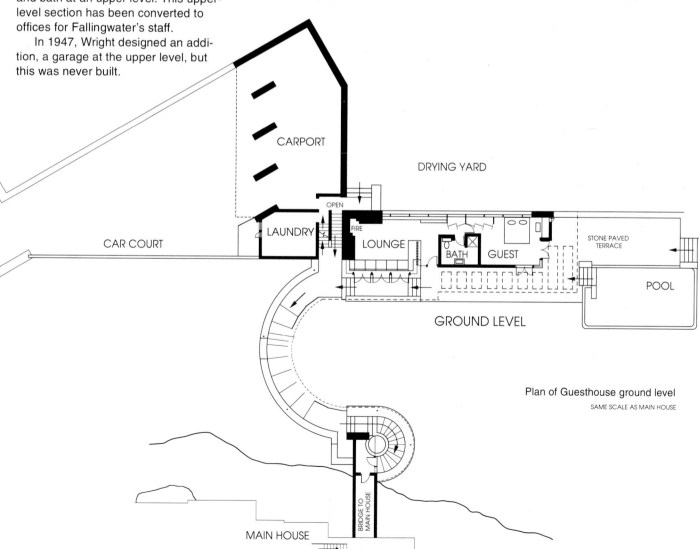

Plan of Guesthouse ground level

SAME SCALE AS MAIN HOUSE

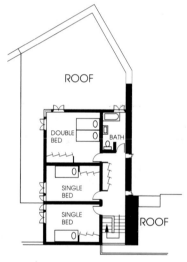

Plan of servant wing of Guesthouse

Kaufmann Office

S.233   T.3704
Edgar J. **Kaufmann,** Sr., **Office**
(1937)
Pittsburgh, Pennsylvania
Moved to the Victoria and Albert
Museum, London, England

Wright's work for the Kaufmann Department Store in downtown Pittsburgh included furniture and paneling. In *The Natural House* Wright noted that sitting is "in itself an unfortunate necessity not quite elegant yet" but admitted that "it is possible now to design a chair in which any sitter is compelled to look comfortable whether he is so or not." Finally, "when the house-interior absorbs the chair as in perfect harmony, then we will have achieved not so minor a symptom of a culture of our

own." To create this harmony in the Kaufmann office, Wright's chairs and other furniture are complemented by a cedar plywood mural in relief.

Carpeting and upholstery were handwoven by Loja Saarinen, wife of Eliel Saarinen, at the Cranbrook Academy of Art near Detroit. The asymmetrical pattern of yellow on off-white is woven into two carpets of hand-knotted woolen pile in a flax base. The upholstery is woven of mercerized (a process involving caustic alkali, to strengthen the fiber and make it more readily dyed, as well as give it a silky luster) cotton, rayon (a synthetic fiber with high gloss) and cotton chenille to achieve its special texture; the colors match the carpet.

The office was dismantled in the late 1950s and given to the Victoria and Albert Museum, London, in 1974. Reconstructed in its entirety, the office has been on display in the Henry Cole Wing of the museum since January 1993.

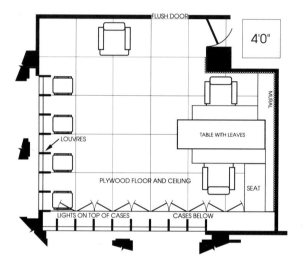

Usonia

"Usonia" (*U*nited, *S*tates, *o*f, *N*orth, America, with an *i* inserted to make the word euphonious), a term attributed to Samuel Butler and supposed to distinguish those in the United States from other Americans on the north and south continents of the western hemisphere, was an ideal to Wright; affordable, beautiful housing for a democratic America.

According to Wright, the first Usonian houses were the California block houses of 1923 (S.214–S.217), but the "Usonian era" is often said to begin with the first Jacobs house (S.234). The Usonian concept was spatial, "the space within to be lived in," not structural. Spatially, the masonry core was important. This "workspace"—kitchen, laundry, utilities, and the like—places the housewife at the heart of domestic activities. Dining space was immediately adjacent for convenience. Active space, the living room, extends the plan in one direction, quiet space, the bedrooms, in another. Typically this meant a 90-degree, or **L**, plan, laid out on a grid of squares, a significant simplification of the Prairie cruciform. Future Usonian development would take this to 120-degree, 180-degree (in-line plan), and other angles, and through more complicated modules, such as hexagons, equilateral triangles and parallelograms, and circular segments.

The principal space is the living room, a room shared by all the family; it may constitute half the area on the floor plan. Usually one side of it is fully glazed, floor to ceiling, a "window wall" (elsewhere called a windowall) which, in the most dramatic instances, is not load-supporting, for the roof was cantilevered. A "gallery," the term preferred by Wright to "hallway," leads to the bedrooms; built-in storage spaces often line one side of this "tunnel," usually lit with clerestory windows. A carport sheltered the auto, but Wright did not waste a client's funds on walls around it, so avoided garages.

A Usonian house's structural characteristics, from 1935 on, include a concrete-slab floor providing gravity heating, the masonry core, and masonry piers terminating the wings. The masonry, often with steel, was called on to support the roof and various cantilevers. In the earliest Usonians, space between these piers was filled with either windowall or dry-wall construction. As Wright used the term, "dry wall" was not contemporary plasterboard, but meant a sandwich type of assembly, a laminate of three layers of wood boards screwed together, producing a modified board-and-batten effect the reverse of Prairie board and batten. Eliminating conventional two-by-four studs, the center, insulating, layer was often plywood. This inexpensive walling was an economic necessity during the Great Depression; it is not inherent to Usonian design. Wright would specify "all masonry" construction when his clients could afford it, and masonry became the standard after World War II.

Finally, the gravity (commonly, but incorrectly, called "radiant") heating is a development of the "Korean room" principle Wright first encountered on a damp winter's eve in the Tokyo house of Baron Okura, the emperor's Imperial Hotel representative. Heat is drawn to a chimney through ducts in floor tiles; Wright's adaption for Usonian construction involved pipes embedded in the slab floor carrying heated water, to generate a springlike environment. (In some late designs, such as a second home for Louis Penfield, S.365, Wright would develop the pure Korean room idea in an air floor heating and air conditioning system.)

Jacobs First Residence

S.234　T.3702
Herbert and Katherine Jacobs First Residence (1936)
Westmoreland, now Madison, Wisconsin
Restored in late 1980s

Wright specifically called this a Usonian house. Many call it the first Usonian house, but Wright, in 1953, gave pride of place to Alice Millard's La Miniatura (S.214). Truly, the Jacobs house advanced concepts tried as early as the California textile block houses (S.214–S.217) and evolved during the Depression in projects for H. C. Hoult and Robert D. Lusk.

Herbert Jacobs was born in Milwaukee; his mother was a college English teacher, his father a Congregational minister. A scholarship allowed him to attend Harvard College, where he graduated in 1926. He then spent an itinerant's life in Paris, Milwaukee, and the French Alps. He worked at the *Milwaukee Journal* as night police reporter from 1931 to 1936, then joined the *Capital Times* in Madison. Here he worked for twenty-six years, finally moving to the San Francisco Bay region, near a daughter and son-in-law who built the first house designed by

the Taliesin Associated Architects after Wright's death.

In this, the first of two residences Wright designed for him (the other, S.283), the active and quiet spaces are joined by a 90-degree angle, creating a typical **L** plan. The whole is drawn on a grid of 2-by-4-foot rectangles. Original drawings suggest a 2-by-2-foot unit, which appears in the final plan only where a 2-foot-wide stair was added for access to basement utilities.

The living room is one-third of the 1,560 square foot plan. Brick is the masonry, and the dry wall uses horizontal recessed 3-inch redwood battens with 9-inch pine boards screwed on to a core of vertical pine boards; there is no specific insulating material. Original cost was $5,500.

When discovered for sale in 1982 by James Dennis, the exterior walls were black with creosote; this has been chemically removed in preference to replacing the boards, though the California Redwood Association supplied new wood as needed without charge. Original 1 1/2-inch iron pipe for gravity heating remains in the bedroom wing, but the living room floor had to be redone with polybutylene pipe. The original roof and several extra layers of asphalt have been replaced with a rubber-membrane roof, free, from Celotex Corp. Restoration, under project architect John A. Eifler, was completed in 1987. The house is listed on the National Register of Historic Places.

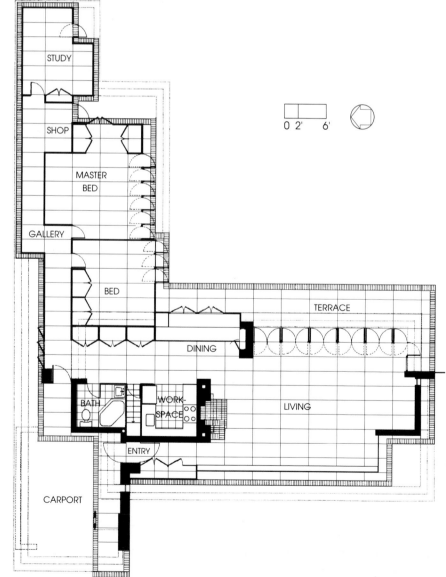

S.235   T.3701
Jean S. and Paul R. **Hanna Residence,** Honeycomb House (1936) and
S.235A   T.4607
Workshop Addition (1950) and
S.235B   T.5634
Residence **Alterations** (1957)
Stanford, California
The living room and workspace are unchanged since original construction, but most of the rest of the house was altered by Wright. There was major earthquake damage in 1989.

The Hanna residence completes the hillside to which it clings, its floor and courtyard levels adjusting to the contours of the hill. It was Wright's first work in the San Francisco region. The Palo Alto campus of Stanford University, including nearby lands where houses such as Paul and Jean Hanna's were built, were laid out by Frederick Law Olmsted. The Hannas found a particularly ingratiating hillside site on which to build their Wright-designed home.

The Hanna house is often called Honeycomb House because the Usonian structure's plan is fashioned on a hexagonal unit system, a module that replaced the octagon from this time on. Taliesin apprentices were

Hanna Honeycomb Residence

Living room

Workspace

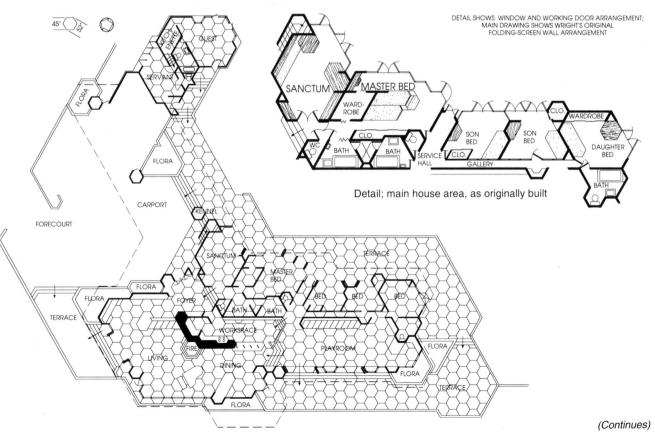

DETAIL SHOWS WINDOW AND WORKING DOOR ARRANGEMENT; MAIN DRAWING SHOWS WRIGHT'S ORIGINAL FOLDING-SCREEN WALL ARRANGEMENT

Detail; main house area, as originally built

Hanna Residence, plan of house as originally built

(Continues)

designing Usonian homes and Cornelia Brierly produced one on a hexagonal unit; the rest is history, for this brought about Wright's break from the square as his basic module.

Wright called this a wooden house. Though it uses common wire-cut San Jose brick inside and out, many of the walls are wood, framed of 1-by-8-inch wall studs on 26-inch centers, twice the basic unit. The hexagon module is clearly marked in the slab floor, each side two units (26 inches) in length, giving a 45.03-inch hexagon altitude. Each redwood board and recessed batten observes the 13-inch unit spacing, interrelating horizontal and vertical elements of design. The ease with which the nonmasonry walls could be assembled or disassembled allowed for considerable alteration of interior space. Individual bedrooms for children needed when the house was first built under master builder Harold Turner's supervision were converted in 1957 by Wright to larger living spaces when the children left. The original copper roof has been replaced with one of Heydite.

This structure has been designated by the American Institute of Architects as one of the seventeen American buildings designed by Wright to be retained as an example of his architectural contribution to American culture.

The house, which is maintained by Stanford University, suffered $1.8 million worth of damage during the Loma Prieta earthquake of October 17, 1989. Stanford University buildings suffered a total of $171 million; repair and seismic bracing ($1.2 million) is promised for the Hanna house, major ownership of which was transferred between 1966 and 1971 from the Hannas to the university. The university has yet to meet the terms of Paul and Jean Hanna's generous gift, which called for the house to be occupied by a prominent visiting professor each academic year. The house is open for visits on a limited basis.

Master bedroom

Master bedroom, reverse view

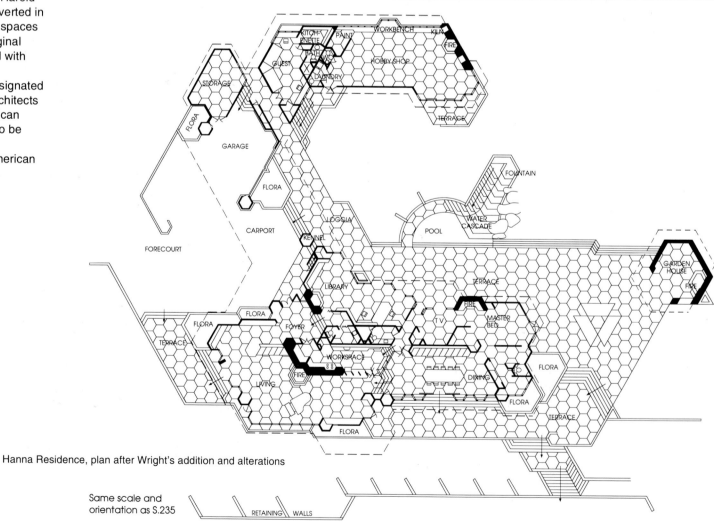

Hanna Residence, plan after Wright's addition and alterations

Same scale and orientation as S.235

Courtyard

Trellis and windowall at TV room and library

Library

Dining room

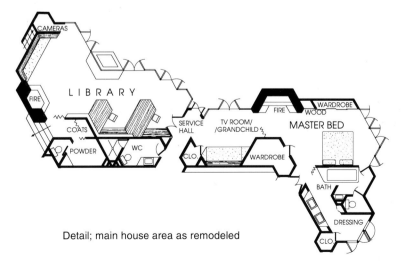

Detail; main house area as remodeled

Guest bedroom

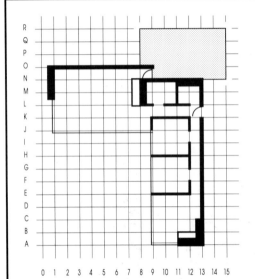

Basic (90°) L plan (with back gallery)

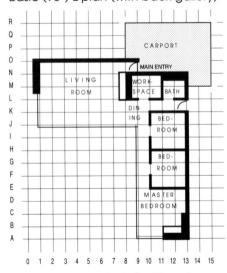

Spaces of an L plan with gallery
at inside of L (front gallery)

Tripartite arrangement of domestic spaces

BASICS OF THE L-PLAN USONIAN HOUSE

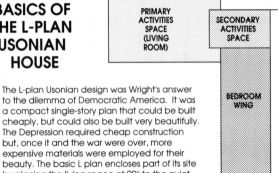

The L-plan Usonian design was Wright's answer to the dilemma of Democratic America. It was a compact single-story plan that could be built cheaply, but could also be built very beautifully. The Depression required cheap construction but, once it and the war were over, more expensive materials were employed for their beauty. The basic L plan encloses part of its site by placing the living space at 90° to the quiet space.

The basic design principle that brought about the Usonian house is the same as that which Wright had established early in his career. The prime activities space, the living room, dominates the design, but even more so here than in his Prairie works. Secondary activities, the workspace (kitchen) in particular, are allotted minimal space, and the bedrooms, upstairs in early work and Prairie designs, are brought to ground level.

The drawings presented here are simplified, to make design principles all the more obvious.

In the plan at the upper left, similar to the first L-plan Usonian, the Jacobs First Residence (S.234), the main entry leads directly only to the living room, without forks to each of the other activities areas, as was the norm in all Wright's designs. Wright allowed this simplification in his least expensive Usonian designs, though a secondary entrance would lead to these areas and actually provide a common center for pedestrian traffic.

The living room of a Usonian home is its largest space. From the workspace, small enough to do all the work by turning, rather than walking, the housewife has a view down the gallery and can be in the dining or living areas quickly.

Usually there is a fireplace in both the living room and master bedroom, as well as any additional guest bedroom. The utilities space may be at level or located below ground. More than this, details are not shown, for it is space, and how it is organically organized for human habitation, that is our prime concern.

In the drawings of Usonian structures here and those that follow, thinnest lines other than the grid lines represent glazed walls, floor to ceiling (or soffit) doors or windows. Thin lines are room partitions, usually of sandwich wall construction. Thick walls are exterior walls, perhaps with transom-level windows. Thick blocks are the masonry masses from which the roofs are cantilevered.

The attempt has been made throughout the Usonian drawings to keep each specific space the same size whatever the unit module or configuration, though the nature of organic design precludes this being made an absolute condition. Throughout all variations, standard elements are kept as regular as is practical, so that underlying design principles may be most easily observed.

Creative detailing, so much a part of Wright's genius, is beyond the scope of these demonstrations of Usonian possibilities. How a simple 90° L can be turned into plans at other angles, or how it can be curved, and how the simple alteration of one area can affect the entire spatial concept, is the creative aspect dealt with here.

If a basic 4' dimension is applied to the unit module for each of the Usonian drawings here and following, each module (except some circular segments) would be 16 square feet, yielding in the basic Usonian L plan on the previous page 1552 sq. ft. and in the Hex below, 1568.

60° Hexagonal plan
(Inside L plan set on hexagonal module)

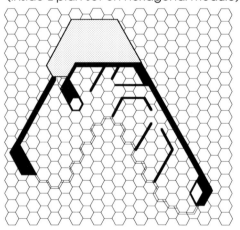

S.236 T.3603
Mrs. **Abby Beecher Roberts**
Residence, Deertrack (1936)
Marquette, Michigan
Copper roofing replaced with composition. Most of the cypress flooring replaced. Terrace enclosed

John and Mary Roberts Lautner often chauffeured Wright in his Cord; when Mr. Wright fell sick with pneumonia, the Lautners were enlisted to speed off to Madison, 40 miles away by country roads, in thirty-six minutes! Why? To obtain fresh fish and champagne for Wright's breakfast, to properly boost his spirits! Into this environment came Abby Beecher Roberts, Mary's mother, for a visit. "Mrs. Roberts bugged him" was John H. Howe's comment. She was a "colonial woman" and, having built three houses herself, felt she knew as much about architecture as Wright did.

This engaging lady once cast Wright's horoscope around the accepted birthdate of 1869. Finding it did not fit the man as she knew him, she discovered that the fit was perfect for 1867, his actual year of birth.

Three miles west of Marquette's Lake Superior shoreline, a long hill slopes southeastward through evergreen forests. Commanding this view is Deertrack, home of Abby Beecher Roberts. Mrs. Roberts wanted pink granite from quarries at nearby Republic; she got Texas brick. The original floor was cypress, most of which has been replaced. A copper roof was laid over Celotex insulation; the Celotex absorbed water, and the roof was replaced with composition.

The original plan is a revision of a Broadacre City model, its flat roof replaced by butterfly for site and client. The terrace has been enclosed, though restoration has begun under Bruce and Karol Peterson. Bruce's father Russell served his building apprenticeship on the house and Karol's father, California architect John Lautner, supervised construction. Further variants on this scheme include the Morris (S.329) and Blair (S.351) residences.

Abby Beecher Roberts Residence

Living room

Gallery

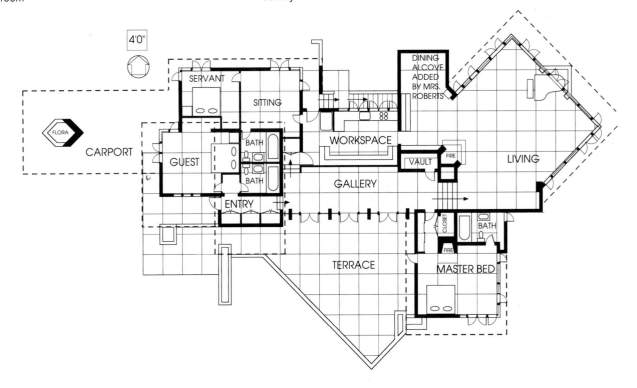

247

Johnson Wax Building with Research Tower to the rear

The main work room

S.237   T.3601
S. C. Johnson & Son Administration Building, **Johnson Wax Building** (1936),
S.237A
Additions (1951) and
S.238   T.4401
Johnson Research **Tower,**
Heliolaboratory (1944) for Herbert F. Johnson, Jr., president, Johnson Wax Company
Racine, Wisconsin

In 1886 Samuel Curtis Johnson purchased the Racine Hardware Manufacturing Company, a business making parquet flooring, from his employer. His first product was a paste wax made from Brazilian Carnauba palm leaves, and this led to floor-care products that outsold the flooring by the turn of the century. In 1917, the S. C. Johnson Company stopped producing floors and became the first in America to share profits with its workers.

Marketing Glo-Coat, a self-polishing floor wax, at the depths of the Depression, Herbert F. Johnson, Jr., grandson of the founder, turned the company's fortunes around. In 1936 he went shopping for a new office building. Despite heated arguments, Wright and Johnson owned Lincoln Zephyrs, the first successful streamlined automobile. That proved enough to keep them talking.

The brick and glass Administration Building that Wright designed for him

and the later Research Tower both became national landmarks. The main office work space is articulated on a 20-foot grid by dendriform (radical calyx) columns capable of supporting six times the weight imposed upon them, a fact Wright had to demonstrate in order to obtain a building permit. The Pyrex glass is not in panes but in tubing, and several layers of different diameters are used to admit light but no view and to fit the vertical unit based on one brick plus mortar. Industrial air pollution caused the tubes to collect dirt; new synthetic resins now permit a permanent seal to be achieved. Gravity heat is used, but there is also an auxiliary ducted system. Engineering was by Mendel Glickman and Wes Peters, with local supervision by Edgar Tafel. Wright designed all the original furniture for the building, including the three-legged secretary chairs, which tip over if one does not sit with correct posture. The tower, also designed to a 20-foot unit, is totally enclosed and has not allowed for horizontal expansion of work space.

Herbert F. Johnson also commissioned Wingspread (S.239). Both the Administration Building and the Research Tower, known popularly as the Johnson Wax Building and Tower, have been designated by the American Institute of Architects as two of seventeen American buildings designed by Wright to be retained as examples of his architectural contribution to American culture. Free tours are conducted during regular business hours.

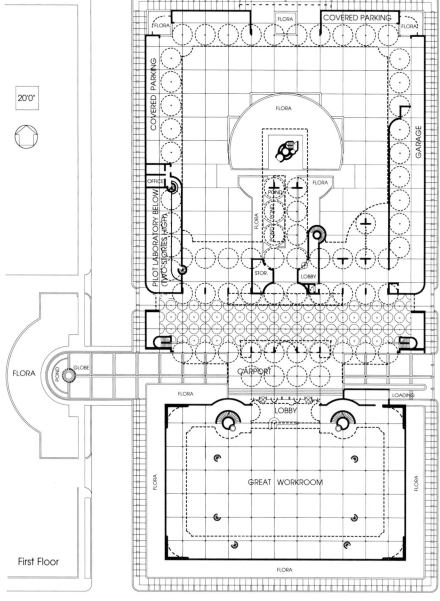

Plan of ground floor, Administration Building

Reception and ceiling of advertising department

Lobby from third level

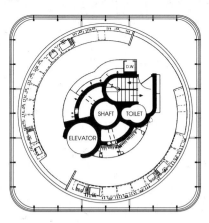

Plan of Tower round floor

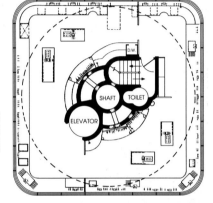

Plan of Tower square floor

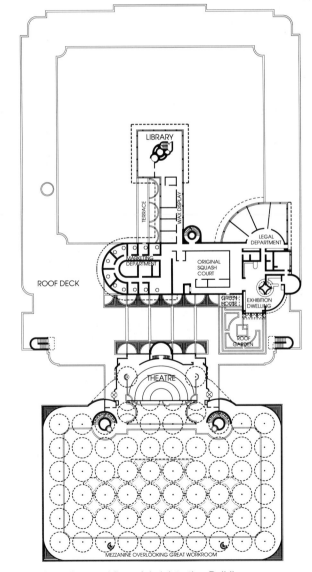

Plan of second floor, Administration Building

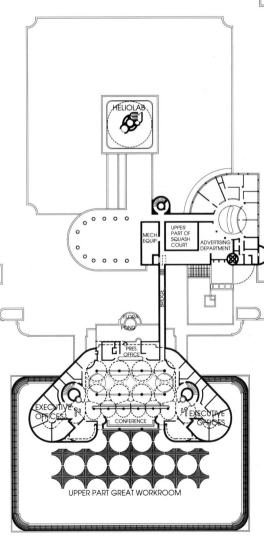

Plan of third floor, Administration Building

Tower, view of north side

249

S.239   T.3703
Herbert F. Johnson Residence,
Wingspread (1937)
Wind Point, Wisconsin

Herbert F. Johnson was the grandson
of S. C. Johnson. His father, Herbert F.
Johnson christened him Hibbert, and
the nickname "Hib" held even after he
changed his name to Herbert. He commissioned Wingspread, his home, and
the Johnson Wax Buildings
(S.237–S.238).

Wingspread, by Wright's own
statement, is the last of the Prairie
houses. Its plan is pinwheel, a form
which precedes the cruciform in
Froebel training, extending from a
central, three-story-high octagon. The
space is zoned; sleeping quarters are
in the north wing, kitchen in the opposite, and so forth. Pink Kasota sandstone, red brick, and cypress are its
primary materials. The side walls of
the swimming pool were undercut so
that they seem to disappear, leaving
only water and reflection.

Herbert F. Johnson Residence, north
(bedroom) wing

Wright considered this his most
expensive and best-built house to
date, and he noted that many had
thought the site undistinguished until
he placed the house on it. West wing
carports (not shown here) have been
converted into office space for the
current occupant, the Johnson Foundation. Master builder Ben Wiltscheck
was involved in supervision of all three
projects for Herbert F. Johnson
(S.237–S.239).

Herbert F. Johnson Residence, south side with swimming pool

Dining level in main teepee

Library area in
main teepee

Music area under
mezzanine

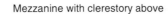
Mezzanine with clerestory above

View from widow's walk through upper terrace trellis to lower level terrace

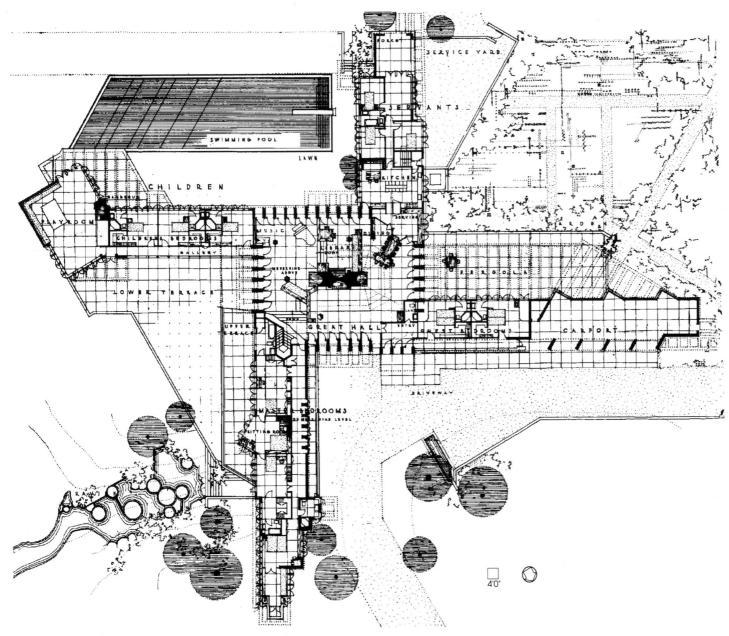

Rebhuhn Residence

S.240 T.3801
Ben Rebhuhn Residence (1937)
Great Neck Estates, New York
Restored after fire in the 1970s

Ben Rebhuhn and his wife "brought up" Ben Raeburn (both names may be pronounced Ray-bun), Wright's publisher at Horizon Press after World War II. Rebhuhn published books to which he believed people ought to have access, on topics such as birth control,

and he went to prison for his principles, while Raeburn went into legitimate book publishing, capitalizing on the acclaim then coming to Wright.

Rebhuhn's house, which cost $35,000, follows a cruciform plan, with a two-story-high living room, similar to the Vosburgh house (S.197), of which it may be considered a Usonian reworking, according to Lloyd Wright. Red tidewater cypress board and batten is employed inside and out, with brick and red roof tile. Master builder Harold Turner was in charge of construction.

A disastrous fire in the 1970s caused scorching of brick and wood. The house was saved by the Great Neck Estates fire department who took great care to put the fire out, not as quickly and safely for themselves as they could, but with as little damage as was practical to the house. Restoration was done by architect Morton Delson, under direction of Rebhuhn's son and his wife Jane. An ancient gentleman, remembered but not named, as a demonstration of his

capabilities, cleaned a 4-by-8-foot area of the burnt cypress in 10 minutes so that it looked better than new, while Delson waited outside. The same gentleman was then hired by Taliesin Associated Architects to salvage the Arizona Biltmore after its fire a few months before its reopening following 1970s restoration. Delson also modernized the kitchen and dining area during the reconstruction.

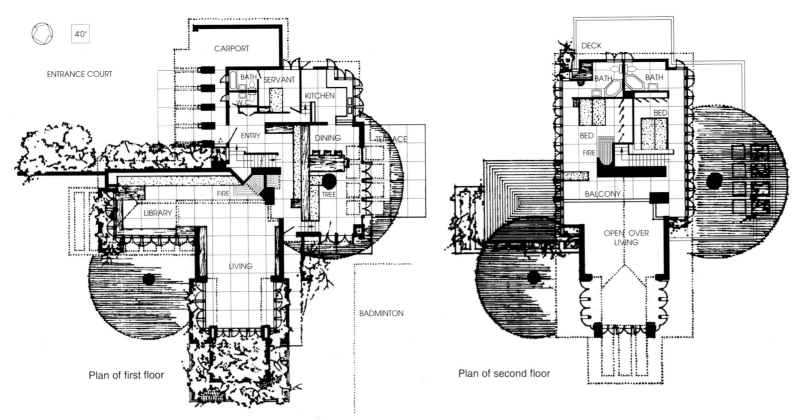

Plan of first floor

Plan of second floor

S.241 T.3803
Frank Lloyd Wright, **Taliesin West**
(1937) including in the main unit Mr.
and Mrs. Wright's quarters, the
Drafting Studio, Kitchen and Dining
Room, Apprentices' Quarters and
Mr. Wright's Office with
S.242 T.3803
Sign (1953),
S.243 T.3803
Cabaret Theatre (1949),
S.244 T.3803
Music Pavilion (1956), and
S.245 T.3709
Sun Trap (1937)
S.245A T.3803
Sun Cottage (1948) remodeling of
Sun Trap
Scottsdale, Arizona
Constantly altered over the years as
Wright's and the Fellowship's needs
changed

Even as Taliesin West seems to
crumble inevitably back, day by day, to
the earth, the stone and the wood from
which Mr. Wright hewed it, it remains
beautiful. Quail and cottontail still
inhabit the grounds more than humans
who, in great numbers, perform a

Taliesin West, Mr. Wright's Office

summer pilgrimage to Taliesin or a
winter one to Taliesin West.

Taliesin West was the name Wright
finally gave this winter home for the
Taliesin Fellowship on Maricopa Mesa
after others, including "Taliesin in the
Desert," failed. The desert offered a
new challenge in materials. The
architect's primary solution was "desert
rubblestone wall" construction, usually
shortened to "desert masonry." There
are many ways of achieving this, but
all involve randomly placing large
stones into forms, then pouring
concrete around the stones while
leaving most of the face next to the
form exposed. In the Bott house
(S.404) wet sand was forced between
form and stone surface before the
concrete was poured. In the Austin
house (S.345) crumpled newspaper

was used instead of sand to keep the
stone faces from being covered with
concrete. At Taliesin West, the mortar
was allowed to seep around the edges
of the stone face, and surplus was
then chipped away to reveal the stone
surface. Often, the stone was washed
with acid to bring out its color.

First there were tents at Maricopa
Mesa. Then a wood and linen structure
for Mr. Wright, Olgivanna, and
Iovanna. When this structure gained a

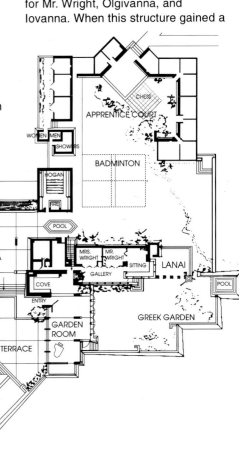

General plan of Taliesin West in its earliest years

(Continues)

View of the main building across Arizona desert

Lighting tower at Taliesin West with the sculptural Sign

Taliesin West Drafting Studio in the 1950s

The living room of Mr. Wright's quarters

linen canvas provided an ideal shield against flash thunderstorms and the sun's glare. Fitted to redwood frames, the material adjusted most effectively, if sometimes noisily, to rapid and wide temperature changes. Fiberglass and steel later replaced much of the original structure.

Following World War II, the Taliesin Fellowship grew as did Mr. Wright's architectural practice. The Cabaret Theatre, a right-angle attachment to Mr. Wright's own office (across the entry patio just north of the drafting room), provided a space for indoor social functions, such as movies and parties. By the early fifties it could no

full concrete slab floor and a hearth, some would say that Taliesin West, as an historical place, was born in the form of Sun Trap, even as the drafting room was in construction. Eventually Sun Trap was transformed into a truly permanent structure, Sun Cottage. A study on the south with an additional bedroom, a separate cottage near the front entry, and other additions were made to the rear sharing the masonry of the main structure, but the hearth, always the symbolic center of any Wright dwelling, remains.

In the dry heat of the Arizona desert, Wright found that stretched

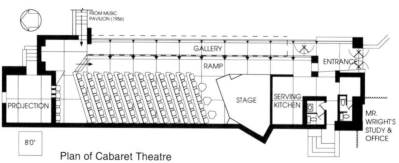

Plan of Cabaret Theatre

Cabaret Theatre with Don Aitken lecturing on Wright's methods of bringing natural light deep into interior spaces, March 1990

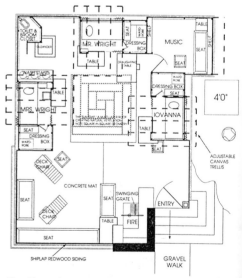

Sun Trap plan

The Music Pavilion at Taliesin West

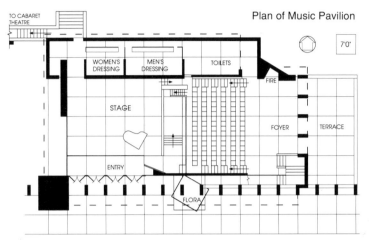

Plan of Music Pavilion

TO CABARET THEATRE

WOMEN'S DRESSING | MEN'S DRESSING | TOILETS

7'0"

STAGE

FIRE

FOYER | TERRACE

ENTRY

FLORA

Midway Barns, lower shed roof awaiting restoration

S.246   T.3802
Frank Lloyd Wright, **Midway Barns**
(1938) with
S.247   T.4730
Dairy and Machine Sheds (1947)
Spring Green, Wisconsin
Sheds, on east side, await rebuilding

longer accommodate the largest social events; the Music Pavilion, which was called a "Movements Pavilion" in early sketches, was built as a right-angle attachment to the Cabaret Theatre.

A single drawing of the Taliesin sign survives, showing a geometric development of Wright's favorite square within a square idea. Here it is created by increasing the length of each second successive side by a unit equal to the first side. It is intended to

be "hung" from a masonry pier. While not done exactly to this drawing's specifications, the sculptural decoration of the Taliesin West light tower is the current expression of this design.

Taliesin West has been designated by the American Institute of Architects as one of seventeen American buildings to be retained as an example of Wright's architectural contribution to American culture. It houses the fellowship the greater part of the year, and a year-round staff for the Frank Lloyd Wright Memorial Foundation. Taliesin apprentices conduct tours throughout the day.

Wright, born in Wisconsin farmland, turned the valley of the Lloyd Joneses to good use. Under the master's guidance, every Taliesin fellow started his apprenticeship by working in and with the earth. Under the care of the apprentices, the rich Wisconsin soil provided much fresh food to the dinner tables shared by the entire Taliesin community. To Wright, no building, whatever its use, was without dignity. Accordingly, he found ways to give beauty and visual interest to these utilitarian buildings. The first barns, located midway between Hillside and Taliesin, and the later dairy and machine sheds served the needs of an expanding architectural community in midwestern Wisconsin.

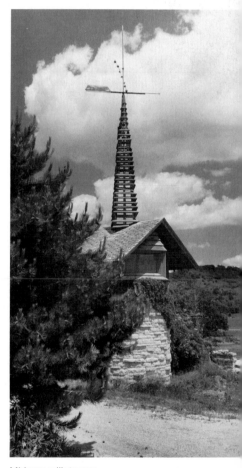

Midway milk tower

The hearth in the Sun Cottage

Exterior of one quadrant

Living room

S.248   T.3906
Suntop Homes (1938) for Otto Tod
Mallery of Tod Company
Ardmore, Pennsylvania
The quadrants, each an individual
housing unit, are identified as follows:
from the northeast clockwise, S.248.1
to S.248.4. Unit S.248.1 rebuilt after
fire in 1941, not to Wright's
specifications. Unit S.248.3 carport
enclosed and interior altered after fire
damage in 1973. Unit S.248.4 has lost
its cantilevered balcony, but this and
S.248.3 are scheduled for restoration
in the 1990s.

The idea of stacking spaces vertically
in quadrants, rather than stacking
single-floor apartments in four stories,
is developed here, in what Wright
called his "Ardmore Experiment." The
building, which houses four families, is
divided into quarters; each 2,300-
square-foot apartment has two stories
and a utilities basement and sunroof.
The ground floor has a carport and a
living room. On the next floor are work
space, dining area, one bedroom with
balcony, and the upper level of the
living room. Above this is the "suntop,"
a roof terrace protected by high wall
(the lapped siding in the photograph)
and additional bedrooms. There were
to have been four of these structures in
Ardmore, built in a row with alternate
units angled identically on their sites.
Only one was built. The exterior is
brick and horizontal lapped cypress

siding (the terrace decks are yellow
pine, the interior trim fir); this siding is
imitated in the wall now surrounding
the structure. Construction was
supervised by master builder Harold
Turner, whose other efforts include
some of Wright's major statements:
residences for Hanna, Affleck,
Armstrong, Christie, Goetsch-Winckler,
and Rebhuhn.

The first apartment (by postal numbering) is the northmost (north-
northeast) unit. In 1941 a fire caused
serious damage. Reconstruction in the
mid-sixties was completed without
necessary steel for the cantilevers, nor
were replacement mullions done to
Wright's design. The second unit is
essentially unchanged from original
construction. The third, or southmost,
has had its carport converted to an
enclosed entry and additional room
after the floor level was lowered. In this
unit, which was reconstructed shortly
after a fire in 1973, ceilings were
raised to 8 feet in the second-level bedroom and the third floor was expanded
to enclose the roof terrace. Additions
include a freestanding carport and
unsightly heat pump equipment on the
roof. The west apartment, entered from
the side street, lost its cantilevered
second-level balcony shortly after construction.

Local residents protested construction of the projected additional three
buildings, and so they were not built. A
white brick colonial has intruded on a
lot at the street corner originally
reserved for another Suntop
Quadraplex.

In 1942, Wright presented much
the same idea as "Cloverleaf Quad-
ruple Housing" to the United States

government for a project near Pitts-
field, Massachusetts. A change in
housing administration and complaints
from local architects that they, not an
"outsider," should be awarded the commissions prevented its construction.
Again in 1957, Wright resurrected this
idea for North Carolina; in the southern
climate, the car was put out at the
road's edge. This allowed the whole
building to be lowered one level, but at
the sacrifice of the two-story high living
room.

Plan; each quadrant shows a different level

Mezzanine

Penthouse

UPPER PART OF LIVING ROOM

SUN TERRACE

DINING

MEZZANINE WINDOWS BELOW   BOYS   CLO.   GIRLS   NURSERY   MASTER BEDROOM   WARD-ROBE   BALCONY

DOUBLE-DECK BEDS   AIR VENT   BATH

WORK AREA   FIRE PLACE

UTILITY ROOM   STORAGE

3'0"   CARPORT   LIVING ROOM

| 248.4 | 248.1 |
| 248.3 | 248.2 |

Basement   ENTRY

Ground Floor

S.249　T.4009
Charles L. Manson Residence
(1938)
Wausau, Wisconsin
Carport enclosed

The Manson house was one of
Wright's attempts to move away from
the **L**-shaped plan by varying the angle
at which the living room intersected
the rest of the house. The diagonal
arrangement achieved here, both with
the living room at one end and the
master bedroom and the carport at the
other, found easier expression when
Wright abandoned the rectangular
modules (a 4-foot square in Manson),
to investigate triangles and parallelograms.

Wright employs 30- and 60-degree
angles to eliminate right-angle corners,
leaving less than half the living room
windowall for floor to ceiling doors. The
plan may seem confusing to a visitor;
the main entrance is immediately next
to the original carport (now made into
an additional room), while a walk
draws one along the southern wall to
an entry at the workspace.

The house, mostly of brick, is
sheathed and partitioned by regular
board-and-batten sandwich walls. A
dropped ceiling is employed in the
children's bedrooms, so that a second-
story darkroom could be accommo-
dated within a height but a few feet
greater than that required for a single-
story structure. This is achieved by
juggling ceiling heights throughout.
The low hall is six board-and-batten,
13-inch units, while other, higher,
ceilings are nine board-and-batten
units. The upper floor is but eight
vertical units, and two of these are
dropped into the boys' room. The living
room is 130 inches high. This gives
a satisfying variety to the interior
spaces.

The carport has been made into a
garage.

Manson Residence

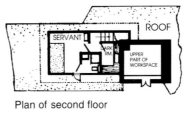

Plan of second floor

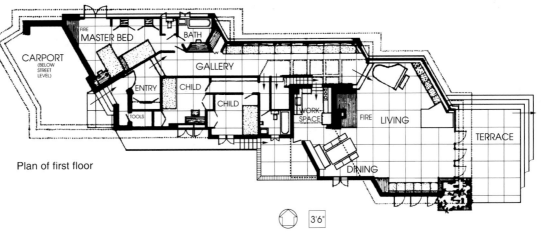

Plan of first floor

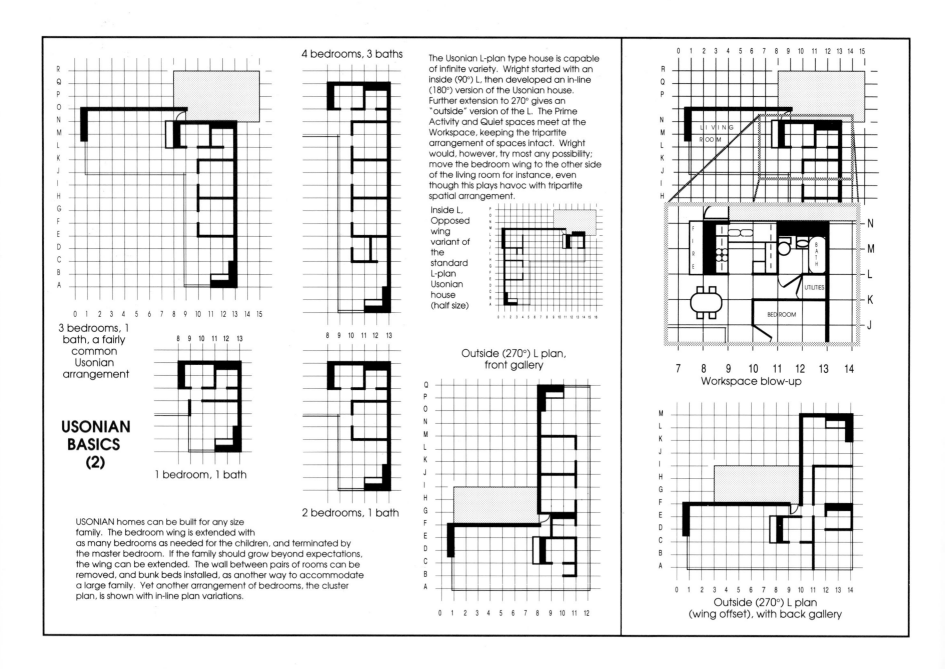

4 bedrooms, 3 baths

The Usonian L-plan type house is capable of infinite variety. Wright started with an inside (90°) L, then developed an in-line (180°) version of the Usonian house. Further extension to 270° gives an "outside" version of the L. The Prime Activity and Quiet spaces meet at the Workspace, keeping the tripartite arrangement of spaces intact. Wright would, however, try most any possibility; move the bedroom wing to the other side of the living room for instance, even though this plays havoc with tripartite spatial arrangement.

Inside L, Opposed wing variant of the standard L-plan Usonian house (half size)

3 bedrooms, 1 bath, a fairly common Usonian arrangement

USONIAN BASICS (2)

1 bedroom, 1 bath

2 bedrooms, 1 bath

Outside (270°) L plan, front gallery

Workspace blow-up

USONIAN homes can be built for any size family. The bedroom wing is extended with as many bedrooms as needed for the children, and terminated by the master bedroom. If the family should grow beyond expectations, the wing can be extended. The wall between pairs of rooms can be removed, and bunk beds installed, as another way to accommodate a large family. Yet another arrangement of bedrooms, the cluster plan, is shown with in-line plan variations.

Outside (270°) L plan (wing offset), with back gallery

Pauson Residence

S.250   T.4011
Rose **Pauson** Residence, Shiprock (1939)
Phoenix, Arizona
Demolished. Chimney mass moved 200 yards south.

Ruins of Shiprock, as it was known, remained after a fire in 1942. These were destroyed in 1980 to make way for an extension of Thirty-second Street. Architect Edward M. Jones relocated the 70-ton chimney mass (9-by-11-foot base, 26 feet high) 200 yards south and incorporated it into his gateway to Alta Vista Park subdivision, which is home to the Boomer (S.361) and Benjamin Adelman (S.344) residences. The original Pauson residence was a desert rubblestone wall, or desert masonry, structure, with lapped redwood siding. The in-line organization featured studio, kitchen, dining, and servant quarters on the lower level, with bedrooms and a balcony overlooking the living room above. Original construction was supervised by Robert Mosher.

Pauson Residence ruins

Pauson fireplace masonry, all that is left today

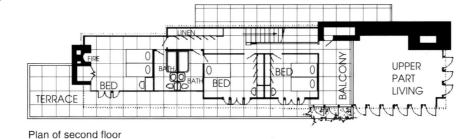

Plan of second floor

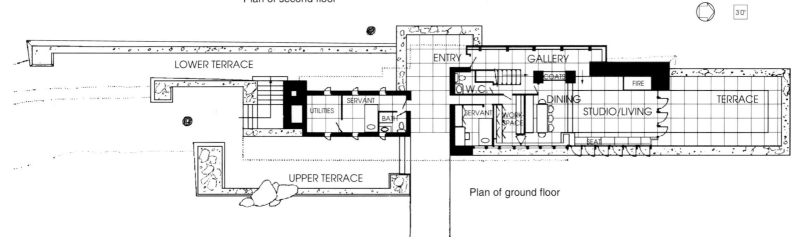

Plan of ground floor

Florida Southern College

Florida Southern College

S.251–S.258   T.3805
Florida Southern College, Child of the Sun, for Dr. Ludd M. Spivey, president (1938–)
Lakeland, Florida

Since Broadacre City never came to fruition, Florida Southern College offers the viewer a rare opportunity; its twelve structures comprise the largest integrated collection of architecture by Wright in the world. The complex takes its name from a quote of Mr. Wright's in which he described his buildings at Lakeland as "out of the ground and into the light, a child of the sun."

In 1938 Wright visited Ludd M. Spivey, president of this Methodist liberal arts college. Spivey shared his dream of a "college of tomorrow" with Wright, who immediately conceived a master plan for a whole college. The realization of individual projects within the master plan spanned two decades.

In the Florida Southern College buildings, reinforced cast-concrete is used for structural members. Sandcast blocks (3 by 9 by 36 inches) are compounded of a semidry mixture of sand, crushed coquina shells (limestone from shells and coral), and concrete, formed in wooden molds, dried under the Florida sun. Many of the blocks are pierced with colored, **L**-shaped glass inserts. Red Tidewater cypress, another native Florida material, is used for all wood members. Copper is used in roofing, and aluminum in the Science and Cosmography Building.

Use of contrasting overall geometric shapes on the basic 6-foot-square unit creates a diversity among the many building types; the Annie Pfeiffer Chapel is a hexagon, while the E. T. Roux Library is a circle (not to be confused with the new one on the northwest corner of the campus). Esplanades link all of Wright's work on the campus, and buildings not so connected are by other architects, such as Nils Schweizer, who completed much of the project following Wes Peters's and Kenn Lockhart's early supervision. These esplanades, or overhanging eaves based on their

design, often create breezeways. The breezeway or some variant of it permeates the design of each building, helping the breezes here, almost 40 miles inland from Tampa's Gulf Coast, cool the buildings. This concept was first employed by Wright in the Gulf Coast bungalows for Louis Sullivan (S.005) and James Charnley (S.007).

New buildings have been added, and inadequate maintenance of Wright's structures led to serious deterioration in recent decades, but a major program of restoration was launched in the late 1980s. Visitors may park in the lot off Johnson Avenue adjacent the Administration Building, where a self-guided walking-tour map is available.

Pfeiffer Chapel from Science
Building Esplanade

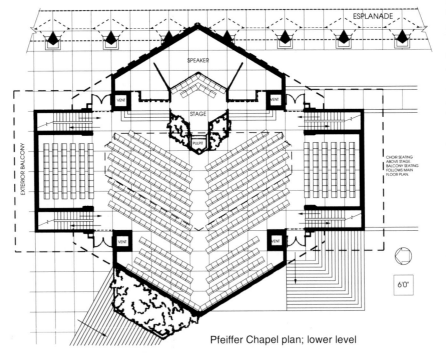

Pfeiffer Chapel plan; lower level

S.251   T.3805A
Annie Merner **Pfeiffer Chapel**
(1938)
Lakeland, Florida
Stage enlarged, seating reduced. Air conditioning added, requiring doors to balconies to be replaced by casement windows

Being a church-related college creates certain expectations in the minds of parents and prospective students. The building of a chapel thus became the first concern in the Florida Southern College project.

The larger plan is a hexagon, but the design is set on the 6-foot square that informs all of Wright's Lakeland spaces. Further, this building provides a link between the unbuilt New Theatre for Woodstock and the Dallas Theatre Center (S.395). The theatre idea is varied by the enormous bell tower, itself a transformation into the vertical dimension of the breezeway found, in some form, in most every Wright-designed campus structure. The tower was such an effective resonant space that local citizens demanded, and got, removal of the carillon. The sandcast block here is well-decorated with colored, **L**-shaped glass.

Originally the Pfeiffer Chapel could seat the entire student body, even when it grew to 800. More recently its "stage" has been enlarged and, with new seats, the seating reduced, and so now only a single class of the nearly 1,800 students can be seated at one time. Full-length doors to side balconies have been replaced by casement windows, and air conditioning ducts installed next to these at sill level.

E. T. Roux Library

Pfeiffer Chapel sanctuary

Florida Southern College

S.252   T.3805G
E. T. Roux **Library** (1941)
Lakeland, Florida
Too small to serve the college's library needs, it is now given over to alternative uses

The E. T. Roux Library (not the new Roux Library on the northwest corner of the campus designed by Nils Schweizer) combines a circle, the student reading room, with a skylit service area. Though the design is dated 1941, the war delayed completion; the building was dedicated in 1945.

The college, having outgrown the capacity of this building's holdings, converted most of the space to administrative uses, retaining the reading room as a meeting area. It is now named the Thad Buckner Building.

Study terrace of
E. T. Roux Library before conversion to administrative uses

Plan of E. T. Roux Library

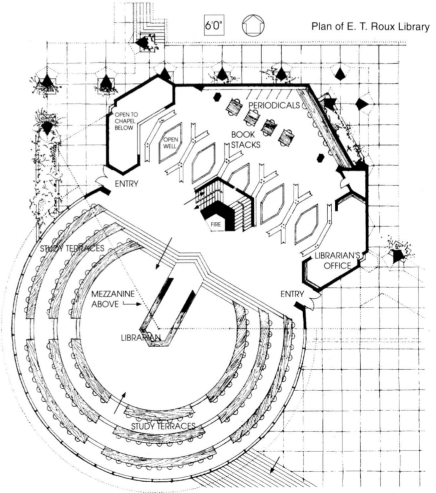

Main circulation desk and cross gallery with fireplace of E. T. Roux Library before conversion to administrative uses

Seminar Buildings and Offices
sheltered by Esplanade

S.253.1-3   T.3805H
Seminar Buildings (1940)
S.253A   T.3805H
Conversion to Offices of Seminar
Buildings (1940–)
Lakeland, Florida
The individual Seminar Buildings, now combined into a single structure but still separately identifiable, should be numbered from west to east S.253.1 to S.253.3.

These three buildings were conceived as seminar buildings, each with two faculty offices and one large classroom. The central seminar building should be investigated by those interested in the test blocks that were made to determine what color was most natural to central Florida. While tan, rose, pink, and gray dominate, the final color that was chosen is closest to honey-colored beige.

The buildings were originally known as the Cora Carter, Isabel Walbridge, and Charles W. Hawkins Seminar Buildings.

Plans at Taliesin show how Wright himself considered the adaptation of these buildings to administrative office use, the way they are employed today.

Bursar's offices and a faculty lounge were made to occupy the two courtyard breezeways that originally separated the three buildings after enclosure.

Plan of Seminar Buildings as converted to office use

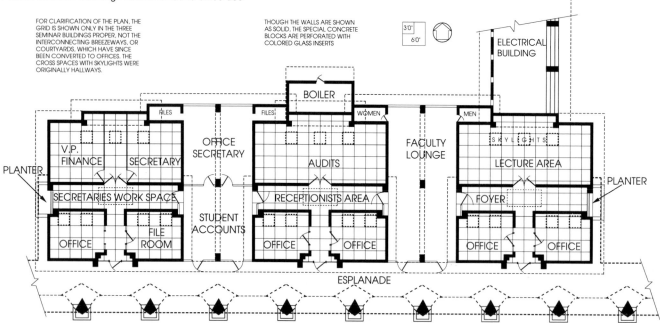

FOR CLARIFICATION OF THE PLAN, THE GRID IS SHOWN ONLY IN THE THREE SEMINAR BUILDINGS PROPER, NOT THE INTERCONNECTING BREEZEWAYS, OR COURTYARDS, WHICH HAVE SINCE BEEN CONVERTED TO OFFICES. THE CROSS SPACES WITH SKYLIGHTS WERE ORIGINALLY HALLWAYS.

THOUGH THE WALLS ARE SHOWN AS SOLID, THE SPECIAL CONCRETE BLOCKS ARE PERFORATED WITH COLORED GLASS INSERTS

Florida Southern College

S.254   T.3805D
Industrial Arts Building (1942)
Lakeland, Florida

Originally designed in 1942 as a
student center, as the main refectory
with its enormous south-facing clerestory still attests, this building was
never used as such. By its construction in 1952, it had been revised to
include wood and metal shops in its
east wing. There is one cross breezeway with one inner courtyard and a
second courtyard created by an
esplanade. A pavilion, now divided into
classrooms and security office, leads
to the circular theatre.

The Industrial Arts Building is now
named the Lucius Pond Ordway
Building.

Refectory of the Industrial Arts Building

Industrial Arts Building

Plan of Industrial Arts Building

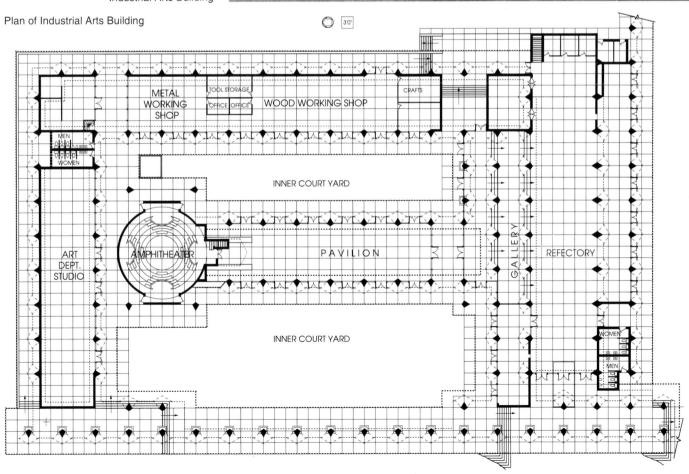

Florida Southern College

S.255 T.3805B
Administration Building Group
(1945), including
S.255A T.3805K
Waterdome (1938, 1948),
S.255B T.3805B
Emile E. **Watson Administration
Building** (1945), and
S.255C T.3805B
Benjamin **Fine Administration
Building** (1945)
Lakeland, Florida
Administration building renovated.
Single large Waterdome pool reduced
to four smaller pools

The Administration Building, completed
in 1948, is actually two structures with
a garden courtyard framed by a double
esplanade, Wright's Gulf Coast
breezeway. The ceiling of the east
section has been fully restored; this is
known as the Benjamin Fine Administration Building. The west portion of
the administration complex is called
the Emile E. Watson Administration
Building.

The Waterdome is shown in
Wright's original campus master plan,
but was not completed until 1948. At
that time it was a large, circular pool.
With construction of the Roux Library,
the pool was threatened with demolition. Nils Schweizer was instrumental
in seeing it converted instead to four
smaller ponds; the original pool
remains outlined by its concrete wall.
This area is now known as the J.
Edgar Wall Plaza.

Administration Building viewed from steps that lead to Waterdome

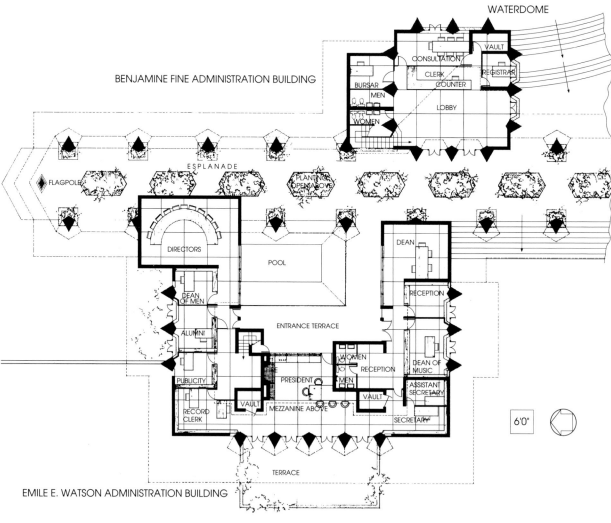

Plan of Administration Building

Ceiling of east wing of Administration Building

Florida Southern College

S.256 T.3805E
Science and Cosmography Building (1953)
Lakeland, Florida
Greenhouses built off originally open esplanades, and breezeways are enclosed

Wright's only built planetarium graces the south end of this three-story structure. Breezeways through the center of each of the two sections of the building are now fully enclosed. Esplanades run along the outer perimeter. The northeast side esplanade is cantilevered from aluminum columns and is given maximal extension by open trellis-work. This has been further extended by greenhouses. It is locally known as the Polk County Science Building.

Planetarium of the Science and Cosmography Building

Aluminum columns, lower level of Science and Cosmography Building

Plan of top floor

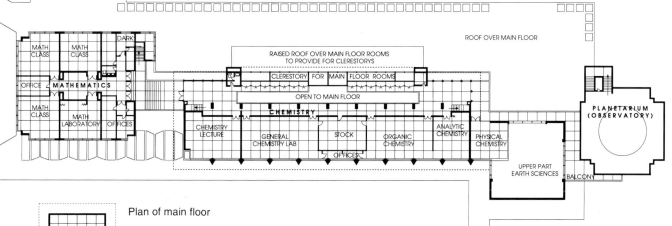

Plan of main floor

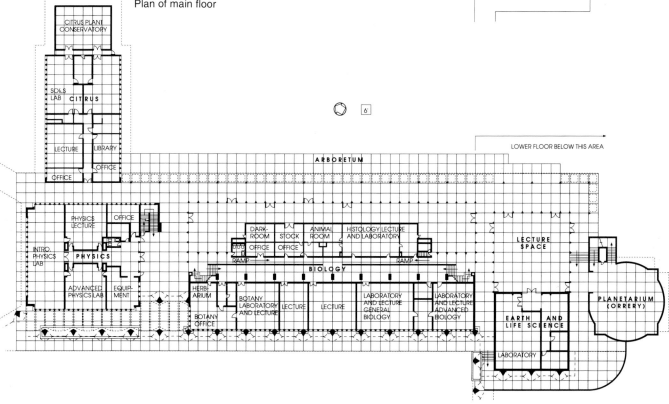

S.258   T.3805F
Minor Chapel (William H. Danforth Chapel) (1954)
Lakeland, Florida
Restored

Minor (Danforth) Chapel

Sanctuary of the Minor Chapel

The Minor Chapel is so oriented on its site that the colored glass windows behind the altar are most effectively lit by the setting sun. This is Wright's only leaded-glass at Florida Southern College. Clerestories help light the interior. Among the first buildings to be fully restored, it is a favorite place for student weddings.

One plan shows the basic grid of 6-foot squares extended from the Pfeiffer Chapel into the Danforth structure. The final plan has the squares rotated 30 degrees to conform to the orientation of the structure.

S.257   T.3805P
Esplanades (1946)
Lakeland, Florida

Usually these esplanades stand free of other structures, but at the Science and Cosmography and Industrial Arts buildings they are an extension of the outer wall, and at the Administration Building, they are doubled, becoming a breezeway uniting the two parts of this building. To keep walkways open to pedestrians yet shield against rain or sun, they are cantilevered from, usually, cast and reinforced concrete piers.

Often, to adjust to the site, which drops through the former sixty-acre citrus grove toward Lake Hollingsworth, the roof makes a **Z**, as shown in the photograph.

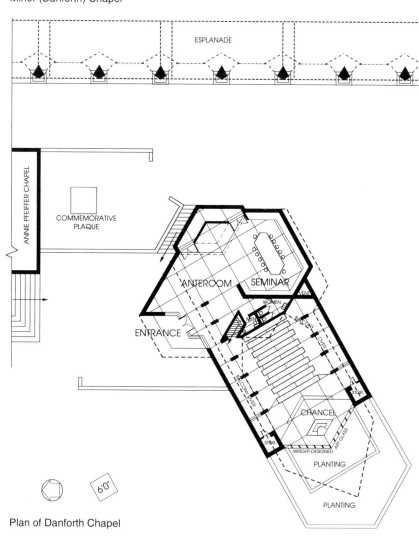

Plan of Danforth Chapel

Esplanade, at northeast corner of the Industrial Arts Building

S.259 T.4002
Sidney **Bazett** (Bazett-Frank) Residence (1939) and
S.259A
Louis and Betty **Frank Playroom/ Studio Addition** to Bazett Residence (1954)
Hillsborough, California

The second house by Wright in the San Francisco region, like its predecessor the Hanna house (S.235), employs the hexagonal module. The result is a version of the Usonian **L** that joins the living room to the bedroom wing at 60 degrees. It is a small house, less than 1500 square feet including the original guest room. The living room, with its undulating glass curtain, faces into the **L** as well as out to the valley and bay beyond under a gabled roof with splayed eaves.

The Bazett's term in the house was short. Betty and Lou Frank moved into the house on August 15, 1945. In the mid-fifties, they asked Wright for more room. A playroom for the boys was added to the original guest room; then this was converted to a studio plus master bedroom arrangement, giving the house four bedroom suites, despite its compact design.

Wright would later decide that the equilateral parallelogram was easier to draw and to construct, as in the Thaxton residence (S.384), when a 60-degree **L** best fitted the site. Blaine Drake was supervisor of construction.

Inside the **L** of the Bazett Residence

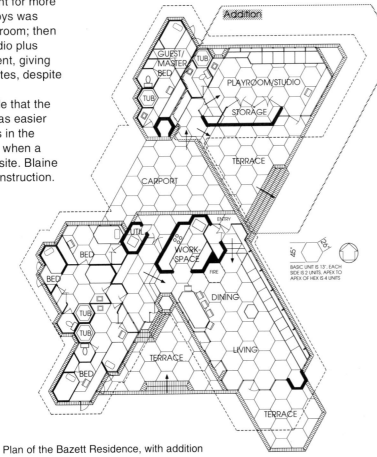

Plan of the Bazett Residence, with addition

Living room

S.260 T.3901
Andrew F. H. **Armstrong**
Residence (1939)
Ogden Dunes, Indiana
Additions by John H. Howe. Perimeter
heating replaces gravity heat

Wright called this house a "dune
dwelling." The organization of the
spaces of this house is an object
lesson in how Wright could fit a structure to a difficult site. Each story of this
house has its own grid of squares,
turned 30 degrees at each change of
level. The top level is the quiet space,
master bedroom looking out to the
Indiana Dunes and Lake Michigan
shoreline on two sides, the morning
sun over a terrace at the hilltop. The
children's bedroom has a southern
exposure. The utilities, a photographic
darkroom, and servant's room are
under the northeast quarter of this top
floor. The 13 foot tall, roughly 24-by-
24-foot living room and workspace are
farther down the sand bank, terraced
to fit. The carport is again a level
lower, with concealed entry not unlike
that of the Palmer house (S.332).

John Peterson bought the property
a year before Wright died; he was the
sixth owner in the two decades of the
house. In 1964 he hired John H. Howe
to restore the building, which had
received little upkeep, and to enlarge
it. Howe designed a bedroom to the
south, reached by a gallery made of
one 4-foot module from the original
children's bedroom. He moved the
workspace wall out one module, then
extended the building east with a new
playroom and screened porch. A separate enclosed garage was located to
the south. In the original children's
bedroom 8-inch **V**-groove cypress was
tried; it was considered unsuitable to
Wright's 13-inch vertical unit system.

Armstrong Residence viewed from southwest, showing
additions and garage by John H. Howe

The Armstrong house, north facade

Fireplace corner in living room

Living room, view toward entry

Five thousand board feet of clear
Philippine mahogany replaced the
cypress; boards were often hand
selected to cover without break the
18-foot side of the living room.
Thermopane replaced quarter-inch
plate glass, and perimeter heating
replaced the gravity heat.

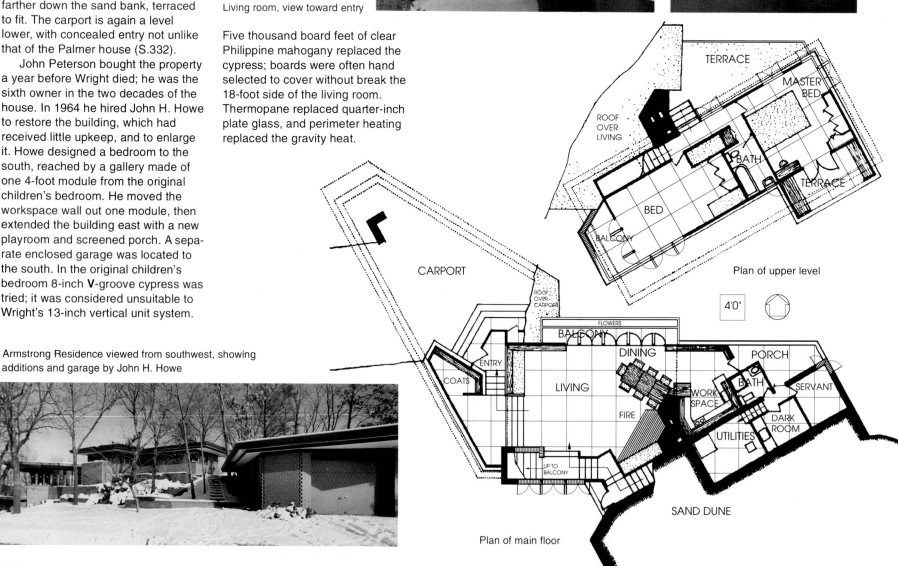

Plan of upper level

Plan of main floor

Auldbrass Plantation

S.261–S.264   T.4015
Auldbrass Plantation (1938–) for
C. Leigh Stevens
Yemassee, South Carolina
Renovated in late 1980s and early
1990s. Fire-destroyed buildings rebuilt

Auldbrass was intended to be a working plantation for owner Leigh Stevens, a time and motion studies specialist. His plantation was to be used for testing ideas about agriculture that might then be transferred to tropical and subtropical areas overseas, especially Africa. One story has it that the plantation was named after the first building on the site, which was supposedly burned by Sherman.

The buildings Wright designed may be seen as a southern version of Taliesin, albeit on a smaller scale. Native cypress, laid at approximately 80 degrees to the horizon, imitate the live oak on the property, while details such as downspouts hint at the hanging Spanish moss. Peter Berndtson supervised initial construction, with later supervision by Wes Peters.

The site was originally a king's grant and had been a rice plantation. It is less than a mile from the Combahee River, the north side of which is swamp. A canal to the river was partially dredged. Wright called for a "clearwater lake," but his presentation drawing shows a typical southern environment. On the lake, guests could ride a dinner barge that would dock at a two-story guesthouse, but neither the guesthouse nor the lake was built.

In the seventies, the buildings passed through a series of owners; most of the furniture was auctioned by Sotheby's. In the mid-eighties, film producer Joel Silver, who had already restored the Storer house (S.215), purchased Auldbrass with the intent of restoring what remains, rebuilding what was destroyed, and completing the two-story guesthouse. Eric Wright, grandson of the architect, was named the project leader. Bennett Strahan was the local architect in charge, and all work was done by a crew assembled in Yemassee by Simon Jinks, who knew Stevens and Auldbrass from its inception.

S.261   T.4015
Stevens Residence (1940, 1951)
with
S.261A   T.4015
Guesthouse (1940, 1993)
Yemassee, South Carolina
Residence restored late 1980s.
Guesthouse to be built 1993 or later

For the Stevens residence and cottages, a hexagon module 2 feet, 6 inches to the side (4 feet, 4 inches between parallel sides, or 5 feet point to point) was employed. Elsewhere squares are the standard module. Each building except the cottages was linked to at least one other building by an esplanade. Wright's plans show a two-story guesthouse (which had not been constructed by the time of Stevens's death in 1962) linked to the main house, at the end of one such esplanade, along which ran a pool. To the other side was a southern swamp lake, heavy with cypress. Wright called it a "clearwater lake" but this would not be indigenous to South Carolina. Black- or red-water lakes (the color caused by tannin) are normal to the Carolinas, where natural lakes are bends in rivers cut off from the main

Stevens Residence, living room (left) and original master bedroom (right)

Stevens Residence completed with correct kitchen connected to main house by gallery dining

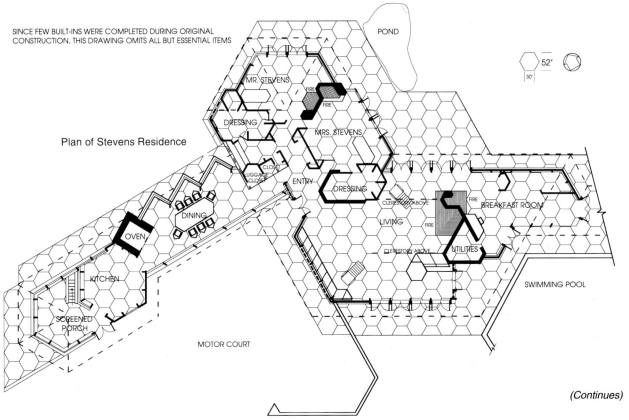

Plan of Stevens Residence

SINCE FEW BUILT-INS WERE COMPLETED DURING ORIGINAL CONSTRUCTION, THIS DRAWING OMITS ALL BUT ESSENTIAL ITEMS

(Continues)

channel. Clearwater lakes are all man-made. In final working drawings, the Auldbrass buildings were mirror-imaged west to east.

Drippings of tannic acid from the live oak and Spanish moss ate through the extremely thin wartime copper-foil roof, the use of such "foil" having been suggested by Lloyd Wright. The breakfast room, enlarged with Wright's approval, served as the main kitchen.

Restoration of the main house constituted phase one of a three-step project for the rebuilding and fulfillment of the Auldbrass design as originally planned. This phase was completed by mid-June 1989. The original workspace was finished, and the breezeway to the house enclosed on one side by plate glass as specified. All wood has been cleaned or replaced with new tidewater cypress, stained to match original boards. Many details, not finished in original construction, have now been done as specified in the drawings.

Construction of the guesthouse (with related glass-bottom boat for cruising the man-made lake) is the last phase of Auldbrass restoration.

Auldbrass cottage

S.262 T.4015
Seven **Cottages**
Yemassee, South Carolina
Two cottages only were built. One cottage renovated 1990.

Original plans called for seven cottages for the plantation workers; only two were built. Each is a hexagon with a veranda that occupies almost half the floor space, so that inhabitants could sleep in a cool breeze. They have since been screened, to keep the area mosquito-free. The interior "room" is quite small, but was sufficient for privacy as needed.

Stevens Residence, living room from gallery, in the 1970s

View along short gallery to living room from entry

Stevens Residence, living room in the 1970s

Stevens Residence, shower stall and bathroom area, as originally built

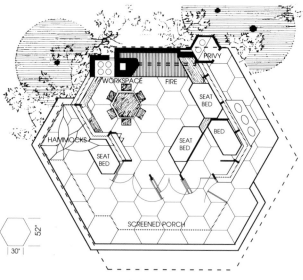

Plan of Auldbrass cottages

Auldbrass Plantation

S.263A   T.4015
Granary **(Barn)** with
S.263B   T.4015
Chicken Runs,
S.263C   T.4015
Shop and
S.263D   T.4015
Caretaker's Quarters
Yemassee, South Carolina
Barn, Shop and Chicken Runs
destroyed by fire, rebuilt 1989–90

The Caretaker's (manager's) Quarters
were at the approximate center of a
group of buildings, between the complex of kennels, stables, and manager's office and the chicken runs and
the barn. All were linked by esplanades which usually clung to one side
of the building structure on its open
side, not as elegant as those of Florida
Southern College (S.251–S.258), but
perhaps even more integrated. Restoration of these buildings is phase
two of the project to finish all of Auldbrass as Wright designed it.

Barn (with ancillary buildings; chicken coops to right)

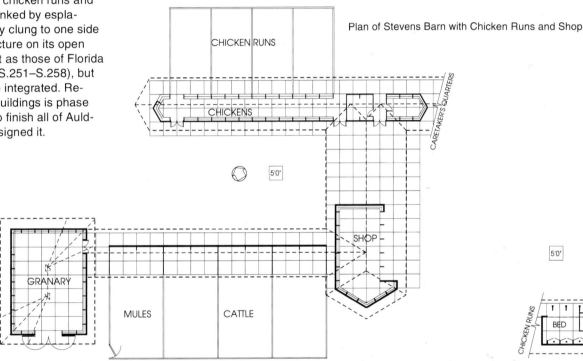

Plan of Stevens Barn with Chicken Runs and Shop

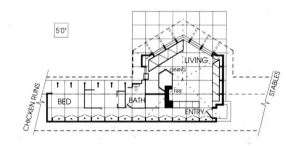

Plan of Caretaker's Quarters

Auldbrass Caretaker's Quarters

Interior of Auldbrass Caretaker's Quarters

Auldbrass Plantation

S.264A   T.4015
Stables with
S.264B   T.4015
Kennels and
S.264C   T.4015
Manager's Office
Yemassee, South Carolina
Restored 1990

The Manager's Office provides a change of direction between the kennels at one end of the group and the stables at the other end, attached to the Caretaker's Quarters (S.263) group. The kennels are of particular interest; each has parallel slats removed from the outside wall with shutters outside, screening inside, for excellent ventilation. Further, there is a fold-down platform so that dogs will not have to lie on the cold cement floors during the chilly winter nights.

Auldbrass Manager's Office,
Stables to the right

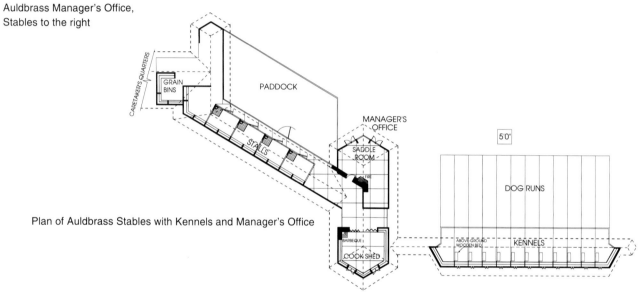

Plan of Auldbrass Stables with Kennels and Manager's Office

Single Auldbrass kennel

Single Auldbrass stable

USONIAN VOCABULARY

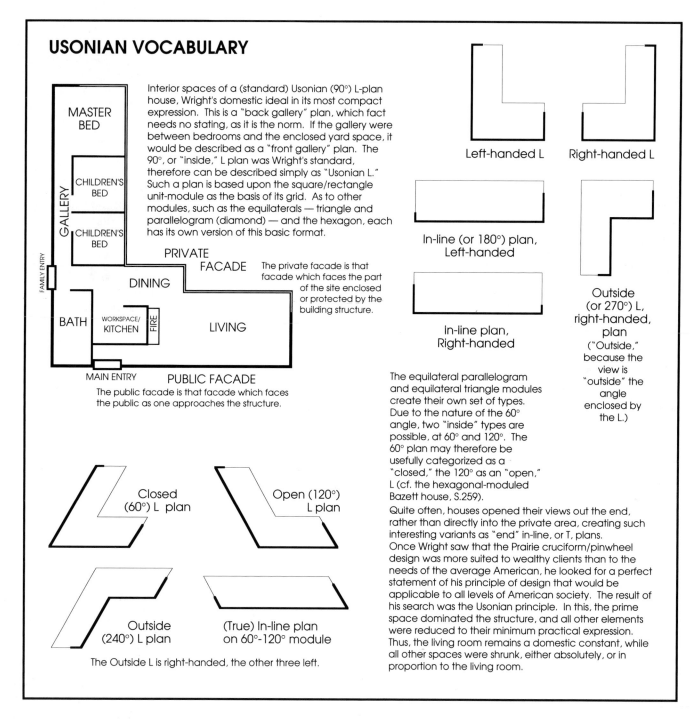

Interior spaces of a (standard) Usonian (90°) L-plan house, Wright's domestic ideal in its most compact expression. This is a "back gallery" plan, which fact needs no stating, as it is the norm. If the gallery were between bedrooms and the enclosed yard space, it would be described as a "front gallery" plan. The 90°, or "inside," L plan was Wright's standard, therefore can be described simply as "Usonian L." Such a plan is based upon the square/rectangle unit-module as the basis of its grid. As to other modules, such as the equilaterals — triangle and parallelogram (diamond) — and the hexagon, each has its own version of this basic format.

MASTER BED

CHILDREN'S BED

CHILDREN'S BED

GALLERY

FAMILY ENTRY

PRIVATE FACADE

The private facade is that facade which faces the part of the site enclosed or protected by the building structure.

DINING

BATH

WORKSPACE/ KITCHEN

FIRE

LIVING

MAIN ENTRY

PUBLIC FACADE

The public facade is that facade which faces the public as one approaches the structure.

Closed (60°) L plan

Open (120°) L plan

Outside (240°) L plan

(True) In-line plan on 60°-120° module

The Outside L is right-handed, the other three left.

Left-handed L

Right-handed L

In-line (or 180°) plan, Left-handed

In-line plan, Right-handed

Outside (or 270°) L, right-handed, plan ("Outside," because the view is "outside" the angle enclosed by the L.)

The equilateral parallelogram and equilateral triangle modules create their own set of types. Due to the nature of the 60° angle, two "inside" types are possible, at 60° and 120°. The 60° plan may therefore be usefully categorized as a "closed," the 120° as an "open," L (cf. the hexagonal-moduled Bazett house, S.259).

Quite often, houses opened their views out the end, rather than directly into the private area, creating such interesting variants as "end" in-line, or T, plans. Once Wright saw that the Prairie cruciform/pinwheel design was more suited to wealthy clients than to the needs of the average American, he looked for a perfect statement of his principle of design that would be applicable to all levels of American society. The result of his search was the Usonian principle. In this, the prime space dominated the structure, and all other elements were reduced to their minimum practical expression. Thus, the living room remains a domestic constant, while all other spaces were shrunk, either absolutely, or in proportion to the living room.

S.265　T.4008
Lloyd Lewis Residence (1939) and
S.266　T.4308
Farm Unit (1943)
Libertyville, Illinois

Mr. Lewis was editor of the *Chicago Daily News* when he commissioned this house for a site over 30 miles north of the Loop. His dwelling, the first "in-line" Usonian plan by Wright, is set on the flood plain of the Des Plaines River. Thus, the living room and balcony of this cypress and brick structure are on the upper story, above the ground-level entrances. The workspace and sanctum, or study, are on one side of the living room, the bedroom wing on the other side, more like the later Erdman Prefab # 1 (S.406–S.411) than the typical L-plan Usonian placement of workspace at the juncture of the living and bedroom spaces. There are two bedrooms, each with its own bathroom, in the wing that falls on the same "spine" as the living room but is a half level below. Separate servant's quarters and guest bedroom are under the living room in what amounts to a split-level arrangement that yields almost 2400 square feet of interior space.

Since living quarters are raised, the heating system pipes had to go through the joists. The plan is laid out on a 4-foot unit module. Detailing is quite fine, with light fixtures and built-in furniture all from Wright's drafting board. To meet Wright's unrealistically low budget, Edgar Tafel, who supervised construction, bid every part of the work separately. The farm unit is a poultry shed.

Lloyd Lewis Residence

Living room

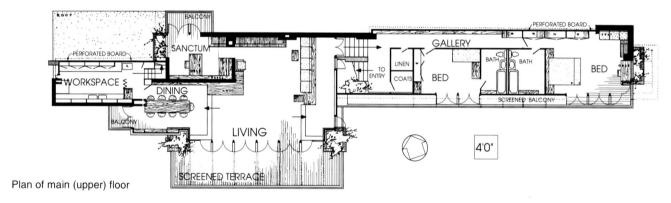

Farm unit

Plan of main (upper) floor

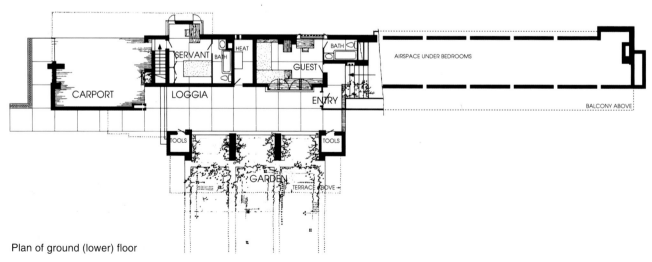

Plan of ground (lower) floor

Rosenbaum Residence

S.267   T.3903
Stanley and Mildred **Rosenbaum
Residence** (1939) and
S.267A   T.4815
Addition (1948)
Florence, Alabama
Restored 1990

Upon the suggestion of their friend
Aaron Green, Professor and Mrs.
Stanley Rosenbaum went to Wright.
Green studied at Taliesin, became a
close friend of Wright's, and later was
associated with him on many San
Francisco area projects.

The Rosenbaum design is an
elaboration of the basic Usonian **L**.
Beyond the masonry, which supports
the extensive cantilevering, at the far
end of the living room is a study with
its own fireplace. The masonry for
cantilever support at the end of the
bedroom wing almost vanishes, turned
parallel to the wing axis. Wright
extends the basic plan, with a second
bathroom exclusively for the master
bedroom. Supervision of construction
was by Burton Goodrich.

In 1948, Wright first extended the
structure opposite the living room,
creating a dormitory for the Rosenbaum's boys. Then a separate gallery,
parallel to the original one, was added
to lead to a guest bedroom. The three
new spaces framed a lanai, since
made into a Japanese garden. Renovation of the entire structure was
completed in 1970 by the Taliesin
Associated Architects. A later restoration provided for the building to be
opened for public visits.

Lanai, view to children's room

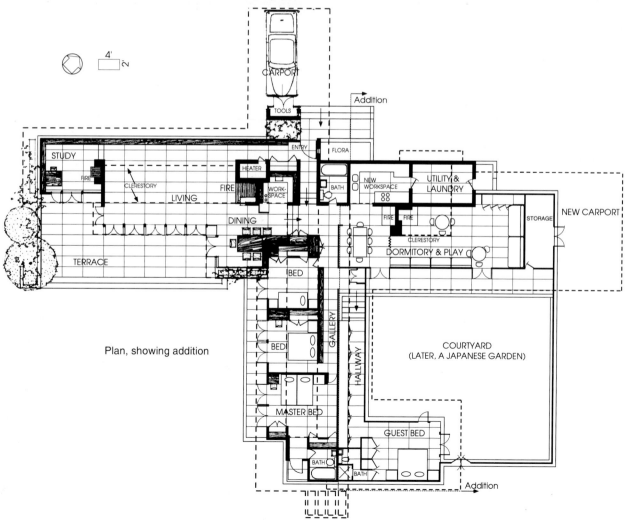

Plan, showing addition

Pope Residence, living-dining wing left, bedroom wing right

S.268   T.4013
Loren B. **Pope** (Pope-Leighey)
Residence (1939)
Falls Church, Virginia
Relocated to Mount Vernon, Virginia, in 1964, where it was improperly oriented and many details of design and construction ignored. Foundation and heating pipes cracked during reconstruction.

On August 18, 1939, Loren Pope, a newsman at the *Washington Evening Star,* wrote Frank Lloyd Wright; "There are certain things a man wants during life, and, of life. Material things and things of the spirit . . . one fervent wish . . . includes both. It is for a house created by you." Wright's September 2 response was, "Of course I am ready to give you a house." Plans for a "Jacobs-style house," an **L**-plan Usonian structure on a 2-by-4-foot rectangular unit module with cypress (true bald cyprus, *Taxodium distichum*) in sunk-batten paneling, were completed by November. Construction, supervised by Gordon Chadwick, went on from June 1940 to the fall of 1941. In November 1946, the Popes sold to the Leigheys.

When extension of Interstate 66 into metropolitan Washington threatened the property in 1963, shortly after Robert Leighey died, Mrs. Marjorie Folsom Leighey offered the house to the National Trust, which took it under their care, moving it to Woodlawn Plantation in 1964. Mrs. Leighey was granted life tenancy in 1969. As relocated, the house was improperly oriented to the sun; even at the original site, reorientation from Wright's first thoughts (in line with the street grid) had been necessary to fit the site topography.

Because of settling and problems incurred during reconstruction, the building requires shoring or relocation. The latter choice was suggested by architect Jonathan Lipman so that the building could be properly oriented on its site, but this program was initially rejected by the National Trust in favor of less costly site stabilization and restoration.

Dining alcove, view to bedroom wing

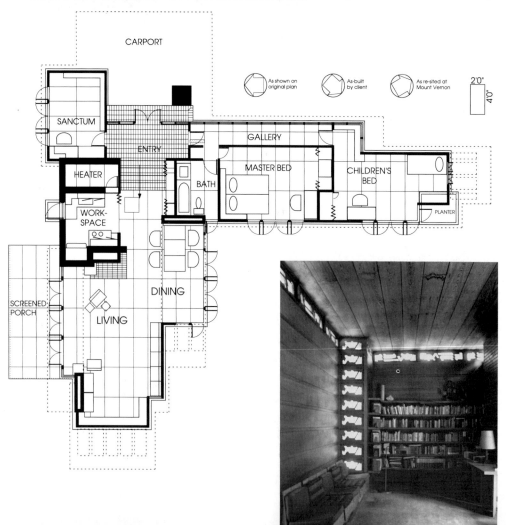

Living room

Goetsch-Winckler Residence

S.269   T.3907
Goetsch-Winckler Residence
(1939) for Alma Goetsch and
Katherine Winckler
Okemos, Michigan
Thermopane replaces plate glass.
Steel added to carport cantilever

On sheet three of the original plans,
Wright corrected "Usonia Two,
Lansing" to "East Lansing" and "House
for the Misses Goetsch and Winckler"
to "The 'Goetsch and Winckler'" which,
for publication, he shortened to "The
Goetsch Winckler." This is the only
house of the original first Usonia
project (see Usonia Homes, S.316–
S.318, for the second Usonia) that was
built in what was to have been a
planned cooperative community for
teachers at Michigan Agricultural
College, now Michigan State University. Misses Goetsch and Winckler
were both from Wisconsin. They joined
with others to acquire a site on Herron
Creek southeast of the campus; banks
refused to finance such modern
designs as Wright had provided his
clients, so the project fell through. The
lady instructors, earning $2000 a year
in 1939, built their home and Erling
Brauner, a latecomer to the community, built a different design (S.312).

In this in-line home on a
4-foot-square unit module, Wright's
use of thin walls as screens to
maintain privacy and masonry to
support extensive cantilevering of
roofs reaches a high point in early
Usonian design. The dry wall construction is a typical Usonian horizontal sunk redwood batten sandwich.
Two bedrooms open onto a lanai,
enclosed for privacy. Off the living
room, actually a studio, is an alcove
with a fireplace. On the other side of
this masonry mass is the workspace.
The cantilever of the carport reaches
18 feet from the workspace support
wall, and 10 feet beyond any side
support. Perforated panels for the
clerestory windows were never built.
Construction began in June 1940, and
the final cost was $6,594.73, or 27¢
below budget.

Master builder Harold Turner was
in charge of construction and "added"
a basement cellar for food storage and
utilities without Wright's approval.
Single-plate glass has been replaced
by Thermopane, and structural steel
has been added to the carport cantilever.

Alcove

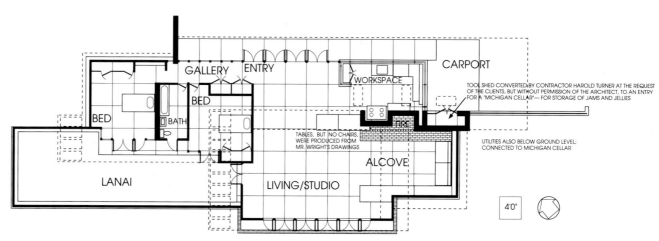

Euchtman Residence

S.270 T.4005
Joseph **Euchtman** Residence
(1939)
Baltimore, Maryland
Exterior altered

This Usonian house carefully shuts out of view its close neighbor to the north and takes maximum advantage of its wedge-shaped lot, which most architects would have shunned. Its view southeast from its main private facade, southwest on the end of the living room, was once across broad boulevard spaces, offering occupants complete privacy; an exterior deck has been added, with plantings to obstruct the view. The rectangular unit grid is angled 30 degrees from north toward the morning sun, while the carport roof line conforms to the east-west lot line. The design is as compact as seems possible, with only two bedrooms in an in-line arrangement. Typically, the flat roof extends well beyond the living room and master bedroom termini in the form of a trellis. The transom-level windows are unadorned in keeping with the low-cost aspect of the building.

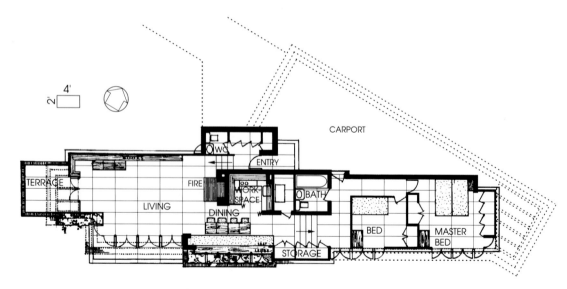

S.271 T.3904
Bernard **Schwartz** Residence
(1939)
Two Rivers, Wisconsin

The September 26, 1938, issue of *Life* magazine published Wright's idea for a house "For a Family of $5000–$6000 Income," and the following year it was built by Bernard Schwartz, a businessman, on the right bank of East Twin River at Still Bend in Two Rivers, Wisconsin. Designed to a nonstandard 42-inch-square unit module, the **T** plan is so angled on its plot as to gain a full view east and south along East Twin River without obstruction from neighboring buildings.

Its two stories suggest a designation never accorded it by the architect himself, "two-story Usonian," for such an idea seems to violate at least a few tenets of basic thirties Usonian design. Yet one must remember that the California block houses (S.214–S.217), which Wright considered Usonian, were multistory. Wright's solution was to place the master bedroom at ground level, then locate two additional bedrooms plus servant's quarters at the second level rather than in a Usonian wing. The Pew house (S.273), with all quiet areas on the second level, will seem to some a neater arrangement.

In this plan there is no "living room," but a "recreation room" opening to a terrace on the south, a sunken court on the north, an arrangement similar to that used in the Pearce house (S.320) a decade later and duplicated in the Gordon house (S.419, 1957). The house is brick and horizontal cypress in a board-and-sunk-batten configuration, with a generous 3000 square feet of space. The patterned clerestory windows deserve special note. Edgar Tafel supervised construction, adding structural steel to the extremely deep carport cantilever. Trellising lightens the load of the recreation room overhang.

Schwartz Residence, south facade private side

Recreation room, view to south facade

Shadow and light; patterns created by clerestory cut-outs

Central bedroom

Recreation room, view from lounge (reverse view from above)

Plan of ground floor

Plan of second floor

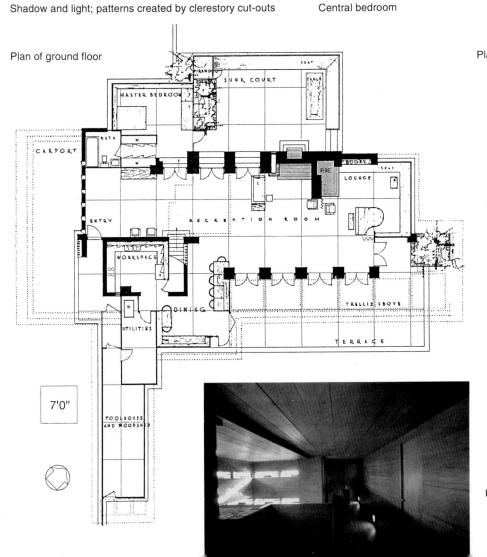

7'0"

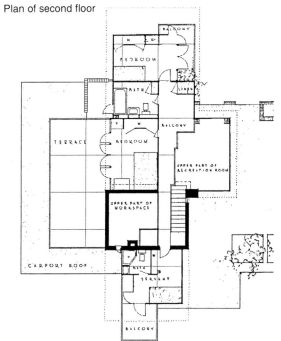

Upper level gallery

S.272   T.3905
George D. **Sturges** Residence
(1939)
Brentwood Heights, California

Most of this house is cantilevered out from its hillside perch. The brick and painted redwood siding (the original was stained) present an appearance of a house without windows; actually the entire east wall, including the living room and bedrooms, opens to a balcony overlooking the street below. That balcony-terrace is nine 6-foot-6-inch-square units long, four for the living room, two each for the bedrooms, one for the side terrace. Workspace, utilities, and bath are behind the bedrooms on the opposite side of the gallery. With an interior space of less than 900 square feet, Wright created a house that seems spacious by intimately relating inside to out by way of the terrace.

Wright chose heart redwood, thinking it would never rot, but a later owner began replacement as the house entered its fifth decade. Wright liked the beauty of redwood and found it a reasonable substitute for cypress, which was not readily available on the West Coast. But it was too soft (only 27 lb./cu. ft. density, the lowest of any wood commonly used by Wright); water penetrates it easily and creates permanent stains.

Supervision was by John Lautner. Wright returned to this design in 1952 for Lawrence Swan in Inkster, Michigan, adding one and a half units for a third bedroom, and doubling the size of the carport for this suburban motor-city client, but that house was never built. The Frank Sander house (S.354) of the same year is a development of this Sturges design.

Sturges Residence

Dining area

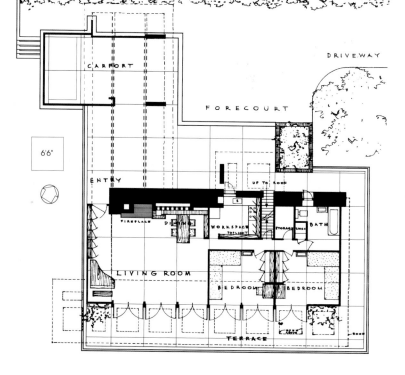

THE IN-LINE PLAN

Wright perfected the Usonian L plan in 1936 with the Jacobs First Residence, S.234. Various experiments in plan organization led, in 1939, to the first in-line plan, the Lloyd Lewis Residence, S.265. In this of Wright's many in-line designs, the wing-mirrored plan is used, with the additional variant that has Living-Workspace areas reversed left for right (grids 1-11 turned 11-1) so that the housewife could view the full living room and the gallery of the bedroom wing from her workspace.

To the right are three in-line plans. The "standard" is at the bottom. By simply mirroring the bedroom wing (flipping north for south in this instance) we get the middle version. The top plan is another simple back gallery variation. One difference between the two back-gallery plans is that one has an unbroken private facade, the other an unbroken public facade.

Like the L-plan Usonian, the in-line can be varied in many ways. The bedroom wing can be extended in the same manner as with the L plan.

Below is a particularly economical in-line floor plan; a short gallery is surrounded by bedrooms in a "cluster" arrangement. In this example, this allows a second bathroom between the children's bedrooms. Another variant on this, used in the Pappas residence, S.392, adds a third child's bedroom in the second bathroom+utilities area and extending an additional unit or two beyond.

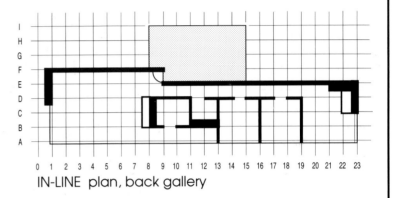

IN-LINE plan, back gallery

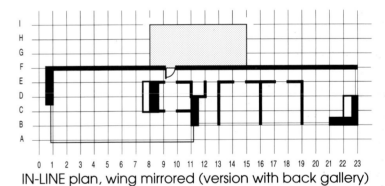

IN-LINE plan, wing mirrored (version with back gallery)

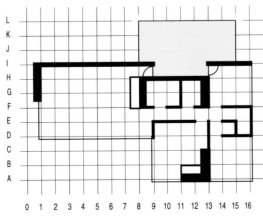

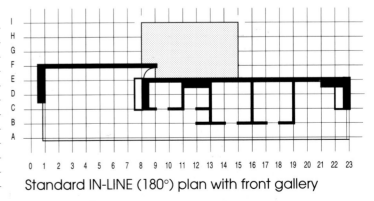

Standard IN-LINE (180°) plan with front gallery

Pew Residence, exposure to Lake Mendota

Pew Residence, soffit detail

Public facade

S.273   T.4012
John Clarence **Pew** Residence (1938)
Shorewood Hills, Wisconsin
Renovated 1989, with flagstone replacing wood-slat floor of the kitchen.

The hillside site slopes gently from Mendota Drive, then drops sharply to Lake Mendota, where the house is perched. With its base on the slope and one wing over the precipice, this limestone-and-cypress structure is able to open its first floor to lake and woods and preserve privacy for its second-story sleeping quarters. The $2,000 lot is cramped between two other houses, but this is not apparent within the 1200 square feet of space that is arranged neatly on a grid of square units. By such details as a lapped wood ceiling, Wright makes the space seem large. Rather than a second wing for the quiet area, Wright here moves the bedrooms and full bathroom upstairs. Full-length piano hinges and accordion-pleated doors are among the standard Usonian features.

General contracting was supervised by William Wesley Peters, who ordered a full train-car load of cypress, split the order and nearly paid for the Pew's part from what was sold. This became necessary as the $6,750 fee (including architect's commission) kept

being exceeded because of changes in lighting fixtures, insulation, and such, leading to the quip, "right house, wrong pew." Many changes were made to Wright's plans during construction, and some of the overhanging roof and trellis features are not to proportions approved by Wright. The Pews became lifelong and close friends of Peters and Wright.

By the early eighties, the Pews had decided they needed to move on to retirement. Their first offer was under $100,000. When they told Wes Peters this, he advised them that it was worth $250,000. So they waited and eventually more than doubled that original offer. Of this, they sent a $1000 check to Wes which, he noted, made up for what he'd lost on the project. They also sent a much larger contribution to The Frank Lloyd Wright Foundation in appreciation for the joy their home had given them over the years. They sold to Dr. John S. and Cynthia Edwards, who rented it out until January 1, 1989. By then, they had sufficient funds to do required renovation. Wood surfaces were cleaned and repaired as needed. Flagstone replaced the wood slat floor in the kitchen and the kitchen skylight was given a cut-out similar to a Wright transom level design.

Plan of upper floor

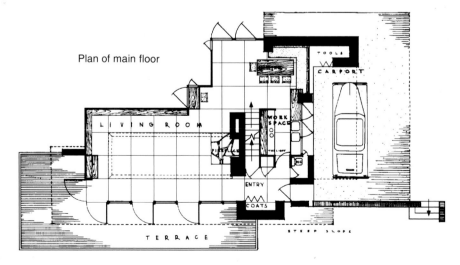

Plan of main floor

Gregor S. and Elizabeth B. **Affleck** Residence (1940)
Bloomfield Hills, Michigan
Restored by Lawrence Institute of
Technology in the 1980s

Part of Gregor Affleck's boyhood was spent on a farm near Spring Green, across the Wisconsin River from Taliesin, and for many years one of his relatives was Wright's secretary. He graduated with a degree in chemical engineering from the University of Wisconsin in 1919. When he and his wife saw drawings and renderings of Fallingwater, they fell in love with all it seemed to represent.

This, the first of two designs for the Afflecks, is taken from the Broadacre City model of a "home for sloping ground." It is a **T** (or outside **L**) plan on a 4-foot-square unit module (incorrectly aligned in all previously published drawings). The living room and its balcony are cantilevered above a ravine, and a glass-covered loggia (it might be open in a warmer climate) separates this from the bedroom wing. The ship-lap cypress siding, each course resting on the one below, used here is a unique feature. Hard-burned shale brick is featured, right-side out (in the Wall house, S.281, it is wrong side out, for a more "romantic" coloring). Harold Turner supervised construction of this 2400 square foot house.

During construction, concrete from the retaining wall foundation was spilled into a basement tunnel.

Affleck Residence

Discovery of the problem came too late for easy correction; leaving the "tunnel" largely impassable.

The house, of course, had a piano, Wright's (and most of his clients') favorite piece of furniture. It did not fit its corner. Wright discovered this on a visit, took a hand saw, and cut off the offending corner of a built-in bookshelf.

The home is now owned by the Lawrence Institute of Technology of Southfield, Michigan. Restoration has proceeded over the years since the

house was placed on the National Register of Historic places through the efforts of Mary and Anthony Gholz, who cared for the house in the years between the death of Elizabeth (1973) and Gregor (1974) and the time when it was acquired as a gift from the client's children, Gregor, Jr., and Mary Anne Affleck Lutomski near the end of the decade. New red Tidewater cypress was obtained from three states and cut to match removed boards, inch for inch.

Living room, view to loggia

Lighting fixture

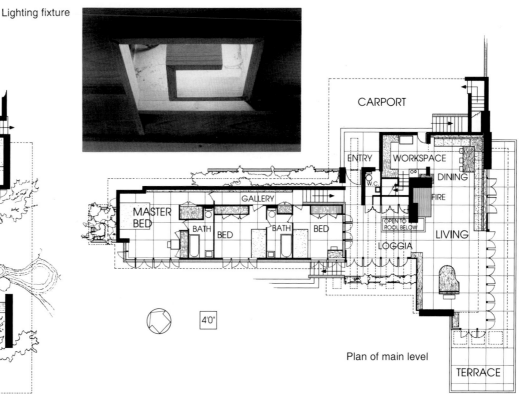

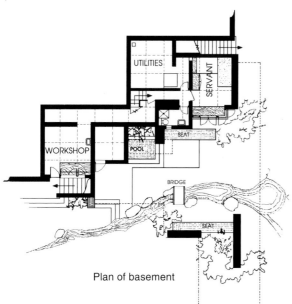

Plan of basement

4'0"

Plan of main level

S.275 T.4112
Arch Oboler Gatehouse Complex (1940),
S.276 T.4112A
Eleanor's Retreat (1941),
S.275A T.4112
Additions to Gatehouse Complex (1944), and
S.275B T.5508
Oboler House (1955)
Malibu, California

Arch Oboler was a major force in the development of 3-D movies, for example, *Bwana Devil*, and author of various novels including *House on Fire*, a Peabody Award Winner considered a "worthy successor to *Rosemary's Baby*!" by the *San Francisco Examiner*. The financial ups-and-downs of his movie ventures prevented construction of the main building, called "Eaglefeather," of an extensive complex that included film processing facilities, stables and paddock, and a large gatehouse. Eaglefeather was one of Wright's crowning achievements, cantilevered magnificently toward the Pacific Ocean from a Malibu mountain precipice. Oboler and his wife, Eleanor, settled for living first in their own gatehouse and later in an alternate house design provided by Wright. Desert masonry construction is used throughout, with horizontal wood siding. Though changes appear to have been made from published plans—simplifications to reduce costs—the basic concept remains intact.

Situated high in the Santa Monica Mountains above Malibu, the retreat, several hundred yards south of the gatehouse, commands a stunning view across mountain wilderness. Having given up on Eaglefeather, Oboler returned to Wright in 1954 for a building on three levels housing a theatre, living room, and separate bedrooms for Arch and Eleanor. This would have been at the end of the partially constructed retaining wall for the pergola, had construction proceeded. Kenn Lockhart was the Taliesin supervisor of the original project. Oboler died in 1987 and his 120 acres of property was sold to a developer.

Oboler Gatehouse, with pergola retaining wall to unbuilt theatre

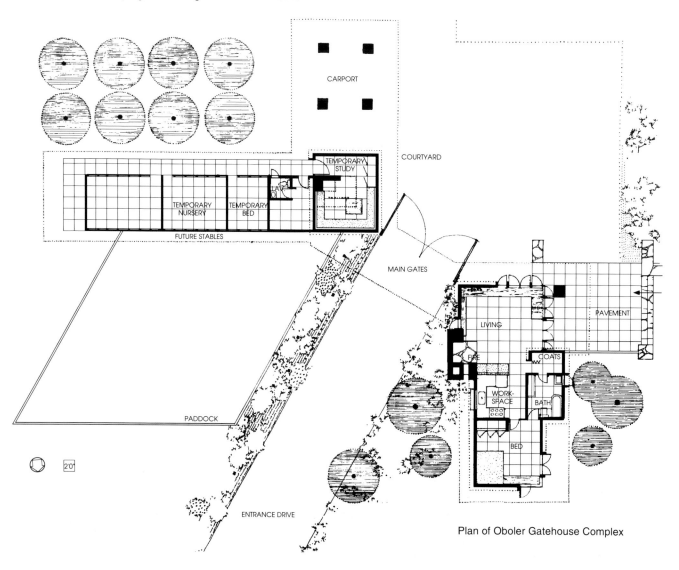

Plan of Oboler Gatehouse Complex

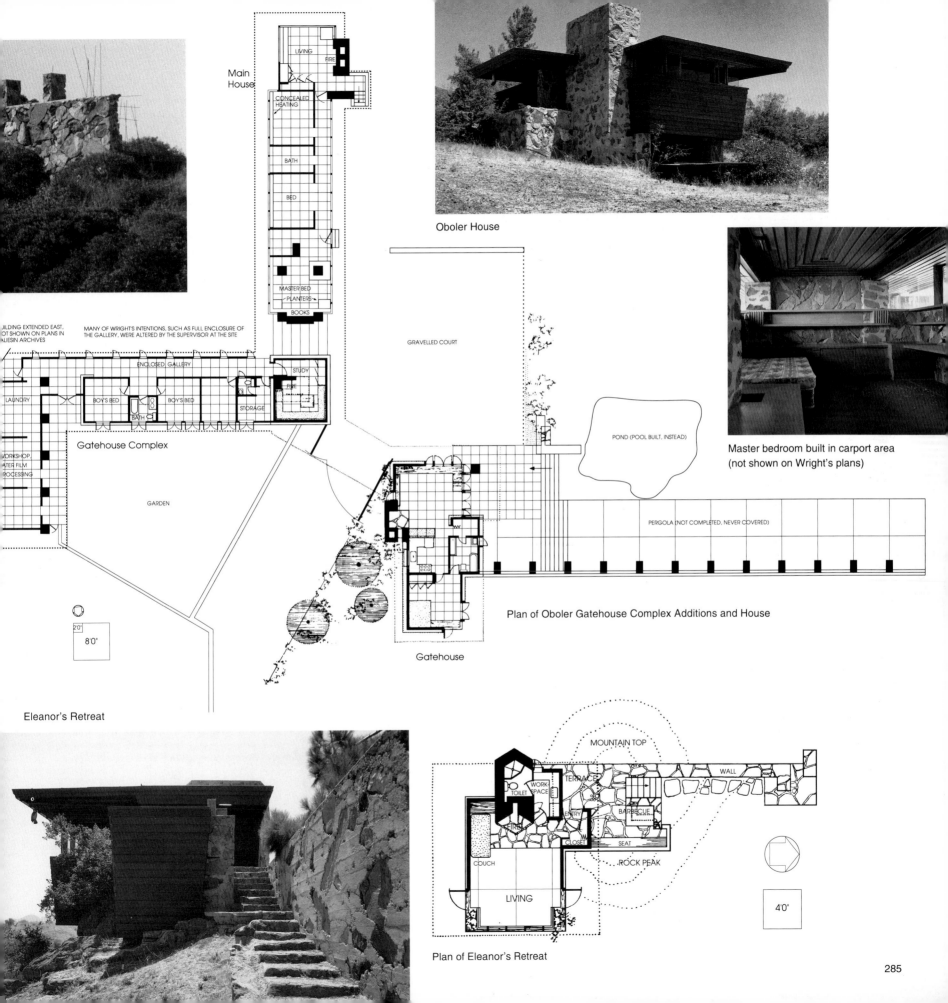

Main House

LIVING

FIRE

CONCEALED HEATING

BATH

BED

MASTER BED

PLANTERS

BOOKS

Oboler House

BUILDING EXTENDED EAST, NOT SHOWN ON PLANS IN TALIESIN ARCHIVES

MANY OF WRIGHT'S INTENTIONS, SUCH AS FULL ENCLOSURE OF THE GALLERY, WERE ALTERED BY THE SUPERVISOR AT THE SITE

ENCLOSED GALLERY

STUDY

FIRE

LAUNDRY

BOY'S BED

BATH

BOY'S BED

STORAGE

WORKSHOP, WATER FILM PROCESSING

Gatehouse Complex

GARDEN

GRAVELLED COURT

POND (POOL BUILT, INSTEAD)

Master bedroom built in carport area (not shown on Wright's plans)

PERGOLA (NOT COMPLETED, NEVER COVERED)

Plan of Oboler Gatehouse Complex Additions and House

Gatehouse

2'0"

8'0"

Eleanor's Retreat

MOUNTAIN TOP

WORK SPACE

TOILET

TERRACE

WALL

BARBECUE

ENTRY

FIRE

SEAT

CLOSET

ROCK PEAK

COUCH

LIVING

4'0"

Plan of Eleanor's Retreat

Baird Residence, from southwest

Baird Residence, from southeast

Detached Shop

S.277 T.4001
Theodore **Baird Residence** with
S.277A T.4001
Detached **Shop** (1940)
Amherst, Massachusetts

Wright's only work in Massachusetts, for Theodore Baird, a college professor, is a Usonian type with brick and horizontal cypress board and sunk batten, Wright's version of dry-wall construction. It is a compact (ca. 1200 square feet) and finely detailed in-line plan on a 2-by-4-foot unit, a Prairie version of the Sturges (S.272) house. Living room and two bedrooms are in line along one facade, workspace, utilities and two bathrooms are the opposite side of the gallery from the bedrooms, and a master bedroom with its own fireplace completes the arrangement at the end of the gallery. Back-to-back fireplaces, one in the living room, help define a small space for a sanctum, or study. A nook, straddling living room and study, is sized for an upright piano.

Financing was a major problem in the war years for most of Wright's clients. In Michigan, for instance, bankers were telling academics in the state capitol region and others trying to build projects near Kalamazoo that their house designs were too radical and would not easily sell if the client defaulted. Ted Baird found a sympathetic patron in the Amherst College president.

William Wesley Peters, the general contractor, notes that this was the only Usonian design for which the walls and glazing were prefabricated at a factory and later assembled rather than cut and built at the site. The prefabricator

was Ted Lyman of Montclair, New Jersey, who also supplied Carl Wall (S.281), James Christie (S.278), and C. Leigh Stevens (S.261–S.264) with materials. This helped speed construction; the Bairds moved in in January 1941. Cary Caraway and Edgar Tafel were also involved in supervision; Caraway suggested the very thick application of mortar between brick courses to align mortar with the recessed batten of the wood walls; the

mortar is not raked, but filled to the brick surface.

An early test of how to repair the gravity heating system when problems arose came with this house. When a leak developed within the floor slab, it was located with a stethoscope.

Bruce Brooks Pfeiffer visited often from nearby Worcester, Massachusetts, before heading west to join the Taliesin Fellowship.

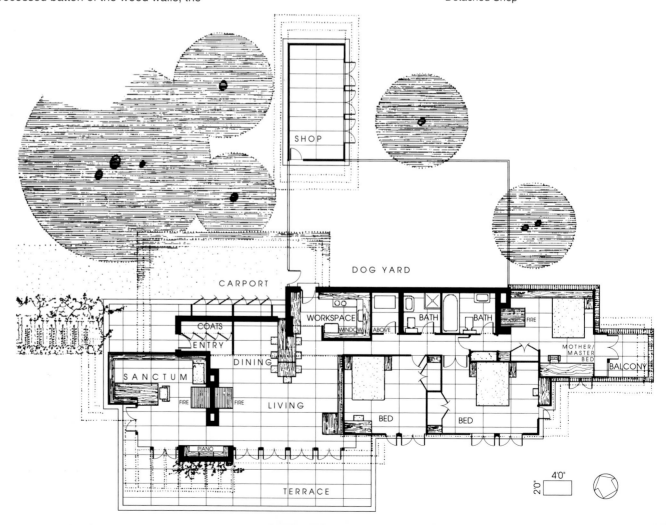

S.278   T.4003
James B. **Christie Residence** and
S.278A   T.4003
Detached **Shop** (1940)
Bernardsville, New Jersey

Local records fail to identify Christie or his connection with what was then rural forested New Jersey. The house was sold within half a decade to Sultan Amerie, a government official from Iran. The published plan, two different plot plans, and two hand-colored perspective drawings in the possession of the sultan's family, who lived in the home for forty years, disagree. Yet there is among them sufficient evidence of what was intended. The main living wing, with living room, workspace, dining area, ground-level utilities space, laundry room, and servant's quarters, is separated from the bedroom wing by a deeply recessed carport and entryway-loggia, all organized on a 2-by-4-foot unit module. The main wing was built as drawn, though with poor methods—no raking of horizontal mortar in the external brickwork and no coloring of the concrete slab floor (with gravity heating) or vertical mortar. Lack of structural steel has resulted in sagging cantilevers and the need for knee braces or other supporting members.

The plan shows three bedrooms, with a tiny master bedroom. As built, the childrens' rooms were combined into a master bedroom. According to the perspective drawings, a fireplace was to have been built beyond the current end wall, facing away from the intended master bedroom; this would have provided the usual end support for that wing's roof cantilever and the

building would have been 32 feet longer. The living room faces northeast to a downhill, wooded view, the bedroom wing northwest, in this reversed 90-degree **L** plan (i.e., the bedrooms face away from the enclosed angle). Thus, neither wing takes advantage of the sun. These and other questions of quality raise doubts about Harold Turner's claim to have been responsible for construction and John H. Howe for supervision. Taliesin makes no claim for any supervision.

The exterior has been painted; interior floors, parts of the bathrooms, as well as some workspace countertops have been covered with linoleum. The original patterned clerestory windows now are replaced with plain, rectangular glass.

Christie Residence, view from north

Living room from dining area

Plan, showing unbuilt portion of bedroom wing

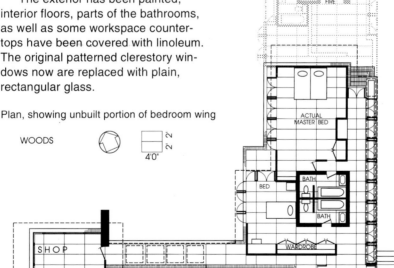
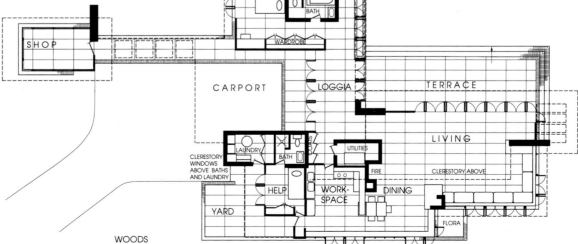

Sondern Residence

S.279   T.4014
Clarence **Sondern** (Sondern-Adler) Residence (1939)
Kansas City, Missouri

If the Jacobs house (S.234) may be called a standard "left-handed" Usonian plan, this house for Clarence Sondern, a chemist, is a "right-handed" version. It is small, with but two bedrooms off its gallery. Though the plan shows a grid of 4-foot squares, rectangles in line with the living room, as in the Jacobs, would not have been out of place. Three masonry rooms, each four units square, complete an implied 5-by-5-unit square, the fourth corner being the entry, and give two options to the visitor: access to the living room or down the gallery to the quiet spaces. The living room faces north, looking over a steep drop to Roanoke Parkway. The dining area and workspace are at the back of the living room, with glazed opening to a southern exposure. This was John H. Howe's first experience in supervising construction. In 1948 Wright provided plans for an addition (S.307).

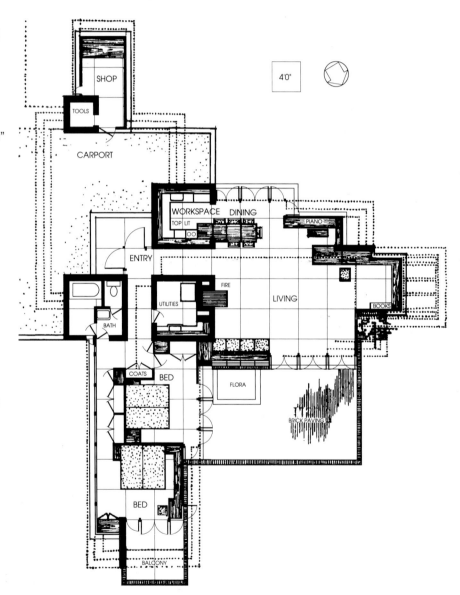

S.280   T.4004
Community Church (1940)
Kansas City, Missouri

This structure as built but vaguely resembles the magnificent concept of Wright's drawings. This is the result of conflict between the architect's advanced ideas for cheap construction and the conservative instincts of local "experts" who had final say over the ambitious project of Rev. Dr. Burris Jenkens. The project was needed to replace the original structure, which had been destroyed by fire. Wright intended to construct with Gunite, a form of pressure-sprayed concrete, to save on costs. It was to be set on rock ballast foundations, a system used in the Johnson buildings in Racine (S.237–S.238); Ben Wiltscheck, who was contractor for those buildings, supervised construction, which proceeded initially without a building permit.

The light tower, which was supposed to be fitted with powerful colored beacons, fell victim to wartime blackouts; it was covered to prevent escape of light from the auditorium, but remains intact. The roof garden that was to have surrounded it was never built.

The structure, located on a main highway in a residential part of Kansas City south of downtown, is designed on an equilateral triangle module, with a unit side of 5 feet, and was to have included a three-level parking garage as well as two large auditoriums. The design combines elements of the little theatre for Woodstock with the Anderton Court (S.356) tower rampway to a roof garden. In his design, Wright, noting the location, gave little concern to the desire for Sunday school space, believing the building would soon be in an urban environment rather than the suburban setting of the forties. The congregation built a separate building for Sunday school use; it is now vacant.

Community Church

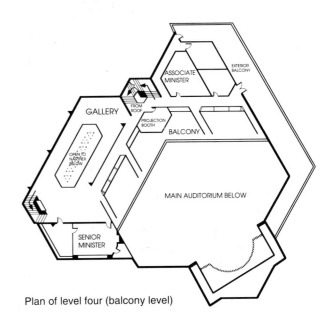

Plan of level four (balcony level)

Auditorium, the sanctuary with interior skylight detail

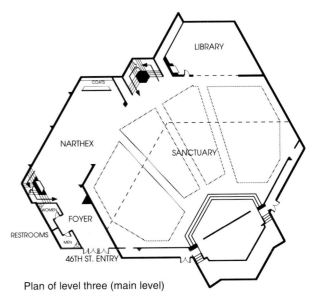

Plan of level three (main level)

Light tower

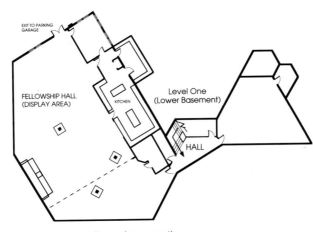

Plan of level one (lower basement)

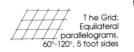

The Grid;
Equilateral
parallelograms,
60°-120°, 5 foot sides

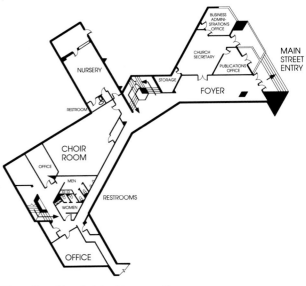

Plan of level two (original basement)

289

Wall Residence

S.281 T.4114
Carlton David and Margaret **Wall**
Residence, Snowflake (1941)
Plymouth, Michigan

Wright, at the first meeting with the Walls, exclaimed, "You're just children." They had recently graduated from Olivet College, and both were in their early twenties.

This brick-and-cypress structure generates a hexagonal living room, workspace, and utility core from the 60–120-degree equilateral parallelogram module of 2-foot altitude, the first such use of this module in Wright's built work. Its hip roof and pierced overhanging trellises create a snowflake form when viewed from above. The living room roof is cantilevered from the masonry core with limited support from steel concealed in the mullions; it stands 18 feet above the workspace floor at a skylight near the roof peak.

The plan is a derivation of an unbuilt design for Lewis N. Bell (which was built, in modified form for Hilary and Joe Feldman 15 years after Mr. Wright's death). It is an outside (240-degree) in-line, with the living room occupying more than half the basic hexagon where the wings meet. The dining room is to the rear of the core, overlooking a courtyard framed by guest and master bedroom wings. The main bedroom wing was extended with a bath and a nursery, under which Carl Wall placed a full basement. A carport and laboratory extend the opposite wing, which houses guest quarters. Direct access to the guest room has been provided by addition of an entry at the tool shed, the first room off the gallery of this wing.

The masonry is hard-burned shale brick, "wrong-side out," obtained at $25 per thousand as an overrun from Michigan Agricultural College (now Michigan State University). Cedar, white pine, and cypress are employed variously. Heating is typically of Usonian gravity type. Harold Turner supervised construction.

In the early 1980s, the house became the property of Thomas Monaghan, who intended to use it for visitors and meetings. In 1989 it was sold and returned to domestic use.

Goldfish ponds in dining area windowall

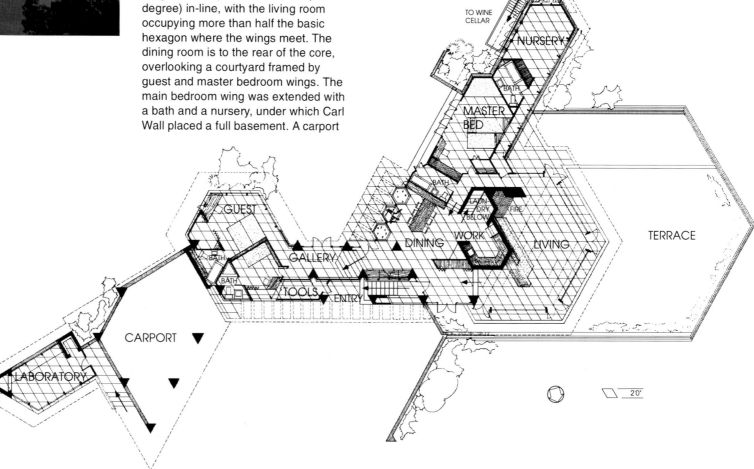

S.282 T.4104
Stuart **Richardson** Residence
(1940)

Glen Ridge, New Jersey
Kitchen remodeled. Accordion-pleated
doors replaced by sliding doors

The residence for engineer Stuart
Richardson and his wife is most notable as an early example of Wright's
use of triangular forms, in the plan of
the living room, derived from a hexagonal concept. The unit module is a
nonstandard 28-inch-sided hexagon
(opposite sides a bit more than 4 feet
apart). This, and a design for Vigo
Sundt, were on the drafting tables at
the same time. Sundt had come to
Wright through Taliesin apprentice
Cary Caraway, who was supervising
construction of the Pew house, in
1940, and an early concrete-block
house design ensued. This did not
satisfy Sundt; he saw the Richardson
plans while at Taliesin in October 1941
and suggested that, with minor revisions, it would serve his needs. Thus,
the often repeated assertion that the
Vigo Sundt project (T.4105) was the
progenitor of a significant number of
plans on triangular and hexagonal
modules is a rewriting of history. It is
the Richardson plan that is the original
and the Sundt that is the mirror-image
version, somewhat scaled-down.

The Richardson project, built on a
different site in 1951, has the building
oriented approximately 120 degrees
from that originally intended (in 1940)
in nearby Livingston; winter sun in the
rotated version warms the interior. The
shape of the new plot prevented the
carport from serving Wright's intended
purpose; the Richardsons made it a
screened porch.

This Usonian dwelling is built
primarily of masonry, with cypress
used as trim more than as walls.
Special brick with 60- and 120-degree
corners was made to fit the hexagonal
unit. The living room ceiling is special;
it slopes 2 feet, 7 inches from the walls
just above the clerestory windows
down to the center point of the room.
This is achieved by allowing each
board to drop its 3/4 inch thickness.
Each room's ceiling is differently
patterned by the same 3/4 inch edges,
though their finished effect is necessarily level because of their lower
basic height.

Richardson Residence

Many changes were made on site
to reduce costs. The windowall doors
to the shallow southeastern patio and
western walled terrace were to have
been pivoted short of their centers;
instead they are standard wood frames
held by full-length piano hinges. The
fascia appears to be incomplete; the
wood is painted. Plans reveal no special detail, but a copper fascia with
surface design, or a dentil mold of triangles, would seem necessary to
complete the scheme. The kitchen,
which has since been remodeled, was
originally installed to a design by the
General Electric Home Bureau. Electric lighting is sunk into the ceiling
except in the living room where above-
deck lighting is used; no space is

well-lit. Many accordion-pleated doors
were replaced with standard sliding
panels. Interestingly, both horizontal
and vertical mortar between bricks is
tinted (Wright specified vertical only)
and deeply raked (Wright's standard
required the vertical mortar to be flush).

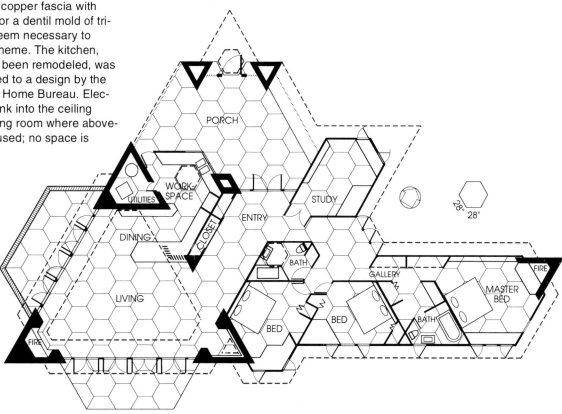

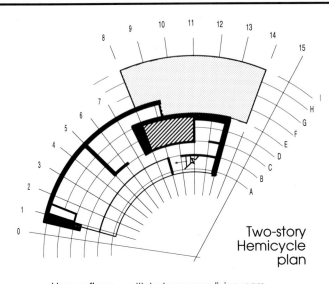

Two-story
Hemicycle
plan

Upper floor   with balcony over living room

THE SOLAR HEMICYCLE

Wright's first Solar Hemicycle, S.283, was the second design by the architect for client Herbert Jacobs. The concave curve of the windowall took advantage of the movement of the sun. Here we have shown an attached carport, though the Jacobs design had none as the public facade was set into a berm to reduce heat loss during cold Wisconsin winters.

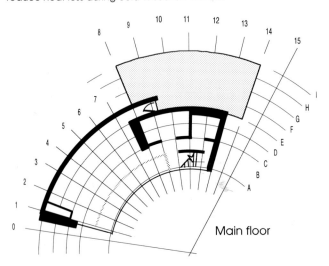

Main floor

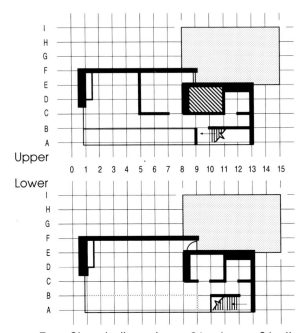

Upper

Lower

Two-Story In-line plan   2 bedroom, 2 bath

Though many people think of Usonian design as limited to single-story structures, Usonia began, by Wright's own statement, with the multistory California block houses. The Schwartz house, S.271, is a two story Usonian design, as are many of the Solar Hemicycles (cf. S.283, S.297, S.358, S.359). Single-story hemicycles may have concave (cf. S.319, S.320, S.360) or convex (cf. S.357) private facades, though the public facades were always convex.

A solar equivalent in rectilinear format is, of course, possible. Consider the problem of a plot of land too shallow for an L, too short for an In-line. Fold the bedroom wing over the main floor living room and workspace, *voilà*, a two-story in-line plan, with upper floor recessed as in the Solar Hemicycle (cf. S.379). With a high living room ceiling on a single-floor design such as the Lovness residence, S.291, gains much the same solar advantages.

Many variants of the hemicycle and two-story in-line shown here are possible. To reveal relationships to other examples of Usonian design, the entry is set on the public facade side, the stairs on the private facade wall; in actual Wright designs, most stairs were to one side of the main entry area.

Jacobs Second Residence

Balcony

S.283 T.4812
Herbert and Katherine **Jacobs** **Second Residence** (1944)
Middleton, Wisconsin

This is the second house Wright designed and built for the Jacobs family. It is the first solar hemicycle, based on circular segments 6 degrees wide, of two stories, with its back set into the earth. Its glassed private facade opens onto a sunken terrace. By placing the bedrooms on a second level, Wright eliminated the tunnel gallery. Here it is transformed into a balcony overlooking the two-story living room. This unifies the interior spaces in a manner contrary to typical Usonian structures with their separate living and quiet zones. This upper level is hung from steel ties themselves suspended from 1-by-12-inch boards spanning from the north wall masonry to the south glazed-wall mullions. One-third of the second level, the balcony, is cantilevered beyond the ties. While the stone is quite beautiful, Jacobs skimped on lumber which, even inside, lacks the beauty usually associated with houses of this period.

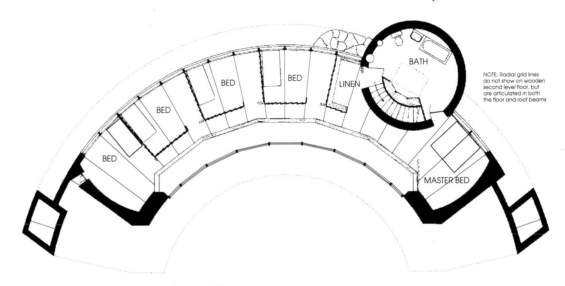

NOTE: Radial grid lines do not show on wooden second level floor, but are articulated in both the floor and roof beams

Plan of second floor

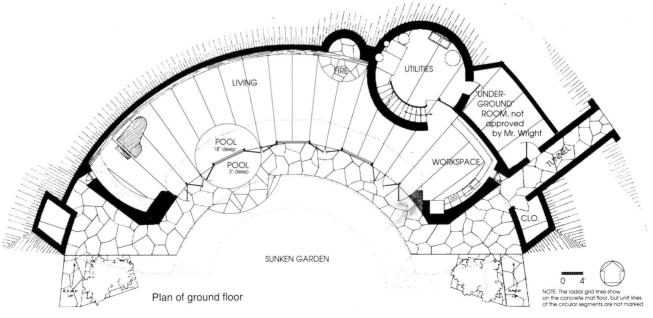

Plan of ground floor

NOTE: The radial grid lines show on the concrete mat floor, but unit lines of the circular segments are not marked

0 4'

Walter Residence

Living room, view southeast

S.284 T.4505
Lowell and Agnes **Walter
Residence**
S.284A
Council Fire and
S.284B
Gate (1945)
Quasqueton, Iowa

Half of the buildings from Wright's imagination that were still standing in 1973 (the date the first edition of *The Architecture of Frank Lloyd Wright: A Complete Catalog* was put into production) were created by 1938, though half of his thousand-plus projects would not be on the drawing boards until the end of World War II. The war

years halted most construction. Only three of Wright's 1941 designs were built, and none from 1942. From his 1943 efforts, the Guggenheim design (S.400) had to wait nearly a decade before the foundation was laid. In 1945 construction activity resumed.

Lowell Walter was born four years before the turn of the century in Quasqueton. He, and his wife Agnes, lived in Des Moines; they had no children. Lowell was head of the Iowa Road Building Company. In 1944 he sold the business and moved "back home," to farmland. His contact with Wright came in 1942, the basic design was completed by 1945, but con-

Living room, view southwest

Pullman bathroom unit

Workspace

Council Fire

Gate

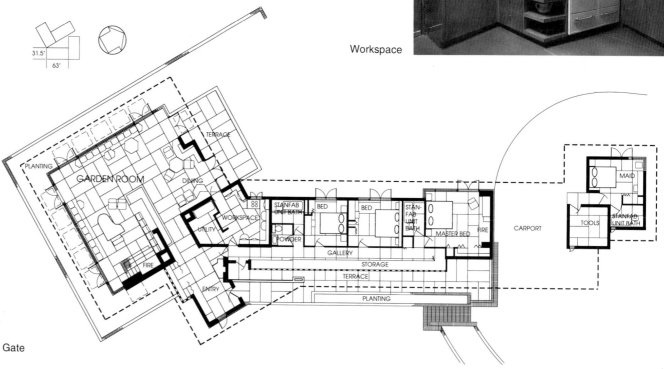

struction could not begin until 1948 because of wartime limitations on building materials. The building was occupied in 1950, and the Walters lived there only when winter was over, staying in Des Moines during the coldest months.

Cedar Rock is part of a limestone bluff on the left bank of the Wapsipinicon River. The main Walter structure derives from the "glass house" for the *Ladies Home Journal* (T.4510). It has a reinforced concrete roof, pierced as a trellis in its overhang, with steel, glass, walnut, and brick elsewhere. The original plan, on a completely regular square module, 63 inches to the side (a unique unit in Wright's work), has three bedrooms. Its living room is a square, slightly ambiguous in orientation with two all-glass walls, and is given focus by a fireplace. A small terrace is beyond. The Walter version names the 900 square foot living room a "garden room" and turns it 30 degrees, taking advantage of the view primarily down the river but also up the river by way of the secondary orientation. Wright called it his "Opus 497," which was a fair guess on his part of the number of designs he had produced by that time. Supervision during construction was by John deKoven Hill, who did the drawings from Wright's very detailed designs.

Typical of Usonian designs, however extensive, the heating used here is a gravity system. Unique, however, are the half-unit slabs set directly on the aggregate in which the heating pipes are laid; these 175 pound slabs can be lifted individually should any problem occur with the pipes. A pullman-type combination of sink, toilet, and bathtub is used for the two bathrooms in the main house and the maid's quarters to the far side of the carport. This idea was apparently not used elsewhere by Wright.

The Council Fire, on a knoll above the house, is an area enclosed by a low, semicircular wall around an outdoor hearth. Wright and some apprentices celebrated completion of the Walter house here.

The Walter residence and River Pavilion (S.285) are public property, having been given by the Walters to the people of Iowa upon his death in 1981. It is now known as Cedar Rock Park.

Walter River Pavilion

S.285   T.4831
Lowell and Agnes Walter River Pavilion (1948)
Quasqueton, Iowa
Restored 1991

The river pavilion, boathouse below, retreat above, is more screened than glazed. Otherwise, materials are the same as in the Walter residence (S.284) further up the hillside site, with reinforced concrete roof imitating that of its neighbor, though with less trellising. The boathouse is designed to withstand river flooding, while the upper-level sun terrace is above the highest-known water level.

A restoration, amounting to complete rebuilding of several walls, was undertaken in 1991.

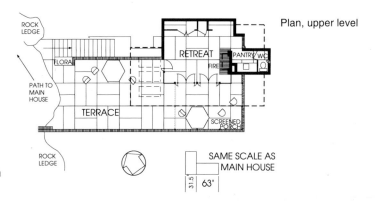

Plan, upper level

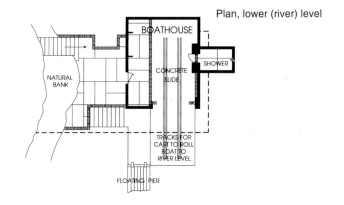

Plan, lower (river) level

S.286 T.4512
Arnold Friedman Vacation Lodge,
The Fir Tree (1945) and
S.286A T.5224
Caretaker's Quarters (1952, 1973)
Pecos, New Mexico

The Fir Tree is well protected from public view by the adjacent Santa Fe National Forest. When working drawings were produced in 1948 by John deKoven Hill and Gordon Chadwick, the original design with atrium had been reduced to a simple in-line plan, with clustered bedrooms at the end of the gallery, all on an equilateral parallelogram. Construction from original plans continued long after Mr. Wright's death. Various additions including a carport eventually created the atrium, and an apartment extended the plan 120 degrees opposite the bedroom wing, creating an outside in-line configuration.

Rough-sawn tongue-and-groove follows a reverse batter in the exterior, set on desert masonry walls. The central "teepee," the living room, is covered with rough cedar shakes. The teepee idea looks back to the Lake Tahoe project of the early twenties; this is the first built version of that teepee type. There is a clerestory where the teepee meets the flared lower roofing (for the effect, see the Davis house, S.324). The furniture features many designs unique to this house, including a two-part deck chair. Pine is used throughout the structure, with rough-sawn boards in a reverse batten inside.

A pool was added in the early seventies (not Wright's design) after Mr. Friedman suffered a heart attack. The caretaker's lodge, extending the stable wing, was built after Wright died, as a summer home.

Arnold Friedman Vacation Lodge

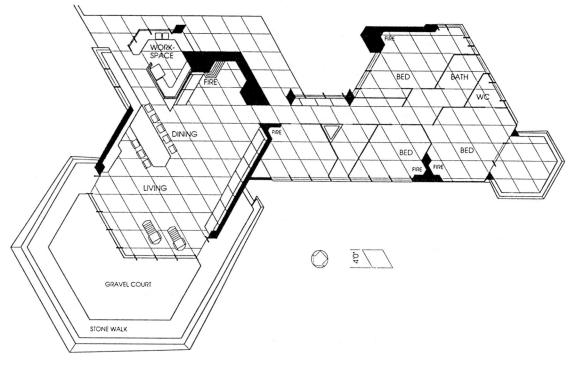

S.287 T.4818
Sara and **Melvyn Maxwell Smith**
Residence (1946)
Bloomfield Hills, Michigan
Addition to bedroom wing by Taliesin
Associated Architects

Mel Smith saw photos of Taliesin in 1938. He read the Detroit Public Library's collection on Wright and became enamored with the 1938 *Architectural Forum* issue on Wright. Mel and Sara were married in 1940; the war took him away, but upon his discharge in 1946, he found a cheap site and sent photographs and a topographic survey of the site to Wright. The plans arrived in December.

Estimates were beyond the teachers' salaries, and so Mel acted as his own contractor, poured over the plans, and learned the techniques necessary to Usonian construction. Eventually construction was started, took thirteen months, and the Smiths occupied their home in May 1950. Mel, told that red Tidewater cypress was impossible to come by, had obtained 14,000 board feet at 27¢ per running foot after an initial quote of 67¢. This and other cost savings were but one expression of Thoreau's philosophy, as stated by Sara, "Make yourself rich by making your wants full." Wright would turn this on its head with "Give me the luxuries of life, the necessities will take care of themselves," similarly expressed by Oscar Wilde, and expressed as "Give us the luxuries of life, and we will dispense with its necessaries" by Oliver Wendell Holmes, which itself is a variation on Plutarch's philosophy.

In this typical Usonian **L**-plan structure brick and cypress board and sunk batten comprise the basic construction materials. The 2-by-4-foot rectangular unit module is laid out in line with the living room, the same as the first Usonian **L** design (S.234); gravity heat in the concrete slab is of standard Usonian type. Structural steel supports the carport cantilever. The house is oriented to take advantage of site and sun. Construction supervision was by John deKoven Hill. The Smith house was enlarged by the Taliesin Associated Architects in 1969–70. The house is here shown in its original

Melvyn Maxwell Smith Residence

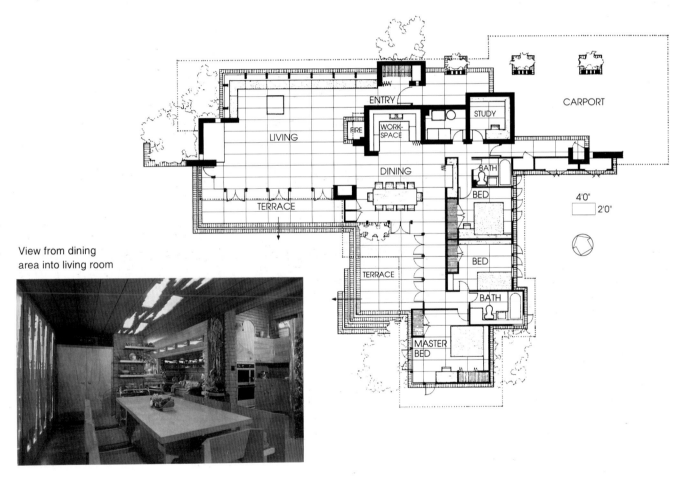

View from dining
area into living room

form; the addition was to the end of the bedroom wing.

This house arguably ends the era of board-and-batten Usonian houses. Board and sunk batten was not an inherent part of Usonian design. Rather, the thin sandwich of wood and insulation that provided non-load-supporting walls between load-supporting masonry was always an economic, rather than preferred aesthetic, solution to construction,

particularly in the Depression. At the end of World War II, with many of his clients gaining special benefits as veterans, others having savings from wartime employment, Wright's suggestion was to build the entire structure in masonry. Thus, we have the "all masonry" Usonian homes of the late forties and early fifties, with wood covering only the interior surface walls. Following the Smith house,

board and batten appeared as full walls only in the less expensive Usonians (e.g., Weltzheimer, S.311; Serlin, S.317; Rubin, S.343; and Brandes, S.350).

S.288 T.4503
Douglas and Jackie **Grant**
Residence (1946)
Marion (now Cedar Rapids), Iowa

When the Grants wrote Mr. Wright asking if it was possible for him to design a home for them, his answer was short: "Dear Grants, Of course its possible." The design he sent them was for a rectangular, two-story house. It is built of Devonian era stone, quarried by the Grants from their own property; because it is quite brittle, the stone breaks with a straight edge. The reinforced concrete roof is 127 feet long with a 20-foot (five-unit) cantilever that soars 8 feet beyond the slim mullions; the roof forms were supported by 150 poplar trees. Local flagstone was to have capped the stonework at roof level, but this seemed not right; Wright agreed to copper and suggested the flagstone for the floors. Steel doors and windows were desired but unavailable, so cypress was used, painted Cherokee/Taliesin red.

Entry to the structure is at the top floor from which one descends to the living room. Glazing is a mix of Thermopane and plate glass; Wright did not like the glass companies capitalizing on his use of Thermopane and raising their prices to him; he told the Grants that "you need Thermopane like a dog needs two tails." Structural steel was unavailable in 1946, delaying construction. Excavation began in September 1949, and the house was occupied fifteen months later.

Grant Residence, living room to left

Living room

Gallery of Grant Residence

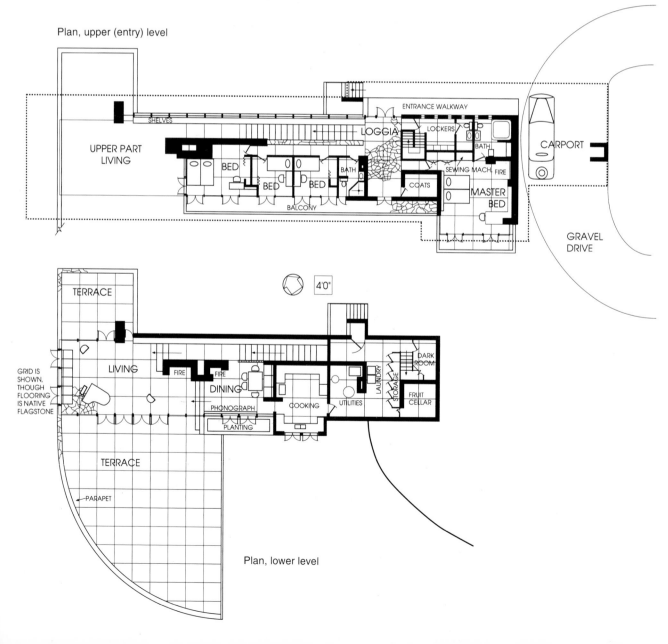
Plan, upper (entry) level

Plan, lower level

Miller Residence

S.289   T.5016
Alvin **Miller** Residence (1946)
Charles City, Iowa
Thermopane has replaced plate glass

This single-story, clerestory-lighted stone and cypress house extends in its terraces and outdoor fireplace to the right bank of the Red Cedar River. Here we have an uncommon example of a "reversed" **L** plan, one in which the living room turns its view away from the angle enclosed by the **L,** into which the other (bedroom) wing looks. This is to take advantage of the river view to the northeast. The house is small, approximately a thousand square feet, for a family without children, with only a master bedroom, bath, and laundry-darkroom in the wing. A study, available as a guest bedroom, projects forward from the gallery opposite the entry suggesting a **T** plan, and providing additional privacy for the living room. Thermopane has replaced plate glass, eliminating Wright's characteristic mitred corner windows.

Wright-designed chair

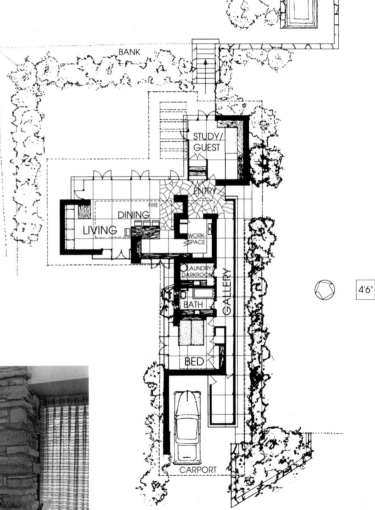

Dining area, clerestory, and entry to workspace

Griggs Residence

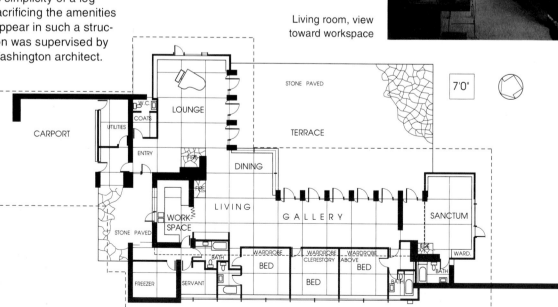

Approach via bridge over Chambers Creek

S.290 T.4604
Chauncey L. and Johanna **Griggs** Residence (1945)
Tacoma, Washington

Chauncey Griggs, a Yale graduate, started the first ski lifts in Washington State and later founded a lumber company named Paxport ("Port of Peace") Mills on the Tacoma tide flats that developed a revolutionary method of sawing hardwood, doubling production with no increase of man-power or loss of grade or footage. With this development, the company concentrated on sawmill activities, rather than exports of northwest hard-woods which had been a mainstay of their business since the end of World War II. Griggs died shortly after his eightieth birthday, in 1989.

Located at the foot of a hill on Chambers Creek, the Griggs house features a two-story facade on the inside of its basic **L** plan. The deeply recessed glass wall opens the gallery to the yard. With glazing just below the eaves on the gallery wing, at the end of the gallery is space for a formal dining room. A lounge, large enough for performance of chamber music, terminates the **L,** which is separated from the workspace and the dining room by the masonry core.

Soaring postwar construction costs caused delays in work. The concrete-slab floor, scored to mark the unusual 7-foot-square unit module, was laid long before the concrete-block core was raised, for a good stone was not available. Siding and roofing are cedar planks, which are arranged diagonally where this follows the slant of the shed

Living room, view toward music studio

Rear of house, showing clerestories

View down gallery

roof. Logs had originally been con-sidered, and this finished product retains the rustic simplicity of a log cabin, without sacrificing the amenities that usually disappear in such a struc-ture. Construction was supervised by Alan Liddle, a Washington architect.

Living room, view toward workspace

300

Unitarian Meeting House

S.291 T.5031
Unitarian Meeting House (1947)
Shorewood Hills, Wisconsin
Education wing added by Taliesin
Associated Architects

Wright's parents were among the earliest members of the Unitarian Society when it was organized in 1879. Wright participated in the church's Contemporary Club as a youth and later signed the membership register. He accepted the commission to design the new edifice in 1946; the church was essentially completed in 1951, often with the help of the Taliesin Fellowship (particularly in the final weeks before dedication), fund-raising speeches by Wright, and an army of parishioners who willingly hauled the limestone from a quarry 30 miles away. Marshall Erdman, who later became involved in Wright's last prefabricated housing projects (S.406–S.412), became the major contractor because local firms, finding Wright's construction methods too radical, did not want to bid on the project.

The module employed is the equilateral parallelogram (popularly called "diamond") with a unit side of 4 feet scored in to the concrete floor. This diamond shape is repeated in the largest forms of the building—the main auditorium with hearth room behind—as well as smaller elements such as the stone piers. The original building covered approximately 11,500 square feet.

The auditorium can seat 252 on Wright-designed single and double benches, removable for concerts and similar events. It faces the morning sun and is triangular in plan, with the minister at the apex, small choir loft behind and above. The hearth room, differentiated from the auditorium by an overhanging low ceiling, which it shares with the entrance lobby, can be employed to enlarge this space when extra capacity is needed. Originally, a

Sanctuary

Foldable chair and table

drape woven by the women of the Society from a design by Wright after a sample provided by Olgivanna allowed these two rooms to be separated. A bronze tablet to the right of the hearth room's fireplace, taken from the Society's first building, proclaims the Bond of Union—the statement of principle of the First Unitarian Society of Madison. On the face of low ceiling over the hearth room, there is an "ancient parable" dictated by Wright; "Do you have a loaf of bread, break the loaf in two and give half for some flowers of the Narcissus for thy bread feeds the body indeed but the flowers feed the soul."

The copper roof rises from the hearth room to a prow (called a belfry on the plans); in later years, Wright would offer that, at the exterior, this

suggests hands held together in prayer. This design also obviated the need for a separate steeple. The copper originally laid on was thinner than specified, to save on cost, and thus led to brown rot infection of the supporting wood members of the hearth room, repaired with new copper in 1977–78. Trim is oak.

A loggia-gallery with Sunday school rooms has been converted to offices. The last Wright-designed part of the building, the west living room, was originally intended to be the living room of a parsonage, though it was never completed as such. The education wing beyond the west living room is by the Taliesin Associated Architects.

This structure has been designated by the American Institute of Architects as one of seven-teen American buildings designed by Frank Lloyd Wright to be retained as an example of his architectural con-tribution to American culture. The building is open for visits weekdays and Saturday as well as for Sunday worship. Tours are offered during summer months. The building is closed during mid-August.

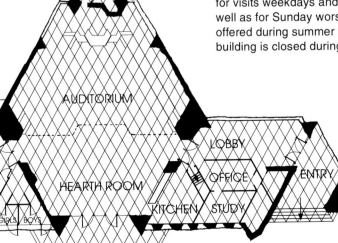

S.292   T.4709

Dr. A. H. **Bulbulian** Residence
(1947)
Rochester, Minnesota

One simple 120-degree angle serves both to fit this cement-brick and cypress structure to the brow of the hill and to orient the living room to take fullest advantage of morning sunlight warmth, looking out the gable end of the roofing, while shielding against hot summer afternoon sun to the side of the gable. The original plan shows a wing short by one bedroom, with only a master bedroom with its own bathroom and a guest bedroom without any lavatory facilities. The house as built has the additional space, constructed on a 32-inch-square unit module.

Wright's original idea was for an all-brick structure, but that was too costly for the client. Cast concrete slabs appear in one plan revision, then the final "Brickcrete" version was developed and built.

Bulbulian Residence

Living room

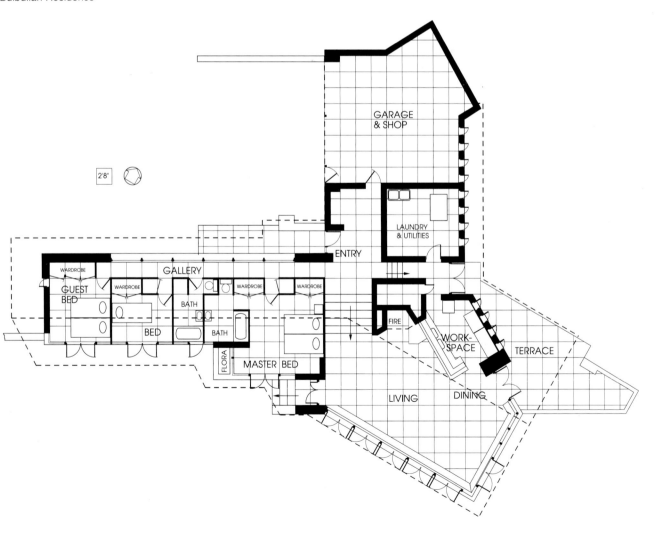

302

S.293   T.4703
Amy **Alpaugh** Studio Residence (1947)
Northport, Michigan
Goat house altered to playroom by Glen T. Arai Associates. Greenhouse altered to bedroom

Halfway up the penninsula from Traverse City to the Alpaugh house, one crosses the imaginary line that is exactly halfway between the Equator and the North Pole. To the west are North and South Manitou islands, the two bear cubs, and Sleeping Bear Dunes National Lakeshore, their mother bear buried under the sand. The islands are visible from the Alpaugh living room–studio, which turns toward Lake Michigan, while the den looks eastward to Grand Traverse Bay.

Though the plans called for construction of four chairs, six hassocks, two desks and two beds, it did not call for goats. Yet they are what Miss Alpaugh was best known for in the region, the goats that would climb her living room roof and look down at visitors. A native of Cincinnati and a Cranbrook graduate, Miss Alpaugh intended to have a second "east house," connected to the built structure only by a low wall, to be used as a weaving studio. Extensive plantings of cherry trees—the annual cherry festival in Leelanau, Benzie and Grand Traverse counties is a major regional event—never provided the hoped-for income needed to support the artistic activities for which the studio residence was designed.

Chicago common brick, seasoned ash and oak in sunk-batten construction, on a concrete slab with gravity heat, constitute the prime materials of this studio residence. The plan is very compact, designed to a 5-foot-square unit module with studio, a 45-degree triangular space, looking southwest though the house is only slightly off a north-south axis. Two bedrooms are behind the kitchen.

The house has been altered by Glen T. Arai Associates with an extension for a playroom where Wright provided an enclosure for goats. The original porch has been converted to an enclosed dining room. Second owners made the greenhouse into a bedroom.

Alpaugh Studio

Combination living-dining-kitchen-studio

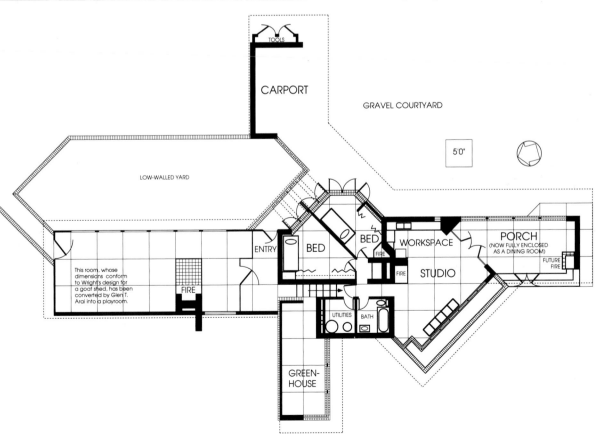

Galesburg Country Homes

S.294–S.297   T.4828

Galesburg Country Homes
Galesburg, Michigan

The Galesburg Country Homes was an idea by a group of friends, many of whom were employed as chemists or biochemists by Upjohn Company in Kalamazoo. Six formed the original group that arrived at Taliesin the day after Olgivanna's daughter, Svetlana, was killed in an accident, yet Wright met with them and suggested they first obtain land. The Acres was their name for 72 acres purchased for less than $65 per acre 10 miles east of Kalamazoo. This seemed a long distance to some, so the group split, some staying in the outskirts of Galesburg, others organizing Parkwyn Village (S.298–S.301) in Kalamazoo. The subdivision plan was drawn up in 1947.

Three of the built structures in Galesburg employ Wright textile block and wood. This method of construction dates to the four California block houses (S.214–S.217), and looks ahead to the Usonian Automatic designs of the mid fifties (see S.344, S.349, S.386–S.389, S.392). Its use shows Wright moving away from original Usonian principles to newer ways of saving on costs, by way of do-it-yourself masonry buildings. Group purchasing helped both associations. The Acres purchased enough rough mahogany from a Grand Rapids lumber yard for all to use and had it milled locally for a cost about that of white pine. Wright often used mahogany, because of its beautiful grain and reddish-yellow color, as a substitute for expensive cypress, even though it had to be imported. Honduras mahogany was preferred, as it is a true mahogany which is relatively hard. Philippine mahogany, or Lauan, is not a true mahogany and is very soft, but was often used to reduce cost.

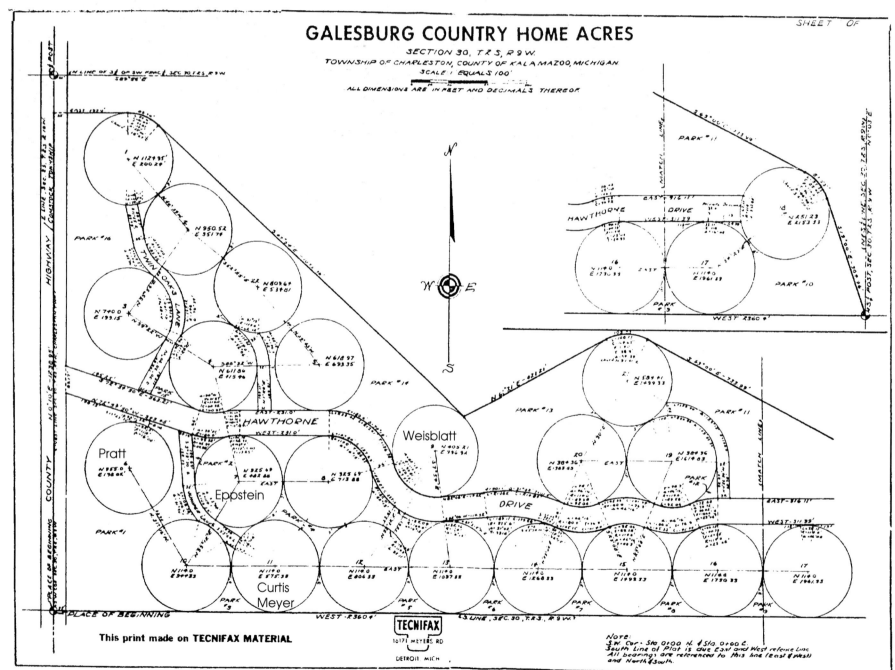

General plan of Galesburg Country Homes

Galesburg Country Homes

Galesburg Country Homes
S.294   T.4918
David I. and Christine **Weisblat**
Residence (1948)
Galesburg, Michigan
House extended with 120-degree wing
by John H. Howe

The Weisblat house was the first of
four structures eventually built at
Galesburg Country Homes. Its living
room roof is cantilevered from side
wall masonry by pairs of 2-by-12-inch
headers over the glazed walls; there is
no structural steel in the roof. Thirty-
four different block shapes were
needed for construction, from 2,075
whole standard blocks to various
inside and outside corner, sill, jamb,
and coping blocks numbering in
hundreds or tens.

In 1960, John H. Howe of the
Taliesin Associated Architects was
responsible for a 120-degree-angled
addition to the compact 4-foot unit
in-line plan (the carport forms an **L** at
the rear). Howe also supervised construction of all four Galesburg country
homes.

Weisblat Residence

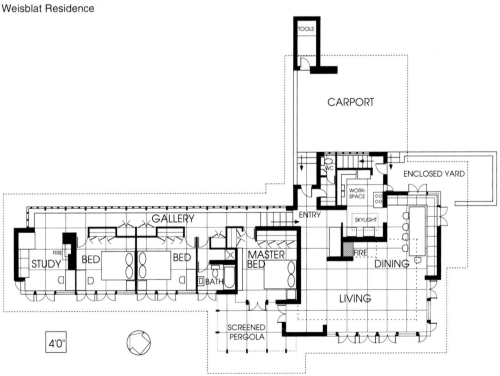

S.295   T.4827
Eric and Pat **Pratt** Residence (1948)
Galesburg, Michigan

Eric Pratt served as purchasing agent for the Acres Association. His long in-line plan house, designed to a 4-foot-square unit module, faces southwest down a long, slow slope. A smaller design came first, but his growing family made it necessary to extend the bedroom wing. Though built in three stages, the complete design was in hand at the start of construction.

The Pratts, as their own contractors, made the sand-colored plain textile blocks. Red-stained mahogany matches the coloring of the slab floor, with its inlaid heating coils for gravity heat. Pratt made minor revisions to enlarge the studio, which he often used as a workshop. Some problems result from incomplete understanding of the unit sytem; thus, half blocks appear to complete corners, and in some places the blocks do not align with the marked grid. The later Staley residence (S.335) is a stone version of this building.

Pratt Residence

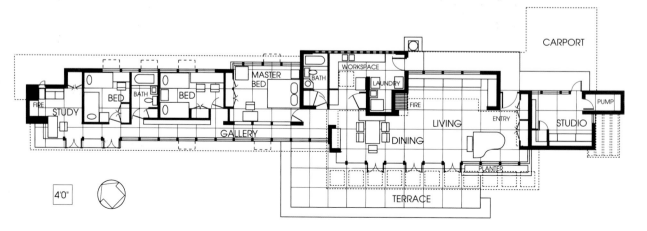

Galesburg Country Homes

S.296   T.4905
Samuel **Eppstein** Residence (1948)
Galesburg, Michigan

Samuel Eppstein wanted to excavate the hill, not just build on it. Wright countered, "If you get enough money, you can excavate the whole hill."

Since this house sits on a rise, the living room can open toward the main road of the Galesburg Country Homes subdivision without reducing privacy. Thus, Wright turns the living room to face away from the bedroom wing, creating an outside **L** configuration for the interior spaces on a 4-foot-square unit module. As built, the quiet zone has a master bedroom, laundry and bath, and four bedrooms with one small bath, and is terminated by a large, approximately square playroom over a basement. This deviates somewhat from Wright's plan, which called for a master bedroom next to a nursery and bath, then three bedrooms with a large bath, and a relatively small study. The original also had a stepped-back living room facade similar to that of the Levin house (S.298).

Eppstein Residence

Eppstein house, north-facing living room and terrace

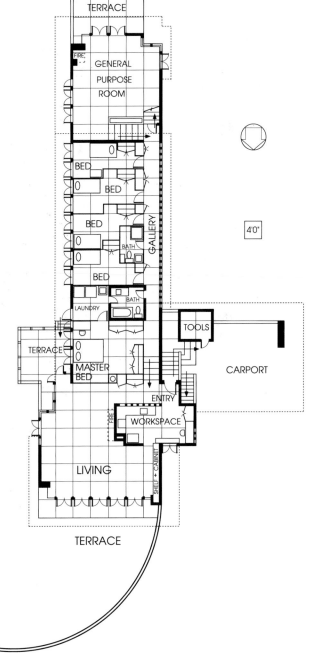

Galesburg Country Homes

S.297   T.5015
Lillian and Curtis Meyer Residence
(1948)
Galesburg, Michigan

It was Lillian Meyer who organized the Wisconsin-bound visitation that led to the Galesburg Country Homes project as well as Parkwyn Village. Six people met with Wright, and two groups of houses, four designs each, resulted from the visitation to Taliesin.

A solar hemicycle facing east down a gentle slope, the Meyer house is designed on a circular segment unit module 7 1/2 degrees wide by 32 inches (2 blocks) deep. The central two-story drum sits in the crest of the hill, enclosing stairs between the lower-floor living room and the upper-level carport and bedrooms. The bedroom "wing" is set over the rear of the living room below, giving it a two-story-high ceiling at the glazed facade. Thus, the master bedroom at the end of the balcony gallery needs no fourth wall, because it gains privacy by its overviewing position; thus this solar has hemicycle almost a "one-room" house configuration. Pairs of 4-by-16-inch concrete blocks in hollow core construction, rather than standard 8-by-16-inch blocks, plus 8-by-8-inch blocks, were used instead of Wright's desired Brickcrete block. Wood trim is mahogany.

Meyer Residence

Dining area, view to living space

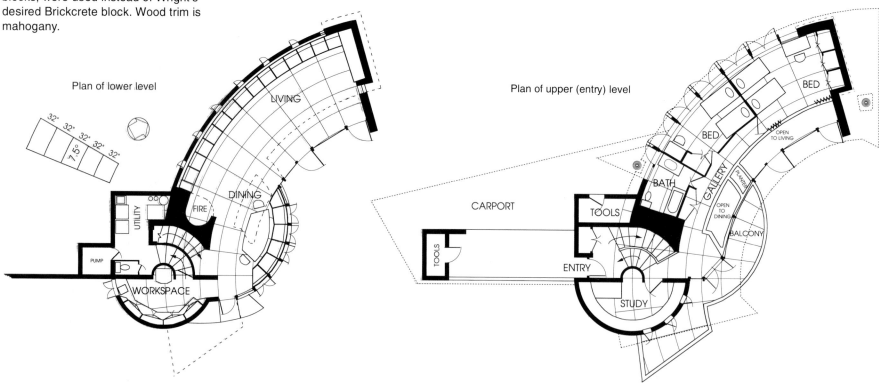

Plan of lower level

Plan of upper (entry) level

Parkwyn Village

S.298–S.301   T.4806
Parkwyn Village
Kalamazoo, Michigan

Several of the original group that formed the Acres in Galesburg (see S.294–S.297) decided that the drive, in the late 1940s, 10 miles east of Kalamazoo was more than they wanted. They found acreage on a bluff over little Lorenz Lake on the southwest side of Kalamazoo, nearer Upjohn Company, where many worked.

A 47-acre orchard formed the major section needed for this community. The subdivision is unique for its absence of street lights as well as power and telephone lines. In the fall of 1949 and spring of 1950, 1100 trees were planted; 300 Chinese elm, 300 red pine, 200 maple, 200 fir, and 100 spruce. Several houses were designed by Wright in its master plan; only four were built.

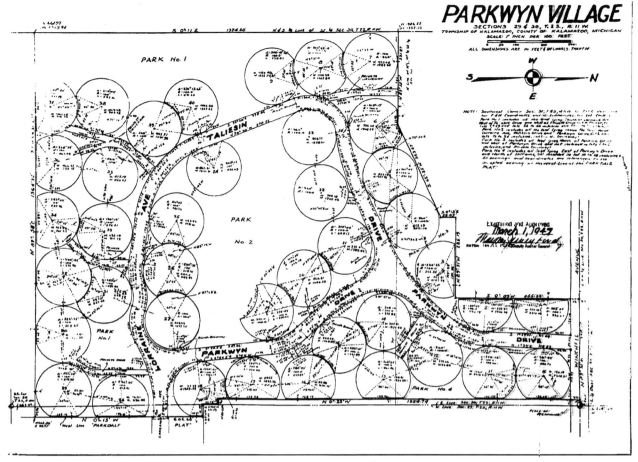

General plan of Parkwyn Village as designed

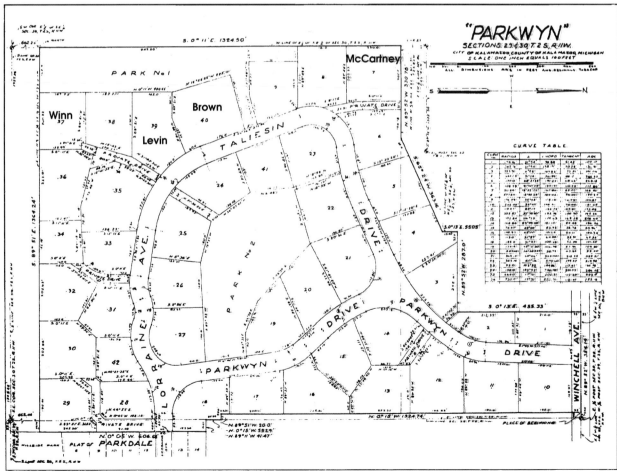

General plan of Parkwyn Village as built

Parkwyn Village

S.298 T.4911
Robert **Levin** Residence (1948)
Kalamazoo, Michigan
Playroom wing with basement below
added by John H. Howe in 1960

The Levin house has an interesting
treatment of its southwest-facing living
room facade; the glazed doors are
stepped out in several bays, each
one-eighth the 4-foot unit in front of the
previous, a design feature continued in
an iron-pipe trellis. The in-line bedroom wing has three bedrooms and
two baths, their windows above the
carport roof. A study is set to the back
side of the gallery at the stairway that
links these quiet spaces to the living
room and workspace several steps
below. Sand-colored textile blocks are
set on a dark tan concrete slab with
gravity heating. Levin made a special
effort and obtained red Tidewater
cypress, Wright's preferred wood for all
the houses. A playroom with basement
was added in 1960 by John H. Howe
of the Taliesin Associated Architects.
Howe also supervised construction of
all the Wright-designed houses in
Parkwyn Village.

Levin Residence with trellis at living room

Dining area, view out to trellis

Plan, upper level

Plan, lower (entry) level

Levin Residence just at completion

310

Parkwyn Village

S.299 T.4912
Helen and Ward **McCartney Residence** (1949) and
S.299A T.4912
Bedroom Wing Addition with
S.299B
Residence **Remodeling** (1956) and
S.299C
Carport Addition
Kalamazoo, Michigan

While a dentist in the Navy, Ward McCartney read Ayn Rand's *Fountainhead.* It is well known that Rand patterned her hero after Wright. What may not be so well known is that Wright never liked the book.

The McCartney house and its conceptual cousin, the Anthony house (S.315), are both developed expressions of a design done originally as a cottage for Wright's sister, Maginel Wright Barney. This is a "one-room" cottage concept on the equilateral parallelogram (later done on a square module as the Peterson Cottage, S.430), with expansion expected. Kitchen core and dining-living room area were built first, and the bedroom wing was added after only four months. Each is in the form of a 30–60-degree triangle. Enclosure of the entry to the north and a carport came later, and were done in Wright textile block and mahogany. The alcove

McCartney Residence before extensions

McCartney Residence with Bedroom Wing Addition

McCartney with carport

Living room, original bedroom corner after alterations

(Continues)

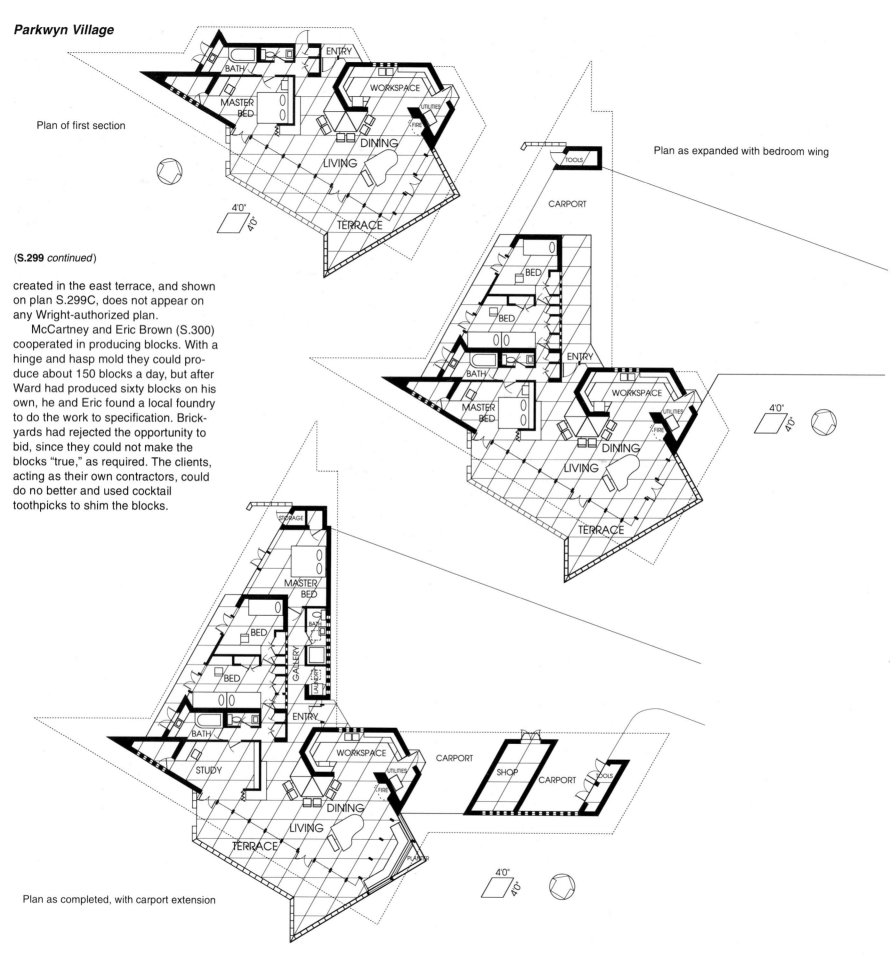

Parkwyn Village

Plan of first section

ENTRY
BATH
MASTER BED
WORKSPACE
UTILITIES
FIRE
DINING
LIVING
TERRACE

4'0"
4'0"

(S.299 *continued*)

created in the east terrace, and shown on plan S.299C, does not appear on any Wright-authorized plan.

McCartney and Eric Brown (S.300) cooperated in producing blocks. With a hinge and hasp mold they could produce about 150 blocks a day, but after Ward had produced sixty blocks on his own, he and Eric found a local foundry to do the work to specification. Brickyards had rejected the opportunity to bid, since they could not make the blocks "true," as required. The clients, acting as their own contractors, could do no better and used cocktail toothpicks to shim the blocks.

Plan as expanded with bedroom wing

TOOLS
CARPORT
BED
BED
ENTRY
BATH
WORKSPACE
MASTER BED
UTILITIES
FIRE
DINING
LIVING
TERRACE

4'0"
4'0"

STORAGE
MASTER BED
BED
BATH
GALLERY
LAUNDRY
BED
ENTRY
BATH
STUDY
WORKSPACE
UTILITIES
FIRE
CARPORT
SHOP
CARPORT
TOOLS
DINING
LIVING
TERRACE
PLANTER

4'0"
4'0"

Plan as completed, with carport extension

Parkwyn Village

S.300   T.5003
Anne and **Eric V. Brown** Residence
(1949) and
S.300A   T.5003
Addition (1950)
Kalamazoo, Michigan

So anxious were Anne and Eric Brown to get construction started that in spring they drove to Arizona with their children and announced to Mr. Wright that they would wait for the working drawings. They waited five days. After one lunch, Mrs. Wright read to them and Mr. Wright from the writings of the mystic, Gurdjieff. Mr. Wright slept; they dared not. They occupied their home in 1950.

Mahogany is employed with textile block in the Eric Brown house, whose uphill roofline is at ground level. The living room and attached terrace look out over broad fields to Lorenz Lake below Taliesin Drive. The plan is in-line to a 4-foot unit module, with work-space behind the fireplace at the back of the living room. The master bedroom is the first space off the tunnel gallery, which leads past a bathroom and a guest bedroom to a dormitory-style children's bedroom. Shortly after construction, a maid's room and additional bathroom were added across the gallery opposite the children's room, and the wing was terminated by a bedroom for the children's grandfather. Total length is 130 feet under gabled roofing.

Eric Brown Residence

Living room

Plan of Eric Brown Residence, as built with addition

Parkwyn Village

S.301   T.4813
Robert D. **Winn** Residence (1950)
Kalamazoo, Michigan

Robert D. Winn, an insurance agent, was a latecomer to the Parkwyn Village group. He had his house designed by Wright because others were doing that, but he seems to have mistrusted Wright's engineering. Set on a half-basement because of the hillside site, the house is based on a mirror-image of the Laurent design done the year before. The site required cantilevering of the porch and the trellis-like pierced roof above, with screen to enclose the space. An incoherent collection of woods was used, and the block painted shortly after construction. Forced air heating was used because the slab floor does not everywhere rest on the ground.

Winn Residence

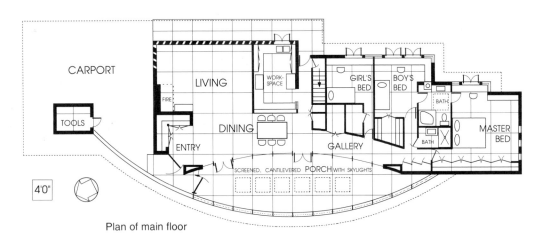

Plan of main floor

Porch

Plan of basement

S.302   T.4914
Herman T. **Mossberg** Residence
(1948)
South Bend, Indiana

To meet local building restrictions
requiring that all homes be two stories,
Wright placed the daughter's bedroom
and bathroom upstairs at one end of a
long hall (with view over the living
room) and the tower above the workspace at the opposite end. A balcony,
facing the street, completed the
charade played on the building commission. On the ground floor, the living
room dominates, one of Wright's great
creations. The main view is to the yard
at the end of the room. At the side the
view follows the roof line down to a
gallery a quarter level below the living
space. This gallery leads to the master
bedroom, entry, dining space and
stairs, and workspace, all in line in the
two-story section, with two bedrooms
and carport in the single-story
extension.

Mossberg Residence from southwest

Mossberg Residence from southeast

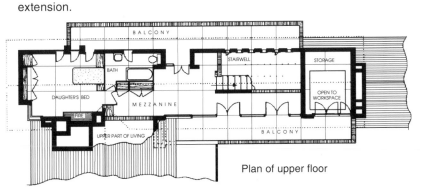

Plan of upper floor

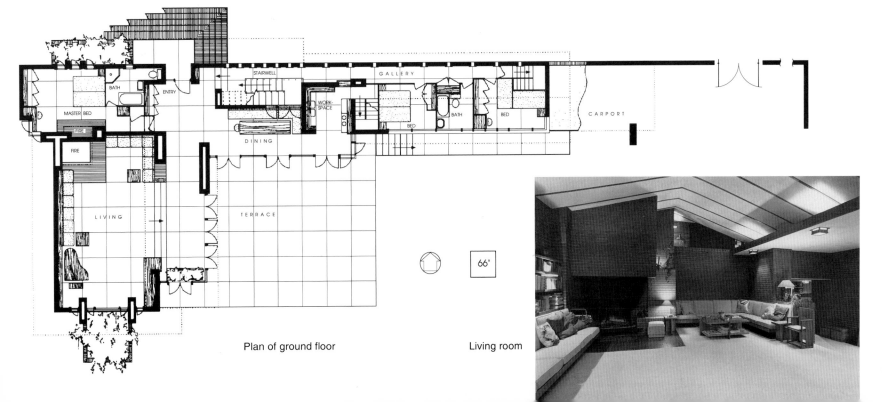

Plan of ground floor

Living room

The Fountainhead wing of the Hughes Residence

grain, and there is one cabinet top of bird's-eye heart wood of particular beauty. The floor is Colorundum, a dry combination of carborundum and color dye, which is trowelled into the concrete after it is sufficiently set to hold ones weight.

Hughes was a wildcat oil driller who experienced feast or famine. The house fell into serious disrepair in the late seventies. Architect Robert Parker Adams restored the Hughes residence in the 1980s. This included leveling of the original concrete mat floor and resurfacing it with a special paint used by the navy on ships, installation of a well-concealed air conditioning system, and completion of the pool below the fountain head.

S.303   T.4908
J. Willis **Hughes** Residence,
Fountainhead (1948)
Jackson, Mississippi
Restored by Robert Parker Adams in
the 1980s

Except for the Sullivan and Charnley efforts (S.005–S.008) on the Gulf Coast, the Hughes Residence is the only Wright building in Mississippi. It and its smaller sibling, the Lamberson house (S.305), were being worked on in the Taliesin drafting room at the same time, both being first drawn to a 4-foot-square unit module. While the Lamberson evolved by rotating this module into three interlocked grids, the Hughes took the more logical course; the working drawings were done with the 30–60-degree triangle, creating a grid of equilateral parallelograms.

The bedroom wing terminates in a fountain over a pool, which gives the structure its nickname, Fountainhead. This carries the 120-degree angled wing out into the glen of the wooded site. Concrete walls and slab floor, horizontal board and batten interior paneling, and copper roof sit well below street level. Wright specified brick after discovering that there was no native stone in Mississippi. The final choice was poured concrete. Since concrete mixing trucks could not go onto the property safely, the concrete had to be mixed in small quantities and brought in by wheelbarrow to the forms. Vandalism during construction led to a surface created by spraying heavy paint and, while it was still wet, spraying beach sand on to it, as well as embedding fine shells in the surface by hand. Wright called for cypress. Mrs. Hughes personally selected heart wood with the finest

The fireplace, with skylight

Plan of Fountainhead

THE FOUNTAIN

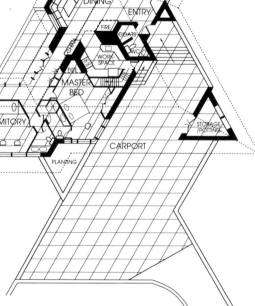

The children's dormitory bedroom

316

Alsop house, view to living room and private facade

S.304 T.4804
Carroll **Alsop** Residence (1948)
Oskaloosa, Iowa

The Alsop house, with its broken-gabled red asphalt-shingled roof, is brick with cypress trim. The plan, on a 5-foot-square unit module, is in-line, with workspace, three bedrooms and bath to the left of the entry, living room down a few steps, fireplace far right at the gable break. If the workspace were behind the fireplace, this plan would be similar to the Erdman Prefab #1 (S.406–S.411) of 1956 in all but its off-angled master bedroom and porch.

Jim De Reus, a local entrepreneur, sought out the builder's contract when he heard that Alsop had commissioned a Wright home. He found the design to be both innovative (particularly in its elimination of the basement and use of a 9-inch concrete mat floor) and cost-saving. Supervision was by John deKoven Hill, later editorial director of *House Beautiful*.

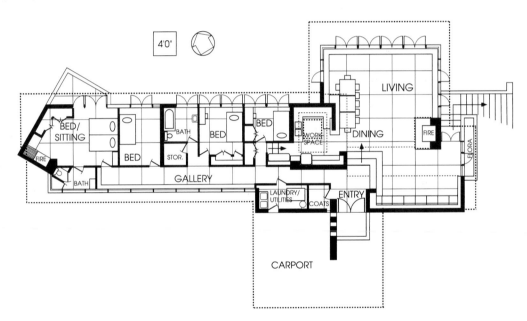

Study, view toward entry hall

Lamberson Residence

Walker Residence, from the beach

Corbelled glazing

S.305   T.4712
Jack **Lamberson** Residence (1948)
Oskaloosa, Iowa

Perched on a gentle hilltop, the red-brick Lamberson home has redwood paneling and trim and asphalt shingles. The bedroom wing is on an east-west axis with its own 4-foot-square grid. The main wing—terrace, living room, workspace, and part of the master bedroom—is set on a separate 4-foot-square grid, at 60 degrees east of north. A third 4-foot-square grid is used for the entry flooring. Extensive use is made of the 30–60-degree triangle on each of these grids, and so corners are typically 120 and 60 degrees, avoiding the squared corner much as does the Hanna residence (S.235), which required the hexagonal module to "eliminate the right angle" from the plan.

This design, however, is a tour-de-force in how to gain a similar effect on the simpler 4-foot-square unit module. It is a smaller twin of the Hughes house in Mississippi, which was, like this, first drawn on a square module but was completed on an equilateral parallelogram. Supervision of construction was by Taliesin fellow John deKoven Hill. This and the Alsop residence (S.304) a short distance away apparently created a local sensation. Nine thousand visitors saw these two houses when they were first constructed in 1951.

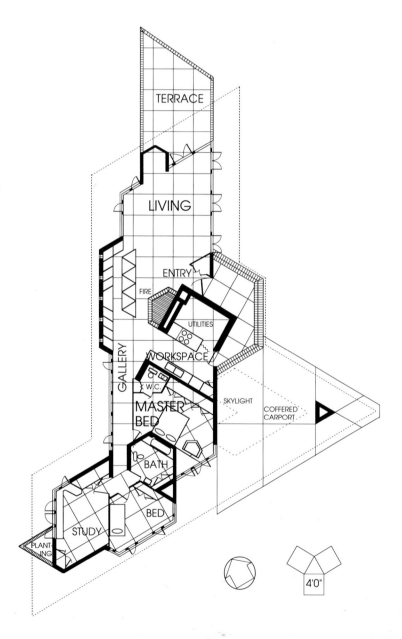

Living room fireplace

View from east beach

S.306   T.5122
Mrs. Clinton **Walker** Residence (1948)
Carmel, California
Addition to master bedroom

This stone structure, built for Della Walker on the beach side of Scenic Road on Carmel Bay, lies mostly below street level, seemingly a natural extension of the rocky promontory at this curve in the beach front. Four thin cast iron columns, reaching from the stone wall to a point halfway from peak to eaves, support the hexagonal cantilevered living room roof, whose anchor is the fireplace on the other side. The glazing blocks a direct breeze, but a gentle current of air is admitted through vent flaps on the underside of the corbelled bands of glass, upon which no weight rests, this idea was first explored in the unbuilt Stuart Haldorn residence of 1945. The workspace fits half within the hexagon, behind the fireplace. The wing to the rear has two guest bedrooms and the master bedroom, all sharing one bathroom. A later enlargement, not by Wright, of the master bedroom included a second bathroom and provided additional security to an otherwise exposed site. Two materials have graced the living room roof, porcelain enamel, then copper. Panels and trim are cedar. The design unit module is an equilateral parallelogram 4 feet to the side.

North side

Sunset

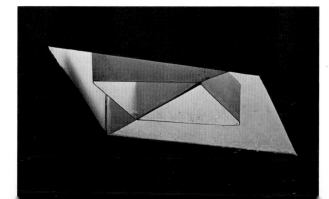

Lighting fixture

Adler Addition to the Sondern Residence

S.307　T.4907
Arnold **Adler Addition** and Alterations to the **Sondern** Residence (1948)
Kansas City, Missouri

When Wright undertook the enlargement of the Sondern residence (S.279) for Arnold Adler, the transformation was complete. The original master bedroom became part of a new living room set a foot lower than the Sondern house radiant-heating mat (and thus gaining a clerestory under the original roof line), with a new dining terrace and kitchen overlooking it, all beyond the walls of the original gallery. The secondary bedroom was enlarged into a new master bedroom. The former tool room and shop, which masonry was a major support for the carport cantilever, was expanded into a heating room. Three masonry rooms, each four units square, which framed the original entry and contained a bathroom, utilities, and workspace, became three bathrooms and servant's quarters, with the entry shifted toward the new wing, its garden, and pool. John deKoven Hill produced the drawings for Mr. Wright.

Living room, the major unit of the Adler Addition

Plan of addition showing addition and alterations to original Sondern Residence

Albert Adelman Residence

S.308   T.4801A
Albert (Ollie and Edie) **Adelman**
Residence (1948)
Fox Point, Wisconsin

In 1945, Wright designed a laundry building for Benjamin Adelman and Son to be erected in Milwaukee, of which Fox Point is a suburb. Though it was never built, two residences were constructed for the Adelman family, this and a home for the senior Adelmans in Arizona (S.344).

The first scheme presented by architect to client was for a large **L**-plan structure on a rather odd unit module, a 7-foot square, with circular elements in the hearths of the two fireplaces and in the terrace and sun court which surround the centrally placed living room. A major revision, dated November 1947, eliminated references to the circle and moved the nursery next to the master bedroom. The basement now included a laundry and playroom along with the heater room; a rooftop playdeck and second-story library, elements held over from the Hein project of 1943, of which this is a derivation, have been eliminated. This second plan is what the Adelmans built: entire plan mirrored, **L** bedroom wing straightened so that it is in line, and gabled roof changed to hip, unit set to 6 feet, 6 inches, dated April 1948. It is buff-colored (integral color) block, stepped out 3/4 inch every second course, cypress, and cedar shakes. The board and batten is on 7- rather than the usual 13-inch centers, requiring twice the labor. Thermopane is used in fixed windows, plate glass in the casements. Quality of construction at every level, structural to details to furniture, is notable.

Living room

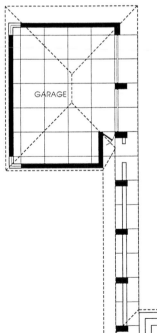

GARAGE

5'6"

The walls feature a reverse batter, not shown here as it would conflict with rooflines. The grid on the walk from house to garage was scored at 63", it is shown here at 66", as designed.

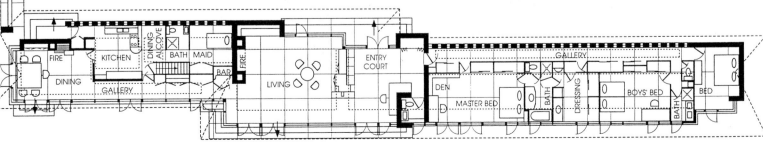

S.309   T.4805

Katherine Z. and Maynard P.
Buehler Residence (1948)
Orinda, California

Maynard Buehler, a tool engineer,
turned his talent to the design of gun
accessories, such as scopes, screws,
and the Buehler safety, and he needed
a large shop in which to develop
products. This became almost a separate unit attached at a right angle
beyond the carport and garage. The
primary entry is at the workspace core,
near the living room of this standard
concrete-block and wood house. The
living space is an octagon set under a
square shed roof, turned 45 degrees to
the 4-foot-square grid, rising toward
the west. The workspace and separate
dining area were altered in shape and
enlarged during construction; underneath is a full basement. The bedrooms, looking out to the swimming
pool and garden, extend southeast,
connecting living-dining-workspace to
the workshop. Other structures on the
grounds employ board and sunk batten
to blend with the one Wright-designed
structure.

Buehler Residence

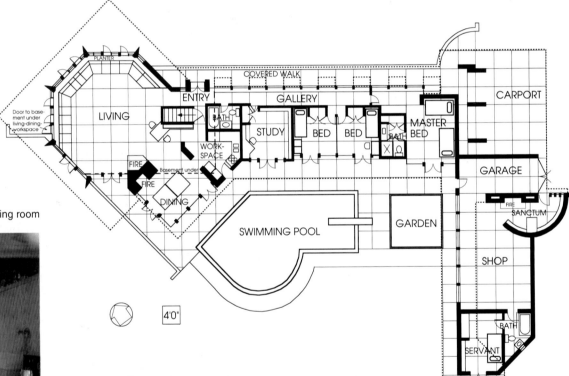

View from workspace into living room

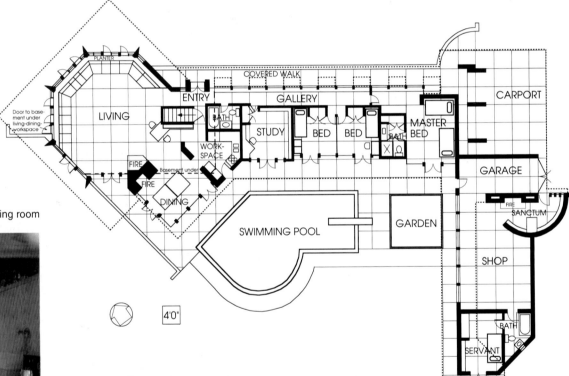

Living room

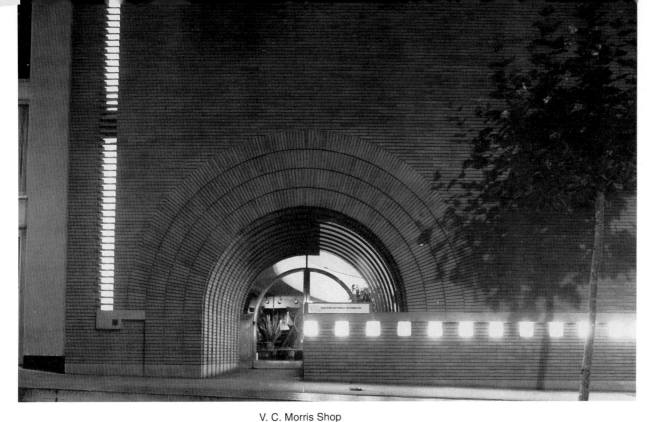

V. C. Morris Shop

Another view, from the upper level, another tenant

S.310   T.4824

V. C. **Morris Gift Shop** (1948)
San Francisco, California

The Morrises first came to Wright in 1944 to obtain a design for a home. This famous yet, sadly, unbuilt project, was a cylinder of three vertically stacked floors on a cliff that dropped 110 feet to the beach from El Camino del Mar on a spit of private land about 500 feet wide between Lincoln Park and the Presidio. Construction of Sea Cliff was postponed, and the Morrises next asked for a design for a gift shop.

The brick facade of the Morris building protects internal contents as it invites visitors to enter the portal. Curvilinear forms are employed inside. Indeed, the circular ramp connecting the two levels hints of the Guggenheim Museum (S.400), the early designs of which date to 1943. Upstairs, a suspended glass screen of translucent circles framed in globes provided soft lighting for the fine crystal, glass, porcelain, silver and gold objects on display when the Morris family occupied the building.

The shop has seen many owners. In 1967 it became the Circle Gallery, which offers guests contemporary paintings, sculpture, and jewelry. Trim and cabinetry is dark walnut, the floor stone. The structure has been designated by the American Institute of

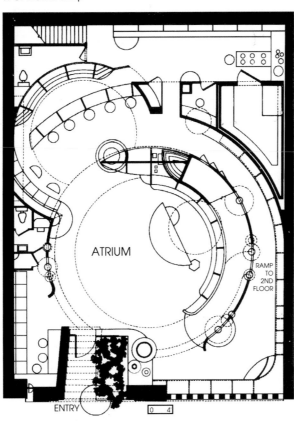

Morris Shop interior from ground floor

Architects as one of seventeen American buildings designed by Wright to be retained as an example of his architectural contribution to American culture. The building is open during regular business hours.

S.311   T.4819
Charles T. **Weltzheimer** Residence
(1948)
Oberlin, Ohio

Each member of the Weltzheimer family was asked to describe for Mr. Wright what he or she wanted in a house. Mom wanted books, one child, dogs, and a piano.

This house is an **L**-plan structure of the Usonian type with walls more of brick than the usual sandwich of boards, here redwood, on plywood. The mortar joints are deeply raked on the horizontal, flush and natural color on the vertical. It is planned to a grid of 2-by-4-foot rectangles. Clerestory detailing and fascia ornamentation are unique among Usonian projects. The first designs were for a typical angular clerestory detail drawn with the 30–60 triangle. Later, three circles on a "branch," perhaps symbolizing the apple orchard on the property, appeared. The final, even more abstract design is composed primarily of circles but also involves some complex curves and is particularly effective in the living room clerestory tower. The fascia molding has large semicircles, perhaps more apples from the orchard.

Many changes executed during construction do not show on Wright's plan, particularly extensions and relocations of walls and entries near the storage space. Removal of alterations inherited from earlier owners and restoration were by Ellen H. Johnson, who retained life tenancy after giving this, her home, to Oberlin College in the 1980s.

Living room, view to fireplace (reverse view of right)

Alcove below clerestory

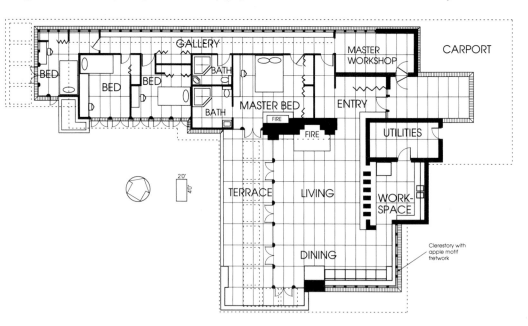

Brauner Residence

S.312   T.4601A
Erling P. and Katherine **Brauner**
Residence (1948)
Okemos, Michigan

The Brauner dwelling is located across Arrow Head Road from the Edwards house (S.313) and only a short distance from the Goetsch-Winckler (S.269) and Schaberg (S.328) houses. Of these, only the Goetsch-Winckler was built as part of Wright's Usonia I, a 1939 project primarily for teachers at what is now Michigan State University. Although the Brauner's original scheme was for that project, what they built was Wright's second scheme, produced after the architect visited the site.

The Brauner house was an attempt to redefine, in masonry, the Usonian house concept. Double hollow-core concrete block, measuring 4 by 8 by 16 inches, replaces brick and dry-wall construction. In the plan, on a 4-foot-square unit module, the wing extension is directly behind the living room, a variant on the in-line plan and one much favored at this time (see S.296, S.306, S.309, S.313, S.328, among others). The master bedroom, called a sitting room by Wright, is attached at the side of the workspace, off a short corridor to the main gallery. A further development of this plan is the Kalil house (S.387). Cypress is the main wood, with birch plywood for cabinetry. The house was constructed in 1949, with Brauner acting as his own contractor.

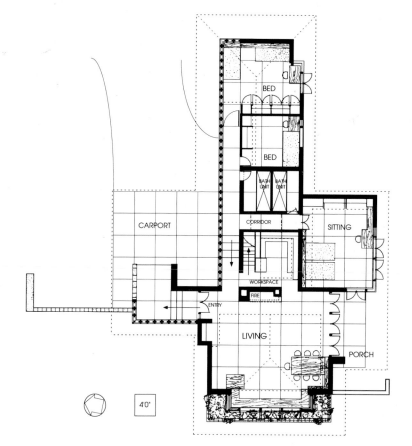

S.313   T.4904

James and Dolores **Edwards**
Residence (1949)
Okemos, Michigan
Wing added at 90 degrees to original
bedroom wing

Jim and Dolores Edwards occupied an
apartment just below Don and Mary
Lou Schaberg (S.328). They had lived
in the Lansing area for a decade,
when they decided to build a Wright-
designed house. Nine months later
Oldsmobile sent their executive
elsewhere.

Brick, Tidewater cypress, asphalt
singles, and concrete floors containing
gravity heat, all were Cherokee red.
The Edwards dwelling is built into a
hillside with its rectangular spaces on
a 4-foot-square unit module. Wright
usually sought a module that would
allow all exterior walls to fall on grid
lines or standard subdivisions thereof.
Here, the living room and entry are
joined to the workspace and bedroom
wing with grids meeting at 60 degrees.
A similar treatment was employed in
the Lamberson house (S.305); in the
Greenberg residence (S.372) two
wings are linked to the living room in
this manner. An earlier instance of this
practice is the Panshin project of 1939,
realized as the Rubin house (S.343).
There is a terrace the full length of the
wing.

The second wing was added in
1968 along with a studio and a garage
by the Taliesin Associated Architects
for F. Jerome Corr; marvelous elevations of this were rendered by David
Dodge. This addition follows the
pattern for such extensions by Wright
as used in the Buehler house (S.309).
The exterior woodwork was refinished
in 1972 by William T. Martin III.

Edwards Residence, entry with cantilevered roof over porch on north side

Edwards Residence, west side

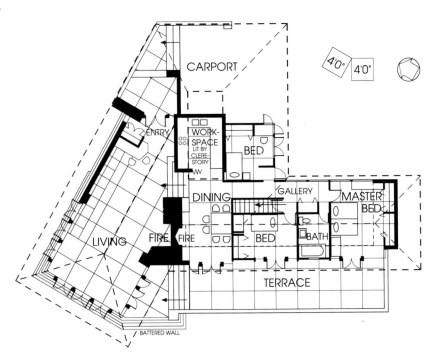

Neils Residence

S.314   T.5020
Henry J. **Neils** Residence (1949)
Minneapolis, Minnesota

Henry J. Neils was involved in both architectural metals and stone, so the use of aluminum window framing (unusual for Wright), scrap marble, larch (a local evergreen that sheds its needles once a year), and cedar shingles in this house on the east shore of Cedar Lake may not be as odd as it seems. It was designed on a unit of 3 feet, 6 inches, reduced from 4 feet to economize on costs, to a 240-degree reversed in-line plan (that is, the living room view is to one side of the main axis, while the bedrooms look to the other, back, side). This makes some passageways rather narrow, but the living room, whose proportions were not affected by the change in the size of the unit, retains its beauty. John Geiger, a veteran of several projects in Michigan (S.287, S.298), started working drawings from Wright's original scheme, and Steve Oyakawa completed them. Wright then redesigned the house on these drawings and Curtis Besinger did new working drawings from which the house was built.

Patricia Neils married Cedric Boulter and built a Wright-designed home in Cincinnati (S.379) in 1954.

Living room

Wright-designed chair in the Neils house

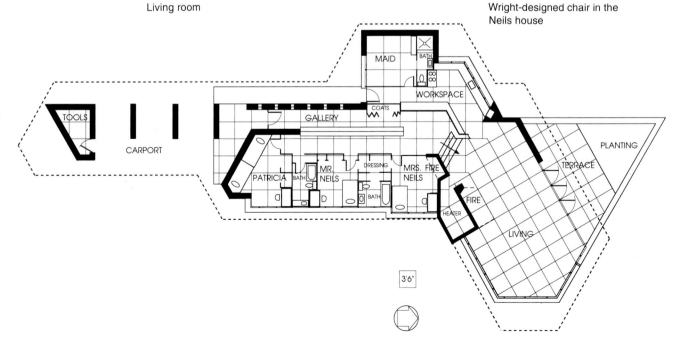

S.315   T.4901

Howard E. and Helen C. **Anthony**
Residence (1949)
Benton Harbor, Michigan

The Anthony dwelling sits above the
right bank of the Saint Joseph River.
Stone is complemented by cypress
and a roof of cedar shingles. The
design is a built version of the cottage
Wright designed for his sister, Maginel
Wright Barney. The main living area is
a mirror image of both the Barney
design and the McCartney house
(S.299A), with living room, workspace, and dining area, plus bedroom
and bath, all on a 4-foot equilateral
parallelogram module. Separation of
private areas from living space is
accomplished by board-and-batten
partitions that rise only to deck level.
Wright reversed the orientation of the
grid when attaching the bedroom and
shop wing, whose 90-degree angle
with the main public facade provides
"arms" signalling the visitor the location
of the entry.
    The soft Madison limestone was
brought to the site on return trips of
trucks shipping Michigan apples to
Wisconsin. The parts of this stone not
protected by overhanging eaves have
weathered badly; harder Indiana limestone was preferred by the client who
was owner of the Heath Company, a
mail order business offering do-it-
yourself electronic equipment kits.
Scott Elliott, of Kelmscott Galleries,
has begun the process of restoration.
The interior needs no work, having
been constructed with the finest materials and workmanship, down to dowel-
covered screws in the board-and-
sunk-batten paneling, but exterior
limestone walls have suffered the
effects of water freezing and
unfreezing throughout the winter.

Anthony Residence

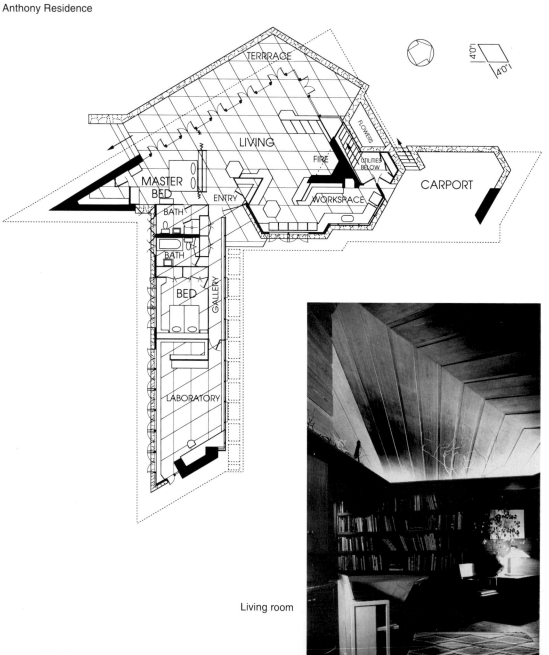

Living room

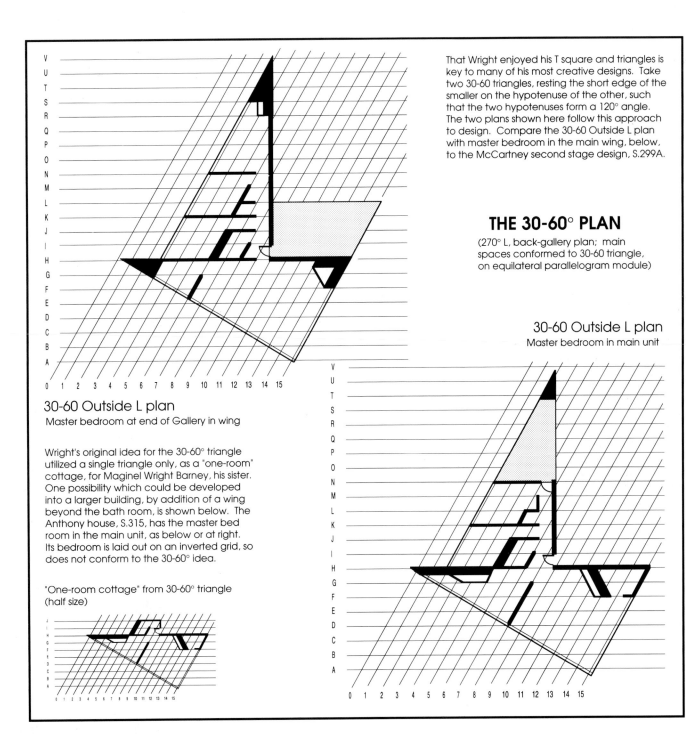

That Wright enjoyed his T square and triangles is key to many of his most creative designs. Take two 30-60 triangles, resting the short edge of the smaller on the hypotenuse of the other, such that the two hypotenuses form a 120° angle. The two plans shown here follow this approach to design. Compare the 30-60 Outside L plan with master bedroom in the main wing, below, to the McCartney second stage design, S.299A.

THE 30-60° PLAN

(270° L, back-gallery plan; main spaces conformed to 30-60 triangle, on equilateral parallelogram module)

30-60 Outside L plan
Master bedroom in main unit

30-60 Outside L plan
Master bedroom at end of Gallery in wing

Wright's original idea for the 30-60° triangle utilized a single triangle only, as a "one-room" cottage, for Maginel Wright Barney, his sister. One possibility which could be developed into a larger building, by addition of a wing beyond the bath room, is shown below. The Anthony house, S.315, has the master bed room in the main unit, as below or at right. Its bedroom is laid out on an inverted grid, so does not conform to the 30-60° idea.

"One-room cottage" from 30-60° triangle (half size)

Usonia Homes

S.316–S.318   T.4720
Usonia Homes (1947)
Pleasantville, New York

With David Henken, a Taliesin apprentice from 1942 to 1944, as prime mover, a group of friends formed the Rochdale Cooperative in 1944. This became Usonia Homes, Inc., in 1945 and, in 1947, the organization purchased 97 acres in Pleasantville, within commuting distance north of New York City. Wright was engaged to design each building or to approve work done by others; he eventually limited his participation to preparation of the site plan and design of a few of the buildings. The site plan initially called for fifty-five circular plots, an acre to each family's house plus an acre for communal use. Circles were eventually adjusted to polygons to satisfy the Board of Assessors. The cooperative developed the overall site with water, electricity, and road systems, as well as fire-fighting capabilities.

Three Wright structures were not built: a Community Center designed on a 5-foot-square unit module and two houses, one on an equilateral triangle module, the other drawn to a hexagonal module. Three others were constructed.

Priscilla Henken, first wife of David, served as historian for Usonia Homes, or Usonia II as it is sometimes known. Usonia I was a title given on the site plan to a group of houses for a cooperative in Okemos, Michigan (see S.269). Similar cooperative arrangements were incorporated in the Galesburg Country Homes (S.294–S.297) and the splinter group that became Parkwyn Village in Kalamazoo, Michigan (S.298–S.301). Whatever its number, Pleasantville was a "Usonia," and its homes Usonian. That they were essentially

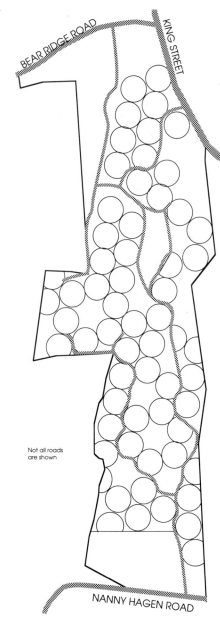

Not all roads
are shown

General plan of Usonia Homes as designed

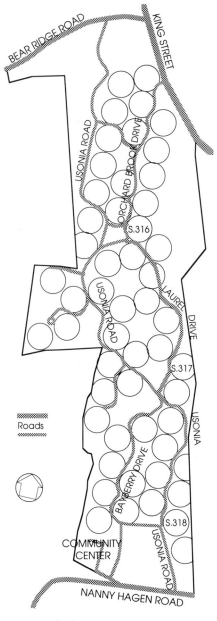

Roads

as revised

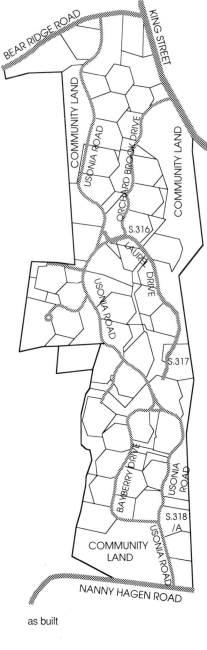

as built

masonry homes, two of them avoiding wood panels in their exterior walls, made them no less Usonian than the others. The choice of wood over masonry was an economic one. With plenty of local stone available, some having to be blasted to make the site suitable for construction, the use of masonry was quite logical, a point too often missed in writing about the Usonian era, which continued through the Usonian Automatic designs of the mid-fifties and beyond.

Usonia Homes

S.316   T.4906
Sol Friedman Residence (1948)
Pleasantville, New York

Three houses were built in Pleasantville's Usonia from Wright's designs, the first being the Sol Friedman house on Toyhill. In geometry, it was the most daring. It is a two-story stone and concrete structure with oak trim, interlocking two cylinders or drums, with a detached mushroom-shaped carport. The smaller of the cylinders contains the workspace and utilities on the main floor and bedrooms above, with a balcony overlooking the living room, which space fills the remainder of the larger, 44-foot outer drum. The geometry is clearly marked in circular segments scored on the concrete floor mat. It may be seen as a circular version of the solar hemicycle (Jacobs II, S.283). The carport roofing harks back to the dendriform columns of the Johnson Wax Building (S.237), and its outline is imitated in the roofing of the two house drums. These roofs are essentially stretched skins, with plywood glued to the rafters. Flitch plates are used in the ridge pole.

Sol Friedman Residence

Lliving room; view to fireplace

Living room;
view from workspace

Plan of upper floor

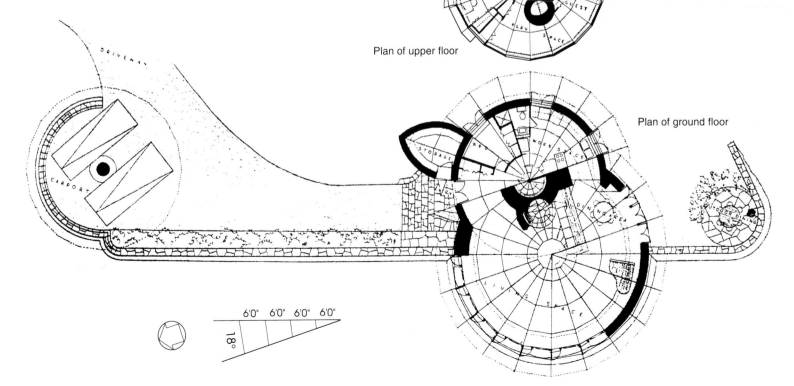

Plan of ground floor

6'0" 6'0" 6'0" 6'0"

18°

Serlin Residence

S.317   T.4917

Edward **Serlin** Residence (1949)
Pleasantville, New York
Additions to the east end by Aaron L.
Resnick

The Serlin house, second of Wright's
Pleasantville projects and the first of
two on which David Henken acted as
general contractor, employs stone, of
mostly local origin, as do its neighbors,
along with horizontal siding. In that
siding, and the title "Usonia Homes,"
this represents a late effort by Wright
in pure Usonian expression, masonry
to support cantilevers, inexpensive
wood paneling between. The Serlins
and Reisleys (S.318) shared a ship-
ment of cypress to save on costs. The
cypress is not configured as board and
batten, but has a simple mitred edge
to provide a **V**-groove at the join, a
system used in the Reisley home, too.
Four fireplaces were designed into the
structure.

Extensions of the building at both
east and west ends were intended to
complete the structure. The west room
was to be a study, with its own fireplace; flues exist in the end wall
beyond the master bedroom. The east
extension was elaborate, including a
large studio unit, carport, and tool
shed; architect Aaron L. Resnick
designed the rooms that now occupy
this area and complete the structure.
Forced-air heat has replaced the
gravity system.

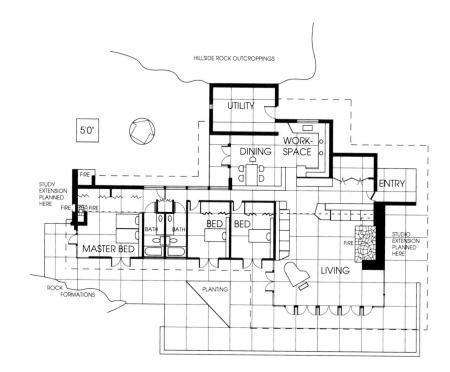

Living room

Usonia Homes

S.318   T.5115
Roland and Ronny **Reisley**
Residence (1951) and
S.318A   T.5115
Addition (1956)
Pleasantville, New York

This last of Wright's Pleasantville projects continues the use of local stone as the basic building material, with cypress wood paneling, trim, and fascia boards, down to a cypress-lined shower. The boards are not screwed, but nailed, the holes filled with putty by Mrs. Reisley. The original structure was a complex small-scaled in-line plan. The main entry is at one end of the carport. A gallery leads to a junction, workspace left, living room ahead, second gallery right. The second gallery leads to the side, then doubles back, dropping off two bedrooms, one used later as a study, with shallow cantilevered balcony and terminating in a bathroom with a special low sink for ease of washing a baby. Off the main gallery is a stairway leading to a basement with photographic darkroom and a wine cellar under the bedrooms. Dining space was to one side of the living room, which looks south over a terrace into hilly, wooded countryside. The floor is covered by a hexagonal rug of unequal sides made to Wright's design in Singapore. The rug reflects the assymetrical nature of a living room slightly altered by Wright from his first design to provide a natural ceiling extension of the speaker system built into one roof corner. Gravity heat is employed, in a brown concrete slab floor scored to show the 4-foot-sided equilateral triangle unit module.

Reisley Residence,
west side balcony
and lower level

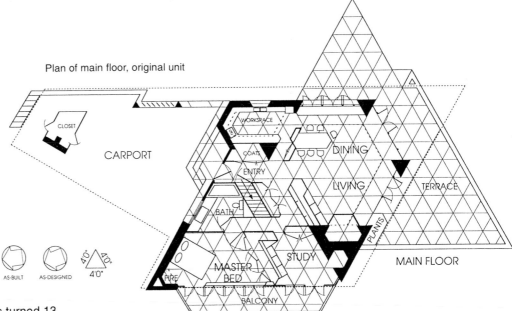

Plan of main floor, original unit

MAIN FLOOR

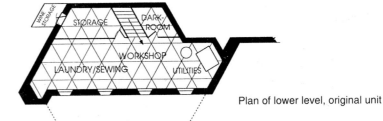

Plan of lower level, original unit

This structure was turned 13 degrees from Wright's site plan to simplify blasting of the rocky hillside. Wright wanted to make the addition climb the hilly site, as the Hanna house (S.235) did, but that would have been expensive. When challenged by the Reisleys, "we don't believe you can do it," Wright "snorted," and produced a workable plan. The addition took no notice of the 13-degree rotation, yet was fitted to the site, at 120-degrees to the original building. Its flooring is terrazzo. It allowed a separate dining space, under the original east soffit. A tunnel gallery leads to three childrens' bedrooms and a bathroom, and is terminated by a playroom. Initial construction was begun in 1951, finished the following year, with the addition being completed five years later.

(Continues)

Reisley Residence, southern terrace outside living room

Living room

Reisley Addition, living room of original building to left

Living room

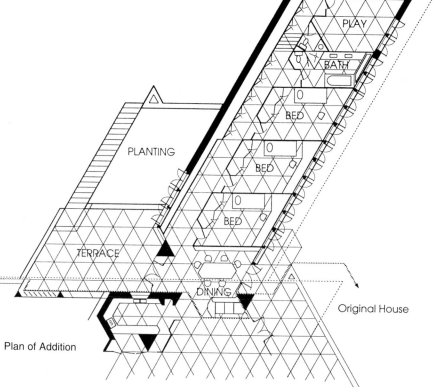

Plan of Addition

S.319 T.4814

Kenneth and Phyllis Laurent
Residence (1949)
Rockford, Illinois
Guest bedroom addition at carport by
John H. Howe

For Kenneth Laurent, a paraplegic, Wright designed a house that presents no obstacles to anyone who must use a wheelchair. The living room space of the Laurent residence opens northwest down a long slope leading to Spring Creek. Segments of circles dominate the plan, interlocking with rectangular spaces (the grid has square modules) in this single-story solar hemicycle.

Wright's first major expression in such segments was the second Jacobs residence (S.283), which had a single center for all radii of the basic structure. In the Laurent dwelling, there are two centers for circles that intersect. Interior spaces are defined by one radius, exterior pool and planting and terrace areas by another. Common brick complements Tidewater cypress. The second concrete seal to the original floor was sprayed on much too late and peeled off like paint.

A bedroom has been added by John H. Howe next to the carport. Refurbishing of the house has included a synthetic membrane roof to replace tar and gravel.

Laurent Residence, private facade

Laurent gallery, workspace to right

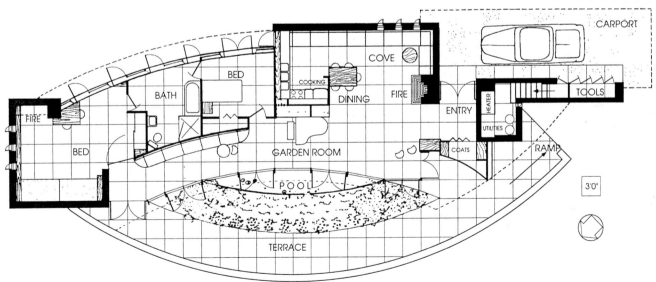

Pearce Residence,
San Gabriel Mountains behind

View from southeast

S.320   T.5114

Wilbur C. **Pearce** Residence (1950)
Bradbury, California

Though in plan the Pearce house superficially resembles the Laurent, site and materials dictated a different architectural expression. The Pearce house commands a location on a foot-hill of the San Gabriel Mountains in the Bradbury Hills. Its living room opens south to the San Gabriel Valley and north to the mountains and the Mount Wilson Observatory. A 3-foot-square unit module is used, with the structure framed on 6-foot centers. The circular segments are constructed with stand-ard concrete block. Roof and carport are cantilevered with steel, the latter being particularly dramatic and requiring two bolts that go through the floor slab as anchors. This concrete slab floor holds Usonian-style gravity heating.

Honduras mahogany provides a warm contrast to the neutral concrete. Douglas fir, a good structural material but of poor appearance, was used for ceiling, rafters and, with mahogany overlay, mullions.

Aaron Green chose to reorient the structure to avoid steep parts of the ridge, thus allowing a 3-foot extension of a utilities space and creating a usable workshop.

View from northeast

Private facade, with terrace wall

Pearce house with San Gabriel Valley behind

Living room, view south toward Los Angeles, showing clerestory

Wright's California houses employ a wide range of woods, including oak in the Barnsdall house (S.208), teak in the Ennis (S.217), redwood in several, as well as mahogany and fir in the Pearce house (S.320). Of the mahoganies, Cuban (caoba) is among the best, with a density (lb./cu.ft.) of 41–45, but the supply was quickly exhausted. Honduran (34–39) was preferred for its beauty, but an infection prevented regrowth. True Philippine mahogany (Shorea negrosensis, 34–39) is generally stronger than readily-available false Philippine, or Lauan (28–41), but the availability of this latter wood and its easy fashioning into door panels, plywood, and such, as well as its beautiful grain structure, made it popular. Of all the woods Wright chose, American white oak (47 lb/cu. ft.) and Teak (45 lb/cu. ft.) had the greatest density.

View of terrace, pond and gallery

Living room, view to fireplace

Plan of Pearce Residence

S.321 T.5012
Thomas E. **Keys** Residence (1950)
Rochester, Minnesota
1971 additions, and conversion of
carport to guestroom, by John H.
Howe.

Keys Residence

Nineteen-fifty was a banner year for
designing; twenty-one projects were
finally constructed. Nine were solutions
for the use of concrete block, although
the Keys residence was first intended
to be stone. Keys and two other
clients, all connected with the Mayo
Clinic, came to Wright within a three-
year period. The design for Dr. B.
Marden Black's house was the most
complex. Dr. Bulbulian built his second
scheme (S.292), as did Keys, librarian
at the clinic.

The house, trimmed with pine, is
based on the berm-type housing first
shown as a $4000 project in
Architectural Forum (1938). A Detroit
project for multiple units was located
outside the city limits on the north side
of Thirteen Mile Road in what is now
Madison Heights. Aaron Green met
with Cooperative Homesteads
members (autoworkers and others) in
1942, and a plot plan and the basic
berm house plans were drawn. Construction was apparently started on
one unit; the foundation was laid but
no utilities were connected when the
spring rains and flooding carried the
building away. Together with the war,
this ended the project.

Additions made in 1971 by John H.
Howe enlarge the living room and
convert the former carport to a
guestroom and bath.

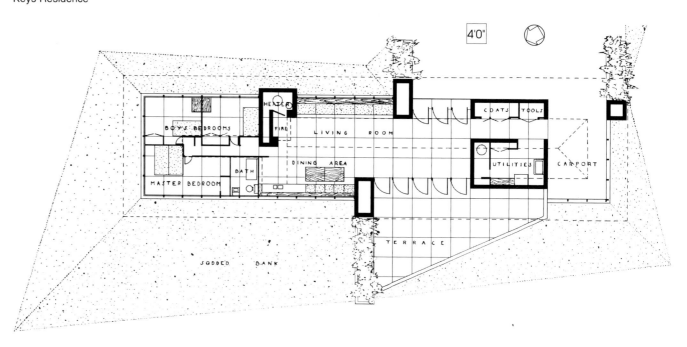

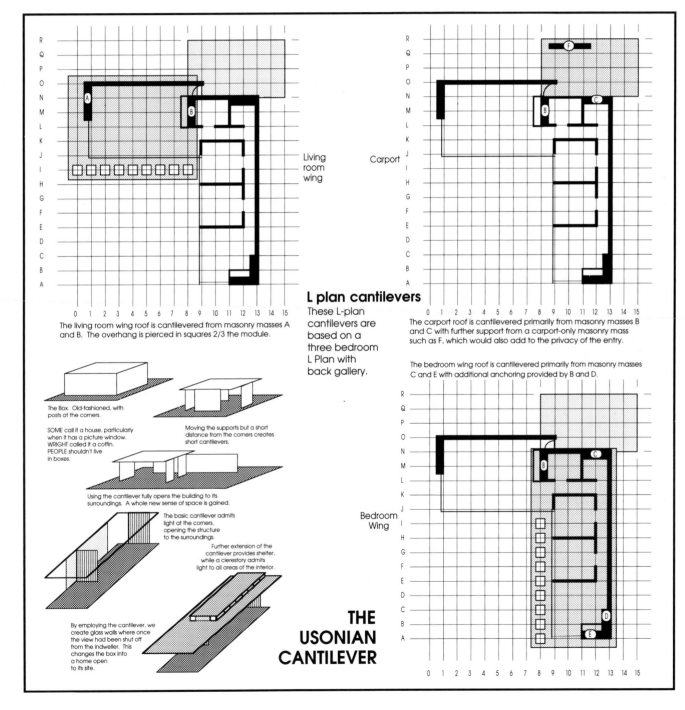

The living room wing roof is cantilevered from masonry masses A and B. The overhang is pierced in squares 2/3 the module.

Living room wing

Carport

Bedroom Wing

L plan cantilevers

These L-plan cantilevers are based on a three bedroom L Plan with back gallery.

The carport roof is cantilevered primarily from masonry masses B and C with further support from a carport-only masonry mass such as F, which would also add to the privacy of the entry.

The bedroom wing roof is cantilevered primarily from masonry masses C and E with additional anchoring provided by B and D.

The Box. Old-fashioned, with posts at the corners.

SOME call it a house, particularly when it has a picture window. WRIGHT called it a coffin. PEOPLE shouldn't live in boxes.

Moving the supports but a short distance from the corners creates short cantilevers.

Using the cantilever fully opens the building to its surroundings. A whole new sense of space is gained.

The basic cantilever admits light at the corners, opening the structure to the surroundings.

Further extension of the cantilever provides shelter, while a clerestory admits light to all areas of the interior.

By employing the cantilever, we create glass walls where once the view had been shut off from the indweller. This changes the box into a home open to its site.

THE USONIAN CANTILEVER

Gladys and **David Wright**
Residence (1950)
Phoenix, Arizona

David Wright, Frank and Catherine's fourth child, was involved in concrete block, its design, manufacture, and promotion (for the association of Portland cement manufacturers). Consequently, when the designs David received from his father for a desert home were not of a construction system consistent with this concern, William Wesley Peters took on the re-engineering of the project for construction in block. The design is a reworking of a generic project "How to Live in the Southwest" (T.5011), which was done by Wright to show how citrus grove treetops could be the "lawn" of a home in the desert. The David Wright home is, in practice, simply the working drawings to Wright's sketches for that "generic" house.

All the living spaces are raised above ground and reached by a spiral ramp, with a 77-foot radius to its outside wall, on a 10-degree circular module. This gives a curved in-line plan, with spaces no longer limited by orthogonal geometry. From the living room, one may look over the almond-shaped pool past the entry ramp and across a carpet of green citrus orchard foliage to the rising sun or nearby mountains. The living room rug, based on a 1926 design with circles interlocking and overlapping to different centers, was woven by V'Soske of Puerto Rico. The heavily reinforced concrete floor, cantilevered from concrete block piers, carries air-conditioning ducts and other appurtenances. The block also features a decorative frieze echoing the plan's circular forms, the one block that is not "standard." Built-in furniture and the curving panels of the ceilings are red Philippine mahogany. The roofing is galvanized steel, covered with copper paint. Concealed lighting, some from outside the house, allows daytime furniture placement to serve after sunset.

A guesthouse to the north is by John H. Howe. To the south is a home for David's son, David Lloyd Wright, designed by elder brother, Lloyd Wright.

Living room, from bedroom gallery

David Wright Residence, "How to Live in the Southwest"

Living room, from entry

Living room exterior

Master bedroom from across garden court and pool

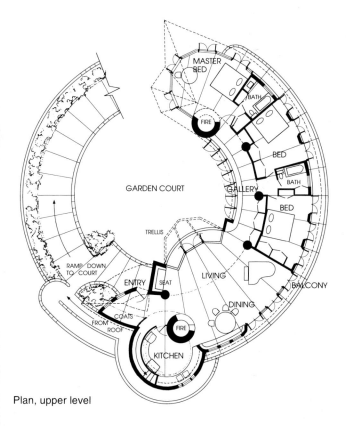

Plan, upper level

0 4'

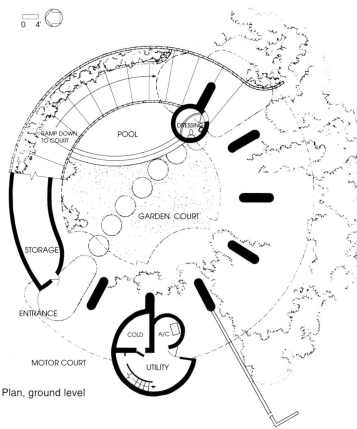

Plan, ground level

Haynes Residence

S.323   T.5110
John **Haynes** Residence (1950)
Fort Wayne, Indiana
Children's rooms converted to drafting room

The Haynes residence is a small Usonian design in brick with gravity heating, its gallery offset to meet the rear of the living room at its center, rather than typically to one side. A music room and three bedrooms drop off this gallery. The plan thus generated is an outside **T**, with living room facing southwest and southeast, bedrooms looking southeast to the morning sun. The gabled roofing is asymmetrical. Plans for a fourth bedroom off the back of the gallery, asked for when Mrs. Haynes again became pregnant, and a tool storage room plus bathhouse and swimming pool at the music room were never realized. With a family grown too large for his house, Haynes built an interesting, if non-Wrightian, circular home on an adjacent site. The two children's rooms have been converted to a drafting room by architect John H. Shoaff.

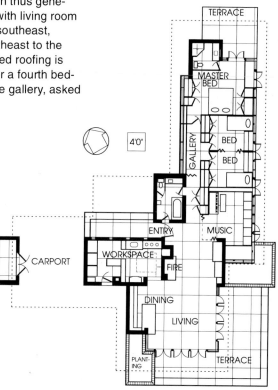

341

S.324   T.5037

Dr. Richard and Madelyn Davis Residence, Woodside (1950) and

0.324A   T.5037

North Bedroom Wing Addition (1954)

Marion, Indiana

Screened porch added at study, later enclosed. Larger kitchen built into study.

Following the Second World War, Wright gave renewed thought to what might be called the "one-room house" concept. In this, all architecturally enclosed spaces would be under one roof, with the barest of partitions to give needed privacy. In practice, this led to a design in which the central masonry core surrounding the work-space would support a roof canti-levered in three, or even in four, directions, with a single bedroom separated by as little as one sandwich-wall partition from the living space.

The McCartney (S.299), Anthony (S.315), and Berger (S.330) homes all fit this description, but each is extended with a bedroom wing for children. The Davis house also fits the description; like the Anthony house, its wing was built immediately as part of the main house, though the teepee could have stood alone. With the McCartney, the added wing brought about changes to the main house space, so this "remodeling" is also numbered with an identifying alpha-betical suffix. Later wings (the carport for McCartney, the north or "second" bedroom wing with basement for Davis) are given further numbers with a suffix. Though the main section of the Berger house was occupied upon its completion, there was no break in construction of the wing, so no suffix applies.

Dr. Davis was a twenty-six-year-old fellow at the Mayo Clinic when Wright arrived with a gall bladder problem and an intestinal obstruction. Wright had Dr. Davis get Dr. Mayo on the phone when he felt good again, and felt afterward that he'd put Dr. Davis in a bind, so he offered to build him a house.

The Davis house is a painted concrete block structure with cedar

Davis Residence, the original unit, with unauthentic screened porch

shingles and Tidewater cypress trim derived from the Lake Tahoe project of 1922, a plan of several cottages and barges based on the concept of the Indian teepee. The first built version of this was the Fir Tree (another image Wright gave to the Tahoe project) for Arnold Friedman (S.286). Then in 1949, for a site at Asheville, North Carolina, Wright did a desert masonry design for Thomas Lea on a square module. Rotated 180 degrees and drawn to a 4-foot-sided equilateral parallelogram unit module, this was built as the residence for Dr. and Mrs. Richard Davis.

The central octagonal teepee section, which rises 38 feet from floor to chimney top, contains living room, dining space, workspace and a studio/bedroom. A three-bedroom wing is included with this basic plan. This, the original house, took two years to build. The second wing with a bomb-shelter basement was constructed shortly after Wright's death. Allen Lape Davison worked with Mr. Wright in preparing the plans and working drawings.

The Davises sold the house in 1966. A screened porch attached to the living space–study juncture of the teepee is not by Wright. It has since been enclosed. Later owners, desiring a larger "kitchen," turned the study into a second kitchen. A museum in Quebec now has the freestanding furniture.

Davis Residence with North Bedroom Wing Addition at the right

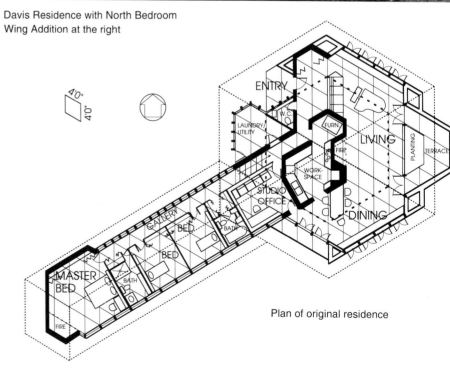

Plan of original residence

The added wing, showing basement windows that were cut in by later owners.

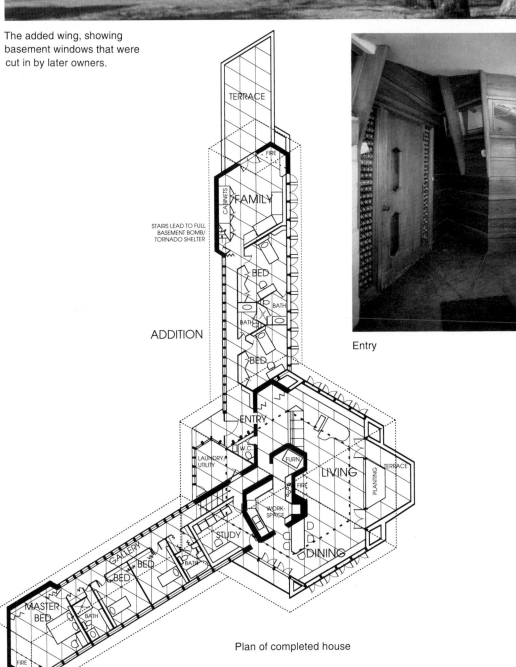

TERRACE

FIRE

CABINETS

FAMILY

STAIRS LEAD TO FULL
BASEMENT BOMB/
TORNADO SHELTER

BED

BATH

BATH

ADDITION

BED

ENTRY

W.C.

LAUNDRY/
UTILITY

FURN.

LIVING

FIRE

TERRACE

PLANTING

WORK-SPACE

STUDY

D

DINING

GALLERY

BED

BED

BATH

MASTER
BED

BATH

FIRE

Plan of completed house

Entry

The teepee living room

LIGHTING WITH A CLERESTORY

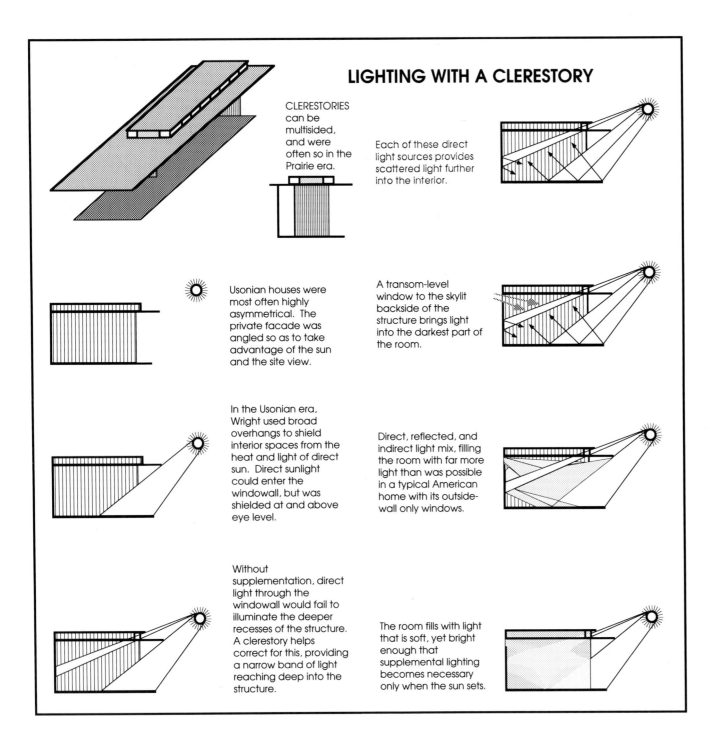

CLERESTORIES can be multisided, and were often so in the Prairie era.

Each of these direct light sources provides scattered light further into the interior.

Usonian houses were most often highly asymmetrical. The private facade was angled so as to take advantage of the sun and the site view.

A transom-level window to the skylit backside of the structure brings light into the darkest part of the room.

In the Usonian era, Wright used broad overhangs to shield interior spaces from the heat and light of direct sun. Direct sunlight could enter the windowall, but was shielded at and above eye level.

Direct, reflected, and indirect light mix, filling the room with far more light than was possible in a typical American home with its outside-wall only windows.

Without supplementation, direct light through the windowall would fail to illuminate the deeper recesses of the structure. A clerestory helps correct for this, providing a narrow band of light reaching deep into the structure.

The room fills with light that is soft, yet bright enough that supplemental lighting becomes necessary only when the sun sets.

Sweeton Residence

S.325 T.5027
J. A. and Muriel **Sweeton**
Residence (1950)
Cherry Hill, New Jersey

In the Sweeton dwelling a red
concrete-slab floor with gravity heat is
complemented by interior red plywood
board and batten. The red roof, originally laid out in board overlapping so
that 2-foot strips ran the length of the
structure to emphasize the horizontal
character of the design, has since
been replaced with asbestos shingles.
Similar emphasis is given in the block:
the vertical grouting fills the joints to
the block surface and the horizontal
grouting is deeply recessed. The compact in-line plan has a 4-foot-square
unit module, with 14 feet of cantilevered, gabled carport roof. There is
also an extension off the master bedroom for additional workshop or study
space. Mahogany was the basic wood,
with redwood plywood panels and pine
for window and door frames.

   Muriel Sweeton designed and wove
the original fabric for drapes and
furniture. She also tracked Wright
down at the Hotel Plaza in New York
City, where he was working on the
Guggenheim design, when plans for
her house did not arrive when she
expected them.

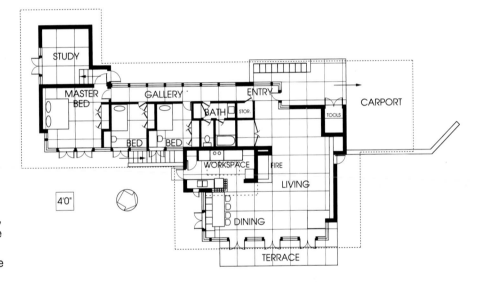

Living room

Carlson Residence shortly after construction

Dining alcove

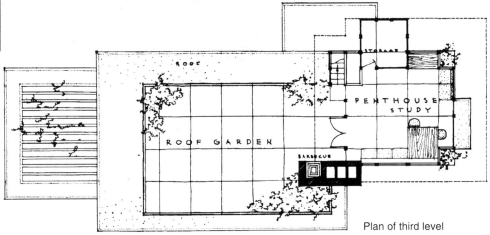

Plan of third level

S.326   T.5004

Raymond **Carlson** Residence (1950)

Phoenix, Arizona
Attached guesthouse added in the 1970s. Main structure restored in the 1980s by Charles Schiffner

This house for the editor of *Arizona Highways* magazine is of post-and-panel construction, using wood posts and insulated cement asbestos (cemesto board) panels. Wright was particularly enamored of this new structural system and the beauty he could create with it. As John H. Howe recalled, "Mr. Wright drew it all up and brought it to the studio, you know, completely drawn up, sections, elevations, plans, everything." Angled southwest to northeast on its corner lot, it rises three stories at its east end. This section has a sublevel kitchen, bedrooms and bath in the middle, and at the top Mr. Carlson's office, which opens to a roof deck. A prominent clerestory in the long living room takes advantage of light from the hot desert sun. To save on costs, the house was largely built by the Carlsons, who were close friends and regular visitors for

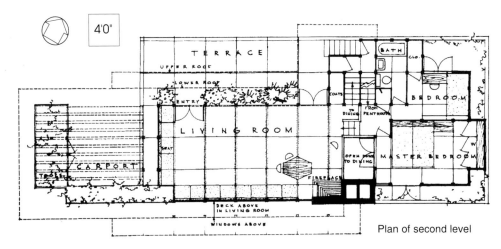

Plan of second level

weekend dinners at Taliesin West. After the party celebrating completion of the house, Wright sent the Carlsons a gift, a piano that cost more than the architect's design fee.

In the 1970s, a guesthouse was added at the southwest corner of the structure. In the 1980s, Charles Schiffner, a former Taliesin apprentice, restored the main structure, which had deteriorated after the original client's death.

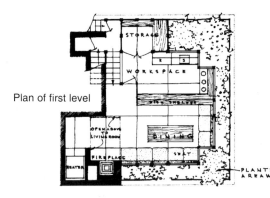

Plan of first level

John O. Carr Residence (1950)

Glenview, Illinois
Living room extended to east and
west, and north at west end

This house is located on level ground
deep in wooded country. Its roof along
the entry sidewalk carefully steps
around a great oak whose branches
shelter the entire structure. It is a **T**-
plan angled 30 degrees west of north
and derived from the Alsop residence
(S.304) by placing the earlier house's
quiet spaces to the rear rather than the
side. Before recent additions, the living
room roof, an asymmetrical gable, thus
angled 240 degrees, admitted delight-
fully changing patterns of light both
morning and evening. Salmon-colored
concrete block and matching concrete
brick (11 5/8 by 3 3/8 inches) are used
inside and out. Patterned concrete
block is used at the west end of the
living room to divide living from kitchen
areas; it rises to deck level, but not to
the ceiling, enhancing the sense of
interior spaciousness.

In the early eighties, two decades
after they bought the house Carol and
Ed Busche decided 1900 square feet
was not enough, and additions more
than doubled the **T**. These include a
conversation room and new master
bedroom with its own bathroom to the
east, ending in a roofline similar to the
original. To the north is a gabled dining
space. West is a sun room facing the
swimming pool. The Busche and
Markson, Inc., additions won Illinois
and National Society of American
Registered Architects awards in 1981
and 1982.

John O. Carr Residence

Original living
room, view toward
workspace

Original workspace

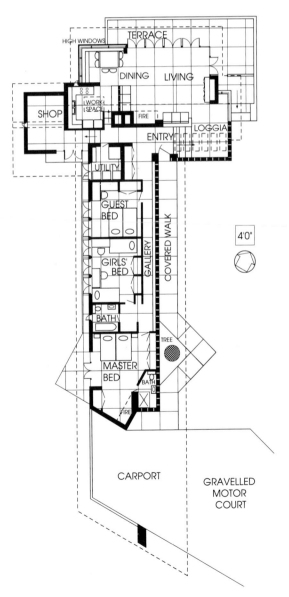

Schaberg Residence

S.328   T.5022
Don and Mary Lou **Schaberg**
Residence (1950)
Okemos, Michigan
Family room and additional bedroom,
to rear, added by John H. Howe

The Schabergs owned a lumber
company, but it is the brick in the
house that fascinates Don, author of a
book on risk investing. The Schaberg
house was built with over 55,000 old
gold hard-burned Maryland bricks
inside and out, in a battered configuration. Mahogany plywood is trimmed
with cypress, and the gabled roof is of
rough cedar shakes.

When he and Mary Lou went to
Wright for a home, they were initially
given a development of the Eric V.
Brown house (S.300), but they persisted in their need for a home that
could accommodate their expanding

family. The plan is basic in-line to a
4-foot-square grid, bedroom wing,
workspace, and dining room (where
the gable reaches forward), then living
room all facing southeast. A carport
extends northwest. This is paralleled
by a family room and bedroom connected to the main house by a second
gallery, designed by John H. Howe,
who supervised the original construction.

View in the living room,
southeast corner

View in the living room, northeast corner

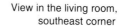

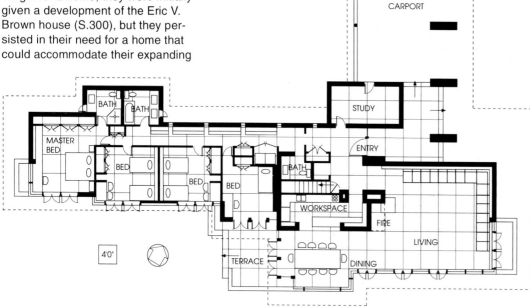

S.329 T.5010

Dr. R. Bradford and Ina Moriss **Harper** Residence (1950)

Saint Joseph, Michigan
Furniture sold at auction 1990. Wood trim painted. A garage has been added to the site, and the carport enclosed

Dr. Harper was a podiatrist. He lived but two years in this $80,000, 1700-square-foot, beautifully appointed gem. It was Mrs. Harper, however, who had read "The Love Affair of a Man and His House" in *House Beautiful,* August 1948, by Loren Pope (see S.268), and thereafter wrote Wright for a "five room 'ranch type' house of approximately twelve to thirteen hundred square feet." The living room of this 45-degree **L**-plan design turns from the bedroom axis to gain a view of Lake Michigan, directly across Old Lake Shore Road. Salmon-colored (sand-mold) brick and cypress are employed throughout the structure. The dining tables and chairs, sold at auction in 1990, are spruce.

To provide privacy on this exposed site, Wright gave the living room a 6-foot wainscoting from the low end of the butterfly roof halfway around its main glazing, where the brick moves out to form a protective wall about the terrace. The end rooms (living room and master bedroom) are set at 45 degrees to the basic 4-foot-square grid, while central rooms (workspace, entry, two bathrooms and the second bedroom) align to the grid. This design is a development of the Abby Beecher Roberts concept (S.236).

Many changes have been made to the house since new owners took possession in about 1990. The freestanding furniture has been sold at auction, and much of the gorgeous cypress has been painted. Prior to this, a garage had been added to the site, and the carport enclosed.

Harper Residence

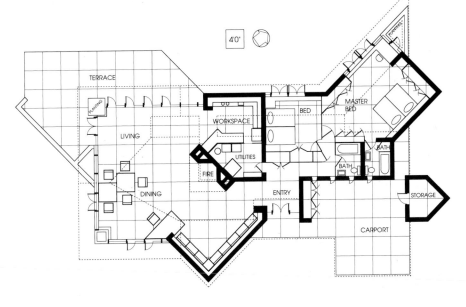

Freestanding dining table

Living room

S.330 T.5039
Robert and Gloria **Berger** Residence (1950)
S.330A T.5039
Eddie's (Dog) **House** for Jim Berger (1956)
San Anselmo, California

Berger Residence, terrace and living room facade

From below, the Berger house rests so deftly on one level ridge of the steep slopes of these north bay hillsides that it can go unnoticed. Fifteen thousand dollars was all the Bergers had to put into their new home, and Bob was an engineer teaching at the College of Marin, and designing his own "box." He decided to go to Wright for something better, but the Korean war interfered. He met Wright in Spring Green on a bus trip as he returned east. The home he gained was truly a Usonian design at the most basic level, though not as "simple" to erect as later Usonian Automatics. Aaron Green guided the Bergers step-by-step and revised the plans as needed for do-it-yourself construction. Bob split the stone (Sonoma or Santa Rosa candy rock). Bucket by bucket, he climbed his ladder and block-and-tackled concrete and stone into place. The head of the local plumbing union volunteered three hours showing him

Public facade, workshop to right, entry center

how to do the plumbing. Robert died in 1973. Gloria could not willingly part with the home whose creation she had lovingly shared.

The building is constructed on a 4-foot-to-the-side 60–120 degree equilateral parallelogram, which generates a lopsided hexagonal living room, with a bedroom in an alcove behind the workspace (á là McCartney, S.299, and Anthony, S.315). This also gives the living room a view in three compass directions. The remaining bedrooms define an in-line configuration.

The Bergers' son Jim thought his dog Eddie ought to have a house and wrote Mr. Wright to ask for one. Wright gladly provided full working drawings.

Living room

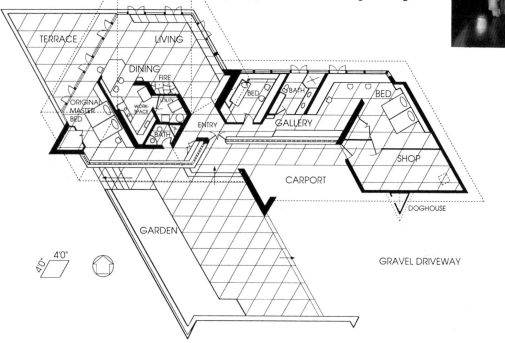

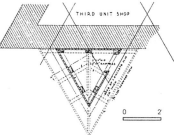

Plan of Eddie's house

Eddie's house, with himself in it

Elevation of Eddie's house   Section of Eddie's house

S.331   T.5013
Arthur C. **Mathews** Residence
(1950)
Atherton, California

Two wings, parallel to each other, originate from the central workspace and dining area of this brick house. With the Mathews house we have moved well beyond simple Usonian design. Board and batten, here redwood, is now relegated to interior paneling, and new modules dominate Wright's plans. The "diamond" module employed here (60–120 degree equilateral parallelogram, with 4-foot side) was Wright's favorite at this point. The living room is at 120 degrees to the workspace, the sleeping area, with three bedrooms and two bathrooms, at 60 degrees. This creates a spacious patio with only "windowalls" separating interior and exterior. The plan, in mirror image, is almost identical to that of the Richard Smith home (S.337); a comparison of the two is instructive. Heating is Usonian gravity type. Mathews completed none of the built-in furniture.

Mathews Residence, the private facade

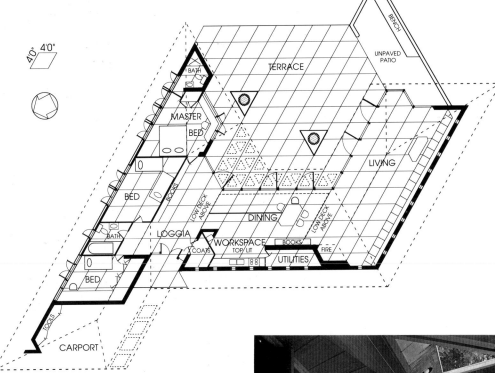

Dining area with workspace beyond

Soffit and awning windows

Corner, showing mitred glass above casement window, with trellised overhang

S.332 T.5021
William and Mary **Palmer**
Residence (1950)
Ann Arbor, Michigan

As a boy, Bill Palmer attended Hollywood High School in California. His grandfather had taken him to see La Miniatura (S.214) at that time, so he had already been introduced to Wright's work. When he and Mary decided to build, they did not know whom to ask. Bill's twin brother suggested Wright, so Mary went to the library at the University of Michigan, where Bill was a professor. She read everything she could find on him, bringing home what she could for Bill to read. They wanted to understand the architectural philosophy before they chose an architect.

Constructed of cypress, sand-mold brick, and a matching block fired the same as the brick, this house grows out of the crest of a hill, opening from its triangular shapes to a curving plateau that welcomes the morning sun. ClayCraft of Columbus, Ohio, produced the brick and block at their Sandusky kiln. Wright noted that he had looked for years for someone to do both. The brick is known as "Cranbrook brick," for it is the basic masonry employed by Eliel Saarinen in his Cranbrook Academy buildings.

The design of the Palmer house is one of Wright's most successful in expressing the possibilities of a single-story dwelling in masonry on a hilly site. The original plan had the living room facing south, but this was turned 120 degrees to northeast, away from summer sun. With this orientation, it exactly fits the ridge. The in-line

Palmer Residence

Living room

plan is generated from an equilateral triangle with 4-foot altitude (a preliminary plan shows this as an equilateral parallelogram). The carport is well below the main level and set at 120 degrees to the main axis. Stairs up to the well-concealed entry enhance the effect of spatial compression followed by expansion in the living room that is a keynote of so many of Wright's designs.

When the clients desired additional space, John H. Howe, who had worked on the original plans, designed a tea-house built down the hill.

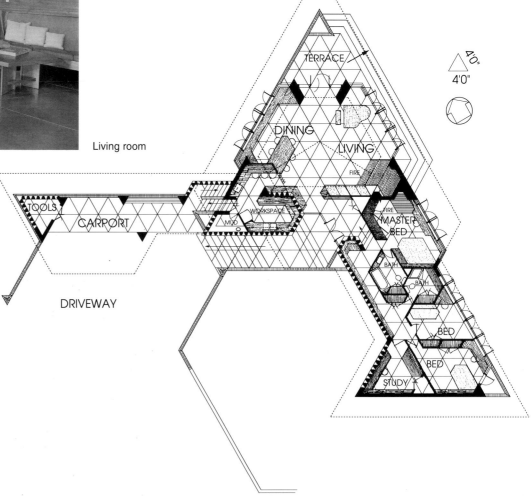

View across dining table into living room

S.333   T.5214

Dr. Isadore J. and Lucille
Zimmerman Residence (1950)
Manchester, New Hampshire
Restored, and opened to the public

A long house with a clerestory lighting the central living quarters, its primary construction materials are red-glazed brick, upland Georgia cypress trim (which has a wider grain and was less expensive than Tidewater cypress), and flat terra-cotta tile for the roof. The true spaciousness of this 1,458 square foot home, designed to a 4-foot-square unit module, is not apparent from the public approach. Two bedrooms are clustered around the workspace, rather than stretched along the usual tunnel gallery. The view is to the southwest over a large yard beautifully landscaped by Wright.

Colorundum, a balanced formulation of nonslip aggregate next to the diamond in hardness, was used in the concrete floor. It was seen by Wright as the ideal solution to uncarpeted areas of plain concrete. Colorundum was trowelled on top of the concrete floor mat. It was not painted or coated, was water repellent, and could not rust or stain, and it was "available in eleven decorator colors."

Wright designed the furniture (though the overall furniture plan fell, typically, to the on-site apprentice-

Zimmerman Residence, private facade

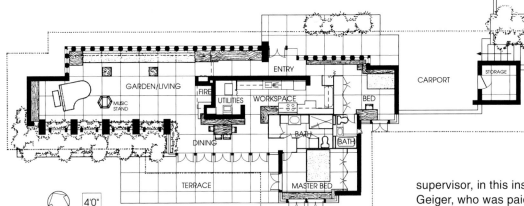

4'0"

Music corner

Living room including hi-fi speaker cabinet (to right, at end of built-in seats)

supervisor, in this instance, John Geiger, who was paid $50.00 a week plus room and board); among the unique pieces is a four-way stand for musicians that so often frequented the 36-foot-long Zimmerman living room. John H. Howe remembers that he, Curtis Besinger, and John deKoven Hill worked on the plans and design of the furnishings, while other sources indicate that Nils Schweizer prepared the working drawings. The Zimmermans first met Wright in August 1949; construction of their home was begun in May 1951, and the Zimmermans occupied the building a year later.

Asphalt shingles replaced the original roofing, and forced air heating was added when the gravity system failed. Dr. Zimmerman died in 1985. Upon Mrs. Lucille Zimmerman's death in 1988, the Courier Gallery of Art took possession, with an endowment from the Zimmerman estate. Restoration was provided by Tilton+Lewis of Chicago. The home, now a museum, is open to visitors by arrangement through the gallery.

353

Muirhead Residence

S.334   T.5019
Robert and Elizabeth **Muirhead**
Residence (1950)
Plato Center, Illinois
Frost-heave damage to concrete mat

The family business is Muirhead Farms; beans, corn, and pigs. The house is surrounded by farmlands, broad open prairie, though no longer covered with prairie grass.

Construction drawings by Allen Lape Davison, who supervised the project, are dated February 1951, and show a basic in-line design extended by a pergola to attached kitchen facilities. In the main unit are five bedrooms, for a son and four daughters, with their own bathroom. A master bedroom with its own bathroom is on the opposite side of the gallery, separated from the living room by the laundry. A closed pergola leads to the unit containing kitchen, dining room, and workshop. Separation isolates noise more effectively from the bedroom wing than the typical Usonian **L**-plan. The shop has an overhead door, but it is not suitable as a garage; a carport is adjacent. An office has been combined with the shop because the original proved too small.

Common brick and cypress plywood are the materials of the dwelling, set on a grid of 4-foot squares. The board-and-batten walls have a 9-inch vertical spacing, with a bevel at the top; mortar between bricks is similarly beveled.

Upon Robert's retirement, grandson Charles moved into the house. Frost-heave damage—buckling of the floor by several inches—had not been corrected in the early 1990s.

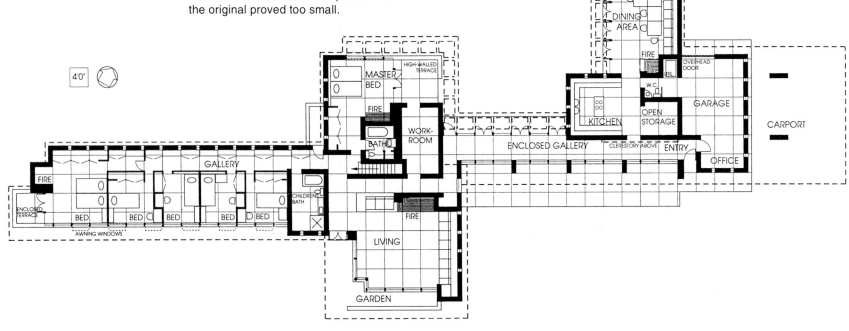

S.335 T.5119
Karl A. **Staley** Residence (1950)
North Madison, Ohio
Renovated in the 1980s

This in-line plan, a version of the Pratt
residence (S.295) in stone, parallels
the nearby Lake Erie shore, southwest
to northeast, with its living room view
to the north. The various stages of
expansion experienced by the Pratts
are clearly shown on the plans for the
Staleys. Shiplap siding is employed in
ceilings and soffits, but not walls.
Elsewhere, a unique lapping of boards,
a wide vertical board alternating with a
narrow, slightly sloping board that
suggests a batten but creates a
ziggurat-like surface, gives special
character to much of the siding.

In the 1980s, Susan and Jack
Turben renovated the house, making
the shop into guest quarters and
restoring the cypress to pristine
condition. While the east end cantilever has sagged, it is stable, and
permits draining without ugly guttering.
Original furniture remains in good
condition.

Living room facade

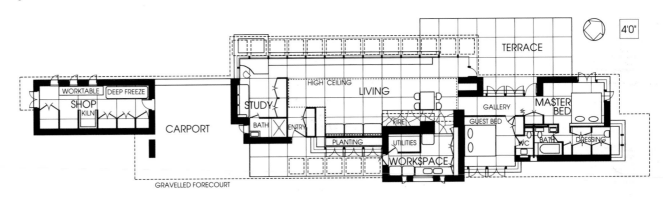

Living room

Elam Residence, main facade

S.336   T.5105
S. P. **Elam** Residence (1950)
Austin, Minnesota

The Elams, who were taking a tour of Taliesin, mentioned to John H. Howe that they wanted to build, and he suggested Mr. Wright. Wright saw them immediately. Later they had a falling out with the architect and had to finish their kitchen without Wright's design.

lever. Cypress is used for board-and-batten siding and ceilings; the roof is cedar shakes. Radiant heating, buried in the broken stone beneath a concrete slab (except in the 5-inch-thick slab where the building is two stories high), follows Usonian standards in a house ample beyond Usonian means.

Entry

Plan of main level

The main floor of this structure is 148 feet long, set on a 4-foot-square unit module, terminated at the east end by a playroom and at the west end by the living room, each configured to a 45-degree triangle. The master bedroom is placed next to the living room, followed by a daughter's bedroom, a bedroom for two boys, and the playroom with kitchenette. Below the living room, workspace, and study are servant's quarters and a workshop. A 40-foot garage extension is also at this level. Massive limestone piers, the stone trucked from a quarry near Taliesin, support the dramatic canti-

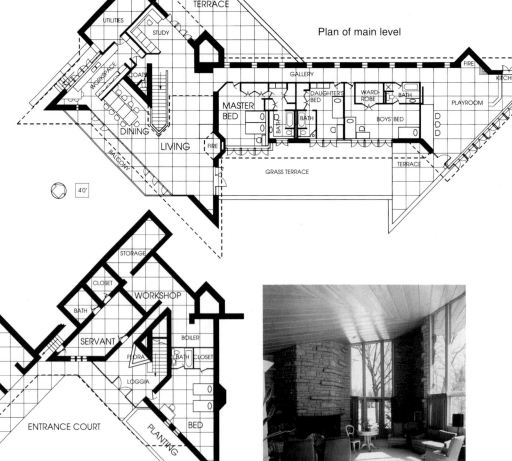

Plan of entry (lower) level

Living room

356

S.337   T.5026
Berenice and **Richard Smith**
Residence (1950)
Jefferson, Wisconsin
Renovated in the early 1990s

This house opens onto a yard just off the Meadow Springs Golf Club. Limestone, plaster, cypress, and cedar shingles are integrated in this structure. The plan is virtually a mirror image of the brick Mathews house (S.331); which was designed first is not certain though some evidence suggests the Smith house may be slightly later. Here Wright called for an equilateral parallelogram module, placing the living room wing at 120 degrees to the workspace and dining area, with the bedroom wing at 60 degrees. This was all oriented to the location of an oak tree embraced by the wings of the house. The result is a home with complete privacy from neighbors and the street, yet open to the sunset.

Because the structure and flooring had deteriorated, the building was renovated during the early 1990s under the direction of John Eifler.

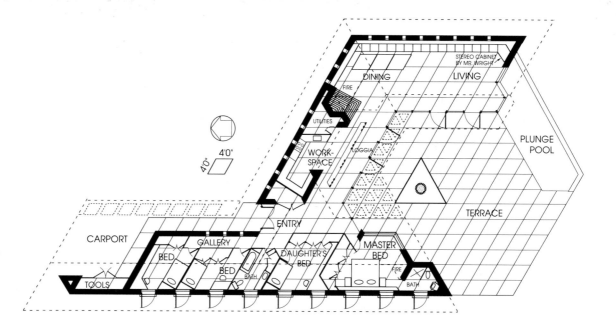

Richard Smith Residence, public facade

Soffit and trellis detail

Trellised walkway to entry

S.338   T.5034

John A. **Gillin** Residence (1950)
Dallas, Texas

John Gillin was a geophysicist, perpetual electronics gadgeteer, and "billionaire" bachelor. After building one Wright design, he commissioned another, Alladin, to be built in the Hollywood hills.

One of Wright's most extensive single-story structures, the Gillin house looks eastward over gently rolling lawns through floor-to-ceiling glass, one of Wright's most extensive windowalls. Three wings spin off a central hexagon at 120 degrees to each other, much as might have happened had Wingspread (S.239) been based on the Gillin equilateral parallelogram module rather than squares. Living and dining spaces are articulated more by the ceiling than by walls, as right angles are avoided, even in the kitchenette facilities of each of the guest rooms. The formal dining room is completely separate from kitchen and living room areas. The grand living room is under a copper roof and ventilator that was specifically copied from the Arizona Biltmore Aztec Theatre. Stone is the primary construction material; it was not cut, but was selected for 30-, 60- or 120-degree angles. Glass, rather than wood, might be considered the secondary material. At the exterior, metal replaces wood; teak is used in the interior. There are also plaster ceilings and soffits. The heating system is a dual radiant and forced-air arrangement, either of which can heat the house by itself as each has its own high-capacity boiler.

Gillin, a self-made man, was admired by Wright and thus allowed to design many details, such as all door hardware including hinges, a vertical broiler, the kitchenettes of stainless steel, tiled bath tubs, electrical switch plates, and even the diving board support. W. Kelly Oliver, Taliesin's representative in Denver, drew the working drawings, supervised construction, and made the drawings for Gillin's custom creations during the three years of construction, which began in 1955.

Gillin Residence, private facade

View into living room

View out of living room

Gillin Residence, public facade, with carport to right

Bedroom

Termination of bedroom wing

Dining room

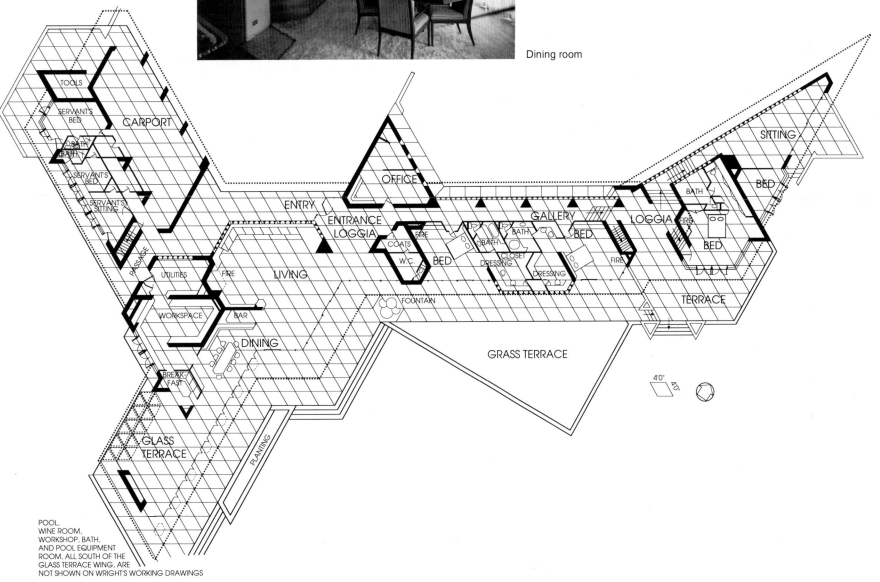

POOL,
WINE ROOM,
WORKSHOP, BATH,
AND POOL EQUIPMENT
ROOM, ALL SOUTH OF THE
GLASS TERRACE WING, ARE
NOT SHOWN ON WRIGHT'S WORKING DRAWINGS

Shavin Residence, private facade

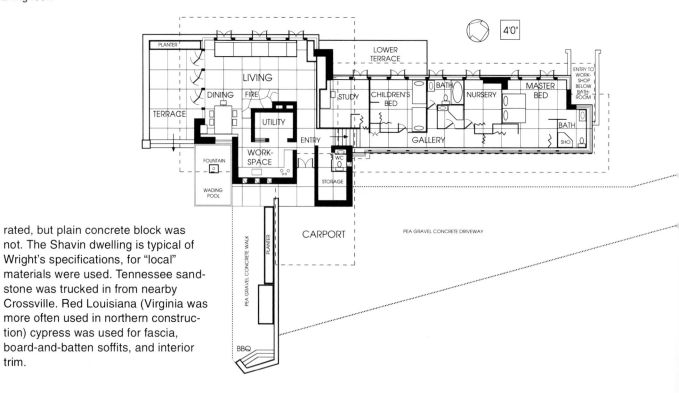

Shavin Residence shortly after construction was completed; terrace, living room, workspace, carport

Living room

Butterfly chair

Dining area

S.339 T.5023
Seamour and Gerte **Shavin**
Residence (1950)
Chattanooga, Tennessee

Wright's only work in Tennessee sits in a hollow on the north end of Missionary Ridge, just high enough to clear a view northward over a two-story home, yet below the hilltop. Emphasizing this is the butterfly roof, leading the eye to the broad panorama of the Tennessee River and framing mountains. The plan is in-line, set on a 4-foot-square grid, with the bedroom wing dropping a half level below the living room to conform to the topography. The first scheme was a front gallery type, but the third major revision moved this to the back, to give the bedrooms a full view of the mountainous countryside.

The Shavin home is an excellent example of an all masonry Usonian home. Usonia was not limited to cheap board-and-batten type designs. It was an architecture for a Democratic America. Wright's basic approach to materials was to tell his clients to buy the best that they could afford. Thus, red Tidewater cypress was preferred over mahogany, which was preferred over redwood. Masonry was preferred for exterior walls over wood, stone over brick; textile block was highly rated, but plain concrete block was not. The Shavin dwelling is typical of Wright's specifications, for "local" materials were used. Tennessee sandstone was trucked in from nearby Crossville. Red Louisiana (Virginia was more often used in northern construction) cypress was used for fascia, board-and-batten soffits, and interior trim.

USONIAN ROOF TYPES

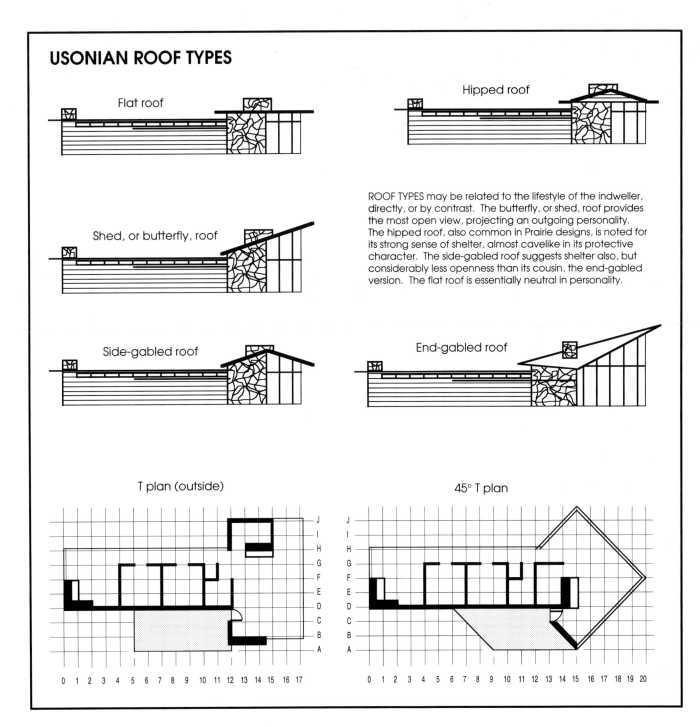

Flat roof

Hipped roof

Shed, or butterfly, roof

ROOF TYPES may be related to the lifestyle of the indweller, directly, or by contrast. The butterfly, or shed, roof provides the most open view, projecting an outgoing personality. The hipped roof, also common in Prairie designs, is noted for its strong sense of shelter, almost cavelike in its protective character. The side-gabled roof suggests shelter also, but considerably less openness than its cousin, the end-gabled version. The flat roof is essentially neutral in personality.

Side-gabled roof

End-gabled roof

T plan (outside)

45° T plan

Kraus Residence, private facade

S.340　T.5123
Russell W. M. and Ruth **Kraus**
Residence (1951)
Kirkwood, Missouri

This artist's house bends around the hill in which it nestles. The plan, using triangular modules, is an interesting variation on the in-line theme. The master bedroom opens directly off the living room, and the second bedroom is down a short gallery. To the opposite side of the living room is the work-space and a gallery that leads to the entry and Mr. Kraus's studio at the southern terminus under the canti-levered roof. The terrace door win-dows, designed by Mr. Kraus, are a geometrical floral pattern stained glass in warm colors, orange predominating. The hilltop is open, while the downhill view is into wooded land. When the power company put a transformer next to the Kraus property, John Ottenheimer designed a fountain whose bubbling sound would mask the hum of the electrical device.

Plan of main floor

Plan of utilities basement

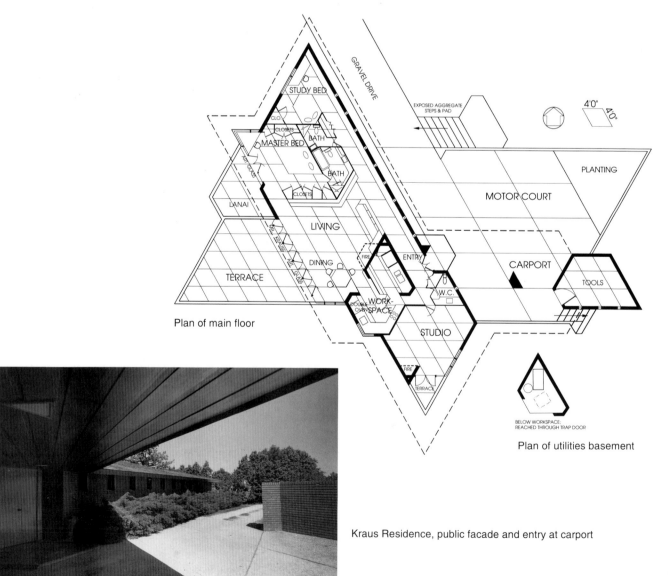

Kraus Residence, public facade and entry at carport

362

S.341   T.5107
Charles F. **Glore** Residence (1951)
Lake Forest, Illinois
Renovated early 1990s

This two-story, pink Chicago common brick, Honduran mahogany, and salmon-colored concrete block structure overlooks a ravine, guardian of the dwelling's privacy to the south. It is an in-line plan, with a children's room opening over the two-story living room; the flues of the fireplaces in both upper and lower rooms share the same masonry core. Other fireplaces warm the opposite end of the dwelling, which is reached by a wider-than-normal gallery that overlooks the terrace. A porch, the living room balcony, and the living room roof are all major cantilevers. The design is set on squares, unit side of a very uncommon 64 inches that possessed a logic of its own, for it made the unit equal to four standard concrete blocks. This was reduced to 56 inches at the time of construction. Unlike the typical Usonian design, the Glore house has a separate dining room and workspace, with servant's quarters, at the entry.

The basic design work and plans were done by John H. Howe, who was to Wright as Wright had once been to Louis Sullivan, the pencil in his hand. Thus, Howe would insist that the design was not his, but Wright's, noting that no plan left the office without Wright's approval, assured by his initials on the red square in a lower corner of the drafting paper.

After falling into severe disrepair, the building was partially renovated in the early 1970s, then fell vacant. In the late 1980s, with seven owners before them in the preceding decade, Larry A. Smith and Vicki Mondae took up the renovation. They removed a greenhouse and added a terrace around a hexagonal deck (Wright's circular pool was not possible given local laws protecting the ravines). A copper roof with strong horizontal emphasis replaced shingles. Three-quarter-inch lapped mahogany siding, stained dark brown, was planed back to its original reddish color with strongly accented grain.

Glore Residence shortly after it received its copper roof

Glore Residence (night photo made during renovation)

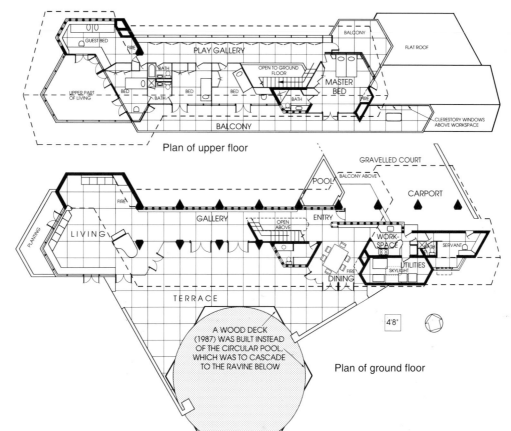

Plan of upper floor

Plan of ground floor

A WOOD DECK (1987) WAS BUILT INSTEAD OF THE CIRCULAR POOL WHICH WAS TO CASCADE TO THE RAVINE BELOW

Living room from second floor

The western (private) facade of the Patrick Kinney Residence.

S.342 T.5038
Margaret and **Patrick Kinney**
Residence (1951)
Lancaster, Wisconsin
Wing addition by John H. Howe

As a college student, Margaret Kinney worked for Wright's sister Jane Porter, so there was little question of who the Kinneys' architect would be. Patrick, a young attorney in a small country town, told Wright that he could afford a $15,000 house; Wright based his fee on that figure, but the house probably cost $20,000 to $25,000. Yet, how can one place a value on one's own labor? Kinney would be up at the crack of dawn and quarry two loads of stone and deliver them to the site in a used 1939 Chevy pickup before heading off to court or the office. The stone was blue hard limestone—very hard he remembers—mostly from a quarry but eight to ten miles out of town where he found two good veins in stone otherwise used in road building.

Kinney was his own contractor, to save on costs, after rejecting Wright's suggestion that he build in concrete block. He dealt with every trade individually, even sweated his own copper tubing. He hired German masons and paid them $1.50 an hour plus room and board. Wright, of course, wanted "stickouts," stones set well out of the basic face of the walls (some of which are battered, others vertical, creating difficult corners for the masons who couldn't read plans), to provide texture. Kinney teased one mason by saying he'd withheld $5 from the paycheck because he had to teach

Tunnel gallery

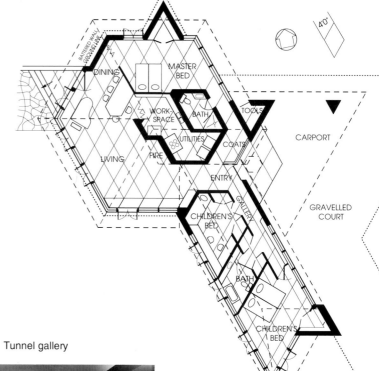

Living room

the mason how to do "schtickouts," as the Germans called them.

Robert Moses, uncle of Mrs. Kinney and czar of many things in New York City, reports on an exchange between the Kinney's and their architect (whom he called "skylark," Wright responding by calling Moses "mole"). Wright had misunderstood the number of children in the Kinney household and, upon discovering it was three rather than two, chided the parents for bringing so many into this world.

The house, a version of the Berger residence (S.330) in mirror image, with the garage at the side, is set on a grid of 60–120-degree (equilateral) parallelograms like those in the Unitarian Meeting House, S.291, notes Mr. Kinney). The living room faces north and west. There is no paneling or veneer inside—stone inside and out. The roof is cedar shingles—not the more expensive and desirable shakes specified—covering a thick rubber membrane (sheets 10 feet square, sealed with mastic) that has prevented leaks.

In 1964, former Taliesin fellow John H. Howe designed a detached northeast wing, which is almost indistinguishable from the main structure.

Entry to workspace

S.343   T.5116
Nathan and Jeanne **Rubin**
Residence (1951)
Canton, Ohio

This plan is a mirror image of the Alexis Panshin house designed in 1939 for the Usonian homes group in Okemos, Michigan (see S.269 for further information), but not built. The Panshin plan was first reworked in 1945 for William Pinkerton in Virginia, then further "perfected" for the Rubins.

Brick and horizontal redwood siding sheathe the building; the sleeping quarters form a 120-degree angle with the remainder of the house, each part on its own 2-by-4-foot grid. The main part of the house is a hexagon, divided roughly in half by the fireplace. Behind the masonry mass is the workspace and to the side a shop. The entry faces west, where Frazer Road was to have been located. Unfortunately, the Market Hills Association changed the routing after the Rubin house was built, placing it east of the structure, thus violating its carefully planned privacy. Allan J. Gelbin not only supervised construction but acted as general contractor throughout the nine-month period in 1953 when this house was built. Salary: $50.00 per week plus room and board with the Rubins. With Gelbin serving in two capacities, bills for construction were paid directly by the client.

Educator Jeanne Rubin has, over the years, studied the history of crystallography. The founder of modern crystal theory, Christian S. Weiss, who was aware of the left- and right-handed nature of crystals, was a teacher of Froebel. Froebel blocks and other gifts operate according to principles of crystal growth. Wright uses the word "crystal" and crystal imagery often in his writings and even in the naming of some projects.

Rubin Residence

Living room

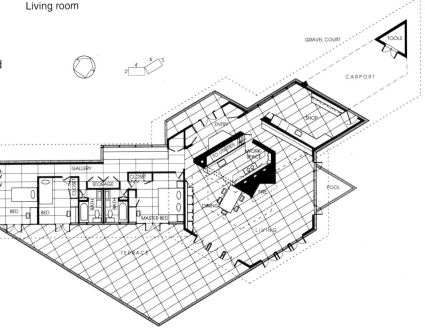

S.344   T.5101
Benjamin Adelman Residence,
including
S.344A   T.5101
Detached **Sitting Room** and
Servant's Quarters and
S.344B   T.5101
Detached **Carport** (1951)
Phoenix, Arizona
Significantly altered to salvage
seriously deteriorated structure

The Benjamin Adelman residence, the
second built for this Milwaukee family
(see S.308), has a two-story living
room and kitchen lighted by the glass
openings in the block pattern. It is
Usonian Automatic in design and
advances concepts that first appeared
in the 1920 textile block houses
(S.214–S.217). Wright was experi-
menting, trying to improve upon the
block houses in Michigan (S.294–
S.296, S.298–S.301), all of which had
wood roofs. His solution was to
suspend the ceiling from concrete
beams. Later he turned to coffered
blocks in a "waffle-iron patterned"
ceiling. The Adelman design came
before that of the Pieper residence
(S.349), but it was built later.

The concept for this house came
from a Minnesota project reworked,
initially, by Taliesin fellow Allan J.
Gelbin. The house is actually two
buildings linked by a covered walkway,
walled on the south side. This partially
enclosed pergola or breezeway idea
also appears in completely enclosed
versions in the Muirhead (S.334) and
Fredrick (S.376) houses. The main
building contains the living room,
workspace, and master bedroom. The
secondary building has guest facilities
and sitting room as well as maid's
room. It employs a 2-foot unit system
with 1-by-2-foot blocks. The living
room wall mural, with gilt and silvered
mirror pieces, is by Eugene Masselink,
who did many such designs for the
Taliesin Fellowship.

Financial difficulties forced sale
of all movable objects, including a
Wright-designed chandelier, in the late
eighties.

Architect Fred Bloch, who worked
under Taliesin fellow Edgar Tafel, took
a building in desperate condition, with
the cantilevered gallery ceiling sagging
beyond simple repair and other structural difficulties, and made it market-
able. This included regularizing spaces

Benjamin Adelman Residence, north side with bedroom wing to the right; much of this area is now filled in with the new bedroom wing

Living room with Eugene
Masselink mural

Workspace

of the existing building, usually
enlarging and squaring-off Wright's
plan. The original design was a rare
instance of Wright's placing the entry
across the living room from the gallery
and workspace. That entry is now
closed, and a new entry near the new
garage at the east end of an enlarged
gallery leads not only to the living room
(left, south), workspace (forward and

to the left), and sitting room wing (far
forward, with enlarged maid's room),
but also a new, sunken master bedroom wing (right) with its own fireplace
and large, tiled bathroom with hot tub.
This new ensemble has been painted
olive grey, hardly Wright's original
desert rose (pink), and crowds a once
open lot.

S.345 T.5102
Gabrielle and Charlcey **Austin**
Residence, Broad Margin (1951)
Greenville, South Carolina

Gabrielle Austin took the train from Greenville to Clemson 30 miles west for two years to study architecture. When she and Charlcey contacted Wright, they were told "I do not design houses on lots. I design homes on acreage. Find suitable acreage and get back in touch." They found a hillside looking at a creek that would flood in springtime.

Desert masonry, more specifically called desert rubblestone wall construction, was used in this house. Stones are dropped between plywood retaining walls, their surfaces having been covered with newspaper before the cement is poured. After the concrete is cured, the plywood is removed, the paper pulled off the stone, and the surface scrubbed with a mild acid cleaning agent like vinegar. In this instance, mica-flecked stones were split in two, to gain maximum color in the exposed stone surfaces.

This is one of the few Wright houses where the sheltering roof is the element first noticed upon approach; it seems to extend the hill out over the house. The entry hall, nestled in the hillside, serves as the spine for the living, cooking, and sleeping quarters. Three bedrooms face downhill off the gallery. There are two full bathrooms, one near the entry, the other next to the master bedroom. There are two 4-inch steps to the bedroom gallery; rather than lower the ceiling, which

Austin Residence

would break the line of the design, Wright chose to raise the floor.

Gabrielle did not like "cheap Usonian materials," so she got a house of desert masonry, solid-core plywood, and all-brass screws. Cypress board, milled in Wisconsin, is 7/8 inch thick, rather than the 3/4-inch standard. The sandwich walls are 7/8 plus 3/4 plus 7/8 inches, or two and a half total. Wall paneling is laid vertically, while the ceiling boards are horizontal under the hip roof. The house has composition shingles because in 1954, when the roof was installed, cedar was not fireproof.

Harold Morton Construction Company, also known as Construction Incorporated, contracted the project, which was supervised by Robert Beharka and Nils Schweizer.

Gallery

In the 1980s, architect Roy Palmer became the owner of the property. He refurbished the house and added a tri-level wood-planked terrace off the dining area below the bedroom wing, using two masons and two carpenters who had worked on the original construction three decades earlier.

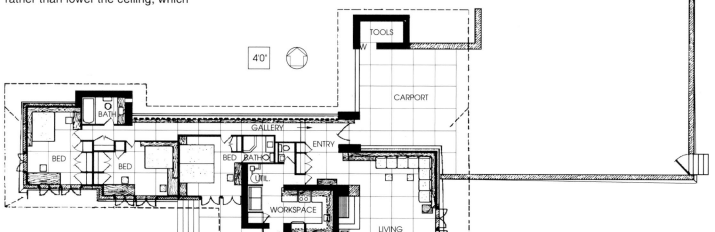

Living room

Chahroudi Cottage

back fireplaces in the living room and master bedroom, providing some warmth when Canadian air cools humid New York summers. The tower is the workspace.

The second owner "improved" the building with aluminum trim, but the third owner restored all wood to its original appearance and, rather than alter the cottage, built separate guest quarters.

S.346   T.5104

A. K. **Chahroudi Cottage** (1951)
Lake Mahopac, New York

Located on the western shore of Petra Island in Lake Mahopac, this structure is the guest cottage to an unbuilt, major plan. Desert masonry construction was employed, with some horizontal wood sheathing. Typical of this method of construction, the walls are battered, here one inch to each foot. The unit module is an equilateral triangle of 4-foot height (which equals a side of 4 feet, 7 and 1/4 inches). The master bedroom opens directly to the living room, separated only by accordion-pleat doors. The wood room partitions rise the usual six vertical units; above this the entire cottage is open to a cathedral-like ceiling. Clearly the building was intended only for summer use since there is no insulation. The chimney serves back-to-

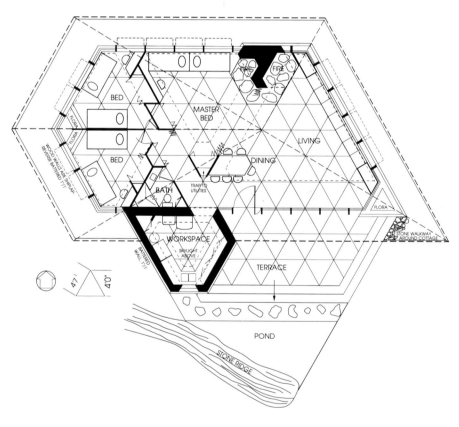

Cathedral ceiling framing, chimney tower to the right

S.347 T.5106
Welbie L. Fuller Residence (1951)
Pass Christian, Mississippi
Demolished by hurricane Camille,
August 17, 1969

This house was in many ways unique among Wright's late works. The structure was exposed standard concrete block and rough-sawn yellow pine stained red. A structural variant on post and beam was used by Wright, post and panel. Walls and ceilings were exposed natural asbestos board sandwich panel with celotex core, placed between structural members; the similarity is to the Carlson house (S.326). The ground floor was red concrete slab scored with a 52-inch-square unit module, main and third floors were heart Southern yellow pine. Plate glass, bronze hardware, and gravel-surfaced flat roof with copper flashing complete the list of materials of this house, which fell to the tidal wave of Camille. Camille killed 256 people and its 200 mph winds, making it a Category 5 cyclone, were even stronger than those of hurricane Hugo (1989), which achieved only Category 4 status.

The main living space was fully above ground level. The entry, workspace, living room, and other spaces opened to balconies, and a canvas-decked terrace extended to an attached guesthouse with its own workspace. A third level was for sleeping quarters. There were bathrooms on all three levels. Furnishings were all Wright designs. Supervision was by Leonard Spangenberg.

Welbie Fuller Residence

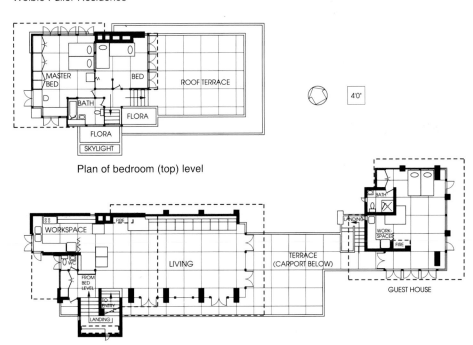

Plan of bedroom (top) level

Plan of main (above ground) level

Living room

Guest house

S.348   T.5117
Roy **Wetmore Auto Service Station Remodeling** (1951)
Ferndale, Michigan
Only partially constructed and not well preserved

Wright designed a complete service station and auto showroom for Wetmore, but they were never built. Later he designed the remodeling of the existing Wetmore facilities. Though some remodeling was done, it merely suggests an attempt to change what was already there to "board and batten" in the style of Wright.

Pieper Residence

Service desk in partially built condition

S.349   T.5218
Arthur **Pieper** Residence (1952)
Paradise Valley, Arizona
Dining room enlarged; air conditioning added

The Pieper house is perhaps the first constructed example of a Usonian automatic house. In building the house, Taliesin West student Arthur Pieper, whose second wife was Iovanna Wright, made the molds for the 3-inch-thick blocks, poured the concrete, knit the blocks together with reinforcing steel rods and grouting, and eventually raised the entire structure, with some help from Taliesin fellow Charles Montooth, whose own house was on the neighboring lot. The "automatic" aspect of construction is that the client can make the project a do-it-yourself home kit. Although two 3-inch-thick walls, as in earlier Wright textile block designs (S.214–S.217), and alternately a Usonian type of sandwich insulating interior wood wall were considered, only one thickness of block was completed. Corner blocks were poured in place, and the regular blocks were shimmed with toothpicks to keep courses level. The roof was not block, but wood beams with Cemesto board (asbestos plus cement) ceiling tile. This economy in construction proved quite unsatisfactory in the desert heat. Air conditioning had to be added, on the roof. An addition was made to the dining room by Arthur Lawton.

Montooth, who had come to Taliesin in 1945, worked on many Wright homes as a laborer, including the David Wright residence (S.322), before forming Horizon Builders with Pieper, with the idea of fabricating block for Usonian Automatic houses. He helped build the Benjamin Adelman (S.344), Boomer (S.361), and Harold Price, Sr. (S.378), houses. The business, formed in 1952, did not grow, and Pieper moved east. Montooth joined the Taliesin Associated Architects in the early sixties.

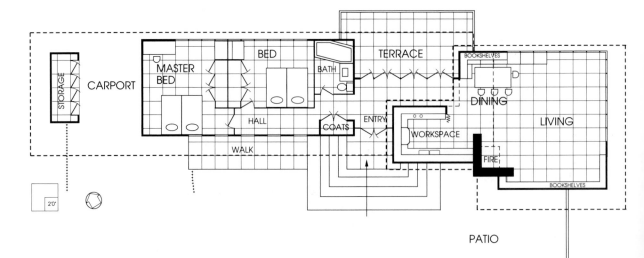

A Last Word on Beauty

A Wright-designed building must be first of all beautiful. "Choose the most beautiful brick (wood, stone, metal, whatever) you can afford" would be a prime dictum from Wright to client.

This actually grants the client great freedom. The beauty of the house resides first in its geometry, its adherence to basic principles of organic spatial design. With Wright this was achieved through use of the unit system, which to this architect was as the staff and bar lines are to a musician, a necessity that grants freedom in the more important matters of artistic composition.

The unit system was augmented by the best, the most beautiful, materials. A poor client could use pine, a richer one Tidewater cypress. The same design could be built in either material and would be beautiful in either because it was organic in its geometry.

This principle of beauty was illustrated to this author by one of Wright's Michigan clients as follows: "We must never forget beauty." That was Commissioner for Development and Cooperation S. K. Dey, who served under Nehru. He was commenting on material improvements in India when asked to do so by University of Michigan professor of economics William Palmer.

Mary and William's close friend was involved in another story that further illustrates a basic Indian, and Wrightian, principle that is operative in the Palmer's Wright-designed home (S.332) and, yes, all other Wright designs.

Looking at the oxen beside and on the road that they were trying to traverse, the professor asked, "Are the females bred for milk, the males for draft?"

"No," came the commissioner's answer, "they must be the right size for the job."

When further queried about this, it was discovered that whatever else was involved, "they must be beautiful."

Form and function are one, but beauty is the first principle.

Brandes Residence, private facade

S.350   T.5204
Ray **Brandes** Residence (1952)
Issaquah, Washington

Mr. Brandes notes the similarity of his own residence to the Goetsch-Winckler house (S.269). The plan is a mirror image, back to front, of the earlier Michigan house, on a 4-foot-square unit module. The house is set on Pine Lake Plateau, surrounded by much heavily wooded acreage. It is sited to take advantage of the afternoon sun in this northwestern climate.

View from living room into alcove

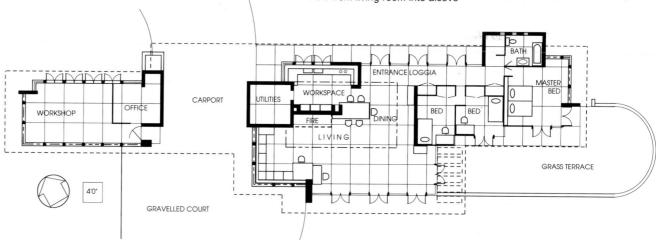

Beyond the two-vehicle carport there is a workshop and office for Mr. Brandes.

The house is constructed with concrete block as its masonry material. The block retaining wall around what was called a grass terrace is only hinted at by Wright in a penciled sketch on the site plan; this is the lanai of the Goetsch-Winckler design.

Brandes was the builder of another Wright house in the Seattle area, the Tracy residence (S.389).

Blair Residence as originally built,
view from south

S.351   T.5203

Quintin and Ruth **Blair** Residence (1952)

Cody, Wyoming
Porch enclosed. Two-car garage added by Bruce Goff. Utility room converted to kitchen, original workspace to a study

The only work of Wright's design in Wyoming is this sandstone and Philippine mahogany house on the plains east of Yellowstone National Park, the home of the owner of Buffalo Bill Village. The rising living room ceiling opens to a view of the entire eastern horizon. The plan, on a 4-foot-square unit module, seems to be generated from the Alpaugh concept (S.293), with its main view away from the bedroom wing. Much of the living room masonry is set at 45 degrees to the main axis and the glazing, thus enlivening the space even though the plan remains a basic **T**. The butterfly roof is supported by steel set three mullions apart and anchored in the masonry workspace core. Thermopane

Gravity heat system in place

Workspace under construction, view across patio

Cantilever beam being set

Framing for the living room glazing

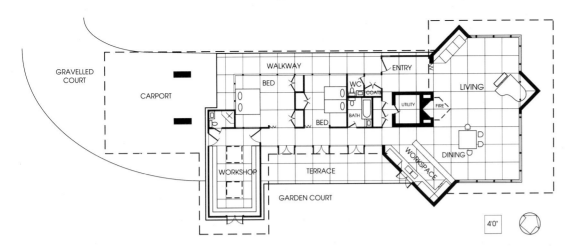

is standard, except where plate glass replaces it to create the mitred corner windows favored by Wright. Philippine mahogany now begins to displace red Tidewater cypress, which becomes scarce and costly, while the imported mahogany was available not only in boards but as plywood and door panels, so that wood could be easily matched throughout the building.

W. Kelly Oliver drew the original plans. The southern porch has been glass-enclosed so it could be used in winter, outside the tourist season, the only time the owners were free to enjoy its use.

Dining table, view toward original workspace and living room fireplace

Aerial view

Teater Studio, public facade

S.352   T.5211
Archie Boyd and Patricia Teater
Studio Residence (1952)
Bliss, Idaho
Renovated in the 1980s by Tom Casey

High on the bluffs above the right bank of the Snake River sits the only work by Wright in Idaho. Archie Teater's fame came as a world-traveling (115 countries) painter. Mrs. Teater's grandmother and Jenken Lloyd Jones were founders of the Browning Society of Chicago.

The Teaters' studio is essentially an 1872-square-foot variant on the "one room house" theme (see Second Erdman Prefab, S.412), generated from a parallelogram module of 5-foot sides (which gives sides 4 feet, 4

Painting, by Teater, of his studio

Dining table

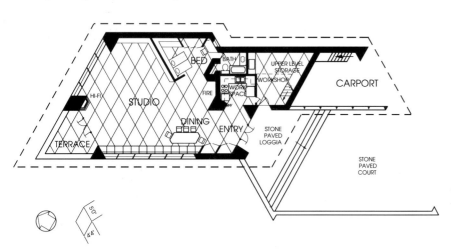

Studio north terrace and roof cantilever with kneebrace before sheathing

inches apart, the typical way Wright specified dimensions for parallelograms), it features an immense studio room whose roof covers three-quarters of the house space with no interfering wall. Quartzite stone from Oakley, concrete slab floor, and native oak enclose the space. Plate glass, the highest 19 feet above the foundation, opens the studio to a painter's northern light, instead of the southern exposure Wright would usually have provided.

A knee brace to the terrace roof is now sheathed in a design by Tom Casey that is reminiscent of the bracket indicated by Wright. Casey was the original supervising Taliesin apprentice, for whom this was his only on-site supervising experience. He became the Taliesin Associated Architects' structural specialist, particularly with respect to Usonian Automatic design and returned to oversee interior alterations and renovations by Henry Whiting II in 1982–84; the house had been virtually abandoned after the artist and his wife died. All exterior woodwork was refinished, and the kitchen and bathroom were redesigned to align with the grid.

Mäntylä, private facade

View from dining area into living room

i-fi cabinet

S.353   T.5208
R. W. **Lindholm Residence,**
Mäntylä (1952)
Cloquet, Minnesota

Mäntylä, Finnish for "house among the pines," is mainly an L plan on 4-foot squares, the quiet wing shifted back and to the side of the workspace, rather than running directly from it. With the carport more enclosed than Wright's typically were, the plan becomes a **T**. It is so situated as to open living and sleeping quarters to the setting sun. At the winter solstice, the sun just reaches bookcases and the foot of the built-in seats at the northmost wall of the living room, while at solar noon in the peak of the summer, the entire living room floor is in shade. Painted concrete block is trimmed with cypress. An 11-inch steel I-beam supports the cantilever. Despite Wright cautioning against "twindows" (Thermopane), it was used at the whispered suggestion of Wes Peters.

The Lindholms went to Wright for a home at the suggestion of their daughter, Joyce, one of whose University of Minnesota professors lived in the Willey (S.229) house. Original bids came in at $80,000 to $100,000, twice what they could afford. Only when they found an Iowa cabinetmaker who bid under $11,000 for his part of the job ($25,000 to $35,000 was the local estimate) did they decide they could build. Plans were drawn by Allen Lape Davison. Supervision was by Joseph Fabris with construction, taking a little over a year, completed May 1, 1956. The Lindholms also built the Broadacre City Service Station (S.414) in downtown Cloquet.

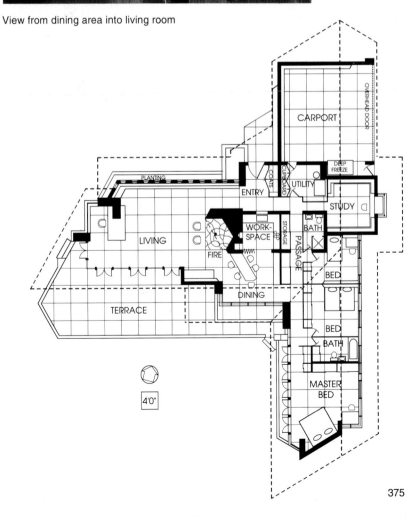

Living room

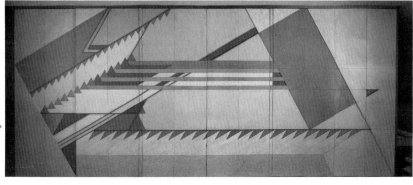

Masselink mural

Sander Residence, with storm windows and screen for autumn weather in place

S.354   T.5304
Frank S. **Sander** Residence,
Springbough (1952)
Stamford, Connecticut
Restored late 1980s into early 1990s

Springbough juts out from a rocky promontory toward the heavily wooded surroundings. Its well-shaded living room and balcony extension face south, the 6-foot cantilever supported by 2-by-12s except at the corners where steel flitch plates help hold the load. The deck is sail canvas laid in white lead, painted red (the standard rule among Taliesin apprentices was, "if you don't know what else to do, paint it red"). Philippine mahogany is used for board-and-batten walls inside, ship-lapped siding outside. Spar maroon varnish originally sealed the wood. The brick coursing exactly matches with the 13-inch batten

centers. Quarter-inch plate glass is used for all glazing. Twenty-four-foot floor joists are covered with fir flooring laid on the diagonal; forced-air heating accordingly replaces the gravity heat found in Usonian houses not using such daring floor cantilevering. The hipped roof is also cantilevered, from the fireplace masonry. Eighty-inch doors are hung on piano hinges.

The Sanders were so eager to begin work that they went to Taliesin West and sat on the walls outside the drafting room awaiting delivery of the working drawings. Their plan is a development of the Sturges (S.272) house, which they asked for; the Sanders unit, however, is 6 by 3 feet. The entrance hallway closet door is surfaced with a mural by Eugene Masselink. Supervision was by Morton Delson, New York representative of Taliesin Associated Architects.

In the late 1980s a four-year program of restoration of the building and new landscaping of the grounds was undertaken.

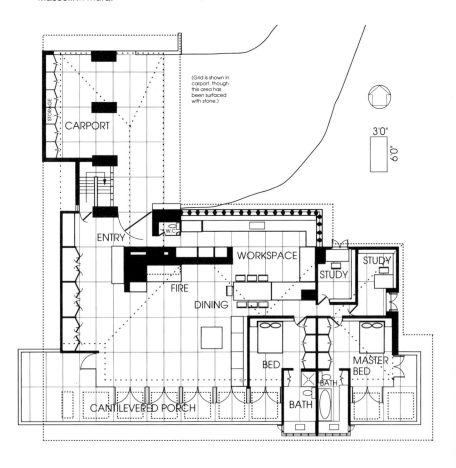

A textile block is 16" square. "Textile," because individual blocks, with surface patterns, are "woven" together by steel rods in edge reveals, into which the grouting is poured. Thus, there is no visible mortar line as with brick or stone. The art of combining the micro pattern(s) of individual blocks into a macro pattern of a wall surface made textile block a favorite masonry material with Wright for his Usonian designs.

TEXTILE BLOCK

6 rows of brick, plus mortar, equals the 16" vertical unit. Raking the horizontal grout, and coloring it, emphasizes the horizontal, in brick or stone.

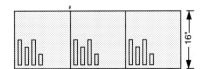

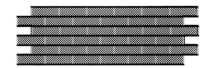

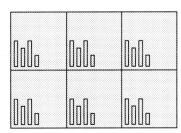

This 4' wide section uses the standard 3 blocks, thus dividing an even unit into odd groups, which provides more interest than division of even by even, 4 x 4.

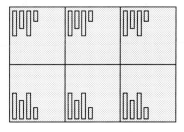

This section uses the standard 3 blocks, with the lower row inverted. This requires two molds, one the mirror of the other.

A wall of 16" x 16" textile blocks. Here, the middle block is plain, and the blocks at either end are rotated to provide a frame.

A great variety of macro patterns is available from a basic pattern and its mirror image.

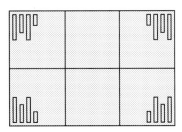

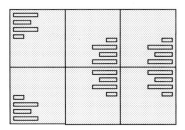

Daytime photograph from southwest; vertical mullions identify the facade to the eight apartment units

Harold Price, Sr., office

S.355   T.5215

Price Company **Tower** (1952) for Harold C. Price, Sr. Bartlesville, Oklahoma

The Prices, father and sons, were good architectural clients, building two homes (S.363 and S.378) and the Price Tower by Wright, as well as a home by Bruce Goff. It was they who gave Wright his one opportunity to make a major statement on what a skyscraper should be. The Price Tower, based on the 1925 Saint Marks Tower project for William Norman Guthrie, stands like a tall tree in the rolling hills of eastern Oklahoma. The superstructure is like that of an ever-green, with a tap root holding a central trunk (elevator and electrical and ventilation facilities) and the floors reaching out like branches. The building is constructed of reinforced concrete with cantilevered floors, copper louvers, copper-faced parapets, and gold-tinted glass exterior. Construction began November 10, 1953, and was completed February 9, 1956.

The building is planned on a 2-foot 6-inch equilateral parallelogram module (e.g., 2 feet, 6 inches across, or 2 feet, 10 and 5/8 inches to the side). Its nineteen floors are seventeen of tower and two of base (with wings extending northeast), plus radio

Night photograph from northwest

Plan of typical office floor with dwelling space

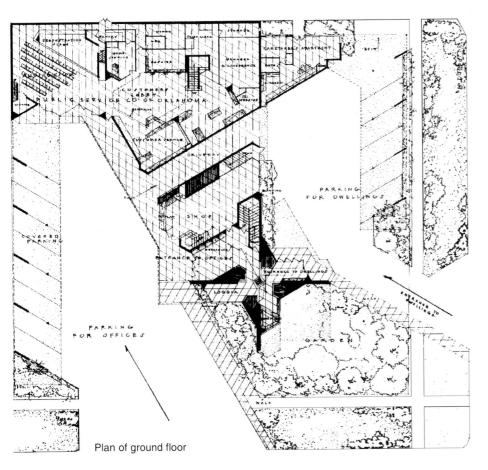

Plan of ground floor

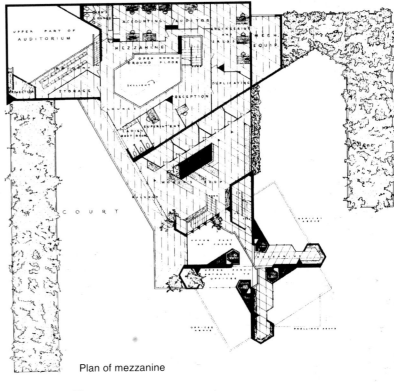

Plan of mezzanine

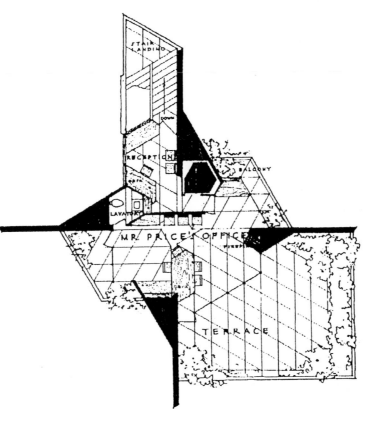

Plan of seventeenth (top) floor

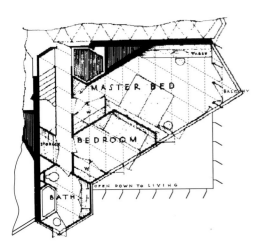

Plan of bedroom level over dwelling space

antenna spire, and contain both offices and apartments in its 37,000 square feet of interior floor space. The larger plan of the tower shows a square overlaid on a pinwheel. The southwest quadrant, however, is itself a rectangle nestled into the pinwheel; this contains eight two-story apartments. The sixteenth floor has a buffet and kitchen with outside terraces including planting areas. The seventeenth floor has a small central office space with a Wright-signed mural plus the living room of the top apartment. Above is the top floor of this apartment and a conference room. The nineteenth floor is not a complete quadrant, but had Mr. Price's own office with a Wright mural and outdoor roof gardens.

Construction was by Haskell Culwell, who built the Arizona Price house (S.378) and Beth Sholom Synagogue (S.373). Electrical and mechanical engineering was by Mendel Glickman, who took his summers from teaching at the University of Oklahoma to work with Taliesin. W. Kelly Oliver did lighting layouts and installed the lighting in the model of the tower that was displayed at Taliesin. This structure has been designated by the American Institute of Architects as one of seventeen American buildings designed by Frank Lloyd Wright to be retained as an example of his architectural contribution to American culture. The Price company was founded in 1921 as a pipeline construction company. This was sold out, and the building purchased, by the Phillips Petroleum Company in 1981–82. In 1983, the tower won the Amerian Institute of Architects 25 Year Award.

Anderton Court Shops

Stairwell

S.356   T.5032
Anderton Court Shops (1952), for Nina Anderton
Beverly Hills, California
Northside galleries extended beyond Wright's protective cantilevers

This group of shops in one building is located in the fashionable downtown section of Beverly Hills on Rodeo Drive. Entrance to all shops is off a ramp that winds its way upwards, in diamond-shaped parallelograms, around a central open well. Four shops were envisioned, with the top space an apartment. Joseph Fabris supervised construction.

The fascia of the third, top, level reveals what should be obvious below; the 8-foot display windows of the north side galleries' extend beyond Wright's nicely proportioned, setback arrangement. Wright showed a clear facade in his plans and was never offered any signs for approval. In more recent years, under management of Petersen Publishing Company, much of this has been cleaned up.

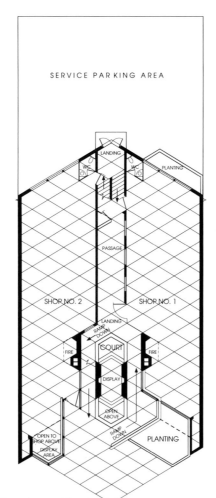

Plan of ground level

Plan of intermediate level

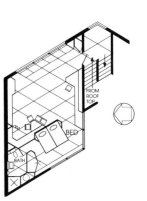

Plan of penthouse

S.357 T.5220
Louis **Marden** Residence (1952)
McLean, Virginia

Louis Marden was an editor with
National Geographic magazine when
he went to Wright for a house design.
Wright wanted his son Robert
Llewellyn to have the site, but no trade
could be arranged, and so the architect gave both his son and Marden
hemicycles. Marden's is in concrete
block and wood and overlooks the
Potomac River from a densely
wooded, steep hillside site.

   The initial plan was derived from a
mirror image of the Pearce residence
(S.320), which called for an opening to
a terrace at the back side of the living
area. The terrace was abandoned,
however, because the site was too
steep, though it would have worked at
Robert Llewellyn's site. Only a row of
transom-level windows pierces that
wall; consequently the living room is
unusually dark except in the morning.
Tom Casey did the working drawings.

Marden Residence

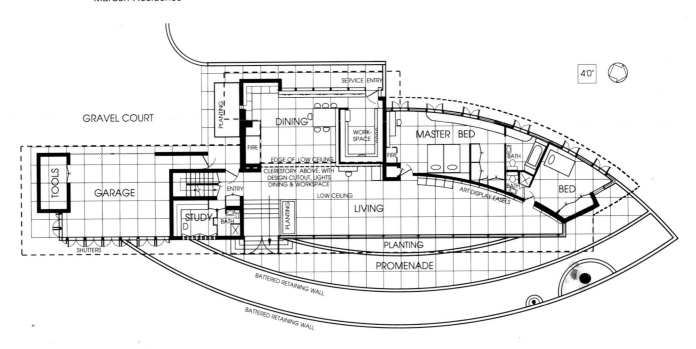

Elizabeth and Robert **Llewellyn
Wright** Residence (1953)
Bethesda, Maryland

Wright's sixth child by his first wife
was known by his middle name,
though he always signed his name
Robert L. Wright. Llewellyn noted
particularly that his father designed a
magnificent house with swimming pool
but when he approached his father
and said a Usonian design would do,
the elder Wright revised the plan to fit
the budget, reducing 86 feet to 65 feet
(the George Lewis house, S.359,
corner to corner measurement is 75
feet).

A two-story hemicycle, this
concrete-block structure is wood-faced
at the second story, where a balcony
continues the hemicircular line. An
elaborate article in *House Beautiful*
(November 1955) shows a plan that is
not accurate, overemphasizing the
garden terrace and cantilevered porch.
The mushroom form on which the
original was to have been built would
have cost as much by itself as did the
final house.

The design that was executed
features a convex private facade and
thus may be seen as a development of
the Curtis Meyer (S.297) plan, with the
circular workspace relocated from the
end to just off center, and the (unbuilt)
carport jutting to the side. While it was
standard practice to place the interior
surface of exterior masonry on the
grid line, a practice observed here, the
unit system for a hemicycle creates
unique dimensional problems. Most
often, Wright specified an angular
dimension in some multiple of 15
degrees, occasionally half that. Here
the grid lines are at 6.9 degrees, but
this is not the specification. Rather, the
unit is 6 feet, or four and a half concrete blocks, on the line at the radius
for the wall that is the public facade.
This 72-inch unit is also twice the
spacing between radius lines. Lloyd
Wright landscaped the grounds in
1960. Usually in such two-story structures, gravity heat was used downstairs, baseboard heat upstairs, but
here air heat is used throughout. The
plans and working drawings were done
by John H. Howe and Curtis Besinger.

Llewellyn Wright Residence, end view

Private facade

View from the ravine, showing
cantilevered porch

Gallery at upper level

Living room from dining area

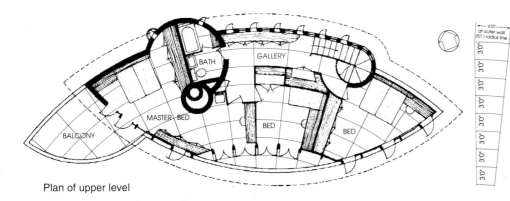

Plan of upper level

Master bedroom

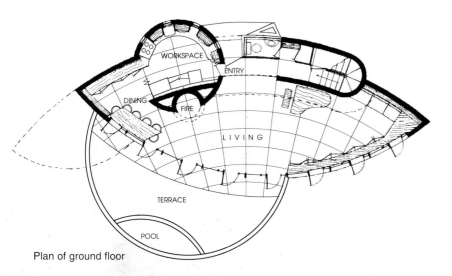

Plan of ground floor

Public facade of George Lewis Residence

S.359   T.5207
Clifton and George **Lewis**
Residence, Spring House (1952)
Tallahassee, Florida

The lower story of this two-story hemi-cycle is concrete block, the upper, wood sheathed. The living room rises two stories. The design is a further development of the Llewellyn Wright house (S.358), with more glazing at the upper level of the public facade and a full two-story glazing of the private facade. Original sketches show a house in stone, with upper-level porches at the extremities; this was simplified to block compounded of

Ocala limestone, crushed, and mixed in with the concrete to create an integral sand-yellow color. Supervision was by Nils Schweizer.

Political activists all their lives in a conservative region, George and Clifton Lewis now find themselves and their home threatened from new sources. The house is seriously encroached upon by development "uphill." A pond created for a sub-division could collapse into the Lewis property. Construction has already dried up the spring, the initial reason for the Lewis's choosing this site. Like many other original clients of Usonian era homes, they are seeking a suit-able, possibly public, use for Spring House, Wright's only built domestic design in Florida.

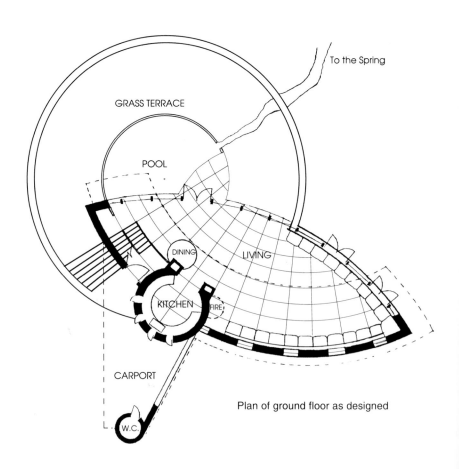

Plan of ground floor as designed

384

Private facade of the George Lewis house

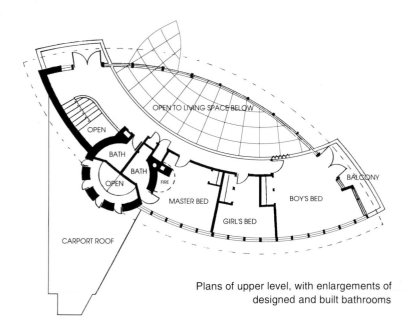

Plans of upper level, with enlargements of
designed and built bathrooms

OPEN TO LIVING SPACE BELOW

OPEN

BATH

BATH

OPEN

FIRE

MASTER BED

GIRL'S BED

BOY'S BED

BALCONY

CARPORT ROOF

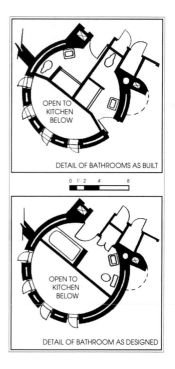

OPEN TO
KITCHEN
BELOW

DETAIL OF BATHROOMS AS BUILT

0 1 2   4'   8'

OPEN TO
KITCHEN
BELOW

DETAIL OF BATHROOM AS DESIGNED

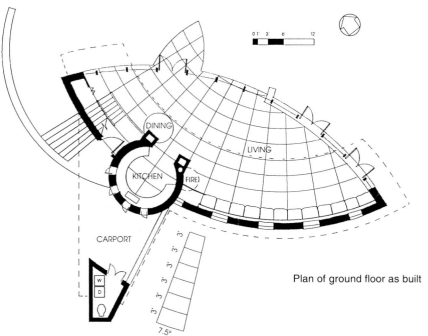

Plan of ground floor as built

0 1' 3'   6'   12'

DINING

LIVING

KITCHEN   FIRE

CARPORT

3'
3'
3'
3'
3'
3'

W
D

7.5°

Living room, view through the windowall

Cooke Residence at night

S.360 T.5219
Andrew B. and Maude **Cooke**
Residence (1953)
Virginia Beach, Virginia
Air conditioning installed and restored
in 1980s

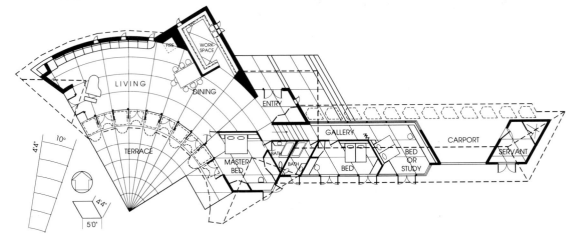

Andrew and Maude Cooke asked for a second, cheaper, design when they saw the plans for this work. Eventually, however, and without Taliesin's knowledge, they built the first design, exactly to specification, completing it in 1959.

The design is a hemicircular version of the Anthony house (S.315), with living room, workspace, and master bedroom all within the basic hemicycle, additional bedrooms in the wing. The points from which the concentric circles of the inner and outer walls of the main living area were drawn are evident in the wedge segments of the patio floor. The module is 10 degrees wide by 5 feet deep. The open space in the living room spans 70 feet; Maude entertained large groups and wanted a suitably commodious living room.

The brick is baked from clay imported from West Virginia, whose color blends with the sand of Crystal Lake, next to which the house stands. It is capped by a copper roof whose cantilevering is nothing short of astonishing. The roof is assembled from 10-degree wide segments which are

much like the stones in a Roman arch, unable to move once the keystone is in place. Here they are anchored at the sides and rear by masonry, and there is no support at the windowall other than the thin, wood mullions.

John H. Howe drew all the plans for this house with its unique blend of two unit systems; circular segments in the 90-degree "wide" living room, 60–120-degree equilateral parallelograms, attached neatly to the final radius, for the quiet space. One side of the parallelogram mates its grid to every other concentric circle. Wright approved the plans without revision.

The house passed to new owners in the 1980s, and a program of restoration was quickly completed. Air conditioning was installed in the roof crawl space above the workspace. Wright called for a pool, flowing over walls to Crystal Lake, but this was not built. Plans now call for installation of a

sauna under the patio just above lake level.

Virginia Beach is in Tidewater country, an area from which red Tidewater cypress, Wright's favorite American-grown Usonian wood, used to come in plentiful supply. Around Auldbrass Plantation (S.261–S.264),

this would be called low country. There is also yellow Tidewater cypress. The color refers to the water in which the trees grow rather than the color of the wood; fresh-cut cypress is usually as white as white pine.

Living room

Boomer Residence north (private) facade

Living room

Workspace

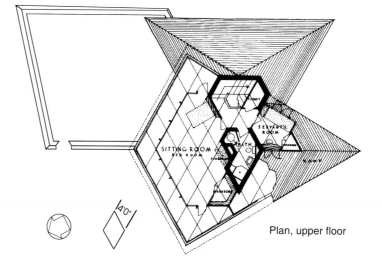

Plan, upper floor

S.361   T.5302
Jorgine **Boomer** Residence (1953)
Phoenix, Arizona

This is a house for a single person, though separate servant's and chauffeur's quarters could make it a family dwelling. It is virtually identical to a design for George Clark for seaside Carmel in 1951, although rotated 180 degrees to turn its back to the desert sun. It is compacted into two stories around a cental chimney flue. Desert masonry construction is employed with some horizontal wood sheathing, notably in the bedroom balcony, all set on an equilateral parallelogram grid.

Miss Boomer was a member of the Dupont family. She donated the building to the Phoenix Art Museum, but it was not suitable to their collections. Lucille Kinter, whose husband had died in the fifties, acquired the property in 1963. As of the early nineties, she had lived in the house three times as long as the original client.

Master bedroom (second level) of the Boomer house

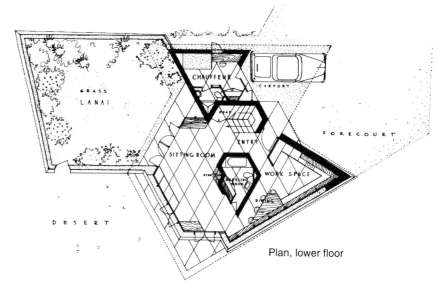

Plan, lower floor

Dobkins Residence

S.362 T.5407
John J. and Syd **Dobkins**
Residence (1953)
Canton, Ohio

The dominant feature of the Dobkins house is the glass facade of the living room, which denies the rectangle in plan and in surface; its module is an equilateral triangle (unit side of 4 feet). The plan is otherwise in-line, with workspace behind the fireplace. Horizontal mortar is deeply raked, though it is not colored to match the deep red brick. Roofing of terne metal plate painted blue-green with Duco enamel was Wright's means of bridging building to the sky above, at a cost much less than copper. Plans were drawn by Allen Lape Davison. Allan J. Gelbin acted both as Taliesin's supervisor of construction and the Dobkins' general contractor for the typical salary of $50 per week, plus room and board. The house was built in about nine months in 1954. The residence is located near the Feiman (S.371) and Rubin (S.343) houses, which were also supervised by Gelbin.

Living room

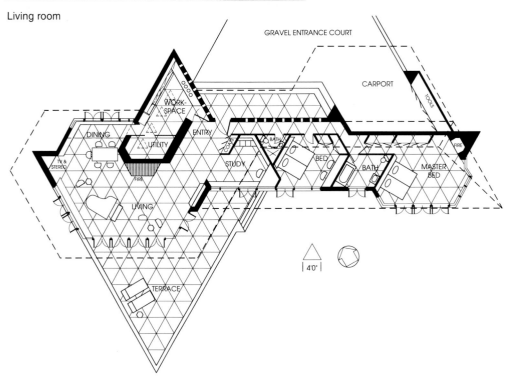

S.363 T.5421

Harold Price, Jr., Residence,
Hillside (1953)
Bartlesville, Oklahoma
Playroom added by William Wesley
Peters

Harold Price, Jr., is the son of Harold
Price, Sr., who commissioned the
Price Company Tower (S.355). Hillside
is a large **L** plan, with a two-story living
room. A balcony off the master bedroom overlooks this space. There is a
separate, formal dining room and,
adjacent to it perhaps Wright's largest
workspace. A hipped roof blends
house and sky. The house went
through considerable revision, and the
built plan is dated August 1954.

There has been an addition, a
playroom by William Wesley Peters,
vice-president of the Frank Lloyd
Wright Foundation at that time. From
original playroom to terrace doors is
114 feet of interior space; the unit
module is a 3-foot square.

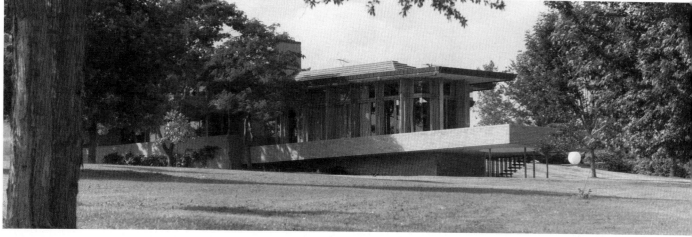

Hillside

Living room

Living room from balcony

Accordion screen

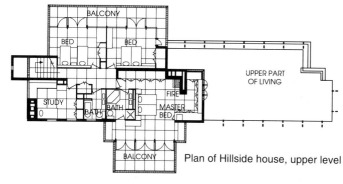

Plan of Hillside house, ground level

Plan of Hillside house, upper level

Goddard Residence

S.364   T.5317
Lewis H. **Goddard** Residence
(1953)
Plymouth, Michigan
Damage to bricks in walls, particularly
the north retaining wall, repaired

Goddard was a friend of Carl Wall and
saw that house (S.281) during its
construction. He purchased several
acres adjacent to the Wall house and
went to Wright for plans.

If the living room were half its size,
the plan, on a 4-foot-square unit
module, could be called a simple **T**.
The living-dining space is lower than
the entry, which is at grade level.
Kitchen and laundry are to one side of
the entry, still in the head of the T, as is
the furnace; there is no utilities basement. There are five bedrooms off a
long tunnel gallery, served by two
bathrooms. This gallery is extended to
the side with a recreation room, then
carport. Philippine mahogany gives a
warm glow to the interior.

Freezing and thawing of brick in
the winter before construction went
unnoticed; as the damage took many
years to become apparent, considerable weakening of the structure
occurred. This was a serious problem
with the north retaining wall below the
living room.

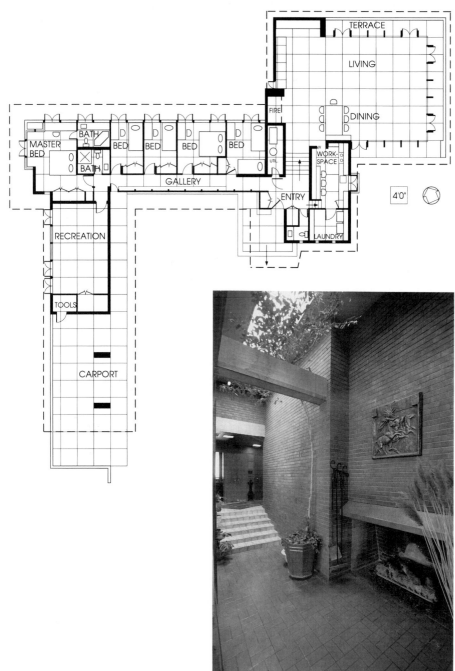

Entry steps to living room and fireplace

S.365   T.5303
Louis Penfield Residence (1953)
Willoughby Hills, Ohio
Repair of exterior paneling begun in
early 1990s

Upon receiving the plans for his house,
Mr. Penfield found it necessary to write
back to Taliesin: "Mr. Wright, I think
there is something I forgot to tell you. I
am 6 feet 8 inches tall." Wright's
standard 13-inch Usonian vertical unit,
which with baseboard gives a 6 foot 8
inch ceiling, was modified to achieve 8
foot bedroom ceilings.

Mr. Penfield's first house by Wright
is concrete block and wood with
cemesto board paneling. The structural
system, then, is the same as that of
the Carlson (S.326) and Welbie L.
Fuller (S.347) houses. Sleeping
quarters are over kitchen facilities. The
two-story living room looks through a
wooded hillside to the Chagrin River in
the valley below and cliffs beyond.

This design as well as that of the
Bachman-Wilson (S.366) and Boulter
(S.379) houses and Turkel Usonian
Automatic (S.388) are all variations on
a two-story in-line theme developed
from two projects, the first for George
Bliss McCallum in 1938 and the
second for Frank A. Rentz in 1939.
From springtime floods, world-noted
masonry specialist Penfield has
gathered stone, intended for the

building of Wright's second house
design for him. It is sited southeast of
the present structure, with construction
planned by Paul Penfield, Louis's son.
This second design features air floor
heating and air conditioning, whereas
the 1953 structure has standard
gravity heating.

Much work to repair exterior
panels, which deteriorated in the
severe winter climate, remains to be
done by the new owner, Penfield's son.

Penfield Residence, private facade

Living room corner

Stair at entry

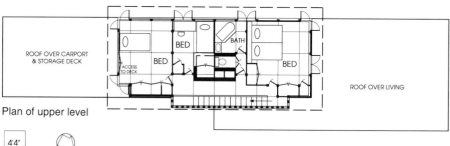

ROOF OVER CARPORT
& STORAGE DECK

ACCESS TO DECK

BED   BED   BATH   BED

ROOF OVER LIVING

Plan of upper level

4'4"

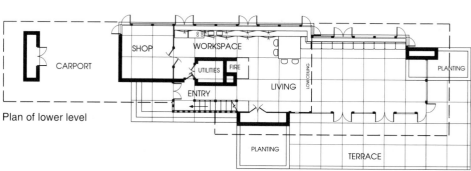

CARPORT

SHOP   WORKSPACE

UTILITIES   FIRE

ENTRY   LIVING   LOW CEILING

PLANTING

PLANTING   TERRACE

Plan of lower level

Wilson Residence, public facade

Wilson Residence, private facade

S.366   T.5402
Gloria Bachman and Abraham
Wilson (Bachman-Wilson)
Residence (1954)
Millstone, New Jersey
Addition north of workspace, now
converted to architectural offices after
restoration of main structure in the
1980s

The original contact with Mr. Wright
was apparently through Mrs.
Bachman's brother. Gloria Bachman,
Wilson's wife, saw her son Marvin off
to Taliesin with a group from
Carnegie-Mellon, including Allan
Gelbin. Marvin was killed in an auto
accident, there was a falling out with
Taliesin, and final work was unsupervised; Morton Delson oversaw early
stages of construction.

Perhaps the idea for this house
dates back specifically to a 1941
project for the Ellinwood family, and
generically to the 1938 McCallum
project. Like the Penfield house
(S.365), it is concrete block and wood
(mahogany, though cypress was specified) with a two-story living room and
sleeping quarters over the kitchen. A
small balcony like those in the Penfield
and Turkel (S.388) houses overlooks
the living room. The recessed entry
and a second balcony opening into the
yard from the master bedroom reveals
this design to be the progenitor of the
second of the two later buildings; the
south end of Turkel is a Usonian
Automatic block version of the Wilson
house.

Living room
(early 1970s)

The structure is angled 45 degrees
east of north on its over-an-acre lot,
which extends from the main road to
the river bank. It is set well back from
the river, however, to avoid possible
flooding; there is no basement and all
utilities are at ground level. The house
was added to in 1970, on the north.
These spaces have been turned
into offices for architect Lawrence
Tarantino, who has restored the building. Restoration required rebuilding
of the roof; the ceilings have been
kept in original wood paneling, but
the addition includes other materials,
providing obvious differentiation
between Wright and later work.

Plan of mezzanine

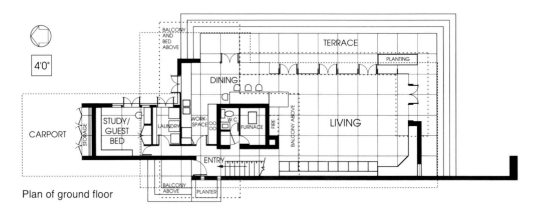

Plan of ground floor

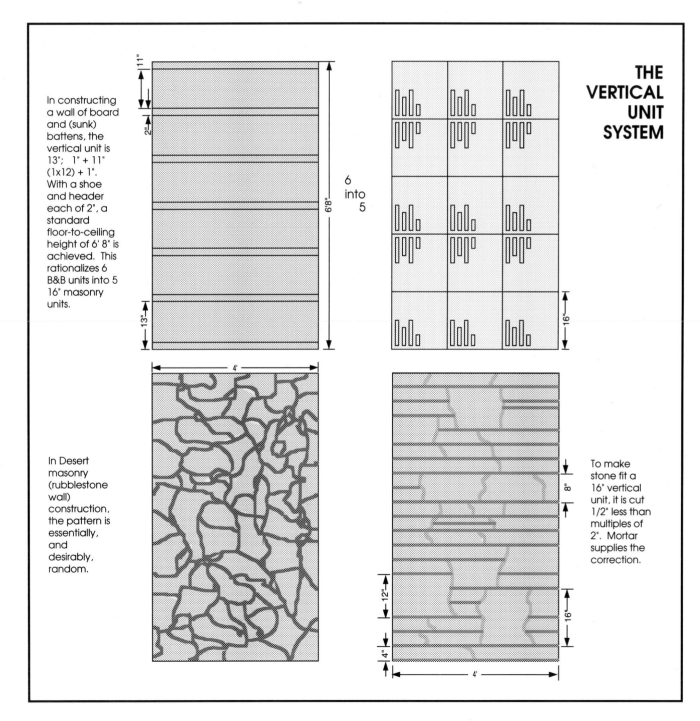

In constructing a wall of board and (sunk) battens, the vertical unit is 13"; 1" + 11" (1x12) + 1". With a shoe and header each of 2", a standard floor-to-ceiling height of 6' 8" is achieved. This rationalizes 6 B&B units into 5 16" masonry units.

THE VERTICAL UNIT SYSTEM

6 into 5

In Desert masonry (rubblestone wall) construction, the pattern is essentially, and desirably, random.

To make stone fit a 16" vertical unit, it is cut 1/2" less than multiples of 2". Mortar supplies the correction.

Southern exposure, public facade,
Frank Lloyd Wright Center at Taliesin

S.367   T.5619
Riverview Terrace Restaurant,
The Spring Green, for Willard H.
Keland, president, Wisconsin River
Development Corporation (1953)
Spring Green, Wisconsin
Now the Frank Lloyd Wright Center at
Taliesin

Perched on a hillside opposite Taliesin
and just above the left bank of the
Wisconsin River, this structure is the
only restaurant designed by Wright
that still stands today. In 1943, Wright
provided Glenn and Ruth Richardson
with a design for this site that included
an auto showroom and service areas
next to a restaurant at ground level,
with living quarters above. Nothing
came of this project, but a decade later
the idea was revived, but the second
time as only the Wisconsin River
Terrace Restaurant, raised to the level
of the previous living quarters for the
view.

Construction was begun in 1957 by
the Taliesin Fellowship, for whom
Wright called it the Taliesin Riverview
Terrace Restaurant. Halted on account
of Wright's death, the project, in a
modified form, was completed by the
Taliesin Associated Architects as the
first building in the Wisconsin River
Development Corporation's planned
resort adjacent to Taliesin. Steel
trusses were obtained from the flight
deck of the aircraft carrier *Ranger*.
Limestone, stucco, and various woods,
including red oak paneling, are used.
In 1993 the building was converted to
use as the Visitor Center for the
Taliesin buildings.

Riverview Terrace Restaurant, view of north facade across the Wisconsin River

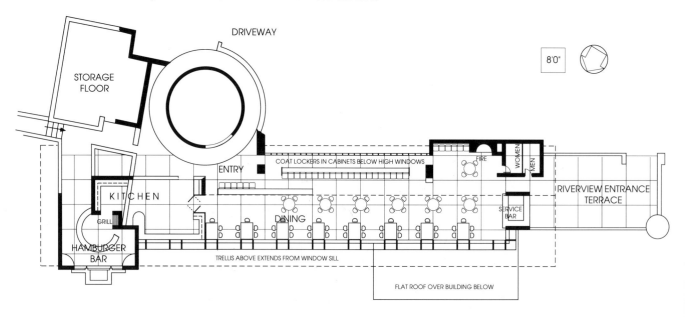

394

S.368 T.5417
Karen Johnson (Johnson-Keland)
Residence (1954)
Racine, Wisconsin
Greenhouse, playroom, and patio
added around the inner courtyard by
John H. Howe in 1961

Karen Johnson Boyd is the daughter of
H. F. Johnson, who built the Johnson
Wax Building (S.237), Heliolaboratory
(S.238), and Wingspread (S.239). Her
first husband, Willard H. Keland,
served as first president of the Wisconsin River Development Corporation,
which completed construction of the
Riverview Terrace Restaurant (S.367);
this house was originally listed in his
name. As the client-partner in whose
ownership the home now resides, it is
now listed in her name.

The various wings of this copper-
roofed structure create an atrium over
which a two-story section dominates,
guest bed and living rooms, with parquet floor upstairs, entry, hall, and
workspace directly below, adjacent the
north-facing living room. This inner
courtyard is, however, as much the
creation of John H. Howe as of Wright,
for it is the product of his playroom,
greenhouse, and patio fountain addi-

Karen Johnson Residence

tion. The usual pattern of master bedroom terminating the quiet space is
here reversed so that the original
children's playroom can have pride
of place with its own terrace. Brick
is used inside and out, while trim,
cabinetry, and other surfaces are
blonde Philippine mahogany. Built-in
cabinets around the living room walls,
plus ample use of board surfaces such
as at the balcony above the living
room, provide space for Mrs. Boyd, an
art dealer, to display paintings and
sculpture. The house has air conditioning and forced-air heating.

Entry

View from living room toward balcony

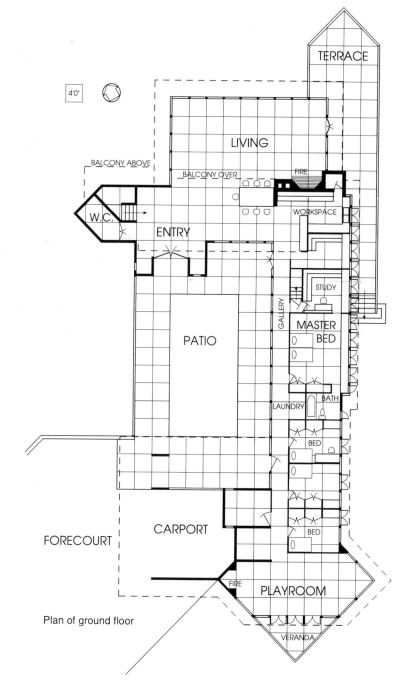

Plan of ground floor

S.369   T.5314
New York Usonian Exhibition House and
S.370   T.5314
Pavilion (1953)
New York, New York
Exhibition house disassembled; sold in parts to benefit the Frank Lloyd Wright Building Conservancy, March 1992

After opening in the Palazzo Strozzi, Florence, and touring Europe, the exhibit Sixty Years of Living Architecture came to New York City. It was housed in the Usonian Exhibition House, on the site where the Guggenheim Museum was begun three years later (S.400). The pavilion was built of pipe scaffolding to a module measuring 7 feet 8 inches by 6 feet 8 inches and covered alternately with layers of corrugated wire glass and 2-inch-thick Cemesto (cement and asbestos) board. Several Taliesin apprentices attached the very heavy Cemesto boards to Wright's specially designed clips, eventually gaining the respect and cooperation of union labor (about whom Wright quipped, "I wouldn't trade your whole . . . union for one of my apprentices"). Of these, Curtis Besinger was the senior apprentice in charge, and John Geiger and Morton Delson stayed on to run the show after the group of seventeen, who slept five to a room in the Croydon Hotel, had repaired the models.

The house, facing into the northeast corner of the pavilion, was designed on a 4-foot square. Chairs for the house were built by Vent-O-

Photograph by Berenice Abbott, courtesy of Scott Elliott of the Kelmscott Gallery

Usonian Exhibition House

Rama. Oak plywood was provided by U.S. Plywood. A Steinway Fiftieth Anniversary piano was supplied free of charge. The Colorado Carnation Society donated so many fresh flowers daily that some had to be given away to visitors. Wright intended for the house to be auctioned and moved at the close of the exhibition, but the winning bidder's site was in a town with painted colonial two-story requirements. David Henken, supervisor of the house and pavilion construction, stored parts in Pleasantville, New York. The building was purchased at a second auction from WNET in New York by Tom Monaghan for $117,500. A third auction sold the parts for $7,850. (See two other houses like the Usonian Exhibition House, Feiman, S.371, and Trier, S.398.)

Plan of house and adjacent pavilion

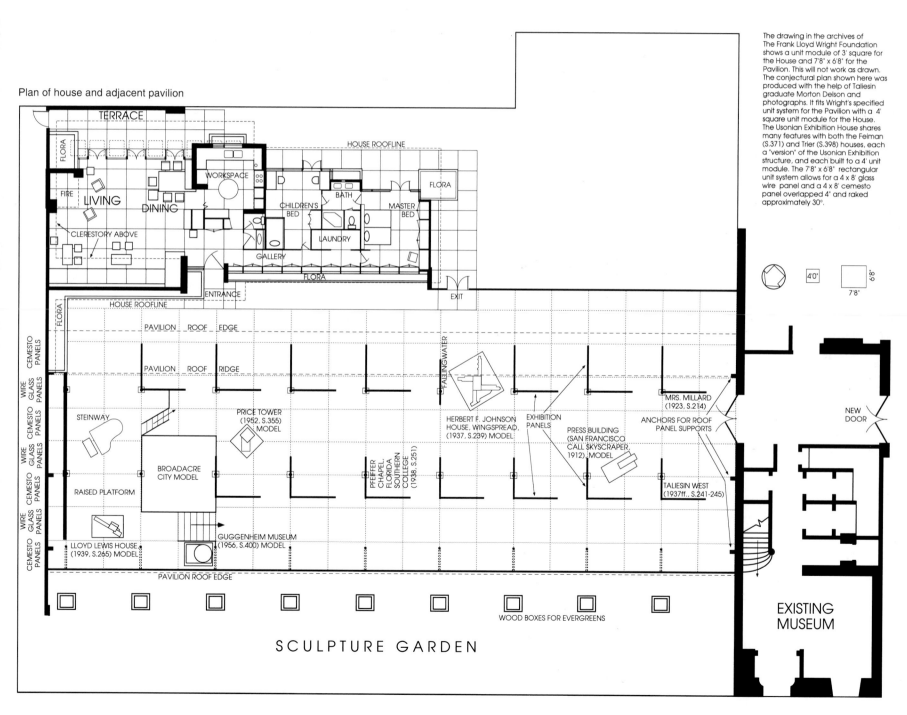

The drawing in the archives of The Frank Lloyd Wright Foundation shows a unit module of 3' square for the House and 7'8" x 6'8" for the Pavilion. This will not work as drawn. The conjectural plan shown here was produced with the help of Taliesin graduate Morton Delson and photographs. It fits Wright's specified unit system for the Pavilion with a 4' square unit module for the House. The Usonian Exhibition House shares many features with both the Feiman (S.371) and Trier (S.398) houses, each a "version" of the Usonian Exhibition structure, and each built to a 4' unit module. The 7'8" x 6'8" rectangular unit system allows for a 4 x 8' glass wire panel and a 4 x 8' cemesto panel overlapped 4" and raked approximately 30°.

4'0"

7'8"   6'8"

TERRACE

FLORA

FIRE

LIVING   DINING   WORKSPACE

HOUSE ROOFLINE

FLORA

BATH

CHILDREN'S BED

MASTER BED

CLERESTORY ABOVE

LAUNDRY

GALLERY

FLORA

ENTRANCE

EXIT

HOUSE ROOFLINE

FLORA

PAVILION   ROOF   EDGE

PAVILION   ROOF   RIDGE

CEMESTO PANELS

WIRE GLASS PANELS

CEMESTO PANELS

WIRE GLASS PANELS

CEMESTO PANELS

WIRE GLASS PANELS

CEMESTO PANELS

STEINWAY

PRICE TOWER (1952, S.355) MODEL

FALLINGWATER

Herbert F. Johnson HOUSE, WINGSPREAD, (1937, S.239) MODEL

EXHIBITION PANELS

MRS. MILLARD (1923, S.214)

ANCHORS FOR ROOF PANEL SUPPORTS

NEW DOOR

BROADACRE CITY MODEL

PFEIFFER CHAPEL, FLORIDA SOUTHERN COLLEGE (1938, S.251)

PRESS BUILDING (SAN FRANCISCO CALL SKYSCRAPER, 1912) MODEL

RAISED PLATFORM

TALIESIN WEST (1937ff., S.241-245)

LLOYD LEWIS HOUSE (1939, S.265) MODEL

GUGGENHEIM MUSEUM (1956, S.400) MODEL

PAVILION ROOF EDGE

WOOD BOXES FOR EVERGREENS

EXISTING MUSEUM

SCULPTURE GARDEN

S.371 T.5408
Alice and Ellis A. **Feiman**
Residence (1954)
Canton, Ohio

Mrs. Alice Feiman and Mrs. Jeanne Rubin are sisters; the Rubin (S.343) house was built by the time the Feimans decided they wanted a Wright-designed home. This wood-trimmed, brick structure is based on the 1953 Usonian Exhibition House (S.369). The Feimans thought they had bought the Exhibition House itself and that it would be carted to Ohio and reassembled.

The plan, though a near copy of the Exhibition House at the living-work-space-entry area, has been enlarged in the bedroom wing (see Trier, S.398). It is a basic in-line type drawn to a 4-foot-square unit module, rather than the 3-foot unit of the Exhibition House. The roof skylight overhang provides summer shade yet has sufficient openness to admit winter light to the living room; the ceiling is lower than in the New York design for this south-facing room, even as the clerestory windows remain unusually tall. A special brick with face dimensions of 11 3/8 x 2 1/4 inches required considerable altering of the brickwork to fit the 4-foot unit, such as in the perforations of the privacy wall, transom-level rear wall of the living room, and the piers supporting the carport. Often one finds 2 to 4-inch shim bricks used to correct a house designed for standard brick. The multi-vehicle carport is not part of

Feiman Residence

the New York design, but specific to this Ohio house.

Counter tops and bathroom sinks are white. Philippine mahogany is used throughout where wood is called for; the ceiling is composed of halved 4-by-8-foot panels, with the grain rotated in adjacent panels to create a pattern. Allan J. Gelbin acted as general contractor as well as construction supervisor during the eight-month period in 1954–55 when the home was built.

Living room

Entry

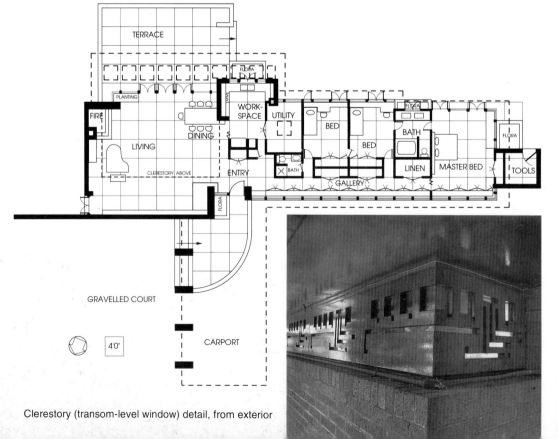

Clerestory (transom-level window) detail, from exterior

S.372   T.5409
Dr. Maurice and Margaret Greenberg Residence (1954)
Dousman, Wisconsin

The Greenberg living room and balcony cantilever out above the treetops of the valley below. Originally designed, like Taliesin, in native stone, it was finally built in brick, concrete, and wood to save on costs.

The plan, like that of the Lamberson house (S.305), is composed on three grids of 4-foot squares. The ancillary services wing is at a 60-degree angle to the living room and the quiet wing at a 30 degree angle, requiring two pivot points to interlock the unit systems. The bedroom wing remains unfinished, and an extension of the carport wing has not been built. Brick sufficient for the entire project was made at the time of original construction.

Of particular interest are the three-dimensional cut-outs for the windows, an idea Wright also employed in the Christian (S.375) and Hoffman (S.390) houses.

Greenberg Residence, approach

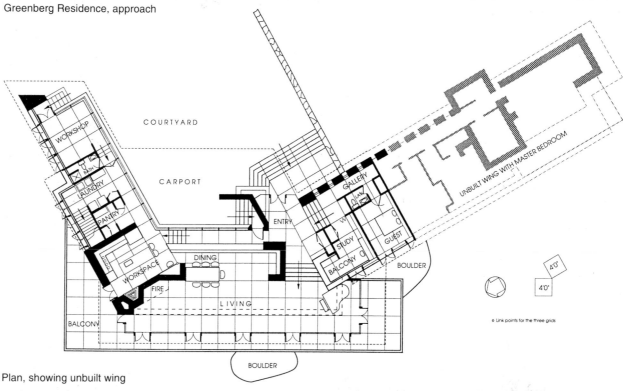

Plan, showing unbuilt wing

Greenberg Residence from below the cantilever

Beth Sholom Synagogue

Detail of Menorahs on ridge

S.373   T.5313
Beth Sholom Synagogue (1954)
Elkins Park, Pennsylvania

Wright gave Rabbi Mortimer J. Cohen credit on the plans as co-designer because of the integration of Jewish symbolism with architectural expression, achieved by cooperation of the two, both men of high principle. Throughout, a hexagon that tends toward an equilateral triangle infuses every element of design. The main sanctuary is suspended from a 160-ton steel tripod frame, each beam 117 feet long, that allows the great hall of the synagogue, with 1,030 seats, complete freedom from internal supports. A double layer of translucent panels, 2,100 square feet of blasted white corrugated wire glass outside and 2,000 square feet of reinforced cream white corrugated fiberglass inside, with a 5-inch air space, transmits soft light to the interior and provides insulation. At night, artificial interior light makes the whole building glow, expressing the idea of the Torah as light, and Mt. Sinai as the mount of light. Aluminum cover strips bind glass to plastic. Aluminum

Great hall for the congregation (decorated for a wedding)

Sisterhood Sanctuary

shells also hold poured concrete. Wood is an oiled walnut stained brown or tan. The separate Sisterhood Sanctuary below the great hall seats 250.

The Arks that hold the Torahs of both sanctuaries incorporate Wrightian design elements. The perforated panels of the Sisterhood Ark suggest late Wright, but the magnificent chandelier that hangs above the congregation, while representing characteristics of God as defined by the Jewish mystics, Kabbalists, reveals Wright returning to Prairie art glass for a traditional statement. The three ridges of the synagogue have abstract representations of seven-branched Menorahs; the entry canopy geometrically

represents the hands of the rabbi joined to pronounce a benediction.

Haskell Culwell, who built the Price Tower, was the general contractor. The synagogue was dedicated on September 20, 1959. This structure has been designated by the American Institute of Architects as one of seventeen American buildings designed by Frank Lloyd Wright to be retained as an example of his architectural contribution to American culture. A booklet explaining the design of the building, particularly the symbolism of architectural elements, is also available.

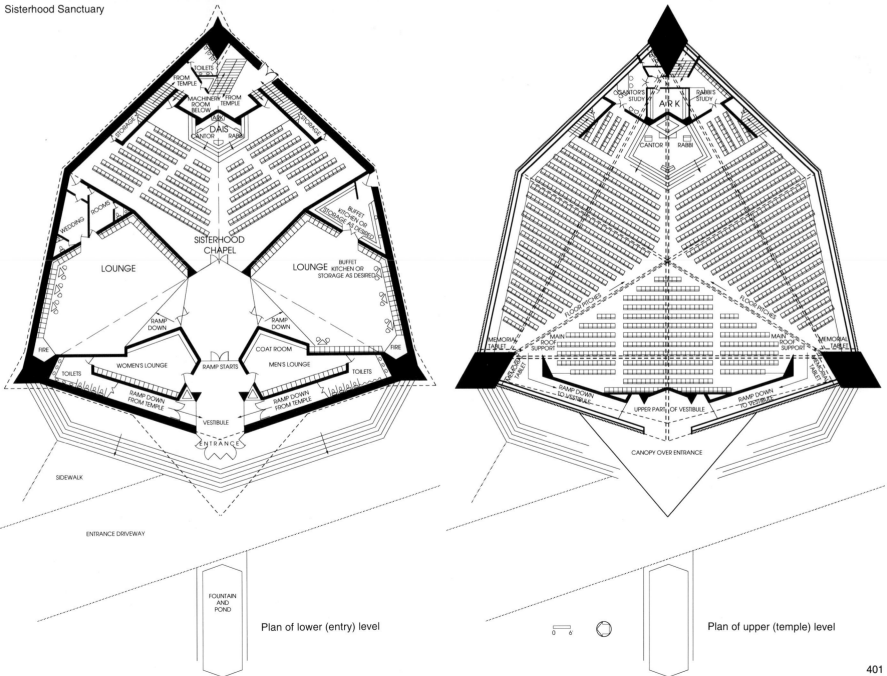

Plan of lower (entry) level

Plan of upper (temple) level

Arnold Residence, living room facade

S.374 T.5401
E. Clarke **Arnold** Residence (1954)
Columbus, Wisconsin
Wing added by John H. Howe in 1959

The Arnold residence is built in native stone from the Sauk City area of Wisconsin, less than 40 miles west of Columbus and only 20 miles from Spring Green. Arnold rejected a 60-degree plan, which Wright then submitted to William Thaxton (S.384). Wright

"straightened it out" to two wings at 120 degrees, on a 60–120-degree equilateral parallelogram module with a 4-foot side. This became a **Y** in 1959 with the addition of a wing by John H. Howe. Typically, the living room is one wing, the bedrooms the other, with the workspace at their juncture. The Allen Friedman house (S.403) is a brick version of this Columbus structure. John Howe notes that this design is based on the principle of the solar hemicycle.

S.375 T.5405
John E. and Catherine **Christian** Residence, Samara (1954)
West Lafayette, Indiana

When the Christians first asked Wright in 1951, "Will you do us a house?" the response was, "How much money have you got?" At Wright's request, Mrs. Christian prepared a booklet of their requirements. They needed to be able to entertain fifty students at one time; Wright understood, telegraphing back that he had "never seen a living room too large." Sixty people can be entertained in the 24-by-24-foot room, for the stairs to one side and those below built-in seats on the other can be used for additional seating. The design process took more than usually long. Christian, author of *Quantitative Pharmaceutical Chemistry* and a professor at Purdue University, did not see the plans until New Year's day, 1955; he and Catherine moved into the house in the fall of 1956.

Throughout, the Christians consulted with the Mossbergs (S.302), whose home was completed by the time they approached Wright. The Christians are "quiet people," so Wright told them they were to have a quiet house, built to a square module, while the Davises (S.324), more extrovert, had been given triangles. Samara is the "winged seed" of the pine tree, and this is the motif cut in the three-dimensional clerestory windows and the stands for the TV dinner tables. The windows use a double-cut stencil; the pattern is cut in boards placed on the inside and the outside, with the glass in between; as one moves around the room, the "winged seed" opens and closes. This single-story brick (stone was Wright's first choice) and Philippine mahogany house sits on a small hill near Purdue Stadium. While the vertical mortar joints are not colored to match the brick, though they are flush with the finish brick surface, all other materials and methods of construction are to Wright's most exacting standards, from mitred corner windows to piano hinges. The plan includes a walled garden on the northeast, a southeast living room, and a central workspace under a clerestory. The walled garden, off the master bedroom, is the only part of this 4-foot-square unit structure to employ a circular segment. The quiet wing has a

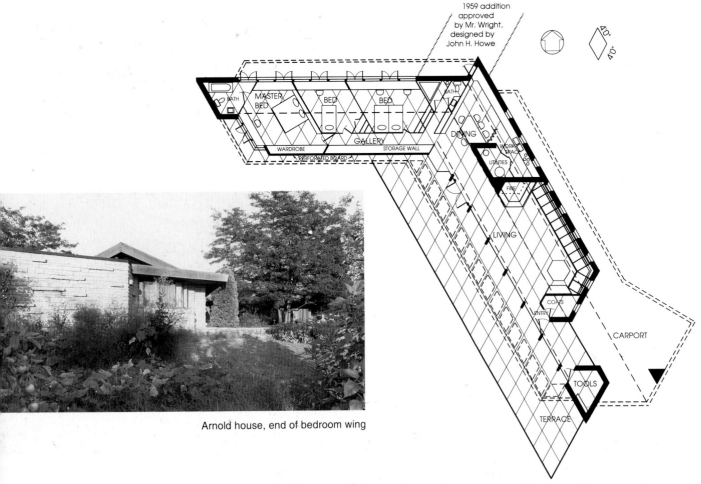

1959 addition approved by Mr. Wright, designed by John H. Howe

Arnold house, end of bedroom wing

Samara before copper fascia

Terrace, before copper fascia

Living room, view from dining area

Living room, view to fireplace

Floor plan labels: TOOLS, BRICK DRIVEWAY, GUEST BED, BATH 2, NURSERY, MASTER BED, GRASS-COVERED LANAI, BATH 1, LAUNDRY, WORKSPACE, UTIL, DINING, FIRE, LIVING, TERRACE, 4'0"

central gallery, with rooms off both sides and the end.

To control the sun's heat, the southeast side of the living room has a 6-foot overhang, while the northeast side has an 8-foot trellis plus a 4-foot covered overhang. In winter, the low-hanging sun reaches in to the fireplace, but in summer no direct sunlight enters. Gravity heat is used in a system considerably more sophisticated than that of the first Usonian houses. The half-inch copper pipes embedded in the floor are 6 inches apart, except at the perimeter windowalls, where

they are 3 inches apart to double the heating capacity. Several exterior sensors control the rate of heat generation. Copper fascia was called for and was finally added in 1991. John deKoven Hill designed the original fabric as well as a 1983 refurbishing.

Clerestory detail

Lanai, copper fascia in place

S.376　T.5426
Louis B. **Fredrick** Residence (1954)
Barrington Hills, Illinois

The Fredrick house commands the top of a hill, nestling just below its crest. The roof line, instead of angling outward as it rises, recedes, to admit light to the living room oriented to the north. Mrs. Fredrick notes that the contractor's placement of the foundation, only a few degrees from Wright's designation, caused the light to shine much deeper into the living (activity) room than had been intended. Three bedrooms are lit by a clerestory on the inside of the gallery. A second gallery leads to a semidetached guest room or playroom. In the 4-foot unit, in-line plan the workspace is at the juncture of the living room and the bedroom wing. The plan is a derivation from, "improvement on" by Wright's standards, the unbuilt project for George Dlesk in Manistee, Michigan. The drawing presented here shows the playroom and the living room as built, but the remainder of the house "as designed" for Dlesk. Original working drawings remain the property of the client, with no copies in any archive.

Fredrick Residence

The Fredricks' meeting with their future architect was at the Blackstone Hotel, Chicago. Wright asked, "What are you doing now?" He meant, not "what is your employment" but "are you free" to go to New York City and see the Usonian Exhibition House (S.369). Had they seen not only the house but the attendant exhibition (S.370), they might have accepted Wright's first design, a Usonian Automatic, rather than a second-hand scheme. The house they erected in 1958 is built with fifty thousand tan-colored, Cranbrook buckskin range bricks, each 11 1/2

inches long, with concrete, wherever used, dyed tan. Only at a later time did these clients see the Parkwyn Village houses (S.298–S.301) and realize that Wright's block had beauty lacking in standard concrete block.

The study, with reverse roof verge

Plan of Fredrick Residence, bedroom wing based on 1955 project for George Dlesk

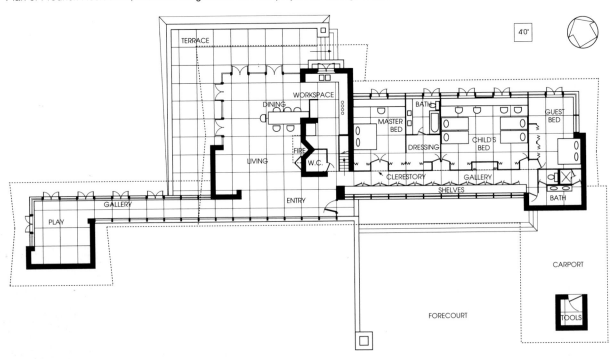

S.377 T.5410
I. N. **Hagan** Residence (1954)
Chalkhill, Pennsylvania
Fire damage fully repaired

Mr. Hagan was in the dairy business in Uniontown; Wright designed an ice cream company building for him, but it was never built. The house Wright created for him is one from which you can see well beyond Uniontown, into West Virginia, Maryland, and possibly Virginia. From just below Kentuk Knob, where to the east 3,213-foot-high Mt. Davis, the highest in the western Pennsylvania highlands, seems to be at eye level, the Hagan house appears to grow out of the hillside, its copper roof blending with the sky. This is where the master bedroom is located. At the opposite extremity, the living room is a ship's prow sailing the Pennsylvania highlands. The house is placed on its site so that, in the winter, sun flows across the living room, although in the summer, none comes in.

The floor stone came from Grantsville, Maryland, whereas the walls are sandstone, split, but not dressed; this allows them to become gray with weathering, like the red Tidewater cypress of the trim. Plate glass was used, though Wes Peters advised the Hagans to get Thermopane if they could afford it. Wright's public posture was that it was cheaper in the long run to have a little more heat in the winter to compensate for the loss through the glass than to pay for Thermopane. Privately, however, Wright did not like the fact that, once he made Thermopane popular, the manufacturer was able to market it without giving him any credit.

The plan was based on a 4-foot 6-inch unit, with standard 13-inch vertical unit. Although the module appears to be a hexagon, it is really an equila-

Hagan Residence

Workspace

Living room, view from fireplace

Living room, view toward fireplace

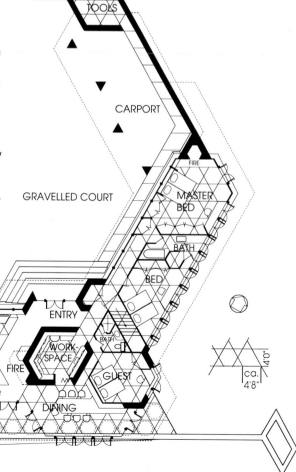

teral parallelogram (which would have been spaced to an altitude of 2 feet were it the design standard). Secondary rulings produce a dominant hexagon and subsidiary equilateral triangles, each one-sixth the area of the hexagon. None of this, however, is obvious, because the living and dining floors are covered with stone, the workspace with cork tile, and the remainder with carpet.

Particularly effective in this design is the workspace, which opens to the entry hall at one end, to the dining area at the other, and has a skylight. All the furniture is by Wright, and there is a screen by Eugene Masselink. John H. Howe did the preliminary drawings, Allen Lape Davison the working drawings. Fire damage has been repaired by the second owner, Peter Palumbo.

Master bedroom

Grandma House from the north

S.378　T.5421
Harold Price, Sr., Residence,
Grandma House (1954)
Paradise Valley, Arizona

This was a retirement home, called
Grandma House, for the elder Prices
(see the Price Company Tower, S.355;
see also S.363).

John H. Howe, who drew the
published perspective, noted that Mr.
Wright took great delight in the house
of which each detail was of concern
and over whose atrium he took great
care in his drawings. The central room,
which divides the plan into in-line
wings, is an atrium. Its roof is raised
above inverted pylon-like concrete
block masses by thin steel pipes,

creating a two-foot high clerestory to
admit fresh breezes. This same roof
provides shade from the desert sun
and shelter from flash thunderstorms,
yet its open skylight admits sun to play
on the water in the central fountain.
The ceiling is framed in steel channels,
major beams, with little steel **T**s in
between which are visible as a detail.
The murals on the atrium doors are by
Eugene Masselink. Common concrete
block is used throughout.

Construction—eight months from
plans to finished house—was by
Haskell Culwell. The survey was off by
10 feet, so one end had to be dug in,
the other required filling. The blue and
turquoise theme was matched to a ring
given by Wright to Charles Montooth,
the associate supervisor, after brown
columns and pyracantha orange detail
did not work. Thin partitions with a plywood core and surface were a refinement of board and batten. In 1956 the
children's play yard was altered into a
master bedroom.

View from southeast, showing pylon-supported atrium roof

Atrium of Price, Sr., Residence

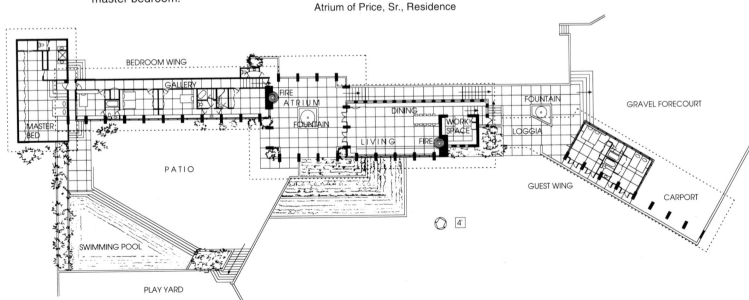

S.379 T.5403
Cedric G. and Patricia **Boulter Residence** (1954) and
S.379A T.5403
Addition (1958)
Cincinnati, Ohio
Carport enclosed

The Boulters were recipients of one of Wright's famous replies. When they wrote asking if he would design them a house, the architect responded "Dear Cedric Boulter, I will" followed by extensive blank space and, at the bottom, "Frank Lloyd Wright."

Lucius or Titus Quinctius Cincinnatus is a legendary Roman patriot of the fifth century B.C. The Society of Cincinnati was formed as a fraternal, patriotic, and nonpolitical organization in 1783 by officers of the Continental army. Losantville was founded in 1788 and was renamed after the Society of Cincinnati in 1790. It is the largest "German" town in America. All this is useful only as narrative leading to the point that Cedric Boulter was a Greek classics scholar.

The Boulter house is concrete block and Philippine mahogany stained Taliesin red; the stair treads, suspended from above, are African mahogany. The mullions in the glazed wall are load-supporting; Douglas fir is used as structural wood. This living room facade is the forerunner of that for Don Lovness (S.391); both were on John H. Howe's drafting tables. The Boulter, however, conceals a second floor to the rear, while Lovness is single story. Thus, the Boulter residence is a near copy of a design for Horace Sturtevant in Oakland, California. The Boulter is a few units longer, and eventually gained a guest bedroom addition beyond the carport. The related perspective drawings are interesting, the California house shown surrounded by evergreens, the Ohio one by hardwoods.

The closeness of this and other two-story rectilinear designs with interior full-length balcony to the solar hemicycle concept may be seen in two projects. Both were for Gibbons Gray Cornwell, the first a 1954 hemicycle (on the drafting boards at the same time as the Boulter drawings), and then a 1955 "straightened" version that was realized from it. Each, however,

Boulter Residence, south windowall, with addition (to the right)

had a circular stairway around ground-floor lavatory and utilities and upper floor mirror-image bathrooms.

As is the common practice in Wright houses, the module is marked out in the Taliesin red-colored concrete floor, here squares equal to three concrete blocks, or 4 feet, on a side. A balcony juts into the two-story-high living room from second-story bedrooms,

held up by stringers from the ceiling; its west extension becomes an exterior balcony. The terrace retaining wall is battered. A technique used in nearly all masonry work on Wright residences is apparent in the laying of the block; mortar in vertical joints is flush with the surface, while in horizontal joints it is

(Continues)

Dining area

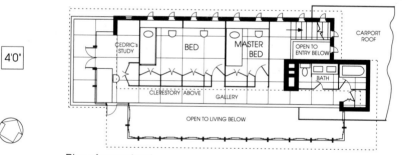

Plan of upper level

Plan of basement

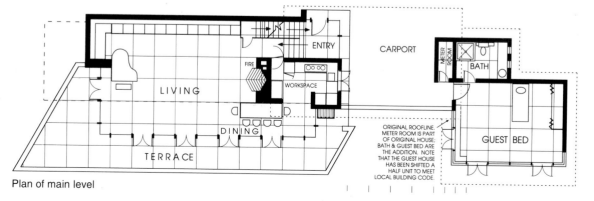

Plan of main level

(S.379 continued)

Living room

Public approach side with berm at main level. Addition is beyond carport

normally recessed. This emphasizes the horizontal nature of the structure. Gravity heating is used at the lower floor, baseboard heating above, though in winter the sun floods into the whole house. Furniture is either original or Wright's via Heritage Henredon. Artificial lighting is by exposed, sausage-shaped clear glass bulbs; they are expensive and last only a year.

Mrs. Boulter is one of two daughters of Henry J. Neils (S.314). Mr. Boulter did not meet Wright until February 1955, when things were at a standstill with the building commissioners. The master bedroom is actually 98 feet square, 2 short of building code requirements. The stairs are 4 feet wide from entry into living room (which is a quarter level down, setting the rear of the house into the hill), 2 feet, 6 inches wide up to the second level, again due to the code. There is an extra 8-inch block course

at both levels, not in Wright's plan, to satisfy the commissioners.

Construction was completed in April 1956. The addition to the house was designed by Wright and shows on the original plan as "future" construction; it reached beyond the property line. Benjamin Dombar, who supervised construction, altered the plan sufficiently to obtain approval from the local building commissioners in 1958. He is also responsible for steel in the roof and retaining wall of the main house.

In 1990, an addition (enclosure of the carport) was undertaken with refurbishing of the exterior.

S.380   T.5622
Hoffman Auto Showroom (1954)
for Maximilian Hoffman
New York, New York
Renovations by William Wesley Peters, Cornelia Brierly, and Morton Delson in 1980s

Hoffman's father was the Rolls-Royce dealer in Vienna. Max left when the Germans arrived. He took to autos quickly, first as an American importer of Volkswagen and Porsche, then the British Jaguar. The showroom is an interior remodeling of the ground-floor northeast corner of a New York City curtain wall skyscraper. It was intended to be for the British product, but before it was completed, Hoffman had moved on to Mercedes-Benz. A large statue of a leaping Jaguar sent from the Coventry, England, factory had to be returned. It was to have been the centerpiece on a turntable which, in

the fifties, could hold an XK-120, a Mark VII, and one other model of the Jaguar line. The showroom design precedes by a year Wright's design for the Hoffman home (S.390).

The ramp curves around the turntable of the display floor. Posts of the skyscraper are surfaced with mirrors (as are some of the walls) to make them seem to disappear. William Short, who had never studied at Taliesin, supervised construction.

Several Wright-designed tables remain in use over thirty years after they were built. Now, over the turntable, the mirror ceiling features the Mercedes three-point star; however handsome and integral to the corporate image, it is not by Wright. Renovations to the space, particularly to provide room for additional sales personnel, were done by Wes Peters, Cornelia Brierly, and Morton Delson in the 1980s.

Hoffman Auto Showroom

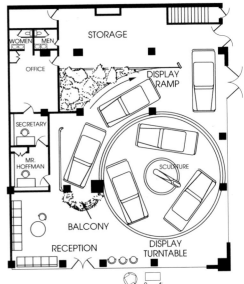

S.381　T.5532
Frank Lloyd Wright, **Hotel Plaza Apartment Remodeling** (1954)
New York, New York
Demolished, 1968

Wright remodeled a three-room apartment suite in the 808-room Hotel Plaza to use for visits to New York City while the Guggenheim Museum and other New York and Connecticut projects were under construction. As apprentices at Taliesin were building the necessary furniture, painted in black lacquer with red edges, Wright was having long red velvet curtains hung the full height of the high-ceilinged rooms. Rose-colored borders framed Japanese gold paper panels on the walls. Circular mirrors became part of the semicircular window arches. Crystal balls were attached to cord pendants which, when pulled, turned on the mirror lights. The Wrights last stayed in this apartment, known to some as Taliesin the Third and to others as Taliesin East, on January 27, 1959.

View from Mr. Wright's desk

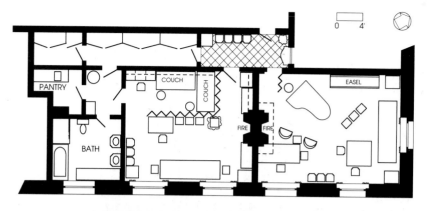

Living room

S.382　T.5427
Municipal Art Gallery (1954)
Los Angeles, California
Mostly demolished, 1969 (garage remains)

Leading to the main entry of Hollyhock House (S.208) is a long, raised, covered pergola or breezeway. Parallel, and east, is a row of pylons that lead to the original door frames, then garage, of the Los Angeles Exhibition Pavilion, always known locally as the Municipal Art Gallery.

In 1951 the exhibit Sixty Years of Living Architecture opened in the Palazzo Strozzi, Florence. From there it went to Zurich, Paris, Munich, Rotterdam, Mexico City, New York City, and, finally, Los Angeles, where a fiberglass exhibition pavilion was built over existing kennels with its entrance from Hollyhock House (Barnsdall, S.208). At the far end was a lecture hall. Wright called it his Los Angeles Exhibition Pavilion to distinguish it from the New York Usonian Exhibition Pavilion (S.370) for the same exhibit on the East Coast.

John Geiger, one of the apprentices who completed the New York exhibit, supervised the Los Angeles installation. To meet Los Angeles building codes, the pipes were welded, rather than set up as scaffolding as in New York. Contractor was Morris Pynoos, and Gene Birnbaum the engineer. Construction took twenty-one days but, the afternoon of the opening, Wright changed the entrance. Quick-set concrete, poured five hours before the formal opening, completed the work.

The lecture hall of the Los Angeles Municipal Art Gallery as viewed from Hollyhock House to its south

The Garage is still standing, as are the stanchions for the Esplanades

S.383   T.5523
John L. **Rayward**
(Rayward-Shepherd) **Residence**,
Tirranna (1955),
S.383A   T.5802
Additions (1958), and
S.383B   T.5747
Victoria and Jennifer **Rayward**
Playhouse (1957)
New Canaan, Connecticut
Workspace enlarged and courtyard
enclosed, greenhouse and connecting
pergola added by Taliesin Associated
Architects. Renovated in the 1980s.

Tirranna—an Australian aboriginal
word meaning "running waters"—is an
intricate intermingling of the ellipse and
a grid of 4-foot squares, a solar hemicycle in its main living, dining, workspace and, originally, master bedroom
space. Standard concrete (not textile)
block is combined with Philippine
mahogany, glass, and Colorundum
flooring to create a house, swimming
pool, and pond wedded to the Noroton
River and its surrounding hills. The
block is standard 16 inch except in
curved surfaces where 8-inch "cubes"
are used. The swimming pool splits in
half the 18-foot drop from living room
to pond, where a dam creates a
waterfall. A series of fish steps at the
far end of the dam provides for
passage of aquatic life through the 20
acres of woodland property. Landscaped by Frank Okamura, landscape
architect of the Brooklyn Botanical
Garden, and Charles Middeleer, the
grounds contain such a quantity and
variety of flora as to qualify as a major
botanical garden. The built-in and
freestanding furniture, fabric pattern,
and carpet layout are Wright's designs,
with the assistance of John deKoven
Hill. Allan J. Gelbin supervised original
construction, with Alfred Elliasson
acting as carpenter foreman. Mark
Heyman, Raj Aderi, Ling Po, and Dick
Stadleman combined to produce the
working drawings.

Like the Anthony house (S.315),
the building was designed, as a main
unit including original master bedroom,
but like the McCartney house (S.299),
it was built in stages, the bedroom
wing following the main unit. Here,
however, the bedroom wing addition
did not bring about changes to the
main space, so it requires no
additional catalog number. A Wright-
designed second wing provided a new

Rayward Residence

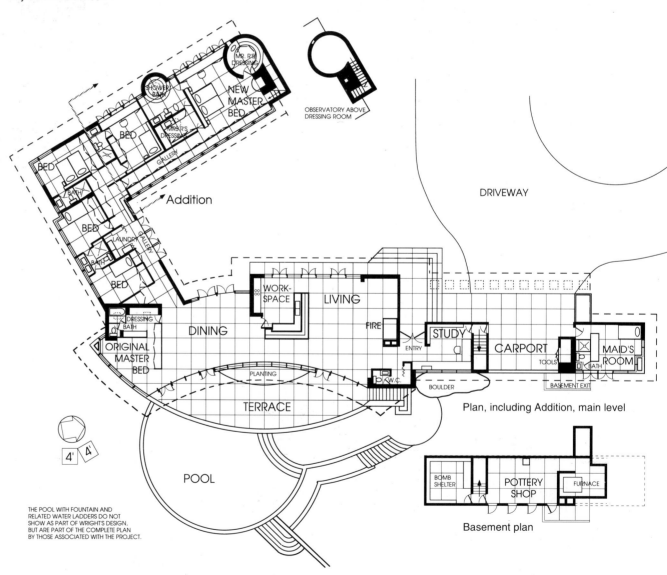

Plan, including Addition, main level

THE POOL WITH FOUNTAIN AND
RELATED WATER LADDERS DO NOT
SHOW AS PART OF WRIGHT'S DESIGN,
BUT ARE PART OF THE COMPLETE PLAN
BY THOSE ASSOCIATED WITH THE PROJECT.

Basement plan

Living room

Dining room

Observatory dome

POND

PENNINSULA

LADDER

TERRACE

Ground level of Playhouse

ROOFTOP

PARAPET

Roof of Playhouse

0   3   6'

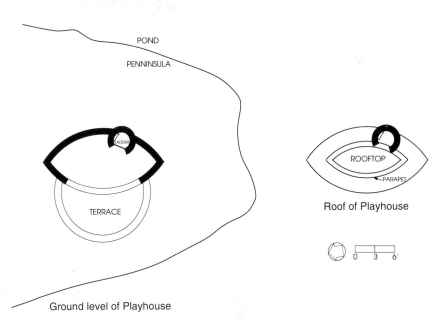

Rayward Playhouse

master bedroom with separate dressing rooms for Mr. and Mrs. Rayward; Mr. Rayward's is surmounted by an observatory.

Wright designed a playhouse with elliptical walls on ten-foot radii (giving nearly 16 feet interior width) for Rayward's daughters, Jennifer and Victoria. It was built on a promontory at the entry point of the stream and provided the children with a place of personal shelter as well as a rooftop deck from which they could survey the pool and other outdoor activities.

Though originally designed for Mr. Rayward, Herman R. Shepherd purchased the house and grounds in 1964 and brought the design to completion, repairing shoddy construction that resulted from Rayward's constant pursuit of the lowest bid. For Shepherd, Taliesin Associated Architects' chief architect, William Wesley Peters provided a major extension

beyond the work room; a curved esplanade leads to a greenhouse with servant and guest quarters, shop and extra carport; greenhouse window details are from the Guggenheim Museum.

Additional work by Taliesin Associated Architects brought about enclosure of the space between original bedroom wing and added master bedroom wing, gaining an atrium and informal living room. With this the workspace was also enlarged. Even later, a circular deck was added above the main pool.

In 1980 Ranko and Susan Santric became the third owners. Finding the building in somewhat rundown condition, they set to cleaning and resurfacing all exposed wood, restoring its original beauty, and replacing fabrics and floor coverings.

411

Thaxton Residence

S.384　T.5414
William L. **Thaxton** Residence (1954)
Bunker Hill, Texas
Significantly altered. Restoration ongoing

Deep among the tall oaks west of Houston sits this battered, concrete-block-walled house, the blocks stepped back every two courses. The original plan, drawn to a 60–120-degree equilateral parallelogram module with 4-foot side as unit, was one first submitted to E. Clarke Arnold (S.374), itself derived from a 1950 project (T.5005) for Robert N. Bush in Palo Alto, California, that was never built. As enlarged for the Thaxtons, the 60-degree **L** plan forms two sides of the swimming pool. Living room and workspace are along the public façade, with carport at the far end. Air conditioning was an integral part of the design for this subtropical southern city. The ductwork is run from the utilities room (next to the workspace) above the decking, which otherwise would serve only to conceal indirect lighting. The detailing in the wood fascia alone contains more than nine hundred pieces of trim.

There is an addition, not by Wright, which is detached from the main dwelling. Other alterations over the years have defaced Wright's façade. Built-in furniture has been gutted. In 1991, threat of imminent destruction—the alternative being removal to another site—brought forth a buyer who agreed to keep the building at its site and restore it, as much as possible, to its original as-built form.

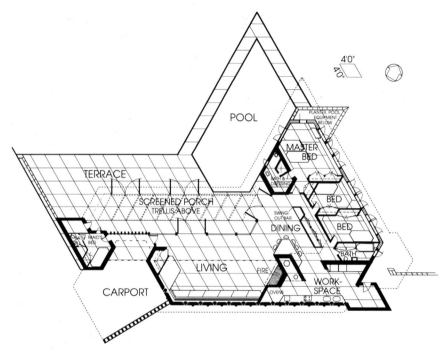

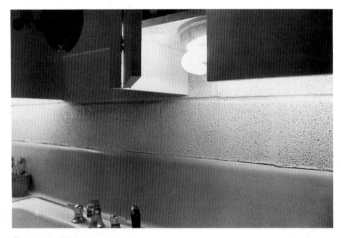

Concealed light detail

S.385　T.5418
Harriet and Randall **Fawcett** Residence (1955)
Los Banos, California

Randall ("Buck") and Harriet Fawcett are numbered among the very few farmers who have Wright-designed houses, and even fewer who have them designed by Frank Lloyd Wright. Fawcett Farms is south of Los Banos in the flat central valley of California. Walnut trees form a green canopy, more attractive to birds than humans.

Battered concrete block and angles of 120 and 60 degrees form the basis of this house. The equilateral triangle module has an altitude of 4 feet, thus, a side of 55 inches. Each of two wings makes a 60-degree angle to the main living space, where the entry is, and features a "walk-in" fireplace. A standing "teepee" arrangement of logs is often needed to draw properly where such a high, cantilevered mantel was designed by Wright. The private facade has a rhythm set up by alternation of doors and fixed glazing, pairs of half bays against full (55-inch) bays. There is no weight on this glass windowall, for the ceiling and trellised soffit overhang are fully cantilevered with structural steel I-beams. The southwest wing contains the quiet spaces, the southeast wing is a playroom and leads to a swimming pool. The floor is brown, rather than the standard Taliesin red. Cedar is used as trim, plexiglass in the clerestory. A modern version of the shallow, circular flower planter so often favored by Wright, softens the edge of the wall that leads visitors to the main entry. To obtain the tapered effect seen on the supporting pier, a special insert was used in the block molds.

The house was sited a short distance from Wright's initial choice, to avoid the humidity of the surrounding walnut orchard. John H. Howe drew the plans. Tom Casey also worked on plans as well as structural and mechanical engineering, areas in which he specialized in more than 50 Wright projects. Robert Beharka spent 18 months supervising construction, then settled in Los Banos to establish his own architectural practice. Taliesin Associated Architects' supervision continued after Wright's death to 1961 completion.

Fawcett Residence public facade

View over pool to private facade

Living room alcove

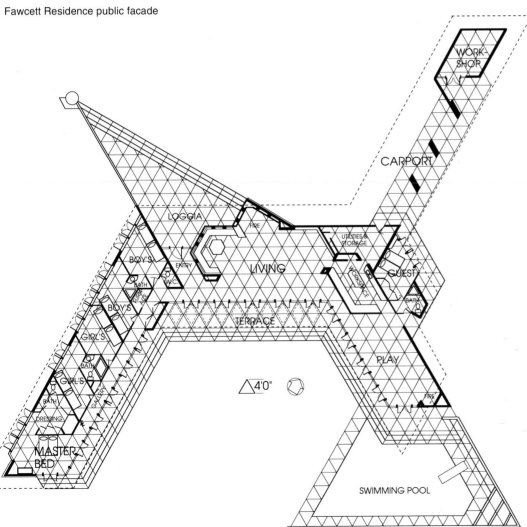

WORK-SHOP

CARPORT

LOGGIA

FIRE

UTILITIES & STORAGE

BOY'S

ENTRY

WC

LIVING

WORKSPACE

GUEST

BATH

BATH

BOY'S

GIRL'S

TERRACE

PLAY

BATH

GIRL'S

FIRE

DRESSING

MASTER BED

△4'0"

SWIMMING POOL

Fireplace

Bathroom

S.386 T.5510
Gerald B. **Tonkens** Residence
(1954)
Amberley Village, Ohio

A major statement in the history of
Usonian Automatic houses, Gerald
Tonkens's residence sits on 6 acres
atop a knoll. Pierced block admits light
to the workspace core as a clerestory.
This core contains heating and cooling
units raised above floor level and other
utilities. One wall of the core is the living
room fireplace.

The plan is "Type G" of seven
Usonian Automatic designs nominally
dated 1956 for Walter Bimson of Valley
National Bank in Phoenix, Arizona, and
at least four other individual clients.
The living room opens to a low-walled
lanai. A bathroom and two bedrooms
are dropped off the tunnel gallery
before the master bedroom and bath
are reached. The carport extends as
an **L** from the second bathroom. The
house is constructed on a 2-foot-
square unit module with the standard
concrete wall block surface of 1 by 2
feet, and 2-foot-square coffered ceiling
blocks weighing 220 pounds each.
Wood for both paneling and furniture is
Philippine mahogany.

The care exercised in this dwelling
over the seventeen months of its
construction is evident. John H. Howe
assisted Wright with the original drawings. Eric Wright, grandson of the
architect, supervised construction from
engineering drawings by William
Wesley Peters. Other supervisors
included John deKoven Hill and
Thomas Casey (fabrics and furniture).
Hill and Cornelia Brierly designed the
landscaping. Engineering of the block
and reinforced-steel ceiling was by

Mendel Glickman, the only non-
Taliesin principal on the project, in
collaboration with Peters and the
architect.

One of Tonkens's enterprises was
the Hamilton Small Loans Company,
for which he had Wright produce an
office design in 1956 that was never
built.

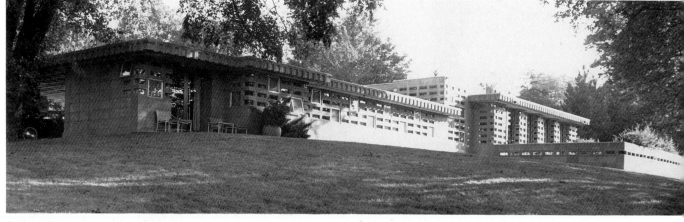

Tonkens Residence, private facade

Dining area, view toward living room

Living room, view toward dining space

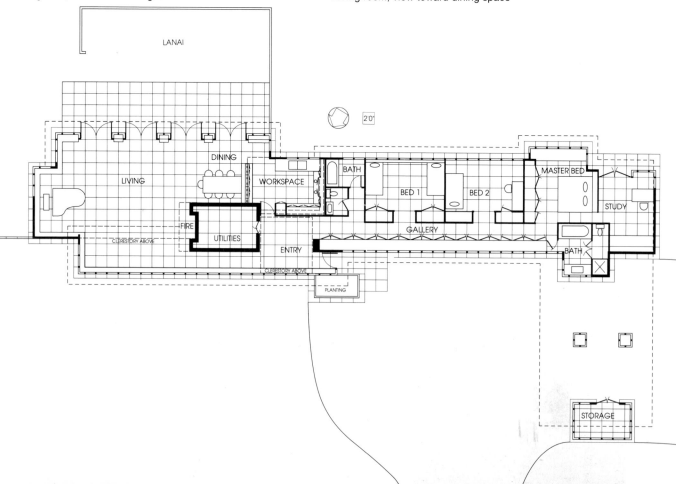

S.387 T.5506

Dr. Toufic H. and Mildred **Kalil** Residence (1955)
Manchester, New Hampshire

This Usonian Automatic design in which concrete block is used not just in the walls but the ceiling as well may be seen as a pierced-block version of the Brauner house (S.312) without its side sitting room. There are no large windows; light is admitted through half-height pierced block, which intensifies the shadow pattern they cast. Mica in the blocks further enhances the quality of light inside the living room whose orientation, due to the pierced block, is the same as the bedroom wing, thus making this an in-line plan.

Dr. and Mrs. Kalil agreed to build the machine to make the blocks and sell it to the next user for the $7,500 cost. Dante Donati, son of an Italian immigrant who made concrete garden animals, went into concrete block manufacturing—Duracrete. He built the steel forms for the twenty-odd shapes required, to a tolerance of 1/64 inch. Basic blocks are two feet long, to fit the 2-foot unit. Each block was made, one by one, under 7000 pounds of pressure, which made it possible for the blocks to be removed from the mold immediately, and the next made in a production-line manner.

As with all Usonian houses, Automatic or otherwise, gravity floor heating is used, but there is also a second, forced-air system for air conditioning which can be used to moderate the gravity system. Trim and partitions are Philippine mahogany. Morton H. Delson, later New York

representative for the Taliesin Associated Architects, was the supervisor of construction. Production of blocks took one winter, raising of the shell (single block wall, not double) the following summer, and finishing of the interior the following winter. The house faces southeast and is located a half-block from the Zimmerman residence (S.333).

Kalil Residence, private side

Living room

Gallery

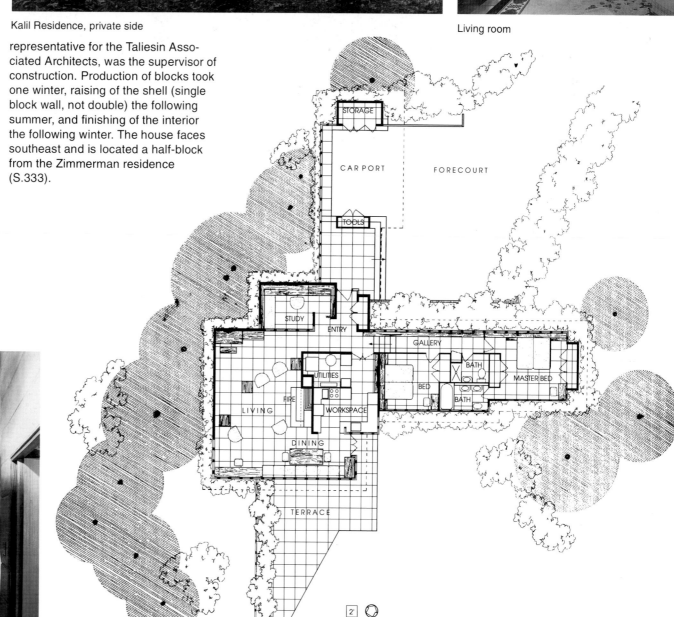

S.388   T.5513

Dr. H. and Dorothy H. **Turkel** Residence (1955)
Detroit, Michigan
Damaged gravity heating system
replaced by forced-air on first floor

This house has always been known
as the home of Dorothy Turkel, for
it was truly hers, a building she loved
and championed. But the extreme
unconventionality of Wright's design
left Dr. Turkel with professional difficulties, which he solved by moving
out.

With the Turkel house, we come
full-circle in Usonian design. Wright
considered La Miniatura (S.214) the
first Usonian home. The group of four
California block houses (S.214–217)
were all two or more stories high,
but the homes most historians call
Usonian (Jacobs, S.234 ff.) are, with
rare exceptions, single-story dwellings.
Thus, this, the only built example of a
two-story Usonian Automatic house, is
of special interest. It features a square
block twice the height of the Kalil
(S.387) house, thus preserving a
proper sense of scale for the larger
structure. Many different block forms
were required, including a special
fascia block and a fascia corner block
used only for that purpose. The living
room, which Wright called a music
room, is the full two stories in height
and has pierced, light-admitting blocks
on two sides, each 16 inches or two-
thirds the 24-inch unit.

Turkel Residence, private facade

Mrs. Turkel's study, the master
bedroom, and four other bedrooms,
plus three bathrooms and a balcony fit
over the lower level workspace, dining,
laundry, utility, and play areas, plus
exterior terrace, in what was originally
an in-line configuration, before the
short **L** of the playroom was added.
The main level was extended into an **L**
to accommodate additional boys' bedrooms and maid's quarters. As built,

the **L** was shortened and made two
stories high. Robert Pond supervised
construction from drawings prepared
by John H. Howe.

The main floor gravity heating
system froze during a freak spring
cold snap while the client-owner was
on vacation; because of the two-story
design, forced air (including air conditioning) was always needed for the
upstairs and to even out the slow
reaction time of the floor system.

The house was purchased by Tom
Monaghan of Domino's Pizza in March
1988; two years later it passed into the
hands of a new owner.

Detail of upper
dentil block

Living room with original furnishings

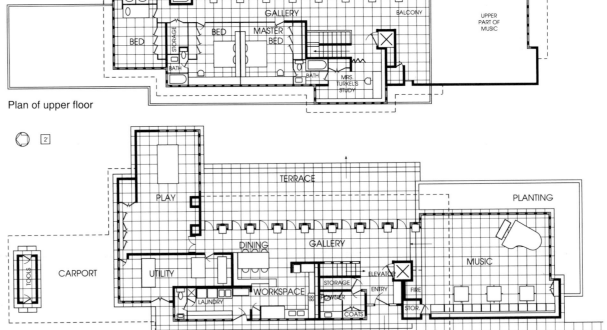

Plan of upper floor

Plan of ground floor

Tracy Residence, private facade

S.389 T.5512
Elizabeth and William B. Tracy Residence and
S.389A T.5512
Detached Garage (1955)
Normandy Park, Washington

This Usonian Automatic house nestles into a rise just above the cliff on the east shore of Puget Sound. Though the blocks appear to be uniform, there are several different ones for inside and outside corners, roof, and walls. The 2-foot blocks were made from the molds first used for the Kalil house (S.387). The in-line plan, laid out on a 2-foot-square unit module, is particularly compact. This is achieved by placing two bedrooms to one side of the gallery opposite the utilities room and workspace, and the master bedroom opposite the bathroom, rather than following Wright's usual practice of having them all off one side of the gallery. Perforated blocks with glass inlays make the columns between French doors appear less structurally significant than they are. The same system of perforation and glass enlivens corners and clerestory. Walls are constructed of block, insulation, and interior paneling. Ceiling block is coffered to reduce its weight. The carport is detached. As with all of the built Usonian Automatics, Thomas Casey provided structural and mechanical engineering and working drawings. Taliesin Associated Architects supervised construction to 1960 completion.

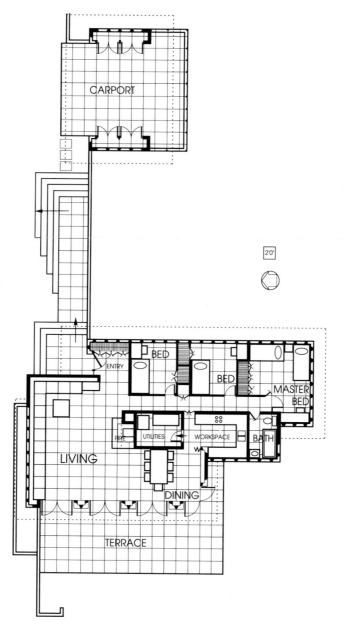

Living room

THE EQUILATERAL PARALLELOGRAM MODULE

Two L-plan Usonian designs were on the Taliesin drafting boards at the same time, the first Jacobs, S.234, and the Hanna, S.235. Original drawings show the Jacobs to have first been done on a 2' square, later redrawn to a 2 x 4' rectangle, while the Hanna was done on a hexagon with 26" side (45" altitude).

The hexagonal unit is time-consuming to draw while the equilateral parallelogram of 60° and 120° is simple and can accommodate anything that would otherwise require the hex. This module is popularly called a "diamond," and is easily drawn with the 30–60° traingle.

120° plans on the equilateral parallelogram module should be called an "open," as opposed to a "closed" 60°, L, and the 240° plans would equate to the 270°, or outside, L. Plans employing interlocked grids of square units would be open Ls at 135° and Outside Ls at 225°. A 45° closed L is possible, but hardly practical.

Double 120° plan, front gallery. This variation gains two additional rooms, each with private bath, over standard 120° plan.

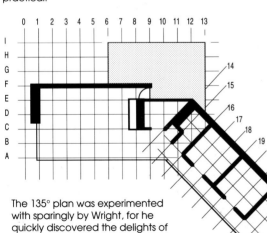

The 135° plan was experimented with sparingly by Wright, for he quickly discovered the delights of the 120° plan on the equilateral parallelogram module.

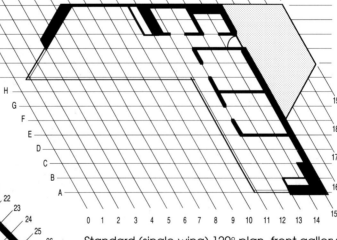

Standard (single-wing) 120° plan, front gallery.

Note the variation shown for the carport which, of course, could be located as in the double 120°. This calls for a single entry and fireplace in its usual place, back-to-back with the workspace. It would also require an additional support for the carport cantilever.

S.390   T.5535
Maximilian **Hoffman Residence** (1955)
Rye, New York
Kitchen wing and new main entry added in 1972 by Taliesin Associated Architects

Mercedes-Benz auto importer (S.380) Maximilian Hoffman accepted this third and least interesting scheme from Wright, who called it a "seashore cottage." The residence is dominated by its living room, 24 feet square between pillars capped by a hipped roof, modeled on the Hillside assembly room at Taliesin only without a mezzanine. Those pillars are among the few clues to break the ambiguity of the spatial orientation of this magnificent room, with its view of Long Island Sound over a swimming pool to the north, over lawn to the east.

Detailing is lavish and construction of high quality. Philippine mahogany (ribbon-stripped) plywood was cut and both flitch- and sequence-matched so that the grain mates at all joints, horizontal and vertical. Due to local restrictions, the roof is of random-thickness slate rather than the copper Wright intended. The fascia, however, is copper, with each 8-inch section cut and stamped in Brooklyn, then soldered to its neighbor on site. Floors are flagstone, which makes the 4-foot unit apparent principally where cabinetry or window mullions articulate the space. The stone, hand-chipped to rectangular proportions, is granite from Yonkers, New York, and is laid with horizontal mortar deeply raked, vertical at the stone surface.

The original dining space was in an alcove at the rear of the living room in what may be seen as an in-line plan, with the workspace behind the fireplace. In the original plan, there were three bedrooms, each with full bath, with a study and dressing room complementing the master bedroom. For privacy on exclusive North Manursing Island, the carport had to be an enclosed garage, extended further into a tool shed and caretaker's quarters.

John H. Howe drew the original plans, Morton H. Delson the working drawings. John deKoven Hill designed the interior. A rug specifically designed for this house was refused by Hoffman, so Wright took it for use in the Taliesin

Hoffman Residence, bedroom wing to living area, private side

living room. The heating is a gravity floor system augmented by forced heat with air conditioning.

In 1972 the Taliesin Associated Architects designed an additional wing. William Wesley Peters at Taliesin West and Morton H. Delson, the original supervisor, in New York were in charge. The new wing off the living room, which serves to close a third side to the driveway-courtyard, provided a den, a new kitchen, laundry, and servant's quarters (all on separate heating and air conditioning). A terrace looking toward the sound is well sheltered for outdoor activity. The new entry in the addition leads directly to the living room, whereas the original entry, under the garage-gateway, required visitors to go the full length of the tunnel gallery to reach the main activities space. Interestingly, this gallery is lit by the only known example of a Wright clerestory that uses (amber) tinted glass. Further, the design is three dimensional (see photo).

As restored and expanded, the house is known as the Emily Fisher Landau Residence.

Hoffman Residence, living room fireplace from original dining area

Light patterns cast by the clerestory

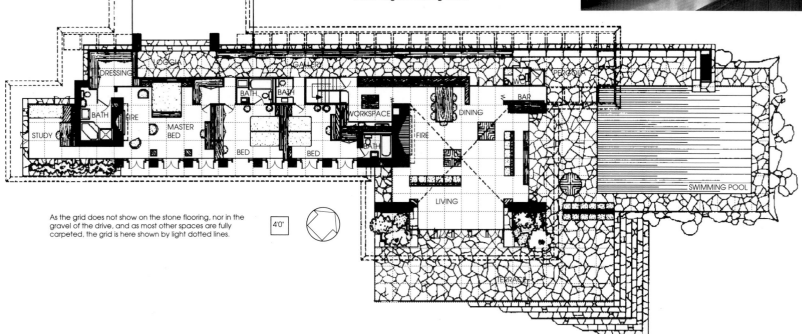

KITCHENETTE
CARETAKER
BATH
TOOLS
GARAGE
COURTYARD

DRESSING
LOGGIA
GALLERY
WC
PERGOLA
BATH
BATH
BATH
BAR
STUDY
BATH
FIRE
MASTER BED
WORKSPACE
DINING
BED
BED
BATH
FIRE
LIVING
SWIMMING POOL
TERRACE

As the grid does not show on the stone flooring, nor in the gravel of the drive, and as most other spaces are fully carpeted, the grid is here shown by light dotted lines.

4'0"

419

Lovness Residence, private facade

Bathroom

Living room

S.391　T.5507
Donald and Virginia **Lovness Residence** (1955)
Stillwater, Minnesota

The residence for Don Lovness, a chemical engineer, and his wife Virginia is notable for its elimination of the usual tunnel gallery without having to add a second floor. The master bedroom is directly off one end of the living room, the daughter's bedroom to the rear near the entry. A fireplace is centered on the back wall. The workspace is separated by deck-high cabinets, at the rear, near the master bedroom. Flitch plates, 2-by-12-inch boards sandwiching a half-inch plate of steel, hold the ceiling and its canti-

lever. Hard limestone, Dolomite, is used; 250 tons at $6 per ton were trucked to the site, about half being usable. The facade, uniformly spaced in the first design, is articulated by fir mullions with full and half-bay plate glass. One interesting feature is the three accordion doors, one by Wright, another by William Wesley Peters, the third by Eugene Masselink.

In 1976 the Lovnesses also built a cottage from plans drawn up by Wright in 1958 and complemented it with furniture constructed from the first designs for the Barnsdall Hollyhock house (S.208).

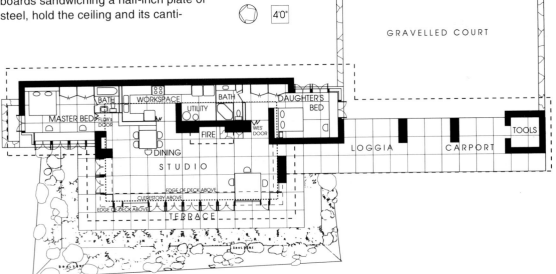

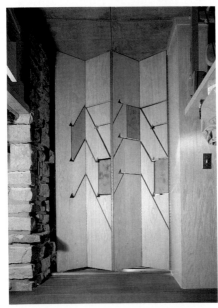

Accordion door to the master bedroom by Wright

S.392 T.5516
Theodore A. and Bette **Pappas**
Residence (1955)
Saint Louis, Missouri

Ted and Bette had lived in Milwaukee after the war; Ted was district manager of 20th Century Fox's Wisconsin division. In Saint Louis he would for a while be public relations director at the Saint Louis Browns. The Pappases never considered themselves wealthy, yet Bette insisted that Wright be the architect of their home even as Ted countered "Wright designs for the very wealthy. He is not in our league. I'm just a poor working boy. You know that Bette." Eventually enough courage was gathered together for a letter to be written to Wright, in 1954. On their visit to Mr. Wright at Taliesin, the architect agreed to design them "a beautiful concrete block home," which sent paroxysms of fear through Bette. Wright's presentation drawings persuaded husband and wife to proceed. The vagaries of life, however, precluded immediate construction. Their two children, Ted, Jr., and Candace, were joined by twin girls. Financial limitations put off start of construction and eventually a new site had to be chosen, one requiring a 180-degree rotation of the plan. Building extended over four years.

In the rolling hills west of metropolitan Saint Louis sits the salmon-tinted block house. It is a Usonian Automatic design whose masonry structure, including the roof, could be built from blocks—Wright called them "stones"—assembled by the client. So this is precisely what the young clients did. Picking up where the prime contractor (Harvey Spigle, who had studied at Taliesin, then Wallace Kimball) left off, with the walls only partly finished, Bette and Ted completed their home, after four years' work, in 1964. They had tried to get accurate molds from which to produce the blocks; only after they had begun building did Wes Peters find the Kalil (S.387) molds at the recently completed Tracy house (S.389) and send them to Saint Louis. Apparently the molds were at the Turkel house (S.388) when the Pappases requested them. The house is air-conditioned, the ducts concealed in the concrete. Two furnaces are used, each serving a different wing. The master bedroom is placed imme-

Pappas Residence, private facade

Living room

Cluster arrangement in bedroom wing

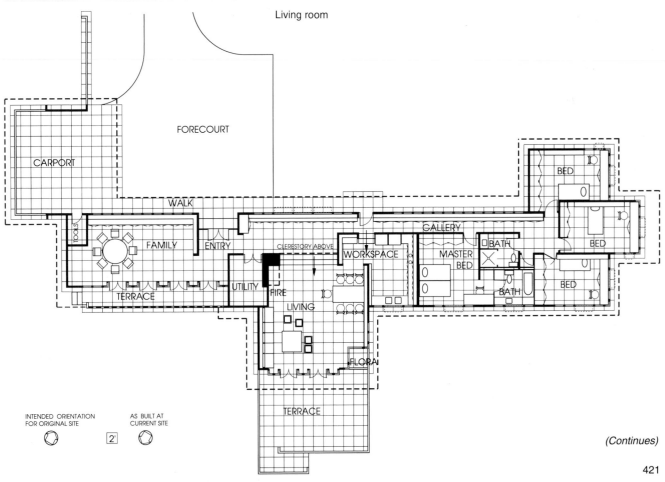

INTENDED ORIENTATION FOR ORIGINAL SITE

AS BUILT AT CURRENT SITE

(Continues)

(**S.392** continued)

Carport cantilever

Sunday Residence

Gallery to playroom, living room fireplace left

diately next to the workspace, and the three children's rooms, clustered side by side (the unique feature of the "E Type" Usonian Automatic in a series done by Wright and his apprentices in 1955–56), complete the bedroom wing without the need of the more usual long tunnel gallery.

Family resemblance among Wright's block houses is strong, even when two dozen different stone forms are employed, as here. The fascia block, otherwise shaped like that of the Tonkens residence (S.386), in this instance opens its "U" design up. The unit employed on the square module is 2 feet; from family room to bedroom terminals is 116 feet. The floors are of Colorundum, as in the Zimmerman house (S.333). The wood is Philippine mahogany. Plate glass, not Thermopane, was used. Birds cannot see the glass and thus fly into it, often killing themselves (this happened during the first meeting of Ted and Bette with Mr. Wright). Accordingly, the Pappases do not clean them; the birds can see the dirt and avoid the glass. The house was placed on the National Register in 1979.

S.393   T.5522
Robert H. **Sunday** Residence (1955)
Marshalltown, Iowa
Formal dining area and family room additions by John H. Howe. Enclosed garage attached to the shop is also a later addition.

Robert Sunday was involved in the sale of building supplies and asked for a brick-and-wood structure. John H. Howe did the preliminary drawings for Mr. Wright. He reformatted the design from a 2-foot block to a 4-foot brick unit system; these plans were signed by William Wesley Peters in June 1959. With Taliesin Associated Architects, Howe supervised construction of the revised design to completion in 1963.

This is an **L**-plan brick structure with blonde Philippine mahogany fascia and trim, possibly the last of the brick Usonian homes. Wright's original concept was for a Usonian Automatic design based essentially on the New York Usonian Exhibition House

(S.369). This in part explains its having forced-air heating and cooling, the latter a necessity for block houses in humid southern climates and often desired by clients elsewhere. (Even when gravity heat was used in the floor slab, some late Usonian houses had forced air as a supplemental system.)

The house as first built had problems, such as a lack of overhangs on one side. So Howe, who, with John Rattenbury, had completed the working drawings, provided an addition in 1969, built in 1970, that "corrected the faults," transforming the **L** into a **T**. The new family room extends the house to the rear at the workspace. Further, a formal dining alcove was built to the other side of the workspace, where it gains the beauty of the setting sun. It faces southwest down its hillside site, and its living room views three compass directions. A smaller building on the same property, mimicking the main house, is not by Wright, nor is the 120-degree addition to the shop of an enclosed garage.

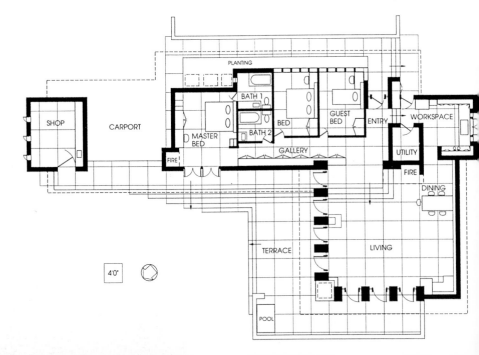

Warren **Scott Remodeling** of the **Isabel Roberts** Residence (1955)

River Forest, Illinois
The Isabel Roberts house, as resurfaced in the 1920s and remodeled inside by Wright.

By the time the Scotts moved into the Isabel Roberts house (S.150), a brick veneer surfacing had been added, sometime in the late twenties. Speculation used to be that this work was done in 1927 by Willliam Drummond, Miss Roberts's neighbor, who had suggested a similar idea to the Coonleys, or that the work may have been Wright's idea. Instead, Harry Robinson was responsible for it, possibly as early as 1926. Wright admitted to Mr. Scott that the house had been cheaply built, but it had been necessary to meet the limited means of his secretary-bookkeeper.

For the 1950s remodeling, with Wright and John deKoven Hill collaborating, a new interior treatment utilizing blonde Philippine mahogany replaced pine as well as some stucco. Further, structural steel was added to correct badly sagging roof cantilevers, and state-of-the-art central air conditioning was installed. The east rooms of the lower level were converted to a study, a pair of rooms above to a single master bedroom. The south

Scott Remodeling of the Isabel Roberts house

porch was enclosed with glass, and work was done on the porch floor to allow the tree growing through it and the ceiling to live another quarter century. Copper, a favorite Wright roofing material, was now placed on the roofs. The kitchen was enlarged and the entry redesigned. Further restorative work was completed in the late eighties, by the son of Warren Scott, Anthony. John G. Thorpe assisted. Once again the British elm in the porch has room to grow another two and a half decades. The exterior photograph shows the house as it appeared, remodeled, in the 1970s.

Living room

Dining room

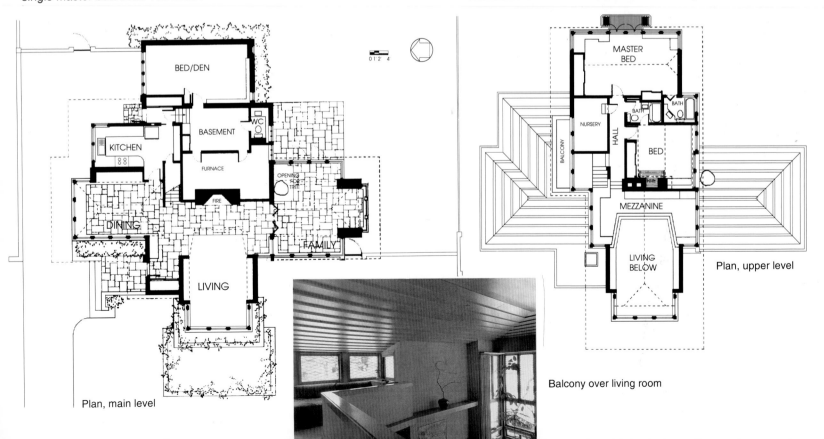

Plan, main level

Balcony over living room

Plan, upper level

S.395   T.5514

Dallas Theatre Center for Paul Baker (1955)
Dallas, Texas
Terrace above foyer enclosed

The Dallas Theatre Center's Kalita Humphreys Theater is a design derived from the New Theatre for Woodstock, New York, of 1931, through a reworking for Florida Southern College in 1938. It is a concrete cantilever construction with a 127-ton concrete stage loft. The circular stage drum, extending well above the rest of the concrete mass, is the focus of the design, which, besides circles, employs a basic grid of equilateral parallelograms. Within the drum, the 40-foot circular stage itself contains a 32-foot turntable divided into thirds, which allows one set to be on stage, one to be struck, and one to be set up for the next scene. The theater can seat 404 people in eleven rows.

Construction was about one-quarter complete when Wright died, and work was finished by the Taliesin Associated Architects. W. Kelly Oliver supervised the project, designing the adjustable stage lighting devices and the furniture, as well as providing theater seats and interior drawings. In 1967, Oliver designed the office and rehearsal hall additions to the building. Thus, the terrace above the foyer is now enclosed, giving a more monumental feeling to the once-light entrance wing. Other alterations have

been made by former apprentice David George.

For the convenience of patrons, the hill is now covered with asphalt to provide close-in parking. For additional office space, a "box" has been constructed next Wright's structure.

The theater is open for visits when no production is in rehearsal.

Kalita Humphreys Theatre

Auditorium with set stage

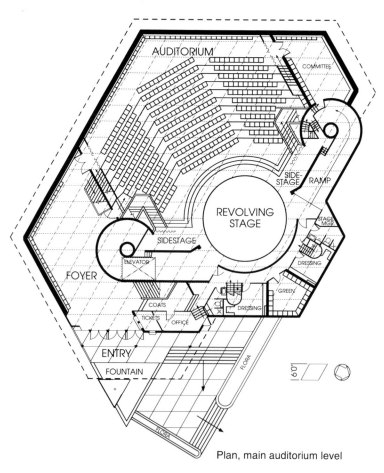

Plan, main auditorium level

S.396 T.5614

Karl **Kundert Medical Clinic** (1955)
for Drs. Kundert and Fogo
San Luis Obispo, California

Dr. Kundert was from the La Crosse area of Wisconsin and went to medical school in Madison. Dr. Fogo was from Richland Center. Wright was, thus, hardly unknown to them. Because Dr. Kundert is tall, 7-foot 4-inch ceilings were required. Construction began in January 1956, and the two doctors moved in on Labor Day.

This clinic of ophthalmology is an **L**-plan with its terrace enclosed by the **L** on two sides and a retaining wall above the adjacent creek bed. Essentially, Wright has taken a Usonian **L**-plan house design and adapted it ingeniously to the specific needs of doctors of eye diseases. The basic form is a long wing with a gallery leading to the parking area and a stubby **L**-wing that encloses the waiting room. Each wing is terminated by a room or rooms without windows for special testing and treatment.

Central to all this is a reception area in the large, triple clerestory-lighted waiting room, derived from the Usonian living room. The clerestory is made of three courses of perforated wood panels with translucent glass insets. Lower clear-glass windows at eye level employ the same cutout. Such panes were used often by Wright to admit patterned light, usually at transom level, as in the Pope residence (S.268). A similar principle underlies the pierced blocks of Usonian Automatic houses, such as the Tonkens and Kalil residences (S.386, S.387); the Kundert Clinic was first conceived in block, then built in brick.

Wright's first plans show a more compact building than was built; the two outside walls were each moved out a unit throughout, two units for part of the main wall, to achieve the more commodious space the doctors considered necessary for successful functioning of the clinic. Mortar is colored both horizontally and vertically to match the brick, and raked deeply on the horizontal. Aaron Green supervised construction from mechanical and structural drawings by Tom Casey.

Kundert Clinic from north (private facade)

Reception room with triple-level clerestory

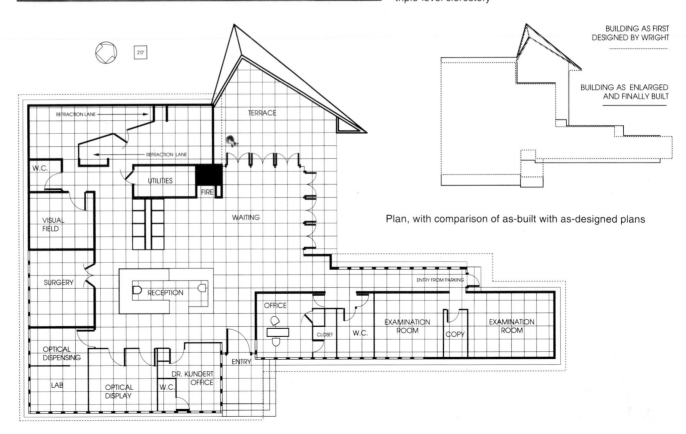

Plan, with comparison of as-built with as-designed plans

Meyers Clinic

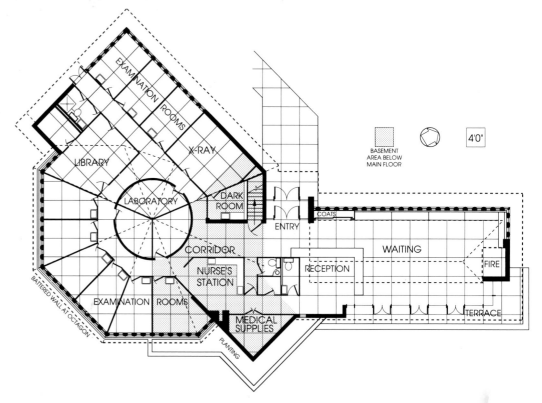

BASEMENT
AREA BELOW
MAIN FLOOR

4'0"

S.397   T.5613
Kenneth L. **Meyers Medical Clinic**
(1956)
Dayton, Ohio
Transom-level windows were not
butted without mortar joints, thus do
not align properly.

Wright apparently had no particularly
strong ideas about how to organize
space in this and other medical clinic
projects (S.396, S.424, S.425). So he
took the program submitted by the
clinic and developed that; in each
instance what resulted was a Usonian
house with bedrooms turned into
doctor-patient offices and the living
room altered into a reception-waiting
space. The Meyers Medical Clinic,
however, gains more offices by meld-
ing the octagon to a basic 225-degree
plan. A rectangular reception room is
linked to doctors' offices (examination
rooms, laboratory, therapy rooms) in
an octagon. A three-eighths segment
of the polygon, set on a separate grid,
is pinwheeled to the side, with medical
library, storage space, and additional
examination rooms. Special bricks
were fired to turn the corner of the
octagon, but the 8-inch standard brick
left no room for mortar with six bricks
to the 4-foot unit. Since mortar joints

were used, the 2-foot-square transom-
level window blocks do not line up
properly where full, mitred panes
should turn the corners.

Wright indicated on his plan the
possibility of extending the pinwheel
section in the future. In 1988, however,
after much local debate, a second
structure was built further out on the
site to handle services for which the
original building was too small. While

this new building seems to pay hom-
age to its neighbor in many details of
design and construction, it is not an
integrated whole nor are its proportions convincing. The later construction
is by a group calling itself the Frank
Lloyd Wright Professional Association,
though it has no official connection
with Taliesin.

S.398 T.5724
Paul J. and Ida **Trier** Residence
(1956)
Johnston, Iowa
Carport area enclosed as playroom.

This, like the Feiman residence
(S.371), is a variant on the New York
Usonian Exhibition House (S.369).
While the living room is smaller than
the New York original (five units
reduced to four), the bedroom wing is
extended with additional work spaces,
storage, and two bedrooms. One bedroom was added by cutting the original
plan on the grid line and inserting the
requisite number of 4-foot units. The
brick is a 12-inch tile type (11 1/2
inches by 3 inches square), and
perimeter, not typical gravity, heat is
used. The clerestory cutout is carried
into shutters for the glass pilasters that
decorate the living room windowall.

The Taliesin Associated Architects,
John Ottenheimer principally, supervised completion of construction in
1960 and provided a playroom, shop,
and storage space by enclosing what
otherwise would have been the carport
of the original design.

Trier Residence, living room facade

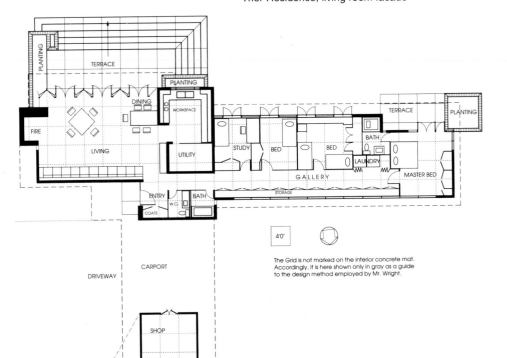

The Grid is not marked on the interior concrete mat.
Accordingly, it is here shown only in gray as a guide
to the design method employed by Mr. Wright.

Living room

427

Annunciation **Greek Orthodox Church** (1956)
Wauwatosa, Wisconsin

The Greek community in Milwaukee, while small, was cohesive in its new American surroundings. When the first Annunciation, "the church bachelors built," was dedicated in 1914, Stasinos Papastasinou had been in Milwaukee barely two years. On July 2, 1961, when Wright's Annunciation was dedicated, Stanley Stacy (the Americanized Stasinos) realized a dream he had sought since he organized the Building Committee in 1952.

The church building is hardly recognizable as such by traditional Greek Orthodox standards, yet it is a masterpiece of form and structure, function and symbolism united in an expression of its religious purpose. A Greek cross inscribed in a circle creates the plan and infuses most elements of detail. The roof structure is a concrete shell dome originally surfaced in blue ceramic mosaic tile and, to withstand extreme temperature changes, supported on thousands of ball bearings. The roof dome rides, then, on these ball bearings set in steel rails, supported by reinforced-concrete cylindrical trussing, visually expressed in the balcony-level fenestration pattern. In turn, the truss is held aloft by four concrete piers that are created by the terminals of the inward-curving concrete walls, forming a Greek cross in the plan at the main level. The balcony further unifies the composition. Its disclike shape (similar to Wright's Prairie era urns) has outer edges that are gravity-supported by the circular truss that it helps to stabilize laterally. This sanctuary space may be seen as the logical circular development of Unity Temple (S.096).

Stained-glass windows by Eugene Masselink were never realized. The metalwork is largely gold-anodized aluminum, then a new process even for its developer, Alcoa. John Ottenheimer supervised construction for the Taliesin Associated Architects. The church was completed in 1963, and problems occurred immediately. The ceiling was gold metalflake on Air-O-Therm asbestos

Annunciation Greek Orthodox Church, main entry

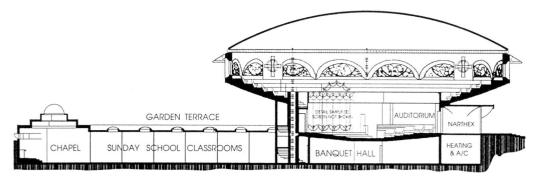

Section

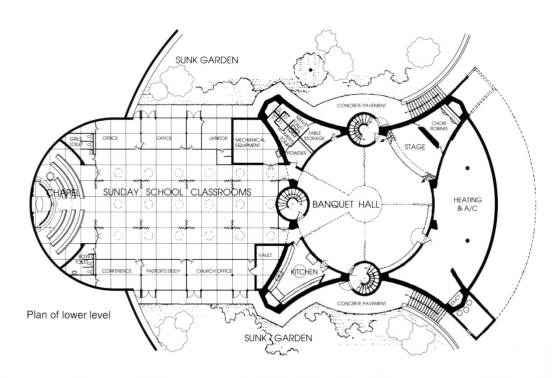

Plan of lower level

thermal and acoustic insulation; it sagged, and some parts even fell. It was replaced with foamed-in-place urethane. Related to the interior ceiling problem was flaking of the exterior roofing tile, which was replaced by a synthetic plastic resin called Neolon. The building was consecrated September 12, 1971; Olga, the three-month-old daughter of Wes Peters and Svetlana Stalin, was baptized there later the same day. The church, which hosted 4000 people on its July 4, 1961, public opening, is open to visitors.

Plan of balcony level

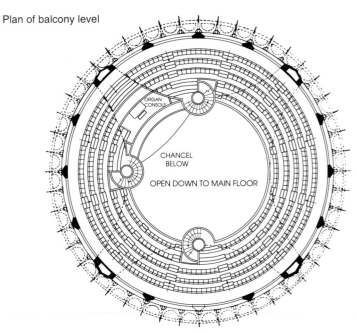

Sanctuary

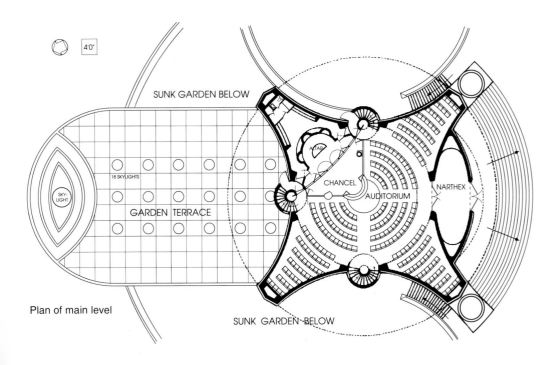

Plan of main level

S.400   T.4305
Solomon R. **Guggenheim Museum**
(1956)
New York, New York
Semi-restored structure opened to
public, June 28, 1992

In 1937 the Solomon R. Guggenheim
Foundation was formed. Hilla Rebay,
spiritual leader of those interested in
nonobjective art (Kandinsky was her
favorite), helped the Guggenheims
form a collection to be called the
Museum of Non-Objective Painting.
Wright was commissioned to provide a
building for the collection.

Wright's original concept, dated
1943, is labeled a "ziggurat," and this
is still evident in the final plan, the
main gallery of which is a continuous
spiraling ramp in concrete. To Wright,
the spiral was symbolic of "organic
process." Wright expected this
incline—actually a decline, since the
architect intended visitors to use the
elevator, which stops one level below
the top of the spiral, then walk down to
the ground floor—to counteract the
usual dominance of right-angled
architecture over the flat plane of a
painting.

Overcoming the restrictions of the
New York City building code took more
time than either design or construction. William Wesley Peters and John
Rattenbury spent a winter revising
details until the New York building
department accepted the design, for
which a foundation had already been
laid. When he received the notice
of construction approval, Wright
announced to those in the Taliesin
drafting room, "I've been designing this
building for others for twenty-five
years; now I'm going to design it for
myself." He did so, incorporating all the
building commissioners' requirements,
while altering the angle of the exterior
walls of the main gallery several times
until he was satisfied that the skylighting would provide proper light for
the paintings. Mendel Glickman, with
William Wesley Peters, re-engineered
the structure to the new design in only
two months. William Short supervised
construction with David Wheatley and
Morton Delson. Lettering for the
incised brass signs was designed by

Guggenheim Museum

John Ottenheimer and used in other
structures such as the Dallas Theatre
Center (S.395). George N. Cohen of
Euclid Construction Company is the
only builder with his name inscribed on
a Wright building.

In 1952 the building was renamed
the Solomon R. Guggenheim Museum.
Wright apparently took little notice of
this in his design, which remained
consistent with the original concept.
On the basis of this change, museum
trustees added sculpture to its collections and, after Wright's death,
accepted the gift of the Justin K.
Thannhauser collection, which is
focused primarily on Impressionist
and post-Impressionist art.

During the 1980s, the museum's
administration seemed to take
umbrage with people who came to see
the building rather than the paintings
and sculpture housed there.

In the mid-eighties New York City
planners approved an architectural
addition to Wright's structure. The
Historic Buildings and Landmarks
Commission failed in late 1989 to grant
historic status to the structure, claiming
that it was a few months short of the

requisite thirtieth anniversary of its
opening (December 1959, though a
published *New York Times* photo
shows all the scaffolding down by
mid-summer); once construction of the
addition was begun, historical status
was granted). Museum trustees sold
major works to finance acquisitions
and the addition—Kandinsky, Chagall,

Modigliani—for profit. Such sales also
financed overseas activities of the
Guggenheim.

There have been other additions
and alterations. The concrete structure
was poorly surfaced to reduce cost,
but never finished in stone as some
evidence indicates Wright had wanted.
A second-level gallery was carved

Plan of lower (lecture room) level

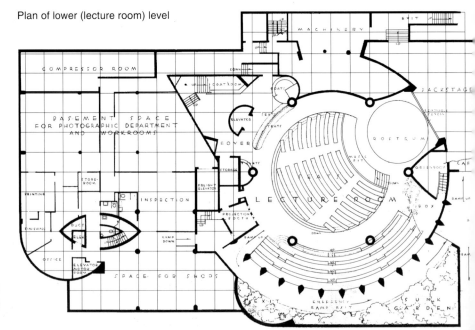

out of office space to house the Thannhauser collection. The driveway, a fifties version of a porte-cochere, has been filled in with a bookstore and cafe; the bookstore remains even after the so-called restoration. The main gallery skylights were covered, destroying Wright's lighting effects. In 1992 the main gallery was restored to Wright's intended design.

The structure has been designated by the American Institute of Architects as one of seventeen American buildings designed by Wright to be retained as an example of his architectural contribution to American culture.

View across galleries, top gallery and 3 levels below

Plan of first level

THOUGH IT IS NOT SCORED INTO THE CONCRETE FLOOR, THE 8' GRID EMPLOYED IN THE DESIGN AND SHOWN ON ALL WORKING DRAWINGS IS HERE SHOWN ON PARTS OF EACH FLOOR TO PROVIDE BOTH A SENSE OF SCALE AND OF THE ORGANIZATION GIVEN TO THE STRUCTURE BY ITS ARCHITECT

8'0"

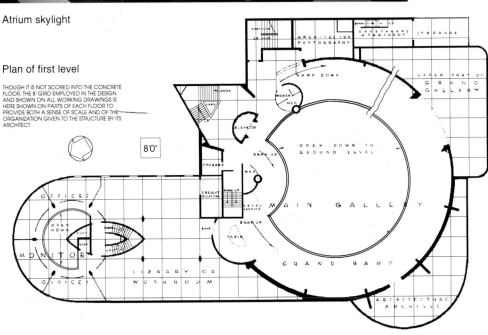

Plan of ground level

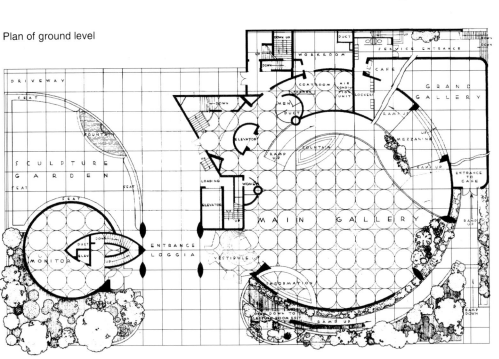

View to floor of gallery, with pool

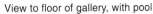

431

Wyoming Valley Grammar School

S.401   T.5741
Wyoming Valley Grammar School
(1956)
Wyoming Valley, Wisconsin

Not far south of Taliesin is the
Wyoming Valley Grammar School, the
only public elementary schoolhouse
built from a Wright design. It is concrete block and redwood with a
shingled roof. Employing 60- and
120-degree angles in its plan, and a
4-foot unit system, it is actually a two-
room school with central loggia. A
great room, convertible to serve as

auditorium or cafeteria, is on the north
side balancing the two classrooms.
The large rooms are skylighted by
the clerestory of the raised central
masonry. Fireplaces enhance the
hallway and great room. Mr. Wright
brought this plan fully drawn to John
H. Howe in the drafting room. The
structure was built essentially without
alterations by Ole Anderson, whose
first work with Mr. Wright was as
carpenter on the first Taliesin. When
the school committee said they could
not afford the architect's fee, Wright
said he would forfeit it. When they said
they could not afford the building,
Wright paid for part of it as a memorial
to his mother.

Main assembly room

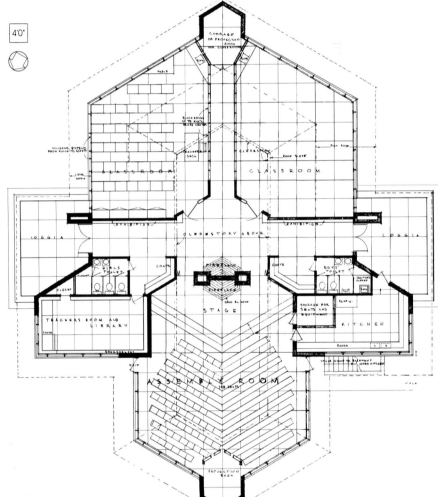

Dudley Spencer Residence

Allen Friedman Residence

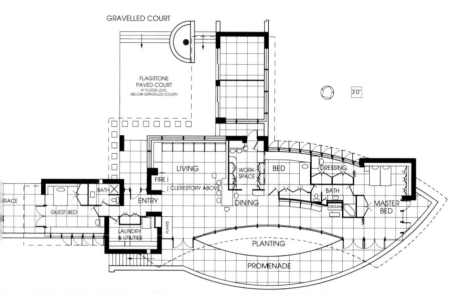

S.402   T.5605
Dudley Spencer Residence (1956)
Wilmington, Delaware
Carport added

The Dudley Spencer house is a solar hemicycle, essentially a mirror image of the Pearce (S.320) house. Stone replaces the block of the Pearce building. This was the second design prepared for the Spencers, the first being a virtual copy of the Shavin (S.339) residence.

S.403   T.5624
Allen Friedman Residence (1956)
Bannockburn, Illinois

This is a 120-degree in-line plan with wing reversed; that is while the bedroom wing faces north, outside the enclosed angle, with its gallery on the south side, the living room looks to the other side of the structure, southwest, into the enclosed angle of the plan. The design started as a version of the Fawcett house (S.385) but, with the playroom wing removed, it became a brick version of the stone Arnold residence (S.374). The carport extends from the workspace and entry area, at 120-degrees to either wing; a garage has been built into the end bays.

The built-in and much of the free-standing furniture is by Wright. Philippine mahogany is used in the built-ins, which include drawers that are shaped as parallelograms, two long sides and two short, that slide out on the 120-

degree angle. Special brick, molded to suit the 120- and 60-degree angles of masonry corners, were both fired and cut from standard bricks. The Friedmans received their final plan revisions, from three to two wings and drawn by John Ottenheimer, just before Wright's death. Construction was supervised by Cary Caraway for the Taliesin Associated Architects to completion in 1960. The original gravity heat has been converted to standard hot water; there has always been a separate air conditioning system, the ducts concealed by the decking that supports indirect lighting.

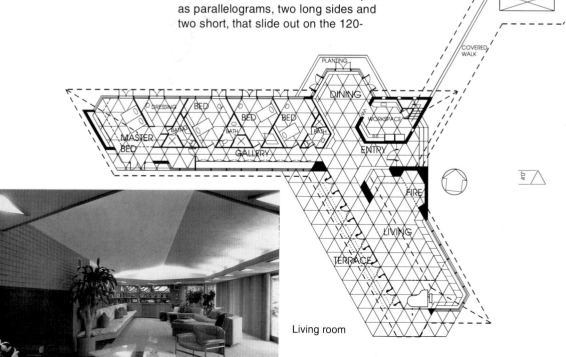

Living room

Bott Residence, view from south

Instead they placed the largest boulders at the bottom, small ones at the top, for the first half of construction. There is structural steel (welded angles) in the mullions. The wood is Honduran mahogany. The 4-by-8-foot boards were first halved, then cut into thirds lengthwise, to produce boards for the board and batten walls. John H. Howe worked on preliminary drawings. The final version and working drawings, completed in January 1960, were done by Cornelia Brierly, who also provided choice of colors in the fabrics for Wright's original furniture. All finish details were designed by April 1961. Construction was completed in 1963, at a cost of $200,000, under supervision of the Taliesin Associated Architects.

Living room

S.404 T.5627
Frank and Eloise **Bott** Residence (1956)
Kansas City, Missouri

Frank Bott's business was to set up dairy cooperatives. When one became financially stable, he would move on to establish another. He met Eloise at Florida Southern College (S.251–S.258).

The terne metal (lead on steel) roof of the Bott residence seems to grow out of the crest of the hill over which one approaches the house. The house is a double cantilever. The living room and balcony cantilever is the most dramatic, reaching far out over the hill toward the Missouri River, affording the Botts a lovely view of Kansas City

and providing complete privacy from neighbors nearby. The plan is a lopsided **T,** on a 4-foot unit system. The workspace is on the entry side of the living room, with a study at the opposite end. Eloise had Wright narrow his first design for the workspace, so that she could do everything by just turning in place. This had been Wright's original idea for all workspaces. A gallery runs the length of this part of the house; a second gallery runs at a 90-degree angle to this, from behind the fireplace masonry to the powder room and master bedroom. Additional rooms are below this main level.

Construction is desert masonry, employing one mile of farmer's wall stone from the nearby flint hills in Kansas. The builders had difficulty adjusting to Wright's required random placing of the stones in the forms.

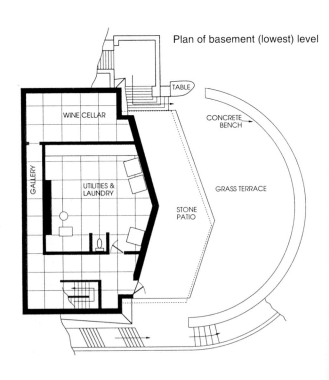

Plan of basement (lowest) level

Plan of main (top) level

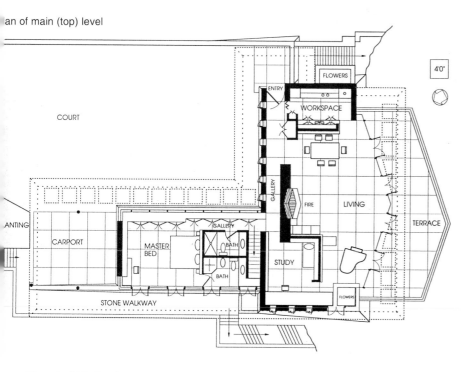

COURT

4'0"

PLANTING

CARPORT

MASTER BED

STONE WALKWAY

Plan of middle level

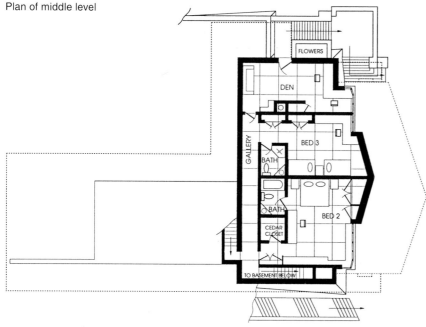

The former studio as used by the Nookers

S.405 T.5604
Clyde **Nooker Remodeling** of the **Frank Lloyd Wright Studio** (1956)
Oak Park, Illinois
Demolished

In the early 1940s, Mr. and Mrs. Clyde Nooker became owners of the Frank Lloyd Wright Residence and Studio. The studio had been separated by a firewall from the home in 1911 to create a duplex. Much of this interior remodeling involved the corridor that once linked Wright's home (S.002) to his studio (S.004). Wright put in a bathroom with shower, vanity, and dressing alcove, in Philippine mahogany, and a new kitchen. Further, he remodeled the original office and the library. All this work was fully documented and then removed in the Frank Lloyd Wright Home and Studio Foundation's restoration of Wright's first lived-in design (see listing S.002–S.004).

Erdman Prefabs

Marshall Erdman and Associates,
Prefab #1 (1956)
Nine sites

Of the three prefabricated house designs that Wright did for the Marshall Erdman company, only two were actually constructed; this is the first of them. The basic plan would be standard in-line except for the placement of the workspace/kitchen not at the juncture of living and bedroom wings, but on the side opposite the living room from that "quiet space." Each house has a masonry core, with painted exterior panel siding of textured Masonite board (5/16-inch thick, 4-by-16-foot Masonite Ridgeline siding) on 2-by-4-inch studs, decorated with horizontal battens on 16-inch centers. Inside this would be 4-by-8-foot mahogany plywood one quarter inch thick. Forced air heating, which could accommodate air conditioning, replaced the gravity heating common to Usonian designs, and probably intended in the earliest concept of this structure. Use of standard Andersen (or Pella) doors and awning windows was a cost-saving feature.

The simplest house, model 1300, was a 2130-square-foot structure with basement and carport; the kit of prefabricated parts was priced at $16,400. A fourth bedroom (model 1400) could be had for an outlay of another $1,200. The garage kit (model 1310/1410) added $400 to the basic kit price, but local purchases such as garage doors raised the total even more. A master bedroom enlarged by one unit raised the price $400. The exposed basement (model number extended with "EB") with windowall was an additional $1,100. Local carpentry and other subcontracts plus options would raise the total further. The Cass, including 3/4 acre site, cost $55,000 total. Four months was normal construction time, with plumbing, heating, wiring, and interior finishing done on the site.

Cedar shakes were a variation for standard asphalt shingles ($569 compared with $640). Wright's architectural fee, per house, was $750.

Continual enlargement—from the broadening of the family room and shifting of family and living room facades by 32 inches for all units after the model home, through a 4-foot extension of the master bedroom, to additions of a full basement (all production units), fourth bedroom and utility room—increased prefab-kit production costs, as well as at-site construction costs, thereby helping doom Erdman's ambitious project.

Van Tamelen Residence, the original model, entry

S.406   T.5518
Eugene **Van Tamelen** Residence (1956)

(Original model, 3 bedroom with carport)
Madison, Wisconsin
Family room expanded and full basement added

In the original Erdman model home, the Van Tamelen residence, the family room was small (10 feet, 4 inches square) and poorly lit; in all later construction it was 12 feet square and fitted with a corner window requiring a steel brace. Living room, family room, and workspace are all three steps below the bedroom wing. Under the bedroom wing, where it meets the living room at the entry, the Van Tamelen house has a utilities basement reached by a stair where Wright's first thoughts were to have a powder room.

The Van Tamelen house was built, at rather high cost, to serve as the Erdman model. It is drawn to a 32-inch-square unit module, or to fit two 16-inch textile/concrete blocks. The vertical unit is half the horizontal unit, or 16 inches, revealing the Prefab's origins in a Usonian Automatic type D design in textile block for Walter Bimson of Phoenix, Arizona.

To gain space, a basement was dug out under the house, and the family room enlarged, by Taliesin Associated Architects.

S.407   T.5518
(3 bedroom with basement)
S.407.1   T.5518
Dr. Arnold and Lora **Jackson** Residence, Skyview (1957)
(Version with optional garage and full, exposed, basement)
Madison, Wisconsin
Removed February 1985 to Beaver Dam, Wisconsin
S.407.2   T.5518
Elizabeth and Don C. **Duncan** Residence (1957)
(Version with carport, basement under all but bedroom wing)
Lisle, Illinois

Lora Zeisel left Elkhart, Indiana, to attend the University of Wisconsin. In Madison, she met Arnold Jackson; the two were married in 1917. After Wright got into a fight on Halloween in 1932, Columbia University and Mayo Clinic–trained Dr. Arnold Jackson repaired the architect's broken nose. A long-term friendship ensued. In 1950, Lora Jackson asked Wright to design a cottage for a site, already named Skyview for its north-facing hillside location, south of Madison. Construction estimates kept well ahead of available funds, even as the Jacksons asked for revisions that enlarged the design. One absolute requirement was a garage—an anathema to Wright, but a necessity for the doctor, who had to be able to start his car in bitter cold weather. When the Erdman Prefab #1 model home (Van Tamelen, S.406) was on public exhibit, the Jacksons saw it and opted to build a version adapted to their needs; this included a garage, and a basement fitted to the sloping site.

The Jackson bedroom had two side-by-side sets of four Andersen Flexvent awning windows stacked vertically in the master bedroom to admit sun to the northwest-facing room and to allow the Jacksons to see any approaching visitors. In the Iber home, this security glazing is reduced to a single set of four awning windows. The flooring, since the prefabs are not set on a concrete slab, is a red tile rubber surface in the workspace where carpeting is not used. Neither the dining table nor most desks, built-ins of

(Continues)

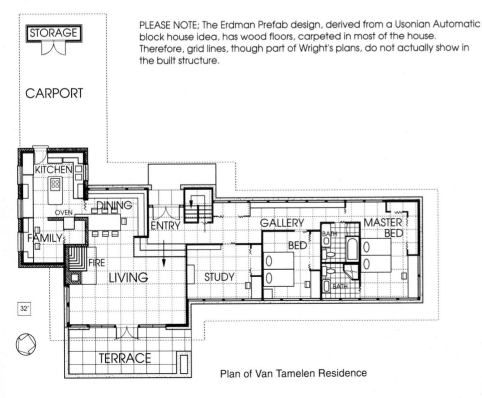

PLEASE NOTE; The Erdman Prefab design, derived from a Usonian Automatic block house idea, has wood floors, carpeted in most of the house. Therefore, grid lines, though part of Wright's plans, do not actually show in the built structure.

Plan of Van Tamelen Residence

Wright's design, were constructed, but the study and bedrooms all have built-in bookshelves.

The Jackson house, after being moved to Beaver Dam by Chris Fecht, was acquired by Andrew and Barbara Spadanuta with Michael and Rebecca Wissell; the latter are Beaver Dam residents, but the building is being reconstructed by all four. The structure was moved onto a new foundation in three sections, the bedroom wing, the living room with dining and entry areas, and the kitchen with family room. Additional structural support was provided for the roof by doubling the framing of alternate beams and by using flitch plates. Tiger stripe mahogany plywood panels at $75 each were obtained to refinish interior surfaces, and some baseboard heat added to supplement the forced air system.

Don Duncan left South Dakota to study radio in Chicago. He then went to work for the telephone company putting up poles, next to Western Electric. During the war, he was assigned to a cruiser in the pacific; Elizabeth was left in Washington, D.C. It was Elizabeth Duncan who wanted Wright as the architect for their house, but Don thought of him as an architect for the rich. The 1956 *House and Home* article on the Erdman prefabs introduced them to the Van Tamelen house. They visited this "model," then the Jackson house, and asked Erdman for the latter. Wisconsin limestone was not affordable, so the home was built in concrete block and with the less expensive carport. The house, sited by David Dodge, was constructed with "no extras" other than cabinets in the dining area for $47,000. The exterior is the same color as the Van Tamelen house, the interior a blonde pigmented bleach on mahogany, with grey block.

The site is near the Danada farms northwest of the Morton Arboretum. This area is shared by Naperville, Lisle, and Wheaton, but was assigned for many years to Wheaton's post office, and only more recently to Lisle's. Since the original contractor lived in Naperville, it has been incorrectly called the Naperville prefab. A bridge, still in place but now unused, had to be constructed across a stream to provide access to the 15-acre site.

Jackson Skyview, master bedroom with security window

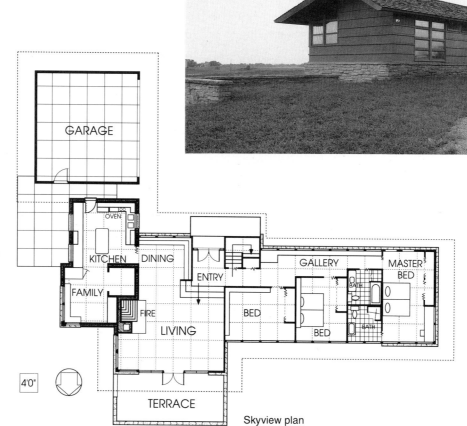

Skyview plan

Duncan Residence

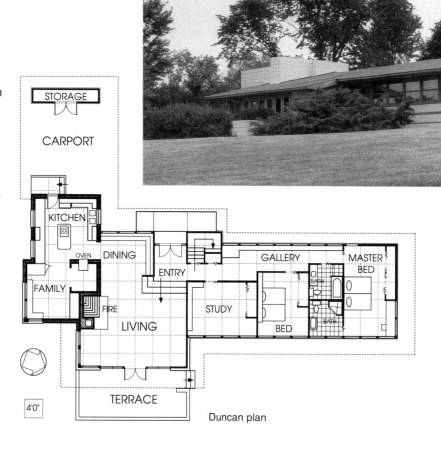

Duncan plan

The Duncans wanted to meet their architect, and so they went out to Taliesin West. They were advised to sit under the bell and enjoy the beauty, for "Mr. Wright will eventually come by." He didn't. Don got tired of waiting. On the way out, he had to pass through Mr. Wright's office. The architect was "very gently" interviewing a Chinese student who had with him some drawings. When the student left, Wright approached Don and shook hands. "Mr. Wright, we never expected to meet you." Mr. Wright's nonagenarian reply: "Young man, you're very lucky."

Erdman Prefab #1

S.408 T.5518
Frank **Iber** Residence (1957)
 (4 bedroom with garage and
exposed basement)
Stevens Point, Wisconsin

The original model features three bedrooms; as built, all others but the
Jackson and La Fond houses have
four, the addition being a mirror of the
middle bedroom placed between it and
the master bedroom. All but the original model, the Duncan, and the
Zaferiou expand the utilities basement
to a full "exposed" basement under the
bedrooms with view opening, by way
of a long windowall, in the same direction as the living room. Generally, the
small space off the family room,
Wright's intended grade-level utilities
space, becomes a powder room,
replacing the one lost to the basement stairs. Limestone is used in the
Jackson, Iber, and Mollica houses;
the Post and Cass employ brick; and
the Van Tamelen, Duncan, Zaferiou,
and La Fond have concrete block,
painted over with a coating of linseed
oil; Wright listed all three masonry
possibilities on the plans, in the order
given here. Gabled-roof variants were
asphalt shingles trimmed with battens
every fifth course (Van Tamelen,
Zaferiou, La Fond) or cedar shakes
(though the Cass has a nonstandard
red terne metal, lead on steel, surface); a flat-roofed version suitable to
Usonian Automatic construction was
never considered for the prefab. Most
often, wood was painted burgundy with
pink trim, or vice versa, though
individual variations were common,
such as the Sauterne or wet sand of
the Zaferiou block. While most of the
exterior paneling of the Iber house is
painted, the fascia and soffits are
blonde mahogany, providing a strong
horizontal band of color between roof
and walls.

Iber Residence, family room corner with garage to left

Iber entry

Iber Prefab, view over terrace from master
bedroom corner

Plan of Iber Prefab

Erdman Prefab #1

S.409   T.5518
(4 bedroom including enlarged master bedroom and exposed basement)
S.409.1   T.5518
Carl **Post** Residence (Borah-Post residence) (1957)
(Version with optional garage)
Barrington Hills, Illinois (formerly S.409)
S.409.2   T.5518
William and Catherine **Cass** Residence, The Crimson Beech (1959)
(Version with standard carport)
Richmond (Staten Island), New York (formerly S.410)
Swimming pool added by Morton Delson

The first four Prefab #1 houses have master bedrooms 12 feet wide, but successive construction made this 16 feet through an extension of the grid one 4-foot unit (the standard for the kit). Van Tamelen, Duncan, Cass, Zaferiou, and LaFond have carports, others the optional 24-by-24-foot garage (the doors obtained locally). The breezeway between kitchen and garage for the Post house is twice as wide as for the Iber; successive plans would make this 12 by 15 feet, and allow for enclosure as a utilities room or shop.

Builder Al Borah erected the Barrington Hills unit and sold it to Carl Post a few months after its completion; it was shown to members of the National Association of Home Builders at their January 1958 annual convention in Chicago. As with most of these prefabs, the built-in furniture, from desks in the bedrooms to dining room table, were not built. The oven is in the original location, with a closet behind.

The Cass house was shown at open houses for Macy's, which furnished the home to Wright's specifications. Its name, the Crimson Beech, refers to a centuries-old Copper Beech tree around which the house was situated; it has since been destroyed by lightning. Morton Delson supervised original construction and designed the swimming pool that was built at the basement level.

Post Residence

Prefab living room (Post Residence)

Prefab family room (Post Residence) viewed from kitchen

PLEASE NOTE: There are dropped ceilings in all the #1 prefabs in the kitchen, over the dining area, at the entry, and over the bath/shower. These are shown only on this drawing, by thin dashed lines.

Plan of Post Residence

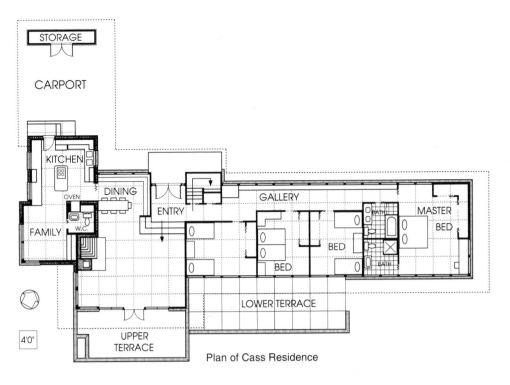

Plan of Cass Residence

Cass Residence, The Crimson Beech, kitchen-family room corner (living room right, family room right center, workspace left center, and carport left)

Zaferiou Residence

S.411   T.5518
(Mirrored plan, with exposed basement and shop or utility room)
S.411.1   T.5518
Joseph **Mollica** Residence (1958)
(4 bedroom with optional garage)
Bayside, Wisconsin
S.411.2   T.5518
Dr. Edward and Lora Jane **LaFond** Residence (1960)
(3 bedroom with standard carport)
Saint Joseph, Minnesota

Two mirror-image houses of the Prefab #1 plan were built, one mostly standard but with the optional mudroom, the other with all options. Builder Joseph Mollica erected his with the optional workshop between kitchen and garage (he used it as a utility room, for laundry and such), and french doors from the kitchen to the backyard, the only Prefab #1 with this feature (LaFond has added this since original construction). Wisconsin limestone is used as facing masonry. Flooring at the entry and around the fireplace is also stone, as are the exposed footings. The fascia and soffits are painted the same pastel green as the exterior walls, softening the horizontal nature of the design. Most of the built-ins that were called for in the bedrooms were not constructed. As the largest of the prefabs, the Mollica house raises the question, Why prefabricate a design if it is not going to reduce construction costs significantly?

The LaFond home on Kraemer Lake is constructed with standard concrete block. It has three bedrooms on the first and a full basement under the entire main floor to accommodate four more bedrooms for the large LaFond family. Window wells in the ground admit natural light. The house is rotated 17 degrees east of south to take advantage of the morning sun and to bring the sun to the rear wall on the long summer days. The contour of the site required that the plan be mirrored. The $20,395 kit was erected by Dr. LaFond's contractor brother, Marcel. Original asphalt shingles with horizontal ribbing have been replaced with "timberline" random asphalt and a wood deck added between terrace and kitchen.

LaFond had little intention of building a Wright-designed home. He was

S.410   T.5518
Celeste and Socrates **Zaferiou** Residence (1961)
(4 bedroom with carport, enclosed basement and mud room/shop)
Blauvelt, New York
This number was formerly assigned the Cass Residence, which is now S.409.2.

The Zaferiou dwelling has the optional 12-by-15-foot workshop or mud room between the kitchen and the carport. Standard 8-by-16-by-8-inch concrete block is used, painted the color of wet sand, as is the Masonite board. This particular site, on a mountainside, required special grading and fill to provide space for the terrace and some yard beyond. Because of the rocky site, the full basement is enclosed, opening only at the end (a later addition) and not out to the hillside. Morton Delson supervised both New York homes; the Zaferiou was begun before the Cass (1959), but finished later due to contractor problems.

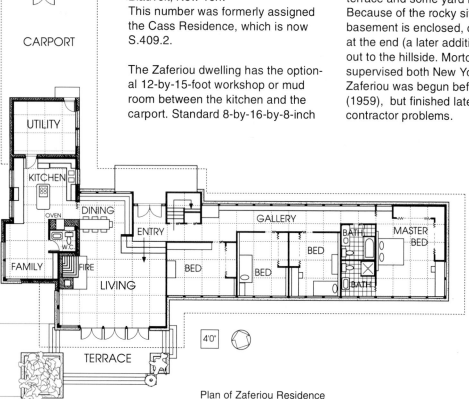

Plan of Zaferiou Residence

Mollica Residence, private facade

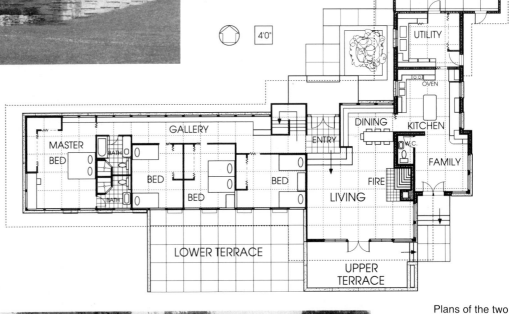

GARAGE

UTILITY

DINING · KITCHEN

ENTRY

MASTER BED · BATH

GALLERY

BED

BED

BED

W.C.

FAMILY

FIRE

LIVING

LOWER TERRACE

UPPER TERRACE

4'0"

visiting the Erdman offices concerning the building of his medical clinic; Erdman is widely known for pre-fabricated medical units, particularly for the Peace Corps in Africa. He saw plans for the Prefab #1 lying on a table, inspected them, and asked about building such a house. Erdman tried to persuade LaFond to build one of his prefabs instead of Wright's, but the doctor persisted.

The Prefab #1 plan is varied by simple additions from the basic Van Tamelen model through versions with basement and optional garage, to inserted fourth bedroom, then enlarged master bedroom, and ending with insertion of workshop or utility room between kitchen and carport/garage. Mirroring significantly alters the relationship to the site, providing yet another variation on the theme. Thus, the LaFond and Mollica are closest relatives, even though it may also be seen as a three-bedroom mirrored plan of the Zaferiou or a mirror of the Duncan house.

Plans of the two mirror-imaged Prefabs

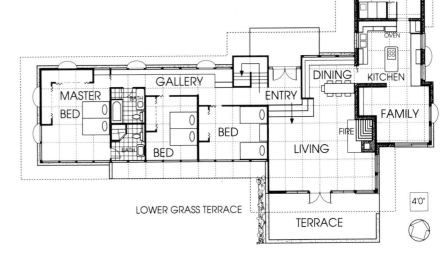

LaFond Residence, public facade

STORAGE

CARPORT

UTILITY

OVEN

MASTER BED

GALLERY

ENTRY

DINING · KITCHEN

BED

BED

BATH

FAMILY

FIRE

LIVING

LOWER GRASS TERRACE

TERRACE

4'0"

LaFond Residence, private facade

Rudin Residence

SQUARE PLANS

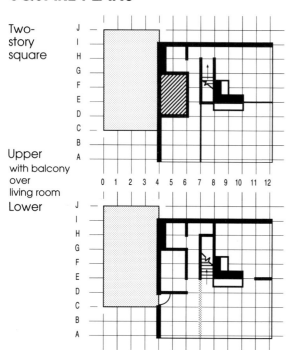

Two-story square

Upper
with balcony over living room

Lower

Master bedroom either down or upstairs. 2 bathrooms

Looking for ways to reduce a house plan to its most compact expression can be an endless pursuit. One attempt was the two-story square or, in its built version, a three-story cube, with full basement including a "play" or family room; see S.412.

Single-story one-bedroom "square"

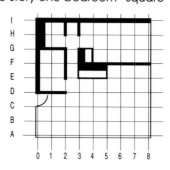

For a single-story one-bedroom cottage, a very compact arrangement can be obtained; this is particularly elegant if one does not encumber it with a carport. A variant of this becomes the "one-room" cottage; see S.430.

S.412   T.5706
Marshall Erdman and Associates, **Prefab #2** (1957)
S.412.1   T.5706
Mary Ellen and Walter **Rudin** Residence
Madison, Wisconsin
S.412.2   T.5706
James B. **McBean** Residence
Rochester, Minnesota

This building was first seen in Madison as part of the Parade of Homes. No others were built in Wisconsin.

The second of the three prefab designs for Marshall Erdman is a version of the "one-room house," a wood structure based on the textile-block Usonian Automatic type A for Walter Bimson of the Valley National Bank, Arizona. The Rudin house is the original model and is situated on a flat site. It is essentially a square plan. A balcony outside the second-story sleeping quarters overlooks the large two-story square living room. The entry separates the kitchen and dining area from utility, bath, and master bedroom. Abandoning his usual injunction against basements, Wright allowed a full lower level with storage, heater, and family room. Windows immediately below the soffit ring the house, making the roof seem to float with no apparent

STORAGE

FAMILY

HEATER

PLANTING

Plan of the basement (lower level) of the Rudin house as built

support. The two units built are both concrete block and painted, with horizontal batten on plywood panels.

The McBean residence is set into a hillside site and so angled as to take maximum advantage of the sun, both morning and afternoon. Since it and the Rudin dwelling have the same floor plan and vary only in minor details such as paint color and siting, they are now listed under the common number of S.412 and differentiated by decimal suffix only. The McBean house was formerly S.413, a number now not used.

The McBean house on its hillside site does not have the planter that was featured in the original design.

McBean Residence

View from McBean balcony

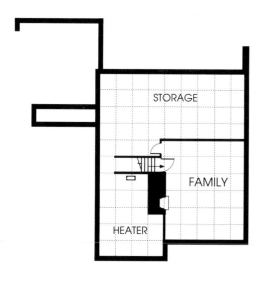

Plan of lower level (basement) McBean version of Prefab #2

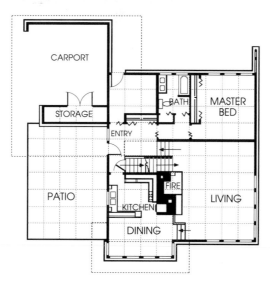

Plan of main (first) floor of McBean version of Prefab #2 (All McBean plans shown with grid)

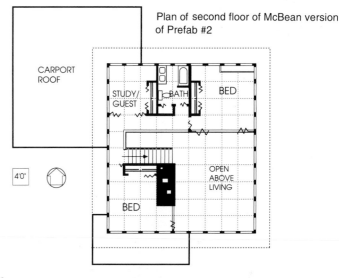

Plan of second floor of McBean version of Prefab #2

Note: the grid does not show on plans and, as the buildings are meant to be carpeted, would not show in the structure. Yet the grid is part of Wright's design, so is shown on this drawing.

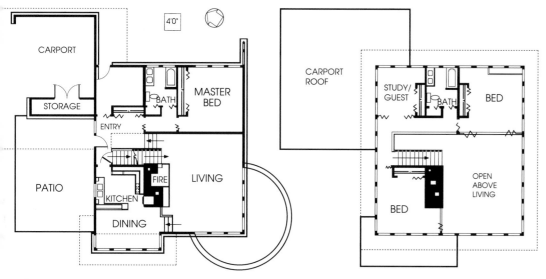

Plan of main (first floor) level of the Rudin house as built

Plan of second floor of the Rudin house as built

View into McBean dining area

445

Lindholm Service Station

S.414　T.5739
R. W. **Lindholm Service Station**
(1956)
Cloquet, Minnesota

The basic design concept for this building derives from the Broadacre City Standardized Overhead Service Station of 1932, which had overhead fuel lines so that the paved surface would be free of obstructions. Local regulations required standard ground-mounted pumps. Otherwise, Wright's cantilevered canopy remains, and the waiting room is still above the attendants' area, while mechanics' working areas are on the ground level and to the side. Construction was of concrete block that is painted, with a terne metal roof. This is the only service station built from Wright's plans. The Lindholms also built a residence (S.353), Mäntylä, four years earlier.

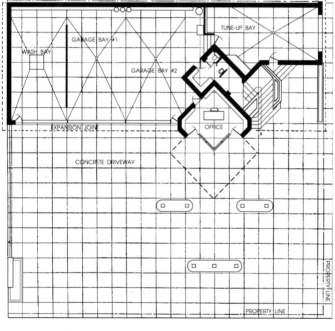

Marin County Civic Center

S.415–S.417　T.5746
Marin County Civic Center (1957)
San Rafael, California

Few were the buildings commissioned from Wright by government agencies, and fewer still those that were built; three are in Marin County. The Marin County Civic Center includes a main Administration Building and contiguous Hall of Justice of similar concrete forms under a roof of cast concrete coated with a polymer paint. The Marin County Post Office, Wright's one completed United States government building, is across the street. Former Taliesin fellow and San Francisco architect Aaron Green supervised all these government projects. Nearby is a Taliesin-designed theater auditorium.

Marin County Post Office

Marin County Civic Center

S.415 T.5746C
Post Office (1957)
San Rafael, California

Wright's only constructed work for the
United States Government is this
building in the Marin County Civic
Center. A nearly circular structure of
concrete block and forms, this post
office sits at the foot of the hill below
the Marin County Administration
Building (S.416). The first, compact,
plan had to be enlarged in the mail-
sorting area, disrupting the original
proportions. Its construction, after
Wright's death, was by the Taliesin
Associated Architects, with completion
in 1962.

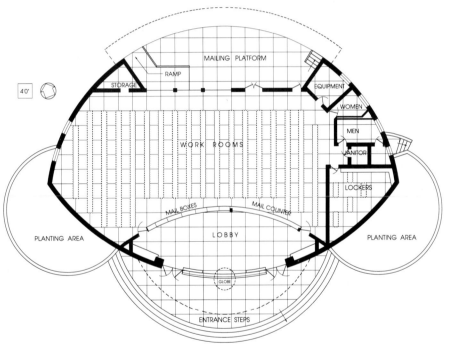

Main lobby of Marin Post Office

Marin County Civic Center

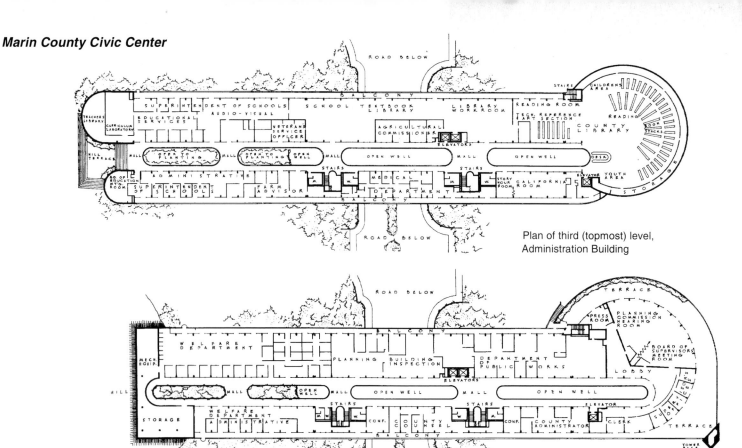

Plan of third (topmost) level, Administration Building

Marin County
Administration Building

Plan of second level, Administration Building

S.416   T.5746A
Administration Building (1957)
and
S.417   T.5746E
Hall of Justice (1957, 1967)
San Rafael, California

The Marin County Administration
Building and contiguous Hall of Justice
are of similar concrete forms, with
roofs of cast concrete coated with a
polymer paint. Reaching out from the
domed library center, behind the
commanding pylon (a ventilation tower
intended by Wright to serve also as a
radio antenna), each of these wings
seeks a distant hill, complementing the
spaces between them. Wright's
drawings were sufficiently detailed for
Aaron Green and William Wesley
Peters to complete necessary working
drawings. Revisions to suit the client
were largely in the area of adjusting
sizes of certain rooms within the Hall

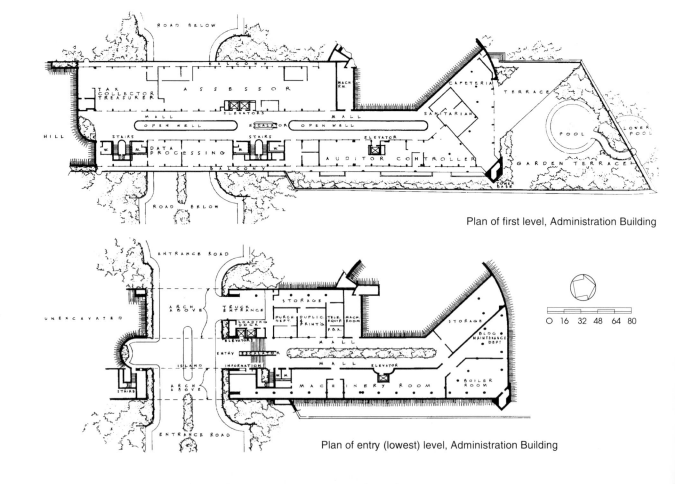

Plan of first level, Administration Building

Plan of entry (lowest) level, Administration Building

Interior galleries of the Marin County Administration Building

of Justice, which features movable walls, to their specific uses and integrating these with the multilevel arcaded format. Green designed the circular court rooms; Bill Schwarz assisted him in completion of the Hall

of Justice. The Administration Building was completed in 1962, the Hall of Justice in 1970, under Taliesin Associated Architects' supervision.

Interior gallery of the Marin County Hall of Justice

Marin County Hall of Justice

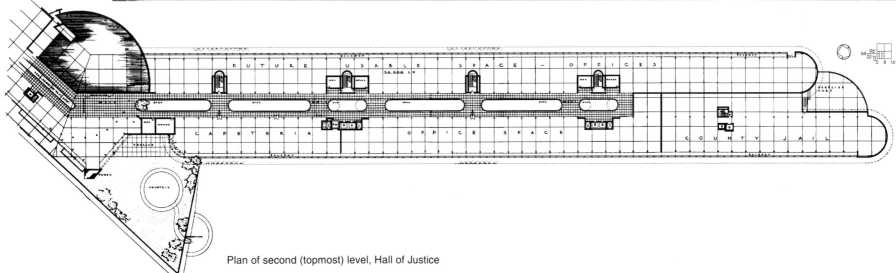

Plan of second (topmost) level, Hall of Justice

Juvenile Cultural Center

Atrium at side of the courtyard of the Center

Faculty Office in north arm of the Center

Classroom in south arm of the Center

S.418   T.5743A
Juvenile Cultural Study **Center**
(1957), Harry F. Corbin Education
Center, for Wichita State University
Wichita, Kansas

Harry F. Corbin was president of the
Municipal University of Wichita and Dr.
Jackson O. Powell was dean and the
moving force in the Juvenile Cultural
Center's construction. These two
persuaded the directors of MUW to
choose Wright as architect for the
College of Education. Two buildings
were planned, a classroom and office
building, the Juvenile Cultural Center
on Wright's plans, and an elementary
laboratory school. Construction of the
former was delayed until 1963 for
lack of funds. Dedication was in June
1964, when it was given the name of
President Corbin, who had fought to
bring MUW into the state university
system and had resigned when his
battle was won. The Kansas Board of
Regents then decided to phase out lab
schools, so the second building, which
might have been the more interesting
of the two in its use of concentric
circular segments as unit modules,
was never built.

Cast concrete, metals, and expan-
ses of glass constitute the rectangular
units either side of the patio. Each
wing is two stories high, with class-

rooms and office space, and courtyards symmetrically placed about the
patio axis, all on an 8-foot-square unit
module. Eleven colors of brick, from
burnt umber to dark orange, are used
in each of the campus buildings;
Wright limited this to a single color for
Corbin, essentially the brick closest
to Taliesin Red.

John H. Howe laid out the original
plan as head of Wright's drafting room;
Howe makes the point that this was
common, that he was "trained by Mr.
Wright to proceed with these designs
and to proceed with them well enough
so Mr. Wright would approve them with
(but) slight changes." Curtis Besinger,
number two man in the drafting room,
supervised construction to completion
in 1964 after preparing the working
drawings, which were signed by
William Wesley Peters as architect for
the Taliesin Associated Architects. The
buildings are open to visitors during
regular university session hours.

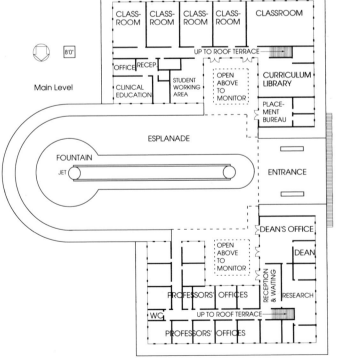

Plan of Juvenile Cultural Center, ground level

S.419 T.5710
**Conrad Edward and Evelyn
Gordon** Residence (1956)
Aurora, now Wilsonville, Oregon

The Gordons wanted to build a house
and had looked at the work of architects in nearby Portland. On a trip to
Phoenix, they visited Taliesin West. Mr.
Gordon, a farmer with lots of land but
little money, mentioned that he was
planning to build. Their tour guide
(they remember Eugene Massellink)
said he'd make them an appointment
with Mr. Wright. At first Wright refused
but, influenced by the fact that he had
never done a home in Oregon and that
architect and former Taliesin apprentice Burton Goodrich had his practice
in Portland, he agreed to produce a
design.

Building was delayed, year after
year, but the dream of building their
Wright house remained with the
Gordons. By then, the Gordon
children, two boys, one girl, had long
since moved on. The house was
completed in 1964 under the guidance
of Taliesin Associated Architects, with
Goodrich as supervisor. Stamberg, the
contractor who was lowest bidder of no
more than five, was so pleased with
the work that he requested an open
house. It was scheduled for only one
weekend, but visitors kept coming
throughout the following week.

The plan of this concrete-block
structure is a **T.** The design may usefully be compared with that of the
Schwartz residence (S.271), of which
this is a variant. The masonry was laid
by one man, with helpers providing
only the manual labor of moving the
wheelbarrows loaded with concrete or
blocks. The two-story living room runs
north toward the right bank of the
Willamette River, opening to both east
and west views. Secondary bedrooms,
with balconies, are in the head of the
T, over the office and the master
bedroom.

Gordon Residence, west side from northwest

Living room of Gordon Residence

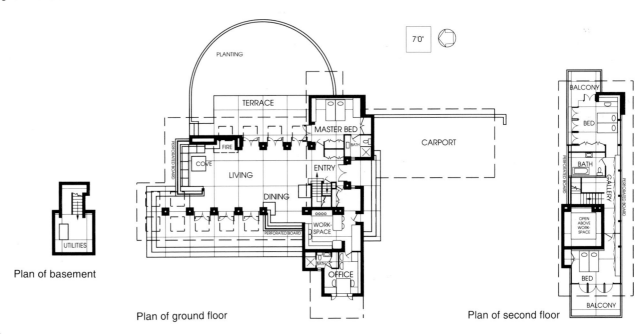

Plan of basement

Plan of ground floor

Plan of second floor

451

Longer view of Duey Wright Residence, bedroom wing to right

Duey Wright Residence, living room left, workspace center

S.420   T.5727

Julia and **Duey Wright** Residence
(1956)
Wausau, Wisconsin

Approximately an **L** plan, the design imitates a musical note; the clients owned Wright's Music Store in Wausau. Common concrete block is used to create the circular section of the living room that commands a panoramic westward view to Rib Mountain from 20 feet above the left bank of the Wisconsin River. The full length of the window curve holds a bench with seating sufficient for 30 people, who come, of course, for chamber music concerts (as many as 112 have fit comfortably into the room). The cut-out for the clerestory and interior decorations represent the rhythm of Beethoven's Fifth Symphony Allegro con brio first theme; "Beethoven builds well," commented Duey Wright. The round window in the workspace is, of course, a whole note. The home, the Wrights' "Wausau Concerto," was occupied in December 1959.

The workspace is adjacent to the living room, while sleeping quarters are in the long wing with carport at its terminus, an arrangement Wright would use in his next two designs (S.421, S.422) as well. Philippine mahogany is used for all trim. Furniture was either designed by Wright or approved by him. There is a basement under all but the bedroom wing. Wright had agreed to a small basement under the music room, but during construction the hillside was found to be of

Workspace

Living room

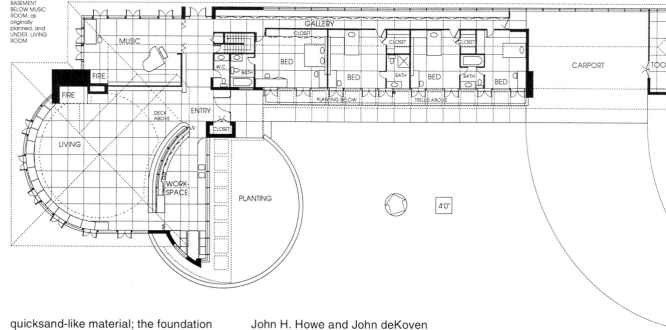

quicksand-like material; the foundation had to be dug to solid ground. The client had the contractor pour a concrete floor in the other excavated area.

John H. Howe and John deKoven Hill worked on the plans, and Hill designed the interior. Duey Wright is not related to the architect.

S.421   T.5623

Dr. Robert G. and Mary **Walton** Residence (1957)
Modesto, California

Situated near the Stanilaus River, this concrete-block house with wood fascia and trim is one of many developments of the New York Usonian Exhibition House concept (S.369). It is an in-line plan on a 32-inch unit (two concrete blocks), facing east, with added master bedroom where a carport would otherwise be.

How do you design for a very large family? The "typical" Usonian design had in its quiet wing but one bathroom near the workspace core (where it could serve both family and visitors), a tunnel gallery leading to the master bedroom, and in-between one additional bedroom for a child or two; bunk beds could expand capacity. It was easy enough to place additional bedrooms in line in this quiet wing, or to cluster them at a common juncture (as in the Pappas house, S.392), if additional children were expected. But what about a *very* large family?

The Walton house is one solution. Run bedrooms in line as far as you dare (four, plus playroom that otherwise would be the master bedroom and eventually was converted to a bedroom), and place a bedroom—in this instance the master bedroom—the other side of the gallery. Wright had already tried this solution for one growing family; when Mrs. Haynes (S.323) became pregnant even as Wright was designing her house, he sketched in a bedroom the other side of the gallery (it was not built). Wright

Walton Residence, public facade

Fascia detail

took full advantage of a necessity, and designed not only a master bedroom with its own bathroom and study, but also a powder room for visitors, in this "attached" wing.

A carport extends the main bedroom wing without making it seem overlong, as an enclosed garage would have. A small gallery overlooks the workspace and provides access to views from the rooftop. Though the fascia is nicely detailed, the transom-level windows, an unusual double row, have only clear glass, no pattern. Perimeter heat and air conditioning were needed for the central valley climate. The Walton house has a fine complement of Wright-designed furniture including a pentagonal table and a full dining room set with straight-backed chairs.

Between Wright's initial 1957 design and completion of construction by the Taliesin Associated Architects in 1961, six units were added between the workspace and the first of the children's bedrooms for a second study and extra bathroom. At roughly 3000 square feet of enclosed space, this is one of Wright's largest single-story homes. A pool has been added, not quite as or where Wright specified.

Private facade, bedroom wing to left

Living room

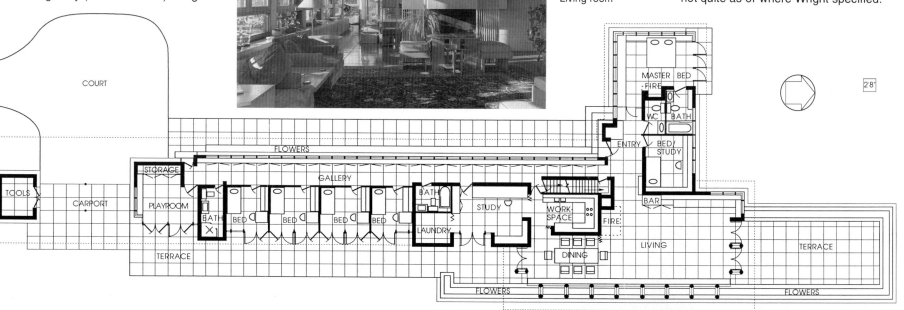

Kinney Residence, private facade

S.422   T.5717
Dorothy Ann and **Sterling Kinney**
Residence (1957)
Amarillo, Texas

Both Mr. and Mrs. Kinney are
attorneys and supporters of community
affairs. They met at the University of
Texas, Austin.

Red-brick walls (90,000 bricks) set
at a 15-degree batter at all but the
living room facades characterize this
house set on the caprock of the west
Texas panhandle. The workspace
separates the living room from children's sleeping quarters, with their
own terrace. A dining area is given its
own space, at the back of the living
room, across from the workspace. The
master bedroom, study, and two bathrooms on the other side of the living
room complete an outside **L** plan with
affinities to the Walton (S.421) layout.
A separate terrace conforms to the **L**
around the west and north facade, into
which the living space looks. Sand is
mixed with paint in those few places it
is used such as ceilings, to provide
texture. The house uses forced-air
ventilation for both heating and cooling.

Construction was completed in
1961 under the Taliesin Associated
Architects and supervised by Allen
Lape Davison.

Living room

Workspace

Dining alcove

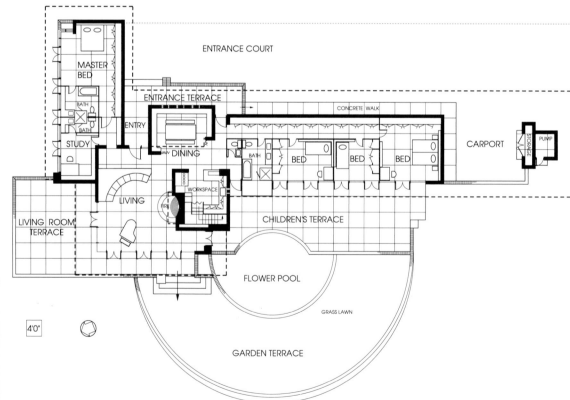

Boswell Residence

S.423   T.5704
William P. **Boswell** Residence
(1957)
Indian Hill, Ohio

Wright produced one preliminary design (T.5526) that would not hold Boswell's "busload of kids." Bank president William P. Boswell rejected revision after revision, so Wright started over with a new design, simpler, if rather large and perhaps relatively undisciplined, in brick rather than the architect's choice of stone. It is an outside (270-degree) **L**-plan with ancillary services in one wing, quiet spaces in the other. The house has a dual forced-air heating and cooling plus radiant heating system. Construction was completed under Taliesin Associated Architects' supervision in 1961.

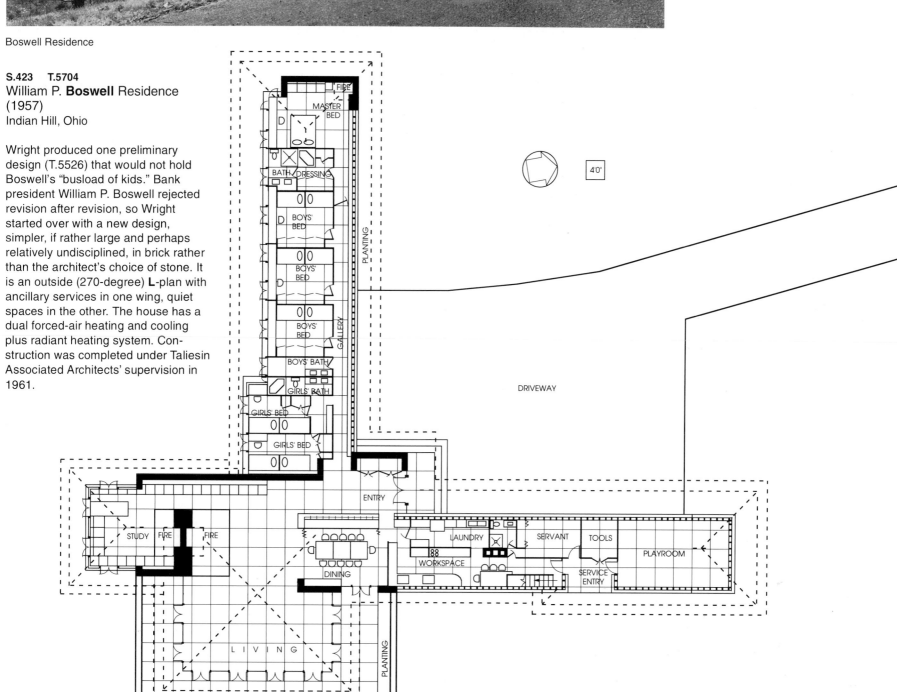

Plan of Boswell Residence, final scheme

S.424 T.5730
Herman T. **Fasbender Medical Clinic,** Mississippi Valley Clinic (1957) for Drs. Werner Fasbender and Frank Cahill
Hastings, Minnesota
Converted from medical to dental clinic

Originally a medical clinic, later a credit union, and more recently dentists' offices, this brick structure is given added character by the draping at the buildings' terminus of its terne metal roof, substituting for copper, which was too expensive. The roof shape and plan are based on a design done in 1941 for a studio-residence for Mary Waterstreet, a close friend of Wright's over the decades.

The reception room occupies one-third of the building. Examination rooms are placed on both sides of a central gallery. Original plans called for an office and four spacious examination rooms each two and one-half by three units; the unit module is a 4-foot square. When the doctor requested more rooms, Wright maintained the total size by reducing three of these four rooms to two by two-and-a-half units, thus gaining two more rooms. The southeast corner room, left

Entry side of the Mississippi Valley Clinic

unchanged, became an emergency surgery room. The tower housed an X-ray room; this has been converted to a records office. The low wall encloses a garden area fully as large as the clinic interior.

The building was erected, more for prestige than profit, by the Graus Construction Company. Tom Olson supervised.

Dr. Fasbender moved when his clinic staff outgrew the space, which allowed for no expansion. Drs. J. K. Kugler and J. W. Thibodo have kept the building much as they received it, altering only for the needs of their dental practice.

South side, view over enclosed garden

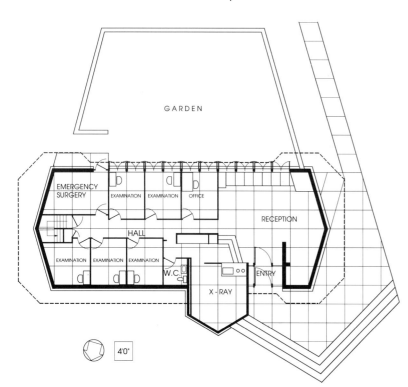

Reception room

S.425 T.5813

Lockridge Medical Clinic, for Drs. Lockridge, McIntyre and Whalen (1958)
Whitefish, Montana
Circular garden eliminated, and interior repartitioned for various office uses

Dr. Lockridge's very large practice was described as "half of Montana." The plan of the clinic is in-line, set on a 4-foot-square unit module. The building is 128 feet long. There are galleries on both sides of the single row of offices set aside for examinations and consultation in the north wing. To the south, the building is twice as deep, to accommodate X-ray facilities. The double clerestory provides for a warm atmosphere in the waiting room, which features a wood mural of the old west by Les Welliver. The lower fascia is concrete, the upper parapet is lapped wood siding.

John H. Howe did the preliminary drawings, Tom Casey the working drawings. Construction, not supervised by Taliesin Associated Architects, was completed shortly after Wright's death; the carpenter came to Taliesin for

Lockridge Medical Clinic, second tenant

"training." Construction was of the highest order, however, with tinted mortar deeply raked on the horizontal joints, flush on the vertical. Philippine mahogany is used for trim.

Dr. Lockridge died a year after occupying the building. It lay vacant for half a year, and then was occupied by the First State Bank. This company removed some load-bearing elements and installed standard truss roof framing. A second rear entry was

added, and windows cut at the south end for drive-in service. The circular garden, which continued into the waiting room, has been eliminated, and many partitions put in to accommodate various businesses. In the late eighties, four partners purchased the building; of these, only Richard G. Brown became a tenant.

Original reception room

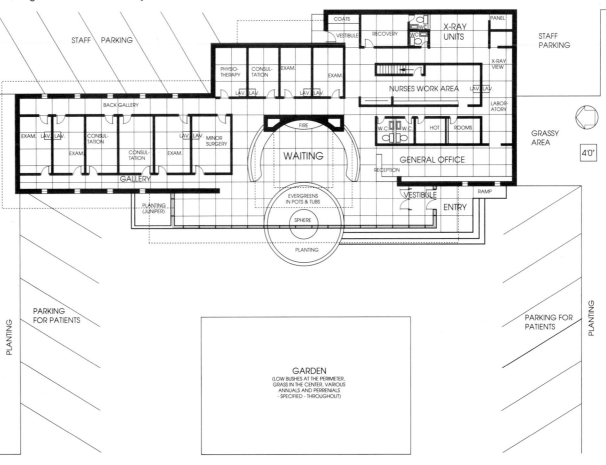

457

Schultz Residence, private facade

Workspace

S.426 T.5745
Carl **Schultz** Residence (1957)
Saint Joseph, Michigan
Master bedroom and guest room
enlarged

Carl Schultz's sister was Emma
Schultz Sauer. Her daughter was Flori
Taylor, wife of Lou Taylor, the second
owners of the Harper house (S.329)
nearby on Lake Michigan.

Nine-pound pavement bricks from
the streets of Benton Harbor combine
with mahogany trim and pink concrete
block transom-level windows in this
house. Its living room terrace cantilevers out over a ravine off the left
bank of the Saint Joseph River, not the
river itself.

The plan is an in-line configuration
on a grand scale, expanded, much like
the contemporaneous Walton and
Sterling Kinney residences (S.421,

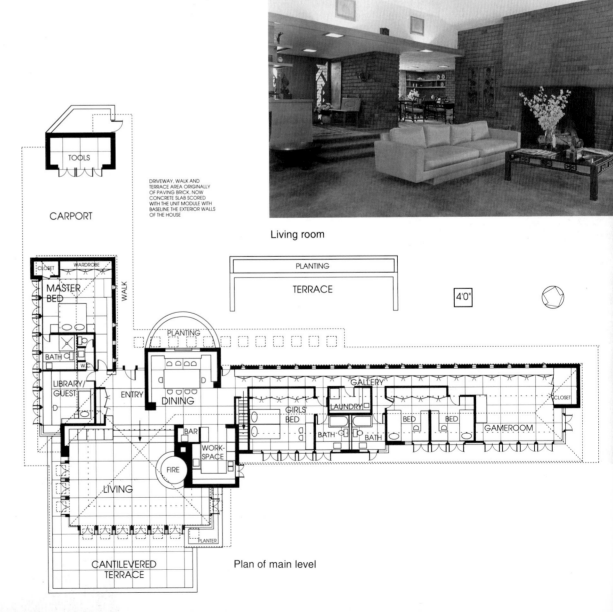

Living room

Plan of utilities and lower basements

Plan of main level

458

S.422). A guest room and master bedroom (each enlarged in 1966) fill space to the carport in what, by the extension, turns this into an outside **L** (270 degree) plan. The living room and its terrace are several feet below the entry level, a favorite device of Wright's in the fifties. A separate dining room is located opposite the workspace next to the entry. The bedroom wing has a dormitory-style girls' bedroom, two other small bedrooms, a laundry room, and two bathrooms off the 56-foot tunnel gallery, and is terminated by a 16-by-20-foot game room. The fascia is given a variation on true dentil molding; 2-inch diameter by 1/2-inch deep circles cut on 3-inch centers.

A utilities basement lies under the workspace. To its side, however, is a set of four steps leading into a grandiose lower basement nearly the size of the living room above; hardheaded German businessman Schultz won out over Wright's objections; he wanted space for a Ping-Pong table!

The unit module is a 4-foot-square with a circular treatment of the fireplace hearth. Construction, with David Wheatley in charge, was completed by Taliesin Associated Architects shortly after Wright's death.

Olfelt Residence, living room facade

S.427   T.5820
Dr. Paul and Helen **Olfelt**
Residence (1958)
Saint Louis Park, Minnesota

The Olfelts met at the University of Minnesota, where Helen had seen Frank Lloyd Wright's architecture fairly presented in art appreciation courses. Vernon Knudson, an architecture student who studied at Taliesin after college, was a friend. Even with this background, the Olfelts approached Wright not expecting him to design for them.

Triangular forms mold the sleeping quarters into a hillside, opening the living room to a view downhill, and fit the whole into the only level part of the site. The gabled roof leads the eye west over the terrain while shielding against summer sun. This sheltering roofline greets the approaching visitor, for it is extended almost to the ground at the carport, providing a dramatic guide to the stairs that lead to the main entry. This roofline is derived from the Austin house (S.345). Another near cousin is the Edwards house (S.313), whose carport roof leads into and covers the living room, but in this earlier work it is done on a square module. Wright-designed furniture, such as hassocks, tables, chairs, complement the design. Construction, under the guidance of John H. Howe and occasional supervision by Vernon Knudson, was completed in 1960 by Taliesin Associated Architects.

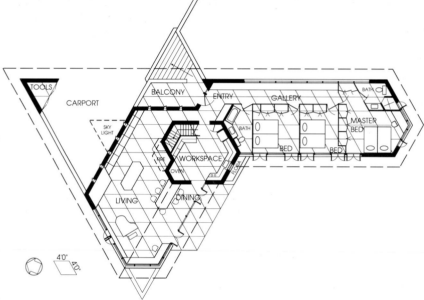

Tunnel gallery

Living room

S.428   T.5812

Dr. George and Millie **Ablin**
Residence (1958)
Bakersfield, California

Salmon-tinted concrete block, cedar shingles (the copper roofing called for was too expensive), and Philippine mahogany are combined in this house on a knoll next to the Bakersfield Country Club. A 48-foot expanse of glazing opens the living room to the southeast, the view protected from nearby development. Its gabled roof is supported by two steel beams reaching from side pillars, two blocks thick at the support points. The plan is an outside **L** (240 degrees on an equilateral parallelogram grid). The master bedroom and a study are in one wing, while childrens' rooms for a growing family, with several bathrooms, the other. The two are spliced together by the large workspace with its pierced light-admitting block, glazed with plexiglass, and the enormous living room.

Between Wright's preliminary design and that brought to completion under Taliesin Associated Architects supervision (Tom Olsen) in 1961 (Wes Peters signed the plans a few weeks after Wright died), the building gained in size. The master bedroom and workspace were deepened a full unit. The children's playroom was widened a full unit. An extension, marked "future maid's room" by Wright became an additional two bathrooms and bedroom serving as a dressing room to the swimming pool. Otherwise, space-

saving was the order of the day, with drawers under beds and other typical Wrightian built-in furniture.

Masonry walls are battered. Vertical mortar joints were filled to the surface, horizontals deeply raked to emphasize horizontality. The mason, however, rubbed all surface-level joints smooth, thus leaving a visible line between textured block; so the masonry was painted to make the whole surface smooth.

Ablin Residence, private facade

Dining area

Ablin Residence, workspace tower at night

Workspace at night

Plan, with comparison of original design and as-built plan

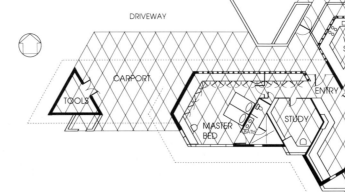

AS ORIGINALLY DESIGNED BY FRANK LLOYD WRIGHT

AS ENLARGED, AND BUILT BY THE TALIESIN ASSOCIATED ARCHITECTS

POOL

COVERED STORAGE

POOL EQUIPMENT

BED
BATH
BED

CHILDREN'S PLAYROOM
BED

BED

DRIVEWAY

WORK SPACE

BATH

DINING

CARPORT

ENTRY
LAUNDRY
UTILITY
FIRE

TOOLS

MASTER BED
BATH
STUDY

LIVING

TERRACE

Stromquist Residence

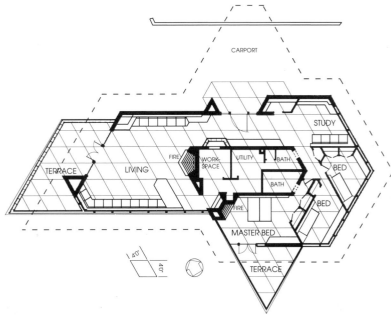

S.429   T.5626
Don M. **Stromquist** Residence
(1958)
Bountiful, Utah
Restored, 1990

Wright's only work in Utah is a
concrete-block structure built on a
4-foot equilateral (60–120 degree)
parallelogram unit module. Trim and
partitions are mahogany. The living
room partakes of the setting sun at this
deep valley site, for the main axis is
300 degrees to north. The study and
children's bedrooms are clustered off
the gallery that surrounds the workspace core, as in the Pappas house
(S.392), except that in this house they
gain the advantage of morning sunlight. This is a major change from the
first scheme for the client, which had
the bedrooms in line in a north wing
and the living room facing southwest.
Here the master bedroom has been
moved to the south side, with its own
triangular balcony. A forced-air heating
system was installed and proved very
noisy.

The design expands the one-room
concept of the Teater studio residence
(S.352) into a space suitable for a
growing family. It was completed in
1963 under Taliesin Associated Archi-

Living room with Wright-designed table

tects' supervision. Shortly thereafter,
Stromquist's employer, U.S. Steel,
ordered him to Pittsburgh; he could not
afford to own two houses. Then, two
years after he sold the house, he
moved back to Ogden, Utah, but was
unable to buy it back. Second owners
let the property deteriorate, but third
owners have provided complete restoration. The original dirt trail is now
hard-surfaced road, and civilization
has crept to adjacent lots.

Fireplace in living room

Shutter, with special cut-out design

S.430 T.5821
Seth Condon **Peterson** Cottage
(1958)
Lake Delton, Wisconsin
Restored 1989–92

Native reddish sandstone, quarried nearby at Rock Springs, and Philippine mahogany plywood panels and trim boards are used in this tiny gem on the ledge above the south shore of Mirror Lake, which was created in 1860 by the damming of Dell Creek. Peterson intended to bring his bride to this secluded 880-square-foot home, Wright's smallest residential design. The fireplace is central to the square plan, its masonry dividing the south half of the interior space in two. By thus using the workspace/kitchen as a space divider, Wright creates something approximating a one-room house; only the bathroom requires a door. The kitchen, walled-in on three sides, is lit by a skylight.

The project was under construction at the time of Wright's death, and work was continued by Taliesin Associated Architects, with Tom Casey supervising. Peterson ran out of funds, and Mackey Adams of Adams Brothers Construction Company in Lake Delton experienced difficulty completing the work as designed. (Another version, with a two-unit roof overhang at the main facade, was built long after Wright's death by Taliesin Associated Architects for Don and Virginia Lovness.) The next owner was Owen Pritchard of Milwaukee, who raised Afghan hounds on the property. At some point, forced-air heating was installed; this is to be replaced with original radiant heating.

The cottage is on a fenced-in western limit of Mirror Lake State Park, where it had been left to deteriorate since its 1966 acquisition by the Department of Natural Resources, State of Wisconsin. It is listed on the National Register of Historic Places. In 1989 a committee was formed by the Mirror Lake Association to preserve and restore the cottage at a cost estimated to be over $200,000. Restoration was by architects John Eifler and Gary Kohn, working for the Seth Peterson Cottage Conservancy. The building is available for rental.

Seth Peterson Cottage before restoration

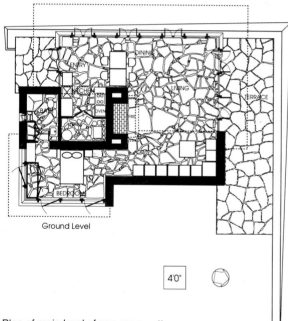

Ground Level

Plan of main level of one-room cottage

Plan of storage (upper) level

Living space of "one-room cottage" before restoration

Congregational Church

S.431 T.5318
Pilgrim **Congregational Church**
(1958)
Redding, California

Desert masonry (desert rubblestone
wall) construction gives this building its
Wrightian flavor. It was designed as a
timber structure, employing telephone
poles. The main roof, as built, is suspended from concrete bents. Wright's
drawings, setting the project on an
equilateral triangle as the module,
show final revision dates of January

and April 1959. There was no on-site
supervision, though John Rattenbury
provided the changes that allowed
construction to begin after Wright's
death. Completion of Taliesin-designed
work was in 1961. Only the fellowship
hall was built, rather than the important
sanctuary or adjacent chapel. It may
be worth noting that redwood pole roof
supports were replaced with structurally more reliable Douglas fir. The
building is usually open during
weekdays.

Fellowship hall used as sanctuary

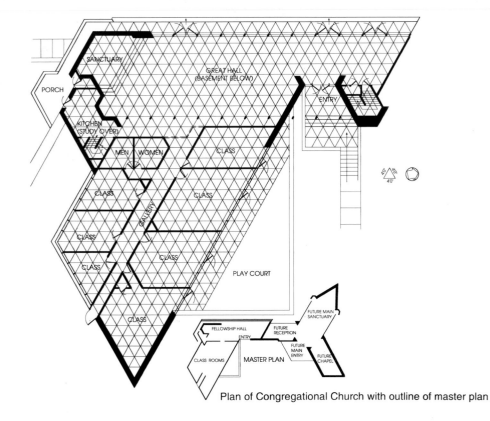

Plan of Congregational Church with outline of master plan

EXTENDING GEOMETRY TO CIRCLES

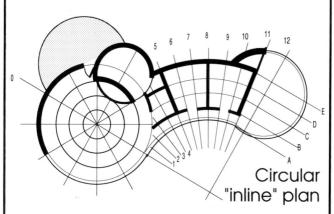

Circular
"inline" plan

That plywood sheets could be soaked in water, then bent into
curved surfaces, helped suggest the use of the circle for
organization of space. Many materials do not curve as nicely as
plywood. The lack of a perfect curved surface could be
disguised in the Second Jacobs Residence, S.283, by use of
stone, but not in the Meyers Residence, S.297, which employs
concrete block. Each of these is of two story hemicycle plan.
Here we show two single-story structures using circles and
circular segments. Compare the circular inline plan with Lykes,
S.433.

One logical variation of the
circle plan is a two-story
version. One such was
built, the Sol Friedman
house, S.316, where,
however, straight lines
connect the circular
module lines
between the
radii, revealing the
use of standard
building materials
rather
than
curved plywood.

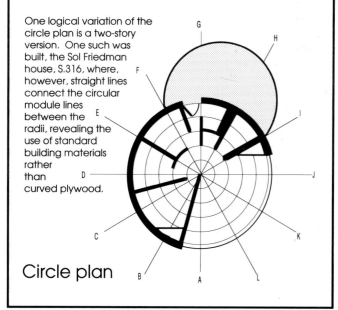

Circle plan

S.432   T.5904

Grady **Gammage Memorial Auditorium** (1959) for Arizona State University

Tempe, Arizona
Stage workshop loading ramp raised to
ground level

The last nonresidential design by
Wright to be constructed is this auditorium that seats 3000 persons in the
continental style (that is, with wide
spacing between rows and no center
aisle) in its three levels (floor, grand
tier, balcony). The grand tier is suspended forward of the rear auditorium
wall on a 145-foot-long steel beam,
providing the space underneath with
the same reverberation characteristics
as uncovered spaces. This effect was
previously achieved only in Adler and
Sullivan's Auditorium, where the
covered space opened into the lobby
behind. The stage is 140 feet wide, the
maximum proscenium opening 64 feet.

There are 50 concrete columns,
cast on the site, and each rises 55 feet
to support the outer roof, whose deck
is gypsum and thin-shell concrete with
a roofing of composition and sprayed-
on asphalt. The exterior walls are brick
and marblecrete (a marblelike composition material) in desert-rose finish;
interior brick and sand-finish plaster
with acoustical tile, walnut trim, and
reinforced-concrete floors complete
the list of major construction materials.
Cost per seat was the lowest achieved
for a multipurpose theater built in the
United States in the 1960s. Engineering and much of the interior
design are by William Wesley Peters,
the architect of record. George Izenour
was the stage designer and Vern O.
Knudsen the acoustics consultant.
John Rattenbury supervised construction. "No smoking" is a design feature;
no ashtrays were provided in either
auditorium or lobby. Half-hour tours are
conducted Saturday afternoons only.

Gammage Auditorium at night

The auditorium

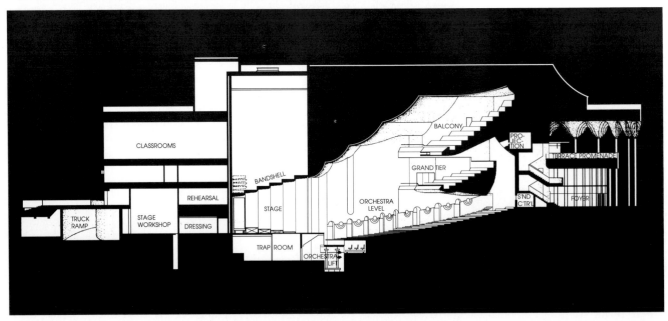

Section

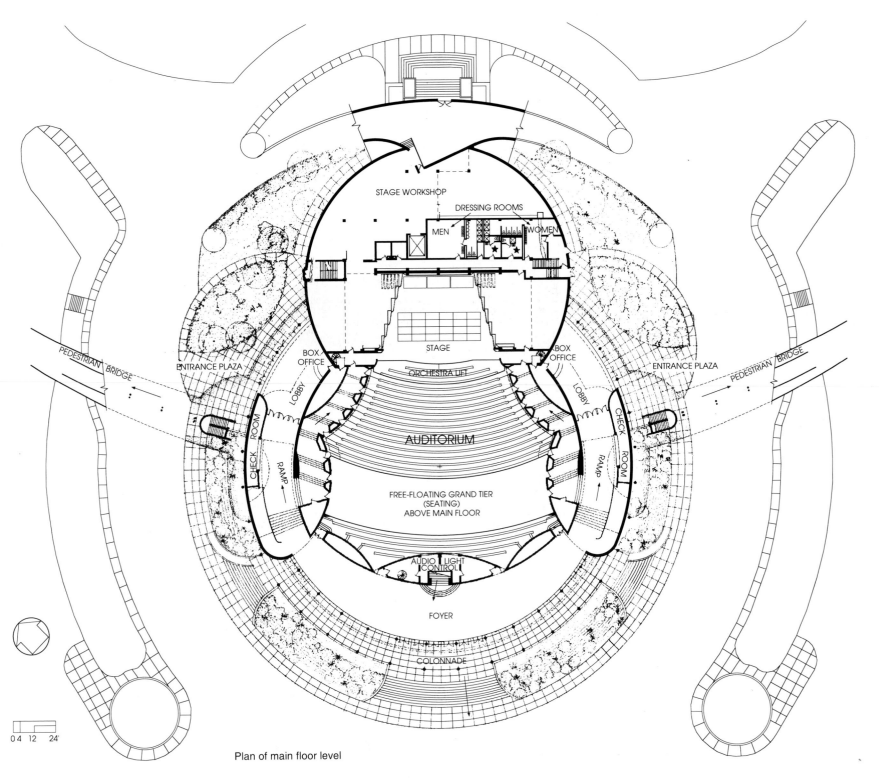

STAGE WORKSHOP

DRESSING ROOMS

MEN WOMEN

PEDESTRIAN BRIDGE

ENTRANCE PLAZA

BOX OFFICE

STAGE

BOX OFFICE

ENTRANCE PLAZA

PEDESTRIAN BRIDGE

ORCHESTRA LIFT

LOBBY

LOBBY

CHECK ROOM

RAMP

AUDITORIUM

CHECK ROOM

RAMP

FREE-FLOATING GRAND TIER
(SEATING)
ABOVE MAIN FLOOR

AUDIO LIGHT CONTROL

FOYER

COLONNADE

0 4 12   24'

Plan of main floor level

S.433   T.5908
Aime and Norman Lykes
Residence (1959/66)
Phoenix, Arizona

Anyone visiting an American seaport is likely to recognize the Lykes name. It appears on commercial vessels sailing the seven seas. It was the Lykes's fate to be given not only a magnificent design, but Wright's last residential design to be built by the original client.

Taliesin fellow John Rattenbury drew both preliminary and working drawings from Wright's sketches, much as had John H. Howe the last two decades of the architect's life. Then he did the detail work and furniture and supervised construction, which took place during 1966–68. Tom Casey, a director of education in structural systems in the Frank Lloyd Wright School of Architecture, did the structural and mechanical engineering. The living room is a circular plan, and all other parts of the total plan are circle segments; five major radius centers were necessary to complete the design. Desert-rose-tinted concrete block and Philippine mahogany are the materials employed. The second-floor study above the workspace drum is an alteration of the plan made by Rattenbury, who is the architect of record.

Lykes Residence

View from master bedroom terrace along bedroom wing to living room "drum"

Living room

Dressing room of master bedroom

Workspace

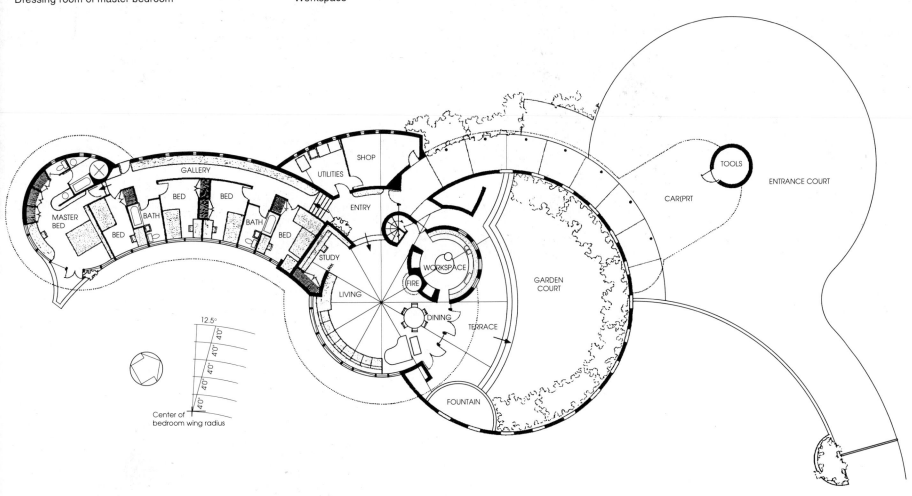

Illustration Credits

Plans

Most plans in this publication are drawn by the author, copyright © 1993 by The Frank Lloyd Wright Foundation.

Many plans were produced from items which are now out of copyright, or from measurements by the author and are copyright © 1993 by William Allin Storrer.

The following is a listing of individuals who were the source for specific measurements, original plans or other information necessary to production of the plans here published. They have rights reserved in said plans as indicated by the Storrer catalog number. For specific copyright information, contact the author.

000 Leslie Nestingen
002–004 Don Kalec
005 Paul Minor
007 Edsel Ruddiman
009 John A. Eifler, AIA
013 John G.Thorpe, AIA
018 Robert C. Spencer, Jr.
020 Vicki and Kenneth Prouty
022 Robert C. Spencer, Jr.
024 HABS
025 Robert C. Spencer, Jr.
028 Robert C. Spencer, Jr.
031 John A. Eifler, AIA
032 Robert C. Spencer, Jr.
033 Henry G. Zimoch, AIA
042 Patty Saltenberger
044 John G. Thorpe, AIA
046 Robert C. Spencer, Jr.
049 Robert C. Spencer, Jr.
051 John Tilton, AIA
052 John A. Eifler, AIA
053 John A. Eifler, AIA
054 John A. Eifler, AIA
067 Kevin Murphy and Karen Brammer
068 Jeanette S. Fields
072 HABS, W. R. Hasbrouck, AIA
074 Jack Prost
079 Kay and John Heep
095 Robert C. Spencer, Jr.
098 Meg Klinkow
101 Patrick Mahoney
105 Nancy Elwood Schmid

106 Donald J. Poore and Staci and Jim Cannon
109 Lois Fineberg
110 Paul and Suzanne Peck-Collier
113 HABS
117 John Tilton, AIA
118 Kathy Hult
127 HABS
128 Maya Moran
129 Darlene Larson
139 Jonathan Lipman, AIA
140 Frank Lucente
147 Karen Brown
148 John Tilton, AIA
150 Anthony Scott
151/B Walter Sobol
160 Robert Ooley
161 John Tilton, AIA
164 HABS
165 Alice Sloan
170 The Journal of the Royal Architectural Institute of Canada
171 Patrick J. Meehan
174 Susan Shipper-Smith
184 Susan Solway, Howard Siegel
193 HABS
194 Meiji Mura
196 HABS
200 City of Milwaukee
201 Jill Arena
202 City of Milwaukee
203.1–3 City of Milwaukee

Photographs and Drawings

The majority of the nearly 1000 photographs in this publication were made by the author in the years 1968–1992. To obtain the most representative photos of many works, a number of photographic images have been obtained from a wide range of sources. These include not only turn-of-the-century publications, but also images made expressly for this publication by contemporary photographers who often have year-round access to structures that are best photographed at only one season or even part thereof.

Photographs licensed for use in this publication are identified by the copyright holder with the picture. All photographs without such identifications were either made by the author, or the author owns the negative from which the print was made, or the items were provided for use by those here named. The list below is intended to give proper credit to those sources whose documentation has proven invaluable in this project.

Individual photographers or collections, and the photos they provided, are indicated by the Storrer catalog number.

001 Henry-Russell Hitchcock
006A Henry-Russell Hitchcock
008B Henry-Russell Hitchcock
018 Henry-Russell Hitchcock (exterior)
029 Henry-Russell Hitchcock
037 Henry-Russell Hitchcock
043 James and Audrey Kouvel
047 Henry-Russell Hitchcock
048 Wilbert R. Hasbrouck, AIA
049 Frank Lloyd Wright Foundation (drawing)
050 Frank Lloyd Wright Foundation (drawing)
051 Jeanette S. Fields (Gray house)
052 Henry-Russell Hitchcock (all)
053 John A. Eifler, AIA
058 The Frank Lloyd Wright Home and Studio Foundation Research Center (view from southeast, billiards room, entry area, dining room)
062 Henry-Russell Hitchcock
064 Brian A. Spencer, architect
068 Jeanette S. Fields (as built)
069 Henry-Russell Hitchcock
077 Todd Lunsford (drawing)
078 The Frank Lloyd Wright Home and Studio Foundation Research Center (interior)
093 Henry-Russell Hitchcock (west facade)

099 Henry-Russell Hitchcock (as built)
112 William Gray Purcell
117 John Tilton, AIA (interior)
129 Friends of Fabyan (both)
130 Geneva Historical Society (photos)
131 Henry-Russell Hitchcock (both)
145 Delton D. Ludwig
147 Karen Brown (exterior)
155 Henry-Russell Hitchcock
156 Henry-Russell Hitchcock
160 Steve Danforth, Wrightian Association (full exterior, living room)
161 John Tilton, AIA (both)
166 Frank Lloyd Wright Foundation
167 Franklin Porter
171 Patrick J. Meehan
172 Henry-Russell Hitchcock
175 Henry-Russell Hitchcock
176 The Frank Lloyd Wright Home and Studio Foundation Research Center (view from southwest, living room)
180 James and Audrey Kouvel (exterior)
180 The Frank Lloyd Wright Home and Studio Foundation Research Center (bandstand, Winter Garden interior)
182 James and Audrey Kouvel
194 The Frank Lloyd Wright Home and Studio Foundation Research Center (promenade)
194 Meiji-mura (interior views exclusive of promenade)
194 Masami Tanigawa (exterior)
206 Shichiro Hayashi (interior)
207 Shiseido Co.
209 Tom Rickard
211 Eleanor Pettersen, AIA
218 Bradley Ray Storrer, AIA (Mr. Wright's bedroom wing)
219 Frank Lloyd Wright Foundation (drawing)
224 Henry-Russell Hitchcock
233 Henry-Russell Hitchcock
234 John M. Dennis (photo by James M. Dennis)
236 Abby Beecher Roberts
241 Dennis C. Schmiedeke, AIA (1950s drafting room)
250 Henry-Russell Hitchcock
269 Bradley Ray Storrer, AIA (exterior)
292 A. H. Bulbulian (exterior)
298 Dennis C. Schmiedeke, AIA (at completion)
299 Bradley Ray Storrer, AIA
302 Dennis C. Schmiedeke, AIA (view from southwest)
302 Bradley Ray Storrer, AIA (view from southeast)
310 Circle Gallery (interior)
314 Patricia Boulter (exterior)
315 Quin and Ruth Blair (all but interior)
318 Roland Reisley (exterior views)
320 Wilbur C. Pearce (two views with San Gabriel Mountains, model)
326 Bradley Ray Storrer, AIA (exterior)
330A Gloria Berger
339 Seamour and Gerte Shavin (shortly after construction)
347 David Lloyd Wright (exterior)
347 Leonard Spangenberg, AIA (living room, guest wing)

352 Archie Boyd Teater (painting)
355 Price Co., public relations department (exteriors)
379A Prof. David Gosling
382 Rothschild Photo, City of Los Angeles Cultural Affairs Department
388 Dennis C. Schmiedeke, AIA (interior)
425 Richard G. Brown (exterior)
429 Don M. Stromquist (all but shutter)
432 Arizona State University (exterior)

Publications (all are out of copyright):

Ausgeführte Bauten (Berlin: Ernst Wasmuth A.-G., 1911), 004 (both), 038 (front), 046, 061A, 070/071 (house and original stable), 072 (all), 078 (exterior), 082 (as built), 093 (all but west facade), 096 (all), 100 (interior views), 101, 105 (interior views and north side exterior), 119 (tennis court view), 127 (3 interior views), 128 (as built without porch pillars), 135 (stairwell, living room), 140 (both), 141 (all), 142 (both), 148 (living room, dining room), 150 (both), 153, 154

Ausgeführte Bauten und Entwürfe von Frank Lloyd Wright (Berlin: Ernst Wasmuth A.-G., 1910), 123, 143

Macintosh Morello Orchards, publicity booklet, 144A

The Official Bluebook of the Jamestown Ter-Centennial Exposition (1909), 132

Various out-of-copyright sources, 010, 019, 045, 075, 106 (as built), 145

"The Work of Frank Lloyd Wright" by Robert C. Spencer, Jr., in *The Architectural Review*, 1900, 025 (as built), 033 (as first constructed), 034 (both), 038 (rear), 054 (entry and rear), 058 (north side showing garage under construction, from west showing pavilion)

Location by ZIP Code

The number following each building's identification is the text entry (Storrer catalog) number, for ease of access to additional information concerning the item listed.

Structures are also listed in the Index by the city in which they are located.

ZIP code ranges, and relevant state listings, are:

00000-09999	Connecticut, Massachusetts, New Hampshire, New Jersey
10000-19999	Delaware, New York, Pennsylvania
20000-29999	Maryland, South Carolina, Virginia
30000-39999	Alabama, Florida, Mississippi, Tennessee
40000-49999	Indiana, Kentucky, Michigan, Ohio
50000-59999	Iowa, Minnesota, Montana, Wisconsin
60000-69999	Illinois, Kansas, Missouri, Nebraska
70000-79999	Oklahoma, Texas
80000-89999	Arizona, Idaho, New Mexico, Utah, Wyoming
90000-99999	California, Oregon, Washington

Foreign listings follow the U.S. listings

Note: This Index by ZIP (Zone Improvement Plan) code of extant buildings by Frank Lloyd Wright is not meant to encourage visits to private homes. Rather, the availability of these addresses places upon the would-be visitor the responsibility of gaining advanced permission from the current owner before entering any private property. The privacy that Wright designed into his clients' residences must be respected.

Buildings that are open to visitors are so noted in the text. Further, phone numbers are given in this list for those buildings regularly open to the public. Be advised that phone numbers and addresses are subject to change; these were accurate at the time of publication.

Massachusetts

01002	Amherst	38 Shays St.	**Baird Residence,** S.277, and **Shop,** S.277A

New Hampshire

03104	Manchester	117 Heather St.	**Kalil,** S.387
		223 Heather St.	**Zimmerman,** S.333; owned by Currier Gallery of Art; (603) 626-4158

Connecticut

06840	New Canaan	432 Frog Town Rd.	**Rayward Residence,** S.383, **Addition,** S.383A, and **Playhouse,** S.383B
06903	Stamford	121 Woodchuck Rd.	**Sander,** S.354

New Jersey

07028	Glen Ridge	63 Chestnut Hill Pl.	**Richardson,** S.282

07924	Bernardsville	190 Jockey Hollow Rd.	**Christie,** S.278
08034	Cherry Hill	375 Kings Hwy.	**Sweeton,** S.325
08876	Millstone	142 S. River Rd.	**Wilson,** S.366

New York

10022	New York City	430 Park Ave.	**Hoffman Auto Showroom,** S.380; now Mercedes-Benz, Manhattan; (212) 629-1666
10028	New York City	Metropolitan Museum Fifth Ave. at 82d St.	**Little Residence II** (living room), S.173; (212) 535-7710
10128	New York City	1071 Fifth Ave.	**Guggenheim Museum,** S.400; (212) 630-3500
10306	Richmond	48 Manor Ct. Staten Island	**Cass,** S.409.2;
10541	Lake Mahopac	Petra Island	**Chahroudi,** S.346
10570	Pleasantville	44 Usonia Rd.	**Reisley Residence,** S.318, and Residence **Addition,** S.318A
		12 Laurel Hill Dr.	**Serlin,** S.317
		11 Orchard Brook Dr.	**Sol Friedman,** S.316
10580	Rye	58 Island Dr., North Manursing Island	**Hoffman Residence,** S.390
10913	Blauvelt	Clausland Mountain Rd.	**Zaferiou,** S.410
11021	Great Neck Estates	9A Myrtle Ave.	**Rebhuhn,** S.240
14047	Derby	6472 Lake Shore Rd.	**Isabel Martin Residence,** S.225, and **Garage,** S.226
14210	Buffalo	Seneca at Larkin	**Larkin Building** (site and ruins), S.093
14214	Buffalo	125 Jewett Pkwy.	**Darwin D. Martin Residence,** S.100; (716) 831-3485
		118 Summit Ave.	**Barton,** S.103
		285 Woodward Ave.	**Darwin D. Martin Gardener's Cottage,** S.090
14216	Buffalo	57 Tillinghast Pl.	**Davidson,** S.149
14222	Buffalo	76 Soldiers Pl.	**Heath,** S.105
14610	Rochester	16 East Blvd.	**Boynton,** S.147

Pennsylvania

15421	Chalkhill	Ohiopyle Rd.	**Hagan,** S.377
15464	Mill Run	State Hwy. 381	**Kaufmann Residence Fallingwater,** S.230, and **Guesthouse,** S.231; Western Pennsylvania Conservancy; (412) 329-8501
18105	Allentown	31 N. Fifth St.	**Little Residence II** (library), S.173; Allentown Art Museum of the Lehigh Valley; (215) 432-4333
19003	Ardmore	152, 154, 156 Sutton Rd.	**Suntop Homes,** S.248.1–.3
		307 E. Spring St.	S.248.4
19117	Elkins Park	Old York Rd. at Foxcroft	**Beth Sholom Synagogue,** S.373; (215) 887-1342

Delaware

19809	Wilmington	619 Shipley Rd.	**Dudley Spencer,** S.402

Maryland

20034	Bethesda	7927 Deepwell Dr.	**Llewellyn Wright,** S.358
21215	Baltimore	6807 Cross Country Blvd.	**Euchtman,** S.270

Virginia

22101	McLean	600 Chainbridge Rd.	**Luis Marden,** S.357

22309	Alexandria	9000 Richmond Hwy Woodlawn Plantation P. O. Box 37 Mount Vernon, VA 22121	**Pope**, S.268; (703) 557-7880
23455	Virginia Beach	320 51st Street	**Cooke**, S.360

South Carolina
29609	Greenville	9 W. Avondale Dr.	**Austin**, S.345
29945	Yemassee	7 River Rd.	**Stevens Auldbrass Plantation**, S.261–264

Florida
32303	Tallahassee	3117 Okeeheepkee Rd.	**George Lewis**, S.359
33801	Lakeland	111 Lake Hollngsworth Dr.	**Florida Southern College**, S.251–258; (813) 680-4116

Alabama
35630	Florence	601 Riverview Dr.	**Rosenbaum Residence**, S.267, and **Addition**, S.267A

Tennessee
37404	Chattanooga	334 N. Crest Rd.	**Shavin**, S.339

Mississippi
39216	Jackson	306 Glenway Dr.	**Hughes**, S.303
39564	Ocean Springs	100 Holcomb Blvd.	**Louis Sullivan Bungalow**, S.005, and **Servant's Quarters**, S.006B
		509 E. Beach	**Charnley Bungalow**, S.007, and
		507 E. Beach	**Guesthouse**, S.008A

Kentucky
40601	Frankfort	509 Shelby St.	**Ziegler**, S.164

Ohio
44057	North Madison	6363 W. Lake Rd.	**Staley**, S.335
44074	Oberlin	127 Woodhaven Dr.	**Weltzheimer**, S.311
44094	Willoughby Hills	2203 River Rd.	**Penfield**, S.365
44709	Canton	452 Santa Clara Dr., N.W.	**Feiman**, S.371
		518 44th St., N.W.	**Rubin**, S.343
44714	Canton	5120 Plain Center Ave., N.E.	**Dobkins**, S.362
45220	Cincinnati	1 Rawson Woods Circle	**Boulter**, S.379, and **Addition**, S.379A
45237	Amberley Village	6980 Knoll Rd.	**Tonkens**, S.386
45243	Indian Hill	9905 Comargo Club Dr.	**Boswell**, S.423
45429	Dayton	5441 Far Hills Ave.	**Meyers Medical Clinic**, S.397
45505	Springfield	1340 E. High St.	**Wescott Residence**, S.099, and **Garage**, S.099A

Indiana
46368	Ogden Dunes	43 Cedar Trail	**Armstrong**, S.260
46601	South Bend	715 W. Washington St.	**DeRhodes**, S.125
46614	South Bend	1404 Ridgedale Rd.	**Mossberg**, S.302
46804	Fort Wayne	3901 N. Washington Rd.	**Haynes**, S.323
46952	Marion	1119 Overlook Rd.	**Davis Residence**, S.324, and **Addition**, S.324A

47906	West Lafayette	1301 Woodland Ave.	**Christian,** S.375

Michigan

48013	Bloomfield HIlls	5045 Pon Valley Rd.	**Melvyn Maxwell Smith,** S.287
		1925 N. Woodward Ave.	**Affleck,** S.274; owned by Lawrence Institute of Technology; (313) 356-0200
48104	Ann Arbor	227 Orchard Hills Dr.	**Palmer,** S.332
48170	Plymouth	12221 Beck Rd.	**Goddard,** S.364
		12305 Beck Rd.	**Wall,** S.281
48220	Ferndale	23459 Woodward Ave.	**Wetmore Auto Service Station Remodeling,** S.348
48221	Detroit	2760 W. Seven Mile Rd.	**Turkel,** S.388
48864	Okemos	2410 Hulett Rd.	**Goetsch-Winckler,** S.269
		2504 Arrow Head Rd.	**Edwards,** S.313
		2527 Arrow Head Rd.	**Brauner,** S.312
		1155 Wrightwind Dr.	**Schaberg,** S.328
49008	Kalamazoo	2662 Taliesin Dr.	**McCartney,** S.299/A–C
		2806 Taliesin Dr.	**Eric V. Brown Residence,** S.300, and **Addition,** S.300A
		2816 Taliesin Dr.	**Levin,** S.298
		2822 Taliesin Dr.	**Winn,** S.301
49022	Benton Harbor	1150 Miami Rd.	**Anthony,** S.315
49053	Galesburg	11036 Hawthorne Dr.	**Pratt,** S.295
		11098 Hawthorne Dr.	**Eppstein,** S.296
		11108 Hawthorne Dr.	**Meyer,** S.297
		11185 Hawthorne Dr.	**Weisblat,** S.294
49085	St. Joseph	207 Sunnybank	**Harper,** S.329
		2704 Highland Ct.	**Schultz,** S.426
49117	Grand Beach	46208 Crescent Rd.	**Vosburgh,** S.197
		46039 Lakeview	**W. S. Carr,** S.199
		47017 Lakeview	**Joseph J. Bagley,** S.198
49461	Whitehall	5318 S. Shore Dr.	**Mr. Thomas H. Gale Summer Residence,** S.088.0
		5324 S. Shore Dr.	**Mrs. Thomas H. Gale Cottage 1,** S.088.1
		5370 S. Shore Dr.	**Mrs. Thomas H. Gale Cottage 2,** S.088.2
		5380 S. Shore Dr.	**Mrs. Thomas H. Gale Cottage 3,** S.088.3
49503	Grand Rapids	450 Madison Ave., S.E.	**May,** S.148; (616) 246-4821
49670	Northport	71 N. Peterson Park Rd.	**Alpaugh,** S.293
49754	Marquette Island	Les Cheneaux Club	**Heurtley Summer Residence Remodeling,** S.075
49855	Marquette	Deertrack, County Hwy. 492	**Abby Beecher Roberts,** S.236

Iowa

50131	Johnston	6880 N.W. Beaver Dr.	**Trier,** S.398
50158	Marshalltown	1701 Woodfield Rd.	**Sunday,** S.393
50401	Mason City	5 W. State St.	**City National Bank Building,** S.155, **Hotel,** S.156, and **Law Offices Remodeling,** S.157
		First St., N.E., at E. State	**Stockman,** S.139
50616	Charles City	1107 Court St.	**Miller,** S.289
52159	Monona	402 N. Page	**Meier,** S.204.4
52326	Quasqueton	Cedar Rock Park	**Walter Residence,** S.284, **Council Fire,** S.284A, **Gate,** S.284B, and **River Pavilion,** S.285; (319) 934-3572
52403	Cedar Rapids	3400 Adel Dr. S. E.	**Grant,** S.288
52577	Oskaloosa	1907 A Ave. E.	**Alsop,** S.304
		511 N. Park Ave.	**Lamberson,** S.305

Wisconsin

53115	Delavan	3455 S. Shore Dr.	**A. P. Johnson,** S.087

		3407 S. Shore Dr.	**Wallis Cottage,** S.079
		3335 S. Shore Dr.	**Fred B. Jones Residence,** S.083, **Gate Lodge,** S.084, and **Barn with Stables,** S.085
		3211 S. Shore Dr.	**Charles S. Ross,** S.082
		3209 S. Shore Dr.	**George W. Spencer,** S.081
53118	Dousman	3902 Hwy. 67	**Greenberg,** S.372
53211	Milwaukee	2420 N. Terrace Ave.	**Bogk,** S.196
53215	Milwaukee	1835 S. Layton Blvd.	**Richards Bungalow,** S.203.1
		2714 W. Burnham Blvd.	**Richards Small House,** S.202
		2720–2734 W. Burnham Blvd.	**Richards Duplex Apartments,** S.201
53217	Fox Point	7111 N. Barnett	**Albert Adelman,** S.308
53217	Bayside	1001 W. Jonathan	**Mollica,** S.411.1
53225	Wauwatosa	9400 W. Congress St.	**Greek Orthodox Church,** S.399; (414) 461-9400
53402	Wind Point	33 E. 4 Mile	**Herbert F. Johnson,** S.239; Wingspread Foundation; (414) 639-3211
53403	Racine	1525 Howe St.	**Johnson Wax Building,** S.237, and **Tower,** S.238; (414) 631-2154
53405	Racine	1425 Valley View Dr.	**Karen Johnson,** S.368
53549	Jefferson	332 E. Linden Dr.	**Richard Smith,** S.337
53562	Middleton	3995 Shawn Trail	**Jacobs Second Residence,** S.283
53581	Richland Center	300 S. Church St.	**German Warehouse,** S.183
53588	Wyoming Valley	Route 23	**Wyoming Valley Grammar School,** S.401
53588	Spring Green	Route 23, Taliesin	**Taliesin Fellowship Complex,** S.228
			Drafting Room, S.228A, and **Theatre,** S.228C
			Romeo and Juliet II, S.037A
			Porter, S.134
			Midway Barns, S.246, with **Dairy and Machine Sheds,** S.247
			Taliesin, S.218, and **Dams,** S.220
		Route 23 at County C	**Riverview Terrace Restaurant,** S.367; now Frank Lloyd Wright Center at Taliesin; (608) 588-7948
		County T near Route 23	**Unity Chapel,** S.000
53703	Madison	22 N. Butler St.	**Lamp Residence,** S.097
53705	Shorewood Hills	3650 Lake Mendota Dr.	**Pew,** S.273
		900 University Bay Dr.	**Unitarian Meeting House,** S.291; (608) 238-2400
53705	Madison	120 Ely Pl.	**Gilmore,** S.146
		110 Martinette Trail	**Rudin,** S.412.1
		5817 Anchorage Rd.	**Van Tamelen,** S.406
53711	Madison	441 Toepfer St.	**Jacobs First Residence,** S.234
53813	Lancaster	474 N. Filmore St.	**Patrick Kinney,** S.342
53916	Beaver Dam	7655 Indian Hills Trail	**Jackson,** S.407.1
53925	Columbus	954 Dix St.	**Arnold,** S.374
53940	Lake Delton	Ferndell Rd.	**Peterson,** S.430; owned by the Seth Peterson Cottage Conservancy, Inc., S1994 Pickerel Slough Road, Wisconsin Dells, WI 53965; (608) 254-6051
54241	Two Rivers	3425 Adams	**Schwartz,** S.271
54401	Wausau	904 Grand Ave.	**Duey Wright,** S.420
		1224 Highland Park Blvd.	**Manson,** S.249
54481	Stevens Point	Springville Dr. at U.S. 5	**Iber,** S.408
54901	Oshkosh	1165 Algoma Blvd.	**Hunt Residence II,** S.203.4

Minnesota

55033	Hastings	State Hwy. 55 at Pine St.	**Fasbender Medical Clinic,** S.424
55082	Stillwater	10121 83d, N.	**Lovness Residence,** S.391,
55414	Minneapolis	255 Bedford St., S.E.	**Willey,** S.229
55416	Minneapolis	2801 Burnham Blvd.	**Neils,** S.314

55416	St. Louis Park	2206 Parkland Lane	**Olfelt,** S.427
55901	Rochester	1229 Skyline Dr., S.W.	**Bulbulian,** S.292
		1243 Skyline Dr., S.W.	**Keys,** S.321
		1532 Woodland Dr., S.W.	**McBean,** S.412.2
55912	Austin	309 21st St., S.W.	**Elam,** S.336
56374	St. Joseph	29710 Kipper Rd.	**LaFond,** S.411.2

Montana

59829	Darby	469 Bunkhouse Rd.	**Como Orchard One-room Cottage,** S.144B, and **Three-room Cottage,** S.144C
59937	Whitefish	341 Central Ave.	**Lockridge Medical Clinic,** S.425

Illinois

60010	Barrington HIlls	265 Donlea Rd.	**Post,** S.409.1
		County Line Rd.	**Fredrick,** S.376
60015	Bannockburn	200 Thornapple	**Allen Friedman,** S.403
60022	Glencoe	790 Sheridan Rd.	**Brigham,** S.184
		850 Sheridan Rd.	**Glasner,** S.109
		1023 Meadow Rd.	**Kissam,** S.192
		1027 Meadow Rd.	**William F. Ross,** S.191
		1030 Meadow Rd.	**Root,** S.189
		1031 Meadow Rd.	**Kier,** S.190
		272 Sylvan Rd.	**Perry,** S.188
		Sylvan Rd.	**Ravine Bluffs Development Sculptures,** S.185.1, S.185.3, and **Bridge,** S.186
		265 Sylvan Rd.	**Booth Residence,** S.187
		239 Franklin St.	**Booth Cottage,** S.178
		Franklin Rd. at Meadow	**Ravine Bluffs Sculpture,** S.185.2
60025	Glenview	1544 Portage Run	**John O. Carr,** S.327
60035	Highland Park	1445 Sheridan Rd.	**Willits Residence,** S.054
		1450 Waverly	**Gardener's Cottage with Stables,** S.055
		1689 Lake Ave.	**Millard,** S.126
		1923 Lake Ave.	**Mary M. W. Adams,** S.108
60043	Kenilworth	205 Essex Rd.	**Baldwin,** S.107
60044	Lake Bluff	231 Prospect Ave.	**Richards Bungalow,** S.203.3
60045	Lake Forest	170 N. Mayflower	**Glore,** S.341
60048	Libertyville	153 Little Saint Mary's Rd.	**Lloyd Lewis Residence,** S.265, and **Farm Unit,** S.266
60091	Wilmette	507 Lake Ave.	**Baker,** S.151
		330 Gregory St.	**Burleigh,** S.203.2
60126	Elmhurst	301 S. Kenilworth Ave.	**Henderson,** S.057
60134	Geneva	1511 S. Batavia Rd. Friends of Fabyan	**Fabyan Remodeling,** S.129; (708) 232-2378
		318 S. Fifth	**Hoyt,** S.120
60170	Plato Center	Rohrsen Rd.	**Muirhead,** S.334
60201	Evanston	2420 Harrison St.	**Charles A. Brown,** S.110
		2614 Lincolnwood	**Oscar A. Johnson,** S.204.3
60202	Evanston	1014 Hinman	**Hebert Remodeling,** S.089
60301	Oak Park	875 Lake St.	**Unity Temple** (Unity Church), S.096; (708) 848-6225
60302	Oak Park	404 Home Ave.	**George W. Smith,** S.045
		Lake St. at Oak Park	**Scoville Park Fountain,** S.094
		138–144 Lake St.	**Francisco Terrace Apartments** (archway only), S.030
		210 Forest Ave.	**Thomas,** S.067
		238 Forest Ave.	**Beachy Remodeling,** S.117
		6 Elizabeth Ct.	**Mrs. Thomas H. Gale Residence,** S.098
		313 Forest Ave.	**Hills Remodeling,** S.051

		318 Forest Ave.	**Heurtley Residence**, S.074
		325 Forest Ave.	**Moore Stable**, S.035
		333 Forest Ave.	**Moore Residence Remodeling**, S.034A
		400 Forest Ave.	**Copeland Residence Alterations**, S.158
		408 Forest Ave.	**Copeland Garage Alterations**, S.159
		951 Chicago Ave.	**Frank Lloyd Wright Residence**, S.002, **Playroom Addition**, S.003, and **Studio**, S.004; (708) 848-1976
		1019 Chicago Ave.	**Parker**, S.017
		1027 Chicago Ave.	**Thomas H. Gale**, S.016
		1031 Chicago Ave.	**Walter M. Gale**, S.020
		1030 Superior St.	**Woolley**, S.023
		334 N. Kenilworth Ave.	**Young Additions** and **Remodeling**, S.036
		611 N. Kenilworth Ave.	**Balch**, S.168
		223 N. Euclid Ave.	**George Furbeck**, S.043
		317 N. Euclid Ave.	**Charles E. Roberts Stable**, S.041
		321 N. Euclid Ave.	**Charles E. Roberts Residence Remodeling**, S.040
		710 Augusta Ave.	**Harry S. Adams Residence**, S.179, and **Garage**, S.179A
		520 N. East Ave.	**Cheney Residence**, S.104
		534 N. East Ave.	**Goodrich**, S.042
		636 N. East Ave.	**William E. Martin Residence**, S.061
		515 Fair Oaks Ave.	**Rollin Furbeck Residence**, S.044, and **Remodeling**, S.044A
		540 Fair Oaks Ave.	**Fricke Residence**, S.059, and **Emma Martin Garage**, S.060
60305	River Forest	Auvergne Pl. at Lake Ave.	**Waller Gates**, S.065
		515 Auvergne Pl.	**Winslow Residence**, S.024, and **Stable**, S.025
		530 Edgewood Pl.	**Williams Residence**, S.033, and **Dormer Remodeling**, S.033A
		603 Edgewood Pl.	**Scott Remodeling**, S.394, and **Isabel Roberts**, S.150
		562 Keystone Ave.	**Ingalls**, S.161
		559 Ashland Ave.	**Davenport**, S.068
		615 Lathrop Ave.	**River Forest Tennis Club**, S.119
		7214 Quick Ave.	**Walter Gerts Remodeling**, S.177
60420	Dwight	122 W. Main St.	**Frank L. Smith Bank**, S.111
60422	Flossmoor	1136 Brassie Ave.	**Nichols**, S.118
60506	Aurora	1300 Garfield Ave.	**Greene**, S.176
60510	Batavia	637 N. Batavia Ave.	**Gridley Residence**, S.121
60521	Hinsdale	121 County Line Rd.	**Frederick Bagley**, S.028
60525	LaGrange	345 Seventh Ave.	**Hunt Residence I**, S.138
		108 S. Eighth Ave.	**Goan**, S.029
		109 S. Eighth Ave.	**Emmond**, S.015
		211 S. LaGrange Rd.	**Clark**, S.013
60532	Lisle	2255 Edgebrooke Dr.	**Duncan**, S.407.2
60546	Riverside	281 Bloomingbank	**Coonley Residence** (main wing), S.135
		300 Scottswood Rd.	**Coonley Residence** (bedroom wing), S.135
		336 Coonley Rd.	**Coonley Coach House**, S.137
		350 Fairbank Rd.	**Coonley Playhouse**, S.174
		150 Nuttall Rd.	**Tomek**, S.128
60604	Chicago	209 S. LaSalle St.	**Rookery Building Remodeling**, S.113
60610	Chicago	1365 Astor	**Charnley Residence**, S.009; (312) 951-8938
60612	Chicago	3005–3017 W. Carroll Ave.	**E-Z Polish Factory**, S.114
		2840–2858 W. Walnut St.	**Waller Apartments**, S.031
60615	Chicago	1322 E. 49th St.	**Blossom Garage**, S.133
		4858 Kenwood Ave.	**Blossom Residence**, S.014
		4852 Kenwood Ave.	**McArthur Residence**, S.011, **Residence Remodeling**, S.011A, and **Stable**, S.011B
		4842 Kenwood Ave.	**Kenwood Dining Room Remodeling**, S.012

		5132 Woodlawn Ave.	**Heller Residence,** S.038, and **Additions,** S.038A
60616	Chicago	3213–3219 Calumet	**Roloson Rowhouses,** S.026
60620	Chicago	9326 S. Pleasant Ave.	**Jessie Adams,** S.048
60626	Chicago	7415 Sheridan Rd.	**Bach,** S.193
60628	Chicago	12147 Harvard Ave.	**Foster Residence,** S.049, and **Stable,** S.050
60637	Chicago	5757 Woodlawn Ave.	**Robie,** S.127; owned by the University of Chicago; (312) 702-8374
60643	Chicago	9914 Longwood Dr.	**Evans,** S.140
		10410 S. Hoyne Ave.	**Guy C. Smith,** S.204.1
		10541 S. Hoyne Ave.	**Hyde,** S.204.2
60644	Chicago	42 N. Central Ave.	**Walser,** S.091
60653	Chicago	700 E. Oakwood Blvd.	**Abraham Lincoln Center,** S.095; owned by Northeastern Illinois University; (312) 268-7500
60901	Kankakee	687 S. Harrison Ave.	**Hickox,** S.056
		701 S. Harrison Ave.	**Bradley Residence,** S.052, and **Stable,** S.053
61008	Belvidere	Harrison at Webster	**Pettit Chapel,** S.116
61114	Rockford	4646 Spring Brook Rd.	**Laurent,** S.319
61606	Peoria	1505 W. Moss Ave.	**Little Residence I,** S.070, and **Stable,** S.071. **Clarke Additions** to the **Little Stable,** S.152
62522	Decatur	2 Millikin Pl.	**Irving Residence,** S.165, and **Garage,** S.165A
62703	Springfield	301–327 E. Lawrence Ave	**Dana Residence,** S.072, and **Stable Remodeling,** S.072A; operated by Dana-Thomas House Historic Site; (217) 782-6776
		231 E. Lawrence Ave.	**White Cottage basement,** S.072B
62704	Springfield	Laurel St. at First	**Lawrence Memorial Library,** S.073; now in the Lawrence Adult Center

Missouri

63122	Kirkwood	120 N. Ballas Rd.	**Kraus,** S.340
63141	St. Louis	8654 Masonridge Rd.	**Pappas,** S.392
64111	Kansas City	3600 Bellview Ave.	**Sondern,** S.279, and **Adler Addition,** S.307
64112	Kansas City	4601 Main St.	**Community Christian Church,** S.280; (816) 561-6531
64116	Kansas City	3640 N.W. Briarcliff Rd.	**Bott,** S.404

Kansas

67208	Wichita	255 N. Roosevelt Blvd.	**Allen Residence,** S.205, and **Garden House,** S.205A; owned by the Allen-Lambe House Foundation; (316) 687-1027
		Yale Ave. at 21st St.	**Juvenile Cultural Center,** S.418; Wichita State University; (316) 689-3737

Nebraska

69001	McCook	602 Norris Ave.	**Sutton,** S.106

Oklahoma

74003	Bartlesville	Silver Lake Rd.	**Harold Price, Jr.,** S.363
		N.E. Sixth St. at Dewey Ave.	**Price Tower,** S.355; visits arranged by the Landmark Preservation Council; (918) 661-7471
74105	Tulsa	3704 S. Birmingham Ave.	**Richard Lloyd Jones Residence,** S.227, and **Garage,** S.227A

Texas

75219	Dallas	3636 Turtle Creek Blvd.	**Dallas Theatre Center,** S.395; (214) 526-8210
75220	Dallas	9400 Rockbrook Dr.	**Gillin,** S.338
77024	Bunker Hill	12024 Tall Oaks	**Thaxton,** S.384
79606	Amarillo	Tascosa Rd.	**Sterling Kinney,** S.422

Wyoming

| 82414 | Cody | 5588 Greybull Hwy. | **Blair,** S.351 |

Idaho

| 83314 | Bliss | Old Hagerman Hwy. | **Teater,** S.352 |

Utah

| 84010 | Bountiful | 1289 Canyon Creek Rd. | **Stromquist,** S.429 |

Arizona

85013	Phoenix	1123 W. Palo Verde Dr.	**Carlson,** S.326
85016	Phoenix	2701 E. Arizona Biltmore Circle	**Arizona Biltmore Hotel,** S.221, and **Cottages,** S.222; (602) 955-6600
		5802 N. 30th St.	**Benjamin Adelman Residence,** S.344, **Sitting Room,** S.344A, and **Carport,** S.344B
		5808 N. 30th St.	**Boomer,** S.361
		5710 N. 32d St.	**Pauson** (ruins), S.250
85018	Phoenix	6636 N. 36th St.	**Lykes,** S.433
		5212 E. Exeter Blvd.	**David Wright,** S.322
85044	Phoenix	Between Mountain Vista Dr. & E. Frye, and 30th & 32d	**Ocatillo Desert Camp** (site), S.224
85253	Paradise Valley	7211 N. Tatum	**Harold Price, Sr.,** S.378
		6442 E. Cheney Rd.	**Pieper,** S.349
85261	Scottsdale	108th St. at Cactus	**Taliesin West,** S.241–245; (602) 860-2700
85281	Tempe	Apache Blvd. at Mill Ave.	**Gammage Memorial Auditorium,** S.432; (602) 965-5062

New Mexico

| 87552 | Pecos | Hwy. 63 | **Arnold Friedman Lodge** S.286, and **Caretaker's Quarters,** S.286A |

California

90027	Los Angeles	4808 Hollywood Blvd.	**Barnsdall Hollyhock House,** S.208, and **Municipal Art Gallery** (garage), S.382; (213) 662-7272 or (213) 485-4580 for groups and non-English speakers
		4808 Hollywood Blvd.	**Barnsdall Residence A,** S.210
		4808 Hollywood Blvd.	**Spring House,** S.209
		2655 Glendower Ave.	**Ennis Residence,** S.217,
		Trust for Preservation of Cultural Heritage	**Chauffeur's Quarters,** S.217A, and **Nesbitt Alterations,** S.217B; (213) 660-0607
90028	Los Angeles	1962 Glencoe Way	**Samuel Freeman,** S.216; (213) 662-7272
90049	Brentwood Heights	449 Skyewiay Rd.	**Sturges,** S.272
90069	Hollywood	8161 Hollywood Blvd.	**Storer,** S.215
90210	Beverly Hills	332 N. Rodeo Dr.	**Anderton Court Shops,** S.356

90265	Malibu	32436 W. Mulholland Hwy.	**Oboler Gatehouse,** S.275, **Additions,** S.275A, and **Eleanor's Retreat,** S.276
91010	Bradbury	5 Bradbury Hills Rd.	**Pearce,** S.320
91103	Pasadena	645 Prospect Crescent	**Mrs. Millard,** S.214
93103	Montecito	196 Hot Springs Rd.	**Stewart,** S.160
93306	Bakersfield	4260 Country Club Dr.	**Ablin,** S.428
93401	San Luis Obispo	1106 Pacific St.	**Kundert Medical Clinic,** S.396
93635	Los Banos	Center Ave.	**Fawcett,** S.385
93921	Carmel	Scenic Road at Martin St.	**Walker,** S.306
94010	Hillsborough	101 Reservoir Rd.	**Bazett,** S.259
94025	Atherton	83 Wisteria Way	**Mathews,** S.331
94108	San Francisco	140 Maiden Lane	**Morris Gift Shop,** S.310
94305	Stanford	737 Frenchman's Rd.	**Hanna Residence,** S.235, **Additions,** S.235A, and **Remodeling,** S.235B; owned by Stanford University; (415) 723-3469
94563	Orinda	6 Great Oak Circle	**Buehler,** S.309
94903	San Rafael	N. San Pedro Rd.	**Marin County Post Office,** S.415, **Administration Building,** S.416, and **Hall of Justice,** S.417; (415) 499-6104
94960	San Anselmo	259 Redwood Rd.	**Berger,** S.330. **Frank Addition,** S.330A
95350	Modesto	417 Hogue Rd.	**Walton,** S.421
96001	Redding	2850 Foothill Blvd.	**Congregational Church,** S.431; (916) 243-3121

Oregon

97070	Wilsonville	303 S.W. Gordon Lane	**Gordon,** S.419

Washington

98027	Issaquah	212th Ave.	**Brandes,** S.350
98166	Normandy Park	18971 Edgecliff Dr. S.W.	**Tracy,** S.389
98467	Tacoma	7800 John Dower S.W.	**Griggs,** S.290

Canada

Ontario

	Sapper Island	Desbarats	**Pitkin,** S.076

Japan

	Tokyo	31-4, Nishi Ikebukuro 2-chome Toshima-ku	**Jiyu Gakuen Girls' School,** S.213
	Tokyo	1-30, Komazawa 1-chome Setagaya-ku	**Hayashi,** S.206
	Inuyama	Museum at Meiji Mura 1, Uchiyama Inuyama-shi, Aichi-ken 484	**Imperial Hotel** (lobby only), S.194
	Ashiya	172 Yamate-cho Ashiya-shi, Hyogo-ken	**Yamamura,** S.212

Index